Among Chekhov's papers the following monologue was found, written in his own hand:

Solomon (alone): Oh! how dark is life! No night, when I was a child, so terrified me by its darkness as does my invisible existence. Lord, to David my father thou gavest only the gift of harmonizing words and sounds, to sing and praise thee on strings, to lament sweetly, to make people weep or admire beauty; but why hast thou given me a meditative, sleepless, hungry mind? Like an insect born of the dust, I hide in darkness; and in fear and despair, all shaking and shivering, I see and hear in everything an invisible mystery. Why this morning? Why does the sun come out from behind the temple and gild the palm tree? Why this beauty of women? Where does the bird hurry, what is the meaning of its flight, if it and its young and the place to which it hastens will, like myself, turn to dust? It were better I had never been born or were a stone, to which God has given neither eyes nor thoughts. In order to tire out my body by nightfall, all day yesterday, like a mere workman I carried marble to the temple; but now the night has come and I cannot sleep . . . I'll go and lie down. Phorses told me that if one imagines a flock of sheep running and fixes one's attention upon it, the mind gets confused and one falls asleep. I'll do it . . . *(Exit)*

Antæus

EDITED BY

DANIEL HALPERN

TANGIER/LONDON/NEW YORK

NO. 66, SPRING, 1991

Publisher
DRUE HEINZ

Founding Editor
PAUL BOWLES

Administrative Director
CHRISTOPHER KINGSLEY

Managing Editor
CATHY JEWELL

Assistant Editor
STEPHEN MORROW

Editorial Assistants

ALEXANDRA FOX   JAMES B. LEE

KATHERINE HEINY   EMMA PRIMAVERA

STEVE HILL   JENNIFER RICHARDSON

Business Manager
SUSAN SHAFTAN

Acknowledgments
THE EDITORS WOULD LIKE TO ACKNOWLEDGE BRIDGET ASCHENBERG,
ANDREAS BROWN, JOHN GUARE, AND HELEN MERRILL FOR THEIR
INVALUABLE ASSISTANCE IN THE PREPARATION OF THIS
COLLECTION OF PLAYS.

ANTÆUS *is published semiannually by The Ecco Press, 26 West 17th Street, New York, N.Y. 10011.
Distributed by W. W. Norton & Company, Inc., 500 Fifth Avenue, New York, N.Y. 10110, Ingram
Periodicals, 347 Reedwood Drive, Nashville, TN 37217, and B. DeBoer, Inc., 113 East Centre St.,
Nutley, N.J. 07110. Distributed in England & Europe by W. W. Norton & Company, Inc.*

Contributions and Communications: ANTÆUS
*American address: 26 West 17th Street, New York, N.Y. 10011
European address: 42A Hay's Mews, London, W1, England
Four-issue Subscriptions: $30.00. Back issues available—write for a complete listing.*

BOOKS FROM THE ECCO PRESS ARE AVAILABLE TO *Antæus* SUBSCRIBERS AT A 10% DISCOUNT. PLEASE WRITE
FOR A CATALOGUE: THE ECCO PRESS, 26 WEST 17TH STREET, NEW YORK, N.Y. 10011.

*ISSN 0003-5319
Printed by Haddon Craftsmen, Inc.
ISBN 0-88001-268-4
Library of Congress Card Number: 70-612646
Copyright © 1991 by* ANTÆUS, *New York, N.Y.
Cover Photograph:
"The Royal Crown Cafe, Boyle, 1983" From* JUKE JOINT *by Birney Imes.
University Press of Mississippi, 1989. Reprinted by permission.
Cover design by Suzanne Noli.
Publication of this magazine has been made possible in part by a grant
from the National Endowment for the Arts.
Logo: Ahmed Yacoubi*

Page 498 constitutes an extension of this copyright page.

CONTENTS

vi / Contents

PREFACE

What follows is a selection of one-act plays by contemporary international authors. I have also included dramatic monologues, which are in some cases part of a longer work, as with the contributions by Sam Shepard and August Wilson, and sometimes complete as they stand, as with Lanford Wilson's *The Moonshot Tape*. Both the play in one act and the dramatic monologue hope to achieve, in a relatively short period of time, a condensed frame of experience. Perhaps these two dramatic forms are to the full-length play what the short story is to the novel, or, prosody disregarded for sake of example, the poem to the story. Regardless of the various differences, each genre certainly hopes to establish an environment that takes readers somewhere they've not yet been, to touch them in a way that feels unique, so that by the final word, regardless of the distance traveled, they are no longer quite as they were before they began. The genres differ most in the time they allow themselves to accomplish this, the degree of compression, the amount of landscape required to complete the experience.

Of the literary genres (poetry, fiction, playwriting, and the essay), it seemed to me as I began assembling this collection, after looking without success for anthologies of one-act plays by contemporary authors, that playwriting is the least likely to find its way into print. This is no doubt due, in part, to the fact that plays are written to be performed, to be *seen*. I want this volume to celebrate the play as an act of "recorded" literature, to be performed, yes, but to be read at leisure, thought over, reconsidered without a second and third price of admission.

Readers, as they make their way through this collection, will notice certain inconsistencies in the typographical format, the presentation of the plays *in type*. I have tried to accommodate the quite varied styles of each writer, while at the same time present an overall uniform and consistent format from play to play.

—Daniel Halpern

/ *ix*

KOBO ABE

TRANSLATED FROM THE JAPANESE
BY DONALD KEENE

The Man Who Turned Into a Stick (death)

CHARACTERS

MAN FROM HELL *A supervisor.*
WOMAN FROM HELL *Recently appointed to the Earth Duty Squad.*
THE MAN WHO TURNED INTO A STICK
HIPPIE BOY
HIPPIE GIRL
VOICE FROM HELL

A hot, sticky Sunday afternoon in June. A main thoroughfare with the Terminal Department Store in the background. Crowds of people passing back and forth. (It is best not to attempt to represent this realistically.) A young man and a young woman sit on the sidewalk curb at stage center front about three yards apart. They are hippies. They stare vacantly ahead, completely indifferent to their surroundings, with withdrawn expressions. (If desired, they can be shown sniffing glue.)

All of a sudden a stick comes hurtling down from the sky. A very ordinary stick, about four feet long. (It can be manipulated, perhaps in the manner of Grand Guignol, by the actor playing the part of the man before he turned into a stick.)

The stick rolls over and over, first striking against the edge of the sidewalk, then bouncing back with a clatter, and finally coming to rest horizontally in the gutter near the curbstone, less than a yard from the two hippies. Reflex action makes them look at where the stick has fallen, then upward, frowning, to see where it came from. But considering the danger to which they have been exposed, their reactions are somewhat lacking in urgency.

MAN FROM HELL enters from stage left and WOMAN FROM HELL from stage right. Both are spotlighted.

HIPPIE BOY   (*Still looking up.*) Goddamned dangerous.

MAN FROM HELL   In the twilight a white crescent moon, A fruit knife peeling the skin of fate.

WOMAN FROM HELL   Today, once again, a man
Has changed his shape and become a stick.

HIPPIE BOY   (*Turns his gaze back to the stick and picks it up.*) Just a couple of feet closer and it would have finished me.

HIPPIE GIRL   (*Looks at the stick and touches it.*) Which do you suppose is the accident—when something hits you or when it misses?

HIPPIE BOY   How should I know? (*Bangs the stick on the pavement, making a rhythm.*)

MAN FROM HELL   The moon, the color of dirty
chromium plate,
Looks down and the streets
are swirling.

WOMAN FROM HELL   Today, once again, a man
Turned into a stick and vanished.

HIPPIE GIRL   Hey, what's that rhythm you're tapping?

HIPPIE BOY   Try and guess.

HIPPIE GIRL   (*Glancing up.*) Look! I'm sure that kid was the culprit!

HIPPIE BOY   (*Intrigued, looks up.*)

HIPPIE GIRL   Isn't he cute? I'll bet he's still in grade school. He must've been playing on the roof.

HIPPIE BOY   (*Looks into the distance, as before.*) Damned brats. I hate them all.

HIPPIE GIRL   Ohh—it's dangerous, the way he's leaning over the edge. . . . I'm sure he's ashamed now he threw it. . . . He seems to be trying to say something, but I can't hear him.

HIPPIE BOY   He's probably disappointed nobody got hurt, so now he's cursing us instead.

STICK   (*To himself.*) No, that's not so. He's calling me. The child saw me fall.

HIPPIE GIRL   (*Abruptly changing the subject.*) I know what it is, that rhythm. This is the song, isn't it? (*She hums some tune or other.*)

HIPPIE BOY   Hmmm.

HIPPIE GIRL   Was I wrong?

HIPPIE BOY   It's always been my principle to respect other people's tastes.

HIPPIE GIRL   (*Unfazed by this, she wiggles her body to the rhythm and goes on humming.*)

(*In the meantime, THE MAN WHO TURNED INTO A STICK is coordinating the movements of his body with those of the stick in HIPPIE BOY's hand, all the while keeping his eyes fastened on a point somewhere in the sky.*)

MAN FROM HELL   (*Walks slowly toward stage center.*)
The moon is forgotten

2 / Kobo Abe

In a sky the color of cement,
And the stick lies forgotten
Down in the gutter.

WOMAN FROM HELL *(Also walks in the same deliberate fashion toward stage center.)*
The stick lies forgotten in the gutter,
The streets from above form a whirlpool.
A boy is searching for his vanished father.

(MAN and WOMAN FROM HELL meet at stage center, several feet behind HIPPIE BOY and GIRL, just as they finish this recitation.)

MAN FROM HELL *(In extremely matter-of-fact tones.)* You know, it wouldn't surprise me if this time we happened to have arrived exactly where we intended.

WOMAN FROM HELL *(Opens a large notebook.)* The time is precisely twenty-two minutes and ten seconds before—

MAN FROM HELL *(Looks at his wristwatch.)* On the button. . . .

WOMAN FROM HELL *(Suddenly notices the stick in HIPPIE BOY's hand.)* I wonder, could that be the stick?

MAN FROM HELL *(Rather perplexed.)* If it is, we've got a most peculiar obstacle in our path. . . . *(Walks up to HIPPIE BOY and addresses him from behind, over his shoulder.)* Say, pal, where did you get that stick?

HIPPIE BOY *(Throws him a sharp glance but does not answer.)*

WOMAN FROM HELL Lying in the gutter, wasn't it?

HIPPIE GIRL It fell from the roof. We had a hairbreadth escape.

WOMAN FROM HELL *(Delighted to have her theory confirmed.)* I knew it! *(To MAN FROM HELL.)* Sir, it was this stick, as I suspected.

MAN FROM HELL *(To HIPPIE BOY.)* Sorry to bother you, but would you mind handing me that stick?

WOMAN FROM HELL I'm sure you don't need it especially.

HIPPIE BOY I don't know about that. . . .

MAN FROM HELL We're making a survey. A little investigation.

HIPPIE GIRL You from the police?

WOMAN FROM HELL No, not exactly. . . .

MAN FROM HELL *(Interrupting.)* But you're not too far off. . . .

HIPPIE BOY Liars! You're the ones who threw the stick at us. And now you're trying to suppress the evidence. You think I'm going to play your game? Fat chance!

(Beating out a rhythm with the stick, he starts to hum the melody HIPPIE GIRL was singing.)

MAN FROM HELL *(In mollifying tones.)* If you really suspect us, I'd be glad to go with you to the police station.

HIPPIE BOY Don't try to wheedle your way around me.

HIPPIE GIRL   *(Looks up.)* You know, I think it was that kid we saw a while ago . . . He's not there anymore.

HIPPIE BOY   You shut up.

WOMAN FROM HELL   *(Animatedly.)* That's right, there was a child watching everything, wasn't there? From the railing up there on the roof. . . . And didn't you hear him calling his father? In a frightened, numb little voice. . . .

HIPPIE GIRL   *(Trying not to annoy HIPPIE BOY.)* How could I possibly hear him? The average noise level in this part of town is supposed to be over 120 decibels, on an average. *(Shaking her body to a go-go rhythm.)*

WOMAN FROM HELL   *(To MAN FROM HELL.)* Sir, shall I verify the circumstances at the scene?

MAN FROM HELL   Yes, I suppose so. *(Hesitates a second.)* . . . But don't waste too much time over it.

(WOMAN FROM HELL hurries off to stage left.)

STICK   *(To himself. His voice is filled with anguish.)* There's no need for it. . . . I can hear everything. . . . In the grimy little office behind the staircase marked "For store employees only" . . . my son, scared to death, surrounded by scabby-looking, mean security guards. . . .

MAN FROM HELL   *(To HIPPIE BOY.)* It's kind of hard to explain, but the fact is, we have been entrusted, for the time being, with the custodianship of that stick. . . . I wish you'd try somehow to understand.

HIPPIE BOY   I don't understand nothing.

HIPPIE GIRL   *(With a wise look.)* This is the age of the generation gap. We're alienated.

STICK   *(To himself. In tones of unshakable grief.)* The child is lodging a complaint. . . . He says I turned into a stick and dropped from the roof. . . .

MAN FROM HELL   *(To HIPPIE BOY.)* Well, let me ask you a simple question. What do you intend to use the stick for? I'm sure you haven't any particular aim in mind.

HIPPIE BOY   I'm not interested in aims.

HIPPIE GIRL   That's right. Aims are out-of-date.

MAN FROM HELL   Exactly. Aims don't amount to a hill of beans. So why can't you let me have it? It isn't doing you any good. All it is is a stick of wood. But, as far as we're concerned, it is a valuable item of evidence relating to a certain person . . .

HIPPIE GIRL   *(Dreamily.)* But one should have a few. People don't have enough. . . .

MAN FROM HELL   Enough what?

HIPPIE GIRL   Aims!

MAN FROM HELL   You're making too much of nothing. It's bad for your health to want something that doesn't really exist. The uncertainty you feel at the thought you haven't got any aims, your mental anguish at the thought you have lost track of whatever aims you once had—they're a lot better proof that you are there, in that particular spot, than any aim I can think of. That's true, isn't it?

HIPPIE GIRL (*To* HIPPIE BOY.) How about a kiss, huh?

HIPPIE BOY (*Gives her a cold sidelong glance.*) I don't feel like it.

HIPPIE GIRL You don't have to put on such airs with me.

HIPPIE BOY I don't want to.

HIPPIE GIRL Come on!

HIPPIE BOY I told you, lay off the euphoria.

HIPPIE GIRL Then scratch my back.

HIPPIE BOY Your back?

(HIPPIE GIRL *bends over in* HIPPIE BOY's *direction, and lifts the back of her collar.* HIPPIE BOY, *with an air of great reluctance, thrusts the stick down into her collar and moves the stick around inside her dress, scratching her back.*)

HIPPIE GIRL More to the left. . . . That's right, there. . . .

HIPPIE BOY (*Pulls out the stick and hands it to* HIPPIE GIRL.) Now you scratch me. (*Bends over toward* HIPPIE GIRL.)

HIPPIE GIRL You don't mean it from the heart. . . . (*All the same, she immediately gives way and thrusts the stick down the back of* HIPPIE BOY's *collar.*) Is this the place?

HIPPIE BOY Yes, there. And everywhere else.

HIPPIE GIRL Everywhere?

HIPPIE BOY (*Twisting his body and emitting strange noises.*) Uhhh . . . uhhh . . . uhhh . . . It feels like I haven't had a bath in quite some time. . . .

HIPPIE GIRL (*Throwing down the stick.*) You egoist!

(MAN FROM HELL *nimbly jumps between the two of them and attempts to grab the stick. But* HIPPIE BOY *brushes his hand away and picks up the stick again.*)

MAN FROM HELL Look, my friend. I'm willing to make a deal with you. How much will you charge for letting me have this stick?

HIPPIE GIRL (*Instantly full of life.*) One dollar.

MAN FROM HELL A dollar? For a stick of wood like this?

HIPPIE BOY Forget it. Not even for two dollars.

HIPPIE GIRL (*To* HIPPIE BOY *in a low voice, reproachfully.*) You can find any number of sticks just like this one, if you really want it.

MAN FROM HELL A dollar will keep you in cigarettes for a while.

HIPPIE BOY Me and this stick, we understand each other. . . . Don't know why. . . . (*Strikes a pose, holding the end of the stick in his hand.*)

HIPPIE GIRL (*With scorn in her voice.*) You look alike. A remarkable resemblance.

HIPPIE BOY (*Staring at the stick.*) So we look alike, do we? Me and this stick?

(Reflects awhile, then suddenly turns to HIPPIE GIRL.) You got any brothers and sisters?

HIPPIE GIRL   A younger sister.

HIPPIE BOY   What was her name for you? *(HIPPIE GIRL hesitates.)* You must have been known as *something*. A nickname, maybe.

HIPPIE GIRL   You mean, the way she called me.

HIPPIE BOY   Precisely.

HIPPIE GIRL   Gaa-gaa.

HIPPIE BOY   Gaa-gaa?

HIPPIE GIRL   No, that's what my brother called me. My sister was different. She called me Mosquito.

HIPPIE BOY   What does Gaa-gaa mean?

HIPPIE GIRL   Mosquito—that's what my sister called me.

HIPPIE BOY   I'm asking what Gaa-gaa is.

HIPPIE GIRL   You don't know what Gaa-gaa is?

HIPPIE BOY   Has it got something to do with mosquitoes?

HIPPIE GIRL   Yes, but it's very complicated to explain.

MAN FROM HELL   Excuse me, but would you . . .

HIPPIE BOY   Yesterday there was a funeral at that haberdashery across the street.

HIPPIE GIRL   *(Looking around at the crowd.)* But it had nothing to do with any of these people, had it?

HIPPIE BOY   But what about Gaa-gaa and Mosquito?

MAN FROM HELL   Wasn't it Gar-gar rather than Gaa-gaa?

HIPPIE GIRL   She died.

MAN FROM HELL   Who died?

HIPPIE GIRL   My sister.

MAN FROM HELL   What happened to her?

HIPPIE BOY   She became a corpse, naturally.

MAN FROM HELL   Of course. That's not surprising.

HIPPIE GIRL   That's why I don't understand anything anymore. Everything is wrapped in riddles.

HIPPIE BOY   What, for instance?

HIPPIE GIRL   Was it Gaa-gaa or Gar-gar?

HIPPIE BOY   You're just plain stupid.

MAN FROM HELL   By the way, in reference to that stick—she says you look like it. Let's suppose for the moment you do look like the stick—the meaning is not what you think it is.

HIPPIE GIRL   Tomorrow people will be calling tomorrow today.

MAN FROM HELL   To begin with, your conceptual framework with respect to the stick is basically—

HIPPIE BOY   I see. Once a human hand grabs something there's no telling what it can do.

HIPPIE GIRL   I missed grabbing it. It's too awful to think that the day after tomorrow will always be tomorrow even hundreds of years from now.

(*WOMAN FROM HELL returns, walking quickly.*)

WOMAN FROM HELL   (*She stops at some distance from the others.*) Sir . . .
MAN FROM HELL   (*Goes up to WOMAN.*) Well, what happened?
WOMAN FROM HELL   We've got to hurry . . .
MAN FROM HELL   (*Turns toward HIPPIES.*) This crazy bunch—I offered them a dollar for the stick, but they refuse to part with it.
WOMAN FROM HELL   The child is coming.
MAN FROM HELL   What for?
WOMAN FROM HELL   Just as I got into the department store I heard them making an announcement about a lost child. The child was apparently raising quite a rumpus. He claimed he saw his father turn into a stick and fall off the roof. But nobody seemed to believe him.
MAN FROM HELL   Of course not.
WOMAN FROM HELL   Then the child gave the matron the slip and ran out of the store, looking for his father.

(*MAN and WOMAN FROM HELL look uneasily off to stage left.*)

STICK   (*Talking brokenly to himself.*) The child saw it. I know he did. I was leaning against the railing at the time, the one that runs between the air ducts and the staircase, on a lower level. I was looking down at the crowds below, with nothing particular on my mind. A whirlpool . . . Look—it's just like one big whirlpool. . . .

(*Actual noises of city traffic gradually swell in volume, sounding something like a monster howling into a tunnel. Suddenly HIPPIE BOY lets the stick drop in alarm.*)

HIPPIE GIRL   What happened?
STICK   (*Continuing his monologue.*) I stood there, feeling dizzy, as if the noises of the city were a waterfall roaring over me, clutching tightly to the railing, when my boy called me. He was pestering me for a dime, so he could look through the telescope for three minutes. . . . And that second my body sailed out into mid-air. . . . I had not the least intention of running away from the child or anything like that. . . . But I turned into a stick. . . . Why did it happen? Why should such a thing have happened to me?
HIPPIE GIRL   What's the matter, anyway?
HIPPIE BOY   (*Stares at the stick lying at his feet with a bewildered expression.*) It twitched, like a dying fish. . . .
HIPPIE GIRL   It couldn't have . . . You're imagining things.
WOMAN FROM HELL   (*Stands on tiptoes and stares off into the distance at stage left.*)

Look! Sir, look! Do you see that child? The little boy with the short neck, prowling around, looking with his big glasses over the ground?

MAN FROM HELL   He seems to be gradually coming closer.

STICK   (*To himself.*) I can hear the child's footsteps . . . bouncing like a little rubber ball, the sound threading its way through the rumblings of the earth shaking under the weight of a million people. . . .

HIPPIE GIRL   (*Steals a glance in the direction of the* MAN *and* WOMAN FROM HELL.) Somehow those guys give me the creeps. . . . Why don't you make some sort of deal with him?

(HIPPIE BOY, *who has kept his eyes glued on the stick at his feet, snaps out of his daze and stands up.* GIRL *also stands.*)

HIPPIE BOY   (*With irritation.*) I can't figure it out, but I don't like it. That stick looks too much like me.

HIPPIE GIRL   (*Her expression is consoling.*) It doesn't really look all that much like you. Just a little.

HIPPIE BOY   (*Calls to* MAN FROM HELL, *who has just that moment turned toward him, as if anticipating something.*) Five dollars. What do you say? (*He keeps his foot on the stick.*)

MAN FROM HELL   Five dollars?

STICK   (*To himself.*) He doesn't have to stand on me. . . . I'm soaked from lying in the gutter. . . . I'll be lucky if I don't catch a cold.

HIPPIE BOY   I'm not going to force you, if you don't want it.

WOMAN FROM HELL   (*Nervously glancing off to stage left.*) Sir, he's almost here.

(THE MAN WHO TURNED INTO A STICK *shows a subtle, complex reaction, a mixture of hope and rejection.*)

HIPPIE BOY   I'm selling it because I don't want to sell it. That's a contradiction of circumstances. Do you follow me?

HIPPIE GIRL   That's right. He's selling it because he doesn't want to. Can you understand that?

MAN FROM HELL   (*Annoyed.*) All right, I guess . . . (*He pulls some bills from his pocket and selects from them a five-dollar bill.*) Here you are. . . . But I'll tell you one thing, my friend, you may imagine you've struck a clever bargain, but one of these days you'll find out. It wasn't just a stick you sold, but yourself.

(But HIPPIE BOY, *without waiting for* MAN *to finish his words, snatches away the five-dollar bill and quickly exits to stage right.* HIPPIE GIRL *follows after him, smiling innocently. She waves her hand.*)

HIPPIE GIRL   It's the generation gap. (*She exits with these words.*)

(MAN *and* WOMAN FROM HELL, *leaping into action, rush to the gutter where the stick is lying. Just then the sun suddenly goes behind a cloud, and the street noises gradually fade. At the very end, for just a second, a burst of riveting is heard from a construction site somewhere off in the distance.)*

MAN FROM HELL   *(Gingerly picks up the dirty stick with his fingertips. With his other hand he takes the newspaper that can be seen protruding from his pocket, spreads it open, and uses it to wipe the stick.)* Well, that was a close one. . . .

WOMAN FROM HELL   Earth duty isn't easy, is it?

MAN FROM HELL   It was a good experience on your first day of on-the-job training.

WOMAN FROM HELL   I was on tenterhooks, I can tell you.

(THE MAN WHO TURNED INTO A STICK suddenly exhibits a strong reaction to something. MAN and WOMAN FROM HELL alertly respond to his reaction.)

WOMAN FROM HELL   There's the child!

(MAN FROM HELL, greatly alarmed, at once hides the stick behind his back. On a sudden thought, he pushes the stick under his jacket, and finally down into his trousers. He stands ramrod stiff for several seconds. Then, all at once, the excitement melts from the face of the MAN WHO TURNED INTO A STICK. MAN and WOMAN FROM HELL, relieved, also relax their postures.)

STICK   *(To himself.)* It doesn't matter. . . . There was nothing I could have done, anyway, was there?

MAN FROM HELL   *(Pulling out the stick.)* Wow! That was a close shave. . . .

WOMAN FROM HELL   But you know, I kind of feel sorry for him.

MAN FROM HELL   Sympathy has no place in our profession. Well, let's get cracking. *(Holds out the stick.)* That crazy interruption has certainly played havoc with our schedule.

WOMAN FROM HELL   *(Accepts the stick and holds it in both hands, as if to make a ceremonial offering.)* I didn't realize how light it was.

MAN FROM HELL   It couldn't be better for a first tryout. Now, make your report, in exactly the order you learned. . . .

WOMAN FROM HELL   Yes, sir. *(Examines the stick from every angle, with the earnestness of a young intern.)* The first thing I notice is that a distinction may be observed between the top and bottom of this stick. The top is fairly deeply encrusted with dirt and grease from human hands. Note, on the other hand, how rubbed and scraped the bottom is. . . . I interpret this as meaning that the stick has not always been lying in a ditch, without performing any useful function, but that during its lifetime it was employed by people for some particular purpose.

STICK   *(To himself. Angrily.)* That's obvious, isn't it? It's true of everybody.

WOMAN FROM HELL   But it seems to have suffered rather harsh treatment. The poor thing has scars all over it. . . .

MAN FROM HELL   *(Laughs.)* Excellent! But what do you mean by calling it a poor thing? I'm afraid you've been somewhat infected by human ideas.

WOMAN FROM HELL   Infected by human ideas?

MAN FROM HELL   We in hell have a different approach. To our way of thinking, this stick, which has put up with every kind of abuse, until its whole body is covered with scars, never running away and never being discarded, should be called a capable and faithful stick.

WOMAN FROM HELL   Still, it's only a stick. Even a monkey can make a stick do what he wants. A human being with the same qualities would be simple-minded.

MAN FROM HELL   *(Emphatically.)* That's precisely what I meant when I said it was capable and faithful. A stick can lead a blind man, and it can also train a dog. As a lever it can move heavy objects, and it can be used to thrash an enemy. In short, the stick is the root and source of all tools.

WOMAN FROM HELL   But with the same stick you can beat me and I can beat you back.

MAN FROM HELL   Isn't that what faithfulness means? A stick remains a stick, no matter how it is used. You might almost say that the etymology of the word faithful is a stick.

WOMAN FROM HELL   *(Unconvinced.)* But what you're saying is too—miserable.

MAN FROM HELL   All it boils down to is, a living stick has turned into a dead stick—right? Sentimentality is forbidden to Earth Duty personnel. Well, continue with your analysis. *(WOMAN remains silent.)* What's the matter now? I want the main points of your report!

WOMAN FROM HELL   *(Pulling herself together.)* Yes, sir. Next I will telephone headquarters and inform them of the exact time and place of the disappearance of the person in question, and verify the certification number. Then I decide the punishment and register the variety and the disposition.

MAN FROM HELL   And what decision have you made on the punishment? *(WOMAN does not reply.)* Surely there can be no doubt in your mind. A simple case like this . . .

WOMAN FROM HELL   You know, I rather enjoy wandering around the specimen room, but I just don't seem to recall any specimens of a stick. *(Shakes her head dubiously.)*

MAN FROM HELL   There aren't any, of course.

WOMAN FROM HELL   *(Relieved.)* So it *is* a special case, isn't it?

MAN FROM HELL   Now calm yourself, and just think . . . I realize this is your first taste of on-the-job training, but it's disturbing to hear anything quite so wide off the mark. . . . The fact that something isn't in the specimen room doesn't necessarily mean it's so rare. On the contrary . . .

WOMAN FROM HELL   *(Catching on at last.)* You mean, it's because sticks are so common!

MAN FROM HELL   Exactly. During the last twenty or thirty years the percentage of sticks has steadily gone up. Why, I understand that in extreme cases, 98.4 percent of all those who die in a given month turn into sticks.

WOMAN FROM HELL   Yes, I remember now. . . . Probably it'll be all right if I leave the stick as it was during its lifetime, without any special punishment.

MAN FROM HELL   Now you're on the right track!

WOMAN FROM HELL   The only thing I have to do is verify the certification number. It won't be necessary to register the punishment.

MAN FROM HELL   Do you remember what it says in our textbook? "They who came up for judgment, but were not judged, have turned into sticks and filled the earth. The Master has departed, and the earth has become a grave of rotten sticks. . . ." That's why the shortage of help in hell has never become especially acute.

WOMAN FROM HELL   *(Takes out a walkie-talkie.)* Shall I call headquarters?

MAN FROM HELL   *(Takes the walkie-talkie from her.)* I'll show you how it's done, just the first time. *(Switches it on.)* Hello, headquarters? This is MC training squad on earth duty.

VOICE FROM HELL   Roger. Headquarters here.

MAN FROM HELL   Request verification of a certification number. MC 621. . . . I repeat, MC 621. . . .

VOICE FROM HELL   MC 621. Roger.

MAN FROM HELL   The time was twenty-two minutes ten seconds before the hour . . . The place was Ward B, thirty-two stroke four on the grid. Stick fell from the roof of Terminal Department Store. . . .

VOICE FROM HELL   Roger. Go ahead.

MAN FROM HELL   No punishment. Registration unnecessary. Over.

VOICE FROM HELL   Roger. Registration unnecessary.

MAN FROM HELL   Request information on next assignment.

VOICE FROM HELL   Six minutes twenty-four seconds from now, in Ward B, thirty-two stroke eight on the grid. Over.

WOMAN FROM HELL   *(Opens her notebook and jots down a memo.)* That would make it somewhere behind the station . . .

MAN FROM HELL   Roger. Thirty-two stroke eight.

VOICE FROM HELL   Good luck on your mission. Over.

MAN FROM HELL   Roger. Thanks a lot. *(Suddenly changing his tone.)* I'm sorry to bother you, but if my wife comes over, would you mind telling her I forgot to leave the key to my locker?

VOICE FROM HELL   *(With a click of the tongue.)* You're hopeless. Well, this is the last time. Over.

MAN FROM HELL   *(Laughs.)* Roger. So long. *(Turns off walkie-talkie.)* That, in general, is how to do it.

WOMAN FROM HELL   Thank you. I think I understand now.

MAN FROM HELL   What's the matter? You look kind of down in the mouth. *(Returns walkie-talkie to WOMAN.)*

WOMAN FROM HELL   *(Barely manages a smile.)* It's nothing, really . . .

MAN FROM HELL   Well, shall we say good-bye to our stick somewhere around here?

WOMAN FROM HELL   You mean you're going to throw it away, just like that?

MAN FROM HELL   Of course. That's the regulation. *(Looks around, discovers a hole in the gutter, and stands the stick in it.)* If I leave it standing this way it'll attract attention and somebody is sure to pick it up before long. *(Takes a step back and examines it again.)* It's a handy size and, as sticks go, it's a pretty good specimen. It could be used for the handle of a placard. . . .

(WOMAN suddenly takes hold of the stick and pulls it from the hole.)

MAN FROM HELL   What do you think you're doing?

WOMAN FROM HELL   It's too cruel!

MAN FROM HELL   Cruel? *(He is too dumbfounded to continue.)*

WOMAN FROM HELL   We should give it to the child. Don't you think that's the least we can do? As long as we're going to get rid of it, anyway . . .

MAN FROM HELL   Don't talk nonsense. A stick is nothing more than a stick, no matter who has it.

WOMAN FROM HELL   But it's something special to that child.

MAN FROM HELL   Why?

WOMAN FROM HELL   At least it ought to serve as a kind of mirror. He can examine himself and make sure he won't become a stick like his father.

MAN FROM HELL   *(Bursts out laughing.)* Examine himself! Why should anyone who's satisfied with himself do that?

WOMAN FROM HELL   Was this stick satisfied with himself?

MAN FROM HELL   Don't you see, it was precisely because he was so satisfied that he turned into a stick?

WOMAN FROM HELL   *(Stares at stick. A short pause.)* Just supposing this stick could hear what we have been saying. . . .

STICK   *(To himself. Weakly.)* Of course I can hear. Every last word.

MAN FROM HELL   I have no specific information myself, since it's quite outside my own specialty, but scholars in the field have advanced the theory that they can in fact hear what we are saying.

WOMAN FROM HELL   How do you suppose he feels to hear us talk this way?

MAN FROM HELL   Exactly as a stick would feel, naturally. Assuming, of course, that sticks have feelings. . . .

WOMAN FROM HELL   Satisfied?

MAN FROM HELL   *(With emphasis.)* There's no room for arguments. A stick is a stick. That simple fact takes precedence over problems of logic. Come, now, put the stick back where it was. Our next assignment is waiting for us.

(WOMAN FROM HELL, with a compassionate expression, gently returns STICK to the hole in the gutter. THE MAN WHO TURNED INTO A STICK up until this point has been

registering various shades of reaction to the conversation of MAN *and* WOMAN, *but from now on his emotions are petrified into an immobile state between fury and despair.)*

STICK   *(To himself.)* Satisfied . . .

WOMAN FROM HELL   But why must we go through the motions of whipping a dead man this way?

MAN FROM HELL   We are not particularly concerned with the dead. Our job is to record their lives accurately. *(Lowering his voice.)* To tell the truth, it is extremely dubious whether or not we in fact exist.

WOMAN FROM HELL   What do you mean by that?

MAN FROM HELL   There is a theory that we are no more than the dreams that people have when they are on the point of death.

WOMAN FROM HELL   If those are dreams, they are horrible nightmares.

MAN FROM HELL   That's right.

WOMAN FROM HELL   Then there's no likelihood that they're satisfied. To have nightmares even though you're satisfied—that's a terrible contradiction, isn't it?

MAN FROM HELL   Perhaps it might be described as the moment of doubt that follows satisfaction. In any case, what's done is done. . . . *(In tones meant to cheer* WOMAN.*)* We'll have to hurry. We have exactly three minutes. If we're late there'll be all hell to pay later on. . . . *(Starts walking, leading the way.)* Don't worry. You'll get used to it, before you know it. I was the same way myself. Sometimes you get confused by the false fronts people put on. But once you realize that a stick was a stick, even while it was alive . . .

WOMAN FROM HELL   *(Still turns to look back at* STICK, *but somewhat more cheerful now.)* Is the next person going to be a stick, too?

MAN FROM HELL   Mmm. It would be nice if we got something more unusual this time.

WOMAN FROM HELL   What do you suppose those kids who tried to keep us from getting the stick will turn into?

MAN FROM HELL   Those hippies?

WOMAN FROM HELL   They didn't seem much like sticks, did they?

MAN FROM HELL   If they don't turn into sticks maybe they'll become rubber hoses.

*(*MAN *and* WOMAN FROM HELL *exit to stage right.)*

STICK   *(To himself.)* Satisfied? Me? Stupid fools. Would a satisfied man run away from his own child and jump off a roof?

(In another section of the stage MAN *and* WOMAN FROM HELL *reappear as silhouettes.)*

MAN FROM HELL   The sky is the color of a swamp, cloudy with disinfectant.
      On the cold, wet ground
      Another man has changed into a stick.

WOMAN FROM HELL   He has been verified but not registered.

He is shut up inside the shape of a stick.

He is not unlucky, so he must be happy.

STICK   *(To himself.)* I've never once felt satisfied. But I wonder what it would be better to turn into, rather than a stick. The one thing somebody in the world is sure to pick up is a stick.

MAN FROM HELL   He has been verified but not registered.

The man's been shut up inside the shape of a stick.

He can't so much as budge anymore, and that's a problem.

WOMAN FROM HELL   Supposing he begins to itch somewhere—

What'll he do? How will he fare?

MAN FROM HELL   I'm afraid a stick would probably lack

The talent needed to scratch his own back.

WOMAN FROM HELL   But anyway, you mustn't mind,

You're not the only one of your kind.

MAN FROM HELL   *(Steps forward and points his finger around the audience.)* Look —there's a whole forest of sticks around you. All those innocent people, each one determined to turn into a stick slightly different from everybody else, but nobody once thinking of turning into anything besides a stick. . . . All those sticks. You may never be judged, but at least you don't have to worry about being punished. *(Abruptly changes his tone and leans farther out toward the audience.)* You know, I wouldn't want you to think I'm saying these things just to annoy you. Surely, you don't suppose I would be capable of such rudeness. . . . Heaven forbid. . . . *(Forces a smile.)* It's just the simple truth, the truth as I see it. . . .

WOMAN FROM HELL   *(Goes up to* THE MAN WHO TURNED INTO A STICK *and speaks in pleading, rather jerky phrases.)* Yes, that's right. You're not alone. You've lots of friends . . . men who turned into sticks.

Curtain.

EDWARD ALBEE

Finding the Sun

Finding the Sun *was written (and copyrighted) in 1983, to satisfy a commission from the University of Northern Colorado. It was first performed there that year, directed by the author (me). It was subsequently performed at the University of California-Irvine (same director) and at the University of Houston (ibid).*

I was making plans for a New York production of the play in 1987 when Tina Howe's Coastal Disturbances *(written or at least copyrighted in 1987) opened off-Broadway. By bizarre coincidence, Miss Howe's play shares a beach setting with* Finding the Sun, *a not dissimilar group of characters and—inevitably—some of the same general preoccupations.*

Gut instinct told me that while the two plays were independent conceptions Miss Howe's had occupied the field—or the beach, to be more exact—and, should mine be then presented some cloudy journalistic minds would deduce that the earlier play (mine) had been substantially influenced by the later one (Miss Howe's).

Life is tough enough these days without any of that nonsense, so I have postponed New York production of Finding the Sun *for a while, at least until the sea air clears.*

I publish it here with pleasure, however, for I am quite proud of it; further, with both texts now available the interested play reader will discover that Miss Howe's play and mine are, in the end, quite different matters.

CHARACTERS

ABIGAIL   *Twenty-three; mousy brown/blond hair, pinched features; not tall; thinnish; not pretty, but not plain.*
BENJAMIN   *Thirty; blond, willowy-handsome; medium height.*
CORDELIA   *Twenty-eight; attractive in a cold way; dark or raven hair; tallish; good figure.*

DANIEL   *Thirty-seven; dark; tall; good-looking.*
EDMEE   *Forty-five, or so; smallish; a together, stylish matron.*
FERGUS   *Sixteen; blond, handsome healthy kid; swimmer's body.*
GERTRUDE   *Sixty; small, gray hair, deeply tanned, thinnish, elegant outdoors woman.*
HENDEN   *Seventy; big, sprawly man; white hair; looks like a retired diplomat.*

SETTING

A beach in bright sun. Eight beach chairs—candy striped or of various colors—spread about, leaving a free area downstage center. A narrow boardwalk upstage with railing.

LIGHT

Bright sun; August, a New England day. Toward the end of the play, a lighting shift; until then, still sun.

COSTUMES

Whatever beach outfits seem most appropriate to each of the characters and the actors playing them. Towels, bags, and the usual beach stuff as well.

The scenes of the play flow into one another without pause, although a tiny "breath" between them—more a new upbeat than anything else—would be nice.

SCENE 1

Rise from black; hold for two seconds. ABIGAIL *and* BENJAMIN *enter; bathing suits, beach stuff.*

ABIGAIL   *(Stretching.)* Ah! Find the sun!
BENJAMIN   *(Nods; pleased approval.)* Find the sun! *(They begin setting up.* CORDELIA *and* DANIEL *enter; bathing suits, beach stuff. They do not see* ABIGAIL *or* BENJAMIN, *nor do they see these two.)*
CORDELIA   Find the sun, you said. *(Smiles, stretches.)*
DANIEL   *(Abstracted smile.)* Did I? "Find the sun?" Well? So? *(They begin setting up.)*

*(*EDMEE *and* FERGUS *enter; same action as above.)*

EDMEE   Finding the sun should always be your first action, Fergus.
FERGUS   *(Feigned puzzlement.)* Not finding a chair with your back to the wall?

EDMEE *(Happy with it.)* Outdoors . . . the sun. *(Looks about.)* Goodness, look at all the people!

FERGUS *(Mock concern.)* Gosh, Mother, will we never be alone!?

EDMEE *(Throaty chuckle.)* Oh, hush! *(They begin setting up.* GERTRUDE *and* HENDEN *enter; same procedures as others.)*

GERTRUDE Oh, Henden! We've found the sun!

HENDEN We've found what? Oh! The sun! *(Sighs.)* You're right: we've found the sun. *(Pause.)*

ALL *(Settling in.)* Ahhhhhhhhh!

SCENE 2

DANIEL *rises, moves down right;* BENJAMIN *sees him, moves to him;* ABIGAIL *has her eyes closed, as does* CORDELIA.

BENJAMIN Is that you!? It is! It's you!

DANIEL I *thought* it was.

BENJAMIN *(Sotto voce.)* What are you *doing* here?

DANIEL . . . though I remember saying to Cordelia—in the car—do you think that's me?

BENJAMIN I mean, I was sitting there and there you were!

DANIEL *(Quick, mirthless smile.)* Seems like old times.

BENJAMIN *(Blurting on.)* Are you here alone? I mean, are you with Cordelia?

DANIEL No: I'm here with a couple of tricks named Jeremy and Phillip I picked up in . . .

BENJAMIN *(Shy smile.)* Oh, come on, Daniel.

DANIEL *(Mimicking.)* Oh, come on, Benjie-wengie!

BENJAMIN *(After a tiny pause.)* So many people here.

DANIEL *(A hand on* BENJAMIN'S *shoulder.)* I miss you.

BENJAMIN *(Shrugs; smiles.)* I love you.

DANIEL *(Nods; removes his hand.)* I love you, *and* I *miss* you.

BENJAMIN *(Giggles.)* I wonder what Abigail will say.

DANIEL Abigail will say . . .

ABIGAIL *(Seeing* BENJAMIN *gone.)* Benjamin!? Where are you!?

DANIEL *That* is what Abigail will say.

SCENE 3

BENJAMIN *and* DANIEL *move back to their places as* EDMEE *and* FERGUS *move down left.*

EDMEE *(As they come.)* Having found the sun—the good sun, the clear, healing heat—having *found* the sun, *then* you put your back to the wall.

FERGUS   *(Imitation of eager student.)* Aha!

EDMEE   The sun is the source of all life: the aminos and all the rest couldn't have done their work with*out* it, you see.

FERGUS   A*ha*!!

EDMEE   Look at your civilizations! Africa!—if you call that a civilization—four? five million years ago, in the hottest of the muck, down there, closest to boiling, the *cradle* of it.

FERGUS   *We* live in New Hampshire.

EDMEE   *(Ignoring? Not having heard?)* And the Mediterranean basin? Greece? Rome? The Parthenon is *not* in Bergin, Norway, my dear. *(Peering.)* I wonder who those people are? Nor does the Appian Way run through Tierra del Fuego.

FERGUS   Nor New Hampshire.

EDMEE   *(Not angry.)* Be civil.

FERGUS   Oh, Mother!

EDMEE   Everything proceeds comparatively, it is true—there is no light without dark, rest without action, and so forth and so on—and a life in the tropics produces a . . . lassitude which leads to an absence of philosophical inquiry, but nor have the Lapps or the Eskimos given us much beyond some charming little carvings—doo-dads, really; no, time in the sun *and* time away: that's the ticket! Everything comparative; everything in season.

FERGUS   Okay.

EDMEE   Why do you dwell on New Hampshire?

FERGUS   We dwell *in* New Hampshire.

EDMEE   You dwell in your own skin. Do you dwell on that?

FERGUS   A life of acne?

EDMEE   This, too, shall pass. *(Sees GERTRUDE rising, coming toward them.)* Is that lady coming to talk to us?

FERGUS   *(Rising.)* To *you*.

EDMEE   *(Sincerely bothered.)* Oh, Fergus! Maybe you'll like her.

FERGUS   *(Moving away.)* Let me know. *(Nods to the approaching GERTRUDE.)* Ma'am.

GERTRUDE   *(Nods.)* Young man. *(To EDMEE.)* Is that yours?

EDMEE   Yes; yes, he is.

GERTRUDE   What is he to you, or am I being nosy?

EDMEE   I beg your pardon? Yes, you probably are.

GERTRUDE   I *always* am. I can't help myself.

EDMEE   *(To get it straight.)* What *is* he to me?

GERTRUDE   Henden says to me, you are the nosiest woman in Christendom, and this in spite of that little gouge above the left nostril, that little gouge where they took the cancer off. Would you believe that I've had four skin cancers removed—all from the sun!—and I still won't stay out of it? Don't go in the sun, Gertrude: You know your propensities.

EDMEE   What *is* he to me? Who is Henden?

GERTRUDE   Or, more to the point, who is *Sylvia?* Henden is my husband, my third; the other two I lost—not through carelessness, but time: I marry older men. Henden is the youngest I have married—in distance from *my* age, I mean to say. Henden is only seventy. What is he to *you;* well, what *is* he to you?—the young boy: Is he your son, your nephew, your ward, your . . . lover?

EDMEE   *(A smile.)* You *should* stay out of the sun.

SCENE 4

EDMEE and GERTRUDE *stay where they are,* GERTRUDE *having sat in* FERGUS's *chair.* ABIGAIL *and* CORDELIA *come down right.*

ABIGAIL   He's such a child; he behaves like . . . such a child!

CORDELIA   *(Eyes closed; absorbing the sun.)* Hmmmmmmmmmmmm.

ABIGAIL   He comes back—when I call him—he comes back, plops himself down in in his chair, and starts blathering on about . . . all the *sail*boats, there *are* no clouds, *are* there!, *where* will we go for dinner . . .

CORDELIA   Hmmmmmmmmmmmm.

ABIGAIL   Not a word! Not one word about running into Daniel . . .

CORDELIA   Hmmmmmmmmmmmm.

ABIGAIL   . . . which meant, naturally, that *you* were here, which information was of interest to *me.* . . .

CORDELIA   Hmmmmmmmmmmmm.

ABIGAIL   Not a word!

CORDELIA   *(Stretching; drawled.)* Well, what would you expect?

ABIGAIL   You would think. . . .

CORDELIA   What do you *really expect*?

ABIGAIL   *(Too brightly innocent.)* I beg your pardon?

CORDELIA   I know them both as well as you know Benjamin—better, probably. Recall I knew them *before* you, and they were *lovers* then. . . .

ABIGAIL   *(Too bright.)* Well, they're not lovers now!

CORDELIA   Because they married us, you mean? Remember the leopard.

ABIGAIL   I beg your pardon?

CORDELIA   Do you not *like* me—or are you like that, I mean . . . naturally?

ABIGAIL   *(Abrupt laugh.)* Whatever do you mean?

CORDELIA   Your tone, baby.

ABIGAIL   *(Haughty.)* I have no idea what you mean.

CORDELIA   Okay. Just remember the leopard.

ABIGAIL   I'm supposed to understand what that means?

CORDELIA *Are* you retarded? Leopard! Leopard: spots. A leopard doesn't change its spots.

ABIGAIL *(Snooty.)* I can't speak for you and Daniel, but Benjamin is home with me every night.

CORDELIA *(Dry.)* How *nice* for him.

ABIGAIL *(Pleased; proud.)* I never let him out of my sight.

CORDELIA They must love you in the men's rooms.

ABIGAIL *(Riding over that.)* You and Daniel may have what is referred to as an "arrangement"—by which is usually implied a moral quagmire—and, to be sure, Daniel may not have . . . adjusted to the world, but Benjamin has seen the follies of his ways, his *former* ways, and . . .

CORDELIA Oh, bullshit!

(Abigail fumes, moves away.)

SCENE 5

HENDEN puttering, FERGUS coming upon him.

FERGUS Hello.

HENDEN Hello.

FERGUS How old are you?

HENDEN What an odd question! I'm seventy.

FERGUS That's what I thought: you're the oldest person here—in the vicinity.

HENDEN I often am.

FERGUS And I'm the youngest. I'm sixteen.

HENDEN Don't be silly.

FERGUS A lot of people say that.

HENDEN There is no such age.

FERGUS Yes, that's what they say. Why are you here?

HENDEN Why am I *anywhere* !? Luck, I guess; or that's what they call it.

FERGUS Who do *you* belong with?

HENDEN *Again* such an odd question! I am *with* my wife, my Gertrude, the one was talking with the lady you arrived with, I believe; that is who I am *with.* As to whether it is Gertrude I *belong* with . . . well, that would take some mulling.

FERGUS Mull away.

HENDEN By which I mean—thank you . . .

FERGUS You're welcome.

HENDEN . . . by which I mean that I am very fond of Gertrude, as wives go —though I've had only two—but whether it is she I *belong* with . . . well, that takes some pondering.

FERGUS What happened to the first one?

HENDEN *(Shrugs.)* She died; after forty-six years of marriage with me she took it into her head to die.

FERGUS Literally?

HENDEN Yes; a brain tumor.

FERGUS Forty-six years is a very long time. *(Afterthought.)* Sorry.

HENDEN Not in retrospect: only during. And I married Gertrude—though I like her very much—I suppose to *be married,* as much as anything: a continuity.

FERGUS Hmmmm. I suspect I'm a little young for a sense of continuity. There's a theory afoot, though, that we young and we old have things in common should bind us together against those in the middle.

HENDEN Heavens! And what *are* those things?

FERGUS I haven't the faintest. Doesn't anybody swim around here?

HENDEN The beginning and the end! An alliance! Well, maybe; might work as well as most. Who do *you* belong with?

FERGUS Well, I'm here with my mother—the lady your Gertrude was talking with—and since I *am* only sixteen and I legally belong *to* her, I daresay I belong *with* her. The day will come, though . . . well, the day will come. Who *are* all these people!?

HENDEN Well, we've accounted for the two of *us,* for Gertrude and your mother; that leaves the other four.

FERGUS . . . of those nearby.

HENDEN Well, surely I'm not to account for the entire coast. The couple over *there (Indicates CORDELIA and DANIEL.)* are Daniel and Cordelia; Daniel is my son—by my first marriage, of course; his wife, Cordelia, is daughter to Gertrude—by one of *her* earliers.

FERGUS My goodness! You know everything! Who are the others? Do you know?

HENDEN The other couple? Abigail and Benjamin.

FERGUS Heaven, you do! Whose daughter and son are *they* !?

HENDEN No one's—well, someone's, naturally, but none of ours.

FERGUS Strangers!

HENDEN Not exactly. Well, perhaps, though they *are* married—to each other! No, the cord binding them to us is, uh . . . . a complex twine.

FERGUS We've heard of that in New Hampshire, I believe.

HENDEN Abigail did not exist before she married Benjamin, but Benjamin . . . well, he and Daniel, before Daniel married Cordelia, he and Daniel were . . . well, how shall I put it . . . ?

FERGUS I don't know!

HENDEN . . . were . . . involved.

FERGUS I beg your pardon?

HENDEN Benjamin and Daniel were "involved."

FERGUS *(Trying to sort it out.)* With one another.

HENDEN Yes.

FERGUS   In a business sense?

HENDEN   How old are you?

FERGUS   Sixteen—but I'm from New Hampshire.

HENDEN   *(Understanding.)* Of course. No; in a . . . personal sense.

FERGUS   Yes?

HENDEN   Benjamin and Daniel were lovers.

FERGUS   *(Long pause.)* With each other?

HENDEN   Yes.

FERGUS   My goodness. *(Considers.)* I believe we've heard of this in New Hampshire. They loved one another?

HENDEN   Certainly.

FERGUS   And gave each other physical pleasure.

HENDEN   As I understand it.

FERGUS   Why are they no longer lovers? Pleasure into pain?

HENDEN   *(Slightly standoffish.)* You'll have to ask them that, young man.

FERGUS   Well, I shall! *(Afterthought.)* I've not been lovers with *anyone*.

HENDEN   Well, you're sixteen.

FERGUS   Romeo was fifteen, they say, but he was Italian.

HENDEN   When you're older.

FERGUS   My hand and I will say good-bye?

HENDEN   Well, will probably develop a more casual relationship.

FERGUS   Oh? Pity.

HENDEN   If you *do* speak to Daniel or Benjamin of their . . . liaison . . .

FERGUS   Yes?

HENDEN   *Do* be cautious.

FERGUS   Oh?

HENDEN   Well, you *are* very young and very . . .

FERGUS   *(Contemptuous.)* Pretty?

HENDEN   *(Gently.)* I was going to say "handsome."

FERGUS   *(Melting.)* Thank you!

HENDEN   But you are . . . young.

FERGUS   That's very true, sir, but don't forget that I'm . . .

HENDEN   *(A hand up.)* I know! You're from New Hampshire.

SCENE 6

HENDEN moves upstage; FERGUS crosses to EDMEE and GERTRUDE.

FERGUS   *(Moving by fast; to EDMEE.)* Have I got things to tell *you*!

GERTRUDE   *(After FERGUS goes.)* Who *is* that?

EDMEE   *(Pause.)* What?

SCENE 7

CORDELIA and DANIEL together.

CORDELIA   I was *so terrible* to Abigail!

DANIEL   *(Reading? Sunning?)* That's nice.

CORDELIA   Do you know what I think it is?

DANIEL   *(Ibid.)* Hmmmm?

CORDELIA   Do you know why I think I'm so terrible to Abigail?

DANIEL   *(Becoming involved.)* Well, let's see: Because she's here? because you don't like her? because she's turning Benjamin into a shell—sucking him dry, you should excuse the expression? because she's a self-obsessed, tedious bore of a woman?

CORDELIA   *(Considers it.) Those* are interesting.

DANIEL   *I* thought so.

CORDELIA   But no; I think I'm terrible to her because there she is with Benjamin and I loathe Benjamin and she *doesn't* control him in *spite* of your lies. . . .

DANIEL   You don't loathe Benjamin.

CORDELIA   The two of you are as close now as you ever were. . . .

DANIEL   What did you do—you and Miss Abbey—marry us as part of a sisterhood solidarity reform movement? And you're falling out among yourselves? You never told me any of this; you should choose your co-conspirators better.

CORDELIA   *(Not to be put off.)* The two of you are as close now as you ever were —which I will probably divorce you for one day. . . .

DANIEL   *(Harsh laugh.)* You wouldn't dare! Your family'd kill you over the publicity: famous former deb, mainline family heirloom—heiress, sorry!— married to fag, files for annulment, names hubby's former hubby as . . .

CORDELIA   The two of you are as close now as you ever were—which I will probably divorce you for one day—and I'm probably taking *that* out on poor Abigail.

DANIEL   Plus you don't like her.

CORDELIA   Why doesn't she make Benjamin take her to live in Peru, or somewhere?

DANIEL   Because, pussycat, then *we'd* have to move to Peru, too, and you *know* how you are with languages. . . .

CORDELIA   Why doesn't she . . . *(Stops.)*

DANIEL   Yes; why doesn't she!

CORDELIA   *(Giggles.)* I accused her of following Benjamin into men's rooms!

DANIEL   *(Giggles.)* You're not *nice*!

CORDELIA   *(Hand out to him; after a beat.)* What *are* we to do?

DANIEL   (*Takes her hand.*) Give it some time.

CORDELIA   It's been three years.

DANIEL   Give it some *time.*

CORDELIA   *Do* you see him secretly?

DANIEL   (*Pause.*) No.

CORDELIA   Do you see *anyone?*

DANIEL   (*Gently.*) Don't probe.

CORDELIA   I love you, you see.

DANIEL   And I love you. (*Pause.*) I've got a very roomy heart. (*Pause; then she begins to laugh; he, too.*)

SCENE 8

CORDELIA and DANIEL *return to their books, or whatever.*

EDMEE   (*Turning to* GERTRUDE, *both still in their beach chairs. Very casual, informal, informational.*) Well, now, to answer your question—your pry, to be more accurate, about Fergus. What he *is* to me is too much. He is my son—he *is:* real mother, real son. And since my husband died—his father—he has been the "man" in my life, so to speak. It's four years now since his father dove off the rocks—showing off, as usual—hit some jutting something underwater wasn't supposed to be there, broke his neck, drowned. (*Shrugs.*) These things happen. I haven't thought of remarrying; perhaps I will, later. I've raised Fergus; he's a good boy. There is, I think—there may be —an attachment transcends the usual, the socially *admitted* usual, that is, by which I mean: given the provocation, Fergus would bed me in a moment. A mother knows these things, even admits knowing them. . . . Sometimes. He doesn't know it, or, if he *does* sense it, is polite or shrewd enough to pretend he does *not.* It is more usual for a son to lust after his mother than a mother for her son, so there is little surprise in the information that my interest in bedding Fergus is minimal. I mean, God! I have birthed him, I have held him, rocked him, comforted him, bathed him, scolded him, dressed him, guided him . . . why on earth would I want to fuck him!? (GERTRUDE *drops whatever she is holding.*)

SCENE 9

EDMEE *and* GERTRUDE *stay where they are; focus on* ABIGAIL *and* BENJAMIN.

ABIGAIL   Cordelia doesn't like me!

BENJAMIN   (*Taking the sun; eyes shut.*) Ohhhhhhh . . .

ABIGAIL   You know perfectly well she doesn't!

BENJAMIN   Well . . .

ABIGAIL   Why don't you tell Daniel to *make* her like me!?

BENJAMIN   Oh, I don't think I . . .

ABIGAIL   Certainly it would make everything easier. I mean, if we're going to live in this proximity, with all the strings and all . . .

BENJAMIN   *(Eyes open.)* Oh, God!

ABIGAIL   . . . having her like me, or at least making a good stab at *pretending* to like me, would be a help. *You* don't help.

BENJAMIN   Oh, God!

ABIGAIL   Nor does "Oh, God" help.

BENJAMIN   Oh, God!

ABIGAIL   You and your sidelong glances, your letters you won't let me read, your odd phone calls, your feeble excuses for getting home late, your . . .

BENJAMIN   *(Rises.)* Oh, God! *(Leaves her area.)*

ABIGAIL   *(Genuine surprise.)* Where are you going?

SCENE 10

HENDEN comes down front.

HENDEN   *(To the audience.)* I get frightened sometimes. Don't you? About dying, I mean? What is the age we become aware of it? That we *know* it's going to happen, even if we don't accept it? It differs with the person, I'm told. The earlier on the better—well, no: I don't mean that young man over there; I don't mean *he* should be burdened with it, not at *his* age, but somewhere in the thirties—forties at the . . . most tardy—it will come on healthy little feet; much later and you're whistling in the . . . light, I suppose. When you reach *my* age you . . . well, you get a little frightened sometimes. Because you're alone. Oh? Really? Wife, if you're lucky? Children? *Grand*children? Yes, certainly, if you're lucky, but you're still . . . alone. *(Taps his head.)* Nobody gets in there with you. Greek peasants have a room they keep their coffin in, ready for the day. *(Shrugs.)* No difference there from keeping it in the back of your head, the back of your mind. Being seventy gives me a few more years, if we're to believe the actuaries —three, four. That's a help, though it isn't a guarantee, and I feel pretty well. Oh . . . I have the usual: one hip not so hot; arthritis in the neck; something uncomfortable down in my lower gut, fairly steadily; a little . . . loss of sensation in my left arm now and again, and I fainted once, last week, tieing my shoes. *(Shrugs.)* The usual. I go to my doctor once every year or so. I ask him; he says, "You're getting old!" Well, I *am*. Still. Nothing to be done about it, but I *do* get . . . just a little . . . frightened now and again. Being alive is . . . so splendid. *(Smiles.)* Ah, well. *(Moves back to his beach chair.)*

SCENE 11

BENJAMIN moves to where DANIEL and CORDELIA are sunning.

BENJAMIN   I can't stand it! Can I move in with you two?
DANIEL   *May* I.
BENJAMIN   *May* I? *May* I move in with you two?
CORDELIA   No.
DANIEL   No.
BENJAMIN   *(A whine.)* Whhhhhyyyy?
CORDELIA   Just because.
BENJAMIN   Aw, come on, guys!
CORDELIA   You made your bed, now sleep in it.
DANIEL   Besides, we *have* someone moving in.
CORDELIA   *(After the briefest catching-on pause.)* Yes; yes, we have.
BENJAMIN   *(Mistrustful.)* Who?
CORDELIA   Well . . . *(Looks to DANIEL.)*
DANIEL   We wrote in to one of those magazines for swingers. . . .
CORDELIA   . . . *Swingers Mag*, it's called. . . .
DANIEL   . . . that's right: *Swingers Mag*, and we saw an ad in there for a bi stud wanted to relocate . . .
CORDELIA   . . . six foot seven, two hundred and thirty-five pounds, wrestler's body . . .
DANIEL   . . . goes both ways, into three-scenes or solos, fully reciprocal, light S and M, no femmes or fatties.
CORDELIA   It seemed like a perfect addition to the house: cheaper than a new playroom, or . . .
DANIEL   He gets here tomorrow; we paid his way, of course.
BENJAMIN   *(After a brief, thinking pause.)* We could do four-sies!
DANIEL   Rub-a-dub-dub, three men and a tub?
CORDELIA   Don't be witty.
BENJAMIN   I don't believe you guys! You wouldn't dare!
DANIEL   *(Haughty.)* And why not, pray?
CORDELIA   Yes, and why not?
BENJAMIN   Because Henden and Gertrude wouldn't put up with it. *(A silence.)*
CORDELIA   He has a point there.
DANIEL   Mmmmmmmmmm; afraid he has.
BENJAMIN   They'd let *me* move in with you, though; they *like me*.
CORDELIA   Tell you what: you go live with *them*.
DANIEL   Right, and we'll send you a subscription to the magazine.
BENJAMIN   *(Moving off.)* You guys are no help.
DANIEL   *(To CORDELIA.)* No help?
CORDELIA   *(To DANIEL.)* Really?

SCENE 12

ABIGAIL and FERGUS. ABIGAIL by herself, talking to herself.

ABIGAIL   *(Practicing.)* Benjamin, this can't go on! Benjamin?, you and I have to have a talk. Benjamin, grow up! *(Faster.)* Who do you think I am, Benjamin? Benjamin, just who do you think you are? I'm leaving you, Benjamin; No, I'll never give you a divorce, you . . . . you . . . ; you're making our lives a shambles, Benjamin; we could have been so happy together. *(Pause.)* Nuts! *(To FERGUS, who is ambling by, listening, really.)* You're not married, *are* you.

FERGUS   Hello!

ABIGAIL   You're not, are you; of *course* you're not; you're . . . you're an adolescent.

FERGUS   I was going to say, my, aren't you pretty! But that word killed it.

ABIGAIL   What word?

FERGUS   Adolescent. If there's one thing an adolescent doesn't want to be called it's an adolescent—even those of us *know* we're adolescents, accept it, we don't want the word used: we don't like the sound of it. Ad-o-les-cent; it's an ugly word.

ABIGAIL   I'm *sorry*!

FERGUS   *(Comforting.)* I *know* you are; I'm *sure* of it.

ABIGAIL   What would you *like* to be called?

FERGUS   Fergus.

ABIGAIL   What a . . . . pretty name. I meant generically.

FERGUS   Young man?

ABIGAIL   *(Considers it.)* Young man. That has a nice sound. *You* are a . . . young man.

FERGUS   My, aren't you pretty! There; you see? One good turn of phrase deserves another.

ABIGAIL   I don't feel particularly pretty right now.

FERGUS   How come?

ABIGAIL   *(Looks about to see if anyone is listening.)* I'm . . . . married.

FERGUS   *(Cheerful.)* I know: to the gentleman over there used to be . . . involved with that other gentleman, who is . . . where? Ah! Over there, with who! —his wife!

ABIGAIL   My God, you know everything, don't you. Do *all* of you know everything?

FERGUS   Who is . . . all?

ABIGAIL   All is too much, most likely.

FERGUS   Have . . . have you and the *other* lady been . . . involved?

ABIGAIL   I beg your pardon!

FERGUS   Have you and the other lady . . .

ABIGAIL   Certainly not!

FERGUS   You make it seem so . . . definite.

ABIGAIL   Well, it *is*!

FERGUS   But why?

ABIGAIL   Cordelia and I are not . . . that *way*.

FERGUS   I see!

ABIGAIL   *(Transparent.)* Nor are Benjamin and Daniel.

FERGUS   I see; yes, I see.

ABIGAIL   Far too much!

FERGUS   Ma'am?

ABIGAIL   Who have you been talking to? To Gertrude? To Henden? Gertrude is Cordelia's mother, you know.

FERGUS   Really?

ABIGAIL   Yes, and Henden is Daniel's father.

FERGUS   My goodness!

ABIGAIL   And Gertrude and Henden are married now.

FERGUS   Gracious!

ABIGAIL   And who's the woman you're with?

FERGUS   Edmee? She's my mother.

ABIGAIL   There's too much family on this beach. I'm the outsider.

FERGUS   *(Considers it.)* Well, that must give you a perspective.

ABIGAIL   It gives me nothing! It gives me the pip!

FERGUS   Pip is given a lot, isn't it.

ABIGAIL   Stay away from Daniel; he's dangerous. *(Afterthought.)* For that matter, stay away from Benjamin, too.

FERGUS   But . . . why?

ABIGAIL   You're very young.

FERGUS   Where is *your* family?

ABIGAIL   They died in a collision.

FERGUS   Oh, I'm so sorry! My mother says the roads are a terrible place.

ABIGAIL   *(Inaudible.)*

FERGUS   Pardon?

ABIGAIL   Not a car! Not roads!

FERGUS   An airplane!

ABIGAIL   No.

FERGUS   *(Puzzles.)* A train, then!

ABIGAIL   No.

FERGUS   *(Awe.)* Boats?

ABIGAIL   *(Inaudible again.)*

FERGUS   Pardon?

ABIGAIL   Balloons.

FERGUS   *(Pause.)* Pardon?

ABIGAIL *(Too loud.)* Balloons! *(Softer.)* Balloons.

FERGUS My goodness.

ABIGAIL *(Still sad and perplexed over it.)* They were in central Texas—anti-quing—and they came upon a town—I don't know, *some*where—and the shops weren't any good, I guess, and they called me, very excited, and said they were going ballooning, that there was an outfit took people up for an hour ride—hot air balloons, you know?

FERGUS I *guess*.

ABIGAIL Be careful, I said. What can happen, they said; what are we going to run into in a hot-air balloon? You never know, I said. Tush, they said, and off they went!

FERGUS And?

ABIGAIL Texas is a big state.

FERGUS Yes.

ABIGAIL Flat.

FERGUS Yes.

ABIGAIL You can see for . . . miles.

FERGUS I don't doubt it. *(Pauses.)* They hit something?

(Abigail shakes her head.)

(Awe.) Something hit *them*?

(Abigail nods.)

My gracious!

ABIGAIL A boy genius! Are you bright? Very bright?

FERGUS I believe so.

ABIGAIL Damn your eyes! A boy genius, building his own rocket—out in all that flatness—building his very own rocket. You'd think he would *see* something in all that flatness, wouldn't you? Sets the fucking thing off—on its way to Mars, I suppose—and it goes right through the bag of the balloon, and the bag deflates, and down like a shot it goes with my appalled mother and father, back to the flat, flat earth, fast, inexplicably . . . and *Splat*!

FERGUS Oh, dear; oh, dear.

ABIGAIL *(Controlled.)* I went down—grief and disbelief; the boy genius had such thick glasses—prisms; enormous hands on such a slight boy; enormous hands and these . . . . prisms. He said he was sorry. *(A sudden explosion of tears.)* And I have to be married to a fairy! *(She runs off.)*

FERGUS *(To her retreating form.)* Yes . . . well . . . *(To himself.)* My goodness.

SCENE 13

FERGUS *(Comes forward; speaks to the audience.)* If you think it's easy being my age, well . . . you have another think coming, as they say. A New England boyhood isn't *all* peaches and cream, maple syrup and russet autumns. I know it *sounds* pretty good—wealthy mother and all, private school, WASP education. ASP, to be precise. *Are* there any black Anglo-Saxons? It all sounds pretty nice, and it *is*. I'm not complaining; it's nice . . . but it isn't always easy. Being corrupted, for example; now, that's important to a young fellow. Whether he takes advantage of it or not. The corrupting influences really should *be* there; all you should have to do is turn a corner and there you are, all laid out for you, so to speak—fornication, drugs, stealing, whatever; it should *be* there. But if you live in Grovers Corners, or wherever, pop. Fifteen hundred and thirty-three, it isn't too easy to come by. You have to . . . search it out. Oh, there's the grocer's youngish widow with her blinds always drawn and the come-hither look, and the mildly retarded girl in the ninth grade has some habits would make a pro blush, *and* the florist with the dyed hair and the funny walk and the mustache for those inclined that way, or at least want to try it. These things are to be *had* in a small town, but not without the peril of observation and revelation. What's missing, I suppose, is . . . anonymity. And there are, after all, some things we'd rather do in private—at least until we're practiced—do them well. The lack of anonymity: Well, in a small New England town, if your family's been there eight hundred years, or whatever, and you're "gentry," *and* you're bright, *and* your mother practically sends out announcements *saying* you're bright and destined for "great things," well, then . . . it's not the same, the nice same, as being able to get it all together behind the barn, so to speak, and then coming out all rehearsed and "ready." "I hear you're getting all A's, Fergus; good for you!" "Your mother says you've decided on Harvard, young fella; well, I hope they've decided on you, ha, ha, ha!" Lordy! Even when I was tiny: "Took his first step, did he!?" "Potty trained is he? Good for him!" Royalty must have it worse, or the children of the very famous. I don't even know what I want to *do* with my life—if I want to do *anything*. If I want to *live* it, even. Do you know what suicide rate has been making the biggest jumps? Kids. Kids my age. I'm not planning to . . . kill myself or anything; don't misunderstand me; I'm happy, ralatively happy, as I understand the term. It's just that . . . well, we kids have all sorts of options. You grown-ups aren't the only ones. Think about *that*. Thank you. *(Bows, moves off.)*

SCENE 14

CORDELIA *(Comes forward; alone. To the audience.)* I would imagine you've been wondering why I married Daniel, considering everything—Benjamin, I mean. I would imagine you've been wondering; heaven knows, *I* have, now and again. My mother—Gertrude, over there—said to me—how many times?—"Why are you *marrying* that person? I warn you, young woman, you're in for a lot of woe." "Oh, Mother," I'd say, knowing full well what she meant. "I warn you: they don't change; you'll find out!" "Oh, Mother!" Back and forth; Ping-Pong. "I had a cousin married one." "Oh, Mother!" "Scandals; driven from one town to another." "Oh, God.!" "Mark my words."

GERTRUDE   *(From where she sits.)* Mark my words!

CORDELIA   *(Out.)* I married him because I love him. Doesn't that seem simple enough? We met; I found him handsome—in his way; sexy—in his way; plus bright plus tender and considerate plus patient plus he cheered me up a lot. I don't mean to suggest that I was greatly in *need* of cheering up; I'm not a manic depressive, or anything. I've had some laughs, some kicks; I've been around—married once before, to a jock, on his way to nowhere, as it turned out. I've been around; I know the scene, the score, whatever. But Daniel was special—*is.* I knew he was gay—right off; some women sense these things; others never get the hang of it. I knew he was gay; I knew he and Benjamin were lovers; and I knew I wanted to marry him. *(Shrugs.)* Well, I'm a grown-up.

GERTRUDE   *(From where she sits.)* Mark my words!

CORDELIA   Oh, Mother! *(Out.)* I knew what the problems would be—*are.* I knew the chances. I *know* Daniel sleeps around; well, I'm pretty sure I know it, and I suspect it's with guys. I *hope* it is: I mean, I *like* being his only woman. I mean, if I turn him straight . . . then he'll start in with girls. This way's better. As long as he's careful.

GERTRUDE   *(From where she sits.)* You're in for a lot of woe! Mark my words!

CORDELIA   *(Laughs.)* Oh, Mother! *(Out.)* Every time we're done making love and we have our cigarettes, Daniel'll turn to me and smile and take my hand and say, "Isn't it nice that we're such good friends." Well, I suppose that isn't *exactly* your usual marriage, isn't precisely *(Imitation of jock.)* "Hey, babe, that was good for me; was it good for you, too?" Not exactly that, but *I* don't mind. I think I prefer it. I think . . . I think perhaps Daniel is more interested in our friendship than our marriage. I mean, he seems . . . happy enough being married to me, certainly no less happy than when he was—married, I suppose, to Benjamin. And if I lose anything, it won't be the way your usual marriage ends—the friendship goes first, and *then* the marriage falls apart. What I mean is, I think I have a friend, and if one day he thinks that our being married is as silly as it *is* . . . well, then I'll lose the marriage, but I think I'll still have a very good friend. *(Shrugs.)* There are worse things in the world to have.

SCENE 15

BENJAMIN, DANIEL, FERGUS. Benjamin and Daniel are standing, separate, stretching. Fergus comes up.

FERGUS Let's play catch.

DANIEL I *beg* your pardon!

FERGUS Let's play *catch*. Here; I have a ball. *(Throws and catches a beach ball.)*

BENJAMIN Hey! Why not?

DANIEL Why *not*? You? Catch something? Herpes is about the only thing you can catch.

FERGUS Who's that?

BENJAMIN *(To DANIEL.)* As opposed to *you*— who comes down with *every*thing: herpes, hepatitis . . .

FERGUS *(Helping.)* Harelip, halitosis. This is fun!

DANIEL *(To BENJAMIN.)* Never mind now; not in front of a child.

BENJAMIN *(Mocking imitation of DANIEL.)* And all I did was go to confession: the wafer must have been contaminated.

DANIEL I said: never mind!

FERGUS May we play?

BENJAMIN Okay! Okay!

DANIEL *(To BENJAMIN.)* Be sure to put your glasses on: you *do* want to catch the ball.

FERGUS *(To DANIEL.)* I'll throw it to you and you throw it to him and he'll throw it to me.

DANIEL *(Mildly sarcastic.)* Won't this be fun!

BENJAMIN It *will* be!

FERGUS Okay; here we go. *(Throws at DANIEL.)* Catch!

DANIEL *(Catching.)* Ow! Jesus!

BENJAMIN *(Parody of baseball player.)* C'mon, guy; heave her over here!

DANIEL *(Disbelief.)* *Heave* her over *here*?

BENJAMIN Come on; have fun!

DANIEL Who ever heard of anybody saying anything like that? *(Underhand toss.)* Here!

BENJAMIN *(Sibilant comment.)* Ooooooh! My gracious! Such force!

FERGUS You guys are *fun*! *(Catches BENJAMIN's fair throw.)* Hey! That's good!

DANIEL *(Jock imitation.)* What's ya name, kid? *(BENJAMIN giggles; FERGUS throws sort of hard to DANIEL.)* Ow!

FERGUS Fergus. Was that too hard?

BENJAMIN *(Jock imitation.)* For a guy like him, kid? You kidding? *(DANIEL throws very hard.)* Ow!

FERGUS You guys *are* fun!

(Natural, casual throwing now; unobtrusive.)

DANIEL   What kind of name is Fergus?

FERGUS   Scots, I believe.

BENJAMIN   I'm Benjamin.

FERGUS   Hi!

DANIEL   And I'm Lucille.

FERGUS   *(No change in friendly tone.)* Hi!

DANIEL   *(Awe at FERGUS's aplomb.)* Wow! No, actually I'm Daniel.

FERGUS   I know. You two are presently married to those ladies over there, although . . . since the two of *you* have been . . . uh . . . intimately involved? . . . there is a question floating around this particular area of the beach as to whether these marriages were made in heaven. I have no opinion on the matter.

BENJAMIN   *(To DANIEL; false sotto voce.)* The "in-laws" have been talking again.

FERGUS   Are you all good friends, you four? You and your wives?

DANIEL   It varies; it varies.

FERGUS   I . . . wondered.

(Pause.)

BENJAMIN   Oh?

DANIEL   Oh?

FERGUS   I was having a little chat with . . . .well, I guess *your* wife, Benjamin; uh . . . Abigail is *yours*?

DANIEL   Oh, yes; Abigail is his and he is Abigail's.

BENJAMIN   Enough!

DANIEL   Desist? Hold? *Basta?*

FERGUS   You guys are really *fun?*

BENJAMIN   What *about* Abigail?

FERGUS   She's . . . *(Tosses ball above his head; catches it.)* . . . well, she's. . . . unhappy?

DANIEL   No kidding!

BENJAMIN   *(Gently.)* I *know.*

FERGUS   I'd take care if I were you.

DANIEL   *(To no one.)* What*ever* can he mean?

BENJAMIN   *(Ignoring DANIEL's tone.)* Whatever *can* you mean?

FERGUS   I'd be careful of her; that's all. *(Quick subject switch.)* Which one of you guys married first?

BENJAMIN   *I* did.

FERGUS   *(Some surprise.)* Really?

DANIEL   I was planning to when this one decided to do something precipitous. "I'll show *you!*"—*that* sort of thing.

BENJAMIN   Untrue! Untrue!

DANIEL   . . . when he realized that I was serious—that Cordelia and I were going to be married. When *that* sank in, he sort of ran out in the street and hooked on to the first gullible girl he could find.

BENJAMIN   Unclean! Unclean!

DANIEL   *(Naggy tone.)* "I'll show you! I'll show you!"

FERGUS   *(To BENJAMIN.)* I'd worry about her a little if I were you.

DANIEL   With any luck she might just . . . walk out of our lives, you mean?

FERGUS   Something like that.

BENJAMIN   *(More or less to himself.)* That *is* something to think about.

FERGUS   *(Starting to leave, still tossing to himself; a kind of "Okay you guys" tone.)* Okay. Okay.

BENJAMIN   Where are you going?

DANIEL   Where are you taking the ball?

FERGUS   You guys don't need the ball; you've got your own game going.

(As FERGUS leaves, a combination of regret and something private and not too nice.)

BENJAMIN and DANIEL   *Aaaaawwwwwwwwwwww* !

SCENE 16

FERGUS moves behind sleeping EDMEE, awakes GERTRUDE and HENDEN.

FERGUS   Have I got things to tell *her* ! *(Moves past, out of their view.)*

EDMEE   *(After a pause; suddenly.)* Who *was* that?

GERTRUDE   Your son . . . .or so you say.

HENDEN   What a nice boy!

EDMEE   My son, or so I say?

HENDEN   Bright, too!

GERTRUDE   I meant no offense.

EDMEE   *(To HENDEN.)* Very bright. *Too* bright?—perhaps.

HENDEN   Oh, come now!

GERTRUDE   *(Singsong.)* No offense at all.

EDMEE   *(Generally.)* There's danger in consciousness, in too much awareness.

HENDEN   We go through it only once, my dear, or so more tell me than don't —better alert than . . . numb, or not comprehending.

GERTRUDE   *(To HENDEN; an old argument.)* You're *certain* of that—that we go *through* it only once.

HENDEN   *(To EDMEE; chuckling.)* Gertrude is of the opinion that a move away from the big bang theory to the notion that the universe has always existed, in whatever form . . .

EDMEE   *(Lazy.)* I don't believe either one.

GERTRUDE   *(Mildly startled.)* Oh? Really?

HENDEN   . . . has—what?—permits the concept of . . . cyclism, I suppose it could be called. . . .

GERTRUDE *(Fingertips to temples.)* Stop it, Henden.

HENDEN What? Oh.

EDMEE *(FERGUS is listening, unbeknownst etc.) (After a tiny pause.)* It's that Fergus is . . . *so* bright I worry for him. Oh, a mother with a dumb one has her own problems—can he find his way *home?* Won't he be embarrassed to be in the third grade at fourteen? Whatever will he *do* with his *life?* Those *are* problems, and I don't envy a woman who *has* them. But Fergus is ready for college and he's just sixteen. We're going to Europe for a year, to Rome, to Athens, to Dendura, to Istanbul, to let him see it all, begin to relate time to place, fact to theory.

GERTRUDE Isn't that nice.

EDMEE You *still* don't think he's my son, *do* you!

HENDEN *(Admonishingly.)* Why, Gertrude!

GERTRUDE *(Too innocent by far.)* I didn't say a word! I haven't said a word for . . . minutes.

EDMEE *(Hard.)* He's not my type, lady! I *told* you that!

GERTRUDE I didn't say a word!

HENDEN *(To placate.)* What a nice boy he is!

(FERGUS turns, pauses, exits just before the end of EDMEE'S next speech.)

EDMEE You know what bothers me most about him, about Fergus—being so special, being so . . . bright, so beautiful and bright? That he'll turn out . . . less than he promises. I don't want to be around when his hair recedes or his body starts its way to fat; I don't want to see the expression in his eyes when he looks at his life and sees it's not going to be quite what it might have been. Tarnish! That's what I don't want to see . . . tarnish.

GERTRUDE *(Cold; to comfort and destroy.)* Well, maybe he'll die young.

EDMEE *(Wistful.)* Maybe.

GERTRUDE Or maybe you won't be around.

EDMEE *(Ibid.)* Maybe.

HENDEN Or, or maybe none of that will happen; maybe he'll . . . *be* . . . everything he might.

EDMEE *(Ibid.)* Maybe.

GERTRUDE *(Caught up in it.)* My goodness! Wouldn't that be something!

EDMEE Yes. Wouldn't it.

SCENE 17

DANIEL and HENDEN, together, HENDEN arriving.

DANIEL Hi, Dad.

HENDEN Hello, son. *(Pause.)*

DANIEL You should keep your head covered.

HENDEN Oh?

DANIEL   Burn.

HENDEN   *Aha* ! *(Pause.)*

DANIEL   Cordelia's over there.

HENDEN   I see; I see she is. *(Pause.)* Gertrude's over there.

DANIEL   Yes; I saw.

HENDEN   *Aha. (Pause.)* How is it going?

DANIEL   What?

HENDEN   It! You, Cordelia, Benjamin, what's-her-name, and all that?

DANIEL   "All that"?

HENDEN   *All* right!! *(Pause.)*

DANIEL   *(Shrugs.)* Not bad.

HENDEN   Good?

DANIEL   *(Harder.)* Not *bad. (Pause.)*

HENDEN   Do you want to talk about it?

DANIEL   You *know* better. *(Pause.)*

HENDEN   I am your father. . . .

DANIEL   *(Explodes.)* Christ! Great, suffering Jesus, do we have to go *on* with this?

HENDEN   *(Hurriedly; mollifying.)* No, no, no, no, now . . .

DANIEL   *(Continuing.) Must* we go on with it? There is no hope! There is . . . going *on*; there is . . . getting through it!

HENDEN   *(Softly.)* All *right.*

DANIEL   *(Continuing.)* There is my *nature* and *Benjamin's* nature, and we are doing what we *can* about it, though I think we're *idiots.* We have fallen between stools, Father; we were better perched on our specialness . . . our disgrace, perhaps. Perhaps not. I don't know—the perch, I mean; not the specialness. I don't know.

HENDEN   I know.

DANIEL   *(Ironic.)* But we are *trying.* Jesus, we're trying!! Benjamin is heart-broken and confused; Abigail—what's-her-name to you—Abigail is close to a collapse of *some* sort; Cordelia is turning tough and brittle at the same time and is beginning to drink just a little too much, though maybe that's *in* her; and *I* . . . *I* can't keep my hands from shaking, *or* shouting at you, dearest man, whom I love above all creatures on this earth. *(Pause.)*

HENDEN   Well.

DANIEL   Yes; well.

(Pause. They embrace; DANIEL *seems to sob;* HENDEN *tentatively hugs him, pats him on the back; they separate, go in opposite directions.)*

SCENE 18

Abigail and Edmee. EDMEE *seated next to a sleeping* GERTRUDE; ABIGAIL *approaches.*

ABIGAIL   May we talk?

EDMEE   I suppose we *could;* I don't really *want* to.

ABIGAIL   *(About to leave; shy.)* I'm sorry.

EDMEE   *(Removing her dark glasses.)* No! *I* am! I'm being rude.

ABIGAIL   Well, a little.

EDMEE   *(None too pleasant.)* I like candor in a girl; next to bitten fingernails, I like candor best.

ABIGAIL   *(Looks to be sure.)* I don't bite my nails.

EDMEE   *(Expansive.)* I don't know what it is about the sea—the beach and the sea: they bring out in me a tristesse I feel no other place. It's not a lugubrious sadness or a grief; no, I described it as I intended.

ABIGAIL   A tristesse?

EDMEE   Yes. I have felt fear in the plains, panic in a church, claustrophobia in the mountains, tearing loss at Christmas with all my lovies around me, implausible sadness on a lovely day, but only here, where the earth and water meet, do I feel this . . . tristesse.

ABIGAIL   *(Shy.)* I see.

EDMEE   We have so much to be thankful for, being alive. *Being alive*!! for one! I've never taken much comfort from "what lies beyond," as they put it. I *doubt* it; I doubt the entire proposition, but even if it does . . . occur, the reports are none too encouraging—hellfire for the wicked and a kind of disembodied cloud sit for the rest? What comfort there! What! No dry martinis? No poetry? No . . . no whatever makes it all worth the effort? Perhaps I could accept an eternity of tristesse, sitting here with a magazine, my mind, and some memories. *(Turns to Gertrude.)* Are you asleep, my dear?

ABIGAIL   *(Wistful; lost.)* The water is . . . lovely.

EDMEE   It's the line where it meets; that's the magic! One element into another, *(Snaps her fingers.)* Just like that! I would love to be able to walk into it —the water—walk down the grade, enter, submerge, walk about, reverse and march right back to my starting point, all erect, all . . . gliding. I would love to be able to breathe both water and air.

ABIGAIL   We can . . . in a way.

EDMEE   *(Scoffing.)* Oh, masks and tanks and things!

ABIGAIL   No; not really. *(Begins to move away.)* Thank you; I enjoyed our talk.

EDMEE   *(To* GERTRUDE's *sleeping form.)* Gertrude? *(To the retreating* ABIGAIL.) Oh! Oh, so did I! I hope I was some . . . *(To herself.)* Well, I hope I was some help.

SCENE 19

ABIGAIL and BENJAMIN; ABIGAIL returning.

BENJAMIN *(Casual.)* Where have you been?

ABIGAIL Where have *you* been?

BENJAMIN Nowhere.

ABIGAIL Me, too.

BENJAMIN Who were you *talking* to?

ABIGAIL *(Indicates.)* That lady.

BENJAMIN Her son is called Fergus; he's . . .

ABIGAIL *(She can't help it.)* . . . a little young for you, don't you think?

BENJAMIN Oh, come *on*! Jesus, can't we even *talk*?

ABIGAIL I'm sorry! *(Softer.)* I *am*; I'm sorry.

BENJAMIN *(Taking her hand.)* How can your *hand* be so *cold*? It's hot out here; how can your hand be so cold?

ABIGAIL *(Withdrawing her hand.)* I'm always cold; I get colder all the time. If you ever held me anymore you'd know.

BENJAMIN *I* hold you.

ABIGAIL Sure!

BENJAMIN *(Anger rising.)* I *hold* you!

ABIGAIL *(A burst of self-propelled anger.)* Yes! *You* hold me! But I hardly know it's *you*, and who are you holding *really*, and why do you want to hurt me in bed, and why are you walking away, and . . . *(BENJAMIN goes.)* . . . and why am I so cold all the time? . . . And *(Raises her hand to the sun; slow, quiet intensity now.)* Why don't you just . . . go out? Burn out? Flare up, sizzle, crackle for a moment, and then . . . just . . . fade . . . bring the ice down on all of us? *I'm* ready; *I'm* cold enough. Go out! I dare you! *(Pause; pain.)* Benjamin! Benjamin!

SCENE 20

EDMEE, GERTRUDE, and HENDEN in their chairs. During this scene ABIGAIL looks off right, gathers her towel and exits, unnoticed by the others.

GERTRUDE *(Waking up; an announcement of subject.)* Am I asleep, my dear.

EDMEE *(Pleased.)* Aha!

GERTRUDE Where is Henden?

HENDEN *(Eyes closed; hat over his face.)* Asleep, my dear.

GERTRUDE Aha. *(To EDMEE.)* I doze; I slip off into sleepettes. Is it tiny strokes, I wonder—the sleepettes? I will be at a dinner party, attentive to my neighbor, and all at once I am aware I have slipped off for a moment. Or

I am reading and it will happen. Tiny strokes? Probably not: Simply that I don't sleep much at night; I cat-prowl. Henden and I still have the same room—the same bed!—and he lies there, a wheezing lump, unconscious.

HENDEN Ah, now . . .

EDMEE *(Literally.)* Tee-hee!

GERTRUDE . . . and I am awake, almost all the night, dozing fitfully until I am awakened by a creak, a chirp, the memory of a dream.

EDMEE *I've* done it.

GERTRUDE I do it as clockwork. I am as familiar with dawn as any farmer, the night as any watchman. I waxed the library table once at three in the A.M., down on my knees in my nightdress doing away at the big claw feet.

HENDEN Looked grand when you were done. *(EDMEE laughs.)*

GERTRUDE And I write long letters in the night—wise, instructive, useful—to our leaders, but I seldom mail them: might change the world; wouldn't do —let bad enough alone.

EDMEE I sleep without moving.

GERTRUDE *(Too bright.)* Who *tells* you?

EDMEE *(Smooth.)* Oh . . . whoever is with me. I have a . . . variety of gentlemen, and one lady, share my night times. I outsleep them; they tell me.

GERTRUDE Why did you wonder if I was awake?

EDMEE *(Mildly corrective.)* I wondered if you were *asleep.*

GERTRUDE Oh. *(Afterthought.)* They are not the same?

HENDEN *(Behind his hat.)* Not exactly.

EDMEE That . . . that girl was talking to me, the young one. I wanted to help.

GERTRUDE Abigail?

EDMEE Is that her name?

GERTRUDE Abigail. She is married to Benjamin. We know all about that.

EDMEE Oh?

GERTRUDE *(Hurrying through it.)* It's so tedious. Abigail is married by mischance to Benjamin, who by mischance was lovers with Daniel, who by mischance is now married to Cordelia. Cordelia is my daughter, and Daniel is Henden's son.

EDMEE Goodness!

GERTRUDE *(Waving it all away.)* They travel in a pack; they are not happy! They worry and bother us.

EDMEE Gracious!

GERTRUDE . . . though we have given up trying to solve it all: too much fate; too much irony.

HENDEN *I* try . . . now and again.

GERTRUDE To any end?

HENDEN You know better.

EDMEE Perhaps it will all resolve itself. I wonder what she wanted.

GERTRUDE (*Shrugs.*) To whine; to explain; to be comforted; to save her soul. Who knows? Perhaps it will all resolve itself? Yes; well, perhaps; and—then again—perhaps not. And so . . . Henden sleeps and I prowl.

EDMEE Jack Sprat!

GERTRUDE (*Laughs.*) Yes; in a way.

HENDEN Jack who?

GERTRUDE Go back to sleep.

(*GERTRUDE and EDMEE laugh, sadly gaily.*)

SCENE 21

BENJAMIN, CORDELIA, DANIEL, EDMEE and GERTRUDE. DANIEL and CORDELIA are stage right, EDMEE and GERTRUDE in their chairs stage left, HENDEN is in his chair, back to front.

BENJAMIN (*Comes down to CORDELIA and DANIEL.*) Hold me, you guys.

DANIEL Another bout?

BENJAMIN (*Still standing.*) Just hold me.

DANIEL Come in between.

CORDELIA (*Shrugs; smiles.*) Why not?

(*The sun goes behind a cloud; the sky becomes gray.*)

GERTRUDE (*To EDMEE.*) Are we losing the sun?

EDMEE Hm?

GERTRUDE I said . . .

EDMEE Why, I think we are.

BENJAMIN There are days when I just don't . . .

DANIEL Forget it.

BENJAMIN Why is the sun going away?

DANIEL (*Sad laugh.*) It's one of those *days.*

BENJAMIN (*A child.*) What if it were to . . . go out?

CORDELIA That'd solve a few things.

DANIEL It sure would. (*Sighs.*)

GERTRUDE (*About the sun.*) Awwwwwwww.

EDMEE So much for skin cancer.

GERTRUDE (*Cheerful.*) Oh, it'll come back.

EDMEE You and I should talk about facelift sometime.

BENJAMIN Let well enough alone, I tell her.

CORDELIA *Well* enough?

DANIEL Indeed.

BENJAMIN What?

DANIEL Let bad enough alone, you mean?

BENJAMIN Something like that.

GERTRUDE   (*To* EDMEE.) Whatever for? Are you planning one?

EDMEE   One likes to think ahead.

GERTRUDE   *I* have the skin of a turtle. *I* don't bother.

BENJAMIN   She says I hurt her in bed.

CORDELIA   (*Gleeful interest.*) Oh? Really?

DANIEL   (*Chuckles.*) Down, girl!

EDMEE   If you're as vain as I am, then you look around the next corner.

GERTRUDE   (*A bit chiding, a bit taunting.*) What would your Fergie say?

EDMEE   (*Laughs.*) Well, then your dreams might come *true*. (*Offhand.*) Where *is* he, I wonder?

BENJAMIN   I think one day it'll have to be just . . . the three of us.

CORDELIA   Only if you'll promise to hurt me.

DANIEL   He'll find a way—one way or another.

BENJAMIN   I'm gentle. How about it, guys? The three of us?

CORDELIA   The *two* of you, you mean.

DANIEL   Oh, come on, baby!

CORDELIA   I'll bow *out*; I *will*.

GERTRUDE   (*To* EDMEE.) Do you think I *should* have it done?

EDMEE   Couldn't hurt.

GERTRUDE   I wonder what Henden would say?

EDMEE   Ask him.

GERTRUDE   (*Looks.*) He's asleep. He probably wouldn't notice.

BENJAMIN   The musketeers.

CORDELIA   (*Looking.*) There's a crowd down there at the water.

DANIEL   A whale, probably; a shark.

CORDELIA   (*Puzzled frown.*) No; no, I don't think so.

DANIEL   Well, why don't you go *see*?

CORDELIA   (*Rising, moving off.*) Yes. Yes, I think I will. (*Exits.*)

DANIEL   (*Imitation of a witch.*) Now we're alone, baby!

BENJAMIN   (*Sincere.*) Oh, Daniel; hold me. (DANIEL *does, gently.*)

EDMEE   There would appear to be two theories about facelift—at least! One is, wait until you're nicely lined and sagged and wattled, and *then* do it. The *other* is, do it often and surreptitiously—never look a day older than when you've begun it.

GERTRUDE   Our skin ages, no matter what you do.

EDMEE   Oh, you have to stay out of the sun.

GERTRUDE   Stay out of the sun? Are you mad?

EDMEE   (*Chuckles; then:*) There are *people* down there.

GERTRUDE   (*Not interested.*) Oh? (*Intense.*) *Why* doesn't the sun come back?

BENJAMIN   Do we have to go on this way? Can't we go back to how we were?

DANIEL   I don't think so.

(CORDELIA *returns with* ABIGAIL's *towel.*)

BENJAMIN   *(Puzzled.)* That's Abigail's towel.

CORDELIA   No beached whale; no shark.

BENJAMIN   That's Abigail's!

DANIEL   *(Eyes narrowing.)* What's wrong?

CORDELIA   *(Looking back toward the water.)* Abigail tried to drown herself. They stopped her. They have her over a barrel—literally; they're pumping the water out of her. She'll live. *(Tosses the towel to* BENJAMIN.) Here; this belongs to you.

BENJAMIN   *(Awe; not moving.)* She tried to drown herself? Why?

DANIEL   *(He and* CORDELIA *chuckle sadly.)* Oh, God.

GERTRUDE   Henden?

BENJAMIN   *(Generally.) Hold* me?

EDMEE   Let him *sleep.*

GERTRUDE   *(Senses something.)* Henden! *(Goes to his chair.)* Henden?

EDMEE   Let him . . . *(She, too, realizes.)* Is he dead?

GERTRUDE   *(Long pause.)* Yes; yes, he is.

EDMEE   Poor him; poor *you.*

GERTRUDE   Poor Henden; poor, dear man.

EDMEE   *(Quiet panic.)* Fergus!

BENJAMIN   *(Not loving.)* I'll have to go to her.

CORDELIA   Let them wring her out. What would you say to her?

BENJAMIN   *(Pause.)* Nothing?

GERTRUDE   *(To* DANIEL, *from where she is.)* Daniel?

DANIEL   *(Pause; soft.)* Yes, Gertrude?

GERTRUDE   You'd better come here.

EDMEE   Fergus?

DANIEL   Is it my father?

GERTRUDE   You know. Yes.

EDMEE   Fergus?

DANIEL   I'll come in a moment.

CORDELIA   Oh, Daniel, poor Daniel.

EDMEE   Fergus?

BENJAMIN   Hold me?

DANIEL   *(Gently.)* Oh, God.

GERTRUDE   Oh, Henden.

EDMEE   Fergus!

BENJAMIN   *Hold me! Someone!*

CORDELIA   Anyone? Here. *(Holds him.)*

EDMEE   Fergus?

GERTRUDE   Oh, my poor Henden.

DANIEL   Oh, God.

EDMEE   *(A frightened child.)* Fergus?

GERTRUDE   He'll come back, my dear; they do. Look! The sun's returning. What glory! What . . . wonder!

(Indeed, the sun is returning.)

BENJAMIN   Daniel?
EDMEE   Fergus?
GERTRUDE   Oh, my Henden.
DANIEL   Oh, God.
EDMEE   Fergus? *(Pause.)* Fergus?

(Pause; slow fade.)

END.

LYNNE ALVAREZ

On Sundays

CHARACTERS

SYLVIA   *A young dancer whom we see during one day of her life.*
JULES   *A dapper man whom we see throughout his life beginning in his late twenties and ending when he is seventy-eight.*
A BEAST

SCENE 1

It is noon on a Sunday in a large, modern city. Traffic is heard, and people's voices as they pass.

Downstage right is a large box with transparent sides. It is open at the top. SYLVIA *is in her bedroom; perhaps there is a pastel-colored makeup table and a mirror, a chair, some fluttery, transparent curtains. She is going through her morning ablutions.*

At her foot is the flipping tail of A BEAST. *It lies still and then twitches as if to brush a fly away. She doesn't notice it.*

JULES enters stage right. He is in his late twenties at this time. He has neatly combed, short, dark hair under his derby hat. He has a thin, neat mustache. He is wearing a summer suit and swings a cane. A newspaper is folded under his arm. He is dapper and charming, with a tinge of sadness. He whistles softly to himself and seems quite happy.

He walks past the box as if it were a window. He catches sight of himself in one of the smooth sides and stops to adjust his hat, his tie, his mustache. He smiles, twirls his cane and continues.

As he passes the side of the box, he catches a glimpse of SYLVIA *and stops abruptly.*

JULES   Ooh la la!

(He is delighted. His actions are exaggerated, mimelike. He looks around cautiously to see if anyone is watching. He backs up and tries to see the entire figure. To do this,

he cranes his neck in all kinds of positions; he stoops, he stands on tiptoe. Finally, he gets down on the floor.)

Impossible!

(He gets up, dusts himself off, and using the smooth side, adjusts his mustache. He smiles at himself and tips his hat to himself.)

Ahh. C'est la vie! *(He tips his hat to* SYLVIA *as he passes the door.)* And a good day to you . . . *(He looks around and adds softly:)* My lovely.

(He exits and immediately reappears. It is later in the afternoon and he looks wilted. His jacket is unbuttoned, his hat slanted over his forehead. He walks slower. There is something defeated in his posture. His newspaper has obviously been opened and refolded, but not carefully.

He walks very slowly across the stage, looking at his feet. As he approaches the door side of the box, he lifts his head. He makes an effort to appear self-composed. He buttons his coat, straightens his posture. He adjusts his hat and walks very purposefully to the box, tips his hat, and starts to move past. He catches himself. He stops and pensively and hopefully addresses SYLVIA.)

Roberta? . . . *(Pause.)* . . . Emily? . . . Blanche? . . . *(His tone becomes more pleading.)* Cynthia? . . . Diane? . . . Joyce? . . . Lillian? Rebecca? . . . Christine? . . . Aurora? . . . Daphne? *(He waits for a response, sighs deeply, and starts to proceed. He stops suddenly, snaps his fingers.)* Ah-ha! *(He returns to the door.)* Sylvia? . . . Sylvia, is that you?

(He almost collapses and rests his head on his arm, pressing against the box.)

SCENE 2

It is noon the following Sunday. SYLVIA *is now preparing breakfast, the* BEAST's *tail is longer.* SYLVIA *is careful to step over it whenever she crosses to set or clear the table. She is preoccupied.*

JULES enters, dressed as he always is, but he is carrying a bouquet of flowers. He approaches the box.

JULES   I'm sorry. I couldn't come before. I want to apologize.

(He looks around self-consciously. He moves closer so he won't be overheard. He faces the audience and speaks over his shoulder, trying to appear nonchalant to passersby.)

I brought you flowers. See?

(He tries to find a place to offer them to SYLVIA. *He holds them to the door, but they are not taken. He puts them on the ground and waits to see if she will reach out. Finally, he throws them over the top into the box.* SYLVIA *finds them and puts them on her morning table.)*

I realize I took advantage of you last Sunday. You probably aren't Sylvia ... You look like Sylvia ... but then perhaps you're not. *(Clears his throat.)* In any event I want to tell you that I am sorry I took advantage of your ... unusual position ... and poured my troubles out like that. I had no right. I'm sorry. *(He waits.)* Of course, I expect that you will hold what I told you in the highest regard and not disclose it to anyone. I hope I can trust you in this respect. *(He waits.)* You seem discreet. You appear to have that quality. *(He waits for a moment.)* In fact, Sylvia ... May I call you Sylvia? You seem to possess more than discretion, much more. *(He becomes more and more passionate in his speech.)* You have an aura of calm. Self-possession, I'd say. Yes. But beyond that ... *(He looks around insidiously.)* May I take the liberty ... Yes, I will take the liberty of saying you project mystery and ... and ...

(He turns and kneels fervently before the door, his hands clasped together near his heart. The BEAST's *tail coils around* SYLVIA's *ankle. She kicks it impatiently.)*

Romance! Yes. Romance.

(He tries to embrace the box. Then he jumps to his feet and adjusts his clothing and his mustache.)

I feel foolish. Thank you for your patience. *(He is about to leave.)* I hope you will let me see you again.

(He takes out a date book from his pocket and flips through the pages, nodding and muttering. After some consideration, he adds:)

Let me see. Let me see ... Ahhhh. Yes. I could come see you on Sundays.

(He tips his hat and exits.)

SCENE 3

JULES comes out with a paper bag with a handle, a Sunday newspaper with the magazine and comic sections, a portable radio, a folding chair, and a tiny, round table.

He is wearing a flower in his lapel and comes out humming.

He puts the table down near the box and opens the chair. He pulls a handkerchief from his breast pocket and flamboyantly opens it and uses it as a tablecloth. Next he takes a paper cup from the bag and a plate. He puts the paper cup in the center of the table and puts the flower from his lapel in it.

JULES Good morning, my love. I've brought brunch and the *News*. The flower is perfectly formed. *Magnifique!*

(As he speaks and gets comfortable, eats and reads the paper, SYLVIA *will be getting dressed to go out. The* BEAST, *which lies at her feet, switching his tail, raises a paw and*

tears whatever she puts on. Her clothes are made of colorful crepe paper. She leaves the shreds on and continues dressing. JULES now takes out a thermos of coffee, another cup, a sweet roll, pats of butter, a plastic knife, sugar, a container of milk and strawberries.)

(He begins to butter the sweet roll and eat strawberries while he chats.) How fresh the strawberries are this time of year. The smallest ones are best, bittersweet. How fragrant this coffee is. It's Hawaiian and Indonesian. A blend. How crisp and sweet is this roll, and how creamy the butter is. It's a tender yellowish white. It makes me think of youth.

(JULES picks up the paper, glances through the comic section quickly. Once in a while he lets out a quick, sharp laugh. When he finishes, he folds it into a paper airplane and shoots it into the box. He sits down and reads another section, the Metropolitan section.)

My, my. Listen to this. "A wounded and lost whale wandered the shores of New York within forty feet of Coney Island beach before a police launch herded the forlorn mammal back to the open sea. The launch got between the whale and the shore and tried to steer him to the open sea as the disoriented whale repeatedly tried to enter several bays. 'He was injured,' the police chief said. 'You could see the cut marks on his back. He nudged the launch like it was his girl. We got worried he was going to try to have some fun with it, if you know what I mean,' the police chief continued." Ahem . . . *(He looks around nervously.)* . . . My . . . my . . . *(Continues.)* "The police launch lost track of the whale but it was reported that the whale will most likely stay in the area for a while. The police chief added, 'They usually hang around. Sometimes they lose a mate and hang around waiting for it to return.'"

(JULES reaches out and touches the box tenderly. It begins to rain, light at first and then harder.)

(He fishes in his bag and takes out a collapsible umbrella, which he opens. He sits sipping coffee, holding the umbrella over his head.)

SCENE 4

SYLVIA, dressed now, tries to leave. The BEAST blocks her way. There are several attempts. JULES comes rushing in. He carries his coat over his arm.

JULES   I hope you'll forgive that I'm late!

(He spreads his jacket on the ground near the door. He sits down there. He is animated, sparkling.)

But I went to the beach! It was delightful! Delicious. Three sea gulls circled the ocean and dove in. Seven women were having a picnic on a pink blanket. Nine couples were laughing on the boardwalk . . . *(Pause.)* I counted them. I like to know what is going on. The world interests me. No! It fascinates me! If only you were there.

(SYLVIA taps on the glass and tries in vain to get JULES's attention. He stands up and takes out a piece of paper from his breast pocket. He unfolds it and takes an oratorical stance, half-facing the box and yet visible to the audience.)

I wrote a poem for you. *(He reads very grandly.)*

"The sea roars and swells
above me
my lone heart leaps
that dolphin part of me."

(He folds the paper and returns it to his pocket. He looks longingly at the box. SYLVIA looks longingly out. He doesn't see her.)

That dolphin part of me.

SCENE 5

During this scene SYLVIA wrestles with the BEAST, who claws her. She bleeds.

It is an overcast Sunday. Years have passed for JULES. This is noted by two things. First, the mirrored sides of the box are streaked with dirt; and second, some flowers, branches, pieces of paper; newspaper, and cloth have accumulated around the bottom of the box as if driven there by wind.

JULES enters. He walks slowly, almost decrepitly, his hat in one hand, leaning on a cane. His hair is unkempt, with visible gray in it. He has a few days' growth of beard; his clothes are rumpled. He walks as if he is physically weak rather than old.

JULES   Well, I'm here. *(He pauses.)* It's been some time now. I don't know precisely how much. But it's been quite some time. You don't look well, I may add. You've changed. *(He pauses.)* Don't worry, though. I've only come . . . This will only be a short visit. For many reasons. *(His voice is tightly controlled.)* You may have noticed that I . . . don't feel too well. It's no wonder with all that's happened. In any event, you've failed to say anything about it. Is that your usual discretion? Well, let me tell you . . . your silence . . .

(He starts to lose control of his voice. As he talks, he absently starts to pick up the trash around the box or will wipe at a streak with part of his sleeve.)

is . . . more . . . than . . . I can . . . tolerate! I will not be treated . . . *(He loses his place. He clears his throat.)* I was ill, you see. A touch of flu. Can you see how pale I've become? How thin? My sources of revenue, my *usual* sources dried up, disappeared and I . . . I was . . . you might say, I was reluctant to leave my home. After all, it is my home, with all my special objects about me, little things I collect, a lifetime, if you wish. And I became afraid to step out. No telling who might come, and I hadn't a cent. Of course, in better health I would have set about . . . set about establishing new sources. Much more stable ones. I had several ideas in fact . . . and . . . *(He clears his throat.)* then these two men burst through the door. Unasked, uncalled for. It was humiliating. I was in my bedclothes . . . indeed, I had retired to my bedclothes some time before, days, perhaps a week . . . Needless to say, I was frightened but maintained a calm presence. "Please leave as you came in," I told them. But they ignored me, in my own house. I would have thrown them out, mind you, although I'm usually quite polite. They were uninvited. I don't know how they knew my name. They read it from a piece of paper and asked me if that was my name. "Why, yes, it is," I answered. "And now will you kindly leave. I'm very tired." But they wouldn't, you know. They looked official. Officious. *(He laughs.)* Like officious ice cream men, really. All in white. It made me laugh. Then one of them said, "Will ya look at this pitiful mess." Now, yes, I was very weak and may have had my eyes closed, but I heard that. *I heard that. (He is quite upset.)* "This pitiful mess" they called it, my home. Who are they to say that? What do they know about beauty, I ask you? But that wasn't the worst. They took me away. It took two of them. But I had worse to contend with. Yes. Your silence haunted me then. Your silence became a burden. All those days upon days. I worried about it. I fretted. Once or twice they told me I screamed out in my sleep. It was agony. *(He steps away from the box.)* And all that time. Not a word, not a note, not a sigh on my account. I paced, I cursed, I spit on you. Yes, I did, and several times. I vowed to come back and end this once and for all just as soon . . . just as soon as I . . . was able.

(He clears his throat and straightens his clothes. He empties his hat and pockets of trash and puts his derby on his head.)

I will no longer be humiliated. I will no longer be ignored.

(He raises his cane and beats the box until he breaks through one side.)

Do you hear? Some response is necessary! Some response is necessary! Some response is necessary! I will no longer tolerate . . . tolerate . . . emptiness!

(He stands back, satisfied with what he has done and stalks off without looking back. SYLVIA is wrestling with the BEAST. She takes its tail and wraps it around its throat and kills it. She lies there breathing heavily.)

SCENE 6

There is a curtain of pastel strips of paper inside the box. We can't see SYLVIA *at all.* JULES *comes in carrying a paper shopping bag over one arm. He is dressed again as before, neatly, although not as precisely as at first. He leans more on his cane and is obviously older. His hair is white. He also carries a broom.*

He approaches smiling. The box looks in sad shape. It is even dirtier, and the glass is cracked. More debris is cluttering around its base. The dead BEAST *lies there, too, discarded.*

JULES *(Looking at the box, walking entirely around it.)* Tsch . . . tsch . . . tsch . . . a little the worse for wear . . . tsch . . . tsch . . . But you know. It is time, time we made our peace. I have had you in my heart all these years . . . as if a sliver from one of these mirrors had entered it and settled there . . . My . . . my . . . *(He puts his bag down and begins to sweep away the debris.)* Yes, a sliver. So I have come back to you . . . my lovely. Do you remember how I called you that? There are many things I must tell you. There are things I must explain to you. . . . Just a minute. *(He sweeps some of the debris offstage and returns.)* It looks better already. No one has taken care of you. Not the way I would have. *(He sweeps, walking all the way around the box. As he reappears, he looks older, perhaps more bent, slower.)* I have made mistakes. Incredible errors for a person who is basically careful, civilized sometimes to a fault. One of which I hope to expiate with you. There are so many things I never told you that would have perhaps . . . perhaps softened things between us. . . . Just a moment . . . *(He sweeps the remaining debris offstage.)* There. Quite an improvement. But that is not all. Voilà!

(He extracts a large bottle of Windex and a rag from his bag. He begins to clean the glass.)

So many things I never ventured to tell you. Never dared to mention because I might disturb some imperceptibly delicate balance. . . . But no matter. Now I can say . . . Now I will say what I please.

(He clears his throat and straightens his derby in the newly cleaned mirror. He makes a face at himself and smiles, tips his hat, almost forgetting his place for a moment.)

Now where was I? Oh, yes . . . Ahem. You see. You may wonder why I never approached you physically. It's not that I don't think that way. Quite the opposite is true. However, physical relationships are . . . I suppose you might say they are difficult for me, but that doesn't mean I haven't admired . . . ardently . . . the smoothness of an arm I have glimpsed . . . *(He tries to peer into the box, slants his hat roguishly.)* or the slenderness of a leg, a length of calf, the velvet flow of hair . . . why even now its perfume wafts, floats to me and makes me drowsy. . . .

(In his cleaning, JULES has turned a corner around the box. He continues talking. When he reappears, he has a slight wispy white goatee.)

(SYLVIA steps out from behind the curtain. She is in tights and a leotard and wears a wreath on her head, streamers.)

And you have inspired me. I have often aspired to be as quiet and accepting as you, not to complain or exclaim, not to pile my emotions and desires against you here as if they were leaves and debris blown in by the wind. I have tried to emulate your steadfastness, your virtuous simplicity.

(He again turns the corner and reappears with a longer beard. Steps back and reviews his work.)

Aha. My lovely. You are once again nearly as I remember you.

(He steps close to wipe a speck away and catches sight of himself. He cannot see SYLVIA, who steps up to the glass. She tries to find an opening in order to leave, but cannot. She is dejected because she can find no way out.)

Oo la la. I have grown old. Who would have thought . . .

(He shakes his head and puts away the Windex. Now he is removing small specks of dirt that only he can see.)

But I must hurry to tell you more. Soon it will be too late.

(A strong wind comes up. We hear it. Then it blows JULES's hat away.)

(Talking over the wind.) I believe . . . in fact I am sure that I have learned from your higher qualities. It has been painful, in fact at times it has been excruciatingly painful to never receive a word of love or feel your affection . . . but now I see that although one may never actually receive tokens of love . . .

(The wind almost blows him over. He holds on to the box. SYLVIA hears the wind; she studies the opening at the top of the box and jumps. Large leaves, as big as he, blow onstage and settle against him or the box.)

(Struggling physically and vocally against the wind.) That doesn't matter. What is left, you see . . . oh, my dear, here is the beauty of it all . . . although you never receive the smallest hint, the vaguest gesture or the slightest trace of love . . . *(His voice rises.)* . . . you can always . . . without fail . . . *give it.* Voilà! That is a life! *(He laughs happily.)* C'est vrai, ma cherie . . . my lovely . . .

(He recovers himself enough to continue polishing the box. For a moment, poised to turn the corner, he tilts his head jauntily, twirls his mustache.)

Now. Let me tell you a joke I overheard. It was quite humorous and I remember it perfectly . . .

(He steps around the corner and his voice is cut off by the wind. He does not reappear this time. The stage begins to fill with huge, gold, orange, and brown leaves. SYLVIA climbs out of the box, looks around, and scampers behind it.)

ROBERT AULETTA

Stops

CHARACTERS

MATTIE   *A woman in her late seventies.*
JEFF   *An old man.*
YOUNG MAN   *Just that.*
IRENE   *A woman in her mid-thirties.*

SETTING

The floor of the stage is littered with small pieces of debris: paper, wood, metal, rope, string, cardboard, etc. Upstage center hangs a traffic light. It contains a red, an orange, and a green signal. They continue blinking throughout the play.

The lights come up on Mattie. She takes three steps, stops, looks at the audience, and smiles.

MATTIE   I'd offer you a fig newton, but I don't have any. I'm all out of 'em. *(She takes three steps, then stops.)* In spite of what I once knew, I go to the house of friends. *(Pause.)* Off in the distance, behind a great hedge. Secluded, comfortable. *(She takes three steps, then stops.)* I have two friends. Nice ones. One like the other. And both like me. *(Calls off into the distance.)* How close we've always been. How sensitive to each other's needs. *(To the audience, lifting up her dress.)* I'm covered with bruises. From head to toe. I fall down a lot. *(Calls off into the distance.)* Don't I? Isn't that true? *(To the audience.)* I often have the need to verify. *(Pause.)* Oh, I've always been clumsy. It's been my way. *(She takes three steps, then stops.)* I have three friends. But one is dead. The two live ones are alive. They're nice. They're like me. The dead one is dead. He's like nothing you've ever seen. He's somewhat awful to remember. But I do. Often. On days like today. On days that contain some mystery. That's when I remember that dead one. *(Calls off into the distance.)* Yoo hoo, yoo hoo. *(To the audience.)* They're hard of hearing, you know. And their hearing aids are badly out-of-date. *(Pause.)* Hard to hear for them that lives over there. In the morning it's better. Sound carries better. Yes, in the morning I often believe that the sound of my voice just reaches them. Even when they've shut their hearing aids off. Even when they've shut their windows and stuck their heads under their pillows. Even then, if I try, I can reach them. *(She stomps her foot.)* Oh, I shouldn't do that. *(Calling off into the distance.)* Did you prepare the hot water for my aching feet? *(To the audience.)* Of course they did. They're sweet dear ones. Like you. You're all sweet dear ones. Even you others who are bastards. You're sweet dear bastards. *(She smiles.)* They're only words that I'm saying. So why not say anything? *(She smiles.)* You know what I mean. And if you don't, you're dumb. *(She takes three steps, then stops.)* Once I had three sweet dear bastards for friends. And on Sundays we would sup together. That is, if we could stand the ordeal. *(Pause, and she loses her balance for a moment.)* I stink the stink of a lousy stinking God. *(She smiles.)* I didn't mean that. You'll vouch for that. I'm sure you'll vouch for that. *(She takes two steps, then stops.)* Oh, how those lousy stinking bastards loved to sup at my table. I used to set a nice table. The nicest on the block. And used to set red flowers everywhere. Hillyhopes, or something of that sort, those red flowers were called. I'll bet they're still called that. Or something of that sort. Even to this day. *(Calls off into the distance.)* Pluck some red flowers for me. *(To the audience.)* They won't. I bet they won't pluck even one. And I want bunches. *(Calls off into the distance.)* I've told on you. I've squealed. *(To the audience.)* They are guilty of outrages of many sorts and assorted kinds. Each more heinous than the other. Just thought I'd let you know. *(Calls off into the distance.)* I just let them know. And by God, are they furious. *(Looks at the audience.)* You've never seen such a miserable bunch of furious bastards in your whole life. They're chewing on their lips. They're spitting blood. *(Smiles.)* Don't worry. I've always been—how might you say it—on the brink, teeter-tottering. *(Pause.)* Teeter-tottering on the brink, my mother used to say. And even if she never said it, it's what she meant to say. The flannel-faced bitch. *(Calls off into the distance, painfully.)* Mother. *(To the audience.)* I only do that to make her think I care. *(Pause.)* Poor thing, so dead. *(Pause.)* She was born dead, my flannel-faced mother. And went through life in that exact same condition until one day the doctor finally made it legal. *(Pause.)* Though we cried real tears. Or something closely approximating them. *(Pause.)* What they were exactly, I'll probably never know. Or never really care to know. Though I am a bit curious to know if their chemistry was truly human or not. Is there a chemist . . . *(She takes two steps, then stops. Calls off into the distance.)* Mother.

(To the audience.) I was going to make a joke about a chemist being in the house. *(Pause.)* And if there is, bless his almighty soul. *(Calls off into the distance.)* Mother, did you really drink iodine before meals, as we children used to say? That's what we thought made you so mean. It's only idle curiosity that impels me to ask you now, Mother. Idle curiosity that forces me back into a land so far away, so gone. Was it iodine, Mother? Or were all us children just dreaming? Tell me, Mother, were your beverages ordinary? And was it our dreams that were extraordinary? *(To the audience.)* Nothing of the kind. My mother drank turpentine. Gallons of it. The north woods variety, designed to kill horses. But with her it produced hardly a hiccup. *(Calls off into the distance.)* Isn't that right, Mother? You were tough, but you were refined. *(To the audience.)* Her beverages were extraordinary. And our dreams were extraordinary. A monstrous brood, each and every one of us. Drunk on each other's vapors. *(Pause.)* And to this day I still remember each and every one of us. Though it would have been grace to have forgotten it all. *(Pause.)* We were a jolly family. Known in and around the neighborhood for our laughter. For it never stopped. Day in and day out. Even to this day we are remembered for it. *(Pause.)* It's hard to kill a jolly family. In fact, it's goddamn near impossible. *(Pause.)* Don't think they didn't try. Oh, they did. Oh, they really did. Droves of them. *(Pause.)* There was always a fryer in the fire. There was always a mat for the car. And a pat on your head. And a kick in the ass to round out the day. *(She takes two steps, then stops.)* In those days families were special. They had an aroma and fragrance so often missing from present-day reality. *(Pause.)* It was the smell of their feet. *(Pause.)* All the members wore filthy feet. And to show contempt for the other members, they very rarely changed their feet. And worse than that, they often took to exhibiting those feet under the noses of the other members. To wreak havoc. To cause discomfort. Their motives were simple but powerful. *(Pause.)* Dark deeds were done in the past. Dark days were lived in the past. *(Pause.)* And may the past be damned. And those that congregated there, may they never know happiness. *(Pause.)* Or light. Or television in the afternoon, when it's snowing outside and your pension check has just arrived and there's honey in the tea. *(She takes a few steps and falls down.)* I keep falling down. I'm always falling down. Why am I always falling down? *(Pause.)* Because I'm a dimwit. Because it's my nature. *(She tries to get up.)* Piss on the high water, said Captain Bligh. And let the low water watch out for itself. *(She gets to her feet.)* Another amazing man, that captain. Though he's probably now dead like the rest of the crew. Under the sea. *(Pause.)* Under the sea. *(She takes two steps, then stops.)* We were a glorious brood. We all had faces like cats. We stuck together. We warmed each other. I remember many times in the early morning watching the snow fall against the window, listening to the brood purr. *(Pause.)* Listen-

ing to the purring brood. *(Pause.)* Listening to the roar of the purring brood. *(Pause.)* Funny, but they always reminded newcomers of ravens. *(Pause.)* Newcomers never stayed long among us. *(Pause.)* We had our ways. And they were the right ways. And even if they weren't, what else could we do? *(Calling off into the distance.)* Yoo hoo, yoo hoo. I'm coming round the mountain. I'm coming *(Pause.)* It is Mattie. It is I. *(To the audience.)* Is there a chemist on the premise? *(Smiles.)* And if there is, bless his almighty chemistry set . . . *(Calling off into the distance.)* It is Mattie. It is I. Do you not remember? *(To the audience.)* In those days I had a different name. It sounded similar to the one I use now. But it meant such different things. *(Pause.)* Sometimes in the morning, when it is clear and still and their hearing aids are working perfectly, I swear, they can hear me. They rise up in their beds and say: It is she! Coming to visit! She of the whitened hair! And then they lock their doors. And bolt them. And double lock them again. And then go back to bed. Pulling the woolen blankets around their ears. *(Pause.)* The old have such difficult ways. But I don't mind. I easily adapt to circumstances. I fit right in. It's my way. *(She takes two steps, then stops.)* I was never a lover. Not in my heart, or in any other place. I guess you might say it was a fault of character, some sort of awkward lack. *(Smiles.)* Don't believe what I say. It's only words. They go their own way. *(Pause.)* It's raining not far from here. On people whom I don't even know. *(Pause.)* I was never a lover. But I consorted with lovers. First-rate lovers, each and every one of them. They wore purple shirts and flowers. Their hair was shiny, their faces flushed, and the wine they drank was exceptionally rare. Mattie, they would say. Mattie, Mattie, they would always say. *(Pause.)* It's a long way to Tipperary. But I think I would hate the place anyway. *(Pause.)* It's where the Irish live. *(Calling off into the distance.)* It is I. The child. *(To the audience.)* They make believe they don't hear me. They look the other way. *(Pause.)* They make believe they don't fear me. They turn their fear the other way. *(Pause.)* But I fear them, indeed I do. In retrospect, and in present-day reality. *(Pause.)* Fear is part and parcel of all the Christmas parcels. *(Cries out.)* Why don't they come for me? Why don't they carry me away? *(Pause.)* Father did not cry real tears when Mum or Mommy or Mom or Ma or Mama or Mother died. What Father cried was simpering music when Mum or Mom or Mama or Mommy died. *(Pause.)* One summer afternoon the sky was splayed by heat lightning. The brood was drunk about the streets. *(Pause.)* And Father cried simpering music. From one room to the next. From morning till night till morning. *(Pause.)* Out of tune. Squeaky. *(Pause.)* I held a red coverlet around me. And underneath I was naked. *(Pause.)* I was a demented young lady. *(Pause.)* I stood on top of the tenement and took the coverlet off. *(Pause.)* From the top of the tenement one could see the tops of other tenements. *(Pause.)* And on the top of each stood a naked young lady watching a red coverlet fall. *(Violently.)* I was always a lover, but there was never anyone left to love. *(Pause.)* The red coverlet fell two hundred feet. *(Pause.)* Mother never knew what hit. Though we had been expecting the worst. Some of us praying against it. Some of us praying for it. *(Pause.)* Nowadays it's hard to sort out who was doing what. *(Pause.)* But one thing is sure, we always got the worst. Each and every one of us. It was our way. *(Pause.)* Father's underwear was shabby. *(Pause.)* He worked by his instincts. But he was not an instinctive man. *(Pause.)* He had little else to go on. *(Pause.)* I offered no help. I was never of any assistance to any of them. *(Pause.)* His shoes were even shabbier than his underwear. Though highly polished. Though strongly polished. You can always tell a man by his shoes, he said, each day of his life. *(Pause.)* I believe that. Even to this day. When there is little else . . . to grab on to. I still believe . . . *(Violently.)* Shoes is true. *(Pause.)* I'm sure. *(Pause.)* He wouldn't lie. *(Pause.)* He wouldn't know how to lie. *(Pause.)* He was a dull man. But with shoes of a high polish. And a straightforward manner. And a keen sense of expectation. That was admired by many. Though it didn't save him. *(Pause.)* Nor did it I. *(She closes her eyes, then opens them.)* *(Calls off into the distance.)* Father, Father, your shoes of a high polish and your face so deathly pale. *(Pause.)* Simper me some music. Simper me some of your sweet music. *(Pause.)* My hand had always been smaller than most. But when it grabbed, it compensated for its lack of size by never letting go. *(She reaches out and grabs.)* Next to my father's hand, my hand growing smaller each second. Next to my father's hand, my hand has almost disappeared. *(She withdraws her hand.)* We did have our times, didn't we? Our ups and our downs. Our ins and our outs. Our dogs and our cats. Our pukes and our vomits. Our summers and our snows. *(Pause.)* Though I never took much of it seriously. Always lighthearted about everything around me. Let it come. Let it go. What's the difference? *(Pause.)* It was only life. They were only people. *(Pause.)* They lived. And they died. And I follow their example. There's not much more to it. *(She takes two steps, then stops.)* On to the house of friends. *(She takes two steps, then stops.)* To the glorious house, of glorious friends. *(Pause.)* A game of monopoly, a tickle of brandy, a laugh and a joke. *(The sound of thunder.)* Oh, dear. *(The lights begin to dim.)* The brood always loved the rain. They moved easily in it. Sometimes they held newspapers over their heads. Sometimes nothing. Water sleeking their backs. Their shoes soggy. Mouths open. Hearts beating. *(Pause.)* They loved it! Their hair hanging in strings and ringlets. Jumping across puddles. Howling across puddles.

(The sound of rain falling.) Jumping into puddles. Howling into puddles. To their knees. To their thighs. To their throats. The sewers overflowing. *(Thunder.)* The sewers gurgling. The brood gurgling. The sky gurgling. *(Pause, then change of tone.)* I would lick the ice cream off his fingers. She

takes two steps, then stops.) Equal in strength. Equal in speed. They would race. *(Thunder.)* Like horses. They would race. *(Pause.)* Like golden, like silver, like black. *(Thunder.)* They would race to the house of friends. *(She takes two steps, then stops.)* But one of the brood slipped and hit his chin on the curb. His face running blood. *(Pause.)* My blood! My blood! *(Pause.)* And the rest of the brood laughed. Then the face, running blood, laughed. And rose up from the gutter and began to race. A bloody, running, laughing face. It raced the brood down. And emerged the victor, emerged the strongest of the brood. Its name was Michael. *(Pause.)* I would lick the ice cream . . . *(Pause.)* Its name was Michael. The face that of a saint. *(Pause.)* Then they entered the radiant house of radiant friends. Music fastened to everything. To the red fire and the red walls. To the black chairs and the black sofa. To the round black table. To the food and the drink. To the beer and the wine and the whiskey. To the ham and the rolls and the sausage and the pickles and the smoked fish and the long, round loaves and the fat, round loaves and the cold roast and the cold chicken and to the six different types of cheese and to the soup and to the salad and to the ice cream and to the coffee steaming clouds through the room and to the pastries of assorted kinds and to the chocolate nougat candies and to the mints. *(Pause.)* To the lovely after-dinner mints. *(Pause.)* The music entered it all, like veins. *(Pause.)* Oh, they all had such lovely hands.

(Thunder.) Which they wiped on their shirts and pants and jackets and on the slipcovers and on the draperies and on the walls and the rugs and on the lamps and on the floors and all over the faces and the bodies and the clothes of the people sitting next to them and even all over the people running away from them, the people running all over the house. *(Pause.)* They were never known for their table manners. They were never loved for their decorum. *(Pause.)* The people running all through the house. With the brood howling behind them. *(Pause.)* They were often overenthusiastic. They often did not know when to stop. *(Pause.)* And they left stains: pickle, salami, mustard, meat, chicken, chocolate stains, ice cream stains, coffee stains, blood stains, urine stains, semen stains everywhere. Everywhere! *(Pause.)* Everything and everybody tottered around heavy with their stains. Reeling with their stains. Half-crazy with their stains. Which never washed off. Which were like acid. Which ate through fabric and furniture and flesh alike. *(Pause.)* Their presence was vividly felt in that radiant room. *(Pause.)* They made their mark. They always made their mark. *(Pause.)* But still they were loved, totally loved. *(Pause.)* Each one of them had known total love. *(Pause.)* The taste and the smell of it. The servitude of it. *(Pause.)* Eternally. *(Calls off into the distance.)* What was it like? What did it feel like? *(To the audience.)* I was never a lover, but neither have I ever denied anyone love. *(She takes two steps, then stops.)* Never!

(Pause.) If there's a man alive that thinks that, let him step forward. Now! *(She looks around. She smiles. She takes two steps forward, then stops. She takes two more steps, then stops. It has stopped raining. The light is brighter. JEFF, an old man dressed in shabby clothes, enters behind MATTIE. He coughs. Mattie hears him but does not turn around.)* Have you come to speak on my behalf? Is that why you have come, as a witness to my life? *(JEFF mutters.)* Then I take it you know the truth. *(To the audience.)* He will tell you the truth of my life. *(JEFF mutters.)* Come to me. Touch me. *(JEFF mutters angrily.)* Come, come touch. You are my witness, aren't you? Thus you have the privilege of intimacy. *(JEFF mutters angrily.)* Are you not a witness? Are you nothing? Are you a stray? *(She turns around.)* I know you not.

JEFF   I'm Jeff.

(She takes two steps toward him, then stops.)

MATTIE   I know no Jeff.
JEFF   Like Mutt and Jeff. Like the comic strip.

(She takes two steps toward him, then stops.)

MATTIE   I know no comic strip.
JEFF   I wander about. *(She takes one step, then stops.)*
MATTIE   Touch me, anyway. *(JEFF laughs.)* Don't do that! *(Pause.)*
JEFF   I've bought a new truss. *(He fiddles with his truss.)*
MATTIE   What?
JEFF   A new truss. At a sale at the surgical store.
MATTIE   Is it a great improvement?
JEFF   Huh?
MATTIE   Is it more comfortable, durable, lighter, more sanitary, does it give you greater freedom?
JEFF   It makes me happy.
MATTIE   Then it's all those things and more. Then it's a good truss.
JEFF   Huh?
MATTIE   Rejoice.
JEFF   I shouldn't wander about.
MATTIE   No.
JEFF   It's bad for me. I can get overexcited.
MATTIE   What?
JEFF   *(Getting overexcited.)* I can get overexcited.
MATTIE   I think I heard you the first time.
JEFF   It's bad for me.
MATTIE   I can see why. *(Pause.)* Tell me what you know, Jeff?
JEFF   I know I shouldn't get overexcited.
MATTIE   Yes. Yes. If only I could have known that. That's truly something important. But what else do you know?

JEFF   I know how to make ends meet.

MATTIE   How does one do that?

JEFF   By cutting corners.

MATTIE   And how does one accomplish that?

JEFF   By doing without.

MATTIE   By doing without what? Exactly what, Jeff?

JEFF   By doing without whatever is not absolutely essential.

MATTIE   And what is the result of all this . . . denial? *(JEFF laughs.)* Come now, tell me, in your own words.

JEFF   The result is . . .

MATTIE   Spit it out.

JEFF   Happiness.

MATTIE   Complete happiness?

JEFF   Yes.

MATTIE   Has it worked for you? Have you attained . . .

JEFF   I am completely happy.

MATTIE   *(Calls off into the distance.)* Why haven't I been told this before? *(Pause; to Jeff.)* It probably would not have worked for me.

JEFF   It works for everybody.

MATTIE   How do you know?

JEFF   I've seen it with my own eyes.

MATTIE   I hope you don't mind me saying this, Jeff, but you don't look completely happy to me. In fact, you look downright miserable.

JEFF   Inside I am a different man. *(He fiddles with his truss. It starts to get dark.)*

MATTIE   And your shoes are not highly polished. *(A siren is heard in the distance.)*

JEFF   Inside I'm altogether different. *(He exits.)*

MATTIE   You can always tell a man by his shoes. Or by his eyes or by his hair or by the words he does not speak. *(She resumes the direction she was going. She takes two steps, then stops. She takes two more steps, then stops.)* Oh, Michael, Michael, you never wore a truss. Ever. *(Pause.)* His back against the window, the window against the light . . . Mother would have had him for herself. *(Calls out.)* Michael. *(Pause.)* It's good you died so early. *(Pause.)* Forgive and forget, I always say. Because it has forgotten you. *(She takes two steps, then stops.)* But it does not let go. Even though the mind wills it. Even though the body pushes it away. *(A YOUNG MAN wearing a white uniform and carrying a broom enters. He begins to sweep up the stage. MATTIE barely notices him. She addresses the audience.)* And look at you! You're so happy, so rested. So sweet, so sweet. *(Pause.)* Once I was the happiest sweet person known. *(Pause.)* But somehow . . . yes, the brood turned against each other. Each one became a dog to the other. *(Pause.)* They ran through the streets like a pack of dogs. *(Pause.)* I am riddled with tooth marks. *(Pause.)* I dropped the red coverlet. Then stood there watching the red coverlet drop. *(Pause.)* I want to drop myself on the dropped red coverlet. *(Pause.)* The brood howled as they ran down the wet streets. Their fur was soaked in blood and water, slobber and beer. They were running to their graves. All decked in holly and slobber. *(Pause.)* Under a lamppost stood a skinny white bitch. The bitch was shivering. And she had a cut paw, which she held up. *(Pause.)* The bitch licked her paw. *(Pause.)* In other words, she licked her blood. *(Pause.)* She liked it. *(The* YOUNG MAN *finishes sweeping, and exits.) (Calls off into the distance.)* I am coming to thee. With my brush and comb. To fix your white hair. *(Pause.)* The red coverlet lay like a heart-shaped drop of blood on the street. In those days there were horses. They reared up and cried out when they saw it. *(Pause.)* I am toothed with riddle marks! *(Pause.)* There were horses! *(The* YOUNG MAN *enters pushing a hospital bed. He places it stage right of the traffic light. Now he walks over to* MATTIE.*)* I stood like a statue on the rim of a building. Because I was never a human child. Nor did I ever live in a human land. *(He puts his arm around her and begins to walk her slowly toward the bed.)* Why was I not pushed? The coverlet lay waiting for me. And I stood above it, about to, about to . . . But I was not pushed! *(Pause.)* I was saved. By an angel. *(They reach the bed. The* YOUNG MAN *helps* MATTIE *to sit on it.)* I wish I could find that angel now. I would speak to him heart to heart, then spit blood and ash into his face. *(The* YOUNG MAN *takes off her shoes, then unbuttons her dress at the throat. Now he helps her get under the covers.) (Calls off into the distance.)* I will only be a moment, just a sweet moment. *(To the* YOUNG MAN.*)* They are the last of the last, the ones who will speak on my behalf. *(He begins tucking her covers in.)* They are probably speaking now, about my life, about the beauty of my life. Listen. It sounds like bees.

YOUNG MAN   Yes, just like them, just like a swarm of bees.

(She grabs his hand and licks his fingers.)

MATTIE   Vanilla. *(He smiles and exits.)* To lie in a red room, to sleep content in a room made glowing red by love . . . *(Suddenly she sits upright. Her face filled with terror.)* Get out of here! Out! Out into the streets! *(Pause.)* Please. *(She sinks back into the bed.)* I'm still in charge. *(Pause.)* I once had a husband. *(Pause.)* I was interested in his betterment. *(Pause.)* He did not understand my concept of betterment. *(Pause.)* I tried very hard to clarify. *(Pause.)* Still he fell behind in all my expectations. *(Pause.)* And this brought much shame to him. *(Pause.)* Much shame. *(To the audience.)* I showed them the human heart. And do you know what they did with it? They ate it! *(Pause.)* My human heart! *(Pause.)* There are things of great beauty in this world that people should not be allowed to touch. *(Pause.)* Let alone eat. *(Calls off into the distance.)* And you have witnessed it! The devouring of the human heart. Come and kneel down, and confess what you've seen. *(Pause.)* They hear me, but they dare not come. *(Pause.)* I moved like a saint among them, among all of them. Even those that hated me. *(IRENE enters.)* Don't come near me. *(IRENE takes a few steps toward her.)* Out! Out into the streets! *(IRENE takes a few more steps.)* You are not my witness. You are nothing to me. *(IRENE rushes to her and tries to embrace her. MATTIE strikes her. IRENE jumps back.)* Nothing. Nothing. *(IRENE rushes out.)* I am consumed. *(She closes her eyes.)* There were horses. And the street was swift with them. And the sky, and the sky . . . *(She opens her eyes. She gets out of bed.)* The frost, the frost . . . *(Pause.)* I scratched it with my fingers from the inside of the window and looked out as they took Mother's body away. *(She takes two steps, then stops.)* I've seen the whole bastard thing with my eyes wide open. And I never flinched or closed my eyes. I gritted my teeth and stared the bastard thing right in the face. *(She takes two steps, then stops.)* And it stared back, believe me. *(Pause.)* I am riddled with tooth marks, from breast to belly to thigh. *(She takes two steps, then stops.)* But I have wept for them. I have wept my heart's blood for all of them. Even for the worst of them. *(She takes two steps, then stops.)* To their graves I have gone. In the cool air, in the cool air . . . By the river, by the river . . . *(Pause.)* The last of the living. *(She takes two steps, then stops.)* In those days there were horses. And they wore bells about their necks. Mother's body followed behind the clomp of horses, the sound of bells. *(She takes two steps, then stops.)* And I danced for them! And I danced for them! As I do now. *(She begins to dance while making the sound of bells. She does well, growing stronger and stronger; then suddenly collapses.)* Why not drop a hook down and swing it into me? Why not hoist me off and dump me into the sea? *(She pulls herself along the ground.)* Once I had a husband, and altogether we brought forth creatures. This is a registered fact. *(She pulls herself along the ground.)* Drop your hook into me! *(She pulls herself along the ground.)* You witnesses. You false witnesses. You are not there. You are dead. *(She pulls herself along the ground.)* Once I had a friend, but now he is dead. But, oh, when he was alive . . . Oh, you should have seen him then. *(She pulls herself along the ground.)* When my husband was away at the store, among the crates and the jars and the cheese . . . *(Pause.)* I got nothing out of it. Nothing at all. I was trod upon. *(Pause.)* Many times. *(Pause.)* Always asking for more. *(She pulls herself along the ground.)* All decked in holly and slobber.

(She lies there quite still. After a few moments the YOUNG MAN enters. He goes to her and picks her up. He carries her to the bed and places her under the covers. Now he takes a strap from the bed and secures her tightly. He exits.)

MATTIE *(To the audience.)* Tell me about your life. Tell me all about it. *(Pause.)* Don't be shy or afraid. Tell me about your beautiful past. Speak it to me. *(Pause.)* About your first feelings and impulses. About how strong and fine they were. How pure. And high-grade. And about how those around you responded. About the gestures. About the faces. What did the hands feel like? And about the hearts. Could you feel their hearts beating beneath their chests? And about the colors. What were the colors like? The colors of the rugs, the walls, the stairs, the sinks, the closets. Tell me all about the colors. And the smells, the smell of the snow. The wonderful smell of the snow. And the sky. The look of it. Tell me. Did it frighten you? And the funny faces you made. Make some of those funny faces now. Don't be afraid. Yes, that's beautiful. Those funny faces you're making are beautiful. And the darkness. Tell me about the darkness. The depth and the intensity of it. Its feel. The grit of it. Of what you lost in it. The black of it. If you died in it. Or if you lived in it. Tell me about it. Speak it to me. Speak the hatred of it to me. Don't be afraid. Spit it on me. Don't hold back. Spit it. That's why I am here. Spit. *(Pause.)* That's good. That's fine. All together. Now we're one together. By the sea for a picnic. In the woods for a romp. Our pretty dresses. Our colored shirts. Sipping cider. Our heads thrown back. Our hair flying. The trees, the sky, the sea, our eyes. *(The traffic light goes out.)* I'm glad, I'm glad. As you are. As we all are. As we all are glad. As we all are one. As we are together. *(Pause.)* Her radiant white hair soft as an animal on the pillow. Her dead eyes . . . *(A crashing metallic sound.)*

AMIRI BARAKA

Jack Pot Melting: A Commercial

CHARACTERS

TVB   *TV brother.*
B   *Brother.*
TVS   *TV sister.*
S   *Sister.*

Score should be a duet for violin and saxophone, each imitating the speech of the couples. Drums should open and close the play and the last words okayed back and forth as a diversely spoken plea, command, question, hope, prediction, confidence, struggle, as a final note of instruction and direction.

TVB   Glad to see you. *(Large head of black man on TV—turned on by brother coming in room.)*

B   Yes. *(Straightening, looking over shoulder.)*

TVB   Glad you're there, dark in half darkness.

B   I gotta get— *(Looks up, continues.)*

TVB   You have to feel the connection. You have to be connected, all right. *(Laughs.)*

B   *(Turns on light.)* Where is that damn manuscript?

TVB   You've got to see the right sun rising . . . is that how they say it? The right sun rising?

B   *(Looks again suddenly at TV.)* Damn . . . that dude *(Stops, double takes.)* When did I do that?

TVB   All right, J.D., Welcome to the gray nasty show, live from the stick's bottom. The wind is here standing, yes, the murderer's eyes. The rattle of the various truths and lost chords.

B   *(Looks.)* What is this? Live? That—me! *(Turns on another light.)* What is this?

TVB   Don't light try to escape? Yes? But we knew older Ethiopians. Welcome, this is live. But first a word from our sponsor.

(Chains and whips with bells and jingles; man jumps on phone, dials.)

B   Hey. *(Lights come up on sister in another apartment.)*
S   I was thinking about you. You s'posed to come by or I'm s'posed to come there?
B   Go turn on Channel 2.
S   What? What . . . ?
B   Turn it on. Go hear—it's weird. . . .
S   *(She leans and turns on set. His image appears.)* What?
B   Yeah— You see that?
S   When'd you do this?
B   I dunno. But listen . . .
TVB   Okay, We're back. Inside the buttons on the leather furniture. With a harmonica and a steam engine. And our hot eyes. Even under the ocean. See the bubbles our hot eyes make. . . .
S   What?
B   Listen.
TVB   Drink Crazy X! Eat Wild Z! Like, yes, here we are, *live* under the monster's thumbnail. We're glad—
S   What kind of joke—
B   Whatever it is I ain't in it.
S   Hey, if this is some TV trick, you can sue them.
B   Yeah, but what's going on. . . .
S   Come on, call the station now—
TVB   Glad the dust mote has spring to its dimensions. There is a life that's going to be here after the next message. The shadow the tip of the look, is alive, we know. And so its future is thrilling and will be here soon. But first . . .
B   *(Phone.)* Hello! Yes, the program on your station, what is it? *The Sidekick Show?* Yeah—well, who is that MC—what's he think he's doing? His name is what . . . Ben?
S   Ben, look at the TV—look.
TVB   Now my first guest this evening. I'm glad and she knows I'm glad as my footprint, the cube's gray sweat.
TVS   Yes, glad would describe them. All my thrills of the corners to be turned! *(Throws up hands.)* Glad! Audience I am here with a sunbeam to speak of the love just around the next . . . *(They embrace.)*
B   *(To s on phone.)* What crazy shit is this?
S   I dunno. What'd the TV people say?
B   They said it was me on the . . . that it was Ben—
S   But the woman—who is that?

TVS Yes, I'm Gloria. Black Wendy arrives posthamburger. *(On TV they embrace, laughing.)* More! All? We—

TVB We are glad to have such health for you. Such love zooming close. Just around the square concrete and its excellent hard evils. The distance . . .

TVB The granulated unmoving. Kept lingerings enshrined and shiny sometimes— We're Glad.

S *(On phone.)* What do you mean her name is Gloria. It's why I'm calling. Because not only does the woman look like me—and that guy like my boyfriend—but they've got our names.

(TVB and s singing a song—background, not clear, in some harmony.)

B What are they telling you?

S They say that those are those people's real names and that they're not made up.

(Now they both, still somewhat dumbfounded, turn and look.)

TVB and s   *(Sing.)* Iron is good
            to eat
            & steel
            & glass
            & sand

(Terrifying unison.) The fires are creeping up backs and necks. The skeletons are tapping on the rain again! Open the matches and collect your ransom, ignorance. We the dancing you.

B Hey—this is too weird. I'll be over . . .

(A knock at door.)

S Yeah. I got a feeling . . . who is that.

(Now a knock at her door.)

      Hey, I've got one too.

B Whatever is goin' on is getting ice cold. *(Suddenly.)* Hey, don't open that door.

S *(To door.)* Who is it? *(Dog starts growling and barking. She is visibly shaken.)* My God, it's some dogs. . . .

B Who's out there? *(Dogs are slowly building up their vicious growling.)* They're dogs outside my door, too. *(They look toward TV.)*

TVB Now it's time for a visit from our best friends. . . . Fame *(A little white puppy bounds onto the set.)* TVS and FORTUNE. *(A little puppy leaps out and into her lap. They begin rocking them . . . on TV . . . like babies and serenading them on and on.)*

TVB Around the next corner—our lives are sweet like open windows.

TVS   We know everyone's glad, or I should say all of us . . . yes, that's a correction. All of us . . . that's in.

TVB   Yes, certainly. Not everyone—that's art.

(Puppies yipping "yip, yip, yip, yip, &c.") (Dogs at B&S doors sound large and vicious—eager to attack!)

B   This is not a joke—no trick VCR, right.

S   I'm so frightened, I'm shaking. What is going on?

TVB   You see at your door golden light from just around the corner.

TVS   *(A finger to her lips.)* Only say nothing *(Instructions lightly.)* & of course, remember nothing.

TVB   Right. Say good-bye to lies! To old slow and the teeth.

TVS   Yes—glad you can do this. Help y'rself. No. Help all us.

TVB   *(They're arrayed in proper-home, peaceful portrait now.)* Are you glad now? Are you watching?

B   *(To S.)* We can't call anybody—I don't want us to get cut off.

S   Who would you call?

B   Hey, we've got friends who'd help. People. Families.

S   Why'd you leave that party early, anyway? I was looking for you. . . .

B   Looking for me—You didn't seem like you were looking for me.

S   God, Ben, you're a terrible male chauvinist. You can talk to any woman— it's okay. But let any other brother pass a few innocent words and you come on like Darth Vader.

TVB   Be Glad! Be Glad!

TVS   Be There for Each Other!

B   Yeah. Why do I always get so uptight. . . .

S   Yeah, and I wish you'd stop it. Even if I wanted to go off with some beautiful man, I have discipline. . . .

B   Discipline? That's all that limits the drama to mouth play? Nothin' else?

S   You mean you never see any woman you're not sexually attracted to . . . ?

B   What?

S   You know! Don't like—

B   But you're talking.

S   What, you mean you can't stand to hear that I might find other men attractive. I had to get used to that with you immediately.

B   Yeah, but you said you knew that was just business.

S   Yeah, until you had that affair.

B   Oh, Gloria, but that was a long time ago.

S   I know! You're *sorry.*

B   Okay, Okay.

(They both look at each other on stage, then turn to look at their two doubles, who are now petting the dogs and crooning.)

TVB   *Fame.*
TVS   *Fortune.*

(Then B and S look at the door—the barking, the snarling.)

B   Okay.
S   Okay.
B   Wow, same exact shit happening to both of us. . . .

(At that moment, a mostly white, blue-ringed "Johnson" dripping red blood bashes through the door of s's apartment. Its "mouth" flaps, turning the dog growls to cries of "Nigger bitch, nigger bitch, nigger bitch . . .")

S   Is your dog usin' a poison animal Johnson as a rapist hatchet?
B   What?
S   Well, it's not quite the same. This dog here is . . . *(Reasoned.)* a mother
      fucker!
B   Sounds like it! *(Shouting.)* I'll be right there!
S   I'ma get . . . Shango, now!
B   Right! I got Obatala here with me. Scientific as a muhfuh . . .
S   Be careful . . . and don't hang up.
B   Hang up? Hell no!
S   And bro—
B   Yeah?
S   Don't try to change the subject like this again!
B   What? Goddamn . . . I didn't think this shit up . . .
S   You the one disappeared. . . .

(As the lights dim, the dogs' bloody barking gets louder.)

CHRISTOPHER DURANG

Naomi in the Living Room

SETTING

A living room. Enter NAOMI, *followed by* JOHN *and* JOHNNA, *an attractive young couple.* JOHN *has a moustache and is dressed in a suit and tie.* JOHNNA *is wearing a dress with a string of pearls.* NAOMI, *though, looks odd.* NAOMI *plants herself somewhere definitive—by the mantelpiece, for instance—and gestures out toward the room.*

NAOMI   And this is the living room. And you've seen the dining room and the bedroom and the bathroom.

JOHN   Yes, I know. I used to live here.

NAOMI   The dining room is where we dine. The bedroom is where we go to bed. The bathroom is where we take a bath. The kitchen is where we . . . cook. That doesn't sound right. The kitchen is where we . . . collect kitsch. Hummel figurines, Statue of Liberty salt and pepper shakers, underpants that say Home of the Whopper, and so on. Kitsch. The kitchen is where we look at kitsch. The laundry room is where we do laundry. And the living room is where Hubert and I do all of our living. Our major living. So that's the living room.

JOHNNA   What do you use the cellar for?

NAOMI   *(Suspicious.)* What?

JOHNNA   What do you use the cellar for?

NAOMI   We use the cellar to . . . we go to the cellar to . . . replenish our cells. We go to the attic to . . . practice our tics, our facial tics. *(Her face contorts variously.)* And we go to the carport to port the car. Whew! Please don't ask me any more questions, I'm afraid I may not have the strength to find the answers. *(Laughs uproariously.)* Please, sit down; don't let my manner make you uncomfortable. Sit on one of the sitting devices; we use them for sitting in the living room.

(There is a couch and one chair to choose from. JOHN and JOHNNA go to sit on the couch.)

NAOMI *(Screams at them.)* Don't sit there, I want to sit there!

(JOHN and JOHNNA stand and look frightened. NAOMI charges over to the couch, and JOHN and JOHNNA almost have to run to avoid being sat on by her.)

NAOMI Shits! Ingrates! It's my house, it's my living room. I didn't ask you, I can ask you to leave.

(JOHN and JOHNNA are still standing and start to maybe edge out of the room.)

No, no, sit down. Please, make yourselves at home, this is the living room, it's where Rupert and I do all our living.

(There's only one chair, so with some hesitation JOHNNA sits in the chair, and JOHN stands behind her.)

(Stretching her arms out on the couch.) Wow. Boy oh boy. I need a big couch to sit on because *I'm a big personality!* *(Laughs uproariously.)* Tell me, are you two ever going to speak, or do I just have to go on and on by myself, or what!

(NAOMI stares at JOHN and JOHNNA intensely. They hesitate but then speak.)

JOHNNA This is a very comfortable chair. I love it.
JOHN Yes, thank you.
NAOMI Go on.
JOHNNA Ummmm, this morning I washed my hair, and then I dried it. And we had coffee in the kitchen, didn't we, John?
JOHN Yes, Johnna, we did.
JOHNNA *(Pause, doesn't know what else to say.)* And I love sitting in this chair.
NAOMI I think I want to sit in it, get up, get up.

(NAOMI charges over, and JOHN and JOHNNA move away from it, standing uncomfortably. NAOMI sits and moves around in the chair, luxuriating in it.)

Hmmmm, yes. Chair, chair. Chair in the living room. Hmmm, yes. *(Looks at JOHN and JOHNNA, shouts at them:)* Well, go sit down on the fucking couch, you morons! *(JOHN and JOHNNA look startled, and sit on the couch. Screams offstage.)* Leonard! Oh, Leonard! Come on in here in the *living room* and have some conversation with us. You don't want me to soak up everything our son says all by myself, do you?

(NAOMI stands and walks over to JOHN and JOHNNA on the couch. She smiles at JOHNNA.)

You probably didn't know John was Herbert's and my son, did you?
JOHNNA Yes, he told me. I've met you before, you know.

NAOMI   Shut up! *(Calls out.)* Hubert! Rupert! Leonard! *(To them.)* I hope he's not dead. I wouldn't know what room to put him in. We don't have a dead room. *(Smiles; screams.)* Aaaaaaaaaaaaaaaaaaahhhhhhhhh! *(Looks at them.)* Goodness, my moods switch quickly.

(NAOMI sees a tiny stuffed pig in a Santa Claus suit perched on the mantelpiece. With momentary interest, she picks it up and looks at it, then puts it down again. Focusing on JOHN and JOHNNA again; a good hostess.)

Tell me all about yourselves, do you have children? *(Sits, listens attentively.)*
JOHNNA   We had five children, but they all died in a car accident. The baby-sitter was taking them for a ride, and she was drunk. We were very upset.
NAOMI   Uh-huh. Do you like sitting on the couch?
JOHN   Mother, Johnna was telling you something sad.
NAOMI   Was she? I'm sorry, Johnna, tell it to me again.
JOHNNA   We had five children. . . .
NAOMI   *(Tries to concentrate, but something impinges on her consciousness.)* Wait a minute, something's bothering me! *(She rushes over to the little stuffed Santa pig, snatches it up and throws it against the wall in a fury.)* This belongs in the kitchen, *not* in the living room. The living room is for living; it is not meant for sincerely designed but ludicrously corny artifacts! Kitsch! *(She sits down again.)* Do you like Hummel figurines?
JOHN   Very much. Now that the children are dead, Johnna and I have begun to collect Hummel figurines, especially little boy shepherds and little girl shepherdesses.
NAOMI   Uh-huh, isn't that interesting? Excuse me if I fall asleep. I'm not tired yet, but I just want to apologize in advance in case your boring talk puts me to sleep. I don't want to offend you. *(Screams.)* Aaaaaaaaaaa-aaaaahhhhhhhhh! I'm just so bored I could scream. Did you ever hear that expression? Aaaaaaaaaaaaaaaaaahhhhhhhhhhh!
JOHN   Excuse me, I want to change my clothes. I'm tired of my color scheme. Do you have a clothes changing room?
NAOMI   No, I don't have a clothes changing room; you certainly are an idiot. Use the bedroom or the bathroom. Really, children these days have no sense. In my day we killed them.
JOHN   *(To JOHNNA.)* Excuse me, I'll be right back.
JOHNNA   Must you go?
JOHN   Darling, I don't feel comfortable in these colors. They're hurting my eyes.
JOHNNA   Well, bring it back.
JOHN   What?
JOHNNA   *(Sincere, confused.)* I'm sorry, I don't know what I mean. *(JOHN exits.)* He's constantly talking about his color scheme. It's my cross to bear, I guess. That and the death of the children.

Christopher Durang / 71

NAOMI So who the fuck are you, anyway?

JOHNNA I'm Johnna. I'm married to your son. All our children recently were killed.

NAOMI Stop talking about your children, I heard you the first time. God, some people can't get over their own little personal tragedies; what a great big crashing bore. Lots of people have it worse, girlie, so eat shit! *(Calls offstage.)* Hey, John, where did you get this turd of a wife, at the Salvation Army? I'd bring her back! *(Laughs uproariously.)* Ahahahahahahahaha!

JOHNNA I think I want to go.

NAOMI Boy, you can't take criticism, can you? Sit down, let's have a conversation. This is the conversation pit. You can't leave the pit until you converse on at least five subjects with me. Starting now, go: *(Waits expectantly.)*

JOHNNA I was reading about Dan Quayle's grandmother the other day.

NAOMI That's one. Go on.

JOHNNA She said there should be prayer in the schools. . . .

NAOMI That's two. *(NAOMI starts to remove her boots, or high-heeled shoes, in order to massage her feet.)*

JOHNNA And that we should have a strong defense . . .

NAOMI That's three.

JOHNNA And that the Supreme Court should repeal the Wade versus Roe ruling that legalized abortions.

NAOMI That's four.

JOHNNA And that even in the case of pregnancy resulting from incest, she felt that the woman should be forced to carry the child through to term.

NAOMI That's four-A.

JOHNNA And then she said she hoped the mother would be forced to suffer and slave over a horrible job and take home a tiny, teeny paycheck to pay for some hovel somewhere and live in squalor with the teeny tiny baby, and that then she hoped she'd be sorry she ever had sexual intercourse.

NAOMI That's still four-A.

JOHNNA Don't you think she's lacking in Christian charity?

NAOMI That's five, kind of. Yes, I do. But then so few people are true Christians anymore. I know I'm not. I'm a psychotic. *(She throws her boot in JOHNNA's direction.)* Get up off the couch. I want to sit there. *(NAOMI rushes over; JOHNNA has to vacate fast. Then NAOMI starts to luxuriate in sitting in the couch, moving sensuously.)* Oh, couch, couch, big couch in the living room. I have room to spread. Couch, couch, you are my manifest destiny. Mmmmm, yes, yes. *(Calls out.)* Edward, hurry out here, I'm about to have an orgasm, you don't want to miss it. *(Back to herself.)* Mmmmmm, yes, couch, couch pillows, me sitting on the couch in the living room, mmmmm, yes, mmmm . . . no. *(Calls.)* Forget it! It's not happening. *(To JOHNNA.)* Tell me, can you switch moods like I can? Let me see you. *(JOHNNA stares for a moment.)* No, go ahead, try.

JOHNNA Very well. *(Happy.)* I'm so happy, I'm so happy. *(Screams.)* Aaaaaaah! Do you have chocolates for me? *(Desperate.)* I'm so sad, I'm so sad. Drop dead! *(Laughs hysterically.)* Ahahahahahahahaha! That's a good one! *(Looks at NAOMI for feedback.)*

NAOMI Very phony, I didn't believe you for a moment. *(Calls offstage.)* Herbert! Are you there? *(To JOHNNA.)* Tell me, do you think Shubert is dead?

JOHNNA You mean the composer?

NAOMI Is he a composer? *(Calls out.)* Lanford, are you a composer? *(Listens.)* He never answers. That's why I sometimes worry he might be dead, and as I said, I don't have a room for a dead person. We might build one on, and that would encourage the economy and prove the Republicans right, but I don't understand politics, do you?

JOHNNA Politics?

NAOMI Politics, politics! What, are you deaf? Are you stupid? Are you dead? Are you sitting in a chair?

(Enter JOHN. He is dressed just like JOHNNA—the same dress, pearls, stockings, shoes. He has shaved off his moustache, and he wears a wig that resembles her hair and has a bow in it like the one she has in her hair. They look very similar.)

JOHN Hello again.

NAOMI You took off your moustache.

JOHN I just feel so much better this way.

NAOMI Uh-huh.

JOHNNA *(Deeply embarrassed.)* John and I are in couples therapy because of this. Dr. Cucharacha says his cross-dressing is an intense kind of codependence.

NAOMI If this Dr. Cucharacha cross-dresses, I wouldn't see him. That's what John here is doing. Too many men in women's clothing; nothing gets done!

JOHNNA *(To JOHN.)* Why do you humiliate me so this way?

JOHN I want to be just like you. Say something so I can copy you.

JOHNNA Oh, John. *(Does a feminine gesture and looks away.)*

JOHN Oh, John. *(Imitates her gesture.)* That doesn't give me much. Say something else.

JOHNNA Maybe it's in your genes.

JOHN Maybe it's in your genes.

(JOHNNA, in her discomfort, keeps touching her hair, her pearls, shaking her head, etc. JOHN imitates everything she does, glowing with glee. His imitations drive her crazy and are undoubtedly part of what has them in couples therapy.)

NAOMI This is a disgusting sight. *(Calls.)* Sherbert, our son is prancing out here with his wife; you should really see this. *(To them.)* I find this uncomfortable. This makes me want to vomit.

JOHNNA Maybe we should go.

JOHN Maybe we should go.

NAOMI *(Upset.)* How come you don't dress like me? How come you dress like her?

JOHN I want to be noticed, but I don't want to be considered insane.

JOHNNA John, please, just stay quiet and pose if you must, but no more talking.

NAOMI Insane? Is he referring to someone in this room as insane? *(Calls.)* Sally! Gretchen! Marsha! Felicity! *(To them.)* I'm calling my army in here, and then we'll have some dead bodies.

JOHNNA Maybe we should go.

JOHN Maybe we should go. *(Keeps imitating JOHNNA's movements.)*

JOHNNA Will you stop that?

(NAOMI, very upset and discombobulated, stands on the couch and begins to pace up and down on it.)

NAOMI Insane, I'll give you insane! What's the capital of Madagascar? You don't know, do you? Now who's insane? What's the square root of 347? You don't know, do you? Well, get out of here if you think I'm so crazy. If you want to dress like her and not like me, I don't want you here.

(NAOMI lies down on the couch in a snit to continue her upset. JOHN begins to stride back and forth around the room, pretending he's on a fashion runway. JOHNNA slumps back in her chair and covers her eyes.)

I can have Christmas by myself, I can burn the Yule log by myself, I can wait for Santa by myself. I can pot geraniums. I can bob for apples. I can buy a gun in a store and shoot you. By myself! Do you get it? *(Stands and focuses back on them.)* You're dead meat with me, both of you. You're ready for the crock pot. You're a crock of shit. Leave here. I don't need you, and you're dead! *(Pause.)*

JOHNNA Well, I guess we should be going.

JOHN Well, I guess we should be going.

(JOHNNA and JOHN, looking the same and walking the same, leave the house. NAOMI chases after them to the door.)

NAOMI Fuck you and the horse you came in on!

(JOHN and JOHNNA exit. NAOMI comes back into the room and is overcome with grief. She sits back on the couch and lets out enormous, heartfelt sobs. They go on for a quite a bit, but when they subside, she's like an infant with a new thought, and she seems to be fairly contented.)

NAOMI Well, that was a nice visit.

RICHARD FORD

American Tropical

SETTING

A house trailer in a trailer park in central Florida. Visible in background is the side of an inexpensive mobile home. Three wooden steps lead to an aluminum door. In the tiny trailer yard an aluminum and nylon lawn chair sits center stage, far forward. Behind it and to the right, near the trailer, a man in his late twenties is seated at a small aluminum table with a ten-year-old girl across from him. They are playing Scrabble, having a jaunty good time, occasionally shrieking laughter at an unexpected word, or else fussing over a disputed one.

It is afternoon, and the light is yellowish, although as the scene develops, light will fall to darkness on all but the single lawn chair. A palm tree is visible in the background of the trailer.

A young woman exits the trailer. She is early twenties, late teens, but with a carriage that implies experience in the world. She wears shortish shorts and a sleeveless blouse. She carries cigarettes, matches, a can of beer, and an ashtray.

She pauses as she approaches the lawn chair and looks judgmentally at the man and the little girl. They look up at her. The man grins crazily.

SID   *(To woman, wildly.)* You hot ticket!

(He turns enthusiastically back to the Scrabble game. The woman looks away indifferently, walks to the lawn chair, and sits, facing audience.)

(She sets down her beer, settles the ashtray in her lap, and lights a cigarette. SID watches her admiringly. She waves smoke away from her face, and now that she's seated, it's apparent her mood is somber and perplexed.)

EVELYN   *(Conversationally, to audience.)* Have you ever been to a poultry house at night? After they were closed? And looked in the windows? Seen all those chickens and ducks in their little cages asleep. Some of them eating, putting their little heads through the wires, pecking up the grain and the water—whatever they can reach out and get. *(Pause.)* Just waiting for tomorrow. *(She takes a drink of her beer and another drag on her cigarette.)*

EVELYN   That's a lot like how I feel. *(Pause.)* I did a bad thing. I've got a humming in my ears all the time now. Huu-umm, huu-umm. Sometime I can't even hear at all. Like the wind came up and blew the sound all away from me. And I'm deaf. *(She looks surprised by all of it.)*

SID   *(Loudly, to her.)* Can you give proper names?

SUZIE   *(Authoritatively.)* We said we could!

SID   *(To EVELYN.)* Does Tommy Dorsey have an 'e' in it? *(EVELYN ignores them moodily.)*

SUZIE   *(To SID, arrogantly.)* S-Y! Just like pussycat!

SID   E! It's *s-e-y.* How'd you know about him? You're too little.

SUZIE   I know a lot of things.

SID   *(Smiling.)* I guess you do.

EVELYN   *(Smoking, to audience.)* We killed a person up in Michigan. It was cra-azy, cra-azy. I regret it now. That's the whole reason we're down here. We're *from* Michigan. A town called Wyandotte. Downriver. From Detroit. We just rent her now. Michigan's a bad place to be in love, let me tell you that.

SID   *(To audience.)* That wind'll knife you up there.

EVELYN   In his *van.* We went in his van to pick up this girl. Penny. I've decided to say her name because she was a friend of mine. We ran together. Ran the streets of Wyandotte all the time. We were going to take her in the van to a party, where she was supposed to be going to meet her boyfriend, whose name is I don't remember what now. *(Vaguely she tries to remember.)* But we were in the van, going. And I said I needed to excuse myself someplace about halfway there. So we stopped in this like park. And I got out and went in the bushes. And I couldn't have been gone only five minutes. Maybe six minutes. But when I came back they were half-undressed back in the comfort chamber. And, well, I just went crazy, and I just started in. And one thing led to another, and she was dead. Penny. I don't know how even.

SID   *(From table.)* She's not mean. She can *be* mean. But it's not really in her.

EVELYN   I've never been mean. I'm not mean.

SUZIE   *(Clamorous.)* Play! Play!

EVELYN   Him and I just drove around town all night after that. Trying to figure out what to do. I don't know what Dean must've thought. Dean was the boyfriend.

SID   *D-e-a-n.*

EVELYN   Finally, we just put her out. Penny out of the van in a woodsy place, and went back to his house. We got Suzie—she's his daughter by a marriage—and started driving. Florida, we thought. Everything in the country flows right to Florida finally, I believe. Like a sink. Plus it's warm. I like the high skies. You can see a long way in any direction you care to look, which relaxes your retinas— I used to work at an optometrist's office. Plus the sunsets don't make me sad, like Michigan did. Though what I *did* makes me sad. And I know tomorrow, maybe, I have to do something about it all. There's this humming in my ears all the time now. Your body doesn't lie to you. It tells you the secret truth.

(SID laughs loudly at something in the Scrabble game. EVELYN glances at him, then back to the audience.)

What's better than a man who'll laugh?

SID   *(To EVELYN.)* Tell about your sister!

EVELYN   No I won't.

SID   Bat shit. Totally bat shit. *(To SUZIE, still playing Scrabble.)* Look at Evelyn smoking, hon. Can you spell *funeral home? Cobalt treatments?*

SUZIE   *A-n-t-i-c-l-i-m-a-x.*

SID   *(Haughty.)* *W-r-i-s-t-w-a-t-c-h.* Wristwatch! *(SID pulls up his sleeve and displays several wristwatches up his arm. He grins crazily.)*

EVELYN   He can make them. He's highly skilled. He could go to work anywhere there's a watch plant.

SID   *(Sarcastically.)* Like Switzerland. *(Gestures at the trailer.)*

EVELYN   He says the secret of a wristwatch is that they're all the same. All of them're alike.

SID   *(From the table.)* Every damn one of them. Longines. Bulovas. Benruses. Timexes. I know about 'em. All of them are made in the same damn place. Upstate New York someplace. Just like automobiles. All that's different is the size and the face. I make the damn things, I oughta know. Or I did make 'em.

EVELYN   *(Abstracted.)* Sometimes we take the short view too much, I think. I used to hope to teach civics someday. That was my best subject at Wyandotte. The Bill of Rights. The Magna Charta. All that. But now I never will because I'm not civic enough myself. The older I get, the more the facts of life are clear to me, I know I'll never teach civics. That's a fact, even though I have experience others don't and I think I have goodwill toward everyone.

SID   *(Smiling.)* That's what everyone thinks.

EVELYN   *(Ignoring him.)* People will talk to you down here in the tropics. A man over there *(Points offstage.)* told me that when they were starting *Candid Camera* they tried to start in Michigan. But no one would talk to them. So they came to Florida. And that's why so many of them had southerners' accents. I don't know what I'd do if people didn't talk to me now. My ears are humming all the time, and it's better when people are talking, or even when I'm talking. I know I lie in bed at night and watch the little window on the clock. Watch the numbers flip down, sometimes all night long. And my ears will be humming, humming. I should go have tests made, though I know well enough what I'm suffering from.

(*SUZIE leaves the table and comes to EVELYN and whispers, then waits for an answer.*)

EVELYN Yes, sweetheart. You certainly may.

(*SUZIE turns and runs toward the mobile home, making a sashay skip past her father, who has turned now to watch EVELYN, smiling in admiration of her. EVELYN takes a drink of her beer.*)

EVELYN I wish I didn't drink these. But I do. (*Pause.*) I always thought kidnapping was the stupidest of crimes. I never knew why anybody'd get interested in it. You always get caught. But at least the *person* gets away, or has the chance to. But killing. *That's* the stupidest crime of them all. Way past kidnapping and the rest. Wyandotte is close to Detroit, so you have a chance to think about it all while you're growing up. I think with killing, apart from the thing itself, the worst is that you *seem* to get away. But no one really goes free.

SID (*From the table.*) She's not really mean. Sometimes women just don't have characters where other women are concerned. It's funny. (*Smiles in wonder.*) My first wife was like that. Exactly the same.

EVELYN I hear God, I think. I saw in a newspaper the other day, it was the *Pennysaver*. I saw a ticket advertised for Holy Rome. Somebody had bought a tour ticket, then couldn't go for some reason at the last minute and was stuck. I thought to myself: Take it. When am I going to see Rome? It's a holy place, and I'm Catholic. See Rome and Die was going to be my motto on the trip.

(*SID leaves the table and comes to the chair beside EVELYN and whispers something to her, then laughs softly, as if it was a private joke between them.*)

EVELYN (*To SID.*) You think I'm a fool? Don't think that, because you'd be wrong.

(*SID laughs good-naturedly, then bends and kisses her on the cheek.*)

SID (*To audience.*) She's a genius, really, isn't she? (*SID walks away toward the mobile home, climbs the steps and passes SUZIE coming back out. SUZIE carries a jar of cold cream in her hands. She heads for EVELYN.*)

EVELYN I read someplace on the way down here about a woman with a brain tumor. They operated on her and took eighty percent of her subconscious mind. She can still walk and talk and think, in a way. She just doesn't keep things much anymore. I thought—seriously—that wouldn't be so bad. Women have characters, no matter what he thinks about the subject. (*Motions at trailer and SID.*) People always like to say it's hard for us to know what we think about things. But I know what I think. And what I think about myself. My mother taught me not to kill another person. And now I've done that in Michigan.

(SUZIE sits on the ground at EVELYN's feet in a posture of apparent adoration. She uncaps the cold cream and begins carefully to rub it into EVELYN's legs, using her hands.)

EVELYN   That's nice, Suzie. That's very nice.

(Light is almost down. The spot illuminates EVELYN and SUZIE. EVELYN gazes up into the dark sky.)

EVELYN   We'll probably get new weather now. That'll make me dizzy. Weather's the only part of Michigan I can honestly say I don't miss, the only part I won't be glad to see when I go back to enter prison.

(SUZIE looks at her strangely, as if each of them is in a trance. EVELYN smokes her cigarette, blows smoke into the darkness.)

EVELYN   *(Conversationally.)* I've always put my faith in men. Maybe that was a mistake and I'll live to regret it. Maybe I'm living that regret right now and have nothing but misery to look forward to. Love is just a loss, isn't it? *(Pause.)* What's the use of making a hunted criminal of yourself? That's a good argument, one I could listen to if I could hear anything but a hum that I'm sure is not just the weather changing and that will only get louder. I wish my friend Penny had said that. But.

(SUZIE stops applying the cold cream and screws the top back on the jar, then sits back, staring at EVELYN.)

EVELYN   I've never disliked being an adult. Never wished I was a young girl again. Yet you feel yourself to be in a position which is the very one you didn't want to be in. That is, come to a bad end. And you can feel like a child about it and wish you could be a child and get out of it. Though that's not so easy anymore, either. I've wished I had my own virginity back more than once in the last month. Sometimes you just start out to do something, and then something else happens. You know? Only you've caused it.

(EVELYN caresses SUZIE's hair. SUZIE puts her head on EVELYN's knee, while EVELYN continues soothing her. A light goes on in the dark trailer.)

EVELYN   Illusion is not my adversary. Definitely. Even though I'm adaptable. Sid has said I'm a clear thinker and hopeful. But I have to go to the phones in a pretty little bit of time now. We need to have good experiences so our memories can be sweet. And we can't live forever. Though it's too bad my family isn't famous; then I would write about what I've done, and people would love it, and somebody'd get rich.

(The porch light goes on at the mobile home. The door opens. SID comes to the screen, look out silently into the dark. EVELYN pats SUZIE to rouse her. SUZIE collects the items on the ground and stands.)

EVELYN *(Softly to SUZIE.)* Take this, sweetheart.

(EVELYN gives SUZIE the beer bottle. SUZIE walks slowly to the mobile home. She enters past her father, who remains at the door watching EVELYN, who stands, holding her cigarettes and ashtray.)

EVELYN Other people don't make you happy or unhappy. You do it all by yourself. Right? So, maybe I've been wrong in putting my faith in men and doing things like killing a girl out of passion. I know eyes are impor- tant to me. I have always trusted people or not due to their eyes. My best friends have trusting eyes. And then one of them wasn't so much. *(Pause.)* So what can you do if you're me? I've always had the feeling of sailing before the storm. And now the storm has caught up with me and all around. *(Pause.)* Just-as-long-as-you're-happy-then-to-hell-with-the-rest is not an especially good motto. I cried when my father died, I know that. *(Shakes her head in wonder.)* What keeps us all from crime. I don't know.

(She turns toward the mobile home, walks toward it, climbs the steps, enters past where SID is standing.)

Dark.

MARIA IRENE FORNES

Springtime

CHARACTERS

RAINBOW *Twenty-nine years old. Slim and spirited.*
GRETA *Twenty-six years old. Slim, handsome, and shy.*
RAY *Twenty-seven years old. High-strung and handsome.*
He wears a dark suit.

SETTING

A small city. The year is 1958.

SCENE 1: *The courtyard of a medical school represented by
a square light on the down-right area of the stage.*

SCENE 2: *Rainbow's bedroom. A small room. On the left wall there is,
upstage, a small door; downstage of the door there is a small window.
Downstage of the window there is a chair. In the upper right corner of the
room there is a small bed with metal foot and headboard. To the left of the
bed there is a night table. On the night table there is a book, a pitcher of
water, and a glass. On the back wall there hangs a painting of a
landscape.*

SCENE 1: FALLING IN LOVE WITH GRETA

*A recording of Al Bowlly's "Bei Mir Bist Du Schoen" is heard. The lights go up on
the courtyard of a medical center. RAINBOW wears a gray duster. She sweeps the floor.
GRETA enters. She wears a white lab coat. She holds a clipboard.*

GRETA You never wear clothes that fit.
RAINBOW This?

GRETA   That's a size too big.

RAINBOW   It's my size.

GRETA   A smock should be smaller.

RAINBOW   Not anymore, madam. Now smocks are not so small. How do you
say that in German?

GRETA   What.

RAINBOW   What I just said.

GRETA   What.

RAINBOW   Now smocks are not so small.

GRETA   *Jetzt sind die ittel nicht mehr so klein.*

RAINBOW   *(Mispronouncing.) Jetzt sind die ittel nicht mehr so klein.*

GRETA   *(Impatiently.) Jetzt sind die ittel nicht mehr so klein.*

RAINBOW   How do you say, "You lose your temper too easily?"

GRETA   Who?

RAINBOW   You.

GRETA   I lose my temper?

RAINBOW   Yes.

GRETA   I don't.

RAINBOW   How do you say it?

GRETA   That I lose my temper?

RAINBOW   Yes.

GRETA   I don't lose my temper.

RAINBOW   How do you say it?

GRETA   *Ich werde niemals hastig.*

RAINBOW   *Ich werde niemals hastig.* . . . I love German! *(She swoons to the floor.)*
. . . I love German.

GRETA   That means "I don't lose my temper." *(Exiting.) Ha!*

SCENE 2: GRETA IS ILL

*RAINBOW's bedroom. The top sheet is accordion-folded at the foot of the bed. On top
of this sheet there is a nightgown. RAINBOW and GRETA have just entered. GRETA takes
off her dress. She is in a slip. She sits on the bed and starts to put on the nightgown.*

RAINBOW   Don't worry, Greta. I know what to do.

GRETA   What, Rainbow? What can you do?

RAINBOW   I'll find some money. Don't worry.

GRETA   How?

RAINBOW   I'll find money, Greta. I can't tell you how.

GRETA   Why not?

RAINBOW   You won't love me anymore if I tell you how.

GRETA   Tell me.

RAINBOW   Please don't make me tell you.

GRETA I don't want you to do anything that would make you ashamed.
RAINBOW I've been in jail.
GRETA Why? What did you do?

(RAINBOW helps GRETA lie down. She covers her with the sheet.)

Tell me.
RAINBOW I've been in jail for stealing.
GRETA Stealing?
RAINBOW Yes. But I don't do it anymore. I haven't done it since I've known you. But now I must do it. You're ill, and we must take care of you.
GRETA No! I don't want you to steal for me. You'll be arrested. You'll go to jail. You mustn't.
RAINBOW I must, my darling.

(There is a silence. GRETA puts her face on the pillow and sobs.)

SCENE 3: STEALING FOR GRETA

GRETA is lying in bed. RAINBOW sits on the chair.

RAINBOW I got it off his pocket. He came out of the store and put it in his pocket. I grabbed it and ran. He ran after me and grabbed me. He tripped. I yanked my arm off, and I threw him. Look. He tore my sleeve. (Putting a wristwatch on GRETA's hand.) He ran after me, but I was gone. Went in a building and hid. Saw him pass. Went to the back of the building and got out through the yard. I was afraid to go in the street. I was afraid he may have gone around the block. There's no one there. I walk to the corner and grab a bus. I didn't look like a thief. Would anyone think I'm a thief? Wasn't out of breath. Sat calmly. (Getting the watch from GRETA.) It's a good watch.
GRETA Get rid of it.
RAINBOW I'll sell it.
GRETA To whom?
RAINBOW I'll find a buyer.
GRETA I'm afraid.
RAINBOW Don't be.
GRETA Just get rid of it.
RAINBOW We need the money. For you. To make you well.

SCENE 4: RAINBOW IS CAUGHT

RAINBOW sits on the chair. She turns her face away from GRETA. Her hand covers her cheek. GRETA lies on the bed.

GRETA   Look at me! Who hurt you like that?

(RAINBOW *turns to face* GRETA.)

Who did that to you?

RAINBOW   The man whose watch I took.

GRETA   I knew you'd get hurt. I knew you couldn't do what you were doing and not get hurt.

RAINBOW   I got careless. I went back where I got the watch.

GRETA   Why?

RAINBOW   He grabbed me and he made me go with him.

GRETA   Where?

RAINBOW   To his place.

GRETA   Oh!

RAINBOW   I tried to get away. He forced me. I resisted, and he pushed me in. He said he'd put me in jail.

GRETA   What did he do to you!

RAINBOW   I had to agree.

GRETA   To what?

RAINBOW   To do something for him.

GRETA   What!

RAINBOW   Meet someone.

GRETA   Who!

RAINBOW   He didn't say.

GRETA   What for?

RAINBOW   He's nasty.

GRETA   Are you afraid?

RAINBOW   Yes.

SCENE 5: GRETA WONDERS IF RAINBOW LOVES RAY

GRETA *lies in bed.* RAINBOW *stands left.*

RAINBOW   He's like a snake.

GRETA   Do you love him?

RAINBOW   Love him? I hate him. He hates me. He hates me for no reason. Not because of the watch. He never cared about that. Just for no reason. He never cared about the watch. That was nothing for him. He hates me. Just because he wants to. I hate him but I have a reason. (RAINBOW *goes to the chair.*) I understand him, though.

GRETA   Why?

RAINBOW   I don't know why.

GRETA   How can you?

RAINBOW   I think in his heart of hearts he's not the way he appears to be.

GRETA   What is he like? He couldn't be good and do what he does.

RAINBOW   Well, he's not what he appears to be. *(Pause. GRETA is convinced.)*

GRETA   . . . Could I have some water?

(RAINBOW pours water. She lifts GRETA's head up and holds the glass to GRETA's lips. When GRETA is done, RAINBOW puts the glass down and sits.)

Didn't you already do what you had to do for him? Didn't you already pay—for the watch? Why do you still have to work for him?

RAINBOW   He's a friend.

GRETA   If I die . . . will you love him then?

RAINBOW   . . . If you die? *(RAINBOW goes to the side of the bed and kneels.)* If you die I'll love *you*. Whether you live or die it's you I love. And if I ever loved anyone else, it would not be Ray. Not Ray. Never Ray. *(GRETA laughs.)*

SCENE 6: RAY GIVES ADVICE TO RAINBOW

RAINBOW stands right, fluffing the pillow. GRETA sits up against the headboard.

RAINBOW   Can you imagine? And I said to him, "It's you who places too much importance on whether I like men or I like women. For me it's not important. What's important is that since I met Greta it's only she I love. *(Placing the pillow behind GRETA.)* That's what's important. *(Taking the bedspread off the bed.)* Why should it be important whether I like men or women? Does it make any difference to anyone? *(Taking the bedspread out the door to shake it.)* If it doesn't make any difference to anyone, why should anyone care? *(Turning to GRETA still holding the bedspread.)* He said, "If it doesn't make any difference, why don't you choose to love a man?" And I said, "It doesn't make a difference to anyone else, but, of course it makes a difference to me." *(Placing the cover over GRETA.)* If I don't like men, why should I pretend that I do? Why should I try to love someone I don't love when I already love someone I love? And besides, do you think it makes a difference to anyone?

GRETA   I suppose it doesn't make any difference to anyone.

RAINBOW   That's right. Why should I force myself. *(Sitting next to GRETA.)* And he said, "What difference does anything make? Live, die, it doesn't make any difference." And I said, "Live or die makes a difference. I want to live and I want to be happy, but I don't care about the things you care about." And he said, "What things?" And I said *(Standing and walking to the chair.)* "The way you see things." And I said that I'm not going to pretend to see life the way he does. And he said, "Why not?" that he thought I should. And he said that I should care about those things, and if I don't, I should pretend that I do. And I said *(Sitting.)* "Why?" And he said that he talks to me as a brother would, for my own good. And I said I thought

he had some nerve, because I thought his life was far from impeccable—
far from it. And I told him that.

GRETA His life is far from impeccable.

RAINBOW I told him he had some nerve.

GRETA Your life is impeccable now. I don't see anything wrong with it.

RAINBOW . . . Neither do I.

GRETA Your life was peccable when you were working for him. But now that
you've paid your debt to him and you don't work for him anymore your
life is impeccable. It was he who made your life peccable.

(RAINBOW laughs.)

Why do you laugh?

RAINBOW How do you say peccable in German?

GRETA Why?

SCENE 7: GRETA WONDERS HOW RAINBOW SEES THINGS

GRETA lies in bed. RAINBOW sits by the window looking out into the yard.

RAINBOW With time they look better and better.

GRETA What, honey?

RAINBOW The flowers.

GRETA How could that be?

RAINBOW Maybe it's the fertilizer I put on the soil.

GRETA What looks better?

RAINBOW The colors. They look healthier.

GRETA How do you see things? Do you see things different from the way I
see them?

(RAINBOW looks at GRETA. She is somewhat alarmed.)

RAINBOW Why do you ask?

GRETA (Smiling.) I just wondered.

RAINBOW Why?

GRETA I worried . . .

RAINBOW That we saw things differently . . . ?

GRETA Yes.

RAINBOW We don't.

SCENE 8: GRETA DISCOVERS WHAT RAINBOW DOES FOR RAY

GRETA *is standing on the chair. She is opening an envelope. She takes out some pictures and looks through them with alarm. She throws them on the floor and stares into space.* RAINBOW *enters. She looks at the pictures on the floor. Then she looks at* GRETA.

GRETA   Is that what you do for him!

(RAINBOW *kneels down to get the pictures.* GRETA *tries to reach for the pictures.*)

Why! Why!

(GRETA *starts pounding on* RAINBOW. RAINBOW *tries to hold her down.*)

Why! Why are you doing that when I asked you not to! Why do you do that! Why do you do that! Why do you do that! You're lying naked with that man! Who is that man! What is he doing to you! Why do you do that! Why do you take your clothes off! Why do you take such pictures!

RAINBOW   I'm sorry! I'm sorry!

GRETA   Why do you do that!

RAINBOW   I have to.

GRETA   Why!

RAINBOW   Because you must have treatment. (GRETA *cries.*) I don't mind. (GRETA *sobs.*) It's for you.

SCENE 9: GRETA ADMIRES THE SUNLIGHT

GRETA *sits upstage of the window. The chair faces front.* RAINBOW *stands next to her.*

GRETA   Could you open the window? (RAINBOW *opens the shutter.*) I like to sit here and see the sun coming in. I like to let it come in through the open window. The sun is brighter that way—or so it seems to me. There are times when I feel disturbed. I feel restless. I feel nasty. And looking at the sun coming in makes me feel calm.

SCENE 10: GRETA THINKS THAT RAY IS IN LOVE

GRETA *stands left of the bed straightening the bed.* RAINBOW *sits on the chair.*

GRETA   Ray was here this afternoon.

RAINBOW   What did he want?

GRETA   He didn't say. He waited for you and then he left. (*She starts moving down as she smooths the covers.*) Does he sound to you like he's in love?

RAINBOW No.

GRETA He sounds to me like he's in love.

RAINBOW Who with?

GRETA I don't know, but he sounds to me like he's in love.

RAINBOW How does a person in love sound? *(GRETA sits on the right side of the bed.)*

GRETA A person in love holds his breath a little after inhaling or while they inhale. They inhale, stop for a moment, and inhale a little more.

RAINBOW I haven't seen him do that.

GRETA *(She lies on the bed.)* I have.

RAINBOW He seems preoccupied to me.

GRETA Yes, I think he sounds preoccupied. Maybe he's lost money in the market.

RAINBOW Maybe he has. Why are you concerned about him?

GRETA I'm not.

RAINBOW You sound concerned.

GRETA He's preoccupied.

SCENE 11: RAINBOW DOESN'T FEEL LOVED ANYMORE

GRETA lies in bed. RAINBOW stands by the door facing her.

RAINBOW Something's wrong. Something's wrong because you're not happy, because you have to keep things from me. I know you don't tell me what you think—not everything. Did you ever keep things from me before? Is this something new, or have you always kept things from me? *(Pause.)* Is it that you don't love me anymore?

GRETA *(Shaking her head.)* No.

RAINBOW For me to love is adoring. And to be loved is to be adored. So I never felt I was loved before. Till I met you. But I don't feel loved anymore.

SCENE 12: RAY WANTS SOMETHING FROM GRETA

GRETA lies in bed. RAY stands to the left of the bed by her feet, facing her.

GRETA I lash out at you because I can't deal with you. I can't even understand what you are.

(RAY moves closer to her and starts to lean toward her. She recoils.)

You're like some kind of animal who comes to me with strange problems, to make strange demands on me. *(She pushes him off. He persists.)* You come in all sweaty and hungry, and you say you want this and you want that. Take your hands away from me! Not again! Not again! Never again!

Don't touch me! Leave me be! I have nothing to give you. Don't tell me that you want these things. Talk about something else. What else can you talk about?

(RAINBOW *enters. She is obviously alarmed. She looks at* GRETA, *then at* RAY; *then at* GRETA *again.* GRETA *turns her head away and sobs.* RAINBOW *and* RAY *look at each other.*)

SCENE 13: RAINBOW LEAVES GRETA

RAINBOW *stands at the door looking out.* GRETA *sits on the bed looking at her. "Melancholy Baby" is heard:*

"Come to me, my melancholy baby.
Just cuddle up and don't be blue.
All your fears are foolish fancy, baby.
You know, honey, I'm in love with you."

(GRETA *moves to the chair. She sits facing* RAINBOW. *She looks down.*)

"Every cloud must have a silver lining."

(GRETA *looks at* RAINBOW.)

"So wait until the sun shines through.
Smile, my honey, dear,
While I kiss away each tear.
Or else I shall be melancholy too."

(GRETA *reaches out and takes* RAINBOW's *hand.* RAINBOW *allows her to hold her hand, but does not respond.*)

"Come sweetheart mine.
Don't sit and pine.
Tell me all the cares
That made you feel so blue.
I'm sorry, hon."

(RAINBOW *faces* GRETA.)

"What have I done.
Have I ever said
an unkind word to you.
My love is true."

(RAINBOW *leans over and puts her head next to* GRETA's.)

"And just for you.
I'll do almost anything

at any time.
Hear when you sigh
or when you cry.
Something seems to grieve
this very heart of mine.

Come to me my melancholy baby.
Just cuddle up and don't be blue."

(RAINBOW *walks to the door slowly and exits while the song plays to the end.* GRETA *lowers her head. Then she turns to the right. After a while she looks up. As the song is ending, she looks down again.*)

SCENE 14: GRETA READS RAINBOW'S LETTER

GRETA *is sitting on the chair opening a book. She takes an envelope from it. She opens the envelope, takes out a letter and reads.*

GRETA   My beloved; I'm sometimes obliged to do things that are dangerous, and to do things that I hate. To befriend people and then betray them. Someday I may be hurt. If this happens and I'm not able to tell you this, I hope one day you'll open this book and find this note. I love you more than anything in the world, and it is to you that I owe my happiness. I always felt that I didn't want to love only halfway, that I wanted to love with all my heart or not at all, and that I wanted to be loved the same way or not at all. With you, I had this, and if anything happens to me, I wanted you to remember this: that you are my angel and I will always love you. Even after death. Forever yours, Rainbow.

(*"Have You Ever Been Lonely" is heard.*)

EDWARD GOREY

Helpless Doorknobs

For an eclectic entertainment, pick—using chance or deliberation or both—twenty or so (of the 2,432,902,069,736,640,000 possible) versions of the text to put on the stage. Six actors are needed; more could be used. Note that ADOLPHUS *is a large black dog.*

ANGUS inherited the grandfather clock from AUNT ADA.
ANGUS concealed a lemon behind a cushion.
ANGUS lost a shoe not far from the folly.
ADELA became disoriented at ALARIC's funeral.
ADELA flung ANGELA's baby from an upstairs window.
ADELA could not find her way out of the woods.
ANDREW came across a horrid secret in ADELA's diary.
ANDREW received a postcard from AMARYLLIS.
AGATHA pedaled to the neighboring village for help.
AGATHA taught ADOLPHUS to do the one-step.
AGATHA finished knitting a scarf for AUGUSTUS.
AMANDA wrote a note to AUGUSTUS.
AMANDA found several unfolded napkins on a back shelf.
ALFRED returned from Novaya Zemlya.
ALBERT left for Peru.
AMBROSE took an overdose of sarsaparilla.
ALETHEA vanished from a picnic.
ARTHUR's outdoor garments turned up in a guest-room closet.
A disguised person came to one of the side doors.
A mysterious urn appeared on the grounds.

RICHARD GREENBERG

Life Under Water

CHARACTERS

AMY-JOY *Early twenties.*
AMY-BETH *Same age.*
KIP *Twenty-one or two.*
JINX *Forty-five.*
HANK *Forty-eight.*

SETTING

Various locations on Long Island's southern fork. Summer.

SCENE 1

The beach. AMY-BETH *and* AMY-JOY.

BETH   So tell me.
JOY   You'll die. I'm bad, I'm so bad.
BETH   What did you do?
JOY   You will just die.
BETH   And what if I don't?
JOY   I'll be very disappointed. But it's not gonna happen, it's just not gon—
BETH   So you went out to allay her fears. . . .
JOY   I went out because the little one, the girl—
BETH   Yes, I know who you mean.
JOY   *Isolde?* Shit, what kind of people name the kids Tristan and Isolde and the dogs Brian and Susan? I mean—

BETH   Your uncle.

JOY   Uncle *Andre*, wouldja believe? Andre Vinegrad as in Abe Weingarten. I mean, the whole family.

BETH   And you went out to allay her fears.

JOY   'Cause she thinks she sees a sea monster. I find out. I go there, I find it out. The other kid—

BETH   Tristan, this is.

JOY   Tristan—you believe that? A name like that he's gonna have serious trouble dating.

BETH   And then what happened?

JOY   And then what happened is like the other kid's a one-of-those-kids-he swims-like-a-fish . . . water baby! Like this article in *People* magazine, and he's in it naked. So he's cool about the whole deal, he's working on her, saying there is no such thing as a sea monster, you know?

BETH   Mm-hm.

JOY   And he's got her just about I would say *half* convinced. And I'm watching and I'm thinking, well nothing for me to do, a child is more likely to respond to a sibling, anyway— I took this family planning course—

BETH   Things are going smoothly.

JOY   Things are going smoothly. And I think—I don't know what came over me—I see this little child, five years old—I see this kid, she looks so goddamn innocent, and I think—wouldn't it be kind of neat to scare her shitless?

BETH   You didn't.

JOY   I did.

BETH   Of course you did.

JOY   Who knows why?

BETH   Sea monsters exist.

JOY   In a big way.

BETH   Amy-Joy—

JOY   Shame on me, I know, I know. But you should see this kid. Too dumb for life. Her eyes look like—

BETH   A simile?

JOY   . . . Big. Very big. The eyes are very big. 'Cause I tell her these sea monsters in the sea—and they eat anybody's ever been in the sea so too late now—and they especially eat little girls who someday intend to have expensive nose jobs—'cause already they're planning it, you can tell. And they especially *especially* eat little girls with stupid names. And they got these big, humongous—this is the best part—these big, humongous—

BETH   Jaws.

JOY   Jaws, you said it. 'Cause like she's got the lunch box? with the shark? with the mouth? with the kid? with the blood?

BETH So right now she's—

JOY Right now she's shitting her pants. But the beauty part is even if she never goes back in the water again, I fixed it so she's terrified. I traumatized her.

BETH Why?

JOY Why? Because. It was something to do. I was bored. Because her father's a fairy antiques dealer.

BETH I wonder what she saw actually . . .

JOY Probably Tristan's little zorch.

BETH Would that have scared her?

JOY It scares you, doesn't it?

BETH I'm another story.

JOY You're telling me . . . Hey.

BETH *(Pause.)* Yes?

JOY You're all right, aren't you? I mean . . . You're all right.

BETH I'm all right.

JOY Good. Let's do something tonight.

SCENE 2

KIP alone in his room, lying on his bed. His mother's voice offstage.

JINX. Kip? . . . Kip! Telephone! . . . It's your father. He's calling from Indianapolis . . . It's long distance, so take your time. Bleed him dry . . . Kip! . . . *(She enters, putting on her earrings, perhaps barefoot—she's getting ready for the evening.)* Are you or aren't you? *(He doesn't respond.)* Do you want to talk about it?

KIP There's a call from Indianapolis. Shouldn't you be on the line?

JINX You're more important.

KIP You just want to frustrate my father. You want him to lose his patience and his money.

JINX He can afford it. The man is not a pauper.

KIP Why don't you talk?

JINX Do you know what he netted last year? *Netted?*

KIP I'm not interested.

JINX Of course, if he's got any of it left, it's a miracle, with that blushing young bride of his.

KIP I don't care.

JINX Twenty-three years old, well, I don't want to talk about it, it's too sickening—

KIP What time is it in Indianapolis, anyway?

JINX And have you heard the latest? Did I tell you? In deference to the new Barbie doll, he's having—it's *too* funny—plastic surgery. Could you—?

94 / Richard Greenberg

(She might exit here to get her shoes, deliver her next line offstage, reenter, sit, put on shoes, etc. The scene should have that kind of activity, that slight distractedness on JINX's *part.)*

KIP I think they're central time, aren't they? Isn't that the time they go by—?

JINX The middle-aged man's recipe for rejuvenation—a nip and a tuck and a youngish fuck.

KIP Mother!

JINX Oh, I'm sorry. I've forgotten your sensibility. An entire generation and I'm stuck with the one member who has a *sensibility*. In any case, he's dead to me now. Talk to him. Get it over with.

KIP No.

JINX Why not?

KIP He's a phony.

JINX I should never have let you read *Catcher in the Rye*. Phony. Your concerns are hopeless.

KIP *(Sitting up; readying himself for the evening.)* I need fifty.

JINX I don't think so.

KIP For tonight. Look, I'll pay you back. I'll mow a lawn or something.

JINX It won't be necessary.

KIP It's a gift, then?

JINX The fifty won't be necessary.

KIP Oh? How do you figure?

JINX You're staying in tonight.

KIP I don't think so.

JINX I'm going out, so you're staying in.

KIP You're going out, so I'm staying in? What is that, physics?

JINX Common sense. I don't want the house to be left alone.

KIP It's a big house, Mother. It can take care of itself. What's the matter? Don't you trust me?

JINX Not since you were sixteen and had that affair with that rock singer—

KIP Folk singer.

JINX Whatever. She had gonorrhea.

KIP Pyorrhea! Pyorrhea! When will you learn? Her gums were infected, not her sex organs. She was a virgin.

JINX Many times over. Listen, I don't want to argue. Your father's on the phone. Sound prosperous and well adjusted and happy that he's gone. There's money in it for you. And merchandise. Maybe a Porsche.

KIP I don't want to talk to him.

JINX That's the spirit. Try to convey that during the conversation if you can. I hate that shirt.

KIP It's tailor-made from England.

JINX Don't lie to me. I know where it's from. And it's all frowsy around the elbows.

KIP Overseas shipping.

JINX Why do you lie the way you do? I mean, I can understand lying in the abstract. For a purpose. But you tell people you summer in Newport instead of the Hamptons. That your father is in steel instead of oil. That's lateral mobility, what does it get you?

KIP It feels more real.

JINX *(Fed up.)* You're such a *problem child*! Change the shirt.

KIP Have I offended you? Did I say something to offend you? What? Tell me.

JINX Kip, please.

KIP I didn't mean to offend you. I never do. It just happens. If you'd just make a list—just make a list—of acceptable things to say and unacceptable things to say, I'd be grateful, I would. I'd study it.

JINX Now, Kip—

KIP Because, mother, I really *don't* mean to offend. I just say what's on my mind sometimes.

JINX I'm leaving. Do what you want about the phone.

KIP Where are you going?

JINX Out.

KIP Who with?

JINX Is that a *significant* question?

KIP Only if it leads to a significant answer.

JINX Hank Renshaw.

KIP It's a significant question.

JINX You over-interpret.

KIP He's *married*.

JINX Drinks, that's all. Maybe a late supper.

KIP Maybe an early breakfast. I can't stand it. It's disgusting to me.

JINX Kip!

KIP Did I do it again? I'm sorry. I didn't mean to offend you.

JINX Don't wait up.

KIP Mother, I'm too old for this. I can't have curfews anymore. I can't have my life run by you. What will I do with my night?

JINX I leave you to your own devices.

KIP No you don't. You strip me of my devices. I need human society.

JINX I don't know why. You're not very good in it.

KIP I'm improving.

JINX Read something. Drink something. *(She kisses his forehead.)* Good night.

SCENE 3

Amy-Joy and Amy-Beth toss around a beach ball intermittently through the scene; Amy-Beth dispiritedly.

JOY You're not being very helpful.

BETH Sorry.

JOY It's fun. Don't you know what fun is?

BETH Yes. Fun is a repetition-compulsion centered on tossing a piece of inflated rubber.

JOY I remember another one.

BETH Who?

JOY The guy I met on Third Avenue.

BETH. The *guy?* Singular?

JOY. No, I mean the sort of classy guy. With the profession. He was a—you know, Security Analyst! Which I still don't know what it means.

BETH Security Analyst. Someone who analyses security. Sort of the opposite of a psychiatrist.

JOY He was a pretty neat guy. Some of them—

BETH You're telling me?

JOY It got pretty bad. You just don't know with the guys you meet. You gotta be so careful.

BETH You do.

JOY In the modern world. Like who knows what's gonna happen? You gotta live as if nothing's gonna happen. You can't go around being careful. You can't be *timid.* 'Cause who knows? You can be hit by a truck any day of the week, am I right?

BETH Of course you're right.

JOY You just gotta be so careful.

BETH Mm-hm.

JOY *Caveat emptor.*

BETH Impressive.

JOY Of course. I've thought about this.

BETH The effort shows. Maybe you should lie down.

JOY 'Cause life is already wearing me out, you know?

BETH Drying you up?

JOY Sort of. I'm hardly ever horny anymore. It's a routine; that's why I want to get married.

BETH That's a terrible idea.

JOY Yeah, but I want to marry someone boring so I don't ever have to think about it.

BETH You lead a ridiculous life.

JOY Some people would think so.

BETH Meaning?

JOY   Don't get tight-ass.

BETH   I'm not getting tight-assed.

JOY   Give me a back rub.

BETH   Forget it.

JOY   Some friend.

BETH   Fuck you.

JOY   Hey, I'll make dinner later. I got lobster and mussels. I got crabs.

BETH   I don't doubt it.

JOY   I mean, *shellfish.* You. I'll make a salad. I got sprouts, mushrooms, radishes, cauliflower, snow pods. Then we can do something later. *(Pause.)* Is there something we can do later? *(Throws her the ball. Pause. Beth throws down the ball.)*

BETH   I hate this game.

JOY   What's to hate?

BETH   It feels like recreational therapy.

JOY   Well . . . I don't know from recreational therapy.

BETH   Meaning?

JOY   Meaning my personal history does not include basket weaving.

BETH   Meaning mine does?

JOY   Meaning nothing. Meaning I said words and forget about it.

BETH   In other words, I'm a neurotic bitch.

JOY   Did I say that? Did you hear me say that?

BETH   We didn't weave baskets. We made lanyards. And we attached whistles to the end of them. There were sixteen people per class. Our instructor was named Sunny. She was the most depressing person I ever met. Are you satisfied?

JOY   They gave whistles to sixteen crazy people? *(BETH turns sharply away.)* Oh, Christ! I'm sick of you being sick.

BETH   It's your own fault for hooking up with a convalescent.

JOY   Why don't you go back to school?

BETH   It started at school. If I go back it will start again. School. People. Masses of people. I need quiet. I need solitude.

JOY   *(Sympathetically.)* You had all that and you freaked again.

BETH   Environments reject me.

JOY   Get a job.

BETH   I had a job. I lost it. I was a receptionist. I was afraid of the telephone. People would drop off packages. They ticked.

JOY   Jesus.

BETH   When I was away, I almost had an affair. With a short-order cook.

JOY   Who couldn't cope with life.

BETH   Well, you see, that was a *tall* order. But what I mean is, shall we compare notes? Would that be a pleasant diversion?

JOY   *(Gently.)* The thing we gotta do is, we gotta find an activity.

(Commotion off.)

BETH *(Looks up.)* What's that?
JOY Oh, my God! Isolde is burying Tristan!

Quick blackout.

SCENE 4

Lights up on KIP's room. It is empty. After a moment, we hear JINX's voice.

JINX Kip! Kip! I'm back. Where are you? Are you in your room? Kip, I'm sorry I made you stay in last night—where are you? I apologize. Humbly. You can come out now. Are you hung over, is that it? Is that why you're not answering me? I'll make you a Prairie Oyster. Kip? Kip? I've got to tell you. Something wonderful happened last night. Mr. Renshaw—Hank —do you know what he said? He said my hair was the color of tea roses. I'll give you the fifty now, Kip! Are you sulking? Are you *sleeping?* At this hour, my God! But I don't care. Sleep the day through, vomit all over the sheets. Get rid of the poisons. I'll clean you up. And I'll give you money. And I'll hold your head. Tea roses. Imagine.

(Lights fade on an empty room. Note: *This scene may be too hard to sustain if JINX remains offstage. In the Ensemble Studio Theatre production, JINX was glimpsed through KIP's window, which was understood to look out on a deck.)*

SCENE 5

The two girls on the beach. KIP comes on, faint, swaying, having walked and drunk all night. He has just arrived. The girls look up from their reading.

JOY Looking for somebody? *(He collapses.)* God!
BETH Who is that?
JOY How do I know?
BETH What are you doing, going to him? He could be dangerous.
JOY I think I can handle myself. *(She kneels beside him, starts shaking him mildly, slapping his face.)* Hey. Hey! Are you all right? Hey! Wake up. Come on, wake up! Jesus, you must have had a night. Do you think he's cute?
BETH Please.
JOY Wake up. *(KIP begins groggily to awaken.)*
KIP What's happening?
JOY Who are you?
KIP What—?
JOY Your name.
KIP Kip.

JOY That's perfect . . . Are you sick?

KIP I've been walking.

JOY Walking where . . . ?

KIP All over. All night. I'm looking for . . .

JOY What . . . ?

KIP Work.

JOY Looking for work? All night? Very few people hire at four A.M.

KIP No . . . I was . . .

JOY What?

KIP Running away.

JOY Are you a fugitive?

KIP In a manner of speaking.

JOY What did you do?

KIP Had a mother.

JOY What? You're running away from home?

KIP I guess so, yes.

JOY Did you bring your skate key and a Twinkie?

KIP It may sound juvenile, but it's not.

JOY No, I'm sure.

KIP God, I must have walked twenty miles. I kept looking for a refuge. I recognized every house. Everybody in every house. They were all members of the club.

JOY Which club?

KIP Whichever. I don't know you.

JOY I'm visiting.

KIP Good. Nice . . . Oh, God! I'm in no condition to face what I have to face.

JOY What's that?

KIP Poverty. I'm penniless. And I'm trying to make my way to the city. Do you have work?

JOY . . . That depends.

KIP I'll do anything. I'll mow your lawn.

JOY There's no lawn. Why can't you just go home and get money?

KIP Never. I can't even go in the vicinity of that place again. I'm not very resourceful. This was a whim, and I've got to stick to it or I'm dead. Dead. Finished. I just want to get to New York.

BETH He's lying.

JOY Hitch.

KIP That's dangerous.

JOY What about a ride from a friend?

KIP I have no friends.

JOY Oh.

KIP Are you sure there's not something I can do?

JOY . . . You can . . . hang out . . .

KIP Excuse me?

JOY Here.

BETH Amy-Joy!

JOY There are all these rooms and no people. Like you can stay here until you find a lawn to mow. You know? I mean—we got these two kids we gotta take care of—my cousins— You can help, we'll pay for that, I mean *I* will.

KIP Is it legitimate work?

JOY Wait till you meet them. They were raised by wolves.

KIP I like children.

JOY *Now* you say that.

BETH Amy-Joy, this is ridiculous!

KIP I don't know your name.

JOY *(When AMY-BETH says nothing.)* Amy-Beth. She'll like you once she gets to know you.

BETH That's never going to happen.

KIP You really will, though. I'm very nice. I'm . . . harmless. I promise, I won't wear out my welcome.

BETH You'll have to leave retroactively.

JOY She doesn't mean it.

KIP Look—I'm sorry—It's just that I can't go back there. Not if I want to be human. And I do. My mother's life is depraved. I like you two. Automatically. Instantaneously. You're not like the people I know. This gives me a lot of hope.

JOY Why don't you go up to the house—

BETH No!

JOY —to the house where people are allowed to stay only because I say so . . . and why don't you clean up? I'll be up in a minute and get you something for your hangover. Be careful of Tristan and Isolde. They're playing Apache.

KIP Which house is it?

JOY The big glass one at the edge of the hill.

KIP Thank you. *(To AMY-BETH.)* We'll get along well. You'll see. *(He exits. AMY-JOY smiles. AMY-BETH glares at her, then looks away. They sit, not looking at each other.)*

BETH Shit.

JOY He'll give us something to do.

SCENE 6

HANK and JINX are seated at a restaurant table drinking a summer drink.

JINX *(Broaching a sensitive topic.)* Hank—

HANK Something rather odd happened the other day. Would you like to hear about it?

JINX   Of course.

HANK   It was at the Princeton Club. I'd had my racquetball and my steam and was drinking a vodka Gibson at the bar when who should tap me on the shoulder but Prescott Fowler?

JINX   Oh, yes.

HANK   Well, you know Press and I are old chums, dating back to Exeter, but I hadn't seen him much lately—only once or twice in the past few years, in fact. Anyway, we got to talking about old times and new times and whatever—and then suddenly—it was the liquor loosening him up, I suppose—he told me the most startling thing.

JINX   What was that?

HANK   Well, let me set it up for you. It seems that over the past few years he's found himself a bit straitened financially. Not critically, of course, just enough to feel the pinch. But Press, it turns out, is quite resourceful.

JINX   How do you mean?

HANK   I don't know if you've seen him lately, but he's in as good a shape as I am. Lean, hard as a rock. We did tennis together at Exeter. And it seems that Press has turned his fitness to economic advantage.

JINX   How is that?

HANK   Apparently—I never knew this before, did you?—there's a woman named Honoria. A very elegant woman named Honoria who operates a most discreet business out of a brownstone on East Sixty-fourth Street.

JINX   Honoria what?

HANK   No last names. Ever.

JINX   My God.

HANK   Not rough trade, of course. Women. Dowagers, even. Lonely and . . . stimulated.

JINX   Press? Really?

HANK   Yes. And not only Press—and this is what cast a whole new light over things. As I said, we did tennis together at Exeter—that was a great bunch of guys. There was a real solidarity among us. And an innocence. Young men, you know.

JINX   And?

HANK   Well, Press whipped out our old tennis photo. At first I thought it was a nostalgic gesture. But there was something strange about this photograph, something dreamlike. My dream. Because in it we had all aged somehow. Gracefully, to be sure, but nevertheless . . . aged. Thickened. Grown tired. And strangest of all, I was missing. From the picture. I was —quite literally—no longer in the picture. As it might well have happened in a dream. And those who *were* . . . in the picture . . . some six or seven of them in all . . . wore unnatural expressions. Gross, somehow. Lurid. Unseemly.

JINX   Well, of course it was—

HANK Yes. A picture of Madame Honoria's stable. My old class at Exeter. My teammates. It seems they had all suffered reversals of one kind or another and one-by-one Press had . . . offered them this solution. You see, Honoria only takes bona-fide social register types. She caters to the sort of woman who will not condescend. Even when all she wants is a good screw.

JINX Doesn't that cause uncomfortable moments? People knowing people, I mean.

HANK Oh, to be sure. But the embarrassment is strictly mutual, making disclosure . . . unlikely.

JINX My God. I just realized. These people you're talking about, they're . . . they must be . . . my friends.

HANK The friends we have in common. I'm not so casual at cocktail parties anymore. And East Sixty-fourth Street has absolutely transformed itself for me.

JINX I'd imagine.

HANK But here's the other extraordinary thing. One of Press's . . . clients . . . the other week—and I think this is the only reason he told me the whole story to begin with—a client he met with just a few days ago . . .

JINX Yes?

HANK Well. They met in a room at the Hotel Carlyle—which I think is dangerous, but never mind. Press and the woman went through the usual protocol. No names. Discreet undressing in separate rooms. Lights out. He took her in his arms. Began. The woman was a wreck. Emaciated. Ravaged face. Nervous eczemous rashes. Press, of course, was tender, sensitive, aware, careful not to show the revulsion he felt for the woman. For her ruined body. And her grief. And he made love to her. Like a gentleman and a scholar. Midway through . . . it . . . she began to sigh in a distinctive way. A kind of little chihuahua yelp. Well, it was like Proust's *madeleine:* a flood of memories. He pulled back, too quickly, and looked at her face, the face of this woman he had been hired to service, and in utter, absolute, blinding shock, he cried out: "Claudia du Plessix!" She closed her eyes then and asked, "Is that you, Press? I thought it might be, but I was afraid to say anything!"

JINX All of which means?

HANK Well, some thirty years ago when he was at Exeter and she at Concord Academy, Claudia du Plessix and Press Fowler lost their virginities to each other. One weekend at a mixer. He was a tennis champion, and she was the prettiest girl at Concord, and after that weekend they never met again.

JINX What did they do when they realized?

HANK They clung to each other for dear life.

JINX And I suppose he declined any fee for his . . . services.

HANK To the contrary. He charged double. *(Pause.)* What I mean is, don't you sometimes think that we're the last moral people on earth? The last people with a sense of the common decencies? Who know about the fitness of things. Who adhere to a standard. *(Pause.)*

JINX Does your wife know about us? Is that what you're saying?

HANK All right, then, yes.

JINX What should we do?

HANK Have I ever told you that your hair is the color of tea roses?

JINX Incessantly.

HANK Does it make you happy?

JINX Yes.

HANK Then what's the problem? *(Pause.)* I mean, I'm not being obtuse. I really don't see the problem. *(They look at each other.)*

SCENE 7

AMY-BETH in chaise lounge, reading. KIP enters, twirling beach ball on his finger.

BETH I thought you were supposed to be working. I haven't seen it.

KIP I've been bathing the kids, feeding them, washing the dishes, Windexing the glass . . . which in this house is a chore, believe me. What kind of people build a glass house on the edge of a hill in front of an ocean?

BETH Rich people.

KIP Why are you playing with that string?

BETH Why not?

KIP Whenever I see you, you've got something . . . string, marbles, a daiquiri glass. Your hands are never unoccupied, why is that?

BETH Do you have money for train fare yet? It can't be more than ten dollars to the city from here.

KIP I've decided to stick around for a while. Until I've got enough to get started. It's not the best idea to arrive in Manhattan empty-handed. Lots of people on the street waiting for you if you do that. Terrible types on the streets of Manhattan. Muggers. Rapists. Mimes. *(AMY-BETH laughs.)* Ah-hah!

BETH That was a spasm.

KIP No, it wasn't.

BETH I promise you it was.

KIP I don't believe you.

BETH I don't care. *(Pause.)*

KIP Amy-Joy tells me you went to Radcliffe for a while. I got kicked out of a lot of schools, too.

BETH I did not get kicked out. I left.

KIP Really? Why?

BETH Reasons. Amy-Joy never understood why I went in the first place. She said, "Once you get in, why bother?"

KIP *(Laughs.)* I like her.

BETH Of course. Everybody does.

KIP I like you, too.

BETH That's a less common reaction.

KIP Why don't you ever talk to me?

BETH Kip, listen. You're here because Amy-Joy wants you here. You're her boy, not mine.

KIP I like you better. I like her a lot, but I like you better. *(Pause.)* What did I say? Did I offend you? I didn't mean to offend you.

BETH I want you to leave soon.

KIP Look—I'm sincere. Utterly. I think we have a lot in common. I have trouble with people, too. I look as if I don't, but I do. *(Pause.)* Do you know before I came here I used to gaze up at this house? I used to wonder about it. There's a green light that burns all night at the end of your dock—

BETH That's the goddamn *Great Gatsby*. I can read! Oh, you sensitive boys with your quotations—I don't trust you as far as I can throw you.

KIP You should. I only tell nice lies. The past five days here I've been looking for a method to approach you. I think unapproachable people like us have a responsibility to seek each other out. The only thing I've come up with is to tell you exactly how I feel. But it's hard to express something like this. You must know how hard it is.

BETH Meaning?

KIP I'd like to get you between the sheets.

BETH I'd like to get you between the eyes.

Blackout.

SCENE 8

KIP's room. KIP is stuffing clothes into a bag. JINX enters in a bathrobe.

JINX The prodigal son returns.

KIP I've come to collect my things.

JINX I'm not giving you money to walk out of here again.

KIP I'm not taking your money.

JINX Sit down and talk.

KIP Why are you wearing your robe in the afternoon? . . . My God—

JINX Oh, leave it alone—

KIP You're disgusting.

JINX There's no one here, why not drop it? *(KIP drops it.)* I've missed you. Everyone talks slowly and in long sentences. Where have you been?

KIP I've been living down the shore. With two girls.

JINX Two girls. Does that mean—?

KIP Orgies every night.

JINX   What are you living on?

KIP   I'm a sort of . . . caretaker at their place.

JINX   Gigolo, you mean?

KIP   You have a sleazy mind. I'll get my things and go.

JINX   Don't be silly. Let's talk. The best part is talking.

KIP   I don't have much time.

JINX   We should get together regularly. I like it. We can be like those people in Henry James who do things so they have something to talk about after.

KIP   I've never read Henry James. *(HANK enters in bathrobe.)* Now that's just . . . great . . .

HANK   Hello, Kip. How are you? *(No answer.)* Huh, Kipper? You doing all right? *(Pause.)* Not talking to me? Okay. Your mom's been frantic.

KIP   Don't come near me.

JINX   Kip—

KIP   This . . . is not my idea of a romantic relationship.

JINX   If you'd just listen—

KIP   Forget it. *(He leaves.)*

JINX   What was the point of that?

HANK   My son knows, why shouldn't yours?

JINX   Skip knows?

HANK   Yes. He saw us someplace.

JINX   What do we do now?

HANK   That question is rapidly becoming monotonous. Come here.

(She goes to him. They kiss.)

Fade.

SCENE 9

Darkness. The sound of the ocean, continuous through the play, more prominent here. After a moment a flashlight, carried by AMY-JOY, switches on, beamed toward the audience.

JOY   Tristan! Isolde! Where are you, you little bastards?

(Another flashlight comes on: KIP's.)

KIP   Tristan! Tristan! Come on out now! Isolde!

BETH   *(Also with a flashlight.)* Tristan! Isolde! Where are you?

JOY   The little sons of bitches, I hope they're dead.

KIP   We should separate.

JOY   Form teams or something. Kip?

KIP   Why don't you take the area around the house?

JOY   Come with me.

KIP   No. It'll be better if we spread out.

JOY   Shit. Those bastards.

BETH   I'll look by the dock.

JOY   Okay. See you later.

KIP   Good luck.

JOY   Does that mean find them or not?

KIP   Find them. *(She exits. KIP shines the flashlight on AMY-BETH.)*

BETH   We should go.

KIP   Wait. *(AMY-BETH shines the light on his face.)*

BETH   Why?

KIP   I want to look at you.

BETH   You're hurting my eyes.

KIP   It's been two weeks. We've talked. We've *failed* to talk. I've told you how I feel about you but you won't believe me. I've told you everything there is to know about me. That didn't take very long. What can I say? Can I make up a story, is there some lie, is there an anecdote I can tell you that will break through?

BETH   I'm squinting in that light.

KIP   You look beautiful.

BETH   Don't say that.

KIP   I mean it. *(AMY-BETH shines the light on his face.)* See?

BETH   It's a weak light.

KIP   I love you.

BETH   "Why did you climb that mountain?" "Because she was there."

KIP   No.

BETH   Why don't you love Amy-Joy?

KIP   That would be ordinary. And very easy.

BETH   Oh.

KIP   She wants me.

BETH   I know.

KIP   She doesn't need me, though.

BETH   And I do?

KIP   Don't you?

BETH   The Salvation Army mentality—save anything that needs it. *(Pause.)*

KIP   It's a beautiful night.

BETH   We should be looking for the children.

KIP   Talk to me. *(Pause.)*

BETH   Turn off the light.

KIP   Why?

BETH   It's hurting my eyes. *(He turns off the light. All we see is KIP's face.)* It didn't happen. It didn't happen anywhere. It didn't happen at school. It didn't happen at home when I escaped from school. It didn't happen when I moved in with Amy-Joy—not even in Manhattan.

KIP   What? What didn't?

BETH   I don't know. Do you? I think Amy-Joy does. Sometimes I think if I could study her like Latin, drilling the way she is, everything would be all right. Her life works somehow. Other people seem to have figured this problem out.

KIP   What problem?

BETH   Don't you know? *(Pause.)* How could you? *(Pause.)* Every gesture it took to live out a day was like some kind of absurd gymnastic event I was too clumsy to perform. You can't imagine what it's like to feel ridiculous all the time. All I could do was watch people. I'd get stomach cramps. I couldn't sleep. Something wanted to jump out of me, but my body contained it. Trapped it. Then one night, when it wouldn't stop raining and I couldn't sleep no matter what I did, I started tearing off my skin. It seemed very hopeful at the time, but I didn't stop until there were deep bloody grooves in my face as if I'd been slashed at with a knife. It's amazing what a little effort can do. I had doctors. A plastic surgeon. He did good work, didn't he? Sealing me up again. *(KIP turns the light on her.)* No, turn that off!

(KIP quickly turns the flashlight off. After a moment, BETH turns the light off him, too. They are in darkness. We hear the water.)

KIP   I love you.

BETH   On an island with no money, you love me. But what about under less desperate circumstances?

KIP   In Manhattan with millions. *(BETH turns the flashlight on his face. He is kneeling now before her, beaming up at her.)*

BETH   What is that, a smile? *(He rises and kisses her. Their faces are ringed in light. She turns the flashlight off.)*

SCENE 10

HANK and JINX in semi-dishabille. Postcoital. HANK cradles a drink in his hand.

HANK   I don't relish the idea . . . !

JINX   What?

HANK   I don't relish the idea of working out my anxieties as a stud on you. And I don't relish the idea of you using me to scratch your itch.

JINX   We're not doing that.

HANK   Love is supposed to make you feel innocent. I don't feel innocent. I feel . . . *uninnocent.* All the people we're hurting. *(Pause.)* Hello, Jinx.

JINX   Hello, Hank.

HANK   Jinx. Jinx and Hank. And Dot. My wife, Dot. And your son Kip and my son Skip. Jinx and Hank and Dot and Kip and Skip. We sound like elves.

JINX Let's go to bed.

HANK I'm not happy in this house.

JINX No. It's your wife's house you're not happy in.

HANK Unhappiness is portable. That's one of its chief characteristics.

JINX Let's go to bed.

HANK Did I ever tell you . . . ?

JINX What?

HANK Did I ever tell you . . . that I *detest* tea roses?

Fade.

SCENE 11

The two AMYS on the beach.

JOY Why are you so happy all of a sudden?

BETH I just am.

JOY That really stinks.

BETH Sorry. Did you visit Tristan?

JOY Yes.

BETH How is he?

JOY Fine. Hardly singed.

BETH You got there in time.

JOY No help from you, thank you very much.

BETH I told you—

JOY Right, right, deep talk, deep talk. *(Pause.)* Shit.

BETH How's Isolde?

JOY I don't know, the shrink's an asshole. He says, like, maybe she's a pyromaniac, like that helps to know or something.

BETH Do you think she's a pyromaniac?

JOY Anybody named Isolde she could be anything. You were no help at all.

BETH I'm not the one who told her the sea monster story.

JOY Yeah, well, who taught her how to build a fire?

BETH That she must have picked up on her own.

JOY Shit. I see this kid sleeping with all those sticks around him, these flames lapping at his feet, the little bitch screaming. "Burn! Burn! Burn!" I almost lost it—I tell you. Meanwhile, you're off getting laid. Well, what the hell, you were hard up.

BETH When are the Vinegrads coming home?

JOY Oh, this is good, get this. Since everything's all right and nobody was hurt, they're gonna stay in Paris two more days until he closes the deal. A sense of responsibility? He's importing antique andirons or whatever-the-fuck; meanwhile, his children are setting each other on fire. They're such Protestants, I swear.

BETH It gives us a couple of more days here, at least.

JOY That's a thrill.

BETH We can go out now. Wherever you want.

JOY I got news. At the best of times, the Hamptons are not a hotbed of activity.

BETH Clubs. Movies.

JOY Jesus.

BETH Are you angry at me?

JOY Disappointed. I am extremely disappointed. That's all. You come here a sick person and you hop into bed with the first man you meet. That's not a solution. I gave you credit for more intelligence than that. I'm just disappointed. But no skin off my nose—you should excuse the expression.

BETH I'm sorry.

JOY Look, that's life.

BETH I guess so.

JOY Everybody's a shit.

SCENE 12

HANK *is doing calisthenics.* JINX *watches.*

JINX That's fascinating, but what's it for? *(Pause.)* Are you in training? *(Pause.)* You're forty-eight years old, and you look sixteen. I'm forty-five and look twelve. When we were thirty, we both looked thirty. Do you think we're receding? *(Pause.)* What do you do with your afternoons? *(Pause.)* Because you're not in your office, I know. I call. *(Pause.)* That was a confession. You can hit me for it. Punch, pummel, strike. Any form of physical contact will be gratefully received. *(Pause.)* The way you're treating me, if I didn't trust you, I'd . . . be much wiser. *(Pause.)* What's going on?

SCENE 13

AMY-BETH *and* KIP *on the beach.*

BETH What happens next?

KIP I've got some money.

BETH You have fifty dollars.

KIP It's something.

BETH Not enough.

KIP You're going back to your parents' house.

BETH For a little while.

KIP I don't suppose that—

BETH No.

KIP No. I didn't think so. *(Pause.)*

BETH You're going home.

KIP No, I won't. I'll do something. I'll mow a lawn.

BETH Lucrative.

KIP Not so far. *(Pause.)* I want to be a responsible person. *(Pause.)* Is there a place where they teach you that? *(Pause.)* I don't know what the hell I'm doing.

BETH That's fine.

KIP I have no money. I don't properly exist.

BETH You're enough.

KIP No. I'm not. *(Pause.)*

BETH After you go home and get money, come to me. I'm leaving home and getting a job. Then I'm going back to school. I'll get an apartment in the city. You can come live with me. There are lots of things you can be.

KIP Like what?

BETH You can be a . . . steward! *(Pause.)*

KIP Maybe I can go back to school, too. I think I'm a high school graduate. I think my father bought me a diploma somewhere.

BETH Good.

KIP It doesn't sound very likely, does it?

BETH Sure it does.

KIP I'll take care of you.

BETH I know. *(Pause.)*

KIP Is there stuff to drink? A lot?

BETH Stop looking as if you've committed a crime.

KIP The thing is—

BETH What? *(Pause.)*

KIP The thing is—

BETH What? *(He looks at her.)*

Fade.

SCENE 14

The porch. A wicker love seat. KIP *is drinking.* AMY-JOY *is with him.*

JOY So tell me. *(Pause.)* Amy-Beth is giving Isolde a bath. I told her to use a blowtorch. That girl is like "Most Likely to Succeed" in a snake pit.

KIP She should be under psychiatric care.

JOY Amy-Beth?

KIP Isolde.

JOY Yeah, her, too.

KIP Why are you two friends?

JOY   Are you kidding? Amy-Beth couldn't live without me. She's my responsibility. You've gotta take care of your friends. We've been bests since forever. First grade.

KIP   Oh.

JOY   She needs somebody like me for protection.

KIP   You don't seem very compatible.

JOY   That's what I mean. Amy-Beth ever met somebody compatible, within the hour they'd be dragging the river for the bodies. Why are you depressed?

KIP   Don't know.

JOY   I mean, finish the wine by all means 'cause I want Uncle Andre to have a connipsh, but what's the problem?

KIP   I made a mistake.

JOY   Yeah, I know.

KIP   I don't know what to do about it.

JOY   That's easy.

KIP   Yeah?

JOY   Go home to Mommy. Some guys are always gonna end up going home to Mommy, no shame in that. What else can you do?

KIP   Nothing.

JOY   At least you got a mother who'll take you. Big maternal instinct, I guess.

KIP   No. Not the way my mother wants things. She really shouldn't have children, she should have a puppy.

JOY   She's got one.

KIP   I guess so.

JOY   Look, so you're bored, you're guilty, you're evil—is that a reason not to be happy?

KIP   What do you mean?

JOY   You make things so goddamn complicated. *(She touches his face.)* I can help. I really can.

SCENE 15

Night. AMY-BETH *alone in a chair, partially in shadow. A long moment. Muffled voices off:* "Go through the patio—" "The what?" "The patio—" "But—" "On tiptoe—" "But just give me the—" "Just go—" KIP *enters, naked. He does not see* AMY-BETH *at first. She says nothing. He notices her. They stare. He walks over to her, kneels beside her, touches her face.*

BETH   *(Quietly.)* Put something on. The children might see you.

Fade.

SCENE 16

The next morning. AMY-BETH *alone, suitcase at her side.* AMY-JOY *enters, gathering stuff from floor, stashing it into a bag.*

BETH So how did it go off?

JOY Please. They're slobbering over the little girl like she did something so *clever*, like it was so *clever* you knew how to set your brother on fire like that, it's to vomit. They're all so fucked up. You think of all the nice people in the world who die in freak accidents . . . You only brought out the one suitcase?

BETH I left the others on the porch, is that okay?

JOY Sure. Maybe Uncle Fartface'll bring 'em down, though I seriously doubt it. Is Kip still here?

BETH No. He left with his mother.

JOY Oh. *(Pause.)* Typical. God, it's a beautiful day, isn't it? I can't wait to get back to New York. You looking forward to Merrick?

BETH Yes.

JOY You're kidding. Hey, you know what I was thinking last night? I was thinking that at the end of the summer I'd either look for a job or go back to school. I think my father's getting a little sick of paying my rent. Or else I'll get married. I'll probably end up getting married.

BETH Oh? Who to?

JOY Who knows? I may draw straws.

BETH That's as good a way as any. *(Pause.)*

JOY So.

BETH So. *(Pause.)*

JOY What time does the train leave, do you remember?

BETH No.

JOY No problem. The schedule's in the house.

BETH Your uncle will drive us to the station.

JOY Sure. Maybe we can eat lunch before, you know? We can get a salad. Seafood.

BETH I don't think so.

JOY Something.

BETH No.

JOY Okay.

BETH Look, do you think your uncle would mind if I took a later train? After you? I'd just like to stay here for a while.

JOY No . . . I guess that'll be all right.

BETH Good. *(Pause.)*

JOY I better get my other suitcases. Old fartface never will.

BETH Sure.

JOY It's been fun. Call me tonight, okay?

BETH If I'm home.

JOY Great. *(She exits.* AMY-BETH *remains.)*

SCENE 17

Lights remain on AMY-BETH *sitting. Lights rise on the other side of the stage:* KIP *and* JINX *together. Evening. Later in the summer.*

KIP *(Looking at photograph.)* I'm glad he doesn't come around anymore.

JINX So, I guess, am I.

KIP Did it just stop? I mean, or what?

JINX More or less.

KIP I don't understand. Why would he send you a picture of all these middle-aged men?

JINX It's a reunion photograph. Of a tennis team. Exeter, Class of Fifty-something.

KIP God. Hank looks awful.

JINX Doesn't he? *(Pause.)* Kip—?

KIP What?

JINX When you were living down the shore . . . Those two girls you spoke about . . .

KIP Yes, Mother?

JINX Did you become . . . involved . . . with one of them?

KIP In a way.

JINX . . . I caught a glimpse from the bottom of the hill when I picked you up. One looked very pretty.

KIP No. It was the other one.

JINX Oh.

KIP Are you cold?

JINX What were their names?

KIP You'd laugh if I told you.

JINX Oh. Cold, no. I don't think so.

KIP Cooler, though.

JINX Well. Fall, soon.

(They sit together. AMY-BETH'S *hand goes up to her face. Slow fade on* KIP *and* JINX. *Slightly slower on* AMY-BETH.*)*

JOHN GUARE

Four Baboons Adoring the Sun

A harpsichord sits at one side of a stage. The harpsichordist plays music from the Baroque.

A messenger dressed as the representative of an eighteenth-century Baroque Italian court appears in white-and-gold livery.

He unfurls a scroll of paper and sings in the impassioned voice of a countertenor the schedule of Alitalia arrivals and departures at Sicily's Palermo Airport.

PHILIP and PENNY MCKENZIE come on, early forties, khaki work clothes, blond, tanned, hard-working. They listen to the flight announcements.

PENNY   Is that us?

PHILIP   They talk so fast—

PENNY   At least they're not on strike.

PHILIP   Can you see the screen?

PENNY   I don't see the flight—oh, Christ! Are they not telling us something! A crash! Please! Make them safe!

PHILIP   No—there it is—via JFK.

PENNY   They came out of Dulles! Is it the right flight? Listen! No—that's Geneva—did it stop? Addis Ababa—Mozambique—it's gone off the screen—no JFK—

PHILIP   Oh, Christ, I hope they're safe—

PENNY   We should have sent them business class.

PHILIP   They have terrorists in business class. I don't think terrorists only terrorize economy. Listen—Milano—is that the flight? Listen—

THE MESSENGER   *(Sings.)*
    The plane from America
    The plane from America
    The plane from America has now arrived!

PHILIP   There it is. On time. On schedule! Over here. By customs—

PENNY   Will they laugh at us? I don't want the kids laughing at us. I want them to see the value of what we're doing.

PHILIP   They'll have a wonderful summer! Wait—announcement—
THE MESSENGER   *(Sings.)*
   The plane from America
   The plane from America
   The plane from America has now arrived!
PHILIP   They'll come through which door? This door? *Grazie—cetta porta*—the
   plane's landed. They're safe!

(The doors open. The kids enter. The "March of the Siamese Children" from The King
and I *plays.* THE MESSENGER *presents the children age nine through fourteen. Four kids
(*WAYNE, LYLE, SARAH, TEDDY*) run to* PHILIP, *screaming with joy.* PHILIP's *kids are
dressed very casually: jogging, surfing, jams. Five kids (*HALCY, JANE, PETER, ROBIN,
ROGER*) run to* PENNY, *screaming with joy. Her kids travel in blazers and gray flannels.*
PENNY *falls to her knees.)*

PENNY   Oh, my arms and legs and eyes and ears and soul. It's been ten weeks.
   Ten weeks!
PHILIP   You're all big and wonderful and healthy. Kiss me. Let me smell you.
   You beauties.
PENNY   You remember Philip.
PHILIP   Kids, this is Penny.
PENNY   How wonderful to meet you!
PHILIP   Wayne. Teddy. Sarah. Lyle.
PENNY   Halcy. Peter. Jane. Robin. Roger.

(The kids size each other up, forming two rival clans.)

PHILIP   Didn't you all get to be friends on the plane?
LYLE   We flew over a volcano.
PENNY   Mount Etna!
SARAH   You brought us to an island with a volcano on it?
PHILIP   We'll drive up there someday.
JANE   We should have been told about a volcano before we agreed to come—
   I'm calling Daddy.
PENNY   Darling, it's a lovely volcano. Lava comes from the word *lover*. Don't
   be afraid of any volcanoes. Now does everybody have their bags? I'm sure
   your father knows Sicily contains Mount Etna.
PHILIP   We can drive up there.
PENNY   I am *saving* the volcano. When we have succeeded in becoming a
   family, when we are forged together, when we have done what we are
   setting out to do, *then* we shall *all* drive up to Mount Etna and look down
   into the mouth of that god Vulcan and show him we are One. That
   volcano is our reward. We will look at Etna. Lava streaming through the
   night, all orange.
PHILIP   Etna's back that way.

116 / John Guare

PENNY   Etna can be anywhere I want it to be. Got your bags?

PHILIP   Where's the car! *Dove e l'auto?*

JANE   Daddy's very happy and didn't send you best greetings or anything.

PETER   Daddy's secretary sleeps in your bed.

PENNY   Hurray for Daddy! We all have what we want. Look me right in the eye. I. Love. You. Pull it together, Roger.

(*THE MESSENGER appears and sings:*)

THE MESSENGER   (*Sings.*)
  Sicilia
  Separated from the mainland of Italia
  Only by the Straits of Messina
  Comprises 9,860 Square miles Sicilia
  A breakwater between the East and West
  Africa and Europe
  Christian and Muslim

SARAH   This is Sicily?

LYLE   I told the kids at school we were coming to pyramids.

PHILIP   That's Egypt. I parked over there.

SARAH   Where's the pyramids?

PETER   I thought this was archaeology.

PENNY   It is. You parked down here.

WAYNE   Where's the temples?

PHILIP   There's the car! *Ecco!* Now we have a long car ride! Halcy, you take the girls to the little girls.

PHILIP   Wayne—the boys follow Wayne.

(*The kids go.*)

PENNY   I don't want the kids laughing at us. I want them to see the value of what we're doing.

PHILIP   We can't expect them all to settle down into a new culture, a new family situation instantly. We're going to have to be strong.

PENNY   I'm *prepared* to be strong. I don't want them *laughing* at us. Beads. Pots. I want them to be thrilled by Sicily. I want them to see Sicily through our eyes. To see its grandeur. Its majesty.

(*The kids return.*)

PHILIP   We set?

PENNY   Before we get in the van. I am so sick of my name. Penelope. And what kind of name is Philip?

PHILIP   It's not much, but it's my name. What do you mean?

PENNY   I was thinking of all the beautiful names—Adonis and Persephone and

Artemis and Dionysus and Semele and Clytemnestra and Zeus and Electra and Minos—

HALCY   What kind of names are those?

(PENNY produces two bags filled with slips of paper.)

PENNY   I've written names and we can each draw a name out and that will become our new Sicilian name and we will find out everything we can about our new name. Girls draw from the girl bowl. Boys draw from the boy bowl. Roger, you take the boy bowl.

(The kids reach in and pick a slip of paper.)

SARAH   I'm Arethusa.

(PENNY produces a thick book.)

PENNY   Now we can look up who that is.

(PENNY finds the right page and passes the book to SARAH.)

SARAH   *(Reads.)* Arethusa is a girl.
PENNY   Say *I*. This is you. *I* am a girl who—
SARAH   *(Reads.)* Was pursued by a river god, and she, I, ran and ran until I could run no more, and I called to Artemis—
HALCY   I'm Artemis!
PENNY   Goddess of the Hunt! Good!
SARAH   I called to Halcy, who changed me into a spring of water that left Greece and bubbled up out in *Sicily*! And she was safe! Thank you, Halcy.
PENNY   We'll look for that spring.
HALCY   *(Takes the book.)* It says here the wicked river god followed her through the tunnel and he came out in Sicily too.
PHILIP   The point is she was *safe*.
PENNY   *And* transformed. Isn't that a dreamy name! Arethusa.
SARAH   I like Sarah.
LYLE   *(To PENNY.)* How come you didn't pick?
PHILIP   Penny doesn't have to. She already has a mythical name. Penelope. The faithful wife who waited and waited and waited and waited for her husband to come home. That's who Penny is.

(PENNY looks askance at PHILIP.)

PENNY   Anything you say, Midas. Get in the car, Artemis! Do you have your sleeping bag, Adonis?
PHILIP   You haven't been here an hour and you already have new names.
WAYNE   Mom said you threw away an empire like the Duke of Windsor.
PHILIP   The archaeology department at the University of Cal—San Luis Obispo is hardly an empire. Everybody got their bags?

WAYNE   Threw away an empire. I like that, Dad.

HALCY   Who's the Duke of Windsor?

PENNY   He gave up the throne of England for the woman he loved.

HALCY   Was he a hero? Were they very beautiful?

WAYNE   I saw a TV movie about them—they were beautiful.

PENNY   TV docudramas have a very slender relation with the truth. Get in get in—*Andiamo! Vite! Vite!*

PHILIP   My good Duchess?

PENNY   Everything fine, my excellent Duke.

WAYNE   My good Duchess. I like that.

HALCY   My excellent Duke.

WAYNE   After you.

HALCY   After you.

(WAYNE and HALCY smile at each other and bow. PHILIP and PENNY happily follow them and their children off.)

THE MESSENGER   *(Sings.)*
    You must always stop at a café by the sea
    You must bask in the sun by this lunatic, crazily blue sea
    You must watch your kids play
    The eternal game of Ringalevio!
    See them running in and out of the water
    See them throwing an orange Frisbee. All the while you drink Bellinis!
    What are Bellinis?
    Champagne and fresh peaches!

(PENNY and PHILIP return, arm in arm, peaceful. They watch their children in the distance.)

PHILIP   Can't tell who's yours.

PENNY   Can't tell who's mine.

(WAYNE and HALCY, the two fourteen year olds, appear. PENNY and PHILIP stand back. The harpsichord plays tremolo.)

PENNY   *(To us.)* I heard the murmuring first. It wasn't a babble like a babbling brook. But it had the quality of clear water running over glittery stones.

PHILIP   Can't tell who's yours. Can't tell who's mine—it's all going to be fine —but then I heard it, too. I heard what? The sound of exotic birds clawing the earth—

WAYNE   —to marry an Etruscan.

HALCY   Mel is a wonderful man. Just does not possess one drop of Etruscan blood. I love him. Our kids. The most *wonderful* kids. I'm happy.

PENNY   Wayne and Halcy whispered to each other. Even though they were down on the beach, the wind carried their voices to our table like a quiet silver gift.

WAYNE   We all have these secret identities hiding inside us.

HALCY   We don't know who we truly are. Or what myth we all belong to.

WAYNE   Is there a moment when all our lives are touched by grace and we discover our true selves?

HALCY   I don't dare.

WAYNE   We have to dare.

HALCY   I've got to get home.

WAYNE   We've been given a gift.

HALCY   I just came into town to have lunch. Things like this don't happen. Not to me.

WAYNE   Not to me.

HALCY   I hate my life.

WAYNE   I hate my life. I can't go on. I'll die if I don't make a change and have love in my life. I'll die.

PHILIP   The breeze changed direction.

PENNY   (*To us.*) What we heard were the contents of letters we had written to each other—of phone calls we made late at night while we were working all this out—they couldn't have been on the phone. They couldn't have been reading our mail. Could they?

THE MESSENGER   (*Sings.*) Am I hallucinating?

PHILIP   I heard it, too.

PENNY   These Bellinis.

PHILIP   No more Bellinis. I think we're just hearing things.

PENNY   Tell me everything is going to be okay.

PHILIP   Tell the gods. They're all around us.

PENNY   Gods! Make them have a better life than we've had.

PHILIP   Till now! Don't forget till now! Okay, kids! Back in the car!

THE MESSENGER   (*Sings.*)

A moment in our lives
When we are touched by grace
We discover our true selves
Is such a moment possible?

(*The family reassembles.* PENNY *and* PHILIP *map out areas with string and place shards of pottery on the earth.*)

PENNY   We're on a dig at La Muculufa. This is where we work!

PHILIP   La Muculufa rises high out of a flat plain, two limestone spires jutting into the sky.

PENNY   Its cliffs are dotted with caves.

PHILIP   The space between the two stone fingers contains the archaeological site lined with trenches

PENNY   and our office and house. We all stay here—

PHILIP   We have six Sicilian workers helping us with the digging. Look at this bead!

PENNY   Exactly! Pure Crete! Rare routes of the Mediterranean. How did this bead, which we know is from Crete, get all the way up here?

PHILIP   We mark off an area with string for the kids to dig.

PENNY   (Waving in the distance.) Buon giorno, Bruno! Si! Le ragazzi! Dice Ciao, bambini. Kids, those are the workers—say hi—well, they're not wildly charming, but they're very good workers. Let me teach you how to hold the equipment.

PHILIP   Wait till you see what work we're part of.

PENNY   What work you're part of.

PHILIP   See these beads! These beads show evidence that the Mesopotamians had traffic as far as this post in the 1200s B.C.!

PENNY   And Philip's being modest. He's identified a bead that might put this site back a hundred years earlier. We'll show you on the computer.

PHILIP   Follow the trade routes! Why did this bead from the island of Crete end up here in Sicily 1100 B.C.? As simple as this—a burial site? Keep digging!

PENNY   This bead. 1100 B.C. Traveled from Crete to this site.

PHILIP   To know why you're here. To identify your true purpose.

SARAH   Beads? You came here for beads?

PENNY   Show them the pottery.

SARAH   Pots and beads?

HALCY   Where's the columns and the statues and the ancient civilization you keep writing about?

PENNY   All under our feet! It's a burial site!

WAYNE   Funerals?

SARAH   Why aren't we in Egypt?

PHILIP   Because we're in Sicily. Penny, I think they're ready to start digging.

(They begin digging. The harpsichord plays furiously.)

PENNY   Now you must be careful. See the layers of earth? An inch of earth can represent hundreds of years' difference from the inch of earth below it.

PHILIP   It's like you're in this incredibly delicate lasagna. All layers. You are in the field!

PENNY   Be careful. It's holy.

SARAH   Is this where you were married?

(The harpsichord stops.)

PENNY   No, darling. We were married in Paris. Step in the trench.

ROBIN   Look! I found this!

PHILIP   Penny! Look!

PENNY   That's wonderful! (PETER finds a piece of pottery.)

PETER   Look!

PHILIP   And Peter has one!

PENNY   This is going to be a valuable day!

SARAH   Beads?

PENNY   We're here for the beads.

SARAH   Beads? You broke up our family for beads?

PHILIP   Now what we do is take it back to the stone hut to the computer.

PENNY   And we trace it and describe it and get all the information out of it we can.

PHILIP   And these satellites scattered above us in the sky make the world one vast archaeological dig. This shard of pottery is found in Sicily, sent to California, and we break the piece down via computer asking all the questions: What was it for? How old is it? What is it? I feed our results into my computers, and we learn by processes of classification stored in the computer that this piece of pottery is not from Sicily—here—but belongs to a division of pottery made in the Late Bronze Age in *Mesopotamia* all these thousands of miles away.

PENNY   Oooooo.

PHILIP   The computer makes the associations. We learn something about trade routes, the structure of the ancient world twelve hundred years before Christ. Our world is a richer place for it. Our work—your work—the Archaeological Computer Conservancy Institute brings the ancient world closer to us.

LYLE   How did you really meet Daddy?

PENNY   Today is about digging. Sarah, I bet if you dug over here you might find—

SARAH   Is it true you lied to us when you said you went to a college reunion and you really went off with Philip?

PHILIP   How are we doing down there?

TEDDY   Daddy, did you lie when you told us you met Penny in April?

PETER   Because you told us March.

PENNY   In that general period. Kids! Look! Here's another piece of pottery sticking right out! Didn't somebody find this? Jane? This is yours.

JANE   When did you meet? April or March?

PENNY   Everything happened so quickly. The divorce. Moving. All this. Down here, kids!

SARAH   March or April?

PHILIP   We met in March.

SARAH   So you lied about April.

PHILIP   In another life we were lovers.

PENNY   Don't make it sound like a reincarnation experience.

PHILIP   It was another life—

PENNY   If young is considered another life—

PHILIP Let me? *(She defers.)* We were lovers in another life. University.

PENNY The sad part. We lost each other.

PHILIP The happy part. We found each other, years later.

PENNY The kind of story everyone loves. Mythic—love lasting over the decades—

THE MESSENGER *(Sings.)*
> The kind of story everyone loves
> Mythic love lasting over the decades
> The centuries
> Into eternity

PHILIP I was an academic.

PENNY Me. Housewife. Exit four. Connecticut Turnpike.

PHILIP One day I flew east and gave a lecture at the Met.

PENNY I attended to see how fat he had become.

PHILIP Fat!

SARAH Daddy fat? Never!

PENNY He came out on that platform at the museum to lecture about Sicily, and my heart stopped. He could've been on television.

PHILIP Television!

PENNY Public television. Archaeology in Action. You made Sicily come alive.

PHILIP Q and A period after.

PENNY Dr. McKenzie, I'd like to . . .

PHILIP *(As her mouth moves.)* My God. Is that—it can't be—Penny? I heard Penny had married some asshole from the business school. Had left archaeology. Had a passel of children, but she's beautiful.

PENNY Using technology to explore the trade routes of the ancient Mediterranean kingdoms.

PHILIP Well . . . Your question bears explanation that would take up time from . . . Could we meet after the session? Next question?

WAYNE Where did you go? When did you meet again?

PENNY Across the street from the Met is a wonderful hotel.

THE MESSENGER *(Sings.)*
> Wonderful hotels have dark corners
> Pianists play love songs from another time
> Night and Day
> Under My Skin is the place I keep you
> Only Make Believe
> Lovers sit in corners

PHILIP Penny, I am an archaeologist who never got into the field. I am head of an archaeology department, and I have never been in the field.

PENNY But you could take your computer anywhere!

PHILIP My wife. My kids. No. No Sicily there. You should go. You had a wonderful knack for the field. That dig in Pennsylvania.

PENNY   We dug up a seventeenth-century sleigh!

PHILIP   Hated the seventeenth century. Too recent. No, the past Past!

PENNY   The blessed beautiful past!

PHILIP   You said you wanted to marry an Etruscan.

PENNY   Mel is a wonderful man. Just does not possess one drop of Etruscan blood. I love him. Our kids. The most *wonderful* kids. I'm happy. Don't tell the kids this part. I snapped the stem of his wineglass. The wine spills over our hands. I mop the wine from his lap with my napkin.

PHILIP   Wouldn't it be crazy if we started up again?

PENNY   You live out west! Don't tell the kids this part. I kissed the napkin.

PHILIP   This can't be my life. I feel like some mutilated Greek statue sitting at a desk. No arms. No face. No legs. No phallus.

PENNY   Oh, but you have a phallus! Don't tell the kids this part.

PHILIP   I hate my life.

PENNY   I hate my life.

PHILIP   Don't tell the kids this part. My wife has a series of lovers. Drugs. Liquor. She's got her own permanent bed at Betty Ford. They won't even take her back anymore.

PENNY   Mel cheats. Womanizes. Why is that the most derogatory word? Womanize. He cheats. I'm stranded. Don't tell the kids this part.

PHILIP   My kids—what's going to become of them? Motorcycles. California.

PENNY   The values. The emptiness. The promise they'll all be on crack. I want my kids to have a life.

PHILIP   We all have these secret identities hiding inside us.

PENNY   We don't know who we truly are.

PHILIP   What myth we all belong to.

PENNY   Occasionally, if we're lucky or grace hits us, we're transformed, and our true self shines through.

PHILIP   Is there a moment when all our lives are *mythic*? Are touched by grace —by God—and we start life? Is it now? Don't tell the kids this part. Penny, look at me.

PENNY   I don't dare.

PHILIP   We have to dare.

PENNY   I've got to get home. Exit four—

PHILIP   We've been given a gift.

PENNY   I just came into town to have lunch. Come to the museum. Things like this don't happen. Not to me.

PHILIP   Not to me.

PENNY   I hate my life.

PHILIP   I hate my life.

PENNY   Philip put a travel folder on the table. It read: Welcome to Sicily.

PHILIP   *Hurray!* It's a year later and we're in Sicily!

PENNY   Married! We made it! We got our divorces! A snap! Kids! Be happy.

PHILIP To do what you dreamed of! All those years behind a desk!

PENNY We were married in Paris! We had dinner on a *bateau mouche* sailing around the Seine by night—a moon—

PHILIP We had some work to do in the archaeological department of the Louvre.

PENNY We saw our favorite piece in the world.

PENNY Four Baboons Adoring the Sun—like this—twenty-fourth dynasty.

THE MESSENGER *(Sings.)* Four Baboons Adoring the Sun

PHILIP But it's from a different period.

PENNY Egyptian.

PHILIP We're Mycean.

PENNY But you should see these four baboons, palms upward, eyes agog.

PHILIP It looked like our divorce, Penny. Me. Your father. Your wife. Four baboons.

PENNY Now it's just us two baboons.

SARAH Why are you being disrespectful of mother?

PHILIP Not baboons.

PENNY Adoring the Mediterranean sun—the sun that shone over Sophocles and Icarus and the oracle at Delphi and the Olympic games and Plato and Achilles and Ulysses and—the same sun blinds you. On all of us!

PHILIP We came to Sicily for a working honeymoon.

PENNY This is going to be our life.

PHILIP Two archaeologists who married each other.

PENNY And it'll be great for you—a new culture, the oldest culture.

PHILIP The divorces worked out fine—all very adult.

PENNY Civilized the way it should be. No baboons we—

PHILIP We each have our kids for the summer—

PENNY in school in America for the winter—their mother—their father—custody fair and square—nobody unhappy.

PHILIP You'll come here—to Sicily—for Christmas and summer and alternate Easters—not baboons. Not baboons at all.

THE MESSENGER *(Sings.)* Four Baboons Adoring the Sun

PENNY You should see them! These four baboons, palms to the sun. I am so happy!

LYLE Did you love our mother?

PHILIP *(To HALCY.)* I love *your* mother deeper than any other human being I've ever known. You're doing very well. Look how well she digs.

JANE Did you love Daddy?

PENNY *(To WAYNE.)* I love your father with all my heart.

PHILIP *(About to be mad.)* Are you little tax accountants?

PENNY Now we are going to take our pottery and march down to the office and turn on the computer and we will plug into the rest of the ancient world and you will see where these beads came from, what they looked like—

PETER   Did we really find them?

JANE   Or did you put them here?

ROBIN   *I* wanted to find them.

PENNY   You *did* find them.

PHILIP   Now all get in line.

PENNY   We are going to march.

LYLE   *(Suddenly all military.)* In line. One two. One two.

PENNY   And we are going to be quiet.

LYLE   No talk!

(They march. The harpsichord plays its tremolo.)

PENNY   And then I heard the sound again. *(She signals PHILIP to halt the kids.)*

(A bed appears. WAYNE and HALCY are in the bed under the covers.)

WAYNE   Penny, all it is, is a challenge—

HALCY   Oh Philip, Philip, Philip! Are we up to it?

WAYNE   I *heard* him say that, too!

HALCY   I heard her say Can she hear you?

WAYNE   I heard him say She's in the other room. Drinking.

HALCY   I heard her say Mel's at the United Nations, so he claims.

WAYNE   I heard him say I wish I was with you.

HALCY   I heard her say We will be. Soon.

WAYNE   I heard him say Soon. I love you.

HALCY   I heard her say I love you, Philip. I hate my life. She said that.

WAYNE   I love you, Penny. I hate my life. We all have these secret identities
    hiding inside us. We don't know who we truly are.

HALCY   Is there a moment when all our lives are touched by grace—by God?

WAYNE   Not to me.

HALCY   Not to me.

WAYNE   I hate my life.

HALCY   I hate my life. *(PENNY and PHILIP gingerly approach the bed.)*

PHILIP   Hi, guys.

PENNY   Anybody home?

PHILIP   I think it's lovely you're getting along

PENNY   but we all have our own beds.

*(PENNY and PHILIP pull back the covers. WAYNE and HALCY look at their parents with
admiration.)*

HALCY   Mommy, you're so very *brave.*

PENNY   Let's go!

WAYNE   Will you let us live together as you—

PHILIP   No!

PENNY   You're kids!

WAYNE Will you let us live together?

PENNY No.

WAYNE You believed! You threw away your lives! You gave up everything! Us—you didn't care what we felt. You loved! Love is the only reality. Love is all. Stronger than anything. Love makes us immortal! You said that.

HALCY The night of the twenty-third of March.

WAYNE And repeated it at eleven P.M. in the evening eastern standard. Eight P.M. California.

HALCY Mom! That's how we met! We realized we were each on the line when you and Philip would talk.

WAYNE You have us to thank for helping you get together.

PENNY You told the kids?

HALCY Everybody knew.

WAYNE We could've got in the way! Refused to come. Refused in general! But your love kept us healthy. I'm off drugs! Sober! Sane! Your love was our love! Is our love!

HALCY We never met till the plane.

WAYNE But we knew each other

HALCY through you.

SARAH We knew everything and we were mad.

WAYNE Kids! Have I been wrong? Listen to me! I want you shaping up! I want you behaving well and supporting these two magnificent people who have given us a life. We will obey them and do everything in our power to help these people begin their lives. That means cleaning up and washing up and listening!

(*The harpsichord plays triumphantly.*)

THE MESSENGER (*Sings.*)
     We will obey them
     We will help them
     That means cleaning up
     Washing up
     Listening!

(PENNY *and* PHILIP *are stunned.*)

PENNY They're just being supportive.

PHILIP What amazing kids!

PENNY They see what we're doing!

PHILIP Talk about blessings!

PENNY But what can we do to protect this?

PHILIP We can't expect them all to settle down into a new culture, a new family situation, instantly. We're going to be strong.

PENNY I'm *prepared* to be strong. I don't want them *laughing* at us. Beads.

Pots. I want them to be thrilled by Sicily. I want them to see Sicily through our eyes. To see its grandeur. Its majesty—listen?

PHILIP   Let's let them see temples. The tourist Sicily. Let them see the flashy stuff so they can focus in on what *we're* doing. They're in love with us! Now let's have them fall in love with Sicily. We're going on a camping trip. Now. Right now.

THE MESSENGER   *(Sings.)*

Agrigento
Solinunte
Monreale
Cefalu
Erice!

(The kids gather around.)

PENNY   And it was evening. Above us, built on sheer cliffs, the town of Erice.

PHILIP   Dedicated to—what goddess?

PENNY   Astarte.

PHILIP   And who is Astarte?

THE MESSENGER   *(Sings.)* Astarte is Venus.

PENNY   Astarte is Venus.

PHILIP   Our crowd, our gang, sits around a fire, bundled up with blankets.

PENNY   Our statement of purpose—

PHILIP   People band together and make families and then those families get strong and they become civilizations.

PENNY   There's no difference between us now and people thousands of years ago.

PHILIP   What your mother and I are doing—what Penny and I are doing—is dealing with history before anybody wrote it down.

PENNY   You see this beautiful temple? Our work goes back further. *Before* there were temples here.

PHILIP   There was a great civilization in Crete ruled by King Minos, and it collapsed. Why? No one knows. There was no written history. How could a great civilization die? We look for clues.

PENNY   It's like being in a mystery story.

SARAH   Who was King Minos?

PHILIP   Glad you asked! Tell her, Penny.

SARAH   I want *you* to tell me.

PHILIP   Who do you think King Minos was?

SARAH   I don't know.

PHILIP   But, my darlings, in Sicily that is the only answer. I *do* not know. Learn that and you have learned the most—the *only*—rule in Sicily. *Omerta*. It means "silence." Say after me. O. Mer. Ta.

KIDS   O. Mer.

PHILIP   *(In a mock rage.) Silence!* You never say *omerta*. *Omerta* is *silence*. One never tells. With the mouth. With the eyes. And you know what the greatest sin is? *Infamita!* There are many ways to commit *Infamita*. The Breaking of the Silence. Say after me. In. Fa. Mit. A.

(The kids start to speak, then realize they should keep mum.)

PHILIP   Smart kids.

PENNY   Remember *omerta*. The most important word. Because King Minos was betrayed by his old, trusted friend who told certain secrets of the kingdom. And King Minos put on a disguise and went all over the world looking for his friend, who betrayed him. He came to Sicily. Right here.

PHILIP   And King Minos saw his old friend who betrayed him. And King Minos made a mistake. He told a young girl he was going to kill this old man. He didn't know the young girl was the daughter of the King of *Here*— where we are—well, this afternoon—and *she* killed King Minos.

SARAH   How?

PENNY   Details aren't important.

SARAH   How?

PENNY   It's all myth.

PHILIP   She poured boiling hot water over him and scalded him to death in his tub.

WAYNE   Dad!

PENNY   *(Quickly.)* The moral of the story is you should never go out seeking revenge.

PHILIP   Or else your civilization will crumble.

PENNY   But where we are now is where civilization was saved!

PHILIP   Daedulus came here after he invented how to fly. Which one of you is Daedulus?

LYLE   I am.

PENNY   And he's the father of who?

WAYNE   Icarus.

THE MESSENGER   *(Sings.)*
   Daedulus came here
   Sat on this beach
   Looked up at those cliffs
   Dreamed of flight

PENNY   We want to find out why the civilization of King Minos collapsed.

PHILIP   Every piece of pottery.

PENNY   Every bead.

PHILIP   Part of a puzzle.

PENNY   Every bead belonged to a person and every person is an opportunity.

PHILIP   We have all these opportunities. We can change everything!

HALCY   Everything?

PENNY   We want to give you a life—not of privilege.

PHILIP   But of possibilities

PENNY   not a life where you can *buy* what's of value.

PHILIP   We want to put all these treasures in you.

HALCY   I have treasures in me?

PENNY   That's why we're here. To release those treasures.

PHILIP   And it'll be great on your college applications that you're not some ordinary kid with brilliant grades.

PENNY   You'll be kids who *lived* in Sicily.

PHILIP   Who were *archaeologists*.

PENNY   You're going to *work with* us.

PHILIP   We're all in the Bronze Age.

PENNY   We're living twelve hundred years before Christ.

PHILIP   You're not in the twentieth century anymore.

TEDDY   Why didn't you ask us to your wedding?

PENNY   The logistics were so difficult. We just got married in Paris and came here.

ROBIN   What did you wear?

PENNY   I sent photos.

ROBIN   Peter and Jane *kept* the pictures.

ROGER   Mommy had a white dress with a veil and white shoes and blue ribbons in her hair.

SARAH   You wore white? That's a laugh.

PENNY   Very good, Roger, darling. Anything you want to know about the wedding, ask Roger. I wrote you all about it. Yes, I did wear white.

LYLE   How did you meet?

PHILIP   Not again—

PENNY   A benefit dance at a museum—

PHILIP   *(To us.)* We climbed into our sleeping bags.

PENNY   *(To us.)* I wanted to be back at our dig in our bed.

PHILIP   *(To us.)* We see in the dark a band of ragged Sicilian children staring at us. I signal the Sicilian kids to join us. We have food left. But the Sicilian kids vanish in the dark.

THE MESSENGER   *(Sings.)*

Tell me everything is going to be okay

Tell the gods

They're all around us

PENNY   How are you? Nobody's asking if everything's all right with you.

PHILIP   We need money. How the hell are we going to raise the money for the workers we need? You should go back to America and have a benefit and raise some money.

PENNY   Apply for a grant?

PHILIP   That means going back to America, but you—well, you could.

PENNY   I could?

PHILIP   I can't leave the dig—

PENNY   I can be spared. I guess it doesn't make any difference what work I do. You seem to think I can easily leave here and all this and you and my children and go back to where I fled and raise tons of cash.

PHILIP   It's not what I meant exactly—

PENNY   Oh, we're into "exactly." What I meant to say— you don't know how much time and energy and sweat and *boredom* it takes to raise that much money. Are you trying to say I'm not a good archaeologist? Because, while we're at it, your work has been more than slightly sloppy the past few days.

PHILIP   I've had things on my mind!

PENNY   The way you processed that Mesopotamian bead without checking it against—

PHILIP   *(To us.)* And then we heard the rumbling.

(The harpsichord plays. The kids sit up, terrified.)

PENNY   Everybody! Hang on!

SARAH   Disneyland!

(PHILIP gathers the kids under his blanket.)

PHILIP   Falling rocks! Cover your heads!

(The harpsichord stops.)

WAYNE   Smell the air.

HALCY   It's burning . . .

PENNY   The air was on fire.

PHILIP   Look! Goats! Sheep! Running along the beach!

ROGER   Was that an earthquake?

PENNY   The cliffs could've caved in!

TEDDY   Are we killed?

PHILIP   We are charmed! We could've been buried!

LYLE   California! The big bang!

PENNY   We're all fine. Models of *corragio*. We're all here. You all behaved very well. Grace under pressure! Are all the children here? Where's Halcy? Wayne?

PHILIP   We've got to get back to the dig.

PENNY   Let's make sure everything is all right here first. Wayne? Halcy?

PHILIP   I want to make sure everything is all right at the dig first.

PENNY   Oh, this comes second? Wayne? Halcy?

(HALCY and WAYNE appear.)

HALCY   Mother. We want to speak to you.

WAYNE   We have something to ask you.

HALCY We want your permission to spend the night together.

WAYNE Your blessing.

PENNY Philip. Would you please handle *this*?

PHILIP *This* can wait.

WAYNE This cannot wait! Suppose we all died?

HALCY So little time. That's what you said to Philip. I saw the letter! April sixteenth.

PENNY What I said to Philip on April sixteenth was my own business.

WAYNE I've never spent the night with anybody. She wants to spend it with me. We could've been buried. Is death always so close?

HALCY Mom? Don't you want me to be as happy as you?

PENNY You have the rest of your life to be happy.

HALCY You hurt Daddy.

PENNY Your father hurt me. He was unfaithful. He put his career over everything.

WAYNE That's what Mom said about *you*, Dad.

PENNY If I stayed with your father one more day, I would have got cancer and suffocated and died.

HALCY That will happen to me if I don't sleep with Wayne.

PENNY That will *not* happen to you if you don't sleep with Wayne.

HALCY Am I so awful and worthless and ugly and stupid I can't touch your precious Philip's son?

WAYNE Aren't I good enough for her, Dad? Am I such an asshole?

PHILIP You are not going to. We are going back to La Muculufa to see if the quake hit the dig. The computers are incredibly delicate.

WAYNE We're not sneaks like you two.

HALCY We want to include you.

PENNY We do not wish to be included. You ask what we think? It's disgusting. You're too young. You're brother and sister. *Fratello e fratella.*

HALCY We are not *fratello e fratella*. We just met on a plane!

PHILIP You want a straight answer? No.

PENNY No no no no no no no!

HALCY I'll call father and ask him.

PENNY You are not to tell your father anything that is going on here. You understand? This is *omerta* in spades.

WAYNE Only the Mafia has *omerta*.

PENNY This is the Mafia.

HALCY We're not the Mafia.

PENNY Oh, yes you are, and you know what the Mafia does to one of its own that breaks the code?

TEDDY *Infamita!*

(*PENNY draws her hand across her throat.*)

132 / John Guare

SARAH   Why did you say she wasn't an archaeologist?

LYLE   Why did you say she should go back home and raise money?

PHILIP   Shut up.

PENNY   And Wayne and Halcy want to be us?

PHILIP   Good Christ, they're us, and we've become Mel and Jeanne. It's just like home.

PENNY   Shut up. It *is* home.

TEDDY   Do you want to know all the card games I can't play? I can't play bridge. I can't play poker. I can't play gin. I can't play canasta. I can't play . . .

(WAYNE and HALCY stand hand in hand and then are gone.)

PENNY   *(To us.)* And in that moment, was it my eyes? Was it the night? Wayne and Halcy vanish?

PHILIP   They step into the dark.

SARAH   They're up there! Going up the cliff!

THE MESSENGER   *(Sings.)*
The children scale the cliffs
The children find a path
The children dig their hands into the earth
They climb higher

(Everyone scatters. PENNY is alone.)

PENNY   Which way to go? Kids! Wait! Let's stay together.

VOICES   —Wayne . . .
—Halcy . . .
—You get back here.

PENNY   Moonlight! The cliffs! I find a path, thick with red flowers. I see Wayne and Halcy in the distance. I see them pulling off their clothes, leaving a trail behind them. I am down on my knees like a guerrilla on their trail. The night air is thick with buzzing of bees, in panic from the earthquake. Heat. The air on fire.

VOICES   —Where are you?
—I'm frightened!

PENNY   Wayne and Halcy ahead of me are naked, in and out of my sight. *Up* the cliff! They vanish behind a stone column. I turn around the column. I swear. This is what I see.

THE MESSENGER   *(Sings.)* Of course, it's by moonlight

PENNY   All that is there is a deer.

THE MESSENGER   *(Sings.)* Wayne?

PENNY   The deer drinks out of a spring, a natural pool of water. Halcy?

THE MESSENGER   *(Sings.)* Halcy?

The moon reflects in the water.
The moon says Yes I am Halcy
I am Wayne
The spring bubbles yes yes yes

(THE MESSENGER draws back a curtain. Blinding light. Music. WAYNE and HALCY, appear transformed, dressed in white and gold. The moon shines behind them in waves of light.)

PENNY   *(Calls, terrified.)* Philip? Hello? *(The harpsichord plays tenderly.)*

HALCY   We understand the joy you have.

WAYNE   We're moving far away.

HALCY   We can't tell you where.

WAYNE   *Addio.* You see we've learned Italian.

HALCY   To live forever! *Vivere Sempre! Sempre!*

WAYNE   *Come tu e* Daddy! *Addio! Sempre!*

HALCY   You'll never hear from us *encore. Te amo!*

WAYNE   Don't look for us. *Addio! Te amo!*

HALCY   We'll make Penny and Philips *dappertutto.* Everywhere! *Addio!*

WAYNE   If we're you, they'll be *more* of you. *Addio!*

(THE MESSENGER draws the silver curtain slowly against them.)

THE MESSENGER   *(Sings.)*
Your eyes have seen into the heart of love
The Beatific Vision blinds you as the sight of God
But this is the second brightest sight
The sight of love
It is easier to adore the sun
Than to look into the heart of love
And now the vision is gone

(WAYNE and HALCY are gone. PHILIP appears, out of breath.)

PHILIP   Where are they?

PENNY   I saw them! They were magnificent! Halcy! My little Halcy! Turned into a spring! And your Wayne—little pimply Wayne—was a deer! There! That spring—that bubbling water!

PHILIP   *(Concerned.)* Penny . . .

THE MESSENGER   *(Speaks.)* They hear singing. There is a procession. What feast day is this? What feast day is this in the middle of the night to make the crowd sing so mournfully. The town celebrates escape from an earthquake. Old men carry an enormous Christ, carved out of wood, writhing in graphic bleeding agony. Altar boys aroused from sleep swing gold thurifers of burning incense. Pregnant women march to the top of cliffs where the temple of Astarte once stood holding rosaries over their bellies. They pray for their children. They pray for unborn children. And at the edge of the cliff, lit by torches and candles of gratitude, stand Wayne and Halcy dressed only in their underclothes, dirty, sweaty, kids, afraid.

(WAYNE and HALCY appear at a height.)

PHILIP   Wayne! You get down here!

THE MESSENGER   Below them. Rocks. Sharp.

PENNY   Kids. Come on. Not so close.

PHILIP   Hi, kids. Now get away from the edge.

THE MESSENGER   The rocks loosen. Pebbles fall, tumbling down the escarpment.

PHILIP   Halcy, you get your ass down here or I'll—

WAYNE   We'll die for our love. We're prepared for that. It's what you'd do. Dad? Isn't it? Halcy, give me your hand. We're going someplace far away and live forever. I'm Icarus. I drew that name out of the bag.

PENNY   It was a game to kill time in the car!

HALCY   It didn't count? It isn't real what you feel for each other? I think you're the most heroic wonderful people who ever lived!

WAYNE   Dad, home with Mom was hell. You've made us a wonderful life. Thank you for Penny! Penny, thank you for making Dad so happy. Kids, we have to obey our parents! You don't know what they've given us— they've made life wonderful for us.

HALCY   Mom! Your courage! Your bravery!

PENNY   We'll go back to your therapist.

PHILIP   We'll work this out.

WAYNE   It is worked out already!

HALCY   We have our destiny!

PHILIP   I don't blame you, Wayne. Halcy is a lovely girl, but you have to define your relationship to her.

WAYNE   I am Philip. She is Penny.

PENNY   It's all jet lag and brand-new, and I appreciate and am touched that you understand what Philip and I are trying to build, but get your asses off that precipice.

WAYNE   You'd die for your love. You said that. We Xeroxed letters from April twenty-third and May eighth. Halcy! Give me your hand!

PHILIP   You get down here.

WAYNE   Will you let us live together as you?

PHILIP   No!

PENNY   Yes!

WAYNE   Are you lying to us?

HALCY   Did you have affairs before each other?

PENNY   No!

PHILIP   Yes!

(The kids appear, one by one from different directions.)

JANE Who?

PHILIP Wanda Hess.

SARAH Mrs. Hess! Ugh!

PHILIP You want truth? Let's get it all out.

PENNY You never told me about any Wanda Hess.

TEDDY Steven Hess's mother? You made me related to Steven Hess?

PHILIP Screwing Wanda Hess does not involve you.

PENNY Who is Wanda Hess?

PETER When did you and Mrs. Hess happen?

PHILIP Four years ago for two horrible years.

PENNY You never told me about Wanda Hess.

PHILIP Some woman in my department.

PENNY An archaeologist?

PHILIP From an entirely different period. The Sumerians.

PENNY I don't know anything about the Sumerians.

PHILIP Neither did Wanda Hess.

JANE Mom, that congressman from Idaho was always phoning you when Dad was away.

LYLE Sending you all those potatoes.

ALL KIDS Yeah! The potatoes!

PENNY That was absolutely nothing.

PHILIP What congressman?

ROBIN What about the man at the gas station you said was so cute?

PENNY I thought that kid at the gas station was cute. Would you all stop looking at us?

PHILIP You will come down here or else—

WAYNE Halcy, give me your hand.

HALCY I'm afraid.

WAYNE Don't you believe! Our parents believed! They threw away their lives! Love is the only reality. Love makes us immortal! They said that.

HALCY May twentieth.

PENNY Halcy, come away from the edge. The rocks are very loose. Come down and help me.

PHILIP We'll drive to Etna! To see the volcano! And the red flowers will be in bloom. To see the poppies—which are the blood of Adonis!

(PHILIP and PENNY advance slowly on them to distract them.)

PENNY Yes, a picnic on the volcano and then we'll go to Siracusa where Aeschylus first performed his play *The Persians*. We'll read the play on the very site where Aeschylus first did it! In 450 B.C.! "With frequent, constant and nocturnal dreams/I have lived, as soon as my son, gathering/His host had gone . . ." Get them!

PHILIP   I rush forward.

(THE MESSENGER and HALCY draw a curtain, burlap this time, rapidly against WAYNE.)

THE MESSENGER   *(Sings.)*
>   Wayne who drew Icarus out of a bag
>   Steps into the sky
>   But it is moonlight and he wears no wings
>   No sunlight melts the wings
>   Wayne falls through the sky
>   The saddest song I ever did hear
>   Dido's lament
>   This is sadder
>   Wayne falls through the sky

ROGER   *(To us.)* Wayne leaps over the side.

SARAH   *(To us.)* We see Wayne against the moon.

THE MESSENGER   *(Sings.)*
>   The saddest song I ever did hear
>   Dido's lament
>   This is sadder
>   Wayne steps over the edge
>   Wayne falls through the sky

(PENNY and PHILIP turn away. PENNY embraces PHILIP.)

PENNY'S CHILDREN   We talked to Dad
>   —he wants us home
>   —he's getting married
>   —he wants us to be part of his new life.

PENNY   I have you for the summer. Daddy has you for the winter. You come here for alternate Christmases. Daddy has you for alternate Easters.

LYLE   We came here on Friday.

JANE   Today is Sunday.

PETER   I thought we'd stay longer.

SARAH   You came here for beads?

LYLE   You threw away our lives for beads?

JANE   Wayne died for beads?

PHILIP   Do they have all their stuff? Whose sleeping bag is this?

PENNY   Is it our fault? How much are we to blame?

PHILIP   *Omerta.* There are questions not to ask.

PENNY   *Omerta.* But I saw them in that spring. That deer—

PHILIP   *Omerta.* I don't know. It's time . . .

SARAH   *(To us.)* We pack up all our gear to go back to the airport.

PENNY   Good-bye, bed. In two thousand years, if archaeologists dig, will they find all the love that was here?

PHILIP   Yes. Yes.

PENNY   So when do you think we'll be back? The workmen want to know if they should stop.

PHILIP   You stay here.

PENNY   Here? I'm coming with you.

PHILIP   My wife—

PENNY   I'm your wife!

PHILIP   Their mother doesn't want you around. She's trying not to drink. She says her life is different. I have to believe her. She's devastated. She's angry. You protect the dig. You stay here—mind the store.

PENNY   I want to be with you.

PHILIP   I'm going to talk to the people back at the university.

PENNY   Look, if it comes down to money, I can raise as much money as we need—

(HALCY appears.)

HALCY   I loved Wayne.

PHILIP   She is not coming back to America.

HALCY   Is Wayne's body going to be on the plane with us? I want to ride with Wayne.

PHILIP   My wife—Wayne's mother—does not want to see you. Because this is what she will ask you. Why didn't you jump?

HALCY   Why am I alive? I should've jumped. I loved him.

PENNY   What are you saying! Both of you!

PHILIP   Are you a coward? You should've jumped!

PENNY   She did not jump because she is not crazy!

PHILIP   Oh. My boy is crazy?

PENNY   She had a moment of sanity. Halcy, go out in the car.

HALCY   I loved him. I'll never get over this. I'll live to be a hundred years old and never get over this. I had one chance to be magic. I had one chance to be a goddess. I had one chance to be special, and now all I'll be the rest of my life is this. I hate this. Mom, I hate this. Me.

PENNY   You don't. Don't say that. You don't.

(HALCY goes.)

PHILIP   Why do you have a child and I don't?

PENNY   Could you say I'm happy Halcy is alive?

PHILIP   I'm not.

PENNY   She's your stepdaughter. Wayne is my stepson. We are all together. Can't tell whose are yours and which are mine. You said that. Grief is like love. It makes us do terrible things. Say terrible things.

PHILIP   I hate emotions. Hate them. Hate them.
PENNY   *(Tenderly.)* Philip . . .
PHILIP   What kind of a name is Halcy?
PENNY   For halcyon. Halcyon days.
PHILIP   You and Mel had halcyon days?
PENNY   Mel and I had halcyon days. . . .
PHILIP   And she was born. Halcyon days.
PENNY   Wayne?
PHILIP   For John Wayne.
PENNY   John Wayne!
PHILIP   Months before he was born he kicked like a cowboy, and we got to calling the unborn baby John Wayne—and when he was born, we realized he already had been named. We had no choice. Even if he was a girl. John Wayne.
PENNY   John Wayne. Not the best name for a girl.
PHILIP   Come with me back to the university?
PENNY   Never! I am here.
PHILIP   Four Baboons Adoring the Sun. Palms upward to the sun. *(He kisses her.)*
PHILIP   There's two kinds of people. Those who do—who love to do.
PENNY   Yes!
PHILIP   And those who love to dream about doing. I was so happy back at the university dreaming about being here. Dreaming about you. You know what I miss? I miss dreaming of all this. It's sort of right, flying back with the kids. Back to my wife. Hating every minute of it. And I'll spend the entire trip dreaming of you. Dreaming of here. Wishing I could have life.
PENNY   But we have it!
PHILIP   But it's not—it's not real.
PHILIP   Who wants to come with me?
PENNY   No one is coming with you!

(PENNY kneels and tries to hold her kids tight. There is absolute chaos as the children run back and forth, trying to decide who stays, who goes.)

PENNY   Let the kids stay here! They have to heal after the grief. Let us be together for the healing part!
JANE   Mom? Let us go?
PENNY   There were court orders!
JANE   Mom.
PENNY   I've given up everything to come here.
PHILIP   No. You gave up everything years ago *not* to come here. You belong here. You actually like making eye contact. No matter what the risks are. No, I didn't see any spring—you saw a spring—you saw a deer—that's it —they weren't anything else.

(PHILIP takes his kids and three of PENNY's. HALCY and ROGER stay with PENNY.)

HALCY   Look at the car drive away. It gets smaller and smaller and smaller and smaller . . .

(In another pool of light, PHILIP is crowded with kids.)

PHILIP   *(To us.)* I sit in the plane. Me with how many kids in my lap look out the window. I see these fingers pointing up into the sky? Is that our dig? A cloud passes and blocks my view. The cloud appears to be in the shape of my first wife. Another cloud in the shape of my university blocks the view. Another cloud in the shape of me prevents my seeing the earth. The kids complain about something—a draft? The attendant passes candy. Kids are sobbing. The coffin is in the hold with my son.

ROGER   Look at that plane! Is that them!

PENNY   *(To us.)* We dig in the trenches. We look up. A plane circles around us and then is lost in the sunset.

PHILIP   *(To us.)* I see Mount Etna spewing out its lava. The plane flies low over the volcano. I see the blazing red flames below melting stones into liquid. The pilot makes one circular passage around the crater, then lifts up and vanishes into the night.

PENNY   Arethusa. Artemis. Diana. Icarus. Adonis . . .

(The lights begin to fade on PENNY and PHILIP each in a separate pool of light.)

THE MESSENGER   *(Sings.)*
        At the end of a perfect day
        In Sicily
        The servant brings a tray
        A tray with a sprig of lavender
        Put the sprig of lavender under your nose
        The scent reminds you of a perfect day
        Time has a perfume
        At least in Sicily
        At least in novels by Giuseppe Lampedusa
        Time has a perfume
        A servant brings a tray of lavender

(THE MESSENGER draws a final curtain against the stage.)

A. R. GURNEY, JR.

The Problem

CHARACTERS

THE HUSBAND *In his thirties.*
THE WIFE *Also in her thirties.*

SETTING

As simple a set as possible: the suggestion of a study. A leather chair with a matching footstool, a reading light behind it. A bookcase.

At curtain, the HUSBAND *is sitting in the chair, feet up on the footstool, reading a book, smoking a pipe, taking notes into a notebook comfortably propped on his knee. After a moment, the* WIFE *comes in from the left, hugely pregnant. She stands looking at him. He continues to read.*

WIFE   Hey.
HUSBAND   *(Not looking at her.)* I'm reading, dear.
WIFE   *(Sticking out her stomach.)* I know. But look at me.
HUSBAND   *(Still reading.)* I'm preparing for a class, dear.
WIFE   I know, but just look. *(She crosses to him, stands by his chair, and sticks out her stomach.)* Just take a gander.
HUSBAND   *(Turns his head and looks right into her stomach. He starts, takes off his glasses, looks again, and then looks up into her face.)* Well, well.
WIFE   Yes.
HUSBAND   Surprise, surprise.
WIFE   Yes.
HUSBAND   Merry Christmas.
WIFE   Exactly. *(Pause.)*

HUSBAND   Why have I never noticed before?

WIFE   Because I wear loose-fitting clothes.

HUSBAND   That's true.

WIFE   Clothes without waists. Merri-mekkos. Sack dresses. Granny gowns.

HUSBAND   That's true.

WIFE   Large, shapeless flannel nightgowns.

HUSBAND   True enough.

WIFE   So only now, tonight, does it seem to show.

HUSBAND   I see. *(Pause. They smile at each other. Then he looks at his watch.)* I've got to teach a class in an hour.

WIFE   Oh, I know. And I've got to go out to a meeting on Open Housing.

HUSBAND   So . . .

WIFE   I just wanted you to know. *(Pause.)* So you could plan.

HUSBAND   Yes. I will. I'll plan accordingly. *(Smiles at her again, puts on his glasses, and returns to his book. She starts off left, and then stops.)*

WIFE   Oh, there's one thing, though.

HUSBAND   *(Reading.)* Mmmmmm?

WIFE   One small problem.

HUSBAND   *(Reading.)* Mmmmmm. And what's that, dear?

WIFE   I don't know whether you've thought about this, or not.

HUSBAND   *(Looking up.)* State the problem. And I'll tell you whether I've thought about it.

WIFE   It's a little tricky.

HUSBAND   Well. We're married, after all.

WIFE   Yes. That's why it's a little tricky.

HUSBAND   Perhaps. But that's also why you should feel free to speak out.

WIFE   All right. *(Pause.)* You see, I'm not absolutely sure that this . . . *(She looks down at her stomach.)* is yours. *(Pause. He marks his place in his book, puts it down carefully, takes off his glasses, and then looks up.)*

HUSBAND   Ah. So that's the problem.

WIFE   Yes. That's the problem.

HUSBAND   I think I'll trust you on this one, dear.

WIFE   That's sweet of you, darling. *(Pause.)* But do I trust myself?

HUSBAND   I think you should. So there we are.

WIFE   But . . .

HUSBAND   But what?

WIFE   The thing is . . . Now how do I put this?

HUSBAND   Speak frankly now.

WIFE   I'll try. The thing is . . . that you and I . . . haven't made love very much. Recently.

HUSBAND   Is that true?

WIFE   I think it is. Not very much. Not recently.

HUSBAND   Hmmm. Define "recently."

WIFE   Well, I mean . . . five years, more or less . . . give or take a month or two.

HUSBAND   Is that true?

WIFE   I think it is. *(Pause.)*

HUSBAND   *(Lighting his pipe.)* My gosh, has it been that long?

WIFE   Oh, yes.

HUSBAND   Well, well. And so . . .

WIFE   And so . . .

HUSBAND   And so you mind, obviously.

WIFE   Mind?

HUSBAND   Mind that we haven't. Much. Recently.

WIFE   Oh, no. Oh, no, no. I don't *mind.* Why should I *mind?*

HUSBAND   Well, then . . .

WIFE   *(Pointing to her stomach.)* I'm just thinking of *this*, that's all.

HUSBAND   Oh, I *see!*

WIFE   *(Smiling.)* You see?

HUSBAND   Of *course.* I see the connection! *(He slaps his head.)* For*give* me. I was thinking about my class.

WIFE   Oh, heavens. I forgive you. You love your work.

HUSBAND   Yes, but I'm with you now. I'm on your wavelength now.

WIFE   Oh, good.

HUSBAND   Yes, yes. I understand now. What you're really saying is . . . now stop me if I'm wrong . . . but what you're really saying is that you think someone else might have impregnated you.

WIFE   More or less. Yes.

HUSBAND   I see, I see, I see.

WIFE   It's possible, after all.

HUSBAND   Yes. It's possible.

WIFE   On these evenings that you have to go teach.

HUSBAND   Yes. When you go out to your meetings.

WIFE   Yes. Exactly.

HUSBAND   So we do have a problem there, don't we?

WIFE   Yes. We really do.

(Pause; he looks at her, looks at her stomach, scratches his head, taps his teeth with a pencil, lights his pipe, twirls his glasses.)

HUSBAND   You know, darling . . . it occurs to me . . . that I should have made love to you more.

WIFE   Oh, no, no. . . .

HUSBAND   I'm kicking myself now.

WIFE   Oh, don't, don't. . . .

HUSBAND   I am. Things would have been much simpler.

WIFE   Oh, sweetheart, stop punishing yourself.

HUSBAND But why didn't I? Darn it! Darn it all!

WIFE Darling, you have your work.

HUSBAND Oh, sure, but . . .

WIFE You have your intellectual life . . .

HUSBAND That's all very well, but . . .

WIFE You had your book to get out . . .

HUSBAND Yes, yes, but, darling, that doesn't really answer the question. The question is, why haven't I made love to you in the past five years? That's the question. *(Pause.)*

WIFE Well. You used to laugh too much, maybe.

HUSBAND Laugh?

WIFE Yes. In the old days. Whenever we started to make love, you'd start to chuckle.

HUSBAND I did, didn't I? I remember now. *(He chuckles.)*

WIFE Yes. You'd chuckle.

HUSBAND *(Chuckling.)* Because the whole thing struck me as being slightly absurd. *(Chuckling.)* When you think about it. *(Chuckling.)* I should learn to control myself. *(He chuckles louder; controls himself stoically; then bursts into loud laughter; then forces himself to subside; looks at her.)* I'm sorry.

WIFE Oh, don't be sorry. I was just as bad.

HUSBAND Did you chuckle?

WIFE No. Actually I'd cry.

HUSBAND I don't remember your crying.

WIFE Well, I'd whimper.

HUSBAND Yes, yes! You would. You'd whimper. *(Chuckles.)*

WIFE Well, I felt so sad! Making love. While all these horrible things are going on in the world.

HUSBAND Yes. So you'd whimper. I remember now.

WIFE Vietnam . . . Urban blight . . . all that. . . . I felt so guilty!

HUSBAND And I felt so absurd.

WIFE Yes. You chuckling, me whimpering. . . .

HUSBAND Yes. Oh, yes.

WIFE And so it wasn't very conducive.

HUSBAND Right. So we gave it up. That answers that. *(Pause; picks up his book and starts to read.)*

WIFE But now there's this. *(Indicates her stomach.)*

HUSBAND *(Reading; taking notes.)* Keep it.

WIFE What?

HUSBAND Keep it. Bear it. Bring it home.

WIFE Oh, darling. . . .

HUSBAND Give it my name. Consider me its father.

WIFE Oh, sweetheart.

HUSBAND   I've let you down. Now I'll make it up. Keep it.

WIFE   But I'm partly to blame.

HUSBAND   But I'm the man.

WIFE   You certainly are! You certainly are the man!

HUSBAND   And now I'm afraid that I must prepare for my class.

WIFE   Yes. And I've got to go to my meeting.

(They smile at each other; then she starts out left; then she stops, and stands reflectively. After a moment, he looks at her.)

HUSBAND   But you're not satisfied.

WIFE   Oh, I am, I am.

HUSBAND   Darling, we've been married ten years. You are not satisfied.

WIFE   You've got a class.

HUSBAND   My wife comes first. Come on. What's the problem now?

WIFE   I'm embarrassed even to bring it up.

HUSBAND   *(Tenderly.)* Come on. Out with it. Tell Daddy.

WIFE   All right. *(Pause.)* What if this . . . *(She looks at her stomach.)* turns out to be black? *(Pause.)*

HUSBAND   Black?

WIFE   Black. Or at least mulatto. Depending on how the chromosomes line up.

HUSBAND   *(Pause. Lights his pipe again.)* Mmmmm.

WIFE   You see? You see the problem?

HUSBAND   *(Nodding.)* Mmmmm.

WIFE   I mean, can you still act as its father if it's black?

HUSBAND   *(Puffing away.)* Mmmmmm. *(Looks at her wryly.)* Yes, well, that puts a different complexion on things.

WIFE   *(Giggling.)* Funny.

HUSBAND   *(Chuckling.)* That's a horse of a different color.

WIFE   *(Laughing.)* Now cut it out. You're awful. *(Stops laughing.)* Try to be serious.

HUSBAND   *(Pause. Settles down.)* Black, eh?

WIFE   I should have told you before.

HUSBAND   No, no. I should have assumed it.

WIFE   It just slipped my mind, I guess.

HUSBAND   I'm glad it did. That says something for America these days.

WIFE   Yes. But it's still a problem.

HUSBAND   In this case, yes. I'd say so. *(Pause.)* So you must let me think it out.

WIFE   But your class . . .

HUSBAND   I'll just be less prepared than I like to be. Which may be good. Which may be very good. Which may make things more lively and spontaneous. So let me think about this other problem. *(Puffs on his pipe; she stands watching him.)* I could still adopt it.

WIFE   How?

HUSBAND   We could tell the world that you had a blue baby. Which died. And then we could bring home the black one. Which we say we adopted.

WIFE   That sounds awfully complicated.

HUSBAND   I know it.

WIFE   Awfully baroque.

HUSBAND   I know it.

WIFE   Besides, the real father might object. He might take pride in it himself.

HUSBAND   Need he know?

WIFE   Oh, yes. Because he'll see it, after all.

HUSBAND   You mean, he'll continue to come around.

WIFE   Oh, yes. After I'm home from the hospital. And capable of sexual intercourse again.

HUSBAND   I see.

WIFE   So that pretty well puts a damper on the adopting idea.

HUSBAND   Yes, it does. *(He thinks.)*

WIFE   But you have your class . . .

HUSBAND   No, no. Now wait a minute. . . . *(He thinks carefully, then suddenly pounds his fist on the arm of his chair.)* Sweetheart, I'm going to be honest with you. *(Points to the footstool.)* Sit down.

WIFE   *(Looking at the footstool.)* I can't sit down. Your feet are there.

HUSBAND   I'll remove my feet. *(He does.)* Now sit down.

WIFE   All right. I'll sit down. *(Sits on the footstool in front of him.)*

HUSBAND   Now don't look at me. Face forward. Because this is going to be hard for me to tell, and hard for you to hear.

WIFE   All right. I won't look at you.

HUSBAND   And if I'm inarticulate about this, you must try to understand that this is a difficult thing for a man to tell his wife. I'm only doing it—I'm only telling you—because it seems to be the only way to solve this problem.

WIFE   *(Smoothing her skirt over her stomach.)* Yes. This problem.

HUSBAND   Now try not to interrupt, darling, unless you have to. Unless you're unclear about anything. Save your remarks and comments for the end. All right?

WIFE   I'll try.

HUSBAND   All right. *(He takes a deep breath.)* Now. To begin with, I've been lying to you this evening.

WIFE   Lying?

HUSBAND   Ssshhh. Lying. I don't have a class tonight. I've never had a class at night. I don't believe in evening classes. All these years I've been lying. The class that I've told you meets at night actually meets on Mondays, Wednesdays, and Fridays at ten A.M.

WIFE   I see.

HUSBAND   You may well ask, therefore, where I go on these nights when I say

I have classes. *(Pause.)* And that is what is so difficult to tell you. *(Pause.)* The fact is, I don't leave this house. Not really. Oh, I leave by the front door, all right. But I immediately circle around in back and go down into the cellar by means of the bulkhead.

WIFE I see.

HUSBAND Now. What do I do in the cellar? You are probably asking yourself that. What do I do in the cellar? . . . Don't look at me, darling! *(Pause; then grimly:)* Here's what I do in the cellar. I make my way to a small space behind the furnace. And in that small space, I have hidden . . . certain things. *(Pause.)* What have I hidden? I'll tell you. *(He counts them off on his fingers.)* Some black theatrical makeup. A woolly wig. A complete change of clothes. And a small mirror. That's what I have hidden in the cellar.

WIFE I see. . . .

HUSBAND Yes. You see, my darling, or you're beginning to. When I go into the cellar, I set the mirror up on an adjacent water pipe. I strip myself to the buff. I daub myself from head to toe with that dusky makeup. I glue on that curly wig. I don those makeshift clothes. I leave the cellar. Go to the front door. Ring the bell. And reappear to you. So you see, my poor darling, I am your Negro visitor, and have been all along.

WIFE You.

HUSBAND Me.

WIFE But—

HUSBAND Oh, I know it sounds implausible. But remember how you always lower the lights. Remember, too, that I played Othello in high school. Somehow I was able to pass. I have deceived you for these past years. Deceived my own wife! Disguising myself as a Negro and capitalizing on the sympathies you naturally feel for that unhappy race!

WIFE But . . . why?

HUSBAND Because I wanted to make love to you. And somehow this seemed to be the only way I could do it. You'll have to admit it worked.

WIFE *(Looking at her stomach.)* Oh, yes. It worked.

HUSBAND So out of all this depravity, at least a child will be born. And I was its father, after all.

WIFE I'm somewhat . . . stunned . . . by all this.

HUSBAND I know you are, darling. *(Gets up.)* Try to assimilate it while I'm gone.

WIFE Gone?

HUSBAND I'm going down to the cellar now.

WIFE To put on your costume?

HUSBAND No. To burn it.

WIFE Burn it?

HUSBAND Yes. It's all over now. Because you know. The mask is off. Any attempt to wear it again would be foolish. I'd be nothing but a self-conscious amateur. Our love life would be as absurd as it was before I found this way around it. So I'm going to destroy my role. *(Pause; he looks at her.)* And when I come back, I want you gone.

WIFE   Gone?

HUSBAND   You must leave me now.

WIFE   No.

HUSBAND   You must. Oh, my darling, this urge to love you is still in me. I don't know what . . . oblique form . . . it will take next. Take the child and go.

WIFE   Never.

HUSBAND   Please. Listen: I don't know what I'll think of next, in the cellar. I've got Genet down there. And a complete de Sade. I'll reread them both, looking for increasingly complicated arabesques of sexual perversion. I may reappear with a whip. Wearing riding boots. Or dressed as a woman. Get out, darling. Run to the suburbs. Give my child a normal home. Go!

WIFE   Normal? Normal? *(She laughs uneasily.)* What is normal?

HUSBAND   You're normal, my love.

WIFE   Me? Oh, my God, how little do you know! *(Grimly.)* Sit down. I have a tale to tell-o.

HUSBAND   Nothing you could say . . .

WIFE   Sit down.

HUSBAND   Nothing . . .

WIFE   I've known all along you were my dark lover!

HUSBAND   *(Sits down.)* You've known?

WIFE   From the beginning.

HUSBAND   But . . . how?

WIFE   Five years ago, when you announced to me that you had scheduled some evening classes, I became suspicious. And so when you left for the first class, I . . . followed you.

HUSBAND   Followed me?

WIFE   Yes. I followed my own husband. Followed you to that tacky little theater-supply shop downtown where you bought your disguise. Followed you back here. Followed you into the cellar, hid behind the hot-water heater, watched you change into your poor, pathetic imitation of a Negro.

HUSBAND   You spied on me. . . .

WIFE   Yes, I spied on you, my darling. Furtively, suspiciously, like some aging matron. But when I saw what you were doing, when I understood that you were doing it for me, my heart went out to you. With a great rush of longing, I dashed back upstairs, eager to receive you, but at the same time terrified that you would see that I recognized you. Frantically, I dimmed the lights, to make things easier for both of us.

HUSBAND   I thought it was because you were romantic.

WIFE   I know you did, darling. And I let you think that. But no: it was simply so I wouldn't give myself away.

HUSBAND   You were acting? The whole time?

WIFE   Yes. Wasn't I good? Pretending that you were someone new and strange? I, I, who am no actress, improvising like a professional during that whole scene!

HUSBAND   *(Shaking his head.)* It's hard to believe. . . . You seemed so . . . excited!

WIFE   I was! I was terribly excited. I'll admit it. That strange, sly courtship, the banter, the give-and-take, with all those peculiar racial overtones. I threw myself into it with a vengeance. But then . . . when you carried me into the bedroom . . . everything changed.

HUSBAND   What do you mean? I was a tiger!

WIFE   You were, darling. You were a tiger. But I wasn't.

HUSBAND   You said you loved me.

WIFE   I was only pretending. I really hated you.

HUSBAND   Hated me?

WIFE   Hated myself. It was awful. I felt so guilty. All my old sexual agonies were magnified, as it were, by a gallery of mirrors. I wanted at least to whimper, as I did normally, with you, when you were white, but now you were black, I had to stifle my own sighs. Worse: I had to pretend, to play, to *fake* the most authentic experience a woman can have! And all the time, I felt like a thing, an object, a creature without a soul, a poor, pathetic concubine in the arms of an Ethiopian potentate. And when you left— finally left—I just lay on the bed, arms folded across my breast, like a stone carving on my own tomb. It took every ounce of energy I could muster to rise and greet you at the door when you returned from your supposed class. *(Pause.)*

HUSBAND   So. For the past five years you have been through hell.

WIFE   No. After that first ghastly evening, I suffered nothing.

HUSBAND   You mean, you grew accustomed . . .

WIFE   I mean, I wasn't there.

HUSBAND   You weren't there?

WIFE   No. I left the house right after you went into the cellar.

HUSBAND   But then who . . . was here . . . with me?

WIFE   I got a substitute.

HUSBAND   I see.

WIFE   Oh, darling, try to understand. I simply could not endure another evening like that. The sham, the pretense—it revolted me. And yet I knew how much it meant to you! All the next day, I racked my brain, trying to figure out something which would satisfy us both. I took a long walk. I wandered all over town. Finally, about an hour before I was due home,

I saw a woman. Who looked a little like me. Same hair, same height . . . roughly the same age. It was at least a chance. Before I really knew what I was doing, I approached her and asked her whether she'd like to sleep with a Negro. Naturally she said she would. And so now, for the past five years, this good woman has come here while you were in the cellar changing your clothes, and in the dim light, she has pretended to be me.

HUSBAND   I see.

WIFE   Do you hate me very much?

HUSBAND   No. I don't hate you. But I must say I'm somewhat . . . surprised.

WIFE   I suspected you would be.

HUSBAND   But what about that? *(Points to her stomach.)*

WIFE   *(Clutching her stomach.)* Ah, this . . .

HUSBAND   Yes. That. Whose is that?

WIFE   Now bear with me, darling. On these nights while you're in the cellar, and while this good woman is preparing herself for your return, I go off with a real Negro. There it is. In a nutshell. His Cadillac pulls up quietly in front. He flashes his lights. And I sneak out and drive off with him into the black ghetto. There, on an old mattress infested with lice, nibbled at by rats, we make love. Love which for the first time in my life I can give myself up to, since I feel that with him I am expiating not only my own guilt but the guilt of all America.

HUSBAND   I see. And so he is the father of that.

WIFE   No.

HUSBAND   No?

WIFE   Somehow, even that relationship wasn't enough. Somehow, in the ghetto, with all that soul music pulsing around me, all that frustration, all that anger, I still felt as if I were not playing my part. So I betrayed my lover for his friend. And his friend for another. And so on and so forth, with Puerto Ricans, Mexican-Americans, and Indians on relief. Oh, darling, for the past five years, I've been offering myself as an ecstatic white sacrifice to anyone with an income of less than five thousand.

HUSBAND   And so the father is . . .

WIFE   Social Injustice, on a large and general scale.

HUSBAND   I see.

WIFE   And now you'll leave me, won't you?

HUSBAND   Me? Leave you now? *(Laughs peculiarly.)* I want to stay more than ever. *(Cleans his pipe carefully.)* What would you say . . . if I said . . . that everything you've told me . . . excites me?

WIFE   Excites you?

HUSBAND   Sets my blood boiling. Gives me strange, wild frissons of desire. . . . What would you say if I said that your ghetto experiences have lit a lurid light in my own loins?

WIFE   Really?

HUSBAND *(Still cleaning his pipe; not looking at her.)* What would you say . . . if I said . . . that I suddenly want to exercise—how shall I put it?— a *droit de seigneur* on you? That I want to steal you from the peasants and carry you into my bedroom and ravage you with the reading lights going full blaze? *(Looks at her carefully.)* What would you say if I said that? *(Pause; she looks at him coyly.)*

WIFE I'd say . . . do it.

HUSBAND Mmmm.

WIFE *(Hastily.)* And let me add this: Let me add that a woman, too, is capable of weird desires. This is hard to say, but looking at you now, slouched in that chair, surrounded by your books and papers, I suddenly have the strange urge to experience the stale comforts of bourgeois married love. They say that Americans in Paris, surfeited by the rich food, yearn for the simple hamburger. So it is with me. For you. Tonight.

HUSBAND *(Getting up slowly.)* Then . . .

WIFE *(Backing away from him.)* But there's still this! *(Indicating her stomach.)* This problem!

HUSBAND *(Moving toward her.)* That's no problem.

WIFE No problem?

HUSBAND That's just the premise to the problem. Now we've solved the problem, we no longer need the premise.

WIFE I fail to follow.

HUSBAND That's just the starting mechanism. Now the motor's going, we no longer need the starter.

WIFE *(Looking down at her stomach.)* Oh.

HUSBAND *(Stalking her.)* That's not really a baby you have in there.

WIFE *(Backing away.)* Not really a baby?

HUSBAND No. That's a balloon you have in there.

WIFE A balloon?

HUSBAND A balloon. Or a bladder. Or an old beach ball.

WIFE It's a baby. I'm practically positive.

HUSBAND No, no. Look. I'll show you. *(Takes the pointed metal prong of his pipe cleaner and gives her a quick, neat jab in the stomach.)* Touché! *(There is a pop, and then a hissing sound. She slowly deflates. They both watch.)* You see? The problem was simply academic. *(Pause.)*

WIFE *(Looking at him sheepishly.)* Aren't we awful?

HUSBAND *(Going to his chair, closing his book, carefully marking the place.)* You started it.

WIFE I know. It was my turn. You started the last one.

HUSBAND *(Neatening his books and papers.)* Well, it's fun.

WIFE Shouldn't we see a psychiatrist?

HUSBAND *(Tapping out his pipe; putting his glasses in his glasses case.)* Why? We're happy. *(Turns off his light. The stage is now lit only from a light off left.)*

WIFE   But we're so de*praved!* *(He looks at her, then throws back his head and gives a long Tarzan-like whoop; then he pounds his chest like a gorilla; she giggles.)* Quiet! You'll wake the children! *(He picks her up in his arms; she pummels him melodramatically; speaks in an English accent.)* No, Tarzan! White men do not take women by force! No, Tarzan! White men *court* their women! They are civilized, Tarzan. It's very complicated. Do you understand what I am saying? Com-pli-ca-ted. . . . Com-pli- . . . *(She giggles and kicks as he carries her off left.)*

Curtain.

DAVID HARE

The Bay at Nice

CHARACTERS

VALENTINA NROVKA
SOPHIA YEPILEVA
ASSISTANT CURATOR
PETER LINITSKY

A large room with a gilt ceiling and a beautiful parquet floor. At the back hangs Guérin's huge oil painting of Iris and Morpheus, *a triumphant nude sitting on a cloud over the body of the King of Sleep. The room is airy and decaying. It is almost empty but for some tables pushed to the back and some gilt and red plush hard chairs. Sitting on one of these is* VALENTINA NROVKA. *She is a lively woman, probably in her sixties, but it's hard to tell. She is dressed in black. Her daughter* SOPHIA *is standing right at the far end of the room, looking out of the main door. She is in her early thirties, much more plainly dressed in a coat and pullover and plain skirt.*

VALENTINA   You don't want to leave an old woman.

SOPHIA   You're not old. (*VALENTINA looks around disapprovingly.*)

VALENTINA   This graveyard! I'm not going to speak to all those old idiots.

SOPHIA   They expect it.

VALENTINA   Nonsense! I'll sit by myself. (*SOPHIA is still looking anxiously out of the door.*)

SOPHIA   I'm afraid we've offended the curator.

VALENTINA   Don't say *we*. I offended him. He was shabbily dressed.

SOPHIA   He wanted you to see the new extension.

VALENTINA   What for? He insults the walls by hanging them with all that socialist realism. Whirlpools of mud. I'd rather look at bare walls. At least they are cleanly painted. I'm tired of looking anyway. "Look, look . . ." (*She smiles, anticipating her own story.*) Picasso lived in a house so ugly—

a great champagne millionaire's Gothic mansion with turrets—that all his friends said "My God, how can you abide such a place?" He said, "You are all prisoners of taste. Great artists love everything. There is no such thing as ugliness." He would kick the walls with his little sandaled foot and say, "They're solid. What more do you want?"

SOPHIA   By that argument, if everything's beautiful, then that includes socialist realism.

VALENTINA   Please. You know nothing of such things. Don't speak of them. Especially in front of other people. It's embarrassing. *(VALENTINA has got up from her seat and is walking to the other side of the room.)* What rubbish do they want me to look at?

SOPHIA   They think they have a Matisse. *(There is a silence. VALENTINA shows no apparent reaction.)*

VALENTINA   You haven't been to see me.

SOPHIA   No. I've been busy.

VALENTINA   Ah, well.

SOPHIA   The work has been very hard. And the children. At the end of the day I'm too tired to do anything. I've said to my employers, as a woman I resent it.

VALENTINA   "As a woman"?

SOPHIA   Yes.

VALENTINA   What does that mean?

SOPHIA   Well . . .

VALENTINA   This fashion for calling people women. Now always "as a *woman*," they say. It was so much more fun when I was young and you could just be a person. Now everyone speaks "on behalf." "On behalf of Soviet women . . ."

SOPHIA   I only meant that I have a family. I also have a job. That's all. And at the school I am taken advantage of.

VALENTINA   They take you for a fool. They know you can never say no.

(SOPHIA is looking across at her back, trying to judge her mood.)

SOPHIA   Who visits you?

VALENTINA   No one. The Troyanofskis, of course. They are terrible people. Madam Troyanofski wants to start a salon. I've told her it's too late. All the artists are dead. The poets are moaners. And the playwrights are worse. Because they're exhausting. People run round the stage. It tires me. In their stories the minute hand is going round like crazy. But the hour hand never turns at all. *(She smiles.)* "Ah well," she said, "if there are no artists worth asking, we can always talk philosophy." No thank you!

SOPHIA   She likes ideas.

VALENTINA   Yes, well, they're Jews. *(She shrugs.)* Tell me, who do you think

I should be seeing? Name anyone in Leningrad who's worth an hour. A full hour.

SOPHIA   Well, of course I enjoy everybody's company. I find something good or interesting in everyone.

(*VALENTINA looks at her mistrustfully.*)

VALENTINA   Yes?

SOPHIA   Shall I get you something to drink?

VALENTINA   Where is this man?

SOPHIA   You frightened him.

VALENTINA   What? So much he's thinking of not showing me the painting?

SOPHIA   I'll go and see.

VALENTINA   No, stay. I want to talk to you.

(*SOPHIA stays, but VALENTINA makes no effort to talk.*)

SOPHIA   The twins both asked me to send you their love.

VALENTINA   How old are they?

SOPHIA   Eight.

VALENTINA   Then plainly you're lying. No eight-year-old asks after adults. Or if they do, they're faking. Why should your children fake?

SOPHIA   I said I would be seeing you, and I suggested . . .

VALENTINA   Ah well, yes.

SOPHIA   . . . they send you their love.

VALENTINA   Now we get the truth of it. Their love was solicited. Like a confession.

SOPHIA   If you insist.

VALENTINA   And Grigor . . . what?

SOPHIA   Grigor is working. He would be here today.

VALENTINA   But?

SOPHIA   But he is working. And he's not interested in art.

VALENTINA   No.

(*There is a pause. SOPHIA looks away, as if anxious to say more, but not daring.*)

Where is the painting?

SOPHIA   They're getting it now. It's in a vault at the bottom of the building.

VALENTINA   Have you seen it?

SOPHIA   Not yet.

VALENTINA   What does it show?

SOPHIA   A window. The sea. A piece of wall.

VALENTINA   It sounds like a forgery.

SOPHIA   They think you will be able to tell.

VALENTINA   How can I tell? I don't know everything he painted. Nobody does.

He got up every morning. He set up his easel, and he started to paint. If at midday he was pleased, then he signed it. If not, then he threw it away and began fresh the next morning. It was said, like a dandy who throws white ties into the laundry basket until he ties one which pleases him. *(She smiles.)* Matisse was profligate.

SOPHIA   So there may be lost work?

VALENTINA   Well, of course. *(She turns away, contemptuously.)* And if there is, what will happen to it? They will put it on the walls of this hideous building. And the state will boast that they own it. And people will gawp at it and say, "What does it mean?" Or "Well, I don't like it." I am told that in the West now people only look at paintings when they are holding cubes of cheese on the end of toothpicks. To me, that says everything of what art has become. *(She smiles.)* Yes, indeed. I sympathize with Grigor. Why be interested in all this gossip and hoopla?

SOPHIA   No, you're wrong. It is painting itself which Grigor dislikes.

VALENTINA   Because you paint? *(SOPHIA looks at her angrily.)*

SOPHIA   I shall look for the curator.

VALENTINA   I have heard all these rumors. Even I. Who have no contact with life except through the Troyanofskis. They are my inadequate means of access to what is happening in the world. Through them everything is admittedly made mean. And yet I have heard of your behavior with Grigor.

SOPHIA   Mother, I don't want to speak about it now.

VALENTINA   Why?

SOPHIA   You will learn in a moment. Soon I shall talk to you.

VALENTINA   When?

SOPHIA   When I have your whole attention.

VALENTINA   Are you choosing your moment?

SOPHIA   No.

VALENTINA   It sums you up. You think everything is a matter of mood.

SOPHIA   I know you better than that.

VALENTINA   You think attitudes are all to do with whim. You understand nothing. Attitudes are all to do with character.

SOPHIA   Please don't lecture me. *(She is turning red with the effort of having to say this.)* If we are to speak, we must speak as equals.

(VALENTINA is looking across at her with sudden kindness and love.)

VALENTINA   Little Sophia, you've used up all your courage already. Come here and tell me what's going on.

(SOPHIA, trembling, doesn't move as VALENTINA opens her arms to her.)

SOPHIA   No, I won't come. I mustn't. I'm determined to be strong with you.

VALENTINA   You've come to make a speech?

SOPHIA Well, yes.

VALENTINA Well, make it.

SOPHIA What, now?

VALENTINA Yes.

(There is an agonizing pause.)

SOPHIA No, I can't.

VALENTINA Why not?

SOPHIA Because I have rehearsed but now I'm frightened. I've said these things to no one.

VALENTINA And yet everyone knows.

(SOPHIA does not move.)

SOPHIA I work. I am sober. I am honest. All day at that school. As you say, always extra duty. I stay long after class. Then I go and stand in line in the shops. I look after the children. I offend no one. And yet if I even have a thought—a *thought* even—it's a crime. Everyone is waiting. Everyone stands ready to condemn me. *(She turns and suddenly rushes to the far side of the room.)* No, it's too cruel.

(She is overwhelmed. She stands facing away from the room. Her mother does not turn. Then in the silence the ASSISTANT CURATOR comes in carrying a canvas which is facing toward him. He is in his mid-thirties. He wears a blue suit. He is nervous.)

ASSISTANT The painting is here.

VALENTINA Where?

ASSISTANT I have it. Madame Nrovka. *(He holds it out, a little puzzled, from the far side of the room.)*

VALENTINA Put it down.

ASSISTANT Where?

VALENTINA Well, over there.

(She gestures at a distant chair. He leans it on the chair, face turned away.)

ASSISTANT Will you view it?

VALENTINA I will look at it later. I'm talking to my daughter.

SOPHIA Forgive me. I'm appallingly rude. *(She wakes up to his embarrassment and walks over to shake his hand.)* I'm Sophia Yepileva.

ASSISTANT I'm the assistant curator.

VALENTINA No doubt your boss has sent you. He is too frightened himself.

ASSISTANT I'm sorry?

VALENTINA If he is frightened, why did he ask me? Why do you need me? Surely you have experts?

ASSISTANT We do. Of all kinds.

VALENTINA What do they say?

ASSISTANT   There is a slight problem. *(He looks nervously to* SOPHIA, *as if not liking them both to be there.)* How shall I put it? There are shades of a dispute. The scientific experts are used to handling *older* paintings.

VALENTINA   Yes, of course.

ASSISTANT   We know a great deal about pigment chronology. We have radio carbon. We have X-ray crystallography. We have wet chemistry. All these are invaluable if the painting is old enough. Because dating is what usually gives the forger away.

VALENTINA   But Matisse is too recent.

ASSISTANT   That's right. *(He smiles, nervous again.)* That is what we—who help run the museum—we are saying this to the scientists, you see. Who do not work for us. They work for the ministry.

VALENTINA   Ah, well.

(There is a pause as the ASSISTANT *appreciates she has understood the problem; then he hurries on.)*

ASSISTANT   Their work is very useful. It is respected. Within certain limits. They have proved that if the canvas was forged, it was forged some time ago. Almost certainly in France. They can establish that. Where and when. That is useful work. But it does—in this case—we believe—stop short of *who*.

VALENTINA   Which you mean is much more a matter of taste.

ASSISTANT   Oh, no . . . not entirely . . . *(He smiles reassuringly at her.)* There is circumstantial evidence. We can guess at motive. We are very suspicious. Obviously. Because Matisse is so recently dead. Only two years ago. If someone were trying—what?—to test the water, this would be an ideal moment. A forger usually offers a cycle of work.

VALENTINA   This would be the first.

ASSISTANT   Exactly. *(He looks to* SOPHIA.) Forgers usually can't resist. Once they have acquired a style, they're reluctant to let go of it.

VALENTINA   No different from painters. Except the very greatest.

ASSISTANT   Vrain Lucas forged manuscripts in the hands of Julius Caesar, the Apostle Paul, and Joan of Arc. A bewildering diversity. But mercifully for us, exceptional.

VALENTINA   And what about the art critics?

ASSISTANT   Yes, a couple have also had a look.

VALENTINA   Well?

(The ASSISTANT *looks hopelessly.)*

ASSISTANT   Adjectives are so subjective, isn't that the problem? "Overdecorative." "Too plastic," they say. "Too cold." "Not fluid." They mean one thing to one man, something quite different to another. *(He pauses a moment.)* So we thought to ask someone who knew the man himself.

(VALENTINA shrugs this off.)

VALENTINA   Surely many people knew him. He even visited this museum, I
   think.
ASSISTANT   I gather, yes. We were honored. Sometime before the war.
VALENTINA   So?
ASSISTANT   It was felt you understand his spirit.
VALENTINA   The experts concede that?
ASSISTANT   Well, no, actually . . .

(VALENTINA smiles, her judgment confirmed.)

Professor Satayev expressly forbade your being asked. He was against it.
He has authenticated the painting, he insists. By scientific methods.
VALENTINA   *(Ironically.)* Well, then?
ASSISTANT   But if he were wrong it would be a major embarrassment.
VALENTINA   For whom? *(There is a slight pause.)* For whom?

(The ASSISTANT looks nervously to SOPHIA.)

You mean for the authorities?
ASSISTANT   Well, perhaps. Yes. For everyone.
VALENTINA   So the white witch is called in.

(She smiles. SOPHIA looks uneasily at the ASSISTANT.)

ASSISTANT   As you know, Matisse himself was fanatic. In his own lifetime. He
   would always go round to check the work being sold under his name. By
   an irony the letters of authentication he then wrote are in themselves
   incredibly valuable. They change hands at three thousand rubles. One or
   two, we think, have already been forged. *(He smiles.)* The whole business
   is way out of hand.
VALENTINA   He would be appalled.
SOPHIA   *(Frowns.)* How do you decide? Finally?
ASSISTANT   There are tests. But these are all negative by nature. They tell you
   if it cannot be Matisse. Dating, pigment, brushwork, so on. If the negative tests are all passed, you are forced to conclude the work must be real.
   The absence of disproof is finally proof. No one ever says "Oh yes, this
   is his . . ." Except . . . *(He pauses.)*
SOPHIA   When?
ASSISTANT   Except when there's someone. I don't know . . . when there's
   someone who knew him quite well.

(There is a pause. VALENTINA seems uninterested, with thoughts of her own.)

SOPHIA   I see.
VALENTINA   My daughter is a painter.

ASSISTANT   Oh really? I'm afraid I don't know your work.

SOPHIA   My mother is exaggerating. I'm an amateur only.

VALENTINA   She tried to paint the sun.

SOPHIA   Yes, Mother.

VALENTINA   The sun can't be painted. Cézanne said, it can be represented, but it can't be reproduced. She tries to prove Cézanne wrong.

SOPHIA   Yes, Mother, but I do it for pleasure.

VALENTINA   Pleasure!

SOPHIA   Yes. I sketch for myself. Not to be in competition with great artists. You think we all want to be Cézanne. Why?

VALENTINA   You should want to be Cézanne. Or else why paint?

SOPHIA   For enjoyment.

VALENTINA   That's nonsense. Painting must be learnt. Like any other discipline. Why go in with no sense of what others have achieved?

SOPHIA   I don't think like that. To me, that's not the point of it.

VALENTINA   Then what is the point of it?

SOPHIA   I paint simply in order . . . (She stops. Then rather feebly, as if knowing how lame it sounds.) . . . to show what is there.

(VALENTINA gestures, her case proved.)

VALENTINA   That is why she can never be good. What you do is called photography. They said of Picasso that he couldn't paint a tree. They were wrong. He was painting trees when he was eight. It quickly came to bore him. He had no interest in trees after that. But he could paint the feeling you had when you looked at a tree. And that is more valuable. Painting is ultimately to do with the quality of feeling. That is why you will never be able to paint.

(The ASSISTANT looks between the two women, embarrassed. But SOPHIA seems unfazed.)

SOPHIA   (Quietly.) I don't know.

ASSISTANT   I can't tell. I'm an academician. My heart is in the catalog.

SOPHIA   Ah, yes.

ASSISTANT   Matisse is a dauntingly complex subject. To be honest, I haven't lately looked at his paintings. I like them. I love them, in fact.

SOPHIA   Well, then, marry them.

ASSISTANT   What?

SOPHIA   No, it's just . . .

(SOPHIA is smiling. So is VALENTINA. A joke shared.)

It's what my son says. I have twins. When my daughter's eating, say, chocolate cake, when she says, "I love this cake" . . . "Well then, marry it." That's what my son says.

(There's a pause. The ASSISTANT *seems bewildered, the women both amused.)*

ASSISTANT   If . . .
VALENTINA   What . . .
ASSISTANT   No . . .
SOPHIA   I'm sorry.
ASSISTANT   No, if . . .
SOPHIA   I'm just being silly.
VALENTINA   To get back to the subject.
ASSISTANT   Yes.
VALENTINA   Where was this found?

(The ASSISTANT *looks anxiously between them.)*

ASSISTANT   It belongs to a count. A czarist.
VALENTINA   I see.
ASSISTANT   He left his home in 1919. He went to live in the south of France. He claims the canvas had been discarded in Matisse's hotel.
VALENTINA   In Nice?
ASSISTANT   Yes. In the Hotel de la Méditerranée. He was a friend of the manager's. The painting had been literally thrown out. I know it's hard to believe.
VALENTINA   I don't think so.
ASSISTANT   He never had it cataloged or valued because of the irregular way in which it was acquired. He was frightened his ownership would then be challenged.
VALENTINA   And how do you come to have it?
ASSISTANT   It's a bequest. The count died earlier this year. In fact, of a disease which has hitherto been diagnosed only in horses. A kind of horse flu, it turned out. The doctors thought he was medically unique.
VALENTINA   My goodness.
ASSISTANT   I mean, he raced a great deal. That's what he did in France all the time . . . all the time the rest of us were here. So to speak. The count bred horses in the Midi. *(There is a pause.)*
VALENTINA   I see.
ASSISTANT   The puzzling thing of course is, since he fled Russia, why he chose to leave us a painting of such value in his will.
VALENTINA   That puzzles you?
ASSISTANT   Yes. Not you?
VALENTINA   No. *(She is suddenly very quiet.)* You've not lived abroad.
ASSISTANT   Well, no . . .
VALENTINA   I was some time in Paris. Oh, many years ago. Before the Revolution.
ASSISTANT   Yes, I know.

VALENTINA   It can pall. Being away. Believe me.
ASSISTANT   Yes, I'm sure.
VALENTINA   We must all make our peace.
ASSISTANT   You mean the Count has made his? By an act of generosity?
SOPHIA   Yes. Or else he's sold you a pup.

(The women smile. The ASSISTANT looks discomfited.)

VALENTINA   Well, that's right.
SOPHIA   I don't understand the legal position. If the Count stole it.
ASSISTANT   "Stole"? I wouldn't say "stole."
SOPHIA   Picked it up.
ASSISTANT   He acquired it.
SOPHIA   Legitimately?
ASSISTANT   Oh, well, really . . . *(He suddenly becomes expansive.)* Apart from
    anything, so much time has gone by. All art is loot. Who should own it?
    I shouldn't say this, but there isn't much justice in these things. If we
    examined the process whereby everything on these walls was acquired
    . . . we should have bare walls.
SOPHIA   My mother was just saying how much she would prefer that.
VALENTINA   Come, what does it show?

(The ASSISTANT makes as if to go and pick it up.)

    No, tell me.
ASSISTANT   Well, it's like a sketch—I'm not speaking technically . . .
VALENTINA   No, I understand.
ASSISTANT   I mean a kind of dry run. For everything that follows. Except the
    foreground is bare. There is no woman. There is no violin. There is no chair.
    (He shrugs.) There is just a wall. A pair of curtains. Wallpaper. Open
    windows. The sea. *(There is a sudden silence. Then he shrugs again.)* It is either
    a copy. Or a beginning.
VALENTINA   Yes. *(She pauses a moment, then she speaks with great finality, as if
    finishing a poem.)* He did them. Then he threw them away. *(She gets up from
    her chair and walks to the far side of the room, where she addresses the ASSISTANT.)*
    You may bring me some tea.
ASSISTANT   Well, I will. I shall leave you some time with the painting. Alone.
    (He looks a moment to SOPHIA who does not move.) I am very grateful. And
    the Curator, I think, would be grateful too for your subsequent discretion.
    Our scientists must not be upset.

(The ASSISTANT smiles and goes out. The women do not move.)

VALENTINA   He's a weak man.
SOPHIA   Yes.

VALENTINA   He doesn't give a fig about painting.
SOPHIA   Do you need time?

(*VALENTINA turns and looks her straight in the eye, level. Then she turns away.*)

VALENTINA   No. I already know. (*There is a pause.* VALENTINA *deep in thought,* SOPHIA *watching her.*) Make your speech.
SOPHIA   What?
VALENTINA   I am ready.
SOPHIA   Now?
VALENTINA   Yes. Isn't that why you're here?
SOPHIA   No. I wanted to come with you. I was interested.
VALENTINA   You want to leave Grigor.

(*SOPHIA hesitates a moment.*)

SOPHIA   How do you know?
VALENTINA   You've wanted to leave since the moment you were married.
SOPHIA   That's not true.
VALENTINA   What else could it be? But now I can see you are hardening. You have the will. It's there. I sense it in you. You have become determined.
SOPHIA   First I want to talk to you.
VALENTINA   Don't lie. Please don't lie. I can tell you've made up your mind. Haven't you?

(*SOPHIA does not answer.*)

   Sophia, please. Talk to me properly.
SOPHIA   Yes.

(*There's a pause.* VALENTINA *is very quiet.*)

VALENTINA   Then I am sure you've met another man.

(*SOPHIA looks down.*)

SOPHIA   Yes.
VALENTINA   You're in love.
SOPHIA   I think less and less of love. What does love have to do with it? What matters is not love, but what the other person makes you. (*SOPHIA turns and walks away to the far side of the room.*) When I stand next to Grigor, it's clear, he is a dutiful man. He's a model servant of the state. Next to him, I look only like a fortunate woman who must struggle every day to deserve the luck she's had in marrying someone so worthwhile. That is my role. In marriages everyone gets cast. The strong one, the weak. The quick one, the slow. The steady, the giddy. It's set. Almost from the moment you meet. You don't notice it, you take it for granted, you think you're just *you*.

Fixed, unchangeable. But you're not. You're what you've been cast as with the other person. And it's all got nothing to do with who you really are.

VALENTINA   Nothing?

SOPHIA   With Grigor, I'm dowdy, I'm scatterbrained, I'm trying to prove myself. All the standards are his. Grigor, of course, has nothing to prove. He's a headmaster at thirty-seven, the party approves of him. He can always find his shirts in the drawer. I usually can. But Usually is no good next to Always. "Usually" becomes a great effort of will. All I can do . . . no, all I can *be* is an inadequate, minor commentary on Grigor's far more finished character. Grigor and Sophia. After ten years we each have our part. Whereas when I'm with . . . this other man . . . then suddenly I'm quite someone else. *(There is a pause.)*

VALENTINA   He is a less good man, I assume from what you're saying. . . .

SOPHIA   Oh no, it's not as easy as that.

VALENTINA   He is less of a challenge, is that right?

SOPHIA   No!

VALENTINA   You've found yourself a mediocrity, so you suffer less by comparison. Is that what you mean?

SOPHIA   Not at all.

VALENTINA   Well, is it? *(She asks this with sudden emphasis. She waits, then, getting no reply, laughs.)* What does he do, this other person with no name?

SOPHIA   He works for the Sanitation Board.

VALENTINA   Well, exactly!

(SOPHIA is pointing at her, bright red with anger.)

SOPHIA   Mother, if you prevent me, I will never forgive you.

VALENTINA   Me? What can I do?

SOPHIA   Withhold your approval.

VALENTINA   My approval?

SOPHIA   Yes.

VALENTINA   From an empty room you never visit?

SOPHIA   I visit you.

VALENTINA   You visit occasionally. Would you really miss that? *(SOPHIA is exasperated.)*

SOPHIA   You don't even like Grigor.

VALENTINA   Well . . .

SOPHIA   It's true. You never did. From the start. You said he was a prig.

VALENTINA   What do I matter? It's not me you have to fear. If you don't know by now, you must face your own conscience. Your children.

SOPHIA   Do you think I've not thought of them? Mother, it's hard. But I have the right to live my own life.

(VALENTINA turns away, smiling.)

VALENTINA   Oh, rights.

SOPHIA   No doubt by will . . . by some great effort of will our marriage may be saved. By will we may grow old together. But I remember once you said to me: Nothing's worth having by will.

VALENTINA   Did I say that?

(SOPHIA looks at her, then moves away, shaking her head.)

SOPHIA   And anyway, it's wrong. There's a principle.

VALENTINA   Oh, really?

SOPHIA   Yes.

VALENTINA   You still believe in that?

SOPHIA   Of course. What do you mean? In their private life, a person must be free to live as they choose.

(VALENTINA raises her eyebrows.)

VALENTINA   My goodness me, your principles are convenient. You call that an ideal?

SOPHIA   Forgive me but I'm afraid . . . yes, well I do.

VALENTINA   How convenient. Goodness. An ideal. Which also coincides with what you want. How perfect. What perfect luck. Run off with this man. Call it "living my own life." "I must be myself, I must do what I want. . . ." *(She smiles.)* I have heard these words before. On boulevards. In cafés. I used to hear them in Paris. I associate them with zinc tables and the gushing of beer. Everyone talking about their entitlements. "I must be allowed to realize myself." For me, it had a different name. I never called it principle. I called it selfishness.

SOPHIA   How can you say that to me?

VALENTINA   Oh yes. Men—your father's friends—used these very same words. Many times. When I was pregnant they said, "Get rid of it. You must live your own life. A child will burden you. You have a right to be happy. Get on with your painting, and realize yourself." You owe your very existence to the fact I did not choose to live my own life.

SOPHIA   Yes, but that's different. . . .

VALENTINA   No, not at all. It's what's involved in facing up to being an adult. Sacrifice and discipline and giving yourself to others, not always thinking of yourself and sometimes . . . yes . . . being harsh. As I am being harsh. . . .

SOPHIA   Oh, how you love that harshness. Nothing can ever be harsh enough for you.

(VALENTINA turns away, but SOPHIA does not relent.)

Well, that's not my fault. It's your fault. You like responsibility? I give it you. It was your fault. It was your life you ruined. You did it. All by yourself. Without consultation. *(She turns away.)* Well, I'm not going to let you now ruin mine.

(Standing at the open door of the room now is PETER LINITSKY. *He is in his mid-sixties, he is bald; he has an unremarkable blue overcoat and carries his hat in his hand. His manner is apologetic.)*

PETER   Excuse me.

SOPHIA   Oh God.

PETER   Am I interrupting?

SOPHIA   No, no, come in.

VALENTINA   Please go away. Who is this?

SOPHIA   It's him.

VALENTINA   What do you mean?

*(*VALENTINA *is genuinely taken aback by* PETER*'s age and his appearance.)*

SOPHIA   It's Peter.

VALENTINA   Peter?

SOPHIA   Yes, Peter, for God's sake. Wake up, Mother. The man with no name.

VALENTINA   It's him?

SOPHIA   Yes.

PETER   What?

SOPHIA   Yes. Goodness. How many times?

PETER   What do you mean, no name?

SOPHIA   Forget it.

VALENTINA   Are you with the Sanitation Board?

PETER   Well, I . . .

SOPHIA   Leave it. You know he is. Don't answer, Peter.

PETER   I didn't get the chance.

SOPHIA   Don't play her game. She contrives to make the words sound like an insult.

PETER   If you . . .

VALENTINA   What words?

SOPHIA   Sanitation Board.

VALENTINA   Did I?

*(*SOPHIA *suddenly turns to her mother with surprising force.)*

SOPHIA   Down here below you, people are forced to be ridiculous. Yes. We lead ridiculous lives. Doing ridiculous things, which lack taste. Like working for a living. For organizations which have ridiculous names. "Oh, I'm from the Department of Highway Cleansing." "Oh, I'm Vegetation Officer in Minsk." That's work. It's called making a living, Mother, it involves silly names and unspeakable people—the mathematics teacher, for me to work beside her, to have lunch, to watch her pick her dirty gray hair from the soup, it's torture, I'd rather lodge beside an open drain. But that's how people live. We have to. We scrabble about in the real world. Because we don't sit thinking all day about art.

(VALENTINA *turns bitterly to* PETER.)

VALENTINA   Is she like this with you?
SOPHIA   Don't answer.
VALENTINA   Peter?
PETER   Like what?
VALENTINA   Self-righteous.
PETER   Er, no.
SOPHIA   Would you two like to be introduced?
VALENTINA   Not especially.
PETER   Good afternoon.
SOPHIA   His name is Peter Linitsky. My mother.
PETER   At last.
VALENTINA   I feel I already know you. Do you have a wife?
SOPHIA   Say nothing.
PETER   I did. (*There is a pause. Finally,* PETER *feels compelled to fill it in.*) She is an extraordinary woman.
VALENTINA   I'm sure. Now you're rid of her. Leningrad is full of aging men praising their wives. Whom they have invariably left. If you hear a man praise his wife in Russia, it means they are no longer together.
SOPHIA   Peter left six years ago.
VALENTINA   Peter left?
PETER   No, seven.
VALENTINA   Oh, seven is one better, of course. Don't miss one. Each one counts. Doesn't each one make it more respectable?
PETER   I have a divorce.
VALENTINA   Well done. It's hard.
SOPHIA   Divorce is possible.
VALENTINA   Yes.

(*There is a pause. Nobody moves.*)

SOPHIA   Mother, it's possible.
VALENTINA   Yes.

(VALENTINA *looks at her a moment with the calm of someone who suddenly knows they have an unanswerable argument.*)

Peter, I know nothing about you. For all I know, you're a kind and decent man. I'm sure you managed a divorce. But I am sure . . . I would stake my life . . . you are not in the party. (*There is a silence.*)
PETER   No.

(*VALENTINA nods very slightly, acknowledging the admission. SOPHIA looks between them.*)

SOPHIA   (*Quietly:*) Mother, neither am I. (*VALENTINA looks at her steadily.*) I have already written to the paper. To place an advertisement.

VALENTINA   Does Grigor know?

SOPHIA   No.

VALENTINA   It means nothing. When did you write? (*She doesn't answer.*)

PETER   She wrote a week ago.

VALENTINA   How long will it take?

PETER   The waiting list is nine months, to get your item in. At the moment. Some people have waited a year.

VALENTINA   Nine months for the advertisement?

PETER   That's right. Unless . . .

VALENTINA   What?

SOPHIA   (*Finishing for him.*) . . . it can be brought forward.

VALENTINA   What? Are you thinking of moving out of Leningrad?

(*PETER and SOPHIA look at one another.*)

SOPHIA   No . . .

PETER   We . . .

SOPHIA   No, there are towns, we know of towns . . . not far away . . . where the queue is not so long for the local paper. And the papers there give more space. A month. Two months. But you must prove residency. You must room there. And . . . there's no question . . . Peter can't leave his job.

PETER   (*Smiles.*) No money.

SOPHIA   And I can't leave mine. I can't take the children.

VALENTINA   Well, here they won't print it. They will ask Grigor first.

SOPHIA   That's not the law.

VALENTINA   They will ask him. He won't agree to publication. Let alone to all the court procedures which follow.

SOPHIA   It doesn't matter. I still have the right.

(*VALENTINA suddenly gets angry.*)

VALENTINA   Don't use that word. You have the *right*? What does it mean? It doesn't mean anything. Be a person. Do what you have to. Don't prattle about rights.

(*SOPHIA looks to PETER for support.*)

SOPHIA   Mother, there are ways. It can be speeded.

VALENTINA   I've never heard of it.

SOPHIA   If you spoke to Grigor.

VALENTINA   If *I* spoke?

SOPHIA   Yes.

VALENTINA   Is this what you came here to ask me?

SOPHIA   If you said you'd seen me . . . and you knew how deeply I felt. You know what the legal criterion is for divorce? It's quite simple. The criterion for divorce is necessity. *(There is a pause.)* Mother, I need to be free.

(VALENTINA smiles.)

VALENTINA   *(Lightly:)* Grigor's not free. You're not free. Child, you've lived thirty-six years. How can you be so naive?

SOPHIA   Is it naive?

VALENTINA   Of course. There's no freedom.

SOPHIA   Oh, really? That's not what I've heard.

VALENTINA   Where? Where do you think there is freedom?

SOPHIA   Well, I've always heard . . . from what you say of Paris . . .

VALENTINA   Don't be ridiculous.

SOPHIA   Your life there.

VALENTINA   I was seventeen!

SOPHIA   With . . . how many lovers? My mother always told me . . . *(She turns to PETER.)*

PETER   Goodness.

SOPHIA   While she was meant to be learning to draw.

VALENTINA   That was Paris. *(She pauses, as if protecting a memory.)* Paris was different.

SOPHIA   Oh, I see. And is Paris the only place where people may be happy? *(She waits a moment. Then quietly:)* Or is it just you who wants it that way?

(There is a silence. SOPHIA waits. But VALENTINA just seems amused.)

VALENTINA   I see. And you think freedom is happiness, do you?

(SOPHIA doesn't answer.)

You think it's the same thing? Do you, Peter?

PETER   Well I . . . I don't know. I'm pressed to make a living. Half goes to my ex-wife. My children are grown up. They work in a factory making bottles. One's doing quite well. The other was born a bit slow. So I am always thinking of him. Most days. Most hours. *(He smiles thinly.)* I'm not an expert on freedom.

VALENTINA   Yes, well, you're wiser than her.

(PETER looks a little nervously to SOPHIA.)

PETER   I only know I've not had much luck in things. I find myself nearly sixty-three. And . . . never really had the chance to take a risk in my life. What else is there now for me but Sophia? I don't mean it unkindly but . . . well, I live alone, I have a room, I'm a great lover of walking; I meet in the park with other model-aircraft collectors. . . .

SOPHIA His aircraft are beautiful.

PETER No, they're . . . quite average. But without Sophia I might as well die. *(He takes another look at her.)*

VALENTINA You didn't think that before?

PETER What do you mean?

VALENTINA Before you met her?

PETER No. I mean, no. Hardly. How could I? But I think it now.

VALENTINA Well, that's love for you, isn't it? Before you met her you were happy.

PETER Not happy, no.

VALENTINA But not "Oh, I'll die" *(She suddenly raises her voice.)* You're Stravinsky's grandfather.

PETER I don't understand.

VALENTINA Stravinsky's grandfather died trying to scale the garden fence on his way to an assignation with his mistress. He was a hundred and eleven years old at the time.

(PETER smiles. VALENTINA laughs. Only SOPHIA is not amused.)

SOPHIA Don't say that of Peter.

VALENTINA And what . . . what, anyway . . . *(She moves suddenly and decisively on to the attack.)* What if you succeeded? What if she uses you to get her a divorce?

SOPHIA I'm not doing that.

VALENTINA What then?

PETER What do you mean?

VALENTINA Love is pain. Am I right? *(He looks mistrustfully, fearing a trap.)*

PETER Not entirely.

VALENTINA Look at you now. You're in torture. You shift from one foot to another . . .

PETER Well, I . . .

VALENTINA You're forever taking sidelong glances at her, checking up on her, seeing she approves of everything you say. Thinking all the time, How does this go down with Sophia? In fiction it makes me laugh when books end with two people coming together. Curtain! At last they fall into one another's arms! The reader applauds. But that's where books should really begin. *(She smiles.)* This fantasy that love solves problems! Love makes you raw. It strips the skin from you. Am I right?

PETER In part.

VALENTINA Suddenly everything has to matter so much. Really, who cares? Suddenly to be aware, to be prey to every exaggerated detail, every nuance of someone else's feelings. How demeaning! What possible point? And then what? What in the future? What will you do? Spend two years in the courts? Two years of little sidelong glances, and oh, is it all right? Is she weakening? Do I love her? Does she love me? And at the end, what? You'll suddenly realize—not a plateau. Oh, no. Not safety. Not if it's love. Really love. Just as likely agony. Oh, yes. A pure gambler's throw. And for this? For *this?* Chuck out everything. Husband. Jobs. Children. Grigor. Yes. Destroy Grigor's life. For a bet placed by two shivering tramps at the racetrack. *(She leans forward.)* And there's nothing guaranteed at the end. *(She gets up, her case proved.)* People should stick. They should stick with what they have. With what they know. That's character.

SOPHIA   You think so?

VALENTINA   Certainly. But these days people just can't wait to give up.

(SOPHIA smiles, as if not threatened by any of this.)

You make such a fuss about everything. I just get on with it. I know what life is. And what it cannot be.

(PETER is puzzled by SOPHIA's calm. Now VALENTINA insults him aimlessly, with no real feeling.)

You're a silly bald man. You're old and you're bald. Your shirt is too young for you. Your trousers are absurd. Is there anything worse than men who can't grow old with dignity? *(She sits at the side of the room, the storm blown out.)* I was promised tea. *(She suddenly shouts, as if she can't think of anything else to say.)* They promised me tea.

PETER   I will get it for you.

SOPHIA   No. Let me go.

(She smiles and goes out. PETER is left standing near the canvas, VALENTINA sitting.)

VALENTINA   She's a good girl. There's no harm in her. She's just weak. And talentless. Her father was a soldier. I knew him three weeks. He claimed there was a war. What did I know? He said his battalion had to move. Perhaps it was true. I never saw his battalion. He said the French had a war to go to in Abyssinia. I've never checked. Was there such a thing?

PETER   I've never heard of it.

VALENTINA   There's no way to tell.

PETER   This was in Paris?

VALENTINA   Yes. Paris and Leningrad. It's all I've known.

(PETER waits a moment.)

PETER   You must have met everyone. I mean, the famous.

VALENTINA   Certainly not. It wasn't like that. I had no interest. I once was asked to a party to meet Ford Madox Ford.

PETER   There you are.

VALENTINA   Him I had heard of. Because they said he was the least frequently washed of all modern novelists. So I didn't go. *(She shakes her head.)* People get it wrong. They have no idea of it. Remember, we were poor. We had no ambitions for ourselves. At school we were a strange group. All penniless. Hungarians, a Chinese, some Americans. Well, Americans have money, but no one else. One boy wanted to pose in the life class. He was one of us. He needed to make money. He said "Well, why not?" All day we looked at naked people. Men, women. "You're not embarrassed," he said, "people come in, take their clothes off. It's fine. Why not me? Why not give me the money?" But we all had a meeting. We said no. A line would be crossed. *(She pauses, deep in thought.)* A naked stranger is one thing. But one of us naked—no. It's all wrong.

(PETER waits respectfully.)

PETER   This was an art school?

VALENTINA   School of painting. At the Sacred Heart Convent. In the boulevard des Invalides.

PETER   Who taught you?

VALENTINA   A man who said he wanted to turn his lambs into lions.

PETER   Who was that?

VALENTINA   Henri Matisse.

(There is a pause.)

PETER   Matisse?

VALENTINA   Yes.

PETER   You mean Matisse?

VALENTINA   I said Matisse.

PETER   Yes, I know.

VALENTINA   Why, you admire him?

PETER   Just the idea that he was alive. And he taught you. It seems unbelievable.

VALENTINA   Well, it's a fact.

PETER   I didn't know he taught.

VALENTINA   He taught for three years.

PETER   Then?

(She turns and looks at him.)

VALENTINA   Then he didn't teach anymore.

(PETER looks down a moment.)

PETER   You mean . . . look, I know nothing—art!—but I've seen some things he's done . . . but what I mean, did he feel there was no point to teaching?

VALENTINA   How would I know? He taught us rules. He believed in them. Not Renaissance rules. Those he was very against. He disliked Leonardo. Because of all that measuring. He said that was when art began to go wrong.

When it became obsessed with measuring. Trying to establish how things work. It doesn't matter how they work. You can't *see* with a caliper. *(She smiles.)* Of course there were rules. He was a classicist. This is what no one understood. He disliked in modern painting the way one part is empha-sized—the nose, or the foot, or the breast. He hated this distortion. He said you should always aim for the whole. Remember your first impression and stick to it. Balance nature and your view. Don't let your view run away of its own accord. For everything he did there was always a reason. No one saw this to begin with. On the walls of Paris, people painted slogans: Matisse is absinthe, Matisse drives you mad. But to meet, he was a German schoolmaster with little gold-rimmed glasses.

PETER   I've seen those drawings he did of himself. I like him in the mirror when he's drawing a nude.

VALENTINA   Yes, it's witty. *(There is a pause.)* Even with color . . . the colors were so striking, people thought, why is this face blue? This is modern. But it wasn't. Each color depends on what is placed next to it. One tone is just a color. Two tones are a chord, which is life. *(She turns a moment, thought-fully.)* It was the same with the body. No line exists on its own. Only with its relation to another do you create volume. He said you should think of the body as an architect does. The foot is a bridge. Arms are like rolls of clay. Forearms are like ropes, since they can be knotted and twisted. In drawing a head never leave out the ear. Adjust the different parts to each other. Each is dissimilar and yet must add to the whole. A tree is like a human body. A body is like a cathedral. *(She smiles.)* His models were always very beautiful. Sometimes he worked with the same model for years. No one drew the body better than him. The lines of a woman's stomach. The pudenda. A few curls. He could make you think of bed. And yet when he was working he said, he took a woman's clothes off and put them back on as if he were arranging a vase of flowers. *(There is a pause.)* He loved going to the mountains. When he was tired, he said it was a relief. Because it's impossible to paint them. You can't paint a mountain. The scale is all wrong.

PETER   That's funny.

(She looks at him, suddenly resuming her original answer.)

VALENTINA   As to teaching, yes, of course, his teaching was inspiring. But it was as if Shakespeare had taught. It gave you an idea. But then when you pick up your own brush, you're faced with the reality of your own talent.

PETER   Frustrating?

VALENTINA   Not always. But how do I say? It's a very different thing. Talking is easy. Oh yes, and Matisse could talk. But genius is different.

(PETER frowns a moment.)

PETER Did it depress you?

VALENTINA No. I went on painting. Although I knew my limitations. I painted by will.

PETER By will?

VALENTINA Yes.

PETER It's odd.

VALENTINA What?

PETER Last night, now, Sophia used that same phrase. "By will."

VALENTINA Yes. She used it to me. *(She looks at him a moment.)* He taught a few years, then he went traveling. He went to Italy, Algeria, Tangiers. By then he was yet more famous. He'd given Picasso one of his paintings. Picasso's friends, who were all very stupid and malicious, used it as a dartboard. But it didn't matter. Matisse's reputation was made. He bought a house in Clamart. People mocked him because it had such a big bathroom. On the ground floor. Too much contact with Americans, that's what people said. He'd developed an interest in personal hygiene. But it wasn't true. Matisse was always clean. *(She smiles.)* I went there a couple of times. Madame Matisse used to cook. She served a jugged hare which was better than anything in Europe. And with it, a wine called Rančio. It's a sort of Madeira. Heavy but excellent. I've never had it since.

PETER I don't know it.

VALENTINA Years later in Berlin, he went for a great exhibition of his work. And waiting for him was the most enormous laurel wreath. "To Henri Matisse, *cher maître*" . . . or whatever. He said, "Why do you give me a wreath? I'm not dead." But Madame Matisse plucked a leaf and tasted it. She said, "This will make the most wonderful soup."

(There is a pause.)

PETER Yes.

VALENTINA It was all one progress. I can't explain. I lost touch with him. I think everyone did. He simply moved out of all our lives. Yet whenever I heard later stories, they fitted. With him, everything belonged.

PETER I can see that.

VALENTINA I've seen photographs of him when he was dying. He's painting on his walls with a brush tied to the end of a long stick. He's too frail to move from his pillows. It's the same man I knew almost fifty years ago. *(She smiles.)* There was only one little—oh, what?—one tiny denial. Which was love. He told me he was too busy. To think of love properly. I mean, to explore it. No, he said. I have no time for that.

PETER I find that strange.

VALENTINA He was asked by an American journalist how many children he had. Four, he said. What are their names? Let me see. There's Marguerite. And Jean. And Pierre. He said suddenly, "No, I have three."

PETER But isn't that . . .

VALENTINA What?

PETER A bit callous?

VALENTINA I think it's admirable.

PETER Why?

VALENTINA Priorities!

(PETER smiles.)

PETER It seems a bit chilly to me.

VALENTINA He loved his family. He painted faces above his bed. He said he slept badly, but he always felt better if he could imagine his grandchildren. So he put them on the ceiling above him. That way he said, "I feel less alone."

PETER But what did they feel?

VALENTINA Does it matter? Marguerite was tortured by the Gestapo. She was in the Resistance. When she came home and told him, he couldn't paint for two weeks. Then he abandoned the work he'd been doing when he heard. Her pain was real to him. He was in anguish. But he could not incorporate her suffering. He didn't want to. He went on painting in just the same way.

(There is a pause.)

PETER What about you?

VALENTINA Me?

PETER Were you like that? Disciplined?

VALENTINA Good Lord, no. No. I wasted my time. Love was *all* I had time for. At least until the twenties.

PETER Sophia said . . . *(He pauses.)*

VALENTINA Yes?

PETER She suggested . . . that for some reason you decided to come home.

VALENTINA That's right. *(She waits.)* What else did she say?

PETER No, nothing, just . . . she said, you didn't have to.

VALENTINA I didn't have to. It was a choice of my own.

(There is a pause. PETER waits.)

I didn't know Matisse well. But I understood him. I understood what's called his handwriting. I love this phrase. Do you know what it is?

PETER No.

VALENTINA It's a painting term. Which is indefinable. It's not quite even signature. It's more than that. It's spirit.

(She looks at him a moment, then SOPHIA returns, silently, with tea in a pot and cups on a tray. She moves round.)

SOPHIA   Here's tea.

VALENTINA   Well, thank you.

SOPHIA   Everyone's vanished. The museum's closed.

VALENTINA   Already?

SOPHIA   It's dark now.

VALENTINA   I didn't notice. What have you done with the assistant curator?

SOPHIA   I told him to wait. *(SOPHIA gives her tea.)*

VALENTINA   Thank you. You've been talking of me, I gather, to Peter here.

SOPHIA   Not in particular. Do you want tea?

PETER   No, thank you.

SOPHIA   We're always short of time. Me and Linitsky. *(She smiles affectionately at him.)* We meet in a café far from our homes. Most of the time we talk about how to meet next. Then when we meet next, how to meet next. And so on.

VALENTINA   It sounds most exhausting.

SOPHIA   In China they say if you want to be taught by a particular professor, you must go to his door every day and ask to be a pupil. And every day for a year, two years, three years, he will close the door in your face. Then one day he will suddenly accept you. He's been testing your endurance. To see if you want the thing badly enough.

VALENTINA   What a sentimental notion.

SOPHIA   It's true.

VALENTINA   I'm sure it's true. *(The hardness of her tone suddenly returns.)* And meanwhile your life has gone by. *(SOPHIA looks a moment to PETER.)*

SOPHIA   So what did you decide?

PETER   Sorry?

SOPHIA   The two of you.

PETER   Oh. *(He pauses.)* About what?

SOPHIA   Peter . . .

PETER   Oh, I see.

SOPHIA   I'm asking, will my mother help us?

PETER   I don't know. She didn't say. *(VALENTINA smiles to herself.)* We didn't get on to the subject. To be honest, we were talking about art.

SOPHIA   Oh, God.

PETER   I know.

SOPHIA   Really, Peter. I asked you . . .

PETER   I know. I'm ashamed.

VALENTINA   Did you give him a mission?

PETER   I got distracted, that's all.

VALENTINA   What was he meant to be asking me?

SOPHIA   *(To VALENTINA.)* Nothing. Mind your own business. *(To PETER.)* Really! Do I have to do everything myself? *(She is at once contrite.)* Oh God, I'm sorry.

PETER   No, no . . .

SOPHIA   Forgive me, I didn't mean to be unpleasant.

PETER   You're not being unpleasant. Really.

SOPHIA   I'm sorry, Peter.

PETER   No, it's my fault.

VALENTINA   Is this how your home life will be? God help us. I think you'd both be better off on your own.

SOPHIA   Well, perhaps. *(She turns to PETER.)* What do you say?

PETER   No, I don't think so. For me it's an adventure, you see. At last something's happening. Even if, as you say, it's unbelievably uncomfortable. It uncovers feelings I didn't know I had. *(He smiles nervously.)* For a start, I'm jealous. It's illogical. Jealous of the past. Of the life Sophia had before I even knew her. The further back, the worse. Even the idea . . . when I think of her as young . . . just young . . . in a short gingham dress, on a pavement, with a satchel, going to school, the idea of her life as an eight-year-old fills my heart with such terrible longing. Such a sense of loss. It makes no sense, it's ridiculous. My brain reels, I can hardly think. Images of someone I never even knew have a power to disturb me, to hurt me in a way which is more profound than anything I've known. *(He looks hopelessly to VALENTINA.)* What can I do? Just abandon her?

SOPHIA   No.

PETER   Just say, "Well, that's it. You've had your glimpse. Now go home and do nothing but glue balsa wood on your own"? *(He shrugs.)* Plainly it's true, I'm not happy. I'm what the textbooks call "seriously disturbed." I wish I were stronger. I wish she didn't so upset me. *(A pause.)* But I think I have to go on.

(There is silence. SOPHIA looks at him a moment.)

VALENTINA   I don't know. Why is that?

PETER   Why?

VALENTINA   Yes, why?

SOPHIA   He just told you.

VALENTINA   Yes. But what he feels will have an effect. On Grigor. On the children.

PETER   I love the children.

SOPHIA   They will live with us.

VALENTINA   Will they? And when will you tell them about the separation?

(SOPHIA does not answer.)

Sophia?

SOPHIA   I already have.

VALENTINA   What?

SOPHIA   Yes. I told them.

VALENTINA   Why did you do that?

SOPHIA   I felt it would be honest.

VALENTINA   Please don't lie to me.

PETER   Sophia . . .

SOPHIA   Also . . .

PETER   (*To* VALENTINA.) I didn't know.

VALENTINA   Tell me your true reason.

SOPHIA   Many things.

VALENTINA   Such as? (*There is a pause.*)

SOPHIA   There would be no going back.

(PETER *is looking across at her, alarmed.* VALENTINA *nods slightly.*)

VALENTINA   Yes. And Grigor? Was Grigor there?

SOPHIA   No. He wasn't with me. I did it this morning. He'll be home about now.

VALENTINA   You told them without asking him.

SOPHIA   Look, Mother, I've asked him often. He always says no. But they must know eventually.

VALENTINA   You told them without his permission?

SOPHIA   He will never give his permission. He claims I'm in the grip of a decadent fantasy. He says I am inflamed by the morals of the West. Mother, he's mad.

VALENTINA   The children won't love you. They will never forgive you.

(SOPHIA *is shaking her head, now very agitated.*)

SOPHIA   All right, I'll be there. I'll go home now. I'll tell him. I'll say "Grigor, the children now know what you and I know." I broke the news because if I didn't, nothing would have happened. Was that wrong? (*She suddenly cries out.*) Mother, don't look at me like that.

VALENTINA   What did the twins say?

SOPHIA   Well . . .

VALENTINA   Tell me.

SOPHIA   Look, what d'you think? Of course it isn't easy.

VALENTINA   Well?

SOPHIA   It's a long process. It's years.

VALENTINA   Just today?

(SOPHIA *pauses a moment.*)

SOPHIA   Nikolai was fine. At once he went back to playing. Alexandra said, would I please go away?

VALENTINA   She's *eight*.

SOPHIA   Mother, don't torture me.

(VALENTINA turns to PETER.)

VALENTINA   Peter, are you shocked?

PETER   No. *(He pauses, uncertain.)* Of course not. It had to be done. Eventually.

VALENTINA   Is there anything worse? Is there anything worse than the weak when they try to be strong? They make such a job of it!

PETER   That isn't fair.

VALENTINA   Oh, I see. Is this how you would have done it?

PETER   I'm not Sophia. I haven't suffered as she has.

VALENTINA   How has she suffered? What does she suffer? Please. I would really like to know.

PETER   Well . . .

VALENTINA   In what way is she different from anyone in Russia? What is her complaint? That she is not *free*? That's what I've been told. Well, who is free? Tell me, am I free?

SOPHIA   No. No, Mother. But it's you who always say I am docile. . . . *(She turns to PETER.)* That's what she tells me. That I'm passive; I'm second-rate, I agree to things too easily. . . .

VALENTINA   I say this?

SOPHIA   Today! Even today you said people take advantage of me. Now when I make a stand, you insult me.

VALENTINA   I do. Because it is doomed. Because it's not in your character.

SOPHIA   No?

VALENTINA   It's just a little spurt. You don't have the character to finish what you've started.

(There is a pause. SOPHIA looks at her, as if finally understanding her objection. Then, with genuine interest:)

SOPHIA   Is that what you fear?

VALENTINA   Yes, it is. You'll fail. You'll lose heart.

SOPHIA   Is that *all* you fear?

(VALENTINA looks slightly shifty.)

VALENTINA   Nor does he. I apologize for saying this. He's ten years from dying.

SOPHIA   Yes, thank you, Mother. Is there anything else? *(She looks calmly to PETER, who seems not remotely upset.)*

PETER   It's all right.

SOPHIA   Perhaps you might explain. I suppose my mother did not tell you anything of her own life.

PETER   Er, no.

VALENTINA   We did not discuss it.

SOPHIA   Valentina does not tell you why she's so hard on me. *(There's a pause, the two women quite still.)* My mother made a choice. Thirty-five years ago.

David Hare / 179

VALENTINA   Yes.

SOPHIA   I was a baby. She carried me in her arms into Russia, in 1921. She brought me here from Paris.

(There is a pause.)

PETER   I see.

(He waits for more, but the two women are still, both looking down. Eventually:)

What . . . I don't see. . . . I don't understand exactly. . . . I mean . . .

SOPHIA   Go on. Please. Yes. Ask.

PETER   Well . . . I suppose I'm wondering . . . do you regret it?

VALENTINA   How do you answer that question? At certain times everything is wrong.

(SOPHIA smiles.)

I was a wayward woman—that's the word. I lay around in beds, in studios, with men, smoking too much and thinking, Shall I grow my hair? I had a child. Oh, I was like Gorki's mother, who stopped for fifteen minutes on a peasants' march to give birth in a ditch. Then she ran to catch up with the marchers. I was the same. I had my little Sophia in an atelier in the Marais, with two jugs of hot water and a homosexual friend who delivered her. And then I thought—well, is this it? This lounging about? This thinking only of yourself? This—what word should I use—*freedom?* Having a child changed everything. I suddenly decided that Paris was meaningless. Indulgence only. I had a Russian daughter. I had to come home. *(She sits back.)* An artist in Russia. Oh, when I came back, of course, everything was possible. *(She smiles.)* But now. I have not exhibited in seventeen years. *(She shrugs slightly.)* Foreign painters are exhibited in all sorts of style. But Russians may have one style only. It does not suit me. That's all there is to say.

(There is another silence.)

SOPHIA   My mother is intolerant of those who complain.

PETER   Yes. Do you ever think . . . you could have left here. . . .

VALENTINA   Exile, you mean?

PETER   Yes.

VALENTINA   It seemed to me cowardly. To give up seems cowardly. Finally that is always the choice. *(She gestures suddenly toward the canvas on the other side of the room.)* A painting, we are told, left by an aristocrat in his will. His last wish, to send it back to Russia. And he left in 1919! *(She laughs.)*

PETER   I don't know, I mean, for myself I've never even thought of it, why should I? But for you . . . with your background . . .

VALENTINA   No, of course not. My life is not happy. I say this to you. But it would also be unhappy if I'd been cowardly. *(She shakes her head.)* Your life is defined by an absence, by what is not happening, by where you can't be. You think all the time about "me." Oh "me"! Oh "me"! The endless "me" who takes over. "Me" becomes everything. Oh, "I" decided. The self-dramatization. Turning your life into a crusade. A crusade in which you claim equal status with Russia. On the one hand, the whole of Russia, millions of square miles. On the other, "I" think and "I" feel. The battle is unequal. That kind of self-advertisement, it seemed to me wrong. And dangerous. And willful. To drink wine or breed horses, and dream of elsewhere. *(Pause.)* I wasn't a Communist. I know what has happened since. I'm still not a Communist. How could I be? But I made a decision.

PETER   And were you right?

VALENTINA   I have no idea.

(There is a silence.)

SOPHIA   Peter. Please. I want to be alone with her.

PETER   What? Oh, of course.

SOPHIA   Please, Peter, she and I need to talk.

PETER   Of course. *(He is upset.)* Now?

SOPHIA   Yes.

(He stands a moment.)

PETER   When shall I see you?

SOPHIA   What?

PETER   See you? We haven't made an arrangement.

SOPHIA   Oh no, that's right.

PETER   Well, er . . .

SOPHIA   Do we have to fix it now?

PETER   Of course we do, yes.

SOPHIA   Sorry, I can't think. You say.

PETER   In three days, do you have . . .

SOPHIA   Yes. Friday. The usual break after lunch.

PETER   Three days.

SOPHIA   Yes.

PETER   I'll see you then. And we'll talk this over. Madame Nrovka, this has been a great honor. *(He goes across to VALENTINA.)*

VALENTINA   I was pleased to meet you.

PETER   To be honest I was scared. Not because of you. But because I care too much. I do crave her happiness.

VALENTINA   Yes. That is clear. *(He stands a moment.)*

PETER   Three days then.

SOPHIA   Yes.

PETER   I must go. *(Without looking at SOPHIA, he turns and goes quickly out.)*

VALENTINA Now it's cold.

SOPHIA Yes.

VALENTINA It's cold suddenly.

SOPHIA They turn the heating off, I suppose.

VALENTINA All the money they must need to heat art. To keep art warm for the public. *(She looks across at SOPHIA.)* Tell me, is it money you want?

SOPHIA Yes, of course.

VALENTINA I guessed that. Peter's embarrassment was on such a scale. I knew you must have told him to ask me for money.

SOPHIA I did.

VALENTINA He's too nice. He would have stood there forever. *(SOPHIA smiles.)* How much do you need?

SOPHIA Two thousand.

VALENTINA When?

SOPHIA Well, after the counseling and the advertisement and the examination in the people's court, finally you need the money for the regional court. But I felt . . . there's no point in my starting if at the end I can't pay.

VALENTINA You should have asked me this morning. Before speaking to the children. But it did not occur to you that I would say no.

(She looks at SOPHIA, who does not answer.)

Why should I give you money when I do not approve?

(There is a silence. SOPHIA just looks at her. VALENTINA turns away.)

You're just unlucky. It's historical accident. In the twenties it was easy.

SOPHIA I've heard.

VALENTINA In the first days of the Soviet Union, you didn't need your partner's consent. You could sue for a divorce by sending a postcard and three rubles. There was to be a revolution of the sexes. I must say I had my doubts at the time. *(SOPHIA smiles as well.)* I had a lover for a while. Or rather I tried to. Another soldier. Like you, we had nowhere to go. After Paris, Russia seemed ridiculous. Because even then, people got upset if you showed your feelings. People disapproved. So we noticed that at stations people may embrace openly because they're always saying good-bye. So he and I used to go and pretend that one of us was catching a train. We embraced on the platform. We said a thousand good-byes. Train after train went without us. Then an official came and said, "You've watched enough trains." *(She pauses, lost in thought.)* And what will you have? A small room in the suburbs of Leningrad. No money. Children who dislike you for taking them away from their father. From prosperity. From someone who belongs. Who fits in. Who is happy here.

SOPHIA Yes.

VALENTINA   Have you thought of the effect the divorce will have on him? A party member?

SOPHIA   Of course. But if I don't I will have no self-respect. *(VALENTINA laughs.)*

VALENTINA   Oh, please. You! No one cares. You have no status here. Be clear. You're a private citizen. Love in a small flat, it's nobody's business. But Grigor—he will lose position. Influence. Friends. He will be discredited. It's a sign of failure.

(SOPHIA looks unapologetically at her.)

SOPHIA   Well, I can't live with the party anymore. *(She shakes her head.)* I've always known . . . after all, in my profession I work with young people. I spread ideas. I can't be considered for promotion unless I am also willing to join. The moment is looming when they will ask me. *(She pauses a moment.)* This way the moment will never arrive.

VALENTINA   Ah, well, I see . . .

SOPHIA   I think the only hope now is to live your life in private.

VALENTINA   So you choose Peter.

SOPHIA   Yes.

VALENTINA   Because he's ineffectual and hopeless and has no ambition. That's clear. You love his hopelessness.

SOPHIA   It seems a great virtue. Is that wrong? After watching Grigor. The way Grigor is. It comforts me that Peter has no wish to get on.

VALENTINA   Yes. That's attractive. But there's a limit.

SOPHIA   You mean Peter is beyond it?

VALENTINA   He is the Soul of No Hope. *(She smiles.)* Everyone here has a vision. How it might be other. We all have a dream of something else. For you it's Linitsky. Linitsky's your escape. How will it be when he becomes your reality? When he's not your escape? When he's your life?

SOPHIA   I don't know.

VALENTINA   Have you thought . . .

SOPHIA   Of course.

VALENTINA   It's possible you'll hate him? As you hate Grigor now.

SOPHIA   No.

VALENTINA   All the things that seem so attractive—that manner, the way he holds his hat in his hands, the gentleness—when they are your life, they will seem insufferable.

SOPHIA   Perhaps. I don't know. How can anyone know? *(VALENTINA smiles.)*

VALENTINA   Everyone here lives in the future. Or in the past. No one wants the present. What shall we do with the present? Oh, Paris! Oh, Linitsky! Anything but here! Anything but now! *(She turns to SOPHIA.)* I had a friend. She loved a violinist. They could rarely meet. He was married. She worshiped him. Eventually he could not play unless he sensed she was in the audience. She went to all his concerts for over three years. She later said to me, rather bitterly, the violin repertoire is remarkably small. The man's wife died. He came to her and said, we're free. It lasted a week. She no longer desired him. *(A pause.)* It seems to me the worst story I know.

(SOPHIA looks at her, holding her gaze.)

What do you feel when he says that he'll die for you? That it's life and death.

SOPHIA   Well . . .

VALENTINA   Is it for you?

(SOPHIA pauses a moment.)

SOPHIA   No. But we're different. I love him. I love what he is.

VALENTINA   Do you wish he loved you less desperately?

SOPHIA   That's how he loves me.

VALENTINA   And is that a good thing?

SOPHIA   Look, how can I say? He's kind to me. He'll never do me harm. I always feel I can rest with him. Yes, there is inequality. If you like, an inequality of need. Finally. But what's wrong with that? If we said, well, I can see this isn't quite perfect, we'd never do anything.

VALENTINA   No. *(There is a pause.)* Even so.

SOPHIA   What is the alternative? I know what you feel. But by your argument, must we put up with everything?

VALENTINA   I have.

SOPHIA   Yes. But now should I?

(VALENTINA turns and looks at her, but does not answer.)

Mother, will you give me the money?

VALENTINA   Of course. *(She laughs.)* Mind you, I don't have it.

SOPHIA   What?

VALENTINA   Two thousand roubles, are you joking?

SOPHIA   I assumed . . .

VALENTINA   Oh, yes, I act as if I'm rich. That seems to me simply good manners. Don't you see through it?

SOPHIA   No.

VALENTINA   Look at my life. How do you think I would have that kind of money? *(SOPHIA begins to laugh.)*

SOPHIA   I thought you were frugal.

VALENTINA   Frugal? I'm poor.

SOPHIA   Oh, Lord, no, I don't believe it. I've been so nervous . . .

VALENTINA   Well, so you should be. But not about money. You mustn't worry. I'll sell my flat.

SOPHIA   Don't be ridiculous.

VALENTINA   Yes. It means nothing. Goodness, if I couldn't throw money away I'd really be tragic.

SOPHIA   No, there's no question . . .

VALENTINA   Yes. I shall do it. To shame you.

SOPHIA   Well, we shall see. *(A pause.)* You'll support me? You think I'm doing right?

VALENTINA   There is no right. Until you see that, you will never have peace. *(She gets up. She walks across the room, decisively.)* I will speak to Grigor. No, not for you. Not to help you. But on behalf of the children, I will persuade him not to oppose you, so that it's quicker in the regional court. He's frightened of women. Most bullies are. *(SOPHIA is about to speak, but VALENTINA interrupts quickly.)* Don't ask me anymore. That's all I can do. Now please go. The man you want to live with is senile. Senile's the word.

SOPHIA   Thank you, Mother.

VALENTINA   You won't be happy. You'll die at forty.

SOPHIA   Good. Well, I'm glad that you're pleased. *(She smiles, genuinely moved.)*

VALENTINA   I'm not pleased.

SOPHIA   Come here.

VALENTINA   No.

SOPHIA   Mother, please. Embrace me.

VALENTINA   Don't be stupid.

(SOPHIA is holding out her arms. VALENTINA doesn't move. So SOPHIA moves across and embraces her. Then she holds her head in her hands.)

SOPHIA   Hey, Mother, hey. *(VALENTINA is about to cry. SOPHIA stops her.)*

VALENTINA   You must go. Give my love to the children. Tell them to visit me.

SOPHIA   Yes.

VALENTINA   Whatever you do, this time you must live with it.

SOPHIA   Yes. I've learnt that from you.

(She looks at her a moment. Then she turns and goes out. There's a moment's silence. Then VALENTINA walks across to the chair and picks up the canvas from the leg against which it is propped. She holds it out at arm's length for five seconds. Then, without any visible reaction, she puts it down. Then she walks across the room and stands alone. Then her eyes begin to fill with tears. Silently the ASSISTANT returns, standing respectfully at the door.)

VALENTINA   You've come back.

ASSISTANT   Yes.

VALENTINA   I didn't hear you.

ASSISTANT   Have you had time to look at it?

VALENTINA   I've examined it. *(There's a pause.)* Yes. It's Matisse. *(Neither of them moves.)* Not, surely, the beginning of a sequence.
ASSISTANT   I'm sorry?
VALENTINA   No, it's just . . . you said . . . there was nothing in the foreground, so you assumed this is where he started. Then later he put in the woman. Or the violin. But no. It was the opposite. He removed the woman. He sought to distill.
ASSISTANT   Oh, I see. Yes. That fits with the scientific dating.
VALENTINA   Yes, it would. You could have saved yourself money.

(The ASSISTANT stands a moment, puzzled by her tone.)

ASSISTANT   Do you need to take another look?
VALENTINA   No. He said that finally he didn't need a model. Finally he didn't even need paint. *He* was there. He was a person. Present. And that was enough.

(The ASSISTANT moves, as if to pick the canvas up.)

The giveaway is the light through the shutters. No one else could do that. The way the sun is diffused. He controlled the sun in his painting. He said, with shutters he could summon the sun as surely as Joshua with his trumpet.
ASSISTANT   Yes. I see what you mean.

(She turns and looks at him.)

VALENTINA   And are you a member?
ASSISTANT   What?
VALENTINA   The party. Do you belong?
ASSISTANT   Oh.
VALENTINA   No. Don't tell me. I know. As surely as if you were a painting. *(She holds a hand up toward him, as if judging him. Then smiles.)* Yes. You belong.
ASSISTANT   In my job you have to. I mean, I want to, as well. If I want advancement. This painting is going to be a great help to me.
VALENTINA   So Matisse did not paint in vain. *(She gathers up her coat.)* I must go. *(Before she is ready, she turns thoughtfully a moment.)* He was once in a post office in Picardy. He was waiting to pick up the phone. He picked up a telegraph form lying on the table and, without thinking, began to draw a woman's head. All the time he talked on the phone, he was drawing. And when at the end, he looked down, he had drawn his mother's face. His hand did the work, not the brain. And he said the result was truer and more beautiful than anything that came as an effort of will.

(She stands a moment, then turns to go.)

ASSISTANT   I'll get you a car.

VALENTINA   No. The tram is outside. It goes right by my door.

(She goes. He stands a moment, looking at the painting. The background fades, and the stage is filled with the image of the bay at Nice: a pair of open French windows, a balcony, the sea and the sky. The ASSISTANT turns and looks to the open door.)

VÁCLAV HAVEL

TRANSLATED FROM THE CZECHOSLOVAKIAN BY
VERA BLACKWELL

Protest

CHARACTERS

VANĚK
STANĚK

SETTING

STANĚK's *Study, Prague*

STANĚK's *study. On the left, a massive writing desk; on it a typewriter, a telephone, reading glasses, and many books and papers; behind it, a large window with a view into the garden. On the right, two comfortable armchairs and between them a small table. The whole back wall is covered by bookcases, filled with books and with a built-in bar. In one of the niches there is a tape recorder. In the right back corner, a door; on the right wall, a large surrealist painting. When the curtain rises,* STANĚK *and* VANĚK *are onstage:* STANĚK, *standing behind his desk, is emotionally looking at* VANĚK, *who is standing at the door holding a briefcase and looking at* STANĚK *with signs of embarrassment. A short, tense pause. Then* STANĚK *suddenly walks excitedly over to* VANĚK, *takes him by the shoulders with both arms, shakes him in a friendly way, calling out:*

STANĚK   Vaněk!—Hello! *(*VANĚK *smiles timidly.* STANĚK *lets go, trying to conceal his agitation.)* Did you have trouble finding it?
VANĚK   Not really—
STANĚK   Forgot to mention the flowering magnolias. That's how you know it's my house. Superb, aren't they?

VANĚK   Yes—

STANĚK   I managed to double their blossoms in less than three years, compared to the previous owner. Have you magnolias at your cottage?

VANĚK   No—

STANĚK   You must have them! I'm going to find you two quality saplings, and I'll come and plant them for you personally. *(Crosses to the bar and opens it.)* How about some brandy?

VANĚK   I'd rather not—

STANĚK   Just a token one. Eh? *(He pours brandy into two glasses, hands one glass to VANĚK and raises the other for a toast.)* Well—here's to our reunion!

VANĚK   Cheers—*(Both drink: VANĚK shudders slightly.)*

STANĚK   I was afraid you weren't going to come.

VANĚK   Why?

STANĚK   Well, I mean, things got mixed up in an odd sort of way— What?— Won't you sit down?

VANĚK   *(Sits down in an armchair, placing his briefcase on the floor beside him.)* Thanks—

STANĚK   *(Sinks into an armchair opposite VANĚK with a sigh.)* That's more like it! Peanuts?

VANĚK   No, thanks—

STANĚK   *(Helps himself. Munching.)* You haven't changed much in all these years, you know?

VANĚK   Neither have you—

STANĚK   Me? Come on! Getting on for fifty, going gray, aches and pains setting in— Not as we used to be, eh? And the present times don't make one feel any better, either, what? When did we see each other last, actually?

VANĚK   I don't know—

STANĚK   Wasn't it at your last opening night?

VANĚK   Could be—

STANĚK   Seems like another age! We had a bit of an argument—

VANĚK   Did we?

STANĚK   You took me to task for my illusions and my overoptimism. Good Lord! How often since then I've had to admit to myself you were right! Of course, in those days I still believed that in spite of everything some of the ideals of my youth could be salvaged, and I took you for an incorrigible pessimist.

VANĚK   But I'm not a pessimist—

STANĚK   You see, everything's turned around! *(Short pause.)* Are you—alone?

VANĚK   How do you mean, alone?

STANĚK   Well, isn't there somebody—you know—

VANĚK   Following me?

STANĚK   Not that I care! After all, it was me who called you up, right?

VANĚK   I haven't noticed anybody—

STANĚK By the way, suppose you want to shake them off one of these days, you know the best place to do it?

VANĚK No—

STANĚK A department store. You mingle with the crowd, then at a moment when they aren't looking you sneak into the washroom and wait there for about two hours. They become convinced you managed to slip out through a side entrance, and they give up. You must try it out sometime! (*Pause.*)

VANĚK Seems very peaceful here—

STANĚK That's why we moved here. It was simply impossible to go on writing near that railway station! We've been here three years, you know. Of course, my greatest joy is the garden. I'll show you around later—I'm afraid I'm going to boast a little—

VANĚK You do the gardening yourself?

STANĚK It's become my greatest private passion these days. Keep pottering about out there almost every day. Just now I've been rejuvenating the apricots. Developed my own method, you see, based on a mixture of natural and artificial fertilizers plus a special way of waxless grafting. You won't believe the results I get! I'll find some cuttings for you later on—

(*STANĚK walks over to the desk, takes a package of foreign cigarettes out of a drawer, brings matches and an ashtray, and puts it all on the table in front of VANĚK.*)

Ferdinand, do have a cigarette.

VANĚK Thanks— (*VANĚK takes a cigarette and lights it: STANĚK sits in the other chair; both drink.*)

STANĚK Well now, Ferdinand, tell me— How are you?

VANĚK All right, thanks—

STANĚK Do they leave you alone—at least now and then?

VANĚK It depends— (*Short pause.*)

STANĚK And how was it in there?

VANĚK Where?

STANĚK Can our sort bear it at all?

VANĚK You mean prison? What else can one do?

STANĚK As far as I recall, you used to be bothered by hemorrhoids. Must have been terrible, considering the hygiene in there.

VANĚK They gave me suppositories—

STANĚK You ought to have them operated on, you know. It so happens a friend of mine is our greatest hemorrhoid specialist. Works real miracles. I'll arrange it for you.

VANĚK Thanks— (*Short pause.*)

STANĚK You know, sometimes it all seems like a beautiful dream—all the exciting opening nights, private views, lectures, meetings—the endless discussions about literature and art! All the energy, the hopes, plans, activities, ideas—the wine bars crowded with friends, the wild booze-ups, the madcap affrays in the small hours, the jolly girls dancing attendance on us! And the mountains of work we managed to get done, regardless! That's all over now. It'll never come back!

VANĚK Mmn— *(Pause. Both drink.)*

STANĚK Did they beat you?

VANĚK No—

STANĚK Do they beat people up in there?

VANĚK Sometimes. But not the politicals—

STANĚK I thought about you a great deal!

VANĚK Thank you— *(Short pause.)*

STANĚK I bet in those days it never even occurred to you—

VANĚK What?

STANĚK How it'll all end up! I bet not even you had guessed that!

VANĚK Mmn—

STANĚK It's disgusting, Ferdinand, disgusting! The nation is governed by scum! And the people? Can this really be the same nation which not very long ago behaved so magnificently? All that horrible cringing, bowing, and scraping! The selfishness, corruption, and fear wherever you turn! What have they made of us, old pal? Can this really be us?

VANĚK I don't believe things are as black as all that—

STANĚK Forgive me, Ferdinand, but you don't happen to live in a normal environment. All you know are people who manage to resist this rot. You just keep on supporting and encouraging each other. You've no idea the sort of environment I've got to put up with! You're lucky you no longer have anything to do with it. Makes you sick at your stomach! *(Pause. Both drink.)*

VANĚK You mean television?

STANĚK In television, in the film studios—you name it.

VANĚK There was a piece by you on the TV the other day—

STANĚK You can't imagine what an ordeal that was! First they kept blocking it for over a year, then they started changing it around—changed my whole opening and the entire closing sequence! You wouldn't believe the trifles they find objectionable these days! Nothing but sterility and intrigues, intrigues and sterility! How often I tell myself, wrap it up, chum, forget it, go hide somewhere—grow apricots—

VANĚK I know what you mean—

STANĚK The thing is, though, one can't help wondering whether one's got the right to this sort of escape. Supposing even the little one might be able to accomplish today can, in spite of everything, help someone in some way, at least give him a bit of encouragement, uplift him a little— Let me bring you a pair of slippers.

VANĚK Slippers? Why?

STANĚK You can't be comfortable in those boots.

VANĚK   I'm all right—

STANĚK   Are you sure?

VANĚK   Yes. Really— (Both drink.)

STANĚK   (Pause.) How about drugs? Did they give you any?

VANĚK   No—

STANĚK   No dubious injections?

VANĚK   Only some vitamin ones—

STANĚK   I bet there's some funny stuff in the food!

VANĚK   Just bromine against sex—

STANĚK   But surely they tried to break you down somehow!

VANĚK   Well—

STANĚK   If you'd rather not talk about it, it's all right with me.

VANĚK   Well, in a way, that's the whole point of pretrial interrogations, isn't it? To take one down a peg or two—

STANĚK   And to make one talk!

VANĚK   Mmn—

STANĚK   If they should haul me in for questioning—which sooner or later is bound to happen—you know what I'm going to do?

VANĚK   What?

STANĚK   Simply not answer any of their questions! Refuse to talk to them at all! That's by far the best way. Least one can be quite sure one didn't say anything one ought not to have said!

VANĚK   Mmn—

STANĚK   Anyway, you must have steel nerves to be able to bear it all and in addition to keep doing the things you do.

VANĚK   Like what?

STANĚK   Well, I mean all the protests, petitions, letters—the whole fight for human rights! I mean the things you and your friends keep on doing—

VANĚK   I'm not doing so much—

STANĚK   Now don't be too modest, Ferdinand! I follow everything that's going on! I know! If everybody did what you do, the situation would be quite different! And that's a fact. It's extremely important there should be at least a few people here who aren't afraid to speak the truth aloud, to defend others, to call a spade a spade! What I'm going to say might sound a bit solemn, perhaps, but frankly, the way I see it, you and your friends have taken on an almost superhuman task: to preserve and to carry the remains, the remnant of moral conscience, through the present quagmire! The thread you're spinning may be thin, but—who knows—perhaps the hope of a moral rebirth of the nation hangs on it.

VANĚK   You exaggerate—

STANĚK   Well, that's how I see it, anyway.

VANĚK   Surely our hope lies in all the decent people—

STANĚK   But how many are there still around? How many?

VANĚK Enough—

STANĚK Are there? Even so, it's you and your friends who are the most exposed to view.

VANĚK And isn't that precisely what makes it easier for us?

STANĚK I wouldn't say so. The more you're exposed, the more responsibility you have toward all those who know about you, trust you, rely on you, and look up to you, because to some extent you keep upholding their honor, too! *(Gets up.)* I'll get you those slippers!

VANĚK Please don't bother—

STANĚK I insist. I feel uncomfortable just looking at your boots. *(Pause. STANĚK returns with slippers.)*

VANĚK *(Sighs.)*

STANĚK Here you are. Do take those ugly things off, I beg you. Let me— *(Tries to take off VANĚK's boots.)* Won't you let me— Hold still—

VANĚK *(Embarrassed.)* No—please don't—no—I'll do it— *(Struggles out of his boots, slips on slippers.)* There— Nice, aren't they? Thank you very much.

STANĚK Good gracious, Ferdinand, what for? *(Hovering over VANĚK.)* Some more brandy?

VANĚK No more for me, thanks—

STANĚK Oh, come on. Give me your glass! -

VANĚK I'm sorry, I'm not feeling too well—

STANĚK Lost the habit inside, is that it?

VANĚK Could be— But the point is—last night, you see—

STANĚK Ah, that's what it is. Had a drop too many, eh?

VANĚK Mmn—

STANĚK I understand. *(Returns to his chair.)* By the way, you know the new wine bar, The Shaggy Dog?

VANĚK No—

STANĚK You don't? Listen, the wine there comes straight from the cask; it's not expensive and usually it isn't crowded. Really charming spot, you know, thanks to a handful of fairly good artists who were permitted— believe it or not—to do the interior decoration. I can warmly recommend it to you. Lovely place. Where did you go, then?

VANĚK Well, we did a little pub crawling, my friend Landovský and I—

STANĚK Oh, I see! You were with Landovský, were you? Well! In that case, I'm not at all surprised you came to a sticky end! He's a first-class actor, but once he starts drinking—that's it! Surely you can take one more brandy! Right?

VANĚK *(Sighs.)*

(Drinks are poured. They both drink. VANĚK shudders.)

STANĚK *(Back in his armchair. Short pause.)* Well, how are things otherwise? You do any writing?

VANĚK   Trying to—

STANĚK   A play?

VANĚK   A one-act play—

STANĚK   Another autobiographical one?

VANĚK   More or less—

STANĚK   My wife and I read the one about the brewery[1] the other day. We thought it was very amusing.

VANĚK   I'm glad—

STANĚK   Unfortunately we were given a rather bad copy.[2] Very hard to read.

VANĚK   I'm sorry—

STANĚK   It's a really brilliant little piece! I mean it! Only the ending seemed to me a bit muddy. The whole thing wants to be brought to a more straightforward conclusion, that's all. No problem. You can do it. (Pause. Both drink. VANĚK shudders.)

STANĚK   Well, how are things? How about Pavel?[3] Do you see him?

VANĚK   Yes—

STANĚK   Does he do any writing?

VANĚK   Just now he's finishing a one-acter, as well. It's supposed to be performed together with mine—

STANĚK   Wait a minute. You don't mean to tell me you two have teamed up also as authors!

VANĚK   More or less—

STANĚK   Well, well! Frankly, Ferdinand, try as I may, I don't get it. I don't. I simply can't understand this alliance of yours. Is it quite genuine on your part? Is it? Good heavens! Pavel! I don't know! Just remember the way he started! We both belong to the same generation, Pavel and I, we've both—so to speak—spanned a similar arc of development, but I don't mind telling you that what he did in those days— Well! It was a bit too strong even for me! Still, I suppose it's your business. You know best what you're doing.

VANĚK   That's right— (Pause. Both drink.)

STANĚK   Is your wife fond of gladioli?

VANĚK   I don't know. I think so—

STANĚK   You won't find many places with such a large selection as mine. I've got thirty-two shades, whereas at a common or garden nursery you'll be lucky to find six. Do you think your wife would like me to send her some bulbs?

VANĚK   I'm sure she would—

STANĚK   There's still time to plant them, you know. (Pause.) Ferdinand—

VANĚK   Yes?

STANĚK   Weren't you surprised when I suddenly called you up?

VANĚK   A bit—

STANĚK   I thought so. After all, I happen to be among those who've still managed to keep their heads above water, and I quite understand that—because of this—you might want to keep a certain distance from me.

VANĚK   No, not I—

STANĚK   Perhaps not you yourself, but I realize that some of your friends believe that anyone who's still got some chance today has either abdicated morally or is unforgivably fooling himself.

VANĚK   I don't think so—

STANĚK   I wouldn't blame you if you did, because I know only too well the grounds from which such prejudice could grow. *(An embarrassed pause.)* Ferdinand—

VANĚK   Yes?

STANĚK   I realize what a high price you have to pay for what you're doing. But please don't think it's all that easy for a man who's either so lucky or so unfortunate as to be still tolerated by the official apparatus and who—at the same time—wishes to live at peace with his conscience.

VANĚK   I know what you mean—

STANĚK   In some respects it may be even harder for him.

VANĚK   I understand.

STANĚK   Naturally, I didn't call you in order to justify myself! I don't really think there's any need. I called you because I like you and I'd be sorry to see you sharing the prejudice which I assume exists among your friends.

VANĚK   As far as I know nobody has ever said a bad word about you—

STANĚK   Not even Pavel?

VANĚK   No—

STANĚK   *(Embarrassed pause.)* Ferdinand—

VANĚK   Yes?

STANĚK   Excuse me— *(Gets up. Crosses to the tape recorder. Switches it on: Soft, nondescript background music. STANĚK returns to his chair.)* Ferdinand, does the name Javurek mean anything to you?

VANĚK   The pop singer? I know him very well—

STANĚK   So I expect you know what happened to him.

VANĚK   Of course. They locked him up for telling a story during one of his performances. The story about the cop who meets a penguin in the street—

STANĚK   Of course. It was just an excuse. The fact is, they hate his guts because he sings the way he does. The whole thing is so cruel, so ludicrous, so base!

VANĚK   And cowardly—

STANĚK   Right! And cowardly! Look, I've been trying to do something for the boy. I mean, I know a few guys at the town council and at the prosecutor's office, but you know how it is. Promises, promises! They all say they're going to look into it, but the moment your back is turned they drop it like a hot potato, so they don't get their fingers burnt! Sickening, the way everybody looks out for number one!

VANĚK   Still, I think it's nice of you to have tried to do something—

STANĚK   My dear Ferdinand, I'm really not the sort of man your friends obviously take me for! Peanuts?

VANĚK   No, thanks—

STANĚK   *(Short pause.)* About Javurek—

VANĚK   Yes?

STANĚK   Since I didn't manage to accomplish anything through private intervention, it occurred to me perhaps it ought to be handled in a somewhat different way. You know what I mean. Simply write something—a protest or a petition? In fact, this is the main thing I wanted to discuss with you. Naturally, you're far more experienced in these matters than I. If this document contains a few fairly well-known signatures—like yours, for example—it's bound to be published somewhere abroad which might create some political pressure. Right? I mean, these things don't seem to impress them all that much, actually—but honestly, I don't see any other way to help the boy. Not to mention Annie—

VANĚK   Annie?

STANĚK   My daughter.

VANĚK   Oh? Is that your daughter?

STANĚK   That's right.

VANĚK   Well, what about her?

STANĚK   I thought you knew.

VANĚK   Knew what?

STANĚK   She's expecting. By Javurek—

VANĚK   Oh, I see. That's why—

STANĚK   Wait a minute! If you mean the case interests me merely because of family matters—

VANĚK   I didn't mean that—

STANĚK   But you just said—

VANĚK   I only wanted to say, that's how you know about the case at all; you were explaining to me how you got to know about it. Frankly, I wouldn't have expected you to be familiar with the present pop scene. I'm sorry if it sounded as though I meant—

STANĚK   I'd get involved in this case even if it was someone else expecting his child! No matter who—

VANĚK   I know— *(Embarrassed pause.)*

STANĚK   Well, what do you think about my idea of writing some sort of protest?

(VANĚK begins to look for something in his briefcase, finally finds a paper, and hands it to STANĚK.)

VANĚK   I guess this is the sort of thing you had in mind—

STANĚK   What?

VANĚK   Here—

STANĚK   *(Grabs the document.)* What is it?

VANĚK   Have a look—

(STANĚK takes the paper from VANĚK, goes quickly to the writing desk, picks up his glasses, puts them on, and begins to read attentively. Lengthy pause. STANĚK shows signs of surprise. When he finishes reading, he puts aside his glasses and begins to pace around in agitation.)

STANĚK   Now isn't it fantastic! That's a laugh, isn't it? Eh? Here I was cudgeling my brains how to go about it, finally I take the plunge and consult you—and all this time you've had the whole thing wrapped up and ready! Isn't it marvelous? I knew I was doing the right thing when I turned to you! *(STANĚK returns to the table, sits down, puts on his glasses again, and rereads the text.)* There! Precisely what I had in mind! Brief, to the point, fair, and yet emphatic. Manifestly the work of a professional! I'd be sweating over it for a whole day and I'd never come up with anything remotely like this!

VANĚK   *(Embarrassed.)*

STANĚK   Listen, just a small point—here at the end—do you think "willfulness" is the right word to use? Couldn't one find a milder synonym, perhaps? Somehow seems a bit misplaced, you know. I mean, the whole text is composed in very measured, factual terms—and this word here suddenly sticks out, sounds much too emotional, wouldn't you agree? Otherwise it's absolutely perfect. Maybe the second paragraph is somewhat superfluous; in fact, it's just a rehash of the first one. Except for the reference here to Javurek's impact on nonconformist youth. This is excellent and must stay in! How about putting it at the end instead of your "willfulness"? Wouldn't that do the trick?— But these are just my personal impressions. Good heavens! Why should you listen to what I have to say! On the whole, the text is excellent, and no doubt it's going to hit the mark. Let me say again, Ferdinand, how much I admire you. Your knack for expressing the fundamental points of an issue, while avoiding all needless abuse, is indeed rare among our kind!

VANĚK   Come on—you don't really mean that—

(STANĚK takes off his glasses, goes over to VANĚK, puts the paper in front of him, sits again in the easy chair, and sips his drink. Short pause.)

STANĚK   Anyway, it's good to know there's somebody around whom one can always turn to and rely on in a case like this.

VANĚK   But it's only natural, isn't it?

STANĚK   It may seem so to you. But in the circles where I've to move such things aren't in the least natural! The natural response is much more likely to be the exact opposite. When a man gets into trouble, everybody drops him as soon as possible, the lot of them. And out of fear for their own positions they try to convince all and sundry they've never had anything to do with him; on the contrary, they sized him up right away, they had his number! But why am I telling you all this, you know best the sort of thing that happens! Right? When you were in prison your longtime theater pals held forth against you on television. It was revolting—

VANĚK   I'm not angry with them—

STANĚK   But I am! And what's more, I told them so. In no uncertain terms! You know, a man in my position learns to put up with a lot of things, but —if you'll forgive me—there are limits! I appreciate it might be awkward for you to blame them, as you happen to be the injured party. But listen to me, you've got to distance yourself from the affair! Just think: Once we, too, begin to tolerate this sort of muck—we're de facto assuming coresponsibility for the entire moral morass and indirectly contributing to its deeper penetration. Am I right?

VANĚK   Mmn—

STANĚK   (Short pause.) Have you sent it off yet?

VANĚK   We're still collecting signatures—

STANĚK   How many have you got so far?

VANĚK   About fifty—

STANĚK   Fifty? Not bad! (Short pause.) Well, never mind, I've just missed the boat, that's all.

VANĚK   You haven't—

STANĚK   But the thing's already in hand, isn't it?

VANĚK   Yes, but it's still open—I mean—

STANĚK   All right, but now it's sure to be sent off and published, right? By the way, I wouldn't give it to any of the agencies, if I were you. They'll only print a measly little news item which is bound to be overlooked. Better hand it over directly to one of the big European papers so the whole text gets published, including all the signatures!

VANĚK   I know—

STANĚK   (Short pause.) Do they already know about it?

VANĚK   You mean the police?

STANĚK   Yes.

VANĚK   I don't think so. I suppose not—

STANĚK   Look here, I don't want to give you any advice, but it seems to me you ought to wrap it up as soon as possible, else they'll get wind of what's going on and they'll find a way to stop it. Fifty signatures should be enough! Besides, what counts is not the number of signatures but their significance.

VANĚK   Each signature has its own significance!

STANĚK   Absolutely, but as far as publicity abroad is concerned, it is essential that some well-known names are represented, right? Has Pavel signed?

VANĚK   Yes—

STANĚK Good. His name—no matter what one may think of him personally —does mean something in the world today!

VANĚK No question—

STANĚK *(Short pause.)* Listen, Ferdinand—

VANĚK Yes?

STANĚK There's one more thing I wanted to discuss with you. It's a bit delicate, though—

VANĚK Oh?

STANĚK Look here, I'm no millionaire, you know, but so far I've been able to manage—

VANĚK Good for you—

STANĚK Well, I was thinking—I mean—I'd like to— Look, a lot of your friends have lost their jobs. I was thinking—would you be prepared to accept from me a certain sum of money?

VANĚK That's very nice of you! Some of my friends indeed find themselves in a bit of a spot. But there are problems, you know. I mean, one is never quite sure how to go about it. Those who most need help are often the most reluctant to accept—

STANĚK You won't be able to work miracles with what I can afford, but I expect there are situations when every penny counts. *(Takes out his wallet, removes two bank notes, hesitates, adds a third, hands them to VANĚK.)* Here— please—a small offering.

VANĚK Thank you very much. Let me thank you for all my friends—

STANĚK Gracious, we've got to help each other out, don't we? *(Pause.)* Incidentally, there's no need for you to mention this little contribution comes from me. I don't wish to erect a monument to myself. I'm sure you've gathered that much by now, eh?

VANĚK Yes. Again many thanks—

STANĚK Well, now, how about having a look at the garden?

VANĚK Mr. Staněk—

STANĚK Yes?

VANĚK We'd like to send it off tomorrow—

STANĚK What?

VANĚK The protest—

STANĚK Excellent! The sooner the better!

VANĚK So that today there's still—

STANĚK Today you should think about getting some sleep! That's the main thing! Don't forget you've a bit of a hangover after last night and tomorrow is going to be a hard day for you!

VANĚK I know. All I was going to say—

STANĚK Better go straight home and unplug the phone. Else Ladovský rings you up again and heaven knows how you'll end up!

VANĚK   Yes, I know. There're only a few signatures I've still got to collect—
it won't take long. All I was going to say—I mean, don't you think it
would be helpful—as a matter of fact, it would, of course, be sensational!
After all, practically everybody's read your *Crash*!

STANĚK   Oh, come on, Ferdinand! That was fifteen years ago!

VANĚK   But it's never been forgotten!

STANĚK   What do you mean—sensational?

VANĚK   I'm sorry, I had the impression you'd actually like to—

STANĚK   What?

VANĚK   Participate—

STANĚK   Participate? Wait a minute. Are you talking about *(Points to the
paper.)* this? Is that what you're talking about?

VANĚK   Yes—

STANĚK   You mean I—

VANĚK   I'm sorry, but I had the impression—

*(STANĚK finishes his drink, crosses to the bar, pours himself a drink, walks over to the
window, looks out for a while, whereupon he suddenly turns to VANĚK with a smile.)*

STANĚK   Now that's a laugh, isn't it?

VANĚK   What's a laugh?

STANĚK   Come on, can't you see how absurd it is? Eh? I ask you over hoping
you might write something about Javurek's case—you produce a finished
text, and what's more, one furnished with fifty signatures! I'm bowled over
like a little child, can't believe my eyes and ears, I worry about ways to
stop them from ruining your project—and all this time it hasn't occurred
to me to do the one simple, natural thing which I should have done in the
first place! I mean, at once sign the document myself! Well, you must
admit it's absurd, isn't it?

VANĚK   Mmn—

STANĚK   Now, listen Ferdinand, isn't this a really terrifying testimony to the
situation into which we've been brought? Isn't it? Just think: Even I,
though I know it's rubbish, even I've got used to the idea that the signing
of protests is the business of local specialists, professionals in solidarity,
dissidents! While the rest of us—when we want to do something for the
sake of ordinary human decency—automatically turn to you, as though
you were a sort of service establishment for moral matters. In other words,
we're here simply to keep our mouths shut and to be rewarded by relative
peace and quiet, whereas you're here to speak up for us and to be rewarded
by blows on earth and glory in the heavens! Perverse, isn't it?

VANĚK   Mmn—

STANĚK   Of course it is! And they've managed to bring things to such a point
that even a fairly intelligent and decent fellow—which, with your permission, I still think I am—is more or less ready to take this situation for

granted! As though it was quite normal, perfectly natural! Sickening, isn't it? Sickening the depths we've reached! What do you say? Makes one puke, eh?

VANĚK Well—

STANĚK You think the nation can ever recover from all this?

VANĚK Hard to say—

STANĚK What can one do? What can one do? Well, seems clear, doesn't it? In theory, that is. Everybody should start with himself. What? However! Is this country inhabited only by Vaněks? It really doesn't seem that everybody can become a fighter for human rights.

VANĚK Not everybody, no—

STANĚK Where is it?

VANĚK What?

STANĚK The list of signatures, of course.

VANĚK (Embarrassed pause.) Mr. Staněk—

STANĚK Yes?

VANĚK Forgive me, but—I'm sorry, I've suddenly a funny feeling that perhaps—

STANĚK What funny feeling?

VANĚK I don't know—I feel very embarrassed— Well, it seems to me perhaps I wasn't being quite fair—

STANĚK In what way?

VANĚK Well, what I did—was a bit of a con trick—in a way—

STANĚK What are you talking about?

VANĚK I mean, first I let you talk, and only then I ask for your signature— I mean, after you're already sort of committed by what you've said before, you see—

STANĚK Are you suggesting that if I'd known you were collecting signatures for Javurck, I would never have started talking about him?

VANĚK No, that's not what I mean—

STANĚK Well, what do you mean?

VANĚK How shall I put it—

STANĚK Oh, come on! You mind I didn't organize the whole thing myself, is that it?

VANĚK No, that's not it—

STANĚK What is it, then?

VANĚK Well, it seems to me it would've been a quite different matter if I'd come to you right away and asked for your signature. That way you would've had an option—

STANĚK And why didn't you come to me right away, actually? Was it because you'd simply written me off in advance?

VANĚK Well, I was thinking that in your position—

STANĚK Ah! There you are! You see? Now it's becoming clear what you really think of me, isn't it? You think that because now and then one of my pieces happens to be shown on television, I'm no longer capable of the simplest act of solidarity!

VANĚK You misunderstand me. What I meant was—

STANĚK Let me tell you something, Ferdinand. *(Drinks. Short pause.)* Look here, if I've—willy-nilly—got used to the perverse idea that common decency and morality are the exclusive domain of the dissidents—then you've—willy-nilly—got used to the idea as well! That's why it never crossed your mind that certain values might be more important to me than my present position. But suppose even I wanted to be finally a free man, suppose even I wished to renew my inner integrity and shake off the yoke of humiliation and shame? It never entered your head that I might've been actually waiting for this very moment for years, what? You simply placed me once and for all among those hopeless cases, among those whom it would be pointless to count on in any way. Right? And now that you found I'm not entirely indifferent to the fate of others—you made that slip about my signature! But you saw at once what happened, and so you began to apologize to me. Good God! Don't you realize how you humiliate me? What if all this time I'd been hoping for an opportunity to act, to do something that would again make a man of me, help me to be once more at peace with myself, help me to find again the free play of my imagination and my lost sense of humor, rid me of the need to escape my traumas by minding the apricots and those damned magnolias! Suppose even I prefer to live in truth! What if I want to return from the world of custom-made literature and the protoculture of television to the world of art which isn't geared to serve anyone at all?

VANĚK I'm sorry—forgive me! I didn't mean to hurt your feelings. Wait a minute, I'll—just a moment.

(VANĚK opens his briefcase, rummages in it for a while, finally extracts the sheets with the signatures, and hands them to STANĚK. STANĚK gets up slowly and crosses with the papers to the desk, where he sits down, puts on his glasses, and carefully studies the sheets, nodding his head here and there. After a lengthy while, he takes off his glasses, slowly rises, thoughtfully paces around, finally turning to VANĚK.)

STANĚK Let me think aloud. May I?

VANĚK By all means—

STANĚK *(Halts, drinks, begins to pace again as he talks.)* I believe I've already covered the main points concerning the subjective side of the matter. If I sign the document, I'm going to regain—after years of being continually sick to my stomach—my self-esteem, my lost freedom, my honor, and perhaps even some regard among those close to me. I'll leave behind the insoluble dilemmas, forced on me by the conflict between my concern for my position and my conscience. I'll be able to face with equanimity Annie, myself, and even that young man when he comes back. It'll cost me my job, though my job brings me no satisfaction—on the contrary, it brings me shame—nevertheless, it does support me and my family a great deal better than if I were to become a night watchman. It's more than likely that my son won't be permitted to continue his studies. On the other hand, I'm sure he's going to have more respect for me that way than if his permission to study was bought by my refusal to sign the protest for Javurek, whom he happens to worship. Well, then. This is the subjective side of the matter. Now how about the objective side? What happens when —among the signatures of a few well-known dissidents and a handful of Javurek's teenage friends—there suddenly crops up—to everybody's surprise and against all expectation—my signature? The signature of a man who hasn't been heard from regarding civic affairs for years! Well? My cosignatories—as well as many of those who don't sign documents of this sort but who nonetheless deep down side with those who do—are naturally going to welcome my signature with pleasure. The closed circle of habitual signers—whose signatures, by the way, are already beginning to lose their clout, because they cost practically nothing. I mean, the people in question have long since lost all ways and means by which they could actually pay for their signatures. Right? Well, this circle will be broken. A new name will appear, a name the value of which depends precisely on its previous absence. And of course, I may add, on the high price paid for its appearance! So much for the objective "plus" of my prospective signature. Now what about the authorities? My signature is going to surprise, annoy, and upset them for the very reasons which will bring joy to the other signatories. I mean, because it'll make a breach in the barrier the authorities have been building around your lot for so long and with such effort. All right. Let's see about Javurek. Concerning his case, I very much doubt my participation would significantly influence its outcome. And if so, I'm afraid it's more than likely going to have a negative effect. The authorities will be anxious to prove they haven't been panicked. They'll want to show that a surprise of this sort can't make them lose their cool. Which brings us to the consideration of what they're going to do to me. Surely, my signature is bound to have a much more significant influence on what happens in my case. No doubt, they're going to punish me far more cruelly than you'd expect. The point being that my punishment will serve them as a warning signal to all those who might be tempted to follow my example in the future, choose freedom, and thus swell the ranks of the dissidents. You may be sure they'll want to show them what the score is! Right? The thing is —well, let's face it—they're no longer worried all that much about dissident activities within the confines of the established ghetto. In some respects, they even seem to prod them on here and there. But! What they're really afraid of is any semblance of a crack in the fence around the ghetto! So they'll want to exorcise the bogey of a prospective epidemic of dissent by an exemplary punishment of myself. They'll want to nip it in the bud, that's all. *(Drinks. Pause.)* The last question I've got to ask myself is this: What sort of reaction to my signature can one expect among those who, in one way or another, have followed what you might call "the path of accommodation." I mean people who are, or ought to be, our main concern, because—I'm sure you'll agree—our hope for the future depends above all on whether or not it will be possible to awake them from their slumbers and to enlist them to take an active part in civic affairs. Well, I'm afraid that my signature is going to be received with absolute resentment by this crucial section of the populace. You know why? Because, as a matter of fact, these people secretly hate the dissidents. They've become their bad conscience, their living reproach! That's how they see the dissidents. And at the same time, they envy them their honor and their inner freedom, values which they themselves were denied by fate. This is why they never miss an opportunity to smear the dissidents. And precisely this opportunity is going to be offered to them by my signature. They're going to spread nasty rumors about you and your friends. They're going to say that you who have nothing more to lose—you who have long since landed at the bottom of the heap and, what's more, managed to make yourselves quite at home in there—are now trying to drag down to your own level an unfortunate man, a man who's so far been able to stay above the salt line. You're dragging him down—irresponsible as you are—without the slightest compunction, just for your own whim, just because you wish to irritate the authorities by creating a false impression that your ranks are being swelled! What do you care about losing him his job! Doesn't matter, does it? Or do you mean to suggest you'll find him a job down in the dump in which you yourselves exist? What? No—Ferdinand! I'm sorry. I'm afraid I'm much too familiar with the way these people think! After all, I've got to live among them, day in day out. I know precisely what they're going to say. They'll say I'm your victim, shamelessly abused, misguided, led astray by your cynical appeal to my humanity! They'll say that in your ruthlessness you didn't shrink even from making use of my personal relationship to Javurek! And you know what? They're going to say that all the humane ideals you're constantly proclaiming have been tarnished by your treatment of me. That's the sort of reasoning one can expect from them! And I'm sure I don't have to tell you that the authorities are bound to support this interpretation and to fan the coals as hard as they can! There are others, of course, somewhat more intelligent, perhaps. These people might say that the extraordinary appearance of my signature among yours is actually counterproductive, in that it concentrates everybody's attention on my signature and away from the main issue concerning Javurek. They'll say it puts the whole protest in jeopardy, because one can't help asking oneself what was the purpose of the exercise: Was it to help

Javurek or to parade a newborn dissident? I wouldn't be at all surprised if someone were to say that, as a matter of fact, Javurek was victimized by you and your friends. It might be suggested his personal tragedy only served you to further your ends—which are far removed from the fate of the unfortunate man. Furthermore, it'll be pointed out that by getting my signature you managed to dislodge me from the one area of operation— namely, backstage diplomacy, private intervention—where I've been so far able to manoeuvre and where I might have proved infinitely more helpful to Javurek in the end! I do hope you understand me, Ferdinand. I don't wish to exaggerate the importance of these opinions, nor am I prepared to become their slave. On the other hand, it seems to be in the interests of our case for me to take them into account. After all, it's a matter of a political decision, and a good politician must consider all the issues which are likely to influence the end result of his action. Right? In these circumstances the question one must resolve is as follows: What do I prefer? Do I prefer the inner liberation which my signature is going to bring me, a liberation paid for—as it now turns out—by a basically negative objective impact—or do I choose the other alternative. I mean, the more beneficial effect which the protest would have without my signature, yet paid for by my bitter awareness that I've again—who knows, perhaps for the last time —missed a chance to shake off the bonds of shameful compromises in which I've been choking for years? In other words, if I'm to act indeed ethically—and I hope by now you've no doubt I want to do just that— which course should I take? Should I be guided by ruthless objective considerations, or by subjective inner feelings?

VANĚK Seems perfectly clear to me—
STANĚK And to me—
VANĚK So that you're going to—
STANĚK Unfortunately—
VANĚK Unfortunately?
STANĚK You thought I was—
VANĚK Forgive me, perhaps I didn't quite understand—
STANĚK I'm sorry if I've—
VANĚK Never mind—
STANĚK But I really believe—
VANĚK I know—

(Both drink. VANĚK shudders. Lengthy, embarrassed pause. STANĚK takes the sheets and hands them with a smile to VANĚK, who puts them, together with the text of the letter of protest, into his briefcase. He shows signs of embarrassment. STANĚK crosses to the tape recorder, unplugs it, comes back and sits down.)

STANĚK Are you angry?
VANĚK No—

STANĚK   You don't agree, though—
VANĚK   I respect your reasoning—
STANĚK   But what do you think?
VANĚK   What should I think?
STANĚK   That's obvious, isn't it?
VANĚK   Is it?
STANĚK   You think that when I saw all the signatures, I did, after all, get the wind up!
VANĚK   I don't—
STANĚK   I can see you do!
VANĚK   I assure you—
STANĚK   Why don't you level with me? Don't you realize that your benevolent hypocrisy is actually far more insulting than if you gave it to me straight?! Or do you mean I'm not even worthy of your comment?
VANĚK   But I told you, didn't I, I respect your reasoning—
STANĚK   I'm not an idiot, Vaněk!
VANĚK   Of course not—
STANĚK   I know precisely what's behind your "respect"!
VANĚK   What is?
STANĚK   A feeling of moral superiority!
VANĚK   You're wrong—
STANĚK   Only I'm not quite sure if you—you of all people—have any right to feel so superior!
VANĚK   What do you mean?
STANĚK   You know very well what I mean!
VANĚK   I don't—
STANĚK   Shall I tell you?
VANĚK   Please do—
STANĚK   Well! As far as I know, in prison you talked more than you should have!

(VANĚK jumps up, wildly staring at STANĚK, who smiles triumphantly. Short tense pause. The phone rings. VANĚK, broken, sinks back into his chair. STANĚK crosses to the telephone and lifts the receiver.)

STANĚK   Hello—yes—what? You mean— Wait a minute—I see—I see— Where are you? Yes, yes, of course—absolutely!—good— You bet! Sure —I'll be here waiting for you! Bye-bye.

(STANĚK puts the receiver down and absentmindedly stares into space. Lengthy pause. VANĚK gets up in embarrassment. Only now STANĚK seems to realize that VANĚK is still there. He turns to him abruptly.)

You can go and burn it downstairs in the furnace!
VANĚK   What?

STANĚK   He's just walked into the canteen! To see Annie.

VANĚK   Who did?

STANĚK   Javurek! Who else?

VANĚK   *(Jumps up.)* Javurek? You mean he was released? But that's wonderful! So your private intervention did work, after all! Just as well we didn't send off the protest a few days earlier! I'm sure they would've got their backs up and kept him inside!

(STANĚK searchingly stares at VANĚK, then suddenly smiles, decisively steps up to him, and with both hands takes him by the shoulders.)

STANĚK   My dear fellow, you mustn't fret! There's always the risk that you can do more harm than good by your activities! Right? Heavens, if you should worry about this sort of thing, you'd never be able to do anything at all! Come, let me get you those saplings—

NOTES

1. Staněk is of course referring to *Audience*.
2. Literary works circulating as *samizdat* text in typescript are understandably often of poor quality. If one gets to read the, say, sixth carbon copy on onion skin, the readability of the script leaves much to be desired.
3. Staněk means Pavel Kohout.

BETH HENLEY

Am I Blue

CHARACTERS

JOHN POLK Seventeen.
ASHBE Sixteen.
HILDA Thirty-five, a waitress.
STREET CHARACTERS: BARKER, WHORE, BUM, CLAREECE

SETTINGS

A bar, the street, the living room of a run-down apartment

TIME

Fall 1968

The scene opens on a street in the New Orleans French Quarter on a rainy blue bourbon night. Various people: a whore, bum, street barker, CLAREECE appear and disappear along the street. The scene then focuses on a bar where a piano is heard from the back room playing softly and indistinctly "Am I Blue?" The lights go up on JOHN POLK, who sits alone at a table. He is seventeen, a bit overweight and awkward. He wears nice clothes, perhaps a navy sweater with large white monograms. His navy raincoat is slung over an empty chair. While drinking, JOHN POLK concentrates on the red-and-black card that he holds in his hand. As soon as the scene is established, ASHBE enters from the street. She is sixteen, wears a flowered plastic rain cap, red galoshes, a butterfly barrette, and jeweled cat eyeglasses. She is carrying a bag full of stolen goods. Her hair is very curly. Ashbe makes her way cautiously to JOHN POLK's table. As he sees her coming, he puts the card into his pocket. She sits in the empty chair and pulls his raincoat over her head.

ASHBE   Excuse me . . . do you mind if I sit here, please?

JOHN POLK   *(Looks up at her—then down into his glass.)* What are you doing hiding under my raincoat? You're getting it all wet.

ASHBE   Well, I'm very sorry, but after all, it is a raincoat. *(He tries to pull off coat.)* It was rude of me, I know, but look, I just don't want them to recognize me.

JOHN POLK   *(Looking about.)* Who to recognize you?

ASHBE   Well, I stole these two ashtrays from the Screw Inn, ya know, right down the street. *(She pulls out two glass commercial ashtrays from her white plastic bag.)* Anyway, I'm scared the manager saw me. They'll be after me, I'm afraid.

JOHN POLK   Well, they should be. Look, do you mind giving me back my raincoat? I don't want to be found protecting any thief.

ASHBE   *(Coming out from under coat.)* Thief—would you call Robin Hood a thief?

JOHN POLK   Christ.

ASHBE   *(Back under coat.)* No, you wouldn't. He was valiant—all the time stealing from the rich and giving to the poor.

JOHN POLK   But your case isn't exactly the same, is it? You're stealing from some crummy little bar and keeping the ashtrays for yourself. Now give me back my coat.

ASHBE   *(Throws coat at him.)* Sure, take your old coat. I suppose I should have explained—about Miss Marcey. *(Silence.)* Miss Marcey, this cute old lady with a little hump in her back. I always see her in her sun hat and blue print dress. Miss Marcey lives in the apartment building next to ours. I leave all the stolen goods as gifts on her front steps.

JOHN POLK   Are you one of those kleptomaniacs? *(He starts checking his wallet.)*

ASHBE   You mean when people all the time steal and they can't help it?

JOHN POLK   Yeah.

ASHBE   Oh, no. I'm not a bit careless. Take my job tonight, my very first night job, if you want to know. Anyway, I've been planning it for two months, trying to decipher which bar most deserved to be stolen from. I finally decided on the Screw Inn. Mainly because of the way they're so mean to Mr. Groves. He works at the magazine rack at Diver's Drugstore and is really very sweet, but he has a drinking problem. I don't think that's fair to be mean to people simply because they have a drinking problem—and, well, anyway, you see I'm not just stealing for personal gain. I mean, I don't even smoke.

JOHN POLK   Yeah, well, most infants don't, but then again, most infants don't hang around bars.

ASHBE I don't see why not, Toulouse Lautrec did.

JOHN POLK They'd throw me out.

ASHBE Oh, they throw me out, too, but I don't accept defeat. *(Slowly moves into him.)* Why it's the very same with my pick-pocketing.

(JOHN POLK sneers, turns away.)

It's a very hard art to master. Why, every time I've done it I've been caught.

JOHN POLK That's all I need is to have some slum kid tell me how good it is to steal. Everyone knows it's not.

ASHBE *(About his drink.)* That looks good. What is it?

JOHN POLK Hey, would you mind leaving me alone— I just wanted to be alone.

ASHBE Okay. I'm sorry. How about if I'm quiet?

(JOHN POLK shrugs. He sips drink, looks around, catches her eye; she smiles and sighs.)

I was just looking at your pin. What fraternity are you in?

JOHN POLK SAE.

ASHBE Is it a good fraternity?

JOHN POLK Sure, it's the greatest.

ASHBE I bet you have lots of friends.

JOHN POLK Tons.

ASHBE Are you being serious?

JOHN POLK Yes.

ASHBE Hmm. Do they have parties and all that?

JOHN POLK Yeah, lots of parties, booze, honking horns; it's exactly what you would expect.

ASHBE I wouldn't expect anything. Why did you join?

JOHN POLK I don't know. Well, my brother—I guess it was my brother—he told me how great it was, how the fraternity was supposed to get you dates, make you study, solve all your problems.

ASHBE Gee, does it?

JOHN POLK Doesn't help you study.

ASHBE How about dates? Do they get you a lot of dates?

JOHN POLK Some.

ASHBE What were the girls like?

JOHN POLK I don't know—they were like girls.

ASHBE Did you have a good time?

JOHN POLK I had a pretty good time.

ASHBE Did you make love to any of them?

JOHN POLK *(To self.)* Oh, Christ—

ASHBE I'm sorry—I just figured that's why you had the appointment with the whore—'cause you didn't have anyone else—to make love to.

JOHN POLK How did you know I had the, ah, the appointment?

ASHBE   I saw you put the red card in your pocket when I came up. Those red cards are pretty familiar around here. The house is only about a block or so away. It's one of the best, though, really very plush. Only two murders and a knifing in its whole history. Do you go there often?

JOHN POLK   Yeah, I like to give myself a treat.

ASHBE   Who do you have?

JOHN POLK   What do you mean?

ASHBE   I mean which girl.

(JOHN POLK gazes into his drink.)

Look, I just thought I might know her is all.

JOHN POLK   Know her, ah, how would you know her?

ASHBE   Well, some of the girls from my high school go there to work when they get out.

JOHN POLK   G.G., her name is G.G.

ASHBE   G.G.—Hmm, well, how does she look?

JOHN POLK   I don't know.

ASHBE   Oh, you've never been with her before?

JOHN POLK   No.

ASHBE   *(Confidentially.)* Are you one of those kinds that likes a lot of variety?

JOHN POLK   Variety? Sure, I guess I like variety.

ASHBE   Oh, yes, now I remember.

JOHN POLK   What?

ASHBE   G.G., that's just her working name. Her real name is Myrtle Reims; she's Kay Reims's older sister. Kay is in my grade at school.

JOHN POLK   Myrtle? Her name is Myrtle?

ASHBE   I never liked the name, either.

JOHN POLK   Myrtle, oh, Christ. Is she pretty?

ASHBE   *(Matter-of-fact.)* Pretty, no she's not real pretty.

JOHN POLK   What does she look like?

ASHBE   Let's see . . . she's, ah, well, Myrtle had acne, and there are a few scars left. It's not bad. I think they sort of give her character. Her hair's red, only I don't think it's really red. It sort of fizzles out all over her head. She's got a pretty good figure—big top—but the rest of her is kind of skinny.

JOHN POLK   I wonder if she has a good personality.

ASHBE   Well, she was a senior when I was a freshman; so I never really knew her. I remember she used to paint her fingernails lots of different colors— pink, orange, purple. I don't know, but she kind of scares me. About the only time I ever saw her true personality was around a year ago. I was over at Kay's making a health poster for school. Anyway, Myrtle comes busting in screaming about how she can't find her spangled bra anywhere. Kay and I just sat on the floor cutting pictures of food out of magazines while she was storming about slamming drawers and swearing. Finally, she found it.

It was pretty garish—red with black and gold-sequined G's on each cup. That's how I remember the name—G.G.

(*As* ASHBE *illustrates the placement of the G's she spots* HILDA, *the waitress, approaching.* ASHBE *pulls the raincoat over her head and hides on the floor.* HILDA *enters through the beaded curtains spilling her tray.* HILDA *is a woman of few words.*)

HILDA   Shit, damn curtain. 'Nuther drink?

JOHN POLK   Ma'am?

HILDA   *(Points to drink.)* Vodka Coke?

JOHN POLK   No, thank you. I'm not quite finished yet.

HILDA   Napkins clean.

(ASHBE *pulls her bag off the table.* HILDA *looks at* ASHBE, *then to* JOHN POLK. *She walks around the table, as* ASHBE *is crawling along the floor to escape.* ASHBE *runs into* HILDA'S *toes.*)

ASHBE   Are those real gold?

HILDA   You again. Out.

ASHBE   She wants me to leave. Why should a paying customer leave? *(Back to* HILDA.*)* Now I'll have a mint julep and easy on the mint.

HILDA   This preteen with you?

JOHN POLK   Well—I— No—I—

HILDA   IDs.

ASHBE   Certainly, I always try to cooperate with the management.

HILDA   *(Looking at* JOHN POLK'S *ID.)* ID, 11-12-50. Date 11-11-68.

JOHN POLK   Yes, but—well, 11-12 is less than two hours away.

HILDA   Back in two hours.

ASHBE   I seem to have left my identification in my gold lamé bag.

HILDA   Well, boo hoo. *(Motions for* ASHBE *to leave with a minimum of effort. She goes back to table.)* No tip.

ASHBE   You didn't tip her?

JOHN POLK   I figured the drinks were so expensive— I just didn't—

HILDA   No tip!

JOHN POLK   Look, miss, I'm sorry. *(Going through his pockets.)* Here, would you like a—a nickel—wait, wait here's a quarter.

HILDA   Just move ass, sonny. You, too, Barbie.

ASHBE   Ugh, I hate public rudeness. I'm sure I'll refrain from ever coming here again.

HILDA   Think I'll go in the back room and cry. *(ASHBE and* JOHN POLK *exit.* HILDA *picks up tray and exits through the curtain, tripping again.)* Shit. Damn curtain.

(ASHBE *and* JOHN POLK *are now standing outside under the awning of the bar.*)

ASHBE   Gee, I didn't know it was your birthday tomorrow. Happy birthday!
    Don't be mad. I thought you were at least twenty or twenty-one, really.
JOHN POLK   It's okay. Forget it.
ASHBE   *(As they begin walking, various blues are heard coming from the nearby bars.)*
    It's raining.
JOHN POLK   I know.
ASHBE   Are you going over to the house now?
JOHN POLK   No, not till twelve.
ASHBE   Yeah, the pink-and-black cards—they mean all night. Midnight till
    morning. *(At this point a street barker beckons the couple into his establishment.
    Perhaps he is accompanied by a whore.)*
BARKER   Hey, mister, bring your baby on in, buy her a few drinks, maybe
    tonight ya get lucky.
ASHBE   Keep walking.
JOHN POLK   What's wrong with the place?
ASHBE   The drinks are watery rotgut, and the show girls are boys.
BARKER   Up yours, punk!
JOHN POLK   *(Who has now sat down on a street bench.)* Look, just tell me where
    a cheap bar is. I've got to stay drunk, but I don't have much money left.
ASHBE   Yikes, there aren't too many cheap bars around here, and a lot of them
    check IDs.
JOHN POLK   Well, do you know of any that don't?
ASHBE   No, not for sure.
JOHN POLK   Oh, God, I need to get drunk.
ASHBE   Aren't you?
JOHN POLK   Some, but I'm losing ground fast. *(By this time a bum who has
    been traveling drunkenly down the street falls near the couple and begins
    throwing up.)*
ASHBE   Oh, I know! You can come to my apartment. It's just down the block.
    We keep one bottle of rum around. I'll serve you a grand drink, three or
    four if you like.
JOHN POLK   *(Fretfully.)* No, thanks.
ASHBE   But look, we're getting all wet.
JOHN POLK   Sober, too, wet and sober.
ASHBE   Oh, come on! Rain's blurring my glasses.
JOHN POLK   Well, how about your parents? What would they say?
ASHBE   Daddy's out of town and Mama lives in Atlanta; so I'm sure they won't
    mind. I think we have some cute little marshmallows. *(Pulling on him.)*
    Won't you really come?
JOHN POLK   You've probably got some gang of muggers waiting to kill me. Oh,
    all right—what the hell, let's go.
ASHBE   Hurrah! Come on. It's this way. *(She starts across the stage, stops, and picks*

up an old hat.) Hey look at this hat. Isn't it something! Here, wear it to keep off the rain.

JOHN POLK *(Throwing hat back onto street.)* No, thanks, you don't know who's worn it before.

ASHBE *(Picking hat back up.)* That makes it all the more exciting. Maybe it was a butcher's who slaughtered his wife or a silver pirate with a black bird on his throat. Who do you guess?

JOHN POLK I don't know. Anyway, what's the good of guessing? I mean, you'll never really know.

ASHBE *(Trying the hat on.)* Yeah, probably not. *(At this point, ASHBE and JOHN POLK reach the front door.)* Here we are. *(ASHBE begins fumbling for her key. CLAREECE, a teeny-bopper, walks up to JOHN POLK.)*

CLAREECE Hey, man, got any spare change?

JOHN POLK *(Looking through his pockets.)* Let me see—I—

ASHBE *(Coming up between them, giving CLAREECE a shove.)* Beat it, Clareece. He's my company.

CLAREECE *(Walks away and sneers.)* Oh, shove it, Frizzels.

ASHBE A lot of jerks live around here. Come on in. *(She opens the door. Lights go up on the living room of a run-down apartment in a run-down apartment house. Besides being merely run-down, the room is a malicious pigsty with colors, paper hats, paper dolls, masks, torn-up stuffed animals, dead flowers and leaves, dress-up clothes, etc., thrown all about.)* My bones are cold. Do you want a towel to dry off?

JOHN POLK Yes, thank you.

ASHBE *(She picks a towel up off of the floor and tosses it to him.)* Here. *(He begins drying off as she takes off her rain things; then she begins raking things off the sofa.)* Please do sit down. *(He sits.)* I'm sorry the place is disheveled, but my father's been out of town. I always try to pick up and all before he gets in. Of course he's pretty used to messes. My mother never was too good at keeping things clean.

JOHN POLK When's he coming back?

ASHBE Sunday, I believe. Oh, I've been meaning to say—

JOHN POLK What?

ASHBE My name's Ashbe Williams.

JOHN POLK Ashbe?

ASHBE Yeah, Ashbe.

JOHN POLK My name's John Polk Richards.

ASHBE John Polk? They call you John Polk?

JOHN POLK It's family.

ASHBE *(Putting on socks.)* These are my favorite socks, the red furry ones. Well, here's some books and magazines to look at while I fix you something to drink. What do you want in your rum?

JOHN POLK Coke's fine.

ASHBE I'll see do we have any. I think I'll take some hot Kool-Aid myself. *(She exits to the kitchen.)*

JOHN POLK Hot Kool-Aid?

ASHBE It's just Kool-Aid that's been heated, like hot chocolate or hot tea.

JOHN POLK Sounds great.

ASHBE Well, I'm used to it. You get so much for your dime it makes it worth your while. I don't buy presweetened, of course, it's better to sugar your own.

JOHN POLK I remember once I threw up a lot of grape Kool-Aid when I was a kid. I've hated it ever since. Hey, would you check on the time?

ASHBE *(She enters carrying a tray with several bottles of food coloring, a bottle of rum, and a huge glass.)* I'm sorry we don't have Cokes. I wonder if rum and Kool-Aid is good? Oh, we don't have a clock, either. *(She pours a large amount of rum into the large glass.)*

JOHN POLK I'll just have it with water, then.

ASHBE *(She finds an almost empty glass of water somewhere in the room and dumps it in with the rum.)* Would you like food coloring in the water? It makes a drink all the more aesthetic. Of course, some people don't care for aesthetics.

JOHN POLK No, thank you, just plain water.

ASHBE Are you sure? The taste is entirely the same. I put it in all my water.

JOHN POLK Well—

ASHBE What color do you want?

JOHN POLK I don't know.

ASHBE What's your favorite color?

JOHN POLK Blue, I guess. *(She puts a few blue drops into the glass—as she has nothing to stir with, she blows into the glass, turning the water blue.)* Thanks.

ASHBE *(Exits. She screams from kitchen.)* Come on, say come on, cat, eat your fresh good milk.

JOHN POLK You have a cat?

ASHBE *(Off.)* No.

JOHN POLK Oh.

ASHBE *(She enters carrying a tray with a cup of hot Kool-Aid and Cheerios and colored marshmallows.)* Here are some Cheerios and some cute little colored marshmallows to eat with your drink.

JOHN POLK Thanks.

ASHBE I one time smashed all the big white marshmallows in the plastic bag at the grocery store.

JOHN POLK Why did you do that?

ASHBE I was angry. Do you like ceramics?

JOHN POLK Yes.

ASHBE   My mother makes them. It's sort of her hobby. She is very talented.

JOHN POLK   My mother never does anything. Well, I guess she can shuffle the bridge deck okay.

ASHBE   Actually, my mother is a dancer. She teaches at a school in Atlanta. She's really very talented.

JOHN POLK   *(Indicates ceramics.)* She must be to do all these.

ASHBE   Well, Madeline, my older sister, did the blue one. Madeline gets to live with Mama.

JOHN POLK   And you live with your father.

ASHBE   Yeah, but I get to go visit them sometimes.

JOHN POLK   You do ceramics, too?

ASHBE   No, I never learned . . . but I have this great pot holder set. *(Gets up to show him.)* See I make lots of multicolored pot holders and sent them to Mama and Madeline. I also make paper hats. *(Gets material to show him.)* I guess they're more creative, but making pot holders is more relaxing. Here, would you like to make a hat?

JOHN POLK   I don't know, I'm a little drunk.

ASHBE   It's not hard a bit. *(Hands him material.)* Just draw a real pretty design on the paper. It really doesn't have to be pretty, just whatever you want.

JOHN POLK   It's kind of you to give my creative drives such freedom.

ASHBE   Ha, ha, ha, I'll work on my pot holder set a bit.

JOHN POLK   What time is it? I've really got to check on the time.

ASHBE   I know. I'll call the time operator. *(She goes to the phone.)*

JOHN POLK   How do you get along without a clock?

ASHBE   Well, I've been late for school a lot. Daddy has a watch. It's 11:03.

JOHN POLK   I've got a while yet.

ASHBE   *(Twirls back to her chair, drops, and sighs.)*

JOHN POLK   Are you a dancer, too?

ASHBE   *(Delighted.)* I can't dance a bit, really. I practice a lot is all, at home in the afternoon. I imagine you go to a lot of dances.

JOHN POLK   Not really, I'm a terrible dancer. I usually get bored or drunk.

ASHBE   You probably drink too much.

JOHN POLK   No, it's just since I've come to college. All you do there is drink more beer and write more papers.

ASHBE   What are you studying for to be?

JOHN POLK   I don't know.

ASHBE   Why don't you become a rancher?

JOHN POLK   Dad wants me to help run his soybean farm.

ASHBE   Soybean farm. Yikes, that's really something. Where is it?

JOHN POLK   Well, I live in the Delta, Hollybluff, Mississippi. Anyway, Dad feels I should go to business school first; you know, so I'll become, well, management minded. Pass the blue.

ASHBE   Is that what you really want to do?

JOHN POLK   I don't know. It would probably be as good as anything else I could do. Dad makes good money. He can take vacations whenever he wants. Sure it'll be a ball.

ASHBE   I'd hate to have to be management minded. *(JOHN POLK shrugs.)* I don't mean to hurt your feelings, but I would really hate to be a management mind. *(She starts walking on her knees, twisting her fists in front of her eyes, and making clicking sounds as a management mind would make.)*

JOHN POLK   Cut it out. Just forget it. The farm could burn down and I wouldn't even have to think about it.

ASHBE   *(After a pause.)* Well, what do you want to talk about?

JOHN POLK   I don't know.

ASHBE   When was the last dance you went to?

JOHN POLK   Dances. That's a great subject. Let's see, oh, I don't really remember. It was probably some blind date. God, I hate dates.

ASHBE   Why?

JOHN POLK   Well, they always say that they don't want popcorn and they wind up eating all of yours.

ASHBE   You mean, you hate dates just because they eat your popcorn? Don't you think that's kind of stingy?

JOHN POLK   It's the principle of the thing. Why can't they just say, yes, I'd like some popcorn when you ask them. But, no, they're always so damn coy.

ASHBE   I'd tell my date if I wanted popcorn. I'm not that immature.

JOHN POLK   Anyway, it's not only the popcorn. It's a lot of little things. I've finished coloring. What do I do now?

ASHBE   Now you have to fold it. Here . . . like this. *(She explains the process with relish.)* Say, that's really something.

JOHN POLK   It's kind of funny looking. *(Putting the hat on.)* Yeah, I like it, but you could never wear it anywhere.

ASHBE   Well, like what, anyway?

JOHN POLK   Huh?

ASHBE   The things dates do to you that you don't like, the little things.

JOHN POLK   Oh, well just the way they wear those false eyelashes and put their hand on your knee when you're trying to parallel park and keep on giggling and going off to the bathroom with their girlfriends. It's obvious they don't want to go out with me. They just want to go out so that they can wear their new clothes and won't have to sit on their ass in the dormitory. They never want to go out with me. I can never even talk to them.

ASHBE   Well, you can talk to me and I'm a girl.

JOHN POLK   Well, I'm really kind of drunk and you're a stranger . . . Well, I probably wouldn't be able to talk to you tomorrow. That makes a difference.

ASHBE   Maybe it does. *(A bit of a pause, and then, extremely pleased by the idea, she says.)* You know we're alike because I don't like dances, either.

JOHN POLK   I thought you said you practiced . . . in the afternoons.

ASHBE   Well, I like dancing. I just don't like dances. At least not like—well, not like the one our school was having tonight. . . . They're so corny.

JOHN POLK   Yeah, most dances are.

ASHBE   All they serve is potato chips and fruit punch, and then this stupid baby band plays and everybody dances around thinking they're so hot. I frankly wouldn't dance there. I would prefer to wait till I am invited to an exclusive ball. It doesn't really matter which ball, just one where they have huge golden chandeliers and silver fountains and serve delicacies of all sorts and bubble blue champagne. I'll arrive in a pink silk cape. *(Laughing.)* I want to dance in pink!

JOHN POLK   You're mixed up. You're probably one of those people that live in a fantasy world.

ASHBE   I do not. I accept reality as well as anyone. Anyway, you can talk to me, remember. I know what you mean by the kind of girls it's hard to talk to. There are girls a lot that way in the small clique at my school. Really tacky and mean. They expect everyone to be as stylish as they are, and they won't even speak to you in the hall. I don't mind if they don't speak to me, but I really love the orphans, and it hurts my feelings when they are so mean to them.

JOHN POLK   What do you mean—they're mean to the orpheens? *(Notices pun and giggles to self.)*

ASHBE   Oh, well, they sometimes snicker at the orphans' dresses. The orphans usually have hand-me-down, drab, ugly dresses. Once Shelly Maxwell wouldn't let Glinda borrow her pencil, even though she had two. It hurt her feelings.

JOHN POLK   Are you best friends with these orphans?

ASHBE   I hardly know them at all. They're really shy. I just like them a lot. They're the reason I put spells on the girls in the clique.

JOHN POLK   Spells, what do you mean, witch spells?

ASHBE   Witch spells? Not really, mostly just voodoo.

JOHN POLK   Are you kidding? Do you really do voodoo?

ASHBE   Sure, here I'll show you my doll. *(Goes to get doll, comes back with straw voodoo doll. Her air as she returns is one of frightening mystery.)* I know a lot about the subject. Cora she used to wash dishes in the Moonlight Café, told me all about voodoo. She's a real expert on the subject, went to all the meetings and everything. Once she caused a man's throat to rot away and turn almost totally black. She's moved to Chicago now.

JOHN POLK   It doesn't really work. Does it?

ASHBE   Well, not always. The thing about voodoo is that both parties have to believe in it for it to work.

JOHN POLK   Do the girls in school believe in it?

ASHBE   Not really; I don't think. That's where my main problem comes in. I have to make the clique believe in it, yet I have to be very subtle. Mainly, I give reports in English class or Speech.

JOHN POLK Reports?

ASHBE On voodoo.

JOHN POLK That's really kind of sick, you know.

ASHBE Not really. I don't cast spells that'll do any real harm. Mainly, just the kind of thing to make them think—to keep them on their toes. *(Blue drink intoxication begins to take over and JOHN POLK begins laughing.)* What's so funny?

JOHN POLK Nothing. I was just thinking what a mean little person you are.

ASHBE Mean! I'm not mean a bit.

JOHN POLK Yes, you are mean— *(Picking up color.)* and green, too.

ASHBE Green?

JOHN POLK Yes, green with envy of those other girls; so you play all those mean little tricks.

ASHBE Envious of those other girls, that stupid, close-minded little clique!

JOHN POLK Green as this marshmallow. *(Eats marshmallow.)*

ASHBE You think I want to be in some group . . . a sheep like you? A little sheep like you that does everything when he's supposed to do it!

JOHN POLK Me a sheep—I do what I want!

ASHBE Ha! I've known you for an hour and already I see you for the sheep you are!

JOHN POLK Don't take your green meanness out on me.

ASHBE Not only are you a sheep, you are a *normal* sheep. Give me back my colors! *(Begins snatching colors away.)*

JOHN POLK *(Pushing colors at her.)* Green and mean! Green and mean! Green and mean! Et cetera.

ASHBE *(Throwing marshmallows at him.)* That's the reason you're in a fraternity and the reason you're going to manage your mind, and dates—you go out on dates merely because it's expected of you even though you have a terrible time. That's the reason you go to the whorehouse to prove you're a normal man. Well, you're much too normal for me.

JOHN POLK Infant bitch. You think you're really cute.

ASHBE That really wasn't food coloring in your drink, it was poison! *(She laughs, he picks up his coat to go, and she stops throwing marshmallows at him.)* Are you going? I was only kidding. For Christ sake, it wasn't really poison. Come on, don't go. Can't you take a little friendly criticism?

JOHN POLK Look, did you have to bother me tonight? I had enough problems without— *(Phone rings. Both look at phone; it rings for the third time. He stands undecided.)*

ASHBE Look, wait, we'll make it up. *(She goes to answer phone.)* Hello—Daddy. How are you? . . . I'm fine . . . Dad, you sound funny . . . what? . . . Come on, Daddy, you know she's not here. *(Pause.)* Look, I told you I wouldn't call anymore. You've got her number in Atlanta. *(Pause, as she sinks to the floor.)* Why have you started again? . . . Don't say that. I can tell it. I can. Hey, I have to go to bed now, I don't want to talk anymore, okay? *(Hangs up phone, softly to self.)* Goddamnit.

JOHN POLK *(He has heard the conversation and is taking off his coat.)* Hey, Ashbe— *(She looks at him blankly, her mind far away.)* You want to talk?

ASHBE No. *(Slight pause.)* Why don't you look at my shell collection? I have this special shell collection. *(She shows him collection.)*

JOHN POLK They're beautiful, I've never seen colors like this. *(ASHBE is silent, he continues to himself.)* I used to go to Biloxi a lot when I was a kid . . . one time my brother and I, we camped out on the beach. The sky was purple. I remember it was really purple. We ate pork and beans out of a can. I'd always kinda wanted to do that. Every night for about a week after I got home, I dreamt about these waves foaming over my head and face. It was funny. Did you find these shells or buy them?

ASHBE Some I found, some I bought. I've been trying to decipher their meaning. Here, listen, do you hear that?

JOHN POLK Yes.

ASHBE That's the soul of the sea. *(She listens.)* I'm pretty sure it's the soul of the sea. Just imagine when I decipher the language. I'll know all the secrets of the world.

JOHN POLK Yeah, probably you will. *(Looking into the shell.)* You know, you were right.

ASHBE What do you mean?

JOHN POLK About me, you were right. I am a sheep, a normal one. I've been trying to get out of it, but now I'm as big a sheep as ever.

ASHBE Oh, it doesn't matter. You're company. It was rude of me to say.

JOHN POLK No, because it was true. I really didn't want to go into a fraternity, I didn't even want to go to college, and I sure as hell don't want to go back to Hollybluff and work the soybean farm till I'm eighty.

ASHBE I still say you could work on a ranch.

JOHN POLK I don't know. I wanted to be a minister or something good, but I don't even know if I believe in God.

ASHBE Yeah.

JOHN POLK I never used to worry about being a failure. Now I think about it all the time. It's just I need to do something that's—fulfilling.

ASHBE Fulfilling, yes, I see what you mean. Well, how about college? Isn't it fulfilling? I mean, you take all those wonderful classes, and you have all your very good friends.

JOHN POLK Friends, yeah, I have some friends.

ASHBE What do you mean?

JOHN POLK Nothing—well, I do mean something. What the hell, let me try to explain. You see it was my "friends," the fraternity guys that set me up with G.G., excuse me, Myrtle, as a gift for my eighteenth birthday.

ASHBE   You mean, you didn't want the appointment?

JOHN POLK   No, I didn't want it. Hey, ah, where did my blue drink go?

ASHBE   *(As she hands him the drink.)* They probably thought you really wanted to go.

JOHN POLK   Yeah, I'm sure they gave a damn what I wanted. They never even asked me. Hell, I would have told them a handkerchief, a pair of argyle socks, but, no, they have to get me a whore just because it's a cool-ass thing to do. They make me sick. I couldn't even stay at the party they gave. All the sweaty T-shirts and moron sex stories—I just couldn't take it.

ASHBE   Is that why you were at the Blue Angel so early?

JOHN POLK   Yeah, I needed to get drunk, but not with them. They're such creeps.

ASHBE   Gosh, so you really don't want to go to Myrtle's?

JOHN POLK   No, I guess not.

ASHBE   Then are you going?

JOHN POLK   *(Pause.)* Yes.

ASHBE   That's wrong. You shouldn't go just to please them.

JOHN POLK   Oh, that's not the point anymore; maybe at first it was, but it's not anymore. Now I have to go for myself—to prove to myself that I'm not afraid.

ASHBE   Afraid? *(Slowly, as she begins to grasp his meaning.)* You mean, you've never slept with a girl before?

JOHN POLK   Well, I've never been in love.

ASHBE   *(In amazement.)* You're a virgin?

JOHN POLK   Oh, God.

ASHBE   No, don't feel bad, I am, too.

JOHN POLK   I thought I should be in love—

ASHBE   Well, you're certainly not in love with Myrtle. I mean, you haven't even met her.

JOHN POLK   I know, but, God, I thought maybe I'd never fall in love. What then? You should experience everything—shouldn't you? Oh, what's it matter, everything's so screwed.

ASHBE   Screwed? Yeah, I guess it is. I mean, I always thought it would be fun to have a lot of friends who gave parties and go to dances all dressed up. Like the dance tonight—it might have been fun.

JOHN POLK   Well, why didn't you go?

ASHBE   I don't know. I'm not sure it would have been fun. Anyway, you can't go—alone.

JOHN POLK   Oh, you need a date?

ASHBE   Yeah, or something.

JOHN POLK Say, Ashbe, ya wanna dance here?

ASHBE No, I think we'd better discuss your dilemma.

JOHN POLK What dilemma?

ASHBE Myrtle. It doesn't seem right you should—

JOHN POLK Let's forget Myrtle for now. I've got a while yet. Here, have some more of this blue-moon drink.

ASHBE You're only trying to escape through artificial means.

JOHN POLK Yeah, you got it. Now, come on. Would you like to dance? Hey, you said you liked to dance.

ASHBE You're being ridiculous.

JOHN POLK (Winking at her.) Dance?

ASHBE John Polk, I just thought—

JOHN POLK Hmm?

ASHBE How to solve your problem—

JOHN POLK Well—

ASHBE Make love to me!

JOHN POLK What?!

ASHBE It all seems logical to me. It would prove you weren't scared, and you wouldn't be doing it just to impress others.

JOHN POLK Look, I—I mean I hardly know you—

ASHBE But we've talked. It's better this way, really. I won't be so apt to point out your mistakes.

JOHN POLK I'd feel great stripping a twelve-year-old of her virginity.

ASHBE I'm sixteen! Anyway, I'd be stripping you of yours just as well. I'll go put on some Tiger Claw perfume. (She runs out.)

JOHN POLK Hey, come back! Tiger Claw perfume, Christ.

ASHBE (Entering.) I think one should have different scents for different moods.

JOHN POLK Hey, stop spraying that! You know I'm not going to—well, you'd get neurotic or pregnant or some damn thing. Stop spraying, will you!

ASHBE Pregnant? You really think I could get pregnant?

JOHN POLK Sure, it'd be a delightful possibility.

ASHBE It really wouldn't be bad. Maybe I would get to go to Tokyo for an abortion. I've never been to the Orient.

JOHN POLK Sure, getting cut on is always a real treat.

ASHBE Anyway, I might just want to have my dear baby. I could move to Atlanta with Mama and Madeline. It'd be wonderful fun. Why, I could take him to the supermarket, put him in one of those little baby seats to stroll him about. I'd buy peach baby food and feed it to him with a tiny golden spoon. Why, I could take colored pictures of him and send them to you through the mail. Come on— (Starts putting pillows onto the couch.) Well, I guess you should kiss me for a start. It's only etiquette; everyone begins with it.

JOHN POLK I don't think I could even kiss you with a clear conscience. I mean, you're so small, with those little cat-eye glasses and curly hair—I couldn't even kiss you.

ASHBE   You couldn't even kiss me? I can't help it if I have to wear glasses. I got the prettiest ones I could find.

JOHN POLK   Your glasses are fine. Let's forget it, okay?

ASHBE   I know, my lips are too purple, but if I eat carrots, the dye'll come off and they'll be orange.

JOHN POLK   I didn't say anything about your lips being too purple.

ASHBE   Well, what is it? You're just plain chicken, I suppose—

JOHN POLK   Sure, right, I'm chicken, totally chicken. Let's forget it. I don't know how, but somehow this is probably all my fault.

ASHBE   You're darn right it's all your fault! I want to have my dear baby or at least get to Japan. I'm so sick of school I could smash every marshmallow in sight! *(She starts smashing.)* Go on to your skinny pimple whore. I hope the skinny whore laughs in your face, which she probably will because you have an easy face to laugh in.

JOHN POLK   You're absolutely right; she'll probably hoot and howl her damn fizzle red head off. Maybe you can wait outside the door and hear her, give you lots of pleasure, you sadistic little thief.

ASHBE   Thief—was Robin Hood— Oh, what's wrong with this world? I just wasn't made for it is all. I've probably been put in the wrong world, I can see that now.

JOHN POLK   You're fine in this world.

ASHBE   Sure, everyone just views me as an undesirable lump.

JOHN POLK   Who?

ASHBE   You for one.

JOHN POLK   *(Pause.)* You mean because I wouldn't make love to you?

ASHBE   It seems clear to me.

JOHN POLK   But you're wrong, you know.

ASHBE   *(To self, softly.)* Don't pity me.

JOHN POLK   The reason I wouldn't wasn't that—it's just that—well, I like you too much to.

ASHBE   You like me?

JOHN POLK   Undesirable lump, Jesus. Your cheeks, they're—they're—

ASHBE   My cheeks? They're what?

JOHN POLK   They're rosy.

ASHBE   My cheeks are rosy?

JOHN POLK   Yeah, your cheeks, they're really rosy.

ASHBE   Well, they're natural, you know. Say, would you like to dance?

JOHN POLK   Yes.

ASHBE   I'll turn on the radio. *(She turns on radio. Ethel Waters is heard singing "Honey in the Honeycomb." ASHBE begins snapping her fingers.)* Yikes, let's jazz it out. *(They dance.)*

JOHN POLK   Hey, I'm not good or anything—

ASHBE   John Polk.

JOHN POLK   Yeah?

ASHBE   Baby, I think you dance fine! *(They dance on, laughing, saying what they want till end of song. Then a radio announcer comes on and says the 12:00 news will be in five minutes. Billie Holiday or Terry Pierce begins singing, "Am I Blue?")*

JOHN POLK   Dance?

ASHBE   News in five minutes.

JOHN POLK   Yeah.

ASHBE   That means five minutes till midnight.

JOHN POLK   Yeah, I know.

ASHBE   Then you're not—

JOHN POLK   Ashbe, I've never danced all night. Wouldn't it be something to—to dance all night and watch the rats come out of the gutter?

ASHBE   Rats?

JOHN POLK   Don't they come out at night? I hear New Orleans has lots of rats.

ASHBE   Yeah, yeah, it's got lots of rats.

JOHN POLK   Then let's dance all night and wait for them to come out.

ASHBE   All right—but, but how about our feet?

JOHN POLK   Feet?

ASHBE   They'll hurt.

JOHN POLK   Yeah.

ASHBE   *(Smiling.)* Okay, then let's dance. *(He takes her hand, and they dance as lights black out and the music soars and continues to play.)*

GERT HOFMANN

Our Man in Madras

CHARACTERS

JIM SIEG
JANE   Secretary.

The office of JIM SIEG. Swivel chair. A telephone with a shoulder rest sits on a large desk, together with an intercom, a pitcher of water, a glass, etc. SIEG is thumbing through a file of reports. After a while he switches on the intercom.

SIEG   Jane.
JANE   Mr. Sieg?
SIEG   Give me our man in Madras.
JANE   Yes, Mr. Sieg.

(SIEG returns to the reports. Soon the intercom buzzes. He switches it on.)

SIEG   Yes?
JANE   Our man in Madras, Mr. Sieg.
SIEG   Thanks, Jane. *(Picks up receiver.)* Hallo, Bob? How's it going? This is Jim speaking. You bet, from the main office, where we, that is HB, the overseas manager, the sales manager, and yours truly have just been discussing you in some detail. If I may be frank, Bob: HB was not very impressed with your last sales report here. Sure, of course—you've picked up a bit from the last quarter—seven-twelfths of a percent, as I pointed out to HB, Bob, but compared with what our men in Australia and Europe are accomplishing, your figures still fall pretty short. Now of course we know, Bob, that you're working under very special conditions down there, which you always write up in your reports in great detail. But, Bob, after all! And since your contract with us expires at the end of the month, anyway—I just happen to have it here in front of me—we now come to the question of

whether we should extend it or, yes, or not. *(He laughs.)* HB—he's in a conference now, no, he hasn't said what he thinks yet, our managers have split opinions, and I'm sympathetically neutral. In order to ease the decision, HB sent you his consulting psychologist two weeks ago. Now, he's one of the really big ones that HB thinks a lot of, and so do I. I also have his testimonial in front of me. He writes, Bob, that within the framework of your activity you can be thoroughly productive but that your potential is greater than what you accomplish. That means that in spite of the salary which HB pays you you're still keeping back a large part of yourself— perhaps the best part. I ask myself: is that fair? What would you say, Bob, if on the first day of next month HB would send only half a check? You'd be sore, wouldn't you? Now you're doing exactly that with HB. I think we ought to hash out this problem of your attitude, and that's why I'm calling you. *(JIM reaches for a cigar.)* Before we come to a final decision about the extension of your contract, I would like to give you the opportunity to explain to me your attitude toward HB. *(He lights a match.)* Do you hear me, Bob? Hallo, Bob. What are you doing? Sometimes you're loud and sometimes you're not. You've what? Burned your hands? *(He extinguishes the match with which he had almost burned his fingers.)* Your skin is peeling? How's that? Not only your hands? What kind of rays, Bob? Can't you speak a little louder? If I've understood you correctly you just said: "Madras has had it." Not only Madras? The whole of southern India? You're putting me on. Did I know? Of course not. I had no idea. Do people know yet who it was? Well, to tell you the truth, I don't know, either, but I'm sure we weren't the ones. And I don't think we could have let it happen unintentionally. Precautions have certainly been taken against such mistakes, on our side in any case. Just a moment, Bob. *(JIM puts his hand on the mouthpiece and switches on the intercom.)* Jane.

JANE   Mr. Sieg?

SIEG   Is HB in his office yet?

JANE   No, Mr. Sieg.

SIEG   Can you just try to find out if he's awake yet? I have something here which might interest him. Check it out for me, Jane.

JANE   Yes, Mr. Sieg.

SIEG   *(Switches off the intercom and speaks again into the telephone.)* Bob, are you speaking from our office? Our office has had it? The whole building is ... The whole quarter, ah! You're speaking from a cellar. That's why your voice sounds so hollow. Your voice . . .

JANE   Mr. Sieg.

SIEG   One moment, Bob. *(He holds his hand on the telephone and switches on the intercom.)* Yes?

JANE   I only wanted to tell you that HB is already awake.

SIEG   And what's he doing?

JANE   They're just putting him in the tub.

SIEG   Ah. Is Fred around?

JANE   Yes, Mr. Sieg.

SIEG   Would you please tell him that I've something here which may interest HB and I would be grateful if he'd keep in touch with me during the next hour?

JANE   Gladly, Mr. Sieg.

SIEG   Let me know when HB leaves his bath. *(Switches off the intercom and speaks again into the telephone.)* Bob, we've been interrupted. What's that? Your hair is falling out. Sorry to hear that, Bob. I hope you know that your health is insured by the firm. You knew it, fine. I just wanted to remind you, because I know from experience that while a guy is healthy, he's liable not to think much about insurance. But as soon as the hospital and the doctor bills come, then it's another story. You can thank God you don't have to worry about the doctor bills, anyway. HB has taken care of that. Just a minute, Bob. *(He puts his hand over the mouthpiece and switches on the intercom.)* Jane.

JANE   Mr. Sieg?

SIEG   Would you please tell Fred that I've been calling to ask him to very cautiously broach the subject to HB, as soon as he's out of the tub, as to whether he shouldn't maybe revise his Asian policy in the light of the newest development there. He's certainly heard about it by now. I see great possibilities in it. You bet I do. And would you ask Fred not to mention that the proposal comes from me until HB makes a positive decision.

JANE   Yes, Mr. Sieg.

SIEG   *(Switches off the intercom and speaks again into the telephone.)* You know you're a lucky dog, Bob. *(Louder.)* I said, you're a lucky dog. *(He yells.)* A *lucky dog*. I was sitting here with your record sheet in hand and was just about to dictate one of my famous farewell letters. I know people who would gladly have a hand chopped off for a chance like this. What kind of a chance? Chrissakes, man, you tell me that all of southern India is gone and you ask me what kind of a chance? If what you're telling me is true, and I hope for your sake it is, then HB has *got* to update his Asian policy. If he does, you've got it made. You know the country. You know the people. You're used to the climate there. Now you can show what you've got on the ball. It's just the situation the old fox has been waiting for. You were saying? Your left ear is wiggling? Don't touch it, Bob. Leave it alone! You know how he enjoys starting something from scratch and then does a really creative job on it, gives it everything he's got, and that's plenty. Hahaha. Why, how often he's looked at me with those big sad eyes and said, "What's with these trifles, Jim? Give me a continent to conquer."

And that's just what we've got now, Bob. A continent. If I understand you correctly, you said there's not much left over there. Just a minute, Bob. *(He puts his hand on the mouthpiece and switches on the intercom.)* Jane!

JANE Mr. Sieg?

SIEG Have you oriented Fred?

JANE Yes, Mr. Sieg.

SIEG Does he want to broach the subject to HB?

JANE Yes, Mr. Sieg. As soon as the masseur is gone.

SIEG Thank you, Jane. *(Switches off the intercom and speaks again into the telephone.)* Bob, if I see the situation correctly, which is not easy, because you don't say much, do you? Your left ear has come off now? Sorry to hear that, Bob. Well, then, it seems to me you're proposing that since the whole place there is gone, nature- and building-wise, HB should shoot in everything he's got and put the country back on its feet in, let's say, two or three years, depending on the contract. Fine, Bob, I'll submit your project to HB. You're speaking from . . . ? *(He makes notes.)* Madras, India. Population: 1,300,000. No kidding. *(JIM puts his hand on the mouthpiece, switches on the intercom.)* Jane, go over to the encyclopedia and look up Madras.

JANE Yes, Mr. Sieg.

SIEG *(Switches off the intercom and speaks again into the telephone.)* Okay, now the extent of the catastrophe, Bob. Tell me. *(He switches on the intercom and puts his hand on the mouthpiece.)* Fire, Jane.

JANE *(Reads.)* "Madras, the capital and chief port of Madras state, India, is situated on the eastern coast of India. Nearly fifty square miles in area, it is the largest town in extent in the Indian republic. The population in 1951 was 1,416,056."

SIEG How many, Jane?

JANE 1,416,056.

SIEG *(Makes a note of it.)* 1,416,056.

JANE "The city can be reached by sea, air, rail, and . . ."

SIEG Just a moment, Jane. *(He switches off the intercom again and speaks into the telephone.)* I admit, Bob, that it's not easy to give a survey of the damage from a cellar hole, but the cellar has got to have a window. Good. Then go to the window. All right, then *crawl*! Hairsplitting, Bob, won't help us at all. Let's just remain objective. *(He switches on the intercom and puts his hand on the mouthpiece.)* Go on, Jane.

JANE *(Reads.)* "Viewed from the air, the city looks quite green, since, even in the most congested parts, there are fine trees, gardens, and parks."

SIEG *(Switches off the intercom. Into the telephone.)* Do you know what one minute of long distance costs HB at this time of day, Bob? Between fourteen and fifteen dollars, Bob. It just now occurred to me. No, no, give yourself time. *(He puts his hand on the mouthpiece and switches on the intercom.)* The industry, Jane.

JANE   (*Reads.*) "Madras possesses some special industries, the most important of which are the films and textiles, engineering and . . ."

SIEG   (*Switches off the intercom and turns again to the telephone.*) You are at the window, Bob? There is a box in front of it? For Chrissakes, then just climb onto it. Or *crawl*, whatever you want. Of course I'll wait. (*He puts his hand on the mouthpiece and switches on the intercom.*) Jane.

JANE   Mr. Sieg?

SIEG   Exports, please.

JANE   (*Reads.*) "The chief exports are seeds, nuts, skins and hides, condiments, textiles, ores, tobacco, and vegetables . . ."

SIEG   (*Switches off the intercom, into the telephone again, pleased.*) Are you up, Bob? Very good. Now tell me what you see. (*He picks up the pencil.*) Nothing? Because what is lying in front of the window? A dead woman? Blocking your view? Sorry, Bob. Can't she be pushed aside, Bob? How do I know what with? You're in a cellar, so just look around a little. A board? Okay, why not a board. Now take it and push her aside. And don't whine like that. I've done a lot of worse things in my life. (*Short pause.*) Do you have the board up? All right, then push. And why doesn't it work? The woman is jammed? Something's on top of her? A what? A *beam*. Fine, Bob, then we'll just have to push the beam out of the way. Firmly now, Bob. (*Short pause.*) And why not? You don't have the strength? I'll tell you what you don't have, Bob. You don't have the . . . You knew the woman? Sorry about that, Bob. I can well imagine how you feel. Just the same, Bob, spit on your hands and push. Push. *What* are you saying? She's your *wife*? She didn't make it to the cellar. (*He changes his tone.*) Bob, do you know what I would like now? I would like to be able to hold your hand. Even if I hardly knew. (*He looks into his papers.*) Martha, that was her name, it wasn't? She was called Elizabeth, Martha was her middle name, so she filled out this form here incorrectly, that's not meant to be a reproach. Even if I hardly knew Elizabeth, Bob, I still remember her clearly. I know what a wonderful person she was and how her absence must hurt you. (*Pause.*) No, Bob, I have to admit I don't remember that little detail. (*Pause.*) Can't quite remember that, either. Unfortunately, in my job I meet very many —far too many women, so that— She had what? Beautiful long dark hair, which is now . . . Sorry about that, Bob. Now that I think about it, I didn't actually know Elizabeth *personally*. No—couldn't possibly have known her, because HB has a rule which says that the wives of our men on overseas duty are introduced only to the overseas director, but not to yours truly, a rule whose wisdom may be doubtful, I'll have to admit. Yes, I should have gotten to know Elizabeth, and now I regret very much that I didn't have a chance at the time. What would you say, Bob, if I would propose to HB to revise this rule so that in the future I would get to personally know *all* the wives of our men on overseas duty? Would that please you, Bob?

Gert Hofmann / 229

Don't you think that it would have also pleased Elizabeth? I think I can do that for you. I'm making a memo on it, Bob. *(He takes no memo.)* What do you want? You want to tell me how *you* met Elizabeth? . . . Sure you can tell me how you met Elizabeth, Bob. I'm listening, Bob! *(He puts his hand on the mouthpiece and switches on the intercom.)* Jane.

JANE   Mr. Sieg?

SIEG   What is HB doing?

JANE   They're just putting him on the table.

SIEG   Thanks, Jane.

JANE   You're welcome, Mr. Sieg.

SIEG   *(Switches off the intercom. Into the telephone, very gently.)* Bob. *(Short pause.)* Bob. *(Short pause.)* Pardon me if I'm interrupting you, Bob. You're a real spellbinder—I could listen to you for hours, but shouldn't we . . . Sure thing, you take your time, Bob. Take all the time you need. *(He puts his hand on the mouthpiece and switches on the intercom.)* Jane.

JANE   Mr. Sieg?

SIEG   The imports.

JANE   *(Reads.)* "The chief imports are coal, coke, food grains, mineral oils, metals, timber, textiles, building materials, machinery, hardware, paper, stationery, and chemical fertilizers."

SIEG   Is that everything?

JANE   Yes, Mr. Sieg. Do you still need the article?

SIEG   No. *(He switches off the intercom. Into the telephone, pleased.)* She's out of the way? Good show! Now what do you see? The street's littered with what? Skip that part, Bob, if you don't mind. These details are too sad. You see . . . I'll take that down. *(He takes notes.)* ". . . wiped out . . . pulverized . . . melted . . . charred . . . suffocated . . . buried. . . ." Are you sure you aren't exaggerating the thing a bit, Bob? No? Good, I believe you. And now let's look in the other direction. What do you see there? But you must see something, Bob! It's suddenly getting dark around you? What time do you have? But how can it get dark at your degree of latitude, at three in the afternoon? Man, I hope you weren't looking just when the thing went off. Do you still see the ruins? No? The window? No? It's getting darker and darker? You can't even see Elizabeth anymore? Sorry about that, Bob. Let's do the following, Bob. *(He does it, too.)* Let's just stretch out our arms straight ahead. *(He moves his hands in front of his eyes.)* Can you see your hands, Bob? What do you mean: just barely? Can you or can't you? You can't. Then let's just move them closer. Can you see them now? Poor old guy. Just a moment! *(He switches on the intercom, puts his hand over the mouthpiece, and speaks.)* Jane!

JANE   Mr. Sieg?

SIEG   Is HB still on the table?

JANE   Yes, Mr. Sieg. They are rubbing him dry.

SIEG   What kind of a mood is he in?

JANE   Fred still wasn't able to see his face.

SIEG   Thank you, Jane.

JANE   You are welcome, Mr. Sieg!

SIEG   *(Switches off the intercom again and speaks into the telephone.)* I just spoke to HB, Bob. I'd be grateful for a second opinion about the extent of the damage. You must know how very much HB needs to feel that he can start something from the bottom up, so that he can completely feel his creativity. I have to be 100 percent convinced things are completely in the red, and I'm not convinced of that yet. No, Bob, I'm sorry. It's impossible for me to rely on the report of an eyewitness, who admits that he can't see his own hands in front of his face. In your idyllic world you have no idea how it is here with us. We don't play golf in the afternoon. We live in a jungle. In my position I sit with my back to the wall, and even then I'm not safe from the daggers of the junior execs. Unfortunately, that's the truth, Bob. We don't want to give them this opening with our plan, do we? Look, Bob —you've lost your wife. You're worried about your job. Maybe your health isn't exactly what it should be. Of course, all this doesn't necessarily speak against you, but in any case it just might impair your judgment, mightn't it? And HB can't reverse his Asian policy on the basis of a judgment colored by personal experiences, can he? So, if you want me to push your project through with HB, you'll have to see to it that somebody confirms your report. It's not necessary that we know the man. It's enough if *you* know. . . . There's *what*? There's nobody left? *(He laughs.)* Now, Bob! You just said yourself that Madras has a population of 1,300,000—actually it's 1,416,056—and now you want to tell me that not one of those people can come to the phone? But, Bob. *(More sharply.)* Please, do me a favor, then, and do something. From here I can't tell you *what*. You're an idea man, aren't you? Well then—*shout. (He makes a face.)* Your voice sounds terrible. As if you had something in your mouth. You *do* have something in your mouth? What do you have in your mouth? You have blood in your mouth? Sorry to hear that, Bob, I thought that you had a hard time talking, but nevertheless, Bob, just yell once more, for *my* sake, Bob! *(Pause.)* Nobody? And you wouldn't like to go out on the street and hunt up somebody yourself? The radiation, I understand. Don't you think that you're a bit too concerned about yourself, Bob? Look, Bob, according to your own information, the thing happened approximately *(He looks at his watch.)* thirty minutes ago. That means that in the meantime a good half hour has gone by. A half hour is a long time, Bob. Nature is able to heal many wounds in a half hour, more than we might imagine. I bet the rays you're afraid of have already been absorbed by dear old Mother Earth and made harmless. Anyway, a certain amount is supposed to stimulate the human organism. *How long* do they last? Ninety-nine years? Just a second, Bob.

(He puts his hand on the mouthpiece and switches on the intercom.) Is HB dry now, Jane?

JANE Yes, Mr. Sieg. He is just being put on the sofa.

SIEG So Fred isn't with him yet?

JANE No.

SIEG *(Switches off the intercom and speaks again into the telephone.)* I consider ninety-nine years a pretty far-out estimate, Bob. Anyway, the whole thing sounds like Communist propaganda. But suit yourself, you must know what your job is worth to you. *(Short pause.)* You want to try to go out, after all? Smart, Bob. Very smart. *(He puts his hand on the mouthpiece and switches on the intercom.)* Jane.

JANE Mr. Sieg?

SIEG Could Fred try to submit the matter to HB as soon as HB has had his oxygen?

JANE I wouldn't recommend sending Fred to HB before he's gotten his hormones.

SIEG Thanks, Jane.

JANE Don't mention it, Mr. Sieg.

SIEG *(Switches off the intercom and speaks into the telephone.)* Do you have another eyewitness now, Bob? No? You weren't even on the street? And why not? You can't see anything now, and you're afraid you couldn't find your way back to your cellar? Well, if you care so much for that damned cellar. Although I find it pretty weird that you can't manage to bring one out of 1,416,056 people to the phone. But please, if you—

JANE Mr. Sieg.

SIEG *(Into the telephone.)* Just a moment, Bob. *(He switches on the intercom.)* Yes?

JANE I just wanted to tell you that Fred is on his way in to see HB.

SIEG Good. And what kind of a mood is HB in?

JANE A bit worn out.

SIEG Is he taking a little nap?

JANE No, Mr. Sieg. They're putting on his clothes.

SIEG Will you keep me in touch?

JANE Sure thing, Mr. Sieg.

SIEG *(Switches off the intercom and speaks again into the telephone.)* We were interrupted, Bob. Still more blood. Sorry to hear that, Bob. Luckily I've better news for you. HB has shown great interest in your project. He's just now in a top-level conference, and I wouldn't be at all surprised if he'll give his immediate okay to the matter, impulsive as he is. Of course, you know what that would mean for you. He might even ask you to take over the whole operation. Of course, if I hadn't pushed it so hard . . . hallo, Bob? Can you still hear? But of course you're getting air. You're getting air terrifically. You're just a pessimist. A *worrywart*, that's what you are.

JANE Mr. Sieg.

SIEG   Yes? *(He covers the mouthpiece and switches on the intercom.)*
JANE   Fred has just broached the subject to HB.
SIEG   And? How did HB take it?
JANE   HB smiled, Mr. Sieg.
SIEG   HB smiled? Really, Jane?
JANE   Yes, Mr. Sieg.
SIEG   I hope Fred won't forget to tell HB that the proposal was mine.
JANE   I'm sure he won't, Mr. Sieg. But HB's just dropped off again for a moment.
SIEG   Dropped off?
JANE   Yes, Mr. Sieg. HB often naps when he's being shaved.
SIEG   You keep me tuned in, Jane?
JANE   Yes, Mr. Sieg.
SIEG   *(Switches off the intercom and speaks again into the telephone.)* The news is getting better and better, Bob. Unofficially, I'm just now getting the cue that HB has already accepted our project. I have seldom seen HB so charged up about something. If he . . . Hallo, Bob, are you still with me? You aren't getting air anymore? Now, do what I say, Bob. This is a tip from my yogi teacher that's done me a world of good. Just lay down flat. Yes, it doesn't matter where. Where? All right, then, lay down on the rats. Relax. Think of something pleasant, Bob. You're still too cramped. Just relax, relax, relax. And now put your fingers on your chest. What do you mean: you don't have fingers anymore? And now just breathe smoothly and regularly, one, two, one, two . . . just count along with me. One, two, one . . .
JANE   Mr. Sieg.
SIEG   *(Switches on the intercom.)* Yes?
JANE   HB is just waking up.
SIEG   And?
JANE   I just wanted to tell you.
SIEG   Thank you, Jane.
JANE   It's a pleasure, Mr. Sieg.
SIEG   *(Switches off the intercom again.)* Yes, Bob, it's a great moment for both of us. Anybody HB is pulling with has got it made. And that seems to be the case with you, you lucky guy. Are you gargling, Bob? You're not gargling? But I very distinctly heard you gargle. You didn't *want* to gargle, aha. I wouldn't be at all surprised if HB should dispatch one of his planes to you today and fly you in tonight for a personal discussion and . . .
JANE   Mr. Sieg.
SIEG   Just a moment, Bob. *(He puts his hand on the mouthpiece and switches on the intercom.)* Yes?
JANE   HB has come to a decision.
SIEG   Yes? And?

JANE HB is against it, Mr. Sieg.

SIEG He is against it?

JANE Yes.

SIEG Why is he against it?

JANE He didn't give a reason. He just shook his head.

SIEG Are you sure, Jane?

JANE Yes, Mr. Sieg.

SIEG You sure he wasn't nodding, Jane?

JANE He shook it sideways, Mr. Sieg.

SIEG Then he's against it.

JANE Yes, Mr. Sieg.

SIEG Did Fred tell HB whose proposal it was?

JANE No, Mr. Sieg.

SIEG Would you ask Fred, then, not to tell HB that it came from me?

JANE Of course, Mr. Sieg.

SIEG Thank you, Jane.

JANE You're welcome, Mr. Sieg.

SIEG *(Switches off the intercom and speaks again into the telephone.)* Bob. This is Jimmy again. I want to go back to the beginning of our conversation. Yes, Bob, to your basic attitude to HB and the firm, which is still not quite clear to me. I'm afraid that our talk couldn't entirely eliminate the unfavorable impression of your last sales figures as well as of your aptitude test, which are here in front of me. The right one came off, too, now? Aha. I do admit that you have an original mind, but sometimes a person can go too far with originality as you've been doing, Bob. You want HB to okay a project, which boils down to investing billions of dollars in a desert, which will be contaminated for more than ninety-nine years. You want to dump our high-quality products on a market which consists of 1,416,056 corpses, Asians at that. Yes, Bob, that's what you want. This proposal of yours, which by the way HB has turned down, isn't too realistic. For example: considering the growing squeamishness of people nowadays, where is HB supposed to get the labor to work in the area? No, Bob, it's no use getting emotional. You were calling for water? Aha. Now I'm still of the opinion that you, Bob, do have original ideas now and then. So look, it won't be difficult for you . . . Bob? Bob. I know you don't have ears anymore. Would you, nevertheless, please try and listen to me one more second. I don't want you to come to me one day and say . . . Hallo, Bob. I don't hear your throat rattling anymore. Hallo, Bob. Are you still there? HB admits, Bob, that you do your very best, but sometimes, Bob, you have to do more than your best if you want to keep your job. I'm sorry, Bob—but we'll just have to let you go. *(He hangs up and closes the file in front of him. Then he switches on the intercom and calls.)* Jane.

JANE Mr. Sieg?

SIEG Do you have our mailing list handy?

JANE Yes, Mr. Sieg.

SIEG Cross off our man in Madras.

TINA HOWE

Teeth

SETTING

A modest one-man dentist's office in midtown Manhattan. An FM radio is tuned to a classical music station. It's March 21, Johann Sebastian Bach's birthday, and Glenn Gould is playing the rollicking Presto from his Toccata in C minor. The whine of a high-powered dentist's drill slowly asserts itself. In blackout . . .

DR. ROSE   Still with me . . . ?

AMY   *(Garbled because his hands are in her mouth.)* Aaargh . . .

DR. ROSE   *(Hums along as the drilling gets louder.)* You've heard his Goldberg reissue, haven't you?

AMY   Aaargh . . .

DR. ROSE   *(Groans with pleasure.)* Unbelievable!

(The drilling gets ferocious.)

AMY   *Ow . . . ow!*

DR. ROSE   Woops, sorry about that. Okay, you can rinse.

(Lights up on AMY lying prone in a dentist's chair with a bib around her neck. She rises up, takes a swig of water, sloshes it around in her mouth, and spits it emphatically into the little bowl next to her. She flops back down, wiping her mouth. She's in her forties. DR. ROSE is several years older and on the disheveled side.)

DR. ROSE   Glenn Gould. Glenn Gould is the penultimate Bach keyboard artist of this century, period! Open, please. *(He resumes drilling.)* No one else can touch him!

AMY   Aarg . . .

DR. ROSE   Wanda Landowska, Roselyn Turek, Trevor Pinnock . . . forget it!

AMY   Aarg. . . .

DR. ROSE   *(Drilling with rising intensity.)* Andras Schiff, Igor Kipness, Anthony Newman . . . no contest!

AMY   Aarg . . .

DR. ROSE   Listen to the man . . . ! The elegance of his phrasing, the clarity of his touch . . . The joy! The Joy! *(He roars.)*

AMY   *(Practically jumping out of her seat.)* Ooooowwwwwwww!

DR. ROSE   Sorry, sorry, afraid I slipped. *(His drilling returns to normal.)* Hear how he hums along in a different key? The man can't contain himself. . . . *(He roars again, then calms down for a spate of drilling. He idly starts humming along with Gould.)* You know, you're my third patient . . . no, make that fourth . . . that's pulled out a filling with candy this week. What was the culprit again?

AMY   *(Garbled.)* Bit O'Honey.

DR. ROSE   Almond Roca . . . ?

AMY   *(Garbled.)* Bit O'Honey.

DR. ROSE   Jujubes?

AMY   *(Less garbled.)* Bit O'Honey, Bit O'Honey!

DR. ROSE   Yup, saltwater taffy will do it every time! Okay, Amy, the worst is over. You can rinse. *(He hangs up the drill.)* *(AMY rinses and spits with even more fury.)*

DR. ROSE   Hey, hey, don't break my bowl on me! *(Fussing with his tools.)* Now, where did I put that probe . . . ? I can't seem to hold on to anything these days. . . . *(AMY flops back down with a sigh.)*

DR. ROSE   *(In a little singsong.)* Where are you? . . . Where are you . . . ? Ahhhhh, here it is! Okay . . . let's just take one more last look before we fill you up. Open. *(He disappears into her mouth with the probe.)* Amy, Amy, you're still grinding your teeth at night, aren't you!

AMY   *(Anguished.)* Aaaaarrrrrrrhhh!

DR. ROSE   You've got to wear that rubber guard I gave you!

AMY   *(Completely garbled.)* But I can't breathe when it's on!

AMY   *(Incomprehensible.)* I feel like I'm choking! I've tried to wear it, I really have, I just always wake up gasping for air. See, I can't breathe through my nose. If I could breathe through my nose, it wouldn't be a problem. . . .

DR. ROSE   I know they take getting used to, but you're doing irreparable damage to your supporting bone layer, and once that goes . . . *(He whistles her fate.)*

(A RADIO ANNOUNCER has come on in the background during this.)

RADIO ANNOUNCER   That was Glenn Gould playing Bach's Toccata in C minor, BWV listing 911. And to continue with our birthday tribute to J. S. Bach, we now turn to his Cantata BWV 80, "Ein Feste Burg," as performed by the English Chamber Orchestra under the direction of Raymond Leppard. *(It begins.)*

DR. ROSE   *(Comes out of her mouth.)* Well, let's whip up a temporary filling and get you out of here. *(He rummages through his tray of tools.)*

AMY   Dr. Rose, could I ask you something?

DR. ROSE   Of course, today's March twenty-first, Bach's birthday! *(Some instruments fall; he quickly recovers them.)* Woops . . .

AMY   I keep having this recurring nightmare.

DR. ROSE   Oh, I love this piece. I used to sing it in college. Mind if I turn it up?

AMY   I just wonder if you've heard it before.

DR. ROSE   *(Turns up the volume, singing along. He returns to his tray and starts sorting out his things, which keep dropping. He quickly retrieves them, never stopping his singing.)*
"*Ein feste Burg ist unser Gott,*
Ein gute Wehr und Waffen. . . . woops.
Er hilft uns frei aus aller, Not,
Die uns itzt hat . . . woops . . . *betroffen.*"

AMY   I have it at least three times a week now.

DR. ROSE   I came this close to being a music major. *This* close!

AMY   I wake up exhausted with my whole jaw throbbing. Waa . . . waa . . . waa!

DR. ROSE   Okay, let's just open this little bottle of cement here. *(He starts struggling with the lid.)*

AMY   You know, the old . . . *teeth-granulating-on-you dream!* *(She stifles a sob.)* You're at a party flashing a perfect smile when suddenly you hear this splintering sound like someone smashing teacups in the next room. . . . ping . . . tock . . . crackkkkkkkkkk . . . tinkle, tinkle. "Well, someone's having a good time!" you say to yourself, expecting to see some maniac swinging a sledgehammer. . . .

(Having a worse and worse time with the bottle, DR. ROSE *moves behind her chair so she can't see him.)*

DR. ROSE   Ugh . . . ugh . . . ugh . . . ugh . . . ugh!

AMY   So you casually look around, and of course there *is* no maniac . . . ! Then you feel these prickly shards clinging to your lips. . . . You try and brush them away, but suddenly your mouth is filled with them. You can't spit them out fast enough! *(She tries.)*

DR. ROSE   *Goddamnit!* *(He goes through a series of silent contortions trying to open it—behind his back, up over his head, down between his legs, etc. etc.)*

AMY   *(Still spitting and wiping.)* People are starting to stare. . . . You try to save face. *(To the imagined partygoers.)* "Well, what do you know. . . . I seem to have taken a bite out of my coffee cup! Silly me!" *(She laughs, frantically wiping.)*

DR. ROSE   *Goddamn son of a bitch, what's going on here?*

AMY That's just what *I* want to know!

DR. ROSE *Is this some kind of conspiracy or what?*

AMY Why me? What did I do?

DR. ROSE They must weld these tops on.

AMY Then I catch a glimpse of myself in the mirror . . .

DR. ROSE *(Starting to cackle.)* Think you can outsmart me . . . ? *(He starts whacking a heavy tool down on the lid.)*

AMY You got it! My teeth are spilling out of my mouth in little pieces. I frantically try and moosh them back in, but there's nothing to hold on to. Then they start granulating on me . . . fsssssssssssssssss. . . . It's like trying to build a sand castle inside an hourglass!

(DR. ROSE is having a worse and worse time. He finally just sits on the floor and bangs the bottle down as hard as he can, again and again.)

AMY My mouth is a blaze of gums. We are talking pink for *miles* . . . ! Magellan staring out over the Pacific Ocean during a sunset in 1520— *(As Magellan.)* "Pink . . . pink . . . pink . . . pink!" *(DR. ROSE starts to whimper as he pounds.)*

AMY What does it *mean*, is what I'd like to know! I mean, teeth are supposed to last forever, right? They hold up through floods, fires, earthquakes, and wars . . . the one part of us that endures.

DR. ROSE Open, damnit. Open, damnit. Open, damnit. . . .

AMY So if they granulate on you, where does that leave you? *Nowhere!*

DR. ROSE *(Curls into the fetal position and focuses on smaller moves in a tiny voice.)* Come on . . . come on . . . Please? Pretty please? Pretty, lovely, ravishing please?

AMY You could have been rain or wind, for all anybody knows. That's pretty scary. . . . *(Starting to get weepy.)* One minute you're laughing at a party and the next you've evaporated into thin air. . . . *(Putting on a voice.)* "Remember Amy? Gee, I wonder whatever happened to her?" *(In another voice.)* "Gosh, it's suddenly gotten awfully chilly in here. Where's that wind coming from?" *(Teary again.)* I mean, we're not around for that long as it is, so then to suddenly . . . I'm sorry, I'm sorry. It's just I have this um . . . long-standing . . . Oh, God, here we go . . . *(Starting to break down.)* Control yourself! Control . . . control!

(DR. ROSE is now rolled up in a ball beyond speech. He clutches the bottle, whimpering and emitting strange little sobs.)

AMY See, I have this long-standing um . . . fear of death? It's something you're born with. I used to sob in my father's arms when I was only . . . Oh, boy! See, once you start thinking about it, I mean . . . *really* thinking about it . . . You know, time going on for ever and ever and ever and ever and you're not there. . . . It can get pretty scary . . . ! We're not talking missing out on a few measly centuries here, but all . . . time! You know, dinosaurs, camel trains, cities, holy wars, boom! and back to dinosaurs again? *(More and more weepy.)* Eternity! . . . Camel trains, cities, holy wars, boom! Dinosaurs, camel trains, cities, holy wars, boom! . . . Dinosaurs, camel trains, cities, holy wars. . . . Stop it Amy. . . . just . . . *stop it!*

DR. ROSE   *(Broken.)* I can't open this bottle.

AMY   *(Wiping away her tears.)* Dr. Rose! What are you doing down there?

DR. ROSE   I've tried everything.

AMY   What's wrong?

DR. ROSE   *(Reaching the bottle up to her.)* I can't open it.

AMY   *(Taking it.)* Oh, here, let me try.

DR. ROSE   I'm afraid I'm having a breakdown.

AMY   I'm good at this kind of thing.

DR. ROSE   I don't know, for some time now I just haven't . . .

AMY   *(Puts the bottle in her mouth, clamps down on it with her back teeth, and unscrews the lid with one turn. She hands it back to him.)* Here you go.

DR. ROSE   *(Rises and advances toward her menacingly.)* You should never . . . *Never do that!*

AMY   *(Drawing back.)* What?

DR. ROSE   Open a bottle with your teeth.

AMY   I do it all the time.

DR. ROSE   Teeth are very fragile. They're not meant to be used as tools!

AMY   Sorry, sorry.

DR. ROSE   I just don't believe the way people mistreat them. We're only given one set of permanent teeth in a lifetime. *One set and that's it!*

AMY   I won't do it again. I promise.

DR. ROSE   Species flourish and disappear, only our teeth remain. Open, please. *(He puts cotton wadding in her mouth.)* You must respect them, take care of them. . . . Oh, why even bother talking about it; no one ever listens to me, anyway. Wider, please. *(He puts in more cotton and a bubbling saliva drain.)* Okay, let's fill this baby and get you on your way. *(He dabs in bits of compound.)* So, how's work these days?

AMY   Aarg . . .

DR. ROSE   Same old rat race, huh?

AMY   Aarg . . .

(During this, the final chorus, "Das Wort sie sollen lassen stahn" has started to play.)

AMY   *(Slightly garbled.)* What is that tune? It's so familiar.

DR. ROSE   "A Mighty Fortress Is Our God."

AMY   Right, right! I used to sing it in Sunday school a hundred years ago.

DR. ROSE   Actually, Bach stole the melody from Martin Luther.

AMY   *(Bursts into song, garbled, the sa-*
liva drain bubbling.) "A Mighty
Fortress Is Our God . . ."

AMY . . . a bulwark never fail- ing . . . Our helper he amid the flood Of mortal ills prevailing. For still our ancient foe, Doth seek to work us woe . . .	DR. ROSE *(Joining her.)* . . . *Und kein' Dank dazu haben,* *Er ist bei uns wehl auf dem Plan* *Mit seinem Geist und Gaben.* *Nehmen sie uns den Leib,* *Gut, Ehr, Kind und Weib. . . .*

(Their voices swell louder and louder.)

Blackout.

GARRISON KEILLOR

Prodigal Son

Sunny piano.

NARRATOR   A happy day, a sunny street, you're young and in love and life is good and you're on your way to lunch, when suddenly a cold shadow falls and *(Loathsome laugh.)* you feel a cold slimy hand touch your face. *(Worse laugh.)* And it's your own hand. *(Worst laugh.)* That's evil. Where does evil come from? Whose fault is it? The American Council of Remorse— a nonprofit organization working for greater contrition on the part of people who do terrible things—brings you: The Prodigal Son.

(Theme.)

DAD   I run a feed-lot operation here in Judea, fattening feeder calves for the Jerusalem market, in partnership with my two sons: my prodigal son, Wally, and my older son, Dwight. One morning about two years ago, I came down to breakfast and—no Wally. Morning, Dwight.

DWIGHT   *(Sitting at table, reading newspaper.)* Morning.

DAD   You see your brother this morning?

DWIGHT   In bed.

DAD   I promised Harry Shepherd I'd be over to his place by seven-thirty. He's got a lost sheep out on the mountain wild and steep.

DWIGHT   Says here that fatted calves are down one and three-quarter shekels on the Damascus market, Dad. Makes me wonder if maybe *lean* calves wouldn't have a higher profit margin, and then we could spend more time in the vineyard— Dad, are you listening to me?

DAD   I'm worried about your brother.

DWIGHT   We can't afford to stand still, Dad. Look at the Stewarts— they're buying up land left and right! You've got to move ahead or you lose ground. . . .

WALLY   (*Thickly.*) Morning, Dad. Morning, Dwight. (*He sits down, groans, puts his head in his hands.*)

DAD   You look a little peaked, son.

WALLY   I donno—it's some kind of morning sickness, Dad. I feel real good at night and then I wake up and hurt all over.

DWIGHT   I noticed a couple empty wineskins behind the fig tree this morning.

WALLY   I dropped them and they spilled! Honest!

DAD   Where were you taking them?

WALLY   I was putting them outside! Wine's got to breathe, you know. And so do I, Dad. I've got a real breathing problem here. I'm worried about my health, Dad. I read an article the other day in *Assyrian Digest* that says bad feelings may be environmental. I donno. Maybe I need to get away for a while, Dad. Get my head straight. Work out some things.

DAD   Well, if that's how you feel, I guess I . . .

WALLY   I was thinking I'd sort of take my share of the farm and head for a far country for a while until I get back on my feet, headwise, and then come back a brand-new guy.

DWIGHT   Dad, could we discuss this?

(*Theme.*)

NARRATOR   And not many days after, the younger son gathered his inheritance together, and took his journey into a far country. . . .

WALLY   (*Walking.*)

I'm walkin' . . . to a far-out land.
I'm talkin' . . . got cash in hand.
I'm hot now . . . don't you understand. (*Yokel voices offstage.*)

You're lookin' at a brand-new man.

(*Foolish virgins enter, harnessed together, led by a wise virgin.*)

Hey! Who's this?
Hey. What's shakin', babes?

WISE   I'm taking these five foolish virgins home, mister. We were supposed to be at a wedding an hour ago, but they're low on oil. You see an oil station that way?

WALLY   Hey, they don't look foolish to me. They look like kinda fun people. Tell you what, they can come with me. I'll buy them oil. My treat.

WISE   Sorry, mister. I've got to look after these virgins myself. They take a lot of supervision. You gotta watch 'em pretty close so they don't bunch up and walk up each other's backs.

(*Crash.*)

WALLY   Whoops—dropped your lamp, huh? Good thing it *didn't* have oil in it.

Well, 'bye! Don't do anything I wouldn't do.

We're movin' . . . down the ole highway.
We're improvin' . . . every day.
We're groovin' . . . and we're okay.

NARRATOR   And he took his journey into a far country, and there wasted his substance in riotous living. . . . *(Enter LOOSE COMPANIONS, dancing, drinking, feasting, whooping. BIMBO on WALLY's arm.)*

WALLY   Take it off! Take it all off! Go for it! Put it on and take it off again! *(To audience.)* Hey, you Pharisees, loosen up—

(To pianist.) Hey, you know "Hey, Judea"?

BIMBO   You're such a wonderful, vital person.

WALLY   *(To "Hey Jude.")*

Hey, Judea—you're a real great place.
You're the best spot in the Bi-i-i-ible. . . .
You're right there by Canaan and Galilee,
You're family, you're tribal.

Hey, publican! Another round of wine for my pals! Put it on my tab! Phhhh! Blaaaaghhhhh! What is this??? Lite wine?

PUBLICAN   You don't like it?

WALLY   Give it to some virgins—and bring me your best.

PUBLICAN   I'll give you a jar to take with you—it's closing time. Time to lock up, Mr. Wally.

WALLY   Hey! I'll pay. Let's party!

BIMBO   Oh, Wally! You're so joyful! So many persons with a farm background, they don't know how to let go and have a good time.

WALLY   Not me, Wanda! Life is a feast if you know where to find it.

PUBLICAN   Here's your bill, Mr. Wally.

BIMBO   That's so beautiful: "Life is a feast." So many people—they place such restrictions on themselves. *(He reads bill, page after page, then searches his pockets and brings out a few coins.)* You have a better sense of who you are. You have that rare quality of trusting yourself. Believing in festivity, not negativity. In a smile, not denial. Sure, rules are good for people who need 'em. But you prefer freedom. You have this tremendous—this great— It's not a structured thing. You know? Your energy is so focused. Like a locust.

WALLY   That's the last of my money. That's all I have left. Amazing.

PUBLICAN   You all right? You need a ride home?

WALLY   No.

BIMBO   Wally—listen. It's been great. Three of the best weeks of my life. Bye.

(The BIMBO, the PUBLICAN, and the LOOSE COMPANIONS leave, one by one.)

NARRATOR   And when he had spent all, there arose across a mighty famine in that land, and he began to be in want. And he went and lived with a farmer who sent him into his fields to feed swine.

FARMER   You ever feed swine before?

WALLY   No, but I fed calves. You just dump the husks and swill down in front of them, right?

FARMER   Lot more to it than that. Usually we require swine feeders to have at least four years of professional experience. But tell you what—I'll put you in my internship program.

WALLY   What does it pay?

FARMER   Pay! I'm offering you a chance to learn the swine business from the mud up.

WALLY   So, you mean I'll sleep out here and eat with the pigs?

FARMER   You want it or not?

WALLY   Fine. Just want to get it clear in my own mind, that's all. C'mon, hogs. Sooo-eyyy! C'mon. C'mon, piggy, piggy, piggy.

NARRATOR   And when he came to himself, he said:

WALLY   How many hired servants of my father's have bread enough and to spare, and I perish with hunger! I will arise and go to my father, and will say unto him: "Father, I have sinned against heaven and before thee, and am no more worthy to be called thy son: make me as one of thy hired servants."

No, that doesn't sound good.

I will arise and go to my father and will say unto him, "Father, it was a great learning experience, and now I'm back, looking for an entry-level position— No. I will arise and go to my father and will say unto him, "Hi, Dad, how you been? Oh, I'm fine. Had a good trip. Say, you got anything to eat around here?"

NARRATOR   And he arose and came to his father.

WALLY   I'm ruined . . . I lost my goods.
　　　　So I'm goin' back to my roots.

SAMARITAN   (Enters and latches on to him.) Here, let me help you!

WALLY   Hey! Let go!

SAMARITAN   Easy. Everything's going to be all right. I'll bind up your wounds here—

WALLY   I don't have any wounds! Let go!

SAMARITAN   Easy.

WALLY   Let go!

SAMARITAN   You sure I can't help?

WALLY   Yes! Let go!

SAMARITAN   Sure you're okay?

WALLY   Yes! Let go.

SAMARITAN   Okay. 'Bye. *(He leaves, reluctantly.)*

WALLY   Boy, sometimes those Samaritans won't take no for an answer.

NARRATOR   And when he was yet a great way off, his father saw him, and had compassion on him, and ran, and fell on his neck, and kissed him. . . .

DAD   Wally! Son! Oh, Wally! *(He shouts offstage.)* Bring some clothes! And a ring! And some shoes! And not those running shoes! The dress shoes! And make that two rings!

(Offstage clamor.)

WALLY   I spent all the money, Dad.

DAD   And bring the fatted calf—let's eat and be merry! My son who was dead is alive again; he was lost and now he is found. Amazing!

WALLY   Mind if I invite some friends too?

(The FOOLISH VIRGINS enter, roped together.)

I met them on the road. They're okay people once you get to know them.

DAD   More rings! More shoes! Another fatted calf! You look good. You look like you've lost weight.

WALLY   I've been on a high-husk diet.

DAD   Dwight! Look who's here! It's Wally!

DWIGHT   *(Enters reluctantly.)* Hi. Nice to see you. *(His DAD turns to WALLY, and DWIGHT shakes both his fists and sticks out his tongue and makes a vulgar gesture.)*

DAD   We're having veal tonight, Dwight! Wally's home.

WALLY   I'm going to go get some of that calf, Dad. Be right back.

DWIGHT   Dad, I don't want this to sound negative in any way, but—how many years have I been working here?

DAD   All your life.

DWIGHT   Have I ever disobeyed you, Dad?

DAD   Never.

DWIGHT   And have you ever given *me* a fatted calf and thrown a big party for me and *my* friends?

DAD   No, but, son—

DWIGHT   But the minute this *bozo* comes hoofing it home—this leaker—

DAD   But your brother was dead and he's alive again! He was lost and now he's found!

DWIGHT   I don't think you're hearing what I'm saying, Dad. You never ran up to me and hugged me— I'd just like to point that out.

DAD   I'm not a hugger, I guess.

WALLY   *(Enters, mouth full.)* Have some calf, you guys. That fat won't keep, you know. Sure is good fatted calf, Dad. Sure beats husks. *(Off.)* Care for another piece, you virgins?

DWIGHT   Ever stop to think who *fatted* that calf, Wally? That was our best calf,

Dad. The *best* one. *(The others slowly leave, talking among themselves.)* Try to think how I feel. I'm hoeing corn all day, come in bone-tired, there's my brother smelling of pig manure, and they got the beer on ice and *my calf* on the barbecue! And MY RING on his hand! *My ring!* You promised it to me, but oh no—can't give it to the son who's worked his tail off for thirty years, oh no, gotta give it to the weasel who comes dragging his butt in the door— Oh great— Wonderful, Dad. Terrific.

Maybe I'll go sleep with the pigs, seeing as you go for that. See ya later, Wally. Help yourself to the rest of my stuff—clothes, jewels, shekels, just take what you want. Take my room. Don't worry about me. I'll be in the pigpen.

(He leaves. Offstage sounds: A stove being kicked, muttered curses, pots and pans being thrown, dishes broken.)

ADRIENNE KENNEDY

She Talks to Beethoven

CHARACTERS

BEETHOVEN
SUZANNE ALEXANDER   Writer.

SETTING

Accra, Ghana; 1961 soon after independence; early evening.

Interior of a bedroom at a house on the campus at Legon, a shuttered room,
a ceiling fan, a bed covered with mosquito netting, a shelf of books over a
small writing table, and a delicate blue phonograph. All windows except
one are shuttered. That window overlooks a winding road. The side of the
room that is shuttered is dim. SUZANNE ALEXANDER listens to a small radio.
She is American, black, a pretty woman in her thirties; part of her arm and
shoulder are wrapped or bandaged in gauze. Placed on a shelf opposite her
bed are a group of X-ray slides, the kind doctors use to analyze a patient's
illness. She studies them, watches the road, and listlessly writes a line or so
in a notebook. On the shelf is a photograph of Kwame Nkrumah, a book
on LUDWIG VAN BEETHOVEN, a wedding photo of SUZANNE and her
husband, David, and a mural displaying various scenes of Ghana's
independence. SUZANNE is dressed in a robe of kinte cloth.

From outside, Ghanains playing stringed musical instruments (as they walk in evening
procession).

SUZANNE   (Reads over notes from published diaries.) "The production of Fidelio
was anticipated by months of increasing tension as the war with Napoleon
escalated. Soldiers were quartered in all suburbs. At nine o'clock houses

were locked and all inns cleared out. At Ulm on twentieth October the Russians conceded defeat to the French. Ten days later, Bernadotte and the French army entered Salzburg. One saw baggage and travel carriages passing. In the afternoon I went with Th(erese) to the Danube. We saw the possessions of the court (being shipped off). . . . The court is sending everything away, even bed warmers and shoe trees. It looks as if they have no intention of ever coming back to Vienna. *Wednesday the Sixth.* After lunch, Eppinger came with the devastating news that the Russians have retreated as far as St. Polten. Vienna is in great danger of being swept over by marauding Chasseurs. . . ." (SUZANNE *suddenly turns to the radio.*)

VOICE ON THE RADIO   I came into this world with the desire to give order to things: My one great hope was to be of the world, and I discovered I was only an object among other objects. Sealed into that crushing objecthood, I turned beseechingly to others. Their attention was a liberation endowing me once more with an agility that I had thought lost. But just as I reached the other side, I stumbled, and the movements, the attitudes, the glances of the others fixed me there. I burst apart. Now the fragments have been put together by another self.

ANOTHER VOICE ON THE RADIO   And that was David Alexander, the American professor of African poetry, here at the University . . . reading from Frantz Fanon. Mr. Alexander is still missing. Alexander travelled with Fanon in Blida. His wife, also American, the writer Suzanne Alexander, is recovering from an unspecified illness. It is known she was writing a play about Ludwig van Beethoven when she was stricken. Alexander was by her side at the hospital when he suddenly vanished two nights ago. Mrs. Alexander has returned to their home on the campus at Legon near Accra.

(Musical passage of African stringed instruments.)

SUZANNE   *(Reading from diaries.)* "The final rehearsal was on May twenty-second, but the promised new overture was still in the pen of the creator. The orchestra was called to rehearsal in the morning of the performance. Beethoven did not come. After waiting a long time, we drove to his lodgings to bring him, but he lay in bed, sleeping soundly. Beside him stood a goblet with wine and a biscuit in it . . . the sheets of the overture scattered on the floor and bed. A burnt-out candle showed he had worked far into the night."

(The room appears out of the darkness. SUZANNE *rises and crosses to* BEETHOVEN *and stands staring at him.)*

RADIO   Although the couple are American, they have lived in West Africa for a number of years and together started a newspaper that was a forerunner to *Black Orpheus*, bringing together poems, stories, and novels by African writers as well as Afro-Americans, some in exile in England. It is known that often Alexander jests with his wife about her continued deep love for European artists, such as Sibelius, Chopin, and Beethoven, and indeed, if anyone in Accra wanted to hear these composers, one had only to pass the windows of the delightful white stucco houses among the flowers on the campus at Legon.

(SUZANNE stares at BEETHOVEN.)

SUZANNE   *(Reading her notes from diary of—)* "Beethoven was the most celebrated of the living composers in Vienna. The neglect of his person which he exhibited gave him a somewhat wild appearance. His features were strong and prominent; his eye was full of rude energy; his hair, which neither comb nor scissors seem to have visited for years, overshadows his broad brow in a quantity and confusion to which only the snakes round a Gorgon's head offer a parallel."

SUZANNE   You worked into the night.

BEETHOVEN   Yes. Tonight is the opening of *Fidelio*.

SUZANNE   Did I awaken you?

BEETHOVEN   I was dreaming of my mother and how every year on St. Magdalene's day, her name and birthday we would celebrate. The music stands would be brought out. And chairs would be placed everywhere and a canopy set up in the room where the portrait of my grandfather hung. We decorated the canopy with flowers, laurel branches, and foliage. Early in the evening my mother retired. And by ten o'clock everyone would be ready. The tuning up would begin, and my mother would be awakened. She would then dress and be led in and seated in a beautifully decorated chair under the canopy. At that very moment magnificent music would strike up, resounding throughout the neighborhood. And when the music ended, a meal was served, and company ate and drank and danced until the celebration came to an end.

(Loud voices from outside.)

BEETHOVEN   That must be the directors of the theater for the new overture. It's not finished.

(He starts toward the door, vanishes.)

SUZANNE   Wait. I want to talk to you. Before David disappeared, he questioned me on passages I wrote about you in Vienna.

(She looks at drawings BEETHOVEN has in his room and sheet music on the floor. Suddenly she runs back to the open window, watching the road for her husband . . . a long passage of the African stringed music from the procession on the road.
BEETHOVEN returns and sits at the piano, composing. He seems to have forgotten SUZANNE. She continues looking out of the window, listening to the African stringed

music, watching the road for her husband, David. The music now changes into the overture BEETHOVEN *is composing.)*

RADIO   Has Alexander been murdered?

SUZANNE   I've been unable to work. David helps me with all the scenes about you.

BEETHOVEN   Perhaps you might seek a retreat in the woods, Suzanne. It makes me happy to wander among herbs and trees.

(He continues composing music.)

SUZANNE   Tell me about your summers in Vienna. . . . I have read life in Vienna during the hot months was not pleasant.

BEETHOVEN   Yes, like tonight here in Accra, it was not pleasant; there were over a thousand horse-drawn cabs and over three hundred coaches of hire traveling across granite cobbles. They raised a terrible dust, which hovered in the air the whole summer and even during part of the winter. It was like a dirty fog. I went to Baden and worked on a symphony. *(Music.)*

SUZANNE   And your fame? I must ask you, are you happy with your fame?

BEETHOVEN   I do not like or have anything to do with people who refused to believe in me when I had not yet achieved fame. My three string quartets were all finished before fame came.

(He composes.
She returns to the window.
He composes
music.)

SUZANNE   *(Reads from diary of—)* "While he was working, he would stand at the washbasin and pour great pitchersful of water over his hands, at the same time howling the whole gamut of the scale, ascending and descending; then pace the room, his eyes fixed in a stare, jot down a few notes and again return to his water, pouring and howling. . . ."

(Music from Fidelio.*)*

BEETHOVEN   You've argued about me?

SUZANNE   Yes. David says many scenes of you are too romantic, that I must read new diaries about you. He gave me one by a baron about this very room.

*(*SUZANNE *reads to* BEETHOVEN.*)*

"I wended my way to the unapproachable composer's home, and at the door it struck me that I had chosen the day ill, for, having to make an official visit thereafter, I was wearing the everyday habiliments of the council of state. To make matters worse, his lodging was next the city wall, and as Napoléon had ordered its destruction, blasts had just been set off under his windows."

RADIO   Has David Alexander been murdered? The outspoken professor at the University of Legon is still missing. As we have reported, Alexander worked with Fanon in Blida and was friends with the late Patrice Lumumba. Now that Fanon may be dying of cancer, Alexander has become highly vocal in keeping Fanon's words alive. We've played you his rendering of Fanon's essays, and now we listen to David Alexander's poetry. It has never been clear, Alexander has said on many occasions, who the enemies of Fanon are, and even though Ghana has won its independence, as Osegefo also continues to remind us: There are still enemies. Alexander was hated by many for his work in the clinics with Fanon and for his statements on the mental condition of the colonized patients. At first it was thought that when Alexander disappeared, he was working with one of the patients at the hospital at Legon, but now it has been revealed he was there waiting to hear the results of his wife's undisclosed surgery. And was indeed by her bedside and disappeared while she slept after surgery. The Alexanders are an inseparable couple who often read their works together and have written a series of poems and essays jointly. It has been learned that at the hospital, while sitting at his wife's side, Alexander made sketches of his wife's illness and explained the progress and surgery procedures to her. *(Music. Passage that BEETHOVEN is composing.)*

(From outside, voices are heard shouting "Karl Karl Karl." BEETHOVEN rushes from the room. SUZANNE stands at the window.
Music from the road.
Voices shouting, "Karl." BEETHOVEN enters.)

BEETHOVEN   My nephew Karl has tried to shoot himself. He's wounded. He's been taken to his mother's house.

SUZANNE   We'll go there.

BEETHOVEN   No, I can't. He told the police he was tormented by me and that is why he tried to kill himself and he does not want to see me. He says he's miserable and he's grown worse because I want him to live his life according to my expectation of him.

(Music.)

SUZANNE   *(Writes in her manuscript.)* "Beethoven's nephew Karl tried to shoot himself; the tension between the two had reached a crisis. The incident left Beethoven in a shocked state. He was the only person Beethoven really loved. To the point of idolatry."

RADIO   And again . . . Alexander . . . reading Fanon . . . still missing . . . where . . . has he been murdered?

SUZANNE   We could still walk to Karl's house near the Danube and look into his window. Perhaps you can call to him.

(Light in room fades.
Now they are walking near the Danube. They look up at what could be Karl's windows.)

(Music.)

BEETHOVEN   *(Shouts.)* Karl Karl Karl.
BEETHOVEN   *(Calls again.)* Karl. *(Silence.)*
BEETHOVEN   We've come far, Suzanne. We won't get back to Dobling until nearly four now.

(Music.)

SUZANNE   *(Writing.)* His nephew refused to see him. We did not get back to Dobling, where Beethoven lived, until seven. As we walked, he started humming, sometimes howling, singing indefinite notes. A theme for the last part of the overture has occurred to me, he said.

(Room appears again. BEETHOVEN enters, running to the pianoforte.)

(Music.)

RADIO   *(Again, David Alexander reading Fanon.)* "Yesterday awakening to the world I saw the sky utterly and wholly. I wanted to rise but fell paralyzed. Without responsibility, nothingness and infinitely I began to weep."

(Music. BEETHOVEN composes.)

SUZANNE   *(Reads from the diary of—)* "Beethoven misunderstood me very often and had to use the utmost concentration when I was speaking, to get my meaning. That, of course, embarrassed and disturbed me very much. It disturbed him, too, and this led him to speak more of himself and very loudly. He told me a lot about his life and about Vienna. He was venomous and embittered. He raged about everything and was dissatisfied with everything, and he cursed Austria and Vienna in particular. He spoke quickly and with great vivacity. He often banged his fist on the piano and made such a noise that it echoed around the room." *(SUZANNE writes while talking to BEETHOVEN.)*
SUZANNE   You must dress now for the opera.
BEETHOVEN   Please go to the theater with me.
SUZANNE   I must watch the road for David.
BEETHOVEN   We'll stay together until David arrives. We'll watch the road and go to the theater together.
RADIO   An hour ago there was an accident near Kumasi that seemed to have

some connection to Alexander, but now that has been discounted. It is now believed that David Alexander, learning of a plot against his life while he sat at his wife's bedside, chose to vanish to protect her, his colleague and fellow writer. Professor Alexander still continues to speak about attaining true independence. So now it is believed he is alive and waiting for the time when he can return home. Included in the next selection are two poems read by the couple together from their recording. The first selection is by Diop.

BEETHOVEN   Is it true that David made drawings of your surgery as he sat by your side so that you would not be frightened?

SUZANNE   Yes.

BEETHOVEN   How very romantic. And do you believe that he vanished to protect you?

SUZANNE   Yes.

BEETHOVEN   And you compose poems and read together?

SUZANNE   Yes.

BEETHOVEN   What scenes did you fight over?

SUZANNE   He wanted a scene where you read your contracts, a scene where you talk about money.

(BEETHOVEN laughs.)

BEETHOVEN   Do you disagree a great deal about your work together?

SUZANNE   No, only over this play. We set out to write it together years ago; then it became mine. Even on the morning of the surgery we argued about it.

(He laughs.)

BEETHOVEN   I feel David will return by morning, perhaps on the road with the musicians, perhaps even in disguise.

SUZANNE   Disguise.

BEETHOVEN   Yes.

RADIO   A body has been found in a swamp in Abijan. Is it Alexander? Has he been murdered?

(SUZANNE begins to unwrap her bandages.)

BEETHOVEN   Why do you unwrap the gauze?

SUZANNE   The bandage is wrapped on my wound. I'm to unwrap it tonight, and if the wound is pale white, I'm still sick.

(BEETHOVEN starts to help her slowly unwrap the gauze.
She does not look at her surgical wound as he unwraps.)

SUZANNE   What color?

BEETHOVEN   The color is pale white.

(Silence.)

How long have you been sick?

SUZANNE   Two and one-half years?

BEETHOVEN   You mustn't worry. I've foreseen my death many times. It will be in winter. In Vienna. My friends will come from Graz.

(He embraces her.
SUZANNE sits at BEETHOVEN's piano. He walks to the window. She reads from the diary of—)

SUZANNE   "Before Beethoven's death I found him greatly disturbed and jaundiced all over his body. A frightful choleric attack had threatened his life in the preceding night. Trembling and shivering, he bent double because of the pains which raged in his liver and intestines, and his feet, hitherto moderately inflamed, were tremendously swollen. From this time on dropsy developed; the liver showed plain indication of hard nodules, there was an increase of jaundice. The disease moved onward with gigantic strides. Already in the third week, there came incidents of noctural suffocation."

(Radio.)

VOICE ON RADIO   *(A recording of Alexander reading David Diop.)*
"Listen comrades of the struggling centuries
To the keen clamour of the negro from Africa to the
Americas they have killed Mamba
As they killed the seven of Martinsville
or the Madagascan down there in the pale light of the prisons. . . ."

(Room fades.)

(They are backstage, BEETHOVEN is dressed formally for the theater.
Music from stage, orchestra rehearsing Fidelio. *They both watch the road.)*

SUZANNE   You must be happy tonight about *Fidelio.* *(He does not speak.)*
BEETHOVEN   Suzanne, because of your anguish I want to share a secret with you. For the last six years I have been afflicted with an incurable complaint. From year to year my hopes of being cured have gradually been shattered, and finally I have been forced to accept the prospect of a permanant infirmity. I am obliged to live in solitude. If I try to ignore my infirmity, I am cruelly reminded of it. Yet I cannot bring myself to say to people, "Speak up, shout, for I am deaf."

(Music from stage, orchestra rehearsing Fidelio.)*

In the theater I have to place myself quite close to the orchestra in order to understand what the actor is saying, and at a distance I cannot hear the high notes of instruments or voices. As for the spoken voice, it is surprising that some people have never noticed my deafness; but since I have always been liable to fits of absentmindedness, they attribute my hardness of hearing to that. Sometimes, too, I can scarcely hear a person who speaks softly; I can hear sounds, it is true, but cannot make out the words. But if anyone shouts, I can't bear it. I beg you not to say anything about my condition to anyone. I am only telling you this as a secret. Suzanne, if my trouble persists, may I visit you next spring?

SUZANNE   I had no idea you were going deaf.

BEETHOVEN   Yes, in fact you must write any further questions in this little conversation book. I've been trying to hide them from you.

(He gives her the conversation books.)

BEETHOVEN   You must write what you want to say to me in them. I cannot hear you.

SUZANNE   Ludwig! *(She embraces him.)*

RADIO   *(Alexander reading from Fanon.)* "At the level of individuals violence is a cleansing force, it frees a man from despair and inaction."

RADIO   *(Interrupts.)* It has been learned that the group who plotted to kill David Alexander has been discovered near Kumasi and has been arrested. It is safe for Alexander to return to Accra. And it is reported that Nkrumah himself met with the revolutionary poet a few hours ago and reported to him the details of his would-be assassins' capture.

SUZANNE   *(Suddenly.)* Ludwig, why is David's handwriting in your conversation books? This poem is in David's own handwriting.

(BEETHOVEN does not answer.)

(SUZANNE studies the conversation books.) Ludwig! There is a message from David. The love poems of Senghn. Whenever he wants to send me a message, he puts a poem inside my papers, in a book he knows I will read.

(Music, orchestra practicing Fidelio. She writes in conversation book and reads.)

"Be not astonished, my love, if at times my song grows dark
If I change my melodious reed for the khalam and the tama's beat
And the green smell of the ricefields for galloping rumble of the tabalas.
Listen to the threats of old sorcerers, to the thundering wrath of God!
Ah, maybe tomorrow the purple voice of your song-maker will be silent
    forever
That's why today my song is so urgent and my fingers bleed on my
    khalam."

(She opens another conversation book.
Music from the stage.)

SUZANNE   *(She reads David's words.)* "Suzanne, please continue writing scenes. Please continue writing scenes we talked about."

(Lights fade backstage.
Lights come up on concert hall.)

256 / Adrienne Kennedy

(BEETHOVEN now goes before orchestra stage center. He waves baton wildly. It is obvious he does not hear.
Music stops.
He starts again. He waves wildly, throwing the singers and orchestra off beat and into confusion.
Silence.
He calls SUZANNE to his side. She writes something in the book. BEETHOVEN buries his face and rushes to the wings, leaving the orchestra.
SUZANNE writes.)

SUZANNE   "Ludwig was still desperately trying to conduct in public and insisted upon conducting rehearsals even though by now, during the concert, the orchestra knew to ignore his beat and to follow instead the Kapellmeister, who stood behind him."

(BEETHOVEN returns stage center; as she speaks, BEETHOVEN conducts music.)

SUZANNE   "At *Fidelio* Ludwig waved his baton back and forth with violent motions, not hearing a note. If he thought it should be piano, he crouched down almost under the podium, and if he wanted faster, he jumped up with strange gestures, uttering strange sounds. Yet the evening was a triumph."

(SUZANNE stands at window, writing. A shadow appears on the road.)

SUZANNE   David! *(The deaf BEETHOVEN turns to her, smiles, conducting violently. Music.)*

SUZANNE   *(From the diary of—)* "As for the musical success of this memorable evening, it could be favorably compared to any event ever presented in that venerable theater. Alas! the man to whom all this honor was addressed could hear none of it, for when at the end of the performance the audience broke into enthusiastic applause, he remained standing with his back to them. Then it was [the contralto soloist] had the presence of mind to turn the master toward the proscenium and show him the cheering throng throwing their hats into the air and waving their handkerchiefs. He acknowledged his gratitude with a bow. This set off an almost unprecedented volley of jubilant applause that went on and on as the joyful listeners sought to express their thanks for the pleasure they had just been granted."

(Concert scene fades.)

(BEETHOVEN's room: SUZANNE stands in the center, staring at BEETHOVEN's grand piano, his chair, manuscript paper.)

SUZANNE   *(From the diary of—)* "Monday the twenty-sixth of March 1827 was a freezing day. From Silesia and the Sudeten peaks, a north wind blew across the Wienerwald. Everywhere the ground lay under a soft blanket of fresh, silent snow. The long winter had been 'raw, damp, cold, and frosty'; on that day it showed no sign of releasing its grip on the land.

"By four o'clock the lights of Vienna, the street lamps, the candles of a myriad rooms, began to pierce the overcast gloom. On the second floor of the Schwarzspanierhaus, the House of the Black Spaniard to the west of the old city walls, lay a man who had all but run his course. In a large, sparsely furnished room of 'sad appearance,' amid squalor and books and manuscript paper and within sight of his prized mahogany Broadwood grand, Beethoven lost hold of life. On a roughly made bed, unconscious, he was at that moment as broken and finished as his piano. The elements continued to rage. Flurries of snow drifted against the window. Then 'there was suddenly a loud clap of thunder accompanied by a bolt of lightning . . . Beethoven opened his eyes, raised his right hand, and, his fist clenched, looked upward for several seconds. . . . As he let his hand sink down onto the bed again, his eyes half-closed. . . . There was no more breathing, no more heartbeat! The great composer's spirit had fled from this world.' So remembered Anselm Huttenbrenner, recording Beethoven's end even more poignantly in the terseness of a diary entry: 'Ludwig van Beethoven's death, in the evening, towards six o'clock, of dropsy in his fifty-seventh year. He is no longer!' "

(She cries.
Sound at the door.
Music, from the road, of African
stringed instruments.
She rushes to the door.)

SUZANNE   David. You sent Beethoven until you returned. Didn't you?
DAVID'S VOICE   *(Not unlike* BEETHOVEN's.*)* I knew he would console you while I was absent.

HARRY KONDOLEON

Linda Her

CHARACTERS

CAROL
MATT
JANET
HILARY

SETTING

The bedroom of a summer house.

TIME

Late summer, the middle of the night.

Center there is a double bed, four pillows, tangled sheets, and Matt, a man in boxer shorts sleeping facedown, some sheet tangled about him. Sitting up is Carol in a shift-like nightgown. There is a white comforter, tangled, draped, half-thrown at the end of the bed.

Upstage of the bed there is a table and on it a medium-large electrical fan with four steel petals spinning with a minimum of racket.

On either side of the slightly askew bed (it is placed almost diagonally) are two, tall white Greek columns.

Barefeet. Moonlight.

CAROL Matt? Wake up, I can't sleep.
MATT (Still half asleep, sitting up only slightly.) What's wrong?

CAROL   The girl you told me about. I can't stop thinking about her.

MATT   What girl?

CAROL   Linda Her. Tell me about her again.

MATT   We were children together. Moved away and something or other happened and now she's gone. Good night. *(His head falls down to sleep again.)*

CAROL   Who told you she died?

MATT   *(Head still down.)* Someone in the post office. *(Slight pause.)*

CAROL   You're not sorry I invited Janet here, are you? We really don't have that much in common. Do you like her, Janet? Matt? Matt.

MATT   *(Muffled voice.)* What?

CAROL   Do you like Janet?

MATT   Yes.

CAROL   But she's no Linda Her. You said everyone loved her.

MATT   Don't tell me you're jealous of a girl I admired in kindergarten.

CAROL   Don't be an ass! *(Slight pause.)* It's just that I picture her so clearly. This very beautiful, bright girl, who everyone likes, with her whole life ahead of her and then one day many years later boom you find out she doesn't exist anymore—isn't that scary? Matt? *(Slight pause.)* Are you sick of me? I'm sick of me. *(Slight pause.)* Matt, can we go home early? I really can't stand it anymore. Let's go home or just away. What do you say? Can we leave in the morning? Matt.

MATT   We only have a week left.

CAROL   That's too much. Say we'll leave tomorrow. Hilary wants to leave, too. I can tell. Matt? Matt? I'm afraid. Matt.

(Enter Janet, a woman in a knee-length white nightgown.)

JANET   Hi.

CAROL   Janet.

JANET   I felt so good I couldn't sleep.

CAROL   I'm glad you're up. I couldn't either and I want to talk and the log I married won't. Come sit by me. Not too close, it's unearthly hot.

JANET   It's not too bad.

CAROL   And you're glad you came for the week?

JANET   Entirely glad.

CAROL   *(Asking truly.)* Do you hate anything, Janet, does anything make you not glad?

JANET   What?

CAROL   Run away with me. I mean it! Remember in junior high school when our fathers once wouldn't let us stay out until one hundred o'clock or whatever it was and we swore to run away? We were going to leave our awful existences behind and join high society. Or low society. Do you remember?

JANET   I don't remember running away.

CAROL   No, that's just it, we never did. Now's the time. I feel it so urgently. We'll take your car and share the driving. I have my passport with me. *(Slight pause.)*

JANET   What did you think of the way I stuffed the tomatoes?

CAROL   Why are you ignoring me, don't you think I'm serious? I'm dead serious, I assure you. I've been thinking about that little girl who was the idol of Matt's elementary school and now she's dead. *(Slight pause.)*

JANET   Run away where? From what? From whom? To go do what? Leave Matt and Hilary? Is that what you're saying, Carol? What time is it?— crazy-chit-chat time?

CAROL   No, you don't remember running away, how could you? I remember now. You were the one who talked us out of going.

JANET   You're really serious. How do you find the nerve to sit two inches from your husband, a man who in my opinion is the nicest guy on earth, and talk of running away from him?

CAROL   He can't even hear me. See? Matt! Matt! *(She slaps his behind.)*

MATT   *(Startled.)* What?!

CAROL   Matt, Janet wants to know what you thought of the way she stuffed the tomatoes.

MATT   The best ever. *(He falls back, facedown, to sleep. Enter HILARY, also in sleep attire, barefoot, no more than ten years old. She combs her own hair repetitiously, tirelessly.)*

CAROL   Oh, Hilary, hurray, you're here, too!—and you've brought your comb. Couldn't you sleep? Do you see, Hilary knows there is no peace in this world. And Hilary, if you're going to stand there getting the benefits of the fan, stand slightly to one side so Janet and I can feel it, too.

JANET   I'm fine.

CAROL   That's right, I keep forgetting. Hilary, wake up your father and tell him you want to go back a week early.

HILARY   No.

CAROL   Hilary, a little girl has died, a little girl has grown up and died.

JANET   Carol, have you lost your mind?! To talk to a child that way!

CAROL   You underrate Hilary, Janet, I promise you. Hilary understands mortality better than you or I, don't you, Hilary?

JANET   I don't recognize you.

CAROL   No, you don't. You don't recognize me because you don't really know me.

JANET   That's a *very* peculiar thing to say to a person who's been your best friend since the seventh grade!

CAROL   Do you remember how we became friends, Janet? You brought me sandwiches. Every day. I thought to myself, why is this girl bringing me sandwiches? Well, maybe she's a lesbian, that's cool. *(HILARY laughs briefly.)*

JANET   Carol!

CAROL   I didn't know yet that that was your method with everything, courtship by nourishment. Even this week you've worked so hard to make yourself indispensable—is that what you do at your office, it's a wonder they can stand you—why doesn't this woman just give herself a vacation, I thought to myself!

JANET   Hilary, go back to your room and I'll make you a paper fan you can use in bed and I'll bring it to you.

CAROL   Hilary's not going anywhere. Once she finds a spot she likes, she sticks to it like a curse.

JANET   So why are we friends, Carol?

CAROL   I've asked myself that.

JANET   Why, then, the phone calls every second or third week? You call me.

CAROL   Well, the way I see it, it gets harder and harder to get rid of things, to just get rid of them. Take this summer cottage, for example, in the middle of nowhere with outlets that don't work—why won't Matt just sell it? Hilary hates it, don't you, Hills? Why?—because Matty was a *boy* here, running back and forth and in circles and it all brings back memories or something and that as we get older I suppose is enough reason not to throw something away.

JANET   And I remind you of your girlhood.

CAROL   I thought you did, but sitting here now, in this light, I must say you remind me of nothing or, worse maybe still, of myself without hope.

JANET   Hope for what?—I'm not sure I want to know—I'm more interested in why this summer you bothered to invite me for a whole week—wasn't your conscience or curiosity free after a ten-minute call?

CAROL   The truth? You started complaining about not having a man-friend or being married or having a child and I felt sorry for you—I did, I'm not saying this maliciously, I felt so sorry for you, you made your life sound so pitiful.

JANET   Well, thank you very, very much!

CAROL   So I thought I'd invite you out here and you'd have a great time, and the really odd thing is you have. You have had nothing but fun. You've gotten along with Matt, whose idea of a vacation is uninterrupted sleep and even with Miss Hilary of the Damned. It's remarkable how well you've fit in.

JANET   You're exaggerating to make me feel self-conscious, your specialty, I might say, since we're taking this time to be so honest.

CAROL   Right. Hilary, tell me what you think of Janet, evaluate her for us. Come on, don't be shy. Hilary is at the top of her class. She reads faster than anyone you or I have ever met, and more impressive still, she can sum up the book—any book—in two or three sentences. Hilary, evaluate Janet.

HILARY   (*No enthusiasm, matter-of-fact.*) She keeps her room tidy and makes her bed right after getting out of it. She pushes her food with a small chunk of bread, which she eats at the end of every meal. She doesn't like sweets but doesn't frown on those who do.

CAROL   More.

HILARY   Her cookies, which she says she made up the recipe to, are the best I've ever eaten.

CAROL   Bravo! *(To JANET.)* There, you see?

JANET   It's none of my business, but if you were nicer to her, I think she would respond to you more.

CAROL   Oh, Janet, you're so dense, you don't read anything for what it is, you're always on the wrong page or something. Hilary, tell Janet what you think of me. Go on, tell her.

HILARY   *(After a pause.)* You're not a phony.

CAROL   You see, there it is. Hilary is a sort of fortune cookie in reverse. *I'm not a phony.* Well, thank you, Hilary, but did you know how sometimes, more than anything, I just wish I were a phony, just one big phony, and then all my problems would be solved!

JANET   I think you should go to sleep.

CAROL   I can't sleep! Isn't that obvious, Janet? I cannot sleep and I cannot rest or relax or take my mind off X, Y or Z and now, in the middle of all *this*, I am confronted with *her*.

JANET   Who?

CAROL   Her. *Her.* Linda Her.

JANET   The girl who died? What, mortality?—everyone's going to die one day. To dwell on it, Carol, is just downbeat.

CAROL   Naturally. Hilary, say something upbeat about mortality to cheer us up.

HILARY   At the science fair in school Mrs. Hoffman fell down the stairs and had to get a cast on her foot, so now when she goes up or down steps she counts them out loud.

CAROL   I can always depend on Hilary for the good news. How vividly I see Mrs. Hoffman taking her fall and from that day on counting her every step. Mrs. Hoffman must know that life is a slippery stairwell.

JANET   I can be gratuitously morbid, too, and say that there's nothing ahead of us but repetitions of old bad days, but I wouldn't believe it!

CAROL   I would.

JANET   Well, then, I have no hope for you! No hope and no kind words!

CAROL   Thank you, that's what I thought. Why don't you stay here, Janet?

JANET   What?

CAROL   You understood exactly what I meant. Stay here with Matt and Hilary.

JANET   The week?

CAROL   Forever. Forever and ever and then a week after that. For good.

JANET   I'm going back to my room.

CAROL   No—stay here and I'll leave.

JANET Hilary, go to your bed.

HILARY No.

CAROL Hilary combs her hair like that all day to hypnotize herself into a state of conformity so she can *excel* and when she graduates from business school her real personality will pop out and she'll bite the heads off of executives like so many chicken heads, won't you, Hilary?

HILARY Maybe.

JANET Would you like me to call a doctor?

CAROL Not unless you feel sick. Do you see, Janet, this is your chance of a lifetime, take it. You say you haven't the knack of meeting men and that family life is both alluring and elusive; here it is, table set. You don't mind Hilary—she's really no less friendly to you than anyone else. My theory on why there are children is so that the minute you finish growing up—you know, that whole period where you feel excluded from everything—they show up to exclude you again.

JANET Is it possible you've become so hard-hearted as to say such horrific things in front of a child!

CAROL First of all, Janet, and you know this as well as I do, Hilary is Matt's child, not mine. And as far as the horrific goes, with Hilary I couldn't hope to compete. Tell Janet, Hilary, what you told me, tell her. *(Slight pause.)* I order you to tell her!

HILARY I think how I have to work very hard in school and get excellent grades so I can become very powerful one day and punish all the people who ever bothered me.

CAROL She saw on one of those talk shows that are on all day a woman who used to be some kind of movie star and became a makeup tycoon and said her whole motivation in life was getting back at people who had mistreated her as a child. So you see, Janet, Hilary's someone you can really work with —and she loves your sandwiches.

JANET Who's bothered you, Hilary, tell me.

CAROL And you do like Matt, you have a real rapport with him, admit it. Admit it. Admit it, Janet.

JANET It's true I find his work interesting.

CAROL Interesting? I have often thought it would be more interesting to be dead than to do what Matt does, but he gets paid so much I feel like a hypocrite when I put it down.

JANET You shouldn't do that.

CAROL I agree with you but I can't help it and he says he doesn't mind but deep down of course he must.

JANET He's not attracted to me.

CAROL I don't think it matters a damn anymore, attraction. It's something you see beyond or into or impose an image on or you just get to a place where you're past caring.

JANET   It's no surprise you're depressed, Carol, when you reduce everything down like that. I may be pathetic but I'm not dead. There's something dead about you.

CAROL   Yes, I know. I'm sure I'd be happier if I could find a plainer, more adaptable self, someone more like you, Janet.

JANET   Even if I were to stay here while you took a vacation—a vacation from I-don't-know-what since your life has always resembled a vacation to me —even if I were to consider something so crazy, how would—

CAROL   You're not getting me, Janet. Listen, then, to Matt. *(She shakes MATT awake.)* Matt, what do I always say about Janet?

MATT   Nothing.

CAROL   There it is, Janet, from the mouth of sleep: I say nothing about you. When we're not talking on the telephone you don't exist for me—why should I for you? Stay here the week and then move into the apartment after that. Cut what dresses you don't like hanging in the closet into square pieces and use them to dust—you like to dust—dust with them.

JANET   In the ninth grade, because it suited your self-image as editor to have some underling there to underline everything you had to say, you let me on the literary magazine even though I couldn't write or draw. But guess what, Carol? You couldn't write or draw, either.

CAROL   That's so true. But you were such a blank, Janet, when I stood next to you I felt exciting and complicated. Now you know.

JANET   In other words you'd take off, just like that.

CAROL   In other words, yes.

JANET   And what about me? I'm supposed to just leave my life behind as if it were a . . . a footprint or something?

CAROL   What will you be leaving behind? Your telephone? You already know my number. Now it's yours. You like to stuff tomatoes, Janet, stuff tomatoes, peppers, eggplants, the empty pots on the porch, the car, the twelve months of the year, stuff everything.

JANET   Very funny. You've always made me feel a little bit tatty and out of the joke, haven't you?

CAROL   Yes.

JANET   And you haven't been a very good friend to me, really at all, after all.

CAROL   No, I suppose I haven't, I'm sorry.

JANET   So, what now?

CAROL   I'll open the door and walk outside of it.

JANET   In your nightgown?

CAROL   Probably. I'll walk along the road until a car passes and picks me up and maybe not the first car or the second car but surely by the third one I'll have found a new life, another ready-made, maybe, and I'll drive to that.

JANET   Is this all because of that little girl, Linda?

CAROL   I don't feel sorry for her. When you're a star like that in kindergarten there's no place left to climb. Hilary, do you want to say something to me? *(Slight pause.)*

JANET   What should I tell Matt?

CAROL   Tell him the place we had lunch today used pancake batter as salad dressing. Tell him I'm looking for a good restaurant. Tell him I've dyed my hair and gone back to kindergarten. Tell him I couldn't sleep. Goodbye. *(CAROL exits. HILARY, frightened, cries. MATT wakes up.)*

MATT   Are you crying, Hilary?

HILARY   No.

MATT   I didn't think so, not such a smart girl like you. Can't you sleep, sweetheart? Come sit by me and I'll tell you a little story.

HILARY   A scary one?

MATT   When I was your age, Hilary, and in school, there was a little girl named Linda Her, and she was the prettiest girl in the whole school.

HILARY   Like me.

MATT   Yes, Hilary, as pretty as you. And she was the smartest, too.

HILARY   But not smarter than me.

MATT   No. And whenever a little boy had a birthday party he would invite Linda, even though these parties were for all boys and she would be the only girl because she was so popular.

HILARY   Then what happened?

MATT   Well, then, my mother—your grandma—moved away and I went to another school and then I went away to yet another school where I met your Mommy and then lots of other things happened and here we are.

HILARY   And Linda?

MATT   She died just like everyone's going to die one day, only sooner. Now, Hilary, that's not a scary story, is it?

HILARY   Mrs. Hoffman at the science fair said that it's cold on the moon.

MATT   When you're an old woman, Hilary, you're going to think back and ask yourself why couldn't I let my father sleep.

HILARY   But I'm afraid.

MATT   I've told you there's nothing to be afraid of. Now just put your head on the pillow and close your eyes and then you'll be asleep. Janet, what are you doing there?

JANET   Nothing, just thinking.

ARTHUR KOPIT

Success

At rise, we see a banquet room in a hotel, lectern downstage center, two chairs downstage right.

At the rear, huge windows. Beyond, an iridescent blue sky. Because of this blazing light, at the moment, the objects on stage are in silhouette.

Beyond the windows, sound of surf can be heard.

Lights come up on the podium, as—

Two people enter from the wings. One is MRS. HOFFENSBERG, *stout, in her sixties at least. In one hand she clutches a book. Her other arm is linked through an arm of* ELIOT ELIZALDE KRUM, *a man of about forty, wearing a wrinkled raincoat.*

Applause greets their entrance. On hearing it, HOFFENSBERG *looks at the audience, then proudly at* KRUM, *smiles, and guides him to one of the two chairs downstage right. He takes off his raincoat, sits, folds the coat neatly across his lap, and stares out with an expression of some alarm—an alarm that grows by the moment.*

HOFFENSBERG *goes to the podium and adjusts some notes she has brought with her. Then she clears her throat and smiles to the assembled throng. Sound of applause is heard again. This time,* KRUM *applauds, too, though only slightly, as if it were merely an imitative action of no meaning by itself.*

HOFFENSBERG   I had the great honor of meeting Eliot Krum two weeks ago at San Francisco State College where he was delivering a . . .

(Her words grow indistinct. The sound of the surf returns.)

(Over this sound, the sound of thunderous applause at whatever MRS. HOFFENSBERG *is now saying. Presently, the sound of applause grows distant; then it and the sound of surf disappear.)*

I found Mr. Krum at that time to be a man of both subtle . . .

(And again her words disappear behind the sound of surf. MRS. HOFFENSBERG *holds up her book and, smiling, glances toward* KRUM. *Then, looking back to her audience, opens the book to its last page, looks soberly out at her audience, then back at the book, and reads what is obviously to her a very moving last paragraph.)*

/ 267

(Finished, she closes the book and looks up at the audience. Not a sound. Not a movement. Then . . . applause.)

(MRS. HOFFENSBERG looks over at KRUM, who does not move. Apparently, she has just introduced him.)

(She says his name again. This time, it is barely audible.
Then it comes through louder. He stirs. He has recognized the sound of his name. She smiles at him and he rises. As he does, she says—
"Eliot Krum!" Wild applause as KRUM assumes the lectern, spreads out his notes, arranges them, then looks over his audience. Smiles. Clears his throat. Opens his mouth.)

(Nothing.)

(Closes his mouth.)

(Frowning, he reaches for a glass of water. Takes a sip. Puts down the glass. Ponders. Opens his mouth. Studies his audience for clues. Finds none.)

KRUM   Would someone be so kind . . . as to tell me . . . what . . . city . . . this is?

(Laughter.)

VARIOUS WOMEN   *(Together.)* Santa Monica!
KRUM   Santa Monica! Well, well—

(Laughter from audience.)

And what . . . *organization* . . . might this be?

(Louder laughter, wild applause.)

HOFFENSBERG   *(To the audience, laughing.)* Mr. Krum has been in such recent demand on the lecture circuit that it seems he no longer knows whereof he speaks!

(Laughter and applause.)

KRUM   Actually, it doesn't really matter. No one seems surprised that I'm here, so apparently I'm in the right place.

(Again, more laughter and applause. He shuffles his notes.)

. . . I thought I'd just ramble on a bit this afternoon, explore a few areas suggested by my book, then open up the floor to relevant and exciting questions, if that meets with the approval of you ladies and— *(He peers around his audience for men; finds one.)* . . . gentleman. First, however, I'd like to thank my gracious host, the lovely Miss, umm—
HOFFENSBERG   *(Sotto voce.)* Mrs.
KRUM   Mrs., ummm—

HOFFENSBERG Hoffensberg.

KRUM Hoffensberg, yes, for bringing me to this delightful spot, wherever it is, and . . . all of *you*, . . . whoever . . . you are. Indeed, had I not had the great fortune to meet Mrs., uh . . . let me write that down.

HOFFENSBERG Hoffensberg.

KRUM "Hoffensberg." Indeed, had I not had the great fortune to meet Mrs.— *(He glances at his note.)*—Hoffensberg some . . . while ago at . . . some . . . place or other, who knows where I'd be today? *(Pause.)* To Mrs. . . . H then, my heartfelt thanks and solid reassurance that in the scrapbook of my mind, she will live forever. Certainly, I shall always cherish the memory of our first conversation. As I recall, immediately, upon taking me aside, she unbuttoned her blouse—

HOFFENSBERG *What? (Long pause.)*

KRUM Ladies, . . . as the former president of a well-known West Coast university once aptly said—sometime, I believe, in the sixties: "It appears I am no longer in possession of my faculties." . . .

Now, I am not particularly *pleased* with this condition. Nor, obviously, are you. Certainly, when you invited me here today, as a leading literary light, you surely did not expect to find the light quite so flickering, if not dim. How has it come about, this dismal state? Well, frankly, it's none of your business.

Nonetheless, I will tell you, it has definitely not been helped by my recent madcap schedule, set up at the behest of my fiendish publisher, a relentlessly charming man, whom I shall try my very best to strangle the next time we meet. You see, for the past several months—six, seven, eight, who can say?—it seems I have been doing nothing but going from one strange place to another talking about this goddamn book of mine—a book I could hardly bear when I was writing, so imagine how I like it now! Which is why, today, I thought I would discuss football. *(He clears his throat.)* Football, as I see it, is one of our most— *(Pause.)* . . . Or is it? *(Pause.)* No! It's not at all, *not at all!* Why would I think it *was? Question! Yes!* No? Thought I saw a hand, clutching, upwards. Ladies, for God's sake, I will give you back my fee, assuming you had planned to give me one, but let me out of this! It is an embarrassment to us all! . . . Except, of course, to Mrs. H, who's shown herself to be beyond embarrassment and whose bizarre bosom has, these last few weeks, played such a vital role in the continuation of my thought processes.

HOFFENSBERG *What?*

KRUM Sorry. Slipped out. Didn't mean to mention it. Forget I ever said a word. So, what shall we talk about? *My book!* Yes. Why not? Ladies, in all candor, the extraordinary popular success of my book has not only taken me completely by surprise, but apparently has taken my mind along with it. Surely, ladies, *surely*, an eight-hundred-and-fifty-page book about suicide— *(He has a sudden and terrible coughing fit; reaches for some water; gains control; takes out a pill, pops it in his mouth, sips some water, puts the glass back down.)* —about . . . suicide . . . would not seem, at first glance, a likely candidate for the best-seller list. And yet!—unless there is some enormous and rather peculiar hoax going on—there it is! Top o' the list! Thirty-fourth straight week! And I am rich. And getting laid like crazy. Mind you, not that sex means that much to me, but in my seven years as a rabbi in Bridgeport and my three as a priest in New Rochelle, I would say I got laid no more than ten, twelve times maximum, and that includes four nuns and a mother superior I ravaged on my last official day, which, as those of you who've read my little volume know, was the first day of Lent, yes, question.

WOMAN IN AUDIENCE   Do you really expect us to sit here and listen to this crap?

KRUM   I'm sorry, I am *very sorry*, but I have not come all this way just to be insulted! To continue. After serving my three years as a priest in a mostly Jewish neighborhood, right on the heels of having served seven as a rabbi in a mostly Catholic, I made the first of my many suicide attempts. Ate seventeen of Mrs. Smith's jumbo apple pies, followed by twelve Sarah Lee pound cakes. When this failed to finish me, I became a psychiatrist. In Mamaroneck.

SAME WOMAN   Mr. Krum!

KRUM   *Question!*

SAME WOMAN   You don't seem to understand: we have all *read* your book. Which means we *know* your background. And your background is *not this*.

KRUM   . . . It's not?

SAME WOMAN   No.

(Silence.)

KRUM   Are you . . . sure we're talking about . . . the *same book*?

SAME WOMAN   *The Gods of War*, by E. E. Krum.

KRUM   Or *"Eeeek,"* as they used to call me in kindergarten!

SAME WOMAN   This *is* your book, then.

KRUM   Definitely. But please, feel free to keep it. To continue! As a psychiatrist, in Mamaroneck—

SAME WOMAN   *Mr. Krum!*

KRUM   Heavens, you're a pest.

SAME WOMAN   According to this book, you never were a rabbi. Never a priest. And never a psychiatrist.

KRUM   *Just what are you trying to say?*

(Pause.)

SAME WOMAN   That . . . you never were a rabbi. Never a priest. And never a psychiatrist.

KRUM   I see. *(Pause.)* Well, this is certainly a very startling piece of news.
SAME WOMAN   To us, especially.
KRUM   Was I a . . . *baseball* player?
SAME WOMAN   No. Sorry.
KRUM   Dentist?
SAME WOMAN   Perhaps you should read your book.
KRUM   What, eight hundred pages, about suicide? You must think I'm mad!
SAME WOMAN   Mr. Krum, frankly, I was very moved by your book. It is really
    a most astonishing account of a man's constant battle against despair.
KRUM   Sounds amusing.
SAME WOMAN   It isn't.
KRUM   Was it illustrated?
SAME WOMAN   Not *my* copy.
KRUM   Well, why'd you read it, then?

(Silence.)

Why'd *any* of you read it?

(Silence.)

I don't understand this. Have you all nothing better to do with your time?

(Silence.)

All right, come now, truthfully, game's over. How many of you actually
read it, raise your hands. Let's go. Hands. Hands. *(He looks at what would
appear to be a sea of hands.)* Well, this makes no sense. No sense at all. And
it's been the same everywhere. *What are you people doing?* I'd *never* buy a
book like that. It's the most lugubrious thing imaginable. You should be
home, fucking. Not reading. You'll ruin your eyes! You wanna go blind?
What's wrong with you people? *I can't take this anymore!* Yes. Question.
Sorry. Thought you had a question. Oh, God, this isn't right, isn't right.
I'm fading, fading . . . *(Pause.)* Fading . . . *(Very long pause.)* Faded.
(Pause.) Ladies . . . Gentleman. Forgive me. But I find I just can't speak
any more today.

(He turns, goes to one of the windows, and opens it.)

*(Sound of surf.
He leaps.)*

*(Lights to original position, with only the iridescent sky lit, all else in silhouette. No
movement.)*

                    Blackout.

CAROL S. LASHOF

Medusa's Tale

CHARACTERS

MEDUSA *A gorgon.*
PERSEUS *A hero.*
POSEIDON *A god.*
ATHENA *A goddess.*
A GIRL

SETTING

The Mediterranean.

TIME

The Mythic Past.

Beneath the opening music, we hear the low murmur of men's voices and the clatter of metal cutlery and plates, which rise in volume until they drown out the music. PERSEUS bangs on the table for attention; as he speaks, the other voices gradually subside.

PERSEUS Listen! *(Pause.)* In this leather pouch is the severed head of Medusa, the gorgon known throughout Greece to be the most loathsome of creatures. Hideous vipers grow from her scalp. They are still alive and writhing, though she is dead. One glance at them and you would turn to stone. Many men perished trying to slay this monster. Then I came to the barren island where she lived in exile.

(A rising wind whistles through a desert landscape. Snakes hiss. MEDUSA *hums a jaunty love song—perhaps "Froggie Went a'Courting." We hear the sound of an armored man running and breathing heavily.)*

MEDUSA   Hey, you!

PERSEUS   What?

MEDUSA   Slow down. You'll catch up with your destiny whether you run or crawl.

PERSEUS   I am the hero Perseus, son of the great god Zeus.

MEDUSA   And I'm Medusa, cast out by gods and kings. You've come to slay me, I presume? *(Pause.)* Cat got your tongue? You warriors, you're all alike. Look at these fellows: civilized young men, from the very best families, but no appreciation whatsoever for the art of conversation. They do make handsome statues, though, don't they?

PERSEUS   It's true, then.

MEDUSA   Of course. Not a word to say, any of them, even when they were living flesh. Just brandish and brazen and then go to it.

PERSEUS   It's true that you turn people to stone just by looking at them?

MEDUSA   So they say.

PERSEUS   Evil monster, beware . . .

MEDUSA   Do I look like an evil monster? Tell me. I want to know.

PERSEUS   Don't think you can trick me into meeting your eyes. Athena has blessed me with wisdom. She has sent me to carry out her will.

MEDUSA   Athena! If you're her slave, then I'll gladly stop your blood dead in your veins.

PERSEUS   I am not her slave. I am her brother. She is the greatest goddess of them all, sprung fully armed from Zeus's noble brow. And I, too, am a child of the almighty Zeus, lord of the heavens.

MEDUSA   You and a few thousand other Greek bastards.

PERSEUS   I am the son of Zeus. Who but he could have slipped through the bars of that tower, a hundred feet high, where she was locked up, my mother. . . .

MEDUSA   And how did Zeus manage this fancy trick? Did he come as a mosquito and buzz in between the bars of her prison window? Did he impregnate her with a sting?

PERSEUS   Blasphemer! He came as a shower of gold.

MEDUSA   *(Pause. Astonished.)* Are you Danae's child? You can't be. She did have a son, but they were both drowned long ago, she and her baby.

PERSEUS   Did you know my mother?

MEDUSA   I knew Danae. *(Pause.)* We were girls together. She used to braid my hair while I told her stories of distant lands. She was hungry for knowledge. But then her father killed her.

PERSEUS   My mother told me we were rescued from the sea when I was a baby.

Carol S. Lashof / 273

MEDUSA   Is she alive? Is she all right?

PERSEUS   Yes. She's fine. She . . . she is the beloved of Zeus! Even now kings beg to marry her and she turns them down.

MEDUSA   But suppose they don't beg or even ask permission? What can she do, then?

PERSEUS   When I've cut off your head and can wield your power, no one will dare to touch her. I'll turn them all to stone if they so much as look at her.

MEDUSA   When you get angry, you knit your brows just the way Danae used to do. No! Don't turn away from me. Close your eyes. Let me look at you. You've got your mother's figure—long and slim.

PERSEUS   Don't touch me, hag! I don't believe you knew my mother. She would never have gone near such a monster as you.

MEDUSA   I was no monster, then. I was honored for my beauty. Poseidon himself was in love with me.

PERSEUS   Liar. Crone! I'll kill you for your evil lies.

MEDUSA   Kill me? You don't even dare to look at me.

PERSEUS   I can see your hateful image in my shield. Athena told me what I was to do.

MEDUSA   It's hard to fight with your back to death.

(MEDUSA laughs as PERSEUS's sword clangs against stone. The sounds of a scuffle ensue.)

Careful! Don't hack away at your fellow heroes. You'll just ruin your blade. Look! I'm right behind you. Oops. You missed. You can't hit a moving target with your eyes squeezed shut. Uh-oh. Watch out for that statue over there.

(There is a loud crash, and PERSEUS gasps in pain.)

All these dead heroes, they get in the way, cluttering up the landscape, falling on top of people.

PERSEUS   My sword!

MEDUSA   Don't worry. I've got it.

PERSEUS   Go ahead if you're going to kill me. One quick thrust will do it. *(Pause.)* What are you waiting for? *(Pause.)* Don't expect me to beg. Even in death I'm the son of Zeus.

MEDUSA   And of Danae. How long before she stops thinking you'll come running off the next boat bursting with pride? *(Pause.)* Swear by her name that you'll leave without trying to harm me and I'll let you go. Even if you are Athena's minion.

PERSEUS   Go? With no proof that I'm a hero? If I were content with that, I'd have stayed at home. I must prove that Danae has received the love of Zeus.

MEDUSA   Why? What good is the love of Zeus?

PERSEUS   I didn't come here to discuss theology. Kill me and be done.

MEDUSA But I want to discuss theology. Do you know what the love of the gods has done for me?

PERSEUS Everyone knows you were cursed by the gods for your crimes.

MEDUSA No one knows! *(Pause.)* If I set you free, will you listen to my story? Will you go home and tell Danae?

PERSEUS I'll never go home unless I can take your bloody head with me.

MEDUSA *(Pause.)* All right. If it has to be that way.

PERSEUS What are you doing? You're crushing my leg.

MEDUSA I'm trying to set you free. Are you going to help or just lie there? That's it. Push! There we go.

(PERSEUS breathes a loud sigh of relief.)

Can you stand on that leg?

PERSEUS Oww.

MEDUSA Well, you might as well sit down, anyway. Put your feet up. I want to tell you a bedtime story.

PERSEUS Where's my sword?

MEDUSA It's safe. You can have it back when the story's over. Listen closely so you may judge for yourself what the love of the gods is worth. Close your eyes. That's a good boy. Now we are in Athens. Look there. On the hill. Above the well. Glaring white against the blue horizon. Athena's sanctuary. See the columns. Tall and strong and straight. Like the goddess herself.

(We can hear water splashing, the creak of buckets being raised from a well, and the murmur of women's voices. An owl hoots.)

And there she is. The goddess of justice. Favorite daughter of Zeus.

(We hear the tread of inhumanly weighty steps. A sea gull cries raucously.)

And here comes Poseidon, Earthshaker. Brother of Zeus and Lord of the Ocean.

ATHENA Honored uncle, what brings you to my blessed city?

POSEIDON Just passing through. How's the olive business?

ATHENA Flourishing. Thanks to the olive tree, all the citizens of Athens enjoy my bounty.

POSEIDON And the women and slaves of Athens enjoy a mule's life.

ATHENA Slaves must drive the mill wheels so their masters may be free to keep the wheels of justice turning. In a just state, each man shoulders his proper burden.

POSEIDON To stand around in front of the courthouse arguing all day—is that the proper burden of a free man?

ATHENA I have given the Athenians the gifts of law and commerce—and they adore me for it.

POSEIDON   They're afraid of Zeus and his thunderbolts, that's all. If they snubbed you, it would make him angry.

ATHENA   You're jealous of the love these mortals bear for me.

POSEIDON   Love! You're far too icy-hearted to know anything about love.

ATHENA   Naturally, I disdain the appetites that drive mere beasts to grunt and thrash.

(Two girls are heard approaching from the distance, chattering and laughing.)

POSEIDON   Now here comes a truly lovable being. Who's she? The dark one with her hair down her back.

ATHENA   She? She's not half so pretty as the other.

POSEIDON   Ugh. I abhor your pale, sickly Athenian girls—their cheeks painted with lead—they look as if they were dying.

ATHENA   The dark one is Medusa. Her father is Phorcys, one of your minor deities, I believe. She's been conducting a faithful pilgrimage to all my temples. She blesses me for protecting her chastity, the wellspring of her freedom.

POSEIDON   Chastity! The emptiest of all the empty virtues.

ATHENA   She loves me with a girl's pure virtuous love.

POSEIDON   Ah, but if she knew the love of a real god . . .

ATHENA   She would spurn you. And your brutish love.

POSEIDON   Do you think so? Let me have just half an hour alone with her.

ATHENA   You may have half of all eternity. Nothing you can do could wrest her love from me.

POSEIDON . We'll see.

GIRL   I don't know what girls are like where you come from, but around here your father would beat you for talking to men in the street.

MEDUSA   My father's much too busy to worry about that sort of thing. He's responsible for the whole of the Aegean sea.

GIRL   Really? What does he do?

MEDUSA   Oh, everything. He manages all the riptides and whirlpools, tends to the undersea forests, stuff like that. When I was a little girl, he used to let me help him. Once I sunk a ship by mistake and I cried and cried, but he just laughed and got the men to shore somehow.

GIRL   I don't believe you really sunk a ship.

MEDUSA   Well, hardly anybody was drowned.

GIRL   Would you show me something?

MEDUSA   Actually . . . no, I can't. I never learned to do much of anything by myself. I just did what Father told me to. And when I got older, he didn't ask me to help him anymore.

GIRL   But he lets you go anywhere and talk to anyone?

MEDUSA   I haven't even seen him in months.

GIRL   But that's horrible. Who will arrange a marriage for you?

MEDUSA   I don't want to get married. At least not until I'm much older, maybe twenty-five or thirty.

GIRL   Nobody will want to marry you then. *(Pause. Whispering.)* Do you suppose the wedding night is fun?

MEDUSA   Probably not half so much fun as being courted.

GIRL   What's fun about that? The man looks you over, he asks your father about the dowry . . .

MEDUSA   I don't mean that part of it.

GIRL   What else is there?

MEDUSA   Oh, you know.

GIRL   Tell me . . .

MEDUSA   Well . . . say for instance, when a man catches your glance in the marketplace and you look away and then look back and he's smiling and you can almost feel his eyes on you.

GIRL   But I would be afraid to look at a man that way.

MEDUSA   Or suppose he pretends to notice that your hair comb is slipping and he buries his strong fingers in your locks and his breath warms your neck.

GIRL   I'd better go. I thought you were chaste or I would never have spoken to you.

MEDUSA   Of course I'm chaste. I'm as chaste as Diana or Athena. I don't want to be stuck like other girls, nursing babies and fetching water. Like that girl, what's-her-name? Chrysis. *(POSEIDON approaches, whistling a sea song.)*

GIRL   But if you're chaste . . . Oh!

MEDUSA   You needn't stand there gaping. It's only Poseidon.

GIRL   Only Poseidon!? Don't you know what they say about him? He's famous —infamous, I mean—for ravishing women. *(Pause.)* He's looking at us. Oh, dear. I think he's coming over here.

MEDUSA   Are you running home to your mother?

GIRL   You should run, too.

MEDUSA   Why? Athena will protect me.

GIRL   Look, he is coming over here.

MEDUSA   *(Calling.)* You forgot your pitcher.

POSEIDON   I hope that I haven't driven your friend away.

MEDUSA   We just met at the well. I don't even know her name.

POSEIDON   And what's your name?

MEDUSA   Medusa. I'm the daughter of Phorcys.

POSEIDON   Phorcys? How dare he make you fetch and carry like an ordinary girl.

MEDUSA   Who says he does?

POSEIDON   Not he? Then what man enthralls you?

MEDUSA   No man has ever enthralled me. *(Pause.)* I met this girl, Chrysis, on the way to the well and we got to talking. She was a young bride, and she was in a great hurry because she wanted to visit her mother. So, since I had nothing better to do, I said I'd fill her pitcher for her and meet her here.

POSEIDON   If she were my young bride, she wouldn't want her mother's arms.

MEDUSA   She was a very young bride. Fourteen at most.

POSEIDON   How old are you?

MEDUSA   Seventeen.

POSEIDON   Too old for a mother's caresses.

MEDUSA   I never knew my mother. She died when I was born.

POSEIDON   You're old enough to be a mother yourself.

MEDUSA   I don't want children. That's why I follow Athena.

POSEIDON   Do you know who I am?

MEDUSA   Of course. You're Poseidon. My father works for you.

POSEIDON   The land and the sea work for me. I command earthquakes and tidal waves.

(There is a great crashing and roaring of water, which rises to a crescendo and then abruptly ceases.)

Wouldn't you like to bear the child of a god?

MEDUSA   No.

POSEIDON   But it's gold laid up in the heavens!

MEDUSA   My friend Danae had a child by Zeus and her father killed her for it. An oracle told him that he'd be killed by his grandson. So he killed the baby and Danae, too, so she wouldn't produce any more sons. He tossed them both in a casket and shoved them out to sea. They must have drowned. Or starved.

POSEIDON   A god would never allow a son of his to come to harm. For all you know, Danae could be seated on a throne on the top of Mount Olympus . . . or lying at the bottom of the sea.

MEDUSA   *(On the verge of tears.)* Well, I can't wait for that girl Chrysis forever. If she's not here by sunset, she'll just have to shift for herself.

POSEIDON   Of course I could easily pay a visit to my brother Zeus and find out about Danae for you.

MEDUSA   Would you?

POSEIDON   For a price.

MEDUSA   Oh.

POSEIDON   Don't you care to know what's happened to your friend?

MEDUSA   What good would it do? I'm sure she's dead.

POSEIDON   All right, then. Be seeing you.

(Whistling, POSEIDON begins to walk away.)

MEDUSA   Wait! *(Pause. Almost a whisper.)* What is your price?

POSEIDON   To intercede on behalf of your friend? What would you give me?

MEDUSA   My hair. I'll cut off all my hair and give it to you. *(POSEIDON laughs.)*

Men always beg me for just one lock. They say they will keep it always, it will be their dearest treasure.

POSEIDON   You have a dearer treasure than your shiny hair. Have you given that away?

MEDUSA   I don't know what you mean.

POSEIDON   Don't you? I think you do. Don't run away!

MEDUSA   You're hurting me. Let me go!

POSEIDON   All I want is a kiss. Hmmm. Don't clench your teeth.

MEDUSA   Stop it! You promised to let me go.

POSEIDON   After a taste of your lips? What did you expect? If you didn't intend to be friendly, you should have run away long ago. Oww! So you bite, do you? Vixen! Oof! And kick, too? That's all right, I like a little spice in my stew. Go ahead. Run to Athena's sanctuary. It's a fine and private place.

(Gasping for breath, MEDUSA scuttles across the stone colonnade. The heavy doors of the temple creak.)

Let me get that door for you, my dear.

(MEDUSA and POSEIDON's voices echo inside the temple.)

MEDUSA   In Athena's name. Please. This is holy ground.

POSEIDON   *(Laughing.)* Wherever I am is holy ground.

MEDUSA   Athena! Please! Save me, Athena!

(POSEIDON laughs. MEDUSA screams. Then there is silence. Finally, we hear MEDUSA sobbing; POSEIDON, whistling, emerges onto the colonnade. The temple doors clang shut, muffling the sound of MEDUSA's sobs.)

POSEIDON   So, Athena, do you still claim the girl as yours? Such a fine creature. What a pity if she'd gone to her grave a virgin.

ATHENA   I didn't count on your brutalizing her within the walls of my own temple. It's an offense against all the gods.

POSEIDON   So run to Zeus, dear little Athena Brighteyes. I know you're his favorite. But even so, he won't punish me merely for taking godly liberties with a mortal girl.

ATHENA   But for profaning a temple . . .

POSEIDON   Who says it was profane? I say it was a holy sacrifice.

ATHENA   There'll be no harmony in the heavens till penance has been done!

POSEIDON   So punish the girl for taking refuge in your sanctuary. Am I to blame because she clung to the feet of your statue while I took her from behind? Hush. Here she is now. Ask her if she still adores you.

(MEDUSA approaches, weeping.)

Come, my dear, don't cry. There's no harm done.

MEDUSA   *(Strangling a scream.)* Stay away from me!

ATHENA Come to me, Medusa. We'll see he pays the proper price for what he's done. There. There. You're tattered and filthy. He's made a beast of you. Phew. You smell like rotting fish.

POSEIDON She smells salty and wet. Like an ocean breeze. What could be more enticing?

MEDUSA Hide me, Athena. Don't let him touch me, please.

POSEIDON That's right, Brighteyes, hide the girl behind your skirts. But you did nothing while we took our pleasure in the heart of your temple. You stood in the doorway and watched. And I'm sure it was a fine sight to see. Hmm?

(Silence.)

MEDUSA Answer him, Athena. Please! Tell me he's lying.

ATHENA What was I to do? Mix in a lustful brawl with Poseidon on the floor of my own temple? I leave such foolery to the likes of Cupid and Aphrodite.

MEDUSA But he raped me!

ATHENA You should have run away before it was too late. It's foolish pride for a mortal girl to have no fear of gods.

MEDUSA But I put my faith in you. *(Pause.)* Don't turn away from me!

ATHENA Can't you clean yourself up a little?

POSEIDON See, Medusa. Athena will have nothing more to do with you. Come, you'll live with me in my golden palace.

ATHENA Stay away from him. *(Pause.)* I'll take you home to your father.

MEDUSA Like this? No. He'd think I was a fool.

POSEIDON Her father won't dare to harbor her. Not if she's lost my favor. And no man will pay a bride's price now for her. I'm generous to take her.

ATHENA You're still lured to her, that's all. Like a dog to its vomit. If you go with him, Medusa, everyone will shun you.

POSEIDON On the contrary. Only as my concubine will she get any respect. *(Seductively.)* And if she's a sweet, tender girl and treats me as a god deserves, then I'll give her jewels and fine sons, and I'll make all my minions bow to her, even her father.

ATHENA You won't have her, Poseidon. No one will have her. Father Zeus. Thunderer. Give me the power to punish this sacrilege.

(There is a deafening crash of thunder, followed by a moment's silence. Then the air is filled with hissing. MEDUSA cries out in anguish.)

MEDUSA What have you done to me? My head's on fire!

ATHENA Zeus has struck you with his lightning. The pain will soon subside. But the vipers will remain, a warning to all vainglorious mortals. Come, look at your reflection. See the penance you have earned.

MEDUSA Poseidon, help me! Help me rip them out!

ATHENA You'll sooner tear your scalp out. And if you try to cut them off, they'll only grow again more hideous still.

POSEIDON Nothing could be more hideous. In all the wild sea I have never seen creatures so vile.

MEDUSA Will you turn from me, too, Poseidon? I was to be your queen.

POSEIDON Never my queen.

MEDUSA *(Almost choking on the words.)* Your concubine, then. I'll go with you. I'll learn to find pleasure in your touch. I'll bear your sons . . .

POSEIDON You would bear me monsters.

MEDUSA But look at me! You found me beautiful. See. My eyes are still bright, my lips still moist, my skin still smooth as cream.

ATHENA Listen to her hawking her wares like any street girl.

MEDUSA If you do not love me anymore, Poseidon, then pity me!

(We hear the tread of heavy steps, then the cry of a sea gull and the beating of wings.)

Don't leave me!

ATHENA Do you dare to turn to him, who ruined you, and beg for pity?

MEDUSA But you turned away from me.

ATHENA Yes. And now every creature on this earth will turn away from you. See those women, hurrying to be home by dark? The story of your infamy will soon be spread among them—and they will learn not to be so unafraid.

MEDUSA There's Chrysis. I was waiting for her. *(Shouting.)* Chrysis! Chrysis! Chrysis, don't look at me like that . . .

ATHENA Don't waste your breath. She'll stand there gaping for all eternity. And any other mortal who lacks the wisdom to turn his back on you or shut his eyes will also turn to stone.

MEDUSA Wait, don't leave me! I'm afraid to be alone. *(Music plays, punctuated by the hoot of an owl as it flaps away.)*

PERSEUS I never really wanted to come here. Let me go—before you cloud my wits completely.

MEDUSA Nobody's keeping you, my young hero. *(Pause.)* Just be careful of your leg—and watch out for the statuary. Here's your sword. You can use it as a cane. Good-bye! Give my regards to your mother. *(Pause.)* What's the matter? Can't you bear to leave me? Or have you forgotten something? Oh, yes, my head. You came for my head, didn't you? You said you couldn't go home without it.

PERSEUS When I was home, the women hissed at my mother on the street and called her names. The boys threw clods of dung at me. Then Athena came to me. She told me I was destined to be a hero. She told me how to find this desolate place. She said you would be asleep. I only had to avoid looking at you—and then I could easily kill you, she said. *(Pause.)* Did you know that she wears your image emblazoned on her armor? Your face is beautiful. The snakes are hideous, but your eyes, your mouth, more beautiful than any woman I've ever seen.

MEDUSA Kiss me. *(Pause.)* Close your eyes and kiss me. Don't worry. It's only looking at me that kills. *(Pause. They kiss.)* Thank you. I've never before been kissed in kindness.

PERSEUS When Athena came to me and called me brother, then I knew I really must be Zeus's son. Suppose you'd borne Poseidon's son, wouldn't you want him to grow up to be a hero?

MEDUSA Do you believe me, then?

PERSEUS I don't know. Athena is my guardian. I must believe in her.

MEDUSA She was my guardian, too. I loved her once.

PERSEUS *(Pleading.)* Athena is wise and just. She would not punish someone who was virtuous.

MEDUSA She failed me. And she punishes me for having seen her failure.

PERSEUS I must kill you. Or else I am nothing.

MEDUSA Yes, I know. But after you have killed me, then what? Will you go home to your mother? Will you tell her my story?

PERSEUS Yes. I'll tell her.

MEDUSA And what will you do with my head?

PERSEUS I'll put it in this leather pouch.

MEDUSA And if anyone makes trouble for you, you'll just whip out my snaky head and turn him into a statue?

PERSEUS I suppose so.

MEDUSA Of course you will. Then after you've made it home safely, leaving a few mute statues in your wake, what next?

PERSEUS I don't know. What difference does it make to you?

MEDUSA I just want to know how the story ends. *(Pause.)* I suppose word will get out quickly of your prowess as a statue maker, so you'll be given a hero's welcome wherever you go. And after your mother is comfortably settled, you'll marry a beautiful princess. Then one day you'll kill your grandfather.

PERSEUS My grandfather?

MEDUSA Yes. Don't you remember? The oracle said you would kill your grandfather, so, naturally, you will.

PERSEUS All right. So I'll kill my grandfather. He's nothing to me.

MEDUSA Even if he were everything to you, you would do it. It's all settled. You're doomed to be a hero.

PERSEUS Yes.

(MEDUSA hums "Froggie Went a'Courting"; PERSEUS's sword whistles through the air and with a thwack cuts off the humming. Silence. Music plays and rises to a scream, then fades into the sounds of a banquet hall where men are still laughing and talking.)

ROMULUS LINNEY

Can Can

CHARACTERS

EX-GI
YOUNG FRENCH WOMAN
AMERICAN HOUSEWIFE
COUNTRY WOMAN

SETTING

Nashville, Paris, Kitty Hawk, rural Kentucky.

TIME

The present and the past.

Four dark wooden stools, upstage and apart.
    Music: the famous Offenbach "Can-Can."
    Balls of light spin in darkness, then vanish as the music ends. Sudden light discovers four people standing by their wooden stools.

EX-GI   I won it in a Dusseldorf crap game! Nine hundred American dollars. Me! Got my leave and took off!

HOUSEWIFE   I went to the beach that day, threw baseballs at bottles, shot wooden ducks and won a bunny rabbit. With the rabbit came a meal ticket, at a country café, so I went there, too.

YOUNG WOMAN   It was the year I entered the Sorbonne. I studied so hard I won a prize and my grandmama tripled it so I had that summer *deux mille francs*, all my own!

COUNTRY WOMAN   The beach had chain swings, a loudspeaker playing can can music, and a shooting gallery with wooden ducks. I shot the ducks and won a prize. It was a bunny rabbit, and I took it with me to work at the café.

EX-GI   I tried Copenhagen first and caught cold. I went to London and couldn't relax. Tried Paris, and all that brandy made me sick. I said, "Oh, hell, I want to go to the beach!" So I took the mistral to the Riviera!

YOUNG WOMAN   I always knew what I would do in my life. Never marry. Be a scientist. Swim every day for my heart and have friends like Prokofiev for my soul. So I went to Avignon to visit my mama, swim, hear concerts, and watch plays in the Palace of the Popes.

HOUSEWIFE   Frenchy's Paris FrenchFry, this place was called. I had the catch of the day. The woman waiting on me saw my bunny rabbit and said, "Win that at the fair?" and I looked up, saying, "Yes," and felt, oh, I don't know, a little funny, she was so homely and countrified.

COUNTRY WOMAN   All by herself she was, sitting there like a doll in a shop, with that rabbit on her table. I took her order and said something and I saw she had a little line of sweat above her lips, like a mustache. Then she smiled at me, and I smiled back.

EX-GI   A buddy in K Company told me, go see Avignon if you can, the countryside looks like French painting, so I stopped off there to sit in the town square, and have a sit-tron press-say!

YOUNG WOMAN   I liked Americans. My friends did not, but I did. And that soldier, that day in the square at Avignon, I liked especially.

HOUSEWIFE   I came back to Frenchy's Fishfry the next day, and I saw her again, all hard work and business, and I said, "Hello. Remember me?"

COUNTRY WOMAN   "You won a rabbit," I said. "So did I. Yes, I remember you."

EX-GI   She looked like a Massachusetts tomboy! Wearing a U.S. lumberjack shirt, flaps out over blue jeans, but she was French, all right, formal a little, and my God, intelligent!

YOUNG WOMAN   He was very agreeable! He didn't talk very much, but when he did, he had good taste. He didn't know it, but he did.

HOUSEWIFE   I went back every day, and every day she waited on me, and I blushed, all the way up through the roots of my hair.

COUNTRY WOMAN   She was just a baby, thinking I was a game she wanted to play, but I saw different, and most near dropped the fried fish on the floor.

EX-GI   She asked me would I come swimming with her friends in a river under a Roman bridge. She was a student at the honest-to-God Sorbonne, studying marine biology. The sea, she said, the sea!

YOUNG WOMAN   So we swam with the others in the river under the Roman bridge, and when he saw me in my bikini, he was no longer interested in the others.

HOUSEWIFE   And what I meant to say was, I want you to touch me, I just do. I don't know why. I was eighteen years old.

COUNTRY WOMAN   It's her Mama, I said to myself. She don't have one, the poor child, but she said no, she had a Mama, that's not what she wanted at all.

EX-GI   We drank brandy that night under a bridge built by soldiers, centuries ago, and we talked, oh, soberly and sensibly.

YOUNG WOMAN   When he took me home, I shook hands with him like a man and said it had been a pleasure and what was he doing tomorrow?

HOUSEWIFE   All her teeth seemed broken. Lines cut everywhere into her face, There were scars on her arms, on the side of her throat, deep shadows made her eyes look hard. When I asked her why she looked like that—

COUNTRY WOMAN   I told her my life was like that, she was a child, was she coming back again tomorrow?

YOUNG WOMAN   And the next day my soldier watched me say good-bye to my mama, getting on the train for Venice to visit my grandmama, and when it moved, he was on it, too, and so then, zut! we ran through the cars like fools in a film, and then there I was with my soldier, never mind my grandmama.

EX-GI   Pale she was! With splotches of crimson high on her cheeks! Like a woman in the kind of painting my K Company buddy said I ought to see. She told me she was the daughter of a French aristocrat, descended from a field marshal of Napoléon, and I said sure, that's why you like soldiers!

COUNTRY WOMAN   I never let her drive me home or see where I lived. But we'd sit on the beach some when I got off work and commence jabbering then, one with the other, and a body couldn't stop.

HOUSEWIFE   I can talk to you! I can talk to you! Like to no one else, ever! Why is that? I'm not a little country-club fool anymore, not with you. Why is that?

(The YOUNG WOMAN moves her stool downstage.)

YOUNG WOMAN   It was my sister who was beautiful, not me. That is the way our mama knew it would be. One with the beauty, one with the brains. But my soldier, he told me Mama was wrong! I had both, and I did! For him, I did!

(The EX-GI moves his stool downstage next to hers.)

EX-GI   I got her off the train at Nice, where it was all fresh air and marble, the sunlight dazzling! hectic! dancing! like the way that GI felt!

YOUNG WOMAN   He took me to Nice, to the Bataille des Fleurs! He would beat me with flowers! I knew he had good taste!

EX-GI   Big floats in the streets at night, covered with flowers and beautiful French-Italian girls, and I mean big strong men slapping each other with tulips!

YOUNG WOMAN People passing in the night, singing and throwing confetti in your face, if they liked what they saw. He got us the last hotel room in Nice!

COUNTRY WOMAN There ain't nothing you can't say, not to me, if you want.

(The HOUSEWIFE moves her stool downstage.)

HOUSEWIFE I know that. It's like in church, in the choir, when I feel wonderful, when great feelings rise up inside me, can you understand that, the singing, all of us together, and she said—

(The COUNTRY WOMAN moves her stool downstage. They are all together now.)

COUNTRY WOMAN I sing like that, too, honey, sometimes. But not in church.

EX-GI Hotel des Anglais, for God's sake! Room with blood-red wallpaper paintings of roses big as cabbages!

YOUNG WOMAN He tore roses off the floats and brought them to me piled high in his arms!

EX-GI I tore roses all to pieces! I scattered them over all that ugly room! Rug, bed, and big old bathtub, which we jumped in together, and I said, "Why are you here, with me?"

YOUNG WOMAN You are my first man. I plan my life, and I picked you for that. As long as I live, I will never forget you. Now give me some soap and kiss me.

HOUSEWIFE Then on a Sunday, when I stood up to sing my solo, "Only A Rose Will Do," I saw somebody come in at the back of the church and oh, God! There she was, in that congregation, like some old black sheep with her broken teeth, watching me.

COUNTRY WOMAN In that spotless place, with the roses and the lilies smelling so sweet and all that perfume and fur pieces, well, I paid it no mind. You commenced to sing, and you were my flower then, my rose, my own.

EX-GI And I kissed her, all right! And the next evening we sailed from Nice over the sea she studied in school on a night boat to Corsica! Where she'd never been, which I'd hardly heard of!

YOUNG WOMAN Where we lived ensemble for a month, in little hotels, on the beaches!

EX-GI Under the Corsican sun, among the palm trees!

YOUNG WOMAN And the flies and the bad wine!

EX-GI And the beautiful cleansing sunsets and winds!

HOUSEWIFE And three months later, after my wedding, I stood there a bride, scatterbrained in taffeta and lace, thinking of nothing in the world but her, and God Almighty, there she came!

COUNTRY WOMAN Scared, not meaning to trouble her, not mad or anything, just having to come, not able to help myself, not right then.

HOUSEWIFE   In a cheap flower-print dress with a pink hat, preposterous, absurd, with dime-store white gloves and all her scars and broken teeth.

COUNTRY WOMAN   The boy you'd married was fixing to dance with you, so I did it proper as I knowed how. I handed you a bottle of whiskey for your wedding night and a silver spoon for your baby.

(For the first time, COUNTRY WOMAN and HOUSEWIFE look at each other.)

HOUSEWIFE   Thank you.

COUNTRY WOMAN   You're welcome.

HOUSEWIFE   Would you like some champagne?

COUNTRY WOMAN   No, I best go. You was just scared about getting married, that was why you done what you done to me, wasn't it. No need, honey. He looks like a fine young man.

HOUSEWIFE   Can I get you some cake?

COUNTRY WOMAN   No. I just want to shake hands with your husband and kiss you and go—

HOUSEWIFE   Some coffee, then?

COUNTRY WOMAN   And I did that and left her and didn't know where I was, not for the longest time.

EX-GI   Come on! Come on! You can do better than that! I'll race you back!

YOUNG WOMAN   All right, all right.

(She chokes, gasps. She presses her hand to her chest. For the first time, YOUNG WOMAN and EX-GI look at each other.)

EX-GI   Hey, now! What's the matter? You all right?

YOUNG WOMAN   Just—a moment—please.

(She smiles, but painfully gets her breath.)

I'm all right now. I just can't go that fast.

EX-GI   But you weren't running, or anything.

YOUNG WOMAN   No.

EX-GI   You got cramps, time of month, that it?

YOUNG WOMAN   No.

EX-GI   So what's the matter with you?

YOUNG WOMAN   *On dit maladie de coeur—tu comprends?*

EX-GI   Heart trouble?

YOUNG WOMAN   Yes, heart trouble. In my family, very spectacular! We live passionate youths, perform miracles, and then our hearts turn to rubber. We say we wore them out, for the great Nap-o-léon! Flap-flop, flap-flop! Flap flop. I will have surgery soon. They tell me I am not so bad as my father was, at this age. So.

EX-GI   He's dead, your father?

YOUNG WOMAN   At forty-one. His father thirty-eight. So, you see, I will live a long, long time.

(Pause.)

EX-GI   Really? This is the truth?

YOUNG WOMAN   *Oui, vraiment.*

HOUSEWIFE   "Who was *that?*" my groom said, laughing, and the hotel orchestra played, and I was swept out onto the ballroom dance floor, away from my mother and my father and my life as a child, to my husband and my children and the day I had to see you again.

COUNTRY WOMAN   Honey, are you sure?

HOUSEWIFE   Yes! Yes!

COUNTRY WOMAN   Best not.

HOUSEWIFE   We must! I'll die.

COUNTRY WOMAN   It'll hurt. You think you know but you don't.

HOUSEWIFE   I won't live! Please!

COUNTRY WOMAN   All right.

EX-GI   What kind of surgery?

YOUNG WOMAN   Open heart. *Le dernier cri.*

EX-GI   It's dangerous?

YOUNG WOMAN   *Bien sur.* You take a knife and go, whop—

(She slides a finger down her chest.)

—and pull it open and say, voilà, Monsieur le Coeur! A-ha-ha-ha! And then you do this and that to it, well, yes, dangerous. Are you sad for me?

EX-GI   Aw, shit, honey.

YOUNG WOMAN   *Oui, vraiment.* Aw, shit, honey.

EX-GI   Well, but what they do now! I mean, doctors do almost anything now, right!

YOUNG WOMAN   Almost.

EX-GI   You got a good doctor?

YOUNG WOMAN   The best.

EX-GI   Hospital?

YOUNG WOMAN   The biggest.

EX-GI   Well, great.

YOUNG WOMAN   So be my budi.

EX-GI   Your what?

YOUNG WOMAN   You know, like soldiers have. I like that, what you call each other. "Hey, boo-*dee.*" Like that.

EX-GI   Buddy.

YOUNG WOMAN   Yes, budi. Remember your old budi.

EX-GI   I will.

HOUSEWIFE   And that's what we did. On beach blankets, in the backseats of cars, through twelve years of motel bedrooms, married to Walter Richards and loving you.

COUNTRY WOMAN   We can stop.

HOUSEWIFE   No, never. We can never stop.

EX-GI   We said good-bye in the train station at Marseille, making jokes, flip and cheerful until we saw the train.

HOUSEWIFE   You came in the motel room without knocking.

YOUNG WOMAN   I was going to be a scientist and have friends like Prokofiev, but when I saw that awful train, zut! Tears!

COUNTRY WOMAN   I couldn't come no sooner.

EX-GI   My God, this is hard! I can't get my breath!

HOUSEWIFE   You're going to leave me!

YOUNG WOMAN   It's hard to breathe, yes. I'll never see you again!

COUNTRY WOMAN   I got to go. It's time.

EX-GI   I was so happy with you! I'll never see you again.

HOUSEWIFE   You can't! I won't let you!

YOUNG WOMAN   It's not in the head or the heart! It's in the stomach, like being beaten there!

COUNTRY WOMAN   Hush, now!

EX-GI   Will we live?

HOUSEWIFE   I will leave my husband! I will leave my children!

YOUNG WOMAN   I think so! I'm not sure!

COUNTRY WOMAN   You know you can't. I wouldn't let you.

EX-GI   You won't forget me?

HOUSEWIFE   I will live on the floor at your feet! I can't love anybody else!

YOUNG WOMAN   No, budi. I won't forget you! I can't!

COUNTRY WOMAN   You got to accept it. For me.

EX-GI   Good-bye.

(Pause. They turn from each other, and face out. Music: the beginning of the gentle waltz from Offenbach's Orpheus in the Underworld.*)*

HOUSEWIFE   All right. For you. Good-bye.

YOUNG WOMAN   My first man. Good-bye.

COUNTRY WOMAN   My little girl. Good-bye.

EX-GI   It was wonderful. You were wonderful.

HOUSEWIFE   For you, I accept. I don't care how it hurts.

YOUNG WOMAN   I'd do it again!

COUNTRY WOMAN   I don't care, neither! I'm glad, too!

(Lights fade, and the spinning balls of light revolve again, now outward, coming from behind them in a stream like time, sweeping them away from the past, into the future.)

EX-GI   You're the best! Best thing ever happened to me!

HOUSEWIFE   *(Simultaneous.)* Best thing ever happened to me!

YOUNG WOMAN *(Simultaneous.)* So are you! The best thing ever happened to me!

COUNTRY WOMAN *(Simultaneous.)* Best thing! *Best* thing!

(Facing out, they wave.)

EX-GI, HOUSEWIFE, YOUNG WOMAN and COUNTRY WOMAN It was wonderful! Good-bye! Wonderful! God bless you! I'll never forget you! Good-bye! Good-bye! Good-bye! God bless you! I'll never forget you! Good-bye! Good-bye!

(The Offenbach waltz swells up, the light goes out on them waving, and the flowing stream of light in the darkness takes them away from us.)

DAVID MAMET

A Life with No Joy in It

CHARACTERS

A   *A man in his mid-fifties.*
B   *A woman of around thirty.*

A   A teaspoon.
B   Is that a teaspoon?
A   Yes. It is.
B   A teaspoon. As if you would say a "*teas*-poon," but for *tea*.
A   Yes.
B   With hinged . . . with *hinges*.
A   Yes.
B   With *jaws*.
A   That open. Yes.
B   And is that where that phrase comes from?
A   Yes. Must be.
B   You think so? Yes?
A   . . . mmm.
B   That our modern *teas-poon* comes.
A   Yes.
B   From a "spoon." Of course, that must be the thing. Then do we resist it?
A   You said "New York"?
B   Like the one we had there.
A   You remembered it there?
B   . . . we had one . . .
A   Yes. *(Pause.)* You remembered it. *(Pause.)*
B   Is it odd that I remembered it?
A   It was so long ago.

B No.

A "Not to *you* . . ."?

B No. Not to me. No. What?

A It was so long ago. Darling. You were so young.

B I, wasn't that you.

A That's what you're saying. No.

B I wasn't that young.

A Yes. I see that. *(Pause.)* I see that. *(Pause.)* Yes. *(Pause.)* Aha. Do you know. As you live, more and more, as you step back from it, you can see more of, if not the *order*, at least, of the *pattern*. Do you think? But perhaps it just means you are removed from it. *(Pause.) Removed* from it. *(Pause.)*

B And, you seen, then, through . . .

A When something shines through . . . when you are *done* with it—it breaks on you, you see. You are done with it. You've put it to rest, and you see the sadness less. And you feel that's true. You feel . . . you've finally achieved "philosophy." Which you sought. And which eluded you. And when you see that it has come upon you, you can feel no *honor* in it. And it signifies no merit, but that you have *lived*. Until a certain time. Where you no longer *desire* those things you desired. And, calling this "philosophy," you question if "philosophy," you see, if it *exists*. Or, or, that it *exists*, but that those who *expounded* it must finally have been other than the tired and the sinful and the confused thing that *I* am. And they must have been *better* than me, who have reached this state of nondesire through dull sloth, and you cannot even say it's *persistence*. No, you say, those men were not as sinful as *I* am. They were *good* and reasoned *purely*. And, further, that that was not the case. They were as sinful as oneself and spoke from nothing other than fatigue and resignation. And this thought destroys philosophy, and what was peace is now only fatigue. The joys are less, the pain is less. But the joys . . . but the pain, you see, has been lessened, but the *joys* have been *obliterated*. "Well," you say . . . *(Pause.)*

B What are you telling me?

A I'm telling you I'm sorry.

B Would you like your tea?

A Yes. Thank you. *(Pause.)* The lassitude. It caused. It drained me.

B The tea did?

A The tea. It enervated me. The afternoons. That we would spend together. I'd try to refrain from drinking it. I wouldn't try to refrain. I would *wish* to refrain. I would not wish to refrain, if I'd wished to do so I would have done so. I would say, "Why do you drink it?" And I would drink it. I sat outside. At this teak set. Of constructed furniture. I suppose much of modern life is in aid of that sort of fashion meant to emphasize stability; as, in an earlier time, we saw emphasis upon the evanescent. *(Pause.)* Didn't we?

B   I don't know.

A   In the postmodern?

B   I don't know.

A   In the . . . in *deconstructivism*? In that "art" which was no way superior to a description given of it? In that which was not art. It was not decor, it was not *politics* . . . what was it? It was assault. It was, if we may use this word, *anger*. We could say "obscenity," but it was not obscene, it was vile. It was vicious—for all that we wrote against it. *(Pause.)* Not that it mattered. *(Pause.)* It *didn't* matter. What do we *not* ascribe purpose to . . . ?

B   I don't . . .

A   . . . and say:

B   . . . I don't understand.

A   "I thought that I was *attacked* . . . and *hated* . . . and I was *humiliated* by that art, that *art*, that which to my mind was not art, but *hurtfulness* and pain seeking a victim. And I was *angered* by it. I *see now* there was a higher purpose! And that very hurt I felt . . ." Do you see?

B   No.

A   ". . . in your treatment of me. When I was so wretched. And I was mistreated. When I was *bereft* . . . when I reached out for comfort and was hurt. And you rejected me. And subjugated me. And trained me to self-hate and to revulsion. And to hatred of the very thoughts I had. And what could I say, being helpless? But to wish to kill or to wish to die or to say . . . 'Ah, Ah. I *see*! I *see* now, that you, who were so powerful.' You who had power over me. That you were *right*!" Do you see?

     "Modern art."

     "I *was*, I *did*, I *was*, I *did mis un der stand you*. I see now . . ."

B   . . . that there was meaning?

A   Yes.

B   . . . when there was not.

A   *As* there was not. There was none in it.

B   I remember watching the rain. From the window. And I said, "I cannot tell if it was raining." And you said, "Two ways are to watch for the *cars*."

A   . . . yes.

B   ". . . and watch their windshield wipers. Or . . ." And gave me to feel that this was the more elegant . . .

A   . . . as it was . . .

B   What was it . . . ?

A   The drops in the puddles.

B   And felt . . . the drops in the puddles—not only . . .

A   . . . as it was.

B   . . . it was more *elegant*, but . . .

A   Yes.

B   Which, perhaps, you meant, if you meant it . . .

A   . . . if I did . . .

B   . . . as the *meaning* of elegance. "Here is a model whereby you may choose the better of two choices. As they come to you: Which is more *basic*? Which of the two is more *natural*? Which is the less *adorned*? Which of the two —perhaps this is most important—could have been employed before the present day—in the *woods*— in the eighteenth *century*? Which, then, avoids the hatedly contrived and the mechanical?" If we could see that, we could live in a world which does not exist but which *perhaps* exists. That world, that basic world below this. *Is this what you meant*? The image of a man I took with me? As per your investiture with all wisdom. Which we give to those we adore. Do we? Good or bad? Is that what you meant? Yes. That I thought that of you. And I remember the teaspoon. And I remember the evenings, and the rain, which I could not say had stopped falling. I remember evenings. And how many times I said, "Don't go," and how guilty you felt. And how I loved you. And how I missed you. And how much I love you. And your worry about modern art. And how you say it all is at an end, and wrack your brain for any evidence that you are wrong, and find none, and look beyond, for any meaning to this end, and resist calling it philosophy, and come to say it is philosophy, but that you are unworthy to enjoy it as such, being worthless, as you think you are, and come to it only through ignorance and pain. I hate this weather. It ain't going to change. *(Pause.)* When are you going back?

A   I'm going back soon.

B   I took the little one to school. I didn't take her to school, I *went* to school. I saw it.

A   How is it?

B   It's fine.

A   She going to like it?

B   Yes.

A   What did you think of Sarah?

B   She was absolutely false.

A   Did you think so?

B   Yes. I know you did, too.

A   I never liked her.

B   No?

A   *(Pause.) People* . . .

B   No. I never liked her, either . . .

A   Why?

B   Because she is *false. (Pause.)*

A   *People* . . .

B   . . . yes?

A   . . . and perhaps you have not seen this. Probably you have not seen enough of them, and why should you have? . . . tend to behave terribly falsely at funerals. I don't know . . .

B . . . yes?

A . . . those that . . . those that. Those that come "up" to one . . .

B . . . I think express themselves quite well.

A Yes. I do, too.

B And laudably, in fact.

A Yes. I do, too. I . . . *truthfully* and with *restraint*, and most importantly . . .

B . . . yes?

A Neither *overcome*, nor . . . that is, overcome *by*, nor, nor . . . *overcoming* their emotions. Those who *speak*, however . . .

B Yes. They're *false*. You . . .

A . . . and we may make allowance for the fact they do not speak in public.

B No.

A . . . with regularity.

B No. I don't like their *disclaimer*. I don't like their *tone* . . . "I hardly *knew* her. . . ."

A . . . yes.

B . . . or, "I hadn't seen her in twenty years, but still . . ."

A Mmm.

B Or, "Two children never were closer." Or, "You must excuse me . . ." Did you see how many began, "You must . . ."

A . . . yes.

B Well. They began with an imperative.

A It's an imperative, yes.

B Why? *(Pause.)* In speaking of the dead?

A . . . no one ever likes the things the clergyman says. . . .

B . . . I'm sure that that's true. But the "bright" and the "sunny" and the stupid Women's Poetry and "like a butterfly" and "The Free Spirit Flying . . ." and her "ever-present cup of tea . . ." Her "endless cups of tea." Well. She Drank *Tea*. She "did" many things. "I never knew *you*, but, in knowing *her*, I feel I know you." You *don't* know me. You don't know me and you didn't know *her, fool*. Who do you think you are? I *suffered* with her for years and spent my waking and sleeping hours trying to understand. And you tell me you "knew" her and she was "a walk in a night's garden" . . . ? And the *other* one . . . what was her name? What are *you* doing there . . . ? And "her love of jazz." "The world was one improvisation to her." Well. How about that? "Just one long melody of thoughts and people. Sand in your Summer Shoes and the crinkle of logs in the wood stove . . ." Thank you. *(Pause.) Thank* you. And endless cups of tea. And how we loved you all. The *three* of you. And we *know* that she is at peace. Well. If she is at peace, then I mistake her. *(Pause.)* As a reward or as a commutation. Then I didn't know her at all. But I *did* know her. They didn't know her. I knew her. Did you know her, too? What shall I say? You're going when? Soon. Yes. A Life of Work.

A   I . . . *(Pause.)*

B   I'm sorry. *(Pause.)* Aren't those the sweetest words? *(Pause.)*

A   But what can bring it back?

B   No, indeed.

A   And we are not those people.

B   Which?

A   The false people.

B   No.

A   We are . . .

B   . . . no . . .

A   We are you and me.

B   . . . isn't that so . . . ?

A   . . . who made a fire in the woods. I understand. I used to think, "Not enough. Not enough." It was not the time. *(Pause.)* It was the trauma. *(Pause.)* Because the time . . . the time would have passed—in *any* case.

GRACE McKEANEY

Chicks

CHARACTER

MISS PHALLON

SETTING

Somewhere in the Midwest there is a kindergarten classroom in a public school that evidences the guidance of a teacher with a wild appetite for life and a healthy analysis bill. . . .

This is MARY MARGARET PHALLON's class, where she has taught for ten years. MISS PHALLON loves other people's children with a zest bordering sometimes on desperation. She has no children of her own. She is thirty-eight or maybe forty-five. . . . The important thing is she is still living at home with an aging father. She has a heart of gold, a sharp Irish tongue, and a weariness now and then born of a yearning for perfection in an imperfect world. . . . She's a little tired of spending her days with people who pick their noses. . . . Life is passing her by. . . . Her humor almost saves her. She'd give anything on earth to be in love.

TIME

The play is a series of four sketches, each taking place on a different school day. The sketches can be connected by music, but it is suggested that if blackouts be used, they be brief: the piece should feel like continuous action. MISS PHALLON speaks to the audience directly, whenever possible, using them as her imaginary students. She is a "Can do" kind of girl on the piano . . . able to pick out snatches of songs when needed for emphasis or fun.

MISS PHALLON enters on a return trip from the principal's office to find the classroom in an uproar. She speaks to twenty-five imaginary kindergarten children who are comprised of the audience.

PUBLIC LIFE

MISS PHALLON   All right, people! People! *(Picking up a paper airplane that glides through.)* That's about *enough of that. (Taking "Mr. Bear" away from someone in the front row.)* Are you supposed to be playing with this now? No! Settle down, settle down, settle down, settle down, settle down, and listen up!

Mr. Felder, why is your hand sticking up in the air like that when Miss Phallon is talking? Are you checking for wind velocity? Well, you can't go right now! We have so much to *do* right now. *(Approaches the piano.)*

This is the musical portion of our afternoon. *(Plays a couple of chords.)* Do what the girls are so masterfully doing. *(Plays a couple of chords.)* Hold it! *(Plays a couple of chords.)* Build character! *(Plays a lavish flourish on the piano.)* Miss Phallon studied piano a thousand years so she could learn how to do that for you this afternoon, and guess what? She's gonna do it again! *(Repeats the flourish, launches into a peppy vamp-for-time piece.)*

It's that time again, kiddies. Time to say howdy to twenty-five new little friends. Think we can get them in the right order today? It's a long way from this to MIT and *(Plays the alphabet song, sings.)* A-B-C-D-E-F-G. *(Stops singing, continues playing.)* Why am I the only one singing?

Gregory Baldoff, is that a finger you have up your nose? You look like you're doing excavation. I said, back up, I think you passed it! On top of everything else, it is *impolite* to eat in front of everyone else, so unless you have enough for the *whole class—and (Continues playing, singing.)* H-I-J-K-L-M-N-O-P- *(Holds note, sings.)*

Paterson, Offbach, Novack—collect your work sheets, rife with error, and contemplate with me for one moment the vast nature and continuing history of all human folly . . . *(Approaching them.)* You all missed question number seven: How much is five plus three?

You all sit surrounding Madeline Fineman, who we all can acknowledge as the self-appointed Smarty Pants in the class, I say that with affection, Madeline, and still you all missed question number seven. Kids, let me hasten to tell you something some very creative accountants have told me repeatedly at tax time, *get the answer any way you can.* And if you are having trouble *seeing the desired* answer, I suggest you march right home this afternoon and tell each of your parents you need your eyesight checked!

Harrison, sit down. Shultz, eyes on me. *(Plays, sings.)* Q-R-S-T-U-V-

Which brings us to Señor Vasquez! *(Plays a snatch of "Fernando's Hide-away.")* Ole!

Señor Vasquez, that is not the purpose towards which end we have been granted the number two yellow lead pencil. I know you are not as yet familiar with our language as you will one day surely become, but for the ongoing time being, *Watchez my lips: no scratchez ze pecker wizzez ze penzil. comprendez?* I don't care if it itches. *Let's get on the program!* The pencil is our link to finer things. The pencil, Señor Vasquez, or its rough equivalent, was held by Donne, Shelley, Ogden Nash. Write a short but apocryphal verse *about* your pecker if a pencil must come into play. But at all costs: *Let's be creative.*

McMillan, turn around. Boswick, are you where you're supposed to be? *(Plays, sings.)* W-X-Y-Z.

Which brings us to Mr. Zorber. *(Plays a few dreadful notes.)* Could everyone turn and relate to Mr. Zorber, who is presently in need of a lot of attention. Are you getting enough focus now, Mr. Zorber? Can we help you by emotionally supporting you in any other way? *(Approaching him.)* I realize you, of all of us, have mastered the complexities of the English alphabet and feel the heady pressure to push on to higher matters, but let's not forget: *We're wrapping up the first week of kindergarten here!* Let's not push it. *(Taking Mr. Bear in her arms.)*

You see, kids, these are the stepping-stones across life's creek we've got here. Let's watch them carefully so that later on we don't find ourselves up life's creek and without a handle. These are the little moments which taken collectively will form the greater part of your personalities, hence the lives you will lead, the happiness or sorrow you will fall heir to, in short, after this: You're cooked. *(Mr. Bear "jumps up" in her arms.)* And Mr. Bear wants us to think about something else. . . . *(Mr. Bear "whispers" in her ear.)*

Well, yes, assuming we are all willing to *dismiss* Eastern religion—and I defy anyone who has truly lived a *Zen day* to write about it in *coherent* essay form— *(Mr. Bear "whispers" again.)* Yes—barring Eastern thought, which I think anyone who is really *serious* has done—we can only believe that *this is it.* We only go around once. And Miss Phallon bets that makes you want to shout something! *(She goes to her scribble easel, flips a page. We see written there: ["Life is short, let's get it right!"]) She takes her pointer and shouts out the line.)* "Life is short. Let's get it right!" Indeed! Let's get it right! You *can* succeed and you *must* succeed. Life's a crap shoot. But with the right attitude, you can *be* and you can *have* anything you want! And you will look back and thank me for being the most positive, illuminating presence in your otherwise drab, pedestrian little li— *(Shock.)*

Paula McFee. I am surprised at you! *(Scrambling.)* Everybody keep your places and turn right back around. *(Approaching Paula.)* Paula, take your hand *out* of *there*. Paula was having a private moment there, forgetting for just an instant that she is in this great public institution, and it's nobody's business, except Paula's and mine—because I am interested in Paula and in helping her to a greater understanding of public life.

All right, let's everybody help clear the air! Let's think of something white. Flour? Good! Sugar? Good! *(She opens her desk drawer, looking for a Valium bottle, then struggles with opening it.)* Ice? Yes! Snow! Yes! Snow! And little snow angels! Little children making little innocent snow angels and children laughing and the world a beautiful place of peace and children laughing! *(She gets the bottle open, takes a pill with a glass of water.)* I feel better. Do you? *(Sees an apple on her desk.)*

Oh, who brought the apple? Playing hard to get, hunh? *(Smiles.)* If Miss Phallon could do anything at all, what do you suppose she would do?

Win the lottery? No, if Miss Phallon won the lottery, she'd still have all the problems she has right now, only a whole lot of money to put between herself and them.

Go to the moon? No, if Miss Phallon went to the moon, she wouldn't be able to take her father for his walks on Sundays; then what would happen to his circulation?

Get married? *(Laughs.)* No, if Miss Phallon got married, then she'd have to put all her faith in one other person, and Miss Phallon is not yet *insane*.

No, if Miss Phallon could do anything at all, she would wrap you each in gossamer blankets and steal you away to come live with her and her father, and she'd love you so much that you'd never develop conflicted personalities or sexual identities or class distinctions. If I could, I'd love you so much, you'd never grow old. . . . *(A kind of weariness floods over her. She smiles tenderly at them.)*

Well, we had a pretty good time this first week, now, didn't we? *(She goes to her desk.)*

Miss Phallon is going to rest her eyes for just a minute, and she wants her buddies to sing the "Merrily Merrily" song for her before the bell rings. *(She puts her head down.)*

What's that, Felder? You don't have to work on your character anymore? That's good. *(Puts her head down.)* It's too late? *(Lifts her head.)* O, it's never really too late, is it, Felder? Felder, talk to me. I want to learn . . . *("Row Row Row Your Boat" plays as the scene shifts. MISS PHALLON changes into a colonial wig and hat; takes up a quill pen and stands at her easel, writing the word: Liberty. A quick blackout may be necessary. . . . At any rate, a gun is dropped in the lap of some poor, unsuspecting audience member. . . .)*

AMERICAN HISTORY *(DAY 2.)*

(Turning from the easel.)

MISS PHALLON   Timothy Knowle: What is that you're brandishing? *(Approaching him.)* Yes, I *did* ask you to bring colonial-related materials for Show and Tell today. *(Realizing.)* Is that a *gun?* Give me that gun. *(Ducking.)* Don't point it at me. Pass it to the end of the line, pass it down and someone bring it to me. *(Taking gun.)*

I want you all to know something: It's Thanksgiving, but I could cry. I have told you about things that used to make me cry. I used to cry when I couldn't tie my shoe, but that doesn't make me cry so much anymore. I *used* to *cry* when my brother Bertie got a bigger slice of cake than me, but with Bertie moved to Toledo, with his own house and his own cake, Miss Phallon now has all the cake she wants. *Different* things make me cry now.

What can make Miss Phallon cry now? Guns! But even more than that! *Children with guns! (Drops gun in the garbage.)* I could cry right now, kids, but instead I'm going to control my feelings and try and put them to more constructive use later when I write a note to your mother, Timothy, asking her if she has *stepped up* to 1985 with the rest of us, if she has any cognitive recollection whatsoever of the sixties, *and* if it is *possible* for her to give a little more thought to the metaphors she is placing at your ready disposal. I'm not blaming you. I'm not even blaming her, but this— *(Points to garbage.)* hurts me! Your hands were meant to hold quicksilver and moonbeams! *(Tears up a bit, wipes her eyes.)*

I'm sorry. Miss Phallon got a little carried away there. *(Does a couple of jumping jacks.)* Let's get back to the past, shall we? Miss Phallon loves the past because it's always there to return to.

Where did we leave off yesterday? *(Takes off colonial hat.)* Ah, yes! We came across the Bering land bridge, didn't we, behind a brash and tawny red man. *(She puts on a cheap Indian headdress and sticks on war paint.)* There's a popular theory making the rounds at present—this will interest *you*, Mr. Bassalman—that the Indians were actually descendants of one of the ancient tribes of Jews migrating southward. Migrating where? *(Laughs.)* Well, toward *Miami*, Alan, where do *you* go every Christmas?

Oh, it's a theory, for God's sake. Your life's going to be lousy with them, so get out of the habit right now of asking so many highfalutin questions. Guess what? Nobody knows anything for sure. I know you find that hard to believe right now, but later in life it's going to be a great comfort. *(Puts on a war-dance record, heavy on the tom-tom beat.)*

I'm anxious to jump ahead or behind, as the case might be, to that thrilling moment in history five hundred years ago. . . . *(She acts out the following story theater style.*) When our Indian friend looked up from the fire he was tending, looked up through the still shadows of cypress and elm, looked out to the distant horizon and saw three ships . . . purposefully creasing what was once the boundless ocean, that singular moment in history when our Indian friend caught sight of three mighty ships reaching inexorably toward a new land and he said to himself, "I'm Fucked!"

What? What was the Indian's name? Why, any name you like. Lance. Lance, the Indian. You don't like Lance the Indian? You don't think it's *Indian* enough? *(Scrambling.)*

See, that's the *whole problem* in a word. *Pigeonholing* now leads to bigger things later on. *(Goes to easel, writes in big letters.)* Who knows what *bigotry* is? Ceil? When a man marries two ladies. No. that's *(Writes.)* *bigamy*, Ceil. How do you know about bigamy? Your father is a bigamist. Oh. Is this in the courts now, Ceil? He's being *arraigned* today . . . ? I'm sorry. Are you staying with your mother, Ceil? Oh, the other lady has moved in with your mother, and they're trying to reach the other three ladies on the West Coast. Wow. What was your dad's job, Ceil? Sexual therapy . . . coast-to-coast, hunh? *(Cheery.)* Hey: want to come home and have some cupcakes with me after school today? We can make turkey center-pieces out of paper plates! Sound good?

After all: it's *November*! And November *always* makes me think of the *Mayflower*! Those were the days, kids! Before everything got all screwed up! The New World! Think of it! How many people would have come across on the *Mayflower* if they could have gotten a seat? *(Counts heads.)* Twenty-four. How many people would have stayed in Europe and enjoyed a life of apoplexy and bearbaiting? *(Counts heads.)* One. Zorber. *(Approaching him.)*

Zorber, why don't you go over and help yourself to those comic books over there in the corner. No, go ahead. Stretch out, lie down, *rot* whatever is *left* of your brain! *Not come over on the* Mayflower! For shame. I'm glad acting president Reagan isn't here right now to hear that! This country wasn't always such a mess, you know. This country was once *very well thought of*. Bernard Shaw spent some time here cutting movie deals. This country once took itself *very seriously*. This country once took itself *so seriously*, it threw Charlie Chaplin *out*! That's how serious this country could be! I know we don't seem very serious right now, but that is why history is so-o-o-o-o important.

I'll tell you one thing we'll never forget: That first Thanksgiving! *(Produces a plastic turkey on a platter with all the trimmings.)* Let me tell you, nobody died and left those Indians chef when it comes to fine cuisine. *(Stirs in a pot.)* How 'bout a big bowl of cornmeal mush. *Yccck*, right.

Let it be known that every Indian right on down to the present day overcooks the *meat*. I mean, the Irish are bad, but the Irish know you only cook the meat to get the *gravy*. This is the foundation of macho Catholicism: Cook the meat to get the gravy, live your life to get into heaven. But the Indians overcook the *gravy*. And if you don't finish everything on your plate, you get a *scalping*! *You bet those pilgrims ate!* Three, four, five helpings! They even ate the turkey legs, which personally I say go right in the trash! They called it *celebrating*. But we know better. You notice the turkey dinner only appears once a year. *(Goes to easel to write.)* This is known as *(Writes.) genetic memory.* For you sometimes Catholic children, that's something very much like original sin. The cells remember. In fear. *(Looks weary suddenly.)*

You don't understand a word I'm saying, do you? This is all going right over your heads. Well, it doesn't matter. *(Removes headdress, war paint.)* Miss Phallon is raving, anyway, due to starvation and premenstrual syndrome. *(Sees an apple on her desk.) Oo, real food.* Who brought the apple? The perfect fruit. *(Takes a bite.)*

Well, okay, there was that little incident back there in Genesis, but it tested our Yankee know-how, didn't it? Look what we learned: Adaptability. Flexibility. Opportunism. Come on in uninvited and take right over. I'm telling you *(Takes another bite.)*, dollars to doughnuts, except for your Quakers and your Catholics who profess to have a little too much *character*, you give this species an opening and they'll take any old *shit* and work it right into the ground plan. It's saved us from certain demise before, and take it from Miss Phallon, it'll pull us out of the crapper once again.

Sasso! I'll break your legs if you do that again! It is important that *you* of all of us take heed of what I'm saying. *(Approaching him.)* You showed some marked scientific aptitude on those state placement tests Miss Phallon gave this fall, which means you might be able to save all our asses from untimely demise in the days ahead. Do us all a little favor and develop some real respect for the nuclear issue *right now*! How? *(Stopped.)* Well, I don't know. I majored in history in college. Miss Phallon doesn't have any gifts for the sciences. Most of the children in here don't have any gifts for the sciences. But if I were you, kid, I'd get on speaking terms with nuclear fission *pronto*; otherwise, it's going to be a lot of innocent bystanders on your conscience and a life wasted in the juvenile courts! *(Waving a tomahawk.)*

Did anyone ever ask me if I wanted a nuclear war? No, they just went ahead and followed their instincts. Better dead than red. . . . Better dead than red. . . . Some of you have probably heard your right-wing fathers mumbling this in their sleep. See, it's all part of this funny little dream they're having in which they come out on top. They like to be on top, so they dream about it. Your mothers like to be in the middle, so they keep having children. Since the bottom was the only opening, that's where you go, until, if you're a boy, you grow up and start dreaming about coming out on top or, if you're a girl, you get caught in the middle. *(Stopped, lies down on her desk.)*

Would it be all right if I lie down a second? Miss Phallon is having one of those blinding little headaches she gets when she sees too many of the far-reaching implications. Oh, my head. Oh, what a banger. Okay, everybody. Six pants and a blow! *(Does breathing exercises from Lamaze.)* That's right, Irene. This is what your mommy did to get ready for that new sister who's come to live with you. No, Miss Phallon is not getting ready for delivery, she just watches entirely too much PBS. The only thing Miss Phallon would like to deliver right now is . . . a tickle. *(Becomes an imp.)* I want you to imagine that Miss Phallon sneaks up behind you right now and tickles . . . and tickles . . . and tickles . . . and tickles . . . and tickles you! *(Smiles.)* There. Look at those smiles. Don't let anybody ever tell Miss Phallon that she doesn't have beautiful Pilgrims. . . . And she forgets all about the far-reaching implications when she sees you smile at her.

(The scene shifts to a new day. Use of music, or a quick blackout.)

BIOLOGY ETC. *(DAY 3.)*

MISS PHALLON holds a couple of sex education dolls.

MISS PHALLON   This is Bill. This is Jill. They want to have a meaningful relationship when they grow up, and so will you. That's why our lesson today is entitled: *"Biology, psychology, sociology, philosophy, romance, pop culture, and you."* You see, kids, there's a lot that goes into this lifelong affair of boys and girls growing up into able-bodied men and women who find each other fascinating and set about forming unions designed for equal profit sharing.

Sasso! If she wanted your finger in her ear, she is perfectly capable of asking.

She did ask.

I see. Okay, let's squeeze a little biology in here while we've got the urge. What do you kids think of when I go like this? *(She pokes the finger of one hand through a fist she makes with the other hand.)* Mr. Knowle: What do you see when I go like this?

The combustion engine.

Okay. Miss McFee, what do you see?

Threading a needle.

Okay. I don't see the point in going any further with this, you kids have the general idea. *(Goes to easel.) Sex* invites a marriage between *business* and *domestic life*. What starts out as fun for everybody winds up needing a lot of corporate planning. Just everybody try and keep those hard facts in mind when you're out there steaming up the windshield in years ahead and they're pushing a lot of recycled Johnny Mathis at you.

And one more thing. And you girls pay special note. Sex screws up everything. That's all I'm gonna say. Just remember you heard it here first. It is the fastest way to make an enemy of a man you are otherwise having a very nice time with. Why? Because *sex* leads to *other things*. You meet somebody perfectly at random and the next thing you know you're fantasizing about moving into his apartment. . . . And how do you think he feels about that, hunh; you think he's ready for *that*? And I think there are a *lot* of men who think sex is yucky because it leads to such unmentionable other things; then they have sex with you and you become yucky; and then they don't call you on the phone the next day.

As a little case in point, Miss Phallon got herself all done up the other night and went down to a bar aptly called the Public Trough, where she found herself having many drinks with a man named Granger and— *(Stops.)*

Oh! You little rascals! You almost had me talking about my *very most private personal life* again. And you *know* what a savage note Miss Phallon got from Mr. Coltrane, the principal, the *last* time she told you a story from her very most private personal life. . . . You see, kids, if other grown-ups get wind I'm leveling with you, it makes them look bad, because then they have to level with you, which for most of them is impossible. Most of your parents, God forgive them, are full of bullshit. I say this with all due respect for the efforts they are making in raising you. But if I were you, I would not allow bullshit in my home. When they start, just go to your room, close the door quietly but firmly, and say: Hey: The bullshit stops here.

What's that, Metcalfe? Is that what I do . . . ? Well, no. But my daddy is old now, and he doesn't talk much anymore . . . and, well . . . don't be too hard on them . . . they don't know what they're doing. . . . They have to try and *appear* to know what they are doing, because they've got these little faces staring at them, when it's all just spit and Scotch tape, however you dress it up. . . . You're the only one with a watch, what time is it, Bassalman? Well, because if it's two-thirty, I have to go to the office. That's right, I go to the office every day at two-thirty because that's when "Tom and Jerry" is over and my daddy likes to talk about what made him laugh. . . . Not time, yet? *(Sits at desk, sighs.)* See, people need other people to talk to about what they like . . . about what's bothering them. . . . When they feel lost . . .

I know you think I've got a lot of nerve talking to you this way, and I do, I do have a lot of nerve. I blame it on my estrogen level, which is really higher than it should be. And I'm not sleeping well. I lie there at night and listen to my father breathing and think: I'm not a little girl anymore. I'm not even a young lady anymore. I'm a woman, kids, and I spell *w-o-m-b*. Does anyone know what a womb is most commonly used to hold? Sasso?

Furniture.

Oh, what do you know? You've just spent time in a womb. You'll never have a womb of your very own. Virginia Wolfe! There, we've had our English lesson. I have a womb. A spare womb. A Womb for Went, as Elmer Fudd might say. And some of the other people in here have wombs, and some of you other people will help them fill them, because nature abhors a vacuum. There, we've had our science lesson. Let's go on to word definitions. Does anyone know what *abhor* means? Patty?

A woman who has sexual relations for money?

Where do you kids get this stuff? How many of you kids watch *Dallas*? Let's get an honest show of hands. *(Counts heads.)* Okay, all right, how many of you kids watch *Dynasty*? *(Counts heads, shocked.)* All right: I want the truth: How many of you kids have seen *Beyond the Green Door*? Where are your parents! Locked in the bedroom, hunh? Making funny noises while they're working on the "Budget"? *(Near tears.)* Well, let me tell you something: Life is not like it is on *Dallas:* People do *not* dress that well. And people do not truly get revenge for wrongs done them . . . and people do not *die* if no one comes along to *love* them. . . . *(Holds back, but wants to cry.)* What's that, Alan? Thank you. It makes me feel a lot better that you would be happy to have me out on a date if you were a little older. Thank you. I *do* have kind eyes, don't I?

What did you say, Zorber? *After* I said I had kind eyes, you said something: You said the kind of eyes I'd like to poke out. *(Breaks down— crying and laughing.)* Zorber made a joke. Which illustrates another point: For in life, when people talk about their problems, they break down at funny moments and talk all around the problem and the dialogue is more baroque. . . . Does anyone know what *baroque* means?

Irene? No money in the checking account.

That's right. Baroque means no money in the checking account. Sometimes that's just what it means. . . .

(Scene shifts . . . music . . . or slight blackout. A Christmas tree is brought on. MISS PHALLON wears a Santa's hat.)

FREEDOM *(DAY 4.)*

MISS PHALLON counts down the minutes.

MISS PHALLON Ten, nine, eight, seven, six, five, four, three, two, one. Ten minutes till Christmas vacation, and I want to talk about freedom. Who knows what Abraham Lincoln did? Offbach? Very good, he set free the slaves. What's a slave, Earl?

A black person forced to work for no pay!

Right! Now here's a tough one for you kids from high-income backgrounds: What's the difference between a slave and a cleaning lady? What's that, Bassalman?

You let the cleaning lady go home.

That's about the size of it, kid. But a little victory is a victory, too. And finding your way home really starts with finding out who you are inside. . . . Mr. Lincoln did a pretty good thing, didn't he, setting those slaves free . . . but before they were set free, they didn't have much to think about, did they . . . their lives were bad, but they were familiar and one day kind of bled into the next. . . . It was *after* they were set free that all the questions started . . . questions always start with personal freedom . . . that's also where fulfillment starts . . . once you get the fear out of the way . . .

Now, take me for example. I've been living alone with my father for many years—you might think what I've said is a contradiction in terms —but it's quite possible to live *alone* with *someone*, especially an older someone who drifts further and further away. . . . I love my daddy. He held me on his knee. But he's really belonged in a different place—a place with people more like him . . . or maybe . . . I don't know . . . Maybe, I've belonged in a different place, more with the living. . . . But so long as there was my father, there was a place for me to hide, and so long as there was a place for me to hide, there was no reason to make a new home for the person I've become. . . . This is very hard for me to do because it is very selfish. But after Christmas vacation, my father won't be living with me anymore. What, Irene?

Is he going to die?

Well, it's a confusing fact, Irene, but all of us are going to die, and some of us haven't lived enough yet to be ready. He'll know that he's cared for, and we'll still take our walks on Sunday. . . . And I'm going to make his house my house. I'm going to bring in plants and change the heavy curtains, and I'm going to bring back my piano. . . . And I'm going to put a mirror by the front door. And I'm going to try and look myself in the eye every day before I go out the door. And I'm going to wish myself something.

What, Paula? What will I wish? I'm going to wish myself—well. That's my Christmas present to me. In January, you'll have a replacement teacher, because Miss Phallon won't be here anymore. This, too, is very hard for me to do.

Where am I going? Alan, I really don't know. No, probably not

Miami. I just know I can't come back and borrow your happiness anymore. I've got to make some of my own. I see the future as a succession of corners to turn . . . with music. . . . I see it as full of clouds and vapors but with something important signaling to me from the other side of fear. . . . This is hard for me to do.

Zorber! Why are you standing on the window ledge? You're going to jump? You're going to jump because you think you've been bad all semester and that's why Miss Phallon is leaving . . . and that's why you brought the apples. . . . *(Takes apple from desk approaching him with great care.)* Zorber . . . if you jump out that window, it's going to hurt Miss Phallon very much. Because . . . then . . . I wouldn't be able to thank you. . . . You see, you think you've been coming every day to school to learn things . . . but I've learned a thing or three myself. . . . Besides: You've got a wonderful mission ahead of you, should you choose to accept it: You're going to teach some effervescent young know-it-all from state teacher's college the meaning of absolute humility by the end of the year. Won't that be fun?

Now, get down and stop acting like an imbecile. I know they don't talk to you like that at home, but they're overeducated. What does your mother have her degree in? The *philosophy of psychology*. I rest my case. I bet she can't butter your toast without courting a cerebral hemorrhage. They *think* too much. And they're *afraid* of you. . . . Because you *know* there are things you can't reason. And you *know* there are things you can't know. And you know that important things just take a leap of some kind. . . . *(Reaching to him.)* . . . but not *that* kind. . . . Come down and be with me for a few more minutes. *(The bell rings. She realizes she is out of time. She slowly gathers things from her desk.)* I hope you have a nice vacation. I hope Santa is good to you. But just you remember: *(Taking apple.)* None of you owes anyone *anything*. . . . Anything you owed has been paid in full, because your skin is soft, and your eyes are clear and your smiles are ready. None of you owes anything. You're a gift all by yourselves. Good-bye, Chicks. *(She takes her bag and goes.)*

Lights down.

TERRENCE McNALLY

Prelude and Liebestod

CHARACTERS

CONDUCTOR   *Magnetic, animal, sexual, charismatic. Makes heads turn.*
CONDUCTOR'S WIFE   *Beautiful, immaculate, somewhat unapproachable.*
Her looks are her defense.
SOPRANO   *Thinks she has all the answers and knows the score. Actually*
terrified of failure.
CONCERTMASTER   *An excellent musician, though loaded with bile and spite.*
MAN   *His personality is defined by his attraction for the* CONDUCTOR. *A*
proto-groupie.

SETTING

The place of the play is various environs of a large concert hall. Though
the setting is necessarily abstract, the individual playing areas should be
sharply defined and specific.

TIME

The time of the play is now.

Lights come up on a conductor's podium, a small, square, raised platform about fifteen
inches high. There is a waist-high railing running the length of the upstage side of it.
Sounds of a symphony orchestra tuning up at random.
Spot up on a beautiful woman in a box seat somewhat upstage of the podium.
She is the CONDUCTOR'S WIFE. *She is perfectly dressed. She looks at her program. She*
looks at her watch. She looks at the orchestra in the orchestra level below her. She looks

up at the higher tiers and balcony above her.

Spot up on a MAN in an orchestra-level seat stage left, also somewhat upstage of the CONDUCTOR's podium. He is looking at the CONDUCTOR's WIFE through a pair of opera glasses. She is not aware of this.

Spot up on the CONCERTMASTER, who is seated in a chair just a little downstage right of the podium. He raps with his bow on his violin stand and gives the note.

An unseen symphony orchestra tunes up to his note.

The CONDUCTOR's WIFE opens her purse and takes out a small box of mints.

The MAN continues to stare at her through the opera glasses. At the same time, he reaches in his breast pocket and takes out a roll of Life Savers.

The houselights dim in the concert hall where the CONDUCTOR's WIFE and MAN are sitting.

At the same time, the lights will come up on the concert stage, that is, the theater itself.

A spotlight hits a door leading to the backstage area. After a longer time than necessary, it is opened by unseen hands, and the SOPRANO enters to strong applause. She is in full regalia.

As SOPRANO moves toward podium, she smiles at the unseen orchestra. The CONCERTMASTER taps his bow on his stand in approval.

SOPRANO turns her back to orchestra (and us, in doing so) and bows deeply to heavy applause.

Now SOPRANO makes a great deal of arranging the panels of her dress and stole as she finally sits in a chair just left and a little downstage of the podium. Her back will be to us, but we will see her in profile as she turns from time to time to take a sip of water from a glass on a low table next to her chair or turns to the other side to smile at the CONCERTMASTER.

Silence.

The spotlight has gone again to the door leading to the backstage area. It waits there. Again the door is opened by unseen hands. No one appears.

Silence in the auditorium. Someone coughs. Someone else shushes them. Door starts to swing shut, then is swiftly pulled wide open as CONDUCTOR hurries through.

Tumultuous applause.

CONDUCTOR moves swiftly to podium and bows deeply. The MAN has risen and is clapping wildly.

MAN   Bravo! Bravo!

(CONDUCTOR's WIFE is applauding. CONDUCTOR leaps off podium and goes to CONCERTMASTER and shakes his hand vigorously. Ovation continues as CONDUCTOR crosses to SOPRANO and kisses her hand, then cheek. MAN continues to stand and applaud.)

MAN   Bravo! Bravo!

(CONDUCTOR's WIFE has stopped applauding. CONDUCTOR has returned to podium for final bow to audience (which means his back is to us) as applause begins to diminish.

MAN *continues to stand and applaud. This time his voice is especially prominent as the general ovation continues to subside.)*

MAN   Bravo! Bravo!

(CONDUCTOR looks to MAN. Eye contact is made. CONDUCTOR'S WIFE looks at MAN. CONDUCTOR looks up at WIFE and smiles, then turns his back to concert-hall audience and faces orchestra (us).
CONDUCTOR *is delighted with his reception. He gives orchestra members a self-deprecating grin and raised eyebrows.*
Silence.
He gets serious. He passes his hands over his face. He takes a deep breath.)

(Shattering the silence:) We love you!

(CONDUCTOR ignores this. Angry shushes from audience. CONDUCTOR reaches to music stand in front of him and closes the score. Gasps and whispers from the audience. He picks up baton. He raises both arms. He waits. He throws the baton onto the music stand and raises both arms again, but this time gives the downbeat almost at once. Wagner's Prelude to Tristan und Isolde *is off and running.)*

CONDUCTOR   *(After the fourth rest.)* I love these pauses. . . . Come on, you suckers, play for me. Play through me, music. Course through me. Surge. Fill me. I am you. This is it. . . . God, that was good. Now we're off and running. I'm up here already. That was quick. I like it up here. The view is glorious. Fill, lungs. Heave, bosom. Burst, heart.

(At this point, the sound of the orchestra is considerably diminished and the CONDUCTOR will seem to be speaking from within his own private place. The music will be more of a "surround" than a presence.)

CONDUCTOR   There were no empty seats. Clean as a whistle. There's no one better than me. Is there? No one even close. God, I love Wagner. That one in the fifth row. I've seen him. Where? In your dreams, asshole. We don't do that anymore. You wanna bet? Oh, shut up! Hey, third cello, look at me! Yes, you! Where did they find you? Yes, you're too loud. You think I'd be looking at you like this if you weren't? Jesus, where was I? Sometimes I think I do this on automatic. There we are, right on target! Somebody up there likes me. Yeah, Wagner, asshole. The big *Kraut in das Himmel* himself. I feel his eyes burning right into my back. He's mentally undressing me. They all are. All 2,187 of them plus the 131 in standing room. Maybe I could steal a look. Are you crazy? She's right up there in a box. She's always right up there in a box. I'd like to see her in a box. It's her box I'm sick of. You don't mean that. I don't mean that. You love her. I love you.

(He looks over his shoulder to WIFE, who is reading something in her program.)

She's reading! The fucking bitch is reading, and you're conducting your fucking ass off. Fuck that shit. Bitch. You wanted to be married. No, you wanted to have children. You have to be married to have children. No, you have to be married to have children if you want to be the principal conductor of a big symphony orchestra with a big stuffy endowment. You're pissed off because you've got the hots for some groupie in the fifth row and *your* goddamn wife is right up there watching every move you make. Eagle eyes. Bionic ears. She can see and hear through lead walls if I'm talking to another man. It's one thing to be straight; it's another to be in a straitjacket.

(Suddenly aware of the CONCERTMASTER.*)*

What are you looking at, asshole? I swear to God, sometimes I think he's calling me an asshole under his breath through the whole concert.

CONCERTMASTER   Asshole.
CONDUCTOR   There! Right now! I'm positive he's doing it. I'd like to see him get up here and conduct, he thinks he's so great. They probably all think they can conduct better than me. Sorry to disillusion you, assholes! That's why I'm up here and you're down there. Whoever said it was right: it is lonely at the top. It's lonely anywhere.
MAN   Look at me. You know I'm here.
WIFE   *(Still looking at program.)* Now that is what I call a stunning outfit. Oscar De La Renta. I should have guessed.
CONCERTMASTER   Asshole!
SOPRANO   Fuck you, too!
CONCERTMASTER   I wasn't talking to you.
SOPRANO   What did I do to him? I'm sorry, but we can't all be Kirsten Fucking Flagstad.
MAN   Turn around. You know you want to.
CONDUCTOR   He's talking to you. Go ahead. This climax. It's a perfect place. Shit! I can't. You blew it, asshole.
MAN   You know what I'd do if I had you alone with me? I have it all planned. I'd undress you. With my teeth. I'd start with a button. This button. *(He touches his collar button.)* Pop!
WIFE   Oh God, I hope Ralph can get away for that weekend when he's conducting in London. I don't think I can stand another week without him. I wonder what he'd do if he knew. Kill me. Punish me through the children. Both.
CONDUCTOR   Turn, turn, turn. To everything there is a season. The Beatles? The Turtles. Ten minutes with someone like that. Less. It doesn't take long. I want you so bad, fifth row.
CONCERTMASTER   Bloody, bleeding, blooming asshole.

CONDUCTOR   If I had a face like yours, I'd kill myself.

SOPRANO   It's nearly me. There's got to be better ways to earn a living.

CONDUCTOR   Why did you have to be out there tonight, fatal beauty, or why did you have to be up there, faithful, adoring wife? Why couldn't tonight be next week in London? I'm doing the Mahler Ninth. I'm always so drained after the Mahler Ninth. Drained and horny.

MAN   Look at me. They say if you stare at someone's left earlobe long enough, eventually it begins to burn a hole and they turn around.

CONDUCTOR   It's all in the music. The longing, the learning. The impossibility. I am loved. I want to love. I've never found anyone as interesting as me. As lovable. As worthy of my undivided attention. Fifth row is one thing; her up there is another. I'm talking about a whole other kettle of fish.

(The Prelude is drawing to an end. The SOPRANO stands and makes ready to sing.)

Good God, it's her turn already. Come on, cow, sing it, swing it, shake it, bend it.

MAN   Maybe it's the right earlobe.

(SOPRANO begins to sing. At first, the music will be at concert-hall volume, then subside to the level of the Prelude. Although her back is to us throughout, it should be clear that the SOPRANO is deeply involved with singing and communicating with her audience out front.)

CONCERTMASTER   You're flat. Get up there, get up there!

WIFE   Now that's a gorgeous voice.

MAN   Sharp as ever.

CONDUCTOR   You're singing through the wrong hole, honey. This is twat music. Listen to it. Listen to the words. God, if I had your instrument!

SOPRANO   Place the tone properly. Support it. Always legato. Thatta girl.

WIFE   If I could sing like that!

MAN   They like her! They actually like her!

CONCERTMASTER   That's more like it.

(Surtitles will appear thoughout.)

SURTITLE   *"Mild und leise wie er lachelt,*
wie das Auge hold er offnet,
seht ihr's, Freunde? Seht ihr's nicht?
Immer lichter, wie er leuchtet,
stern-umstrahlet hoch sich hebt?
Seht ihr's nicht?"

CONDUCTOR   Do you know what the words mean? Sing it like you know what it meant. It's about love. It's about dying. It's about trans-fan-fucking-figuration. Sing it like you meant it.

SURTITLE   *"Wie das Herz ihm mutig schwillt,*

voll und hehr im Busen ihm quillt?
Wie den Lippen, wonnig mild,
susser Atem sanft entweht,
Freunde! Seht! Fuhlt und seht ihr's nicht?"

CONDUCTOR This is not enough. Conducting it is not enough. Singing it is not enough. Writing it is not enough. Experience it. Love-death. Love-death. *Liebestod.*

CONCERTMASTER What is he doing?

CONDUCTOR You're behind, honey, catch up, catch up!

SOPRANO This is not the tempo we agreed—!

WIFE That man looks like Ralph.

MAN He's losing you, lady.

CONDUCTOR Who do you love the most? Who do you love the best?

SURTITLE *"Hore ich nur diese Weise*
die so wundervoll und leise,
Wonne klagend, alles sagend,
mild versohnend aus ihm tonend,
in mich dringet, auf sich schwinget,
hold erhallend um mich klinget?
Heller schallend, mich umwallend,
sind es Wellen sanfter Lufte?
Sind es Wogen wonniger Dufte?"

CONDUCTOR What is transfiguration but an orgasm coupled with a heart attack?

SURTITLE *"Wie sie schwellen, mich umrauschen,*
soll ich atmen, soll ich lauschen?
Soll ich schlurfen, untertauchen?
Suss in Duften mich verhauchen?"

CONDUCTOR Wagner knew a lot about fucking. I bet that guy in the fifth row does, too. My wife knows nothing about fucking. I'd like to fuck the entire world. No, I'd like to fuck every attractive man, woman, and child in the world. Child over eleven. No, fourteen, fifteen, fifteen. Fuck it.

SURTITLE *"In dem wogenden Schwall, in dem tonenden Schall,*
in des Welt-Atems wehendem All
ertrinken, versinken—
unbewusst, hochste Lust—"

CONDUCTOR It's over already. Shit. I don't even remember it beginning.

(Long pause as music fades to silence.)

WIFE Oh, shit, now the Bruckner Fourth.

CONCERTMASTER Oh shit, now the Bruckner Fourth.

SOPRANO Isn't anybody going to clap?

MAN Now he's got to turn around.

(Ovation begins. A tremendous one. CONDUCTOR *doesn't move. Instead, he remains with his back to concert-hall audience.* SOPRANO *accepts ovation with great humility.)*

MAN *(Above all the others.)* We love you!

*(*CONDUCTOR *picks up baton and raps with it.)*

CONDUCTOR Again! From the top!

CONCERTMASTER But—!

*(*CONDUCTOR *gives downbeat.* SOPRANO *looks startled but takes her seat.* MAN *sits.* WIFE *remains standing in her box, looking concerned, but will eventually sit. The* Tristan Prelude *will seem very loud at first. It will finally settle at same level of volume as previous rendition of it.)*

CONDUCTOR Give them profile. Feed it to them. They love your profile. Move the body. They come for body movement. Those fabulous, famous, far-reaching shoulders. Magnificent arms on a mighty torso. High flying adored. You and Evita! Wiggle your ass. Tight, firm buttocks worthy of someone half your age. Make them think about your cock and balls. Are they large? Is he clipped? Is he good? I'm terrific, baby. Ask her. Ask him. Ask anyone who's had the pleasure of my acquaintance. It's them who don't measure up. It's them who fail me. They're fucking me. Taking. Drawing my strength. Where's my equal? My match? I'm so alone. Up here. Everywhere. I really love this pause. What is this music really about? What is anything really about? I don't think this is such a great theme. I've written better, but he's Richard Wagner—big fucking deal—and I am Marie of Romania—big fucking deal. This music always makes me think of certain kinds of sex. Hot late-afternoon damp sheets sweaty grunting people outside blinds drawn dark dirty make it last as long as you can come crazy, scream, rip the sheets, howl like a werewolf, hurt him, hurt her, ouchy kind of sex. This will be in all the papers tomorrow. For twenty-four hours I'll be the most famous person in the world. Forty-eight maybe. Seventy-two. Then next week, when the magazines come out, there will be a new spurt of fame. Then a gradual subsiding until the first major memorial service. A plaque will go up somewhere. Probably outside the hall. God knows, no one ever, anywhere, ever again will listen to this music without thinking of me. *(He glances at* WIFE. *Their eyes meet and hold.)* You had the most beautiful skin and breasts and throat and everything when we met. They weren't enough. Nothing has ever been enough. The children. They're not real. Real in themselves but not real to me. Nothing, no one is real enough. I am the only person in the world, and I cannot bear the pain of being so alone. I'm only alive when I come—the way I want to be alive—ecstatic, half-conscious, eyes closed, brain flaring, words, thoughts inadequate. *(He glances at the* MAN.*)* The only satisfying sexual experience I ever had was with a man.

MAN   Finally.

CONDUCTOR   The kind of sexual experience this music is about.

CONCERTMASTER   This is more like it.

WIFE   Go on.

SOPRANO   I hate it when they look at me.

CONDUCTOR   I was twenty-two years old, studying in Milan, already made my debut in Salzburg that summer, an instant sensation, the old fool got sick, I took over, the Bruckner Fourth and the *Pathetique*. . . . God, that would have been next on the program, I loathe Bruckner! Who couldn't conduct the *Pathetique*? The toast of Europe. God, I was handsome that year. I could spend hours in front of the mirror talking to myself. I'd make faces. Scowl, smile. Flirt with myself. I could even get myself hard. This bastard —what was his name?—he was a journalist, political. . . . The apartment was near the Piazza della Republica. . . . It was over a pharmacy. . . . The steps were exhausting . . . deep, steep Renaissance steps. . . . There was a terra-cotta Madonna in the apartment. . . . He said it was a Lucca della Robbia, and I wanted to believe him. . . . God, I was already so famous, but I was still so easily impressed! . . . What the fuck was your name?

MAN   Giorgio, Piero, Giacomo, Giuseppe, Gaetano.

WIFE   Does it matter?

CONCERTMASTER   Asshole!

MAN   Carlo, Mario, Fausto, Arturo, Vittorio, Fred.

CONDUCTOR   Guglielmo! Guglielmo Tell. Kidding, kidding. No, I'm not. Guglielmo Bianchini. He knew who I was. He must have. Everyone did. My picture was everywhere that summer. I was so beautiful that year—I was perfect—I was all I wanted—all anyone could ever possibly want—and this cocksucker, this arrogant wop, this goddamn glorious dago, he led me on and on and on. A touch, a glance, a brush of thigh, but no more. I wasn't even sure he was queer. Weeks went on like this. Torture. No one knew why I was staying in Milan. I'm doing research. What research? You know everything. It's true. I did. About music. But the promise of this person kept me on.

WIFE   My poor darling.

MAN   After the concert, when I ask for your autograph, I will pass you a slip of paper with my telephone number on it. No name, just a number. You'll know what to do with it.

SOPRANO   I better be paid twice for this. And I'm certainly not singing the *Tannhäuser* for an encore.

CONCERTMASTER   Asshole, asshole, asshole.

CONDUCTOR   Finally, there was a weekend when his father, a widower and some sort of famous judge or lawyer, would be out of town at their place in Como. I went to the apartment. The door was ajar. There was no sign of him. I wandered through the empty apartment. It had been a palazzo.

Everything was huge—molded, sculpted, ornate. I went into a bedroom —it must have been the father's—yes, that is where the Lucca della Robbia was and I stood looking at this enormous bed, and then I felt—I feel!— hands on me from behind. I didn't turn around. Don't want to.

(The SOPRANO *stands and begins to sing the* Liebestod *again. Only this time the surtitles will be in English.)*

Hands here, hands there. Hands over my eyes, hands over my mouth. Four hands. Someone else is there. I didn't struggle. My clothes are being taken off—were being taken off— I don't know what tense I'm in—what tense I want to be in— The past is too painful, the present too forlorn—and I am being stripped and stroked and I am blindfolded and I am led to the bed and my cock is so hard and I am put on the bed and I let myself be tied spreadeagle to it— No one has ever done this to me and I do not resist— And when it is done I am left there for what seems like hours and my hard-on will not subside and once even it threatens to explode and I pray to the unseen Della Robbia Madonna above me not to let me come and I know this is blasphemy and I know that she forgives and understands because she is a good mother—all mothers are good mothers—and oh, it is so unimaginably intense to be there like that with him.

SOPRANO   "How gently and quietly he smiles,
how fondly he opens his eyes!
See you, friends? Do you not see?
How he shines ever higher,
soaring on high, stars sparkling around him?
Do you not see?
How his heart proudly swells
and, brave and full, pulses in his breast?
How softly and gently from his lips
sweet breath flutters:—
see, friends! Do you not feel and see it?
Do I alone hear this melody
which, so wonderous and tender
in its blissful lament, all-revealing,
gently pardoning, sounding from him,
pierces me through, rises above,
blessedly echoing and ringing around me?"

CONDUCTOR   And after a while I am unblindfolded and see my captors—Guglielmo and a young woman who can only be his twin sister; she is a feminine mirror image of him—and they are both nude and more beautiful than anyone I have ever seen—more beautiful than even I was that summer—and she straddles me and lowers herself on my cock very slowly just once and I almost come but I pray and then he—Guglielmo—what an absurd name!—put his mouth on my cock and moves it up and down the length of it just once and again I almost come and have to pray and then they both just looked at me and I said, "Please, make me come." "*Prego, farmi morire*" is what I said. "Please make me die." I didn't know the Italian for "come," you see. "*Prego, farmi morire.*"

SOPRANO   "Resounding yet more clearly, wafting about me,
       are they waves of refreshing breezes?
       Are they clouds of heavenly fragrance?
       As they swell and roar round me,
       shall I breathe them, shall I listen to them."

CONDUCTOR   And they just smiled at each other. He kissed one of her breasts. She touched his cock. I knew they weren't really twins. I wondered if they were even brother and sister. She took her panties, pink, and ran them the length of my body, toe to head. Then she very slowly pushed them into my mouth, gagging me with them. I didn't resist. The whole time our eyes held. He blindfolded me again. I felt their hands on me, their mouths. Everywhere. And then I heard the door close. After a while I stopped thinking about the Madonna and praying to her, and when I thought of Guglielmo and Francesca—I'd named her by then, you see; I have a great need to know the name of things—adoring me, I couldn't hold back any longer. I didn't want to, and I came with an intensity that amazes me to this day and that I have never since even remotely equaled. I could feel my own semen on my lips, on my eyes, in my hair. Guglielmo and Francesca.

MAN   What are your secrets?

WIFE   I only deceive him sexually.

CONCERTMASTER   This is beautiful. I'll grant him that.

SOPRANO   "Shall I sip them, plunge beneath them,
       to expire in sweet perfume?"

CONDUCTOR   Of course, after I came I lost all interest in the game and wanted to be free. More importantly, I lost all interest in them. I lay there feeling the flood of semen grow watery, then dry and caked on my stomach, chest, and face. Hours passed. I could not free myself. The blindfold, the gag, held firm. Once, I relaxed enough to mentally relive the episode, and I immediately got hard and came again, though not nearly so much this time. The next thing I knew I heard a strange woman's scream, a man's angry voice, and pretty soon I'm unblindfolded and the room is filled with people, most of whom are police, and an irate, bewildered couple in their sixties who had returned to their apartment after an outdoor performance of *Nabucco* in the Piazza del Duomo, and who was I, how did I get there, what was I doing? Translation: What had I done? I never saw Guglielmo or Francesca again. It wasn't their apartment, of course. Were they even real? The orgasm was.

SOPRANO   "In the surging swell, in the ringing sound,

in the vast wave of the word's breath—
to drown, to sink
unconscious—supreme bliss!"

CONDUCTOR Once I asked her to tie me to the bed and sit on me. She loved it.

WIFE This is so beautiful.

CONDUCTOR Once I tied her. She loved it.

CONCERTMASTER I gotta hand it to you, asshole.

CONDUCTOR Once I let a fan—someone like you, sweetheart—try it, but I'd had too much to drink or he'd had too much to drink or he smelled funny or he said something I didn't like—like Nixon wasn't such a bad president —or he was too big or too little or one of the ten million other things that don't let you connect perfectly with another person. That afternoon in Milan when I was young and first famous and still thought the answer to a good life was in my work, in other people, in success, seems so long ago. There is no other person. There is a woman in a box who is my wife and bore me two children. There is a man in the fifth row who entertains fantasies about someone who he thinks is me. There is a concertmaster who detests me but not half as much as I detest myself. There is a cow guest soprano who sings music that has no meaning for her in a perfectly ravishing voice. And so it goes. There are a lot of people. Five billion of us, I read just this morning, and pretty soon there will be six billion and the only time I ever felt connected to any of them was when I was twenty-two years old and tied spreadeagled to a retired Milanese optometrist's bed wanting to be made love to by two people I'm not even sure exist.

(The last measures of the Liebestod *are sounding.* CONDUCTOR *takes a small Japanese seppuku blade from the music stand in front of him.)*

I know why I'm doing this. Wagner knew. Tristan and Isolde knew. That's four of us. Fuck the rest.

(He plunges the blade into his abdomen. Blood spurts onto the music stand. CONDUCTOR's *face is transfigured. Another standing ovation has begun.* SOPRANO *bows deeply to the audience in the concert hall. The* MAN *is already on his feet.)*

MAN Bravo! Bravo! We love you!

*(*WIFE *rises in her box, afraid.* CONDUCTOR *continues to stare straight ahead, blood spurting from him onto the music stand, the transfigured, ecstatic expression on his face. The ovation is mounting. The* CONCERTMASTER *is busily gathering his music, ready to leave the stage.)*

CONCERTMASTER Asshole.

Fade to black.

JOSEPH McPHILLIPS

ADAPTED FROM A STORY BY JANE BOWLES

Camp Cataract

SCENE 1

SADIE *(Seated at dining-room table, finishing a letter, smiling as she signs.)* "Your loving sister, Sadie" . . . Now, I hope Harriet appreciates this. *(Reading aloud.)* "Dear Sister, you are still at Camp Cataract visiting the falls and enjoying them. I always want you to have a good time. This is your fifth week away. I suppose you go on standing behind the falls with much enjoyment like you told me all the guests did. Here everything is exactly the same as when you left. The apartment doesn't change. I wonder, of course, how you feel about the apartment once you are by the waterfall. Also, I want to put this to you. Knowing that you have an apartment and a loving family must make Camp Cataract quite a different place than it would be if it were all the home and loving you had. There must be wretches like that up there. If you see them, be sure to give them loving because they are the lost souls of the earth. I fear nomads. I am afraid of them and afraid for them, too. I don't know what I would do if any of my dear ones were seized with the wanderlust. When you are gone, I get afraid about you. I think that you might be seized with the wanderlust and that you are not remembering the apartment very much. Particularly this trip . . . but then I know this cannot be true and that only my nerves make me think such things. Remember, the apartment is not just a row of rooms. It is the material proof that our spirits are so wedded that we have but one blessed roof over our heads. There are only three of us in the apartment related by blood, but Bert Hoffer has joined the three through the normal channels of marriage, also sacred. I know that you feel this way, too, about it and that just nerves make me think Camp Cataract can change anything. May I remind you also that if this family is a garland, you are the middle flower; for me you are, anyway. Maybe Evy's love is now flowing more to Bert Hoffer because he's her husband, which is natural. I wish they didn't think you needed to go to Camp Cataract because of your spells. Haven't I always tended you when you had them? Bert's always taken Evy to the Hoffers', and we've stayed together, just the two of us, with the door safely locked so you wouldn't in your excitement run to a neighbor's house at all hours of the morning. I hope you haven't got it in your head that just because you are an old maid you have to go somewhere and be by yourself. Remember, I am also an old maid. I must close now, but I am not satisfied with my letter because I have so much more to say. I know you love the apartment and feel the way I feel. You are simply getting a tourist's thrill out of being there in a cabin, like all of us do. I count the days until your sweet return. Your loving sister, Sadie" Oh! I can talk to her so much better than I can put it in a letter. I'll send it, but that is not enough . . . I'll go *(She is overcome with joy.)* I will. *(She stands up.)* I will journey to Camp Cataract. *(She suddenly becomes confused, but then brightens up.)* I will not mention my decision to Evy and Bert. It will be easier to write a note. I'll pack my valise and walk out tomorrow afternoon while they're at business. They can get their own dinners for a few days. Maybe I'll leave a great big meat loaf. *(Eyes shining like stars.)*

BERT *(Entering.)* Goddamned velours. It's the hottest stuff I ever sat on.

SADIE Next summer we'll get covers with a flower pattern if you like. What's your favorite flower? *(BERT looks at SADIE as if she's taken leave of her senses.)*

SADIE I'll fix you a canned pineapple salad for supper. It will taste better than heavy meat on a night like this.

BERT If you're going to dish up pineapple salad for supper, you can telephone some other guy to come and eat it. You'll find me over at Martie's Tavern eating meat and potatoes, if there's any messages to deliver.

SADIE I thought because you were hot.

BERT I was talking about the velvet, wasn't I? I didn't say anything about the meat.

EVELYN *(Entering and staring at her husband and SADIE with distaste.)* You both look ready for the dump heap, not for the dining room. Why do we bother to have a dining room . . . is it just a farce?

SADIE How was the office today?

EVELYN *(Looking at SADIE in closer scrutiny.)* What's the matter with you? There's something wrong besides your dirty apron. You look crazy. What's the matter with you? You look so crazy I'd be almost afraid to ask you to go to the store for something. Tell me what's happened!

SADIE I'm not crazy. I'll go get the dinner.

Blackout.

SCENE 2

EVELYN   When I find out why Sadie looks like that if she isn't going to be crazy, then I'll eat. *(Folding her arms across her chest.)*

SADIE   I'm not crazy.

EVELYN   *(Crossly.)* There's a big danger of your going crazy because of Grandma and Harriet. That's why I get so nervous the minute you look a little out of the way, like you do tonight. It's not that you get Harriet's expression . . . but then you might be getting a different kind of craziness . . . maybe worse. She's all right if she can go away and there's not too much excitement . . . it's only in spells, anyway. But you—you might get a worse kind. Maybe it would be steadier.

SADIE   *(Apologetically.)* I'm not going to be crazy.

EVELYN   Why don't you ask me why *I'm* not going to be crazy? Harriet's my sister and Grandma's my grandma just as much as she is yours, isn't she? *(SADIE's eyes have a faraway look.)* If you were normal, you'd give me an intelligent argument instead of not paying any attention. Do you agree, Hoffer?

BERT   Yes, I do.

EVELYN   *(Stiffening her back.)* I'm too much like everybody else to be crazy. At a picture show, I feel like the norm.

EVELYN   Take my plate and put it in the warmer, Hoffer. I won't eat another mouthful until Sadie tells us what we can expect. If she feels she's going off, she can at least warn us about it. I deserve to know how she feels. . . . I tell every single thing I feel to her and Harriet. . . . I don't sneak around the house like a thief. In the first place, I don't have any time for sneaking. I'm at the office all day! Is this the latest vogue, this sneaking around and hiding everything you can from your sister? Is it? *(Staring at BERT, widening her eyes in fake astonishment—BERT shrugs.)* I'm no sneak or hypocrite and neither are you, Hoffer, you're no hypocrite. You're just sore at the world, but you don't pretend you love the world, do you?

SADIE   *(Light-headed, with embarrassment, mumbling.)* Only for a few days . . . and then I'll be right back here at the table.

EVELYN   *(In consternation.)* What do you mean by announcing calmly how many days it's going to be? *(Shouting.)* "That's really sacrilegious! Did you ever hear of such a crusty sacrilegious remark in your life before?" *(Turning to BERT looking horror-stricken.)* "How can I go to the office and look neat and clean and happy when this is what I hear at home . . . when my sister sits here and says she'll only go crazy for a few days? How *can* I go to the office after that? How can I look right?

SADIE   *(Sorrowfully.)* I'm not going to be crazy.

EVELYN   You just said you were going to be crazy, didn't she, Bert?

BERT   Yes, she did say something like that. . . .

EVELYN   Now, tell me this much, do I go to the office every day looking neat and clean, or do I go looking like a bum?

BERT   You look okay.

EVELYN   Then why do my sisters spit in my eye? Why do they hide everything from me if I'm so decent? I'm wide open, I'm frank, there's nothing on my mind besides what I say. Why can't they be like other sisters all over the world? One of them is so crazy that she must live in a cabin for her nerves at *my* expense, and the other one is planning to go crazy deliberately and behind my back. (*Exasperated and screaming.*) I can't stand it, and I won't stand it.

SADIE   Why don't we leave the space all on one side when there's no company?

EVELYN   (*Vehemently shoving table till she knocks over one chair.*) Leave it there, leave it there till doomsday. (*Stomps out to living room.*)

BERT   What about dessert?

SADIE   Leftover bread pudding without raisins.

EVELYN   (*Summoning them from living room.*) Come here, both of you. I have something to say. I could be normal and light in any other family. I'm normally a gay, little girl . . . not a morose one. I like all the material things.

BERT   What do you want to do tonight? Do you want to be excited, or do you want to go to the movies? (*EVELYN sits with eyes shut, then suddenly gets up and walks abruptly out of the room.* BERT *follows.*)

SADIE   I'm glad Evy and Bert have gone to a picture show. Evy gets high-strung from being at the office all day. (*Walks back to dining room.*) Looks like the train went through here.

SADIE   (*Leaning against table and speaking to audience.*) I'll call up tomorrow and find out when the buses go, or maybe I'll take the train. In the morning I'll buy three different meats for the loaf, if I don't forget. It won't go rotten for a few days, and even it it does, they can eat at Martie's, or else Evy will make bologna and eggs. . . . She knows how, and so does Bert. (*Lights dim, showing only* SADIE'S *outline.*)

SADIE   (*Whispering.*) Would you like it so much by the waterfall if you didn't know the apartment was here? How much more I'll be able to say when I'm sitting right next to her. (*Pause.*) And then we'll come back here.

Fade to black.

SCENE 3

(*At Camp Cataract, where* HARRIET *is finishing reading Sadie's letter to her friend Beryl.*)

HARRIET   Sister Sadie is a great lover of security.

BERYL   She must be.

HARRIET   I have no regard for it whatsoever . . . *none*. In fact, I am a great admirer of the nomad, vagabonds, gypsies, seafaring men. I tip my hat to them; the old prophets roamed the world, for that matter, too, and most of the visionaries. *(Folding her hands in her lap with an air of satisfaction, then clearing her throat as if for a public address.)* I don't give a tinker's damn about feeling part of a community, I can assure you. . . . That's not why I stay on at the apartment . . . not for a minute, but it's a good reason why she does. . . . I mean, Sadie, she loves a community spirit, and she loves us all to be in the apartment because the apartment is in the community. She can get an actual thrill out of knowing that. But of course I can't. . . . I never could, never in a thousand years. *(Tilting her head back and half-closing her eyes.)* Now, we can come to whether I, on the other hand, get a thrill out of Camp Cataract. *(Pausing.)* Actually, I don't, but if you like, I will clarify my statement by calling Camp Cataract my tree house. You remember tree houses from your younger days. . . . You climb into them when you're a child and plan to run away from home once you are safely hidden among the leaves. They're popular with children. Suppose I tell you point-blank that I'm an extremely original woman, but also a very shallow one . . . in a sense, a very shallow one. I am afraid of scandal. *(Assuming a more erect position.)* I despise anything that smacks of a bohemian dash for freedom; I know that this has nothing to do with the more serious things in life. . . . I'm sure there are hundreds of serious people who kick over their traces and jump into the gutter; but I'm too shallow for anything like that. . . . I know it and I enjoy knowing it. Sadie, on the other hand, cooks and cleans all day long and yet takes her life as seriously as she would a religion . . . myself and the apartment and the Hoffers. By the Hoffers, I mean my sister Evy and her big pig of a husband Bert. *(Making a wry face.)* I'm the only one with taste in the family, but I've never even suggested a lamp for the apartment. I wouldn't lower myself by becoming involved. I do, however, refuse to make an unseemly dash for freedom. I refuse to be known as "Sadie's wild sister Harriet." There is something intensively repulsive to me about unmarried women setting out on their own . . . also a very shallow attitude. You may wonder how a woman can be shallow and know it at the same time, but then, this is precisely the tragedy of any person, if he allows himself to be gripped. *(Pausing and looking into darkness with fierce light in her eyes.)* Now let's get back to Camp Cataract. *(With renewed vigor.)* The pine groves, the canoes, the sparkling purity of the brook water and cascade . . . the cabins . . . the marshmallows, the respectable clientele.

BERYL   Did you ever think of working in a garage?

HARRIET   No, why should I?

BERYL   *(Shifting her position in her chair.)* Well, I think I'd like that kind of work better than waiting on tables. Especially if I could be boss and own my garage. It's hard, though, for a woman.

HARRIET   *(Staring at her in silence.)* Do you think Camp Cataract smacks of the gutter?

BERYL   No, sir . . .

HARRIET   Well, then, there you have it. It is, of course, the farthest point from the gutter that one could reach. Any blockhead can see that. My plan is extremely complicated and from my point of view rather brilliant. First, I will come here for several years. . . . I don't know yet exactly how many, but long enough to imitate roots. . . . I mean to imitate the natural family roots of chidhood . . . long enough so that I myself will feel: Camp Cataract is habit, Camp Cataract is life, Camp Cataract is not escape. Escape is unladylike; habit isn't. As I remove myself gradually from within my family circle and establish myself more and more solidly into Camp Cataract, then from here at some later date I can start making my sallies into the outside world almost unnoticed. None of it will seem to the onlooker like an ugly, impetuous escape. I intend to rent the same cabin every year and to stay a little longer each time. Meanwhile, I'm learning a great deal about trees and flowers and bushes. . . . I am interested in nature. *(She is quiet for a moment.)* It's rather lucky, too, that the doctor has approved of my separating from the family for several months out of every year. He's a blockhead and doesn't remotely suspect the extent of my scheme nor how perfectly he fits into it. . . . In fact, he has even sanctioned my request that no one visit me here at the camp. I'm afraid if Sadie did, and she's the only one who would dream of it, I wouldn't be able to avoid a wrangle, and then I might have a fit. The fits are unpleasant; I get much more nervous than I usually am and there's a blank moment or two. *(Glancing sideways at BERYL for a reaction, but BERYL is impassive.)* So you see my plan, complicated, a bit dotty, and completely original . . . not like my sisters. . . . oddly enough I don't even seem to belong socially to the same class as my sisters do. I am somehow *(Hesitating.)* more fashionable. *(Glancing out window.)* Do you think I'm a coward?

BERYL   No, sir. If you were, you wouldn't go out paddling canoes solo, with all the scary shoots you run into up and down these rivers. . . .

HARRIET   *(Twisting her body impatiently with sudden desire to be alone.)* Good-bye. *(Rudely.)* I am not coming to supper.

BERYL   *(Rising from chair.)* I'll save something for you in case you get hungry after the dining room's closed. I'll be hanging around the lodge like I always am till bedtime.

Blackout.

SCENE 4

(DRIVER arrives with SADIE at Camp Cataract.)

DRIVER   This shingled building is the main lodge. The ceiling in there is three times higher than average, if you like that style. Go up on the porch and just walk in. You'll get a kick out of it. *(SADIE reaches into pocketbook for money.)* My wife and I come here to drink beer when we're in the mood. If there's nobody much inside, don't get panicky; the whole camp goes to the movies on Thursday nights. The wagon takes them and brings them back. They'll be along soon.

SADIE *(Walking in, spots a fat woman sitting in the distance.)* She doesn't even know I'm here. Because the rain's so loud, she probably didn't hear me come in. *(Calling over to fat woman.)* Do you have anything to do with managing Camp Cataract?

ROVER No, I don't. Why? *(Pause as SADIE remains silent.)* Do you think I look like a manager? *(Pause.)* I suppose you might think I was manager here, because I'm stout, and stout people have that look; also I'm about the right age for it. But I'm not the manager. . . . I don't manage anything, anywhere. I have a domineering cranium, all right, but I'm more the French type. I'd rather enjoy myself than give orders.

SADIE French . . .

ROVER Not French, French *type*, with a little of the actual blood. *(Silence.)* Individuality is my god. That's partly why I didn't go to the picture show tonight. I don't like doing what the groups do, and I've seen the film. *(Dragging her chair forward.)* The steadies here—we call the ones who stay more than a fortnight steadies—are all crazy to get into birds-of-a-feather-flock-together arrangements. If you look around, you can see for yourself how clubby the furniture is fixed. Well, they can go in for it if they want, but I won't. I keep my chair out in the open here, and when I feel like it, I take myself over to one circle or another. . . . There's about ten or twelve circles. Don't you object to the confinement of a group?

SADIE We haven't got a group back home.

ROVER I don't go in for group worship, either, any more than I do for the heavy social mixing. I don't even go in for individual worship, for that matter. Most likely I was born to such a vigorous, happy nature I don't feel the need to worry about what's up there over my head. I get the full flavor out of all my days whether anyone's up there or not. The groups don't allow for that kind of zip . . . never. You know what rotten apples in a barrel can do to the healthy and nervous. *(ROVER gets up and walks toward exit. Just as she approaches it, BERYL enters and walks over to SADIE.)*

BERYL I can show you rooms, unless you'd rather wait till the manager comes back from the movies.

SADIE Well, you see, I'm looking for my sister. Her name is Harriet.

BERYL *(With a scowl.)* What? You must be Sadie. Harriet didn't tell me you were coming.

SADIE It's a surprise. I meant to come here before. I've been promising Harriet I'd visit her in camp for a long time now, but I couldn't come until I got

a neighbor in to cook for Evy and Bert. They're a husband and wife
. . . my sister Evy and her husband Bert.

BERYL I know about those two. Harriet's told me all about them.

SADIE Will you please take me to my sister's cabin?

BERYL I thought you folks had some kind of arrangement. I thought you folks
were supposed to stay in the apartment while she was away at camp.

SADIE Bert Hoffer and Evy have never visited Camp Cataract.

BERYL You bet they haven't. That's part of the arrangement. They're supposed to stay in the apartment while she's here at c: ip; the doctor
said so.

SADIE They're not coming up.

BERYL I'll tell you what. Instead of taking you down there to the Pine Cones
—that's the name of the grove where her cabin is—I'll go myself and tell
her to come up here to the lodge. She's got some nifty rain equipment, so
she won't get wet coming through the groves like you would . . . lots of
pine trees out there.

SCENE 5

HARRIET (At BERYL's arrival.) Beryl, what are you doing here? Are you drunk?
I'm certainly not hacking out a free place for myself in this world just in
order to cope with drunks.

BERYL Your sister Sadie's up at the lodge.

HARRIET What are you saying?

BERYL Your sister Sadie's up at the lodge, your sister Sadie who wrote you the
letter about the apartment.

HARRIET But she can't be! She can't be! It was all arranged that no one was
to visit me here.

BERYL That's what I told her.

(HARRIET paces up and down, taking deep breaths, making strange sounds.)

BERYL Take it easy . . . take it easy.

HARRIET Dash some water in my face.

(BERYL is too transfixed to move. HARRIET goes to basin and after several dashes of water,
wipes her face and resumes pacing.)

It's the boorishness of it that I find so appalling. If she's determined to
wreck my schemes, why doesn't she do it with some style, a little bit of
cunning? I can't picture anything more boorish than hauling oneself onto
a train and simply chugging straight up here. She has no sense of scheming,
of intrigue in the grand manner . . . none whatever. Anyone meeting only
Sadie would think the family raised potatoes for a living. Evy doesn't make

a much better impression, I must say. If they met her, they'd decide we were all clerks! But at least she goes to business. . . . She doesn't sit around thinking about how to mess my life up all day. She thinks about Bert Hoffer. Ugh!

BERYL   When did you and Sadie start fighting?

HARRIET   I don't fight with Sadie. I wouldn't dream of fighting like a common fishwife. Everything that goes on between us goes on undercover. It's always been that way. I've always hidden everything from her ever since I was a little girl. She's perfectly aware that I know she's trying to hold me a prisoner in the apartment out of plain jealousy, and she knows, too, that I'm afraid of being considered a bum, and that makes matters simpler for her. She pretends to be worried that I might forget myself if I left the apartment and commit a folly with some man I wasn't married to, but actually she knows perfectly well that I'm as cold as ice. I haven't the slightest interest in men . . . nor in women, either, for that matter; still, if I stormed out of the apartment dramatically the way some do, they might think I was a bum on my way to a man . . . and I won't give Sadie that satisfaction, ever. As for marriage, of course I admit I'm peculiar and there's a bit wrong with me, but even so, I shouldn't want to marry: I think the whole system of going through life with a partner is repulsive in every way. Don't you imagine, however, don't you imagine that just because I'm a bit peculiar and different from the others that I'm not fussy about my life. I *am* fussy about it, and I *hate* a scandal.

BERYL   To hell with sisters! Give 'em all a good swift kick in the pants.

HARRIET   (*Collapsing on the bed, burying her head in her hands and sobbing uncontrollably.*) I can't anymore. I can't. . . . I'm old. . . . I'm much too old.

BERYL   (*Moving next to her.*) You are not old . . . you are beautiful.

HARRIET   (*Stops crying, looks up and says:*) Beryl, you must run back to the lodge right away.

BERYL   Sure will.

HARRIET   Go back to the lodge and see if there's a room left up there, and if there is, take her grip into it so that there will be no question of her staying in my cabin. I can't have her staying in my cabin. It's the only place I have in the whole wide world . . . and if there's no room?

BERYL   Then I'll put her in my place. I've got a neat little cabin all to myself that she can have, and I'll go bunk in with some dopey waitress.

HARRIET   Well, then, go, and hurry! Take her grip to a room in the upper-lodge annex or to your own cabin before she has a chance to say anything and then come straight back here for me. I can't get through these pine groves alone . . . now . . . I know I can't.

BERYL   All right. I'll be back in a jiffy, and don't you worry about a thing.

SCENE 6

BERYL comes in, snatches SADIE's suitcase, and exits without a word.

SADIE   I feel like I was sitting at my own funeral. *(Pause.)* I hope nothing bad
  happens. . . . *(HARRIET and BERYL enter.)*

HARRIET   *(Shouting.)* Not a night fit for man or beast.

SADIE   *(Staring, then getting up to embrace her sister, backs away.)* Have you put
  on fat?

HARRIET   I'll never be fat. I'm a fruit lover, not a lover of starches.

SADIE   Yes, you love fruit. Do you want some? I have an apple left from my
  lunch.

HARRIET   *(Looking aghast.)* Now! Beryl can tell you that I never eat at night;
  in fact, I never come up to the lodge at night, *never*. I stay in my cabin.
  I've written you all about how early I get up . . . I don't know anything
  about the lodge at night.

SADIE   You don't?

HARRIET   No, I don't. Are you hungry, by the way?

BERYL   If she's hungry, we can go into the Grotto Room, and I'll bring her the
  food there. The tables in the main dining room are all set up for tomorrow
  morning's breakfast.

HARRIET   I despise the Grotto.

SADIE   I'm not hungry. I'm sleepy.

HARRIET   Well, then, we'll sit here for a few minutes and then you must go to
  bed. *(Pausing.)* I really do despise the Grotto. Actually I don't hang
  around the lodge at all. This is not the part of Camp Cataract that interests
  me. I'm interested in the pine groves, my cabin, the rocks, the streams, the
  bridge, and all the surrounding natural beauty . . . the sky also. Now, tell
  me about the apartment. . . . What's new, how are the dinners coming
  along, how are Evy and Bert?

(Before SADIE can answer, ROVER enters.)

HARRIET   Rover, come and sit with us. My sister Sadie's here.

ROVER   It's a surprise to see you up at the lodge at night, Hermit.

HARRIET   You see! I was not fibbing, was I? How are Evy and Bert? Is the
  apartment hot? *(SADIE nods.)* I don't know how long you plan to stay, but
  I'm going on a canoe trip the day after tomorrow for five days. We're going
  up the river to Pocahontas Falls. . . . I leave at four in the morning, too,
  which rather ruins tomorrow as well. I've been looking forward to this trip
  ever since last spring when I applied for my seat, back at the apartment.
  The canoes are limited, and the guides . . . I'm devoted to canoe trips, as
  you know, and can fancy myself a redskin all the way to the falls and back,
  easily. *(SADIE doesn't answer.)* There's nothing weird about it. It's in keep-

ing with my hatred of industrialization. In any case, you can see what a chopped-up day tomorrow's going to be. I have to make my pack in the morning, and I must be in bed by eight-thirty at night, the latest, so that I can get up at four. I'll have only one real meal, at two in the afternoon. I suggest we meet at two behind the souvenir booth; you'll notice it tomorrow. *(SADIE sits in silence, then leaps to her feet in terror.)*

HARRIET   What is it? Why do you look like that? Are you mad? *(SADIE relaxes.)* Why did you jump up? Is it because you are at Camp Cataract and not at the apartment?

SADIE   *(Wearily.)* It was a long and dirty train trip. I had only one sandwich all day long, with no mustard or butter . . . just the processed meat. I didn't even eat my fruit.

HARRIET   Beryl offered to serve you food in the Grotto! Do you want some now or not? For heaven's sake, speak up!

SADIE   No . . . no. I think I'd best go to bed. Take me to your cabin. . . . I've got my slippers and my kimono and my nightgown in my satchel.

HARRIET   Beryl's got you fixed up in one of the upper-lodge-annex rooms. You'll be much more comfortable up here than you would be down in my cabin. We all use oil lamps in the grove, and you know how dependent you are on electricity. . . . I get up terribly early, and my cabin's drafty, besides. You'll be much more comfortable here. You'd hate the Boulder Dam wigwams as well. Anyway, the wigwams are really for boys, and they're always full. There's a covered bridge leading from this building to the annex on the upper floor, so that's an advantage.

BERYL   We put old ladies here mostly because they can get back and forth to the dining room without going outdoors. . . . Then, also, we don't like the old ladies dealing with oil lamps, and here they've got electricity.

HARRIET   The cabins are much draftier. . . . You'll be more comfortable in the annex.

SADIE   I think I've got to go to sleep wherever. I can't stay awake anymore.

HARRIET   All right, but don't forget tomorrow at two by the souvenir booth. . . . You can't miss it. I don't want to see anyone in the morning because I can make my canoe pack better by myself . . . it's frightfully complicated. . . . But if I hurried, I could meet you at one-thirty; would you prefer that? *(SADIE nods.)* Then I'll do my best. . . . You see, in the morning I always practice imagination for an hour or two. It does me lots of good, but tomorrow I'll cut it short.

BERYL   Okay, folks, let's get going.

HARRIET   Good night. Is there anything I forgot to ask you about the apartment?

SADIE   No. You asked everything.

Blackout.

SCENE 7

(HARRIET bursts in the next morning to lodge where BERYL is seated.)

HARRIET   I can't make my pack.

BERYL   *(Removing her pipe and swinging her leg around to get out of chair.)* I'll make your pack. I would have come around this morning, but you said last night you wanted to make it alone.

HARRIET   It's Sadie . . . it's that cursed lunch with Sadie. . . . I can't go through with it. . . . I know I can't. I shouldn't have to in the first place. She's not even supposed to be here. . . . I'm an ass. . . .

BERYL   To hell with sisters. Give 'em all a good swift kick in the pants.

HARRIET   She's going to stop me from going on my canoe trip. . . . I know she is.

BERYL   No, she isn't.

HARRIET   Why not?

BERYL   She'd better not try anything . . . ever hear of jujitsu? Come on, we'll go make your pack.

HARRIET   Will you go with me to the souvenir booth? I don't want to meet her alone.

BERYL   I'll go with you, but let's stop at my cabin on the way so I can change into my uniform. I'm on duty soon.

Blackout.

SCENE 8

(SADIE, standing by souvenir booth, glances around for HARRIET. Thinking she sees HARRIET, she moves toward the image of her sister.)

SADIE   I'm pleased the diners will see us together. They'll realize that I'm no vagrant but a decent woman visiting her sister. *(Approaching image of HARRIET.)* I thought you would come out of the pine grove. I kept looking that way. I know you told me that's the way you ordinarily come. . . . Oh, Harriet, did you really make a reservation for a table? That's why you went to the terrace first, to find a more suitable table for us to talk, and you ordered Turkish pilaf. You knew it was my favorite, and you went there early because you thought it might run out. *(Studying HARRIET's face.)* You look so much refreshed . . . the night's sleep must have done you a world of good. I know we had better hurry because afterwards I do want to buy souvenirs for Evy and Bert . . . and maybe for Flo and Carl and Bobby, too. . . . Wait a minute, Harriet. . . . Look, look at the three men eating hamburgers and corn on the cob. They've put their napkins in their collars. Bert Hoffer's careful of his clothes, too. Don't you think men look different sitting all by themselves without women? . . . Okay, I'm coming now. I know you don't want them to give our table to someone else. . . . Harriet, I don't like men. *(Suddenly stops, looking wildly around for HARRIET.)* Harriet, Harriet . . . no, I'm not feeling ill. I'm not trying to look like a gorilla. *(Grabbing for HARRIET's hand.)* Come, come with me. I've got something to tell you. It's hot because the pine trees shut out all the wind. Don't mind the flies. . . . I wonder why they're here. *(Suddenly planting both feet apart.)* Let's not go back to the apartment. Let's not go back there. Let's you and me go out in the world . . . just the two of us. *(Covering her face, sobbing, looking terrified into HARRIET's face.)* You hate me, don't you? You hate me. Go away . . . go away . . . or I'll suffocate. Go away, please go away. . . . I'll suffocate.

Blackout.

SCENE 9

INDIAN CHIEF in full regalia at souvenir booth where SADIE is standing.

INDIAN CHIEF   What can I do for you?

SADIE   I'm leaving, so I want souvenirs. . . .

INDIAN CHIEF   Take your choice; you've got birchbark canoes with or without mailing cards attached, Mexican sombrero ashtrays, exhilarating therapeutic pine cushions filled with regional needles . . . and banners for a boy's room.

SADIE   There's no boy home.

INDIAN CHIEF   How about cushions . . . or canoes? . . . Which do you want?

SADIE   Both.

INDIAN CHIEF   How many?

SADIE   Eleven.

INDIAN CHIEF   Eleven of each?

SADIE   Yes . . . yes, eleven of each.

INDIAN CHIEF   You sure don't forget the old folks at home, do you?

SADIE   *(Shifting glance from his hands to his face, then suddenly looking away.)* They'll see it. . . . they'll see it, and they'll know that I've seen it, too. They must never know I've seen it. . . . *(Whispering.)* Quickly. Go out your little door and meet me back of the booth. . . . Listen! We must hurry. . . . I didn't mean to see you. . . . I'm sorry. . . . I've been trying not to look at you for years. . . . for years and years and years. . . . *(Gaping.)* Why are you standing there? We've got to hurry. . . . They haven't caught me looking at you yet, but we've got to hurry. *(Clutching at packages of souvenirs, back off toward the increasingly loud noise of the waterfall.)*

Blackout.

SCENE 10

HARRIET *(To* BERYL *as they approach souvenir booth.)* Perhaps she's been here and gone back to the lodge for a minute. I'll find out. . . . Was there a woman waiting here a while ago, Timothy?

INDIAN CHIEF A dark middle-aged woman?

HARRIET That's right.

INDIAN CHIEF She was here for an hour or more, never budged from this stall until about fifteen minutes ago.

HARRIET She couldn't have been here an hour! Not my sister. . . . I told her one-thirty, and it's not yet two.

INDIAN CHIEF Then it wasn't your sister. The woman who was here stayed more than an hour, without moving. I noticed her because it was such a queer-looking thing. I noticed her first from my chair at the bridge, and then, when I came up here, she was still standing by the booth. She must have stood here over an hour.

HARRIET Then it was a different middle-aged woman.

INDIAN CHIEF That may be, but anyway, this one left about fifteen minutes ago. After standing all that time, she turned around all of a sudden and bought a whole bunch of souvenirs from me. . . . Then, just when I was punching my belt for the change, she said something I couldn't understand—it sounded like Polish—and then she lit out for the bridge before I could give her the souvenirs or a penny. That woman's got impulses. If she's your sister, I'll give you her change in case she don't stop here on her way back. . . . But she sounded to me like a Polack.

HARRIET Beryl, run across the bridge and see if Sadie's behind the waterfall. I'm sure this Polish woman wasn't Sadie, but they might both be back there. . . . If she's not there, we'll look in the lodge. *(*BERYL *leaves stage, but returns shortly obviously in state of shock.* HARRIET *stares at Beryl's dead white face as she returns.)* Beryl? *(Shouting.)* Beryl? *(Grabbing* BERYL*'s shoulders and shaking her hard, screaming.)* Beryl!

Blackout.

CASSANDRA MEDLEY

Waking Women

The setting is a closed-in porch of a neat A-frame house in a working-class black neighborhood in a midwestern city. At rise the porch is empty. Sunshine streams through the screen windows, glistening on the potted and hanging plants that are placed on the banister in great profusion. Birds can be heard as well as the barking of unseen nearby dogs and the occasional passing of a car.

The sound of banging is heard as if someone is knocking on the screen door. MS. EDIE enters as if coming from the direction of the street. She is a black woman in her mid to late fifties, dressed in a plain housedress and slippers. She is carrying a rattan hand fan in one hand to beat off the heat and a potted plant tied with a white ribbon in the other. Her hair is done up in curlers with a hair net tied securely on her head. She has a sorrowful expression on her face as she addresses the unseen woman before her. Throughout the monologue she speaks to the audience as if speaking directly to her close friend and confidante, Lucille.

MS. EDIE Lucille! . . . I was *so* sorry to hear about it! Girl, you *know* I was gonna make it over soon as I could, you *know* I was gonna be over to see 'bout you just as soon as I was able . . . honey, I was so surprised! Gina Hawthorne just called me just now and *told* me! I said to her, I said, "*Passed?*" Whose husband done passed? . . . "Well, when did it happen?!"

My goodness. 'Cause seem to me that I saw Coleman out working in the yard just last week, seem to me, and he looked to be so *healthy*, and now you tell me he done passed! have mercy! and when's the funeral? *(Pauses.)* Oh, I see . . . *(Pauses, listening.)* Well, where your in-laws spring from? ah, so his people from Ohio! Ah-so . . . you don't say . . . and you gonna have the wake at night . . . *(Nods her approval.)* Well, that's good, that's good. Well, sir, I was *so* sorry to hear . . . *(Points to herself.)* Me? *(She leans back and fans herself vigorously.)* Aw, girl, I'm all right, I guess I'll do. *(She is frowning and scowling.)* Chile, it's just that I'm so outdone so, till I don't know *what* to do! *(Pauses.)* Hon-nee, I just can't tell you! *(Pauses.)* Well, what time is it . . . ? Okay, well, hon-nee, get ready for this.

. . . Pinkie's in labor! *(Fanning herself with indignation.)* that's *right*! Yeah, girl, Pinkie done been in labor since . . . well, she went in at four this morning and here it is what . . . ? Twelve-thirty? Okay, so she's still, yeah, chile . . . well, you know they say that first baby is always the hardest. So she's in there now and uh . . . took her down at four o'clock, her water broke at three-thirty . . . um-hum . . . Oh, yeah, that's what they say . . . that first one . . . yep . . . count on that to be the hardest. Well, now, course with me, they just "dropped" . . . I was real lucky . . . 'cause I weren't in there *no* time and 'fore I knew nothing, I was just opening up m'legs and look like my boys just "dropped" out the barrel, but hon-nee, poor Pinkie, she's up in there now and she's having a time of it. . . . *(Pauses, then with disapproval as if answering a question.)* . . . "De-troit General." . . . Yeah, that's where . . . um-hum . . . yeah *(Fans vigorously.)*

(She pauses abruptly and with scowling reacts to the unseen woman's question.)

Girl, don't ask! and ain't no sense in me troubling you with *my* trouble in *your* time of trouble! I don't even want to bother you. Naw-naw, you just rest. Never mind 'bout Pinkie, you just take it easy yourself . . . Naw-naw, never mind . . . *(Suddenly.)* Well, chile, it's just a shame! Just a sin and a shame, and that's *all* I'm gonna say!

(She seems to have closed the subject for a few beats; then she suddenly launches into a tirade.)

Shooo! That silly sister-in-law of mine! that Gladys! best good common sense my brother ever had was to *leave* that woman . . . girl, the way she brought up that poor Pinkie! *(Pause.)* Say what? Now, girl, you mean to tell me you been living in this neighborhood all this time and you *don't* know? Ha! "Paulette." yeah! "Paulette," but we been calling her Pinkie ever since she first drew breath, 'cause she was such a pretty lil "pink" thing when she come. *(Pause.)* Oh, chile, I just don't even wanna get into it 'cause you got *enough* on your mind as it is, but hon-nee, do you know, that Pinkie, that child ain't *never* been to a picture show in her *life*! Now you know that's a shame! That's the gospel truth! Fifteen years old and ain't never *ever* been to the movies in her life! I ain't telling no tale. Cause my damn sister-in-law, 'scuse my French, cause my sister-in-law Gladys just keeps Pinkie all locked up in the house *all* the time! Oh, I don't know *what* be going through Gladys's mind! She think she be sheltering Pinkie or "protecting" her or I don't know what. Keeps Pinkie in the house *all* the time! Don't let her go *nowhere*. Don't let her go out shopping with her little friends . . . *parties?* You better forget it! *Sleepovers?* Forget it! *Dances?* Forget it! Join a club? Forget it! After-school home games and whatnot? *(She waits for Lucille to silently answer back "forget it," and she nods "correct.")* You got it! And like I told Gladys, I said, "Gladys," we was sitting out on the porch and I said, "Gladys" . . . 'cause you know me, I speak my mind, if that's one thing about me, I'm gonna pull your coat from the jump. I said, "Gladys you just can't keep your daughter locked up under lock and key in the house like that," I said, "Gladys, that ain't right! 'cause *you* know and I know we was all young once, and Gladys, you just can't keep Pinkie under your nose all the damn time."

Now I know for myself, see I'm gonna tell ya, when I was young, see, I was "fast." I'm gonna tell you like it is; I was "fast." And here I was dark skinned and considered "ugly" and the boys was after me? And here Pinkie is, light skinned and with straight hair! Well, now, you *know* the boys gonna be after her! And here she can't even go to the picture show and ain't never been in her life! And I told Gladys, I said, "Gladys," "Gladys," I said, "You know that now we have got to face reality. It ain't like when we was coming up, no, it ain't. It ain't like back when they didn't talk about nothing and you weren't supposed to know nothing and when your first time of the month first come on you, you thought you was bleeding to death and all that, 'cause you didn't know no better and all, like y'know, when we come up. After all, this is 1991 and my goodness, and things have changed and you gotta face up to it!" And I told my ole silly sister-in-law, "Gladys, you just can't rule that girl like that!" I've told Gladys time and time again, "We have got to face re-ality here, and we have got to tell these kids 'bout birth control and whatnot," and hon-nee, ooohhh! What did I want to say that for? Chile, do you know she looked at me like I was the devil's own *slut*? Oh, yes, she did!

(Pause. She studies Lucille, nodding as to answer a retort.)

Well, now, I know, I *know* that, hon-nee, I know what you mean 'bout "sin," and I'm as religious as the next one, I'm as upstanding as any one of the rest of your friends, Lucille, but keeping these kids *ignorant* ain't keeping them from "sin." How's *that* s'pposed to "keep 'em from sin" . . . ? *(Pauses.)* See what I'm saying? *(Pauses.)* I mean, I mean, yeah, I see what *you* saying, but do you see what *I'm* saying? . . . So anyway, okay . . . so I said to myself right there and then, I said, *all right! so be it! lemme just shut up and back off, lemme just shut my mouth!* so I shut my mouth.

Yessir, here I am trying to plead with that ole sanctified heifer—'scuse my talk, Lucille, in your time of sorrow, but it just makes me so "outdone" and dang-blasted put-out so, till I don't know what! naw, naw, Gladys just gonna make Pinkie stay up in that house all the damn time; make her come home from school and lock her up in that house and not let her go *nowhere*.

Well, course, now, my brother? I blame him as much as anybody. He just *had* to go 'head and marry and father a child by that ole light-skinned dumb bunny—I mean y'know, hey . . . let's just admit it and call the card like it is—just 'cause he thought she was educated and pretty and proper and holy! Well! He left her and left poor Pinkie *with* her, and you see what happened, don't you? Gladys call herself keeping Pinkie pure, and Pinkie *still* ended up here with the big belly! In *my* family! a relative of *mine*, a relation to *me* with *my* family name and ending up out of wedlock and "big"!

See, 'cause these here kids these days, they gonna get out here, they are curious. And a young girl like that? Huh! Pretty as she is? You *know* she gonna be wanting to find out and to experiment and whatnot . . . with what it's like to have a boy kissing her and—and holding her and hon-nee, . . . humph! *(Fans herself vigorously.)* That's just nature, wanting somebody to be rubbing up 'gainst ya and thing. . . . Course, now that ole fool I married, well, *my* time is now dried up. . . .

(Suddenly she stops, throws her hand to her mouth, gasps in embarrassment and running on in such a way.)

Oh, my goodness, chile, listen to me carrying on at "this" time! Why didn't you stop me; oughta be 'shamed of myself . . . ! *(Pauses.)* Darlin', Lord ha-mercy, forgive me, pardon me, this ain't the time for none of this kinda talk. . . . Naw-naw, I ain't going no further. Let me stop, let me just stop. *(Pauses.)* Yeah, you may *think* you "okay" and that it "don't bother you," but I'm gonna just *stop*.

(Silence for several beats; she folds her hands in her lap.)

(Unable to contain her frustration.) But you *see* what I'm saying, though! I mean this chile is young, fine, "new minted" and shuuuu!! *(Nodding in agreement with Lucille.)* Who you telling? That age you be *wanting* to be held and have your toes curl up and . . . whew! yes ma'am! And see, when you raising these here kids nowadays, you got to face it! face that fact! things are *not* like when we was coming up. See and Gladys wanna get sour faced with me when I tell her like it is. See 'cause, I ain't gonna hold back, you know me girl, if it's gotta be *looked at* then I'm gonna make you lay it out flat in the sun and take a good look at it, yessir, whatever it is! I'm gonna get you told about it!

Well, now, I'll tell you how it went down, see . . . Here all these weeks and weeks and carrying on, see, and I'm steady coming over visiting Gladys, and here I'm noticing that Pinkie up here always got on the *same* top, day after day, week after week, the same kinda blouselike thing, like a navy blue, you know like them navy blue nylon button-down things, like a jacket, and she's wearing this thing day in and day out, from "can't see to can't see," and I'm steady coming over. Well, one day, Gladys is out of earshot, and I say to Pinkie, "Say, Pinkie? honey, you gotta change that top, girl, I think you gonna have to wash that blouse, 'cause you know how 'navy' is now, that 'navy' gets that funk in it, and you can't wash it out. . . ." I said, "Well, Pinkie, uh, you gotta change your blouse *sometime* uh . . ." and I'm thinking to myself, well what is going on? And Gladys ain't saying nothing, and I'm waiting for her to notice or say something or *something*. I guess she ain't seen it, 'cause she ain't said nothing. Gladys got her head so stuck in them prayer books—'scuse me for saying so, Lucille, on such a sad occasion—but she can't half see no way. I mean— I mean, the Lord said for us to "pray," well, okay, but not to go deaf, dumb, and blind in doing it! And then if I try and say, "Gladys, ain't Pinkie got another jacket or something to put on?" Then Gladys think I'm trying to talk bad about her, and she wanna rile up and jump up in *my* face and jump bad with me. And look like to me every time I turn round here come Pinkie in that same navy blouse, jacket-type blouse thing, so I'm thinking, *What is* with *this child?* and I said to Gladys finally, I said, "Gladys, Pinkie's wearing that thing out"! And Gladys come talking 'bout *(Imitating a high-pitched voice.)* "Well, if that's what she wants to wear, then that's what she wants, what you trying to make something of it? what you trying to start?" so I said to myself, "Well, hell, I'm gonna just let well enough alone then!" And what happened? The next thing I know Bernadette from 'cross the street come calling me, calling *my* house, talking 'bout how her daughter Carol, who's Pinkie's best friend, told *her* that Pinkie up at the school told *Carol* that she thought she *may* be pregnant and that Pinkie told Carol "not to tell nobody," but that Carol just now *told* her! Well, I said, *"Whaaaaa?"* Say *what?!* Well, hon-nee, I said to myself, *Let me go down here to Gladys's* and see what is what, see just *what* is going on here!" Well, so, hon-nee . . . I couldn't get out m'house fast enough! My phone come ringing off the hook, and who's on it but Gladys, weeping and wailing and having conniptions and pleading with me as the "Auntie" to come over and "have a word with Pinkie." Uh-hum! *See!?* And far be it for me to say, "I told you so," far be it from me to say, "I told you the pony was gonna jump the stable!"

See, and she wanna jump all up in my face when I was trying to *tell* her something way back, but now, now when it come down to the get-go, you *see* who she called on, now don't you! *(Pauses in fury.)* I'm telling, you, girl! see, now that the monkey's out the bag, now that she finds out the cards done *already* been shuffled, *then* she come calling on me "to deal!"

Hon-nee, I was so outdone! So I come over there to the house, I come over saying to myself, "Oh, Lord ha-mercy! Oh, Lord!" 'Cause you know, honey, I been *seeing* that navy blue top day in and day out. . . .

Well, honey! Get down to the house and what do I find? Gladys sitting up there with Pinkie looking all long face and looking like she been nailed to the cross and Pinkie's all wide-eyed and mystified! And Gladys acting like she ain't never left Sunday school, just hedging and swallowing and ducking and dodging! Don't know what's *with* that woman; act like she ain't never see the "wee-wee" on a dog! Don't know *how* my brother ever got a child with that woman, my goodness—that's that ole sanctified church mess. They ain't like *our* kind of Christian; them people crazy—way she act you'd think she ain't never seen herself "down there," I swear! You shoulda seen her, *(Imitating a high-pitched, awkward voice.)* "uh . . . uh, P-P-P-P-P-P-Pinkie? P-P-P-P-P-P-Pinkie?" She wanna beat round the bush and hesitate and germinate and I don't know what else. "P-P-P-P-P-P-Pinkie . . . have you—have you *done* . . . have you been doing anything?" And Pinkie she just stares at Gladys wide-eyed and shakes her head back and forth *(She shakes her head in no response.)* "Un-uh" . . . Shit, girl!!— 'Scuse me, 'scuse me, Lucille, this is not the place and this is not the time, but I was so outdone, I said, Well, hell! I mean hell! later for all this! Let's get it all out here in front and the hell with beating round the bush and carrying on and acting all prettified and citified. I said, Well, hell, let's just get it out in the open. I said, "Pinkie have you *fucked?!*" I mean, you know, *Let's just get it out here!*

Well, her Mama wanted to have a seizure, but I ain't studyin' that woman. I said to Pinkie, I said, "Pinkie, well, when was your last time you had your period?" I mean, you know, let's call a "trump card" a "trump," let's say it like *is*, let's bring it all out here! Later for all this shucking and jiving and ducking and dodging and conniving and hiding and carrying on!

Well, hon-nee, I am here to tell you, Pinkie went up to that calendar and hon-nee, them pages of that calendar went to . . .

(She illustrates with her hands flipping the air.)

. . . flipping and ah flipping and ah flipping and ah flipping and ah flipping . . . *(Her voice trails off.)* And I said, uh-oh, oh, Lord! oh, Lord ha-mercy! well, well sir, I walked up to her and hon-nee, I lifted up that ole navy blue blouse, jacket, whatever the hell it was, and that belly was ah sitting up there just as pre-tee!

And see Gladys all this time wanna keep hiding Pinkie way from the world and keeping her at home and keeping her under lock and key and keeping her all closed up and keeping her way from the boys and what happened? You *see* what happened! And I said to her, "Pinkie, when did this happen?" Well, it turns out she was sneaking some little boy round here, right in the very house of her so sanctified mama! Honey, it's the gospel truth! *(She throws her hands in the air.)* If I'm lying, Lord choke me! Right there in the basement, right under own noses. I was probably sitting up there, too, with Gladys upstairs, probably watching tee-vee with her and here Pinkie supposed to be following Gladys's ole-timey rules and regulations, supposed to be "in the bed." Ha, she was "in the bed," all right, "in the bed" down in the basement with that boy!"

And Gladys wanna act all horrified and carrying on. She wanna come talking 'bout, "If your father was still living here, if your father was still right with the Lord, then this never would have happened." I said, "Gladys, Gladys, the Lord ain't got nothing to do with it! You can't keep locking the girl up under lock and key and anyway, 'The fox has got the hen' *now*, so what we carrying on about?" And I dunno what Gladys getting all upset for, anyway, 'cause see *(She whispers very low.)* girl, I had to bite my tongue, see, 'cause Gladys don't know that I know, but I know, 'cause see my brother *let me* know, that 'fore she married my brother, the "stork had already given notice as to Pinkie," if you know what I mean. . . .

So anyway . . . yeah . . . Pinkie's laying up there now, she's laying up there in labor, and I'll tell you one thing, my dear. . . . Now she's fifteen and having this baby. . . . Oh, Gladys is gonna help take care of it, and Gladys and me we gonna hog whip that chile if she don't *stay* in school. . . . But honey . . .

(Her face is suddenly a portrait of sadness, foreboding, and old hidden recollections.)

Her childhood is *over* . . . her childhood is up! Them days of being a little carefree little girl? She can just lock 'em up . . . !

(She struggles to fight back tears.)

. . . 'Cause raising up a baby and raising up a child and being a child your own self and with no man? Trying to raise yourself plus raise something all by yourself? *(Pause.)* Talk about being "grounded in the house"? Now she *really* gonna be "grounded"! *(Pauses.)* she's on the killing ground now . . . yes, Ma'am!! Pinkie's gonna be a mama! She's on the killing ground now . . . ! *(Pauses and recovers herself.)*

So anyways, Lucille, I was so, so sorry to hear that Coleman passed . . . and now what day is the viewing of the body? Oh, that's good. Let him be laid out for a couple days. That way everybody that wants to can pay they respects; that's good. . . .

(Her voice trails off, she nods to Lucille's remarks as the lights fade.)

That's good . . . right . . . right. . . . . Amen. . . . .

Fade out.

ARTHUR MILLER

The Last Yankee

CHARACTERS

LEROY HAMILTON
FRICK

SETTING

A hospital waiting room.

The visiting room of a state mental hospital. LEROY HAMILTON *is seated on one of the half-dozen chairs, idly loafing through an old magazine. He is forty-eight, trim, dressed in subdued Ivy League jacket and slacks and shined brogans.*

    MR. FRICK *enters. He is sixty, solid, in a business suit. He looks about, glances at* LEROY, *just barely nods, and sits ten feet away. He looks at his watch, then impatiently at the room.* LEROY *goes on leafing through the magazine.*

FRICK   *(Pointing right.)* Supposed to notify somebody in there?

LEROY   *(Indicating left.)* Did you give your name to the attendant?

FRICK   Yes. 'Seem to be paying much attention, though.

LEROY   They know you're here, then. He calls through to the ward. *(Returns to his magazine.)*

FRICK   *(Slight pause.)* Tremendous parking space down there. 'They need that for?

LEROY   Well, a lot of people visit on weekends. Fills up pretty much.

FRICK   Really? That whole area?

LEROY   Pretty much.

FRICK   'Doubt that. *(He goes to the window and looks out. Pause.)* Beautifully landscaped, got to say that for it.

LEROY   Yes, it's a very nice place.

FRICK   'See them walking around out there it's hard to tell. 'Stopped one to ask directions and only realized when he stuck out his finger and pointed at my nose.

LEROY   Heh-heh.

FRICK   Quite a shock. Sitting there reading some thick book and crazy as a coot. You'd never know. *(He sits in another chair. LEROY returns to the magazine. He studies LEROY.)* Is it your wife?

LEROY   Yes.

FRICK   I've got mine in there, too.

LEROY   Uh, huh. *(He stares ahead, politely refraining from the magazine.)*

FRICK   My name's Frick.

LEROY   Hi. I'm Hamilton.

FRICK   Gladameetu. *(Slight pause.)* How do you find it here?

LEROY   I guess they do a good job.

FRICK   Surprisingly well kept for a state institution.

LEROY   Oh, ya.

FRICK   Awful lot of colored, though, ain't there?

LEROY   Quite a few, ya.

FRICK   Yours been in long?

LEROY   Going on seven weeks now.

FRICK   They give you any idea when she can get out?

LEROY   Oh, I could take her out now, but I won't for a couple weeks.

FRICK   Why's that?

LEROY   Well, this is her third time.

FRICK   'Don't say.

LEROY   I'd like them to be a little more sure before I take her out again.

FRICK   That fairly common—that they have to come back?

LEROY   About a third, they say. This your first time, I guess.

FRICK   I just brought her in last Tuesday. I certainly hope she doesn't have to stay long. They ever say what's wrong with her?

LEROY   She's a depressive.

FRICK   Really. That's what they say about mine. Just gets . . . sort of sad?

LEROY   It's more like . . . frightened.

FRICK   Sounds just like mine. Got so she wouldn't even leave the house.

LEROY   That's right.

FRICK   Oh, yours, too?

LEROY   Ya, she wouldn't go out. Not if she could help it, anyway.

FRICK   She ever hear sounds?

LEROY   Oh, ya. Like a loud humming.

FRICK   Same thing! Ts. What do you know! How old is she?

LEROY   She's forty-four.

FRICK   Is that all! I had an idea it had something to do with getting old. . . .

LEROY   I don't think so. My wife is still—I wouldn't say a raving beauty, but she's still . . . a pretty winsome woman. They're usually sick a long time before you realize it, you know. I just never realized it.

FRICK   Mine never showed any signs at all. Just a nice, quiet kind of a woman. Always slept well. . . .

LEROY   Well, mine sleeps well, too.

FRICK   Really?

LEROY   Lot of them love to sleep. I found that out. She'd take naps every afternoon. Longer and longer.

FRICK   Mine, too. But then about six, eight months ago she got nervous about keeping the doors locked. And then the windows. I had to air-condition the whole house. I finally had to do the shopping, she just wouldn't go out.

LEROY   Oh, I've done the shopping for twenty years.

FRICK   You don't say!

LEROY   Well, you just never think of it as a sickness. I like to ski, for instance, or ice-skating . . . she'd never come along. Or swimming in the summer. I always took the kids alone. . . .

FRICK   Oh, you have children.

LEROY   Yes. Seven.

FRICK   Seven! I've been wondering if it was because she never had any.

LEROY   No, that's not it. You don't have *any*?

FRICK   No. We kept putting it off, and then it got too late, and first thing you know . . . it's just too late.

LEROY   For a while there I thought maybe she had too *many* children. . . .

FRICK   Well, I don't have any, so . . .

LEROY   Yeah, I guess that's not it, either.

FRICK   I just can't figure it out. There's no bills; we're very well fixed; she's got a beautiful home. . . . There's really not a trouble in the world. Although, God knows, maybe that's the trouble. . . .

LEROY   Oh, no, I got plenty of bills, and it didn't help her. I don't think it's how many bills you have.

FRICK   What do you think it is, then?

LEROY   Don't ask me, I don't know.

FRICK   When she started locking everything, I thought maybe it's these Negroes, you know? There's an awful lot of fear around; all this crime.

LEROY   I don't think so. My wife was afraid before there were any Negroes. I mean, around.

FRICK   Well, one thing came out of it—I finally learned how to make coffee. And mine's better than hers was. It's an awful sensation, though—coming home and there's nobody there.

LEROY   How'd you like to come home and there's seven of them there?

FRICK   I guess I'm lucky, at that.

LEROY   Well, I am, too. They're wonderful kids.

FRICK   They still very young?

LEROY   Five to nineteen. But they all pitch in. Everything's clean, house runs like a ship.

FRICK   You're lucky to have good children these days. I guess we're both lucky.

LEROY   That's the only way to look at it. Start feeling sorry for yourself, that's when you're in trouble.

FRICK   Awfully hard to avoid sometimes.

LEROY   You can't give in to it, though. Like tonight—I was so disgusted I just laid down and . . . I was ready to throw in the chips. But then I got up and washed my face, put on the clothes, and here I am. After all, she can't help it, either, who you going to blame?

FRICK   It's a mystery—a woman with everything she could possibly want. I don't care what happens to the country, there's nothing could ever hurt her anymore. Suddenly, out of nowhere, she's terrified! . . . She lost all her optimism. Yours do that? Lose her optimism?

LEROY   Mine was never very optimistic. She's Swedish.

FRICK   Oh. Mine certainly was. Whatever deal I was in, couldn't wait till I got home to talk about it. Real estate, stock market, always interested. All of a sudden, no interest whatsoever. Might as well be talking to that wall over there. . . . Your wife have brothers and sisters?

LEROY   Quite a few, ya.

FRICK   Really. I even thought maybe it's that she was an only child, and if she had brothers and sisters to talk to . . .

LEROY   Oh, no—at least I don't think so. It could be even worse.

FRICK   They don't help, huh?

LEROY   They *think* they're helping. Come around saying it's a disgrace for their sister to be in a public institution. That's the kind of help. So I said, "Well, I'm the public!"

FRICK   Sure! It's a perfectly nice place.

LEROY   They want her in the Rogers Pavilion.

FRICK   Rogers! That's a couple of hundred dollars a day minimum. . . .

LEROY   Well, if I had that kind of money I wouldn't mind, but . . .

FRICK   No-no, don't you do it. I could afford it, but what are we paying taxes for?

LEROY   So they can go around saying their sister's in the Rogers Pavilion, that's all.

FRICK   Out of the question. That's fifty thousand dollars a year. Plus tips. I'm sure you have to tip them there.

LEROY   Besides, it's eighty miles there and back, I could never get to see her. . . .

FRICK   If they're so sensitive, you ought to tell *them* to pay for it. That'd shut them up, I bet.

LEROY Well, no—they've offered to pay part. Most of it, in fact.

FRICK Whyn't you do it, then?

LEROY *(Holding a secret.)* I didn't think it's a good place for her.

FRICK Why? If they'd pay for it . . . It's one of the top places in the country. Some very rich people go there.

LEROY I know.

FRICK And the top doctors, you know. And they order whatever they want to eat. . . . I went up there to look it over; no question about it, it's absolutely first-class, much better than this place. You should take them up on it.

LEROY I'd rather have her here.

FRICK Well, I admire your attitude. You don't see that kind of pride anymore.

LEROY It's not pride, exactly.

FRICK Never mind, it's a great thing, keep it up. Everybody's got the gimmes, it's destroying the country. Had a man in a few weeks ago to put in a new shower head. Nothing to it. Screw off the old one and screw on the new one. Seventeen dollars an hour!

LEROY Yeah, well. *(Gets up, unable to remain.)* Everybody's got to live, I guess.

FRICK I take my hat off to you—that kind of independence. Don't happen to be with Colonial Trust, do you?

LEROY No.

FRICK There was something familiar about you. What line are you in?

LEROY *(He is at the window now, staring out. Slight pause.)* Carpenter.

FRICK *(Taken aback.)* Don't say. . . . Contractor?

LEROY No. Just carpenter. I take on one or two fellas when I have to, but I work alone most of the time.

FRICK I'd never have guessed it.

LEROY Well, that's what I do. *(Looks at his watch, wanting escape.)*

FRICK I mean you're whole . . . your way of dressing and everything.

LEROY Why? Just ordinary clothes.

FRICK No, you look like a college man.

LEROY Most of them have long hair, don't they?

FRICK The way college men used to look. I've spent thirty years around carpenters, that's why it surprised me. You know Frick Supply, don't you?

LEROY Oh, ya. I've bought quite a lot of wood from Frick.

FRICK I sold out about five years ago. . . .

LEROY I know. I used to see you around there.

FRICK You did? Why didn't you mention it?

LEROY *(Shrugs.)* Just didn't.

FRICK You say Anthony?

LEROY No, Hamilton. Leroy.

FRICK *(Points at him.)* Hey, now! Of course! There was a big article about you in the *Herald* a couple of years ago. Descended from Alexander Hamilton.

LEROY That's right.

FRICK Sure! No wonder! *(Holding out his palm as to a photo.)* Now that I visualize you in overalls, I think I recognize you. In fact, you were out in the yard loading plywood the morning that article came out. My book-keeper pointed you out through the window. It's those clothes—if I'd seen you in overalls I'd've recognized you right off. . . . Well, what do you know. *(The air of condescension plus wonder.)* Amazing thing what clothes'll do, isn't it. . . . Keeping busy?

LEROY I get work.

FRICK What are you fellas charging now?

LEROY I get seventeen an hour.

FRICK Good for you.

LEROY I hate asking that much, but even so, I just about make it.

FRICK Shouldn't feel that way; if they'll pay it, grab it.

LEROY Well, ya, but it's still a lot of money. My head's still back there thirty years ago.

FRICK What are you working on now?

LEROY I'm renovating a colonial near Waverly. I just finished over in Belle-ville. The Presbyterian church.

FRICK Did you do *that*?

LEROY Yeah, just finished Wednesday.

FRICK That's a beautiful job. You're a good man. Where'd they get that altar?

LEROY I built that.

FRICK That altar?

LEROY Uh-huh.

FRICK Hell, that's first-class! Huh! You must be doing all right.

LEROY Just keeping ahead of it.

FRICK *(Slight pause.)* How'd it happen?

LEROY What's that?

FRICK Well, coming out of an old family like that—how do you come to being a carpenter?

LEROY Just . . . liked it.

FRICK Father a carpenter?

LEROY No.

FRICK What was your father?

LEROY Lawyer.

FRICK Why didn't you?

LEROY Just too dumb, I guess.

FRICK Couldn't buckle down to the books, huh?

LEROY I guess not.

FRICK Your father should've taken you in hand.

LEROY *(Sits with magazine, opening it.)* He didn't like the law, either.

FRICK Even so. —Many of the family still around?

LEROY Well, my mother and two brothers.

FRICK   No, I mean of the Hamiltons.

LEROY   Well, they're Hamiltons.

FRICK   I know, but I mean—some of them must be pretty important people.

LEROY   I wouldn't know. I never kept track of them.

FRICK   You should. Probably some of them must be pretty big. Never even looked them up?

LEROY   Nope.

FRICK   You realize the importance of Alexander Hamilton, don't you?

LEROY   I know about him, more or less.

FRICK   More or less! He was one of the most important founding fathers.

LEROY   I guess so, ya.

FRICK   You read about him, didn't you?

LEROY   Well, sure, . . . I read about him.

FRICK   Well, didn't your father talk about him?

LEROY   Some. But he didn't care for him much.

FRICK   Didn't care for *Alexander Hamilton*?

LEROY   It was something to do with his philosophy. But I never kept up with the whole thing.

FRICK   *(Laughing, shaking his head.)* Boy, you're quite a character, aren't you.

(LEROY is silent, reddening. FRICK continues chuckling at him for a moment.)

LEROY   I hope to God your wife is cured, Mr. Frick. I hope she never has to come back here again.

FRICK   *(Sensing the hostility.)* What have I said?

LEROY   This is the third time in two years for mine, and I don't mean to be argumentative, but it's got me right at the end of my rope. For all I know, I'm in line for this funny farm myself by now, but I have to tell you that this could be what's driving so many people crazy.

FRICK   What is!

LEROY   This.

FRICK   This what?

LEROY   This whole kind of conversation.

FRICK   Why? What's wrong with it?

LEROY   Well, never mind.

FRICK   I don't know what you're talking about.

LEROY   Well, what's it going to be, equality or what kind of country? I mean am I supposed to be ashamed I'm a carpenter?

FRICK   Who said you . . . ?

LEROY   Then why do you talk like this to a man? One minute my altar is terrific and the next minute I'm some kind of shit bucket.

FRICK   Hey now, wait a minute . . . !

LEROY   I don't mean anything against you personally, I know you're a successful man, and more power to you, but this whole type of conversation about my clothes—should I be ashamed I'm a carpenter? I mean everybody's talking "labor, labor," how much labor's getting; well, if it's so great to be labor, how come nobody wants to be it? I mean, you ever hear a parent going around saying, *(Mimes thumbs pridefully tucked into suspenders.)* "My son is a carpenter"? Do you? Do you ever hear people brag about a bricklayer? I don't know what you are, but I'm only a dumb swamp Yankee, but . . . *(Suddenly breaks off with a shameful laugh.)* Excuse me. I'm really sorry. But you come back here two, three more times and you're liable to start talking the way you were never brought up to. *(Opens magazine.)*

FRICK   I don't understand what you're so hot about.

LEROY   *(Looks up from the magazine. Seems to start to explain, then sighs.)* Nothing. *(He returns to his magazine.)*

(FRICK shakes his head with a certain condescension, then goes back to the window and looks out.)

FRICK   It's one hell of a parking lot, you have to say that.

JOYCE CAROL OATES

Tone Clusters

CHARACTERS

FRANK GULICK   *Fifty-three years old.*
EMILY GULICK   *Fifty-one years old.*
VOICE   *Male, indeterminate age.*
*These are white Americans of no unusual distinction, nor are they in any
self-evident way "representative."*

Tone Clusters *is not intended to be a realistic work; thus, any inclination
toward the establishment of character should be resisted. Its primary effect should
be visual (the dominance of the screen at center stage, the play of lights of
sharply contrasting degrees of intensity) and audio (the* VOICE, *the employment
of music—"tone clusters" of Henry Cowell and/or Charles Ives and electronic
music, etc.). The mood is one of fragmentation, confusion, yet, at times, strong
emotion. A fractured narrative emerges that the audience will have no difficulty
piecing together even as—and this is the tragicomedy of the piece—the characters*
MR. *and* MRS. GULICK *deny it.*

In structure, Tone Clusters *suggests an interview, but a stylized interview
in which questions and answers are frequently askew. Voices trail off into silence
or may be mocked or extended by strands of music. The* VOICE *is sometimes
overamplified and booming; sometimes marred by static; sometimes clear, in an
ebullient tone, like that of a talk-show host. The* VOICE *has no identity but must
be male. It should not be represented by any actual presence on the stage or
within view of the audience. At all times, the* VOICE *is in control: the principals
on the stage are dominated by their interrogator and by the screen, which is
seemingly floating in the air above them, at center stage. Indeed, the screen
emerges as a character.*

*The piece is divided into nine uneven segments. When one ends, the lights
dim, then come up again immediately. (After the ninth segment lights go out*

completely, and darkness is extended for some seconds to indicate that the piece is ended: it ends on an abrupt cut off of lights and images on screens.) By degree the GULICKS *become somewhat accustomed to the experience of being interviewed and filmed but never wholly accustomed; they are always slightly disoriented, awkward, confused, inclined to speak slowly and methodically or too quickly, "unprofessionally," often with inappropriate emotion (fervor, enthusiasm, hope, sudden rage) or no emotion at all (like "computer voices"). The* GULICKS *may at times speak in unison (as if one were an echo of the other); they may mimic the qualities of tone-cluster music or electronic music (I conceive of their voices, and that of the* VOICE, *as music of a kind); should the director wish, there may be some clear-cut relationship between subject and emotion or emphasis— but the piece should do no more than approach "realism," and then withdraw. The actors must conceive of themselves as elements in a dramatic structure, not as "human characters" wishing to establish rapport with an audience.*

Tone Clusters *is about the absolute mystery—the* not knowing—*at the core of our human experience. That the mystery is being exploited by a television documentary underscores its tragicomic nature.*

Lights up. Initially very strong, near-blinding. On a bare stage, middle-aged FRANK *and* EMILY GULICK *sit ill at ease in "comfortable," modish cushioned swivel chairs, trying not to squint or grimace in the lights (which may be represented as the lights of a camera crew, provided the human figures involved can be kept shadowy, even indistinct). They wear clip-on microphones to which they are unaccustomed. They are "dressed up" for the occasion, and clearly nervous: they continually touch their faces or clasp their hands firmly in their laps or fuss with fingernails, buttons, the microphone cords, their hair. The nervous mannerisms continue throughout the piece but should never be too distracting and never comic.*

Surrounding the GULICKS, *dominating their human presence, are TV monitors and/ or slide screens upon which, during the course of the play, disparate images, words, formless flashes of light, are projected. Even when the* GULICKS' *own images appear on the screens they are upstaged by it: they glance at it furtively, with a kind of awe.*

The monitors always show the stage as we see it: the GULICKS *seated, glancing uneasily up at the screen. Thus there is a "screen within a screen."*

The employment of music is entirely at the director's discretion. The opening might be accompanied by classical tone-cluster piano pieces—Henry Cowell's "Advertisement," for instance. The music should never be intrusive. The ninth scene might well be completely empty of music. There should certainly be no "film music" effect. (The GULICKS *do not hear the music.)*

The VOICE, *too, in its modulations is at the discretion of the director. In a way, I would like* Tone Clusters *to be aleatory, but that might prove too radical for practicality. Certainly at the start the* VOICE *is booming and commanding. There should be intermittent audio trouble (Whistling, static, etc.); the* VOICE, *wholly in control, can exude any number of effects throughout the play—pomposity, charity, condescension, bemusement, false chattiness, false pedantry, false sympathy, mild incredulity (Like that of a television MC), affectless "computer talk." The GULICKS are entirely intimidated by the VOICE and try very hard to answer its questions.*

Screen shifts from its initial image to words: "In a Case of Murder"—large black letters on white.

SCENE 1

VOICE   In a case of murder (taking murder as an abstraction) there is always a sense of the Inevitable once the identity of the murderer is established. Beforehand there is a sense of disharmony. And humankind fears and loathes disharmony. Mr. and Mrs. Gulick of Lakepointe, New Jersey, would you comment?

FRANK   . . . Yes I would say, I think that.

EMILY   What is that again, exactly? I . . .

FRANK   My wife and I, we . . .

EMILY   Disharmony . . . ?

FRANK   I don't like disharmony. I mean, all the family, we are a law-abiding family.

VOICE   A religious family, I believe?

FRANK   Oh yes. Yes, We go to church every

EMILY   We almost never miss a, a Sunday, for a while, I helped with Sunday school classes the children, the children don't always go, but they believe, our daughter Judith, for instance, she and Carl.

FRANK   Oh, yes, yessir

EMILY   And Dennis, they do believe they were raised to believe in God and, and Jesus Christ.

FRANK   We raised them that way because we were raised that way.

EMILY   there *is* a God whether you agree with Him or not.

VOICE   "Religion" may be defined as a sort of adhesive matter invisibly holding together nation-states, nationalities, tribes, families for the good of those so held together, would you comment?

FRANK   Oh, oh yes.

EMILY   For the good of . . .

FRANK   Yes, I would say so, I think so.

EMILY   My husband and I, we were married in church, in

FRANK   In the Lutheran church.

EMILY   In Penns Neck.

FRANK   In New Jersey.

EMILY   All our children,

BOTH   they believe.

EMILY   God sees into the human heart.

VOICE   Mr. and Mrs. Gulick from your experience would you theorize for our

Joyce Carol Oates / 351

audience: is the Universe "predestined" in every particular or is man capable of acts of "freedom"?

BOTH   . . . .

EMILY   . . . I would say, that is hard to say.

FRANK   Yes. I believe that man is free.

EMILY   If you mean like, I guess choosing good and evil? Yes

FRANK   I would have to say yes. You would have to say mankind is free.

FRANK   Like moving my hand. *(Moves hand.)*

EMILY   If nobody is free it wouldn't be right would it to punish anybody?

FRANK   There is always hell. I believe in hell.

EMILY   Anybody at all

FRANK   Though I am not free to, to fly up in the air am I? *(Laughs.)* because well, I'm not built right for that am I? *(Laughs.)*

VOICE   Man is free. Thus man is responsible for his acts.

EMILY   Except, oh, sometime if, maybe for instance if
        A baby born without

FRANK   Oh one of those "AIDS" babies

EMILY   poor thing

FRANK   "crack" babies Or if you were captured by some enemy, y'know and tortured Some people never have a chance,

EMILY   But God sees into the human heart, God knows who to forgive and who not.

Lights down.

SCENE 2

Lights up. Screen shows a suburban street of lower-income homes; the GULICKS stare at the screen and their answers are initially distracted.

VOICE   Here we have Cedar Street in Lakepointe, New Jersey neatly kept homes (As you can see.) American suburb low crime rate, single-family homes suburb of Newark, New Jersey population twelve thousand the neighborhood of Mr. and Mrs. Frank Gulick the parents of Carl Gulick Will you introduce yourselves to our audience please? *(Houselights come up.)*

FRANK   Go on, you first

EMILY   I, I don't know what to say

FRANK   My name is Frank Gulick, I I am fifty-three years old that's our house there 2368 Cedar Street

EMILY   My name is Emily Gulick, fifty-one years old,

VOICE   How employed, would you care to say? Mr. Gulick?

FRANK   I work for the post office, I'm a supervisor for

EMILY   He has worked for the post office for twenty-five years

FRANK   . . . The Terhune Avenue branch.

VOICE   And how long have you resided in your attractive home on Cedar Street?

(Houselights begin to fade down.)

FRANK   . . . Oh I guess, how long if this is this is 1990?
EMILY   *(Oh just think: 1990!)*
FRANK   We moved there in, uh Judith wasn't born yet so
EMILY   Oh there was our thirtieth anniversary a year ago,
FRANK   wedding no that was two years ago
EMILY   was it?
FRANK   or three, I twenty-seven years, this is 1990
EMILY   Yes: Judith is twenty-six, now I'm a grandmother
FRANK   Carl is twenty-two
EMILY   Denny is seventeen, he's a senior in high school No none of them are living at home now
FRANK   not now
EMILY   Right now poor Denny is staying with my sister in
VOICE   Frank and Emily Gulick you have been happy here in Lakepointe raising your family like any American couple with your hopes and aspirations until recently?
FRANK   . . . Yes, oh yes.
EMILY   Oh for a long time we *were*
FRANK   oh yes.
EMILY   It's so strange to, to think of The years go by so
VOICE   You have led a happy family life like so many millions of Americans
EMILY   Until this, this terrible thing
FRANK   *Innocent until proven guilty*—that's a laugh!
EMILY   Oh it's a, a terrible thing
FRANK   Never any hint beforehand of the meanness of people's hearts. I mean the neighbors.
EMILY   Oh now don't start that, this isn't the
FRANK   Oh God you just try to comprehend
EMILY   this isn't the place, I
FRANK   Like last night: this carload of kids drunk, beer drinking foul language in the night
EMILY   oh don't, my hands are
FRANK   Yes but you know it's the parents set them going And telephone calls our number is changed now, but
EMILY   my hands are shaking so we are both on medication the doctor says,
FRANK   oh you would not believe, you would not believe the hatred like Nazi Germany
EMILY   Denny had to drop out of school, he loved school he is an honor student
FRANK   everybody turned against us

EMILY   My sister in Yonkers, he's staying with

FRANK   Oh he'll never be the same boy again, none of us will.

VOICE   In the development of human identity there's the element of chance, and there is genetic determinism. Would you comment please?

FRANK   The thing is, you try your best.

EMILY   oh dear God yes.

FRANK   Your best.

EMILY   You give all that's in your heart

FRANK   you can't do more than that can you?

EMILY   Yes but there is certain to be justice. There *is* a, a sense of things.

FRANK   Sometimes there is a chance, the way they turn out but also what they *are*.

EMILY   Your own babies

VOICE   Frank Gulick and Mary what is your assessment of American civilization today?

EMILY   . . . it's Emily.

FRANK   My wife's name is,

EMILY   it's Emily.

VOICE   Frank and *Emily* Gulick.

FRANK   . . . The state of the civilization?

EMILY   It's so big,

FRANK   We are here to tell our side of,

EMILY   . . . I don't know: it's a, a democracy

FRANK   the truth is, do you want the truth? the truth is where we live Lakepointe it's changing too

EMILY   it has changed

FRANK   Yes but it's all over, it's terrible, just terrible

EMILY   Now we are grandparents we fear for

FRANK   Yes what you read and see on TV

EMILY   You don't know what to think,

FRANK   Look: in this country half the crimes are committed by the, by half the population against the other half. *(Laughs.)* You have your law-abiding citizens,

EMILY   taxpayers

FRANK   and you have the rest of them. Say you went downtown into a city like Newark, some night

EMILY   you'd be crazy if you got out of your car

FRANK   you'd be dead. That's what.

VOICE   Is it possible, probable or in your assessment *im*probable that the slaying of fourteen-year-old Edith Kaminsky on February 12, 1990 is related to the social malaise of which you speak?

FRANK   . . . "ma-lezz"?

EMILY   . . . oh it's hard to, I would say yes

FRANK . . . whoever did it, he

EMILY Oh it's terrible the things that keep happening

FRANK If only the police would arrest the right person,

VOICE Frank and Emily Gulick you remain adamant in your belief in your faith in your twenty-two-year-old son Carl that he is innocent in the death of fourteen-year-old Edith Kaminsky on February 12, 1990?

EMILY Oh yes,

FRANK oh yes that is the single thing we are convinced of.

EMILY On this earth.

BOTH With God as our witness,

FRANK yes

EMILY Yes.

FRANK The single thing.

Lights down.

SCENE 3

Lights up. Screen shows violent movement: urban scenes, police patrol cars, a fire burning out of control, men being arrested and herded into vans; a body lying in the street. The GULICKS *stare at the screen.*

VOICE Of today's pressing political issues the rise in violent crime most concerns American citizens Number-one political issue of Mr. and Mrs. Gulick tell our viewers your opinion?

FRANK In this state, the state of New Jersey

EMILY Oh it's everywhere

FRANK there's capital punishment supposedly

EMILY But the lawyers the lawyers get them off,

FRANK you bet There's public defenders the taxpayer pays

EMILY Oh, it's it's out of control (like that, what is it "acid rain"

FRANK it can fall on you anywhere,

EMILY the sun is too hot too:

BOTH the "greenhouse effect")

FRANK It's a welfare state by any other name

EMILY Y'know who pays:

BOTH the taxpayer

FRANK The same goddamn criminal, you pay for him then he That's the joke of it *(Laughs.)* the same criminal who slits your throat *(Laughs.)* He's the one you pay bail for, to get out. But it sure isn't funny. *(Laughs.)*

EMILY Oh God.

FRANK It sure isn't funny.

VOICE Many Americans have come to believe this past decade that capital punishment is one of the answers: would you comment please?

FRANK   Oh in cases of actual, proven murder
EMILY   Those drug dealers
FRANK   Yes *I* would have to say, definitely yes
EMILY   I would say so yes
FRANK   You always hear them say opponents of the death penalty "The death penalty doesn't stop crime"
EMILY   Oh that's what they say!
FRANK   Yes but *I* say, once a man is dead he sure ain't gonna commit any more crimes, is he. *(Laughs.)*
VOICE   The death penalty *is* a deterrent to crime in those cases when the criminal has been executed
FRANK   But you have to find the right, the actual murderer.
EMILY   Not some poor innocent some poor innocent

Lights down.

SCENE 4

Lights up. Screen shows a grainy magnified snapshot of a boy about ten. Quick jump to a snapshot of the same boy a few years older. Throughout this scene images of Carl Gulick appear and disappear on the screen, though not in strict relationship to what is being said, nor in chronological order. Carl Gulick in his late teens and early twenties is muscular but need not have any other outstanding characteristics: he may look like any American boy at all.

VOICE   Carl Gulick, twenty-two years old the second-born child of Frank and Emily Gulick of Lakepointe, New Jersey How would you describe your son, Frank and Emily
FRANK   D'you mean how he looks or . . . ?
EMILY   He's a shy boy, he's shy Not backward just
FRANK   He's about my height I guess brown hair, eyes
EMILY   Oh! no I think no he's much taller Frank he's been taller than you for years
FRANK   Well that depends on how we're both standing. How we're both standing Well in one newspaper it said six feet one inch, in the other six feet three inches, that's the kind of
EMILY   accuracy
FRANK   reliability of the news media you can expect!
EMILY   And oh that terrible picture of, in the paper that face he was making the police carrying him against his will laying their hands on him
FRANK   handcuffs
EMILY   Oh that isn't *him*
BOTH   that isn't our son *(The GULICKS respond dazedly to snapshots flashed on screen.)*

EMILY   Oh! that's Carl age I guess about

FRANK   four?

EMILY   that's at the beach one summer

FRANK   only nine or ten, he was big for

EMILY   With his sister Judith

FRANK   that's my brother George

EMILY   That's

FRANK   he loved Boy Scouts,

EMILY   but Oh when you are the actual parents it's a different

FRANK   Oh it is so different! from something just on TV

VOICE   In times of disruption of fracture it is believed that human behavior moves in unchartable leaps History is a formal record of such leaps but in large-scale demographical terms in which the individual is lost Frank and Emily Gulick it's said your son Carl charged in the savage slaying of fourteen-year-old shows no sign of remorse that is to say, *awareness* of the act: thus the question we pose to you Can guilt reside in those without conscience, or is memory conscience, and conscience memory? can "the human" reside in those devoid of "memory"

EMILY   . . . Oh the main thing is, he is innocent.

FRANK   . . . Stake my life on it.

EMILY   He has always been cheerful, optimistic

FRANK   a good boy, of course he has not forgotten

BOTH   He is innocent.

EMILY   How could our son "forget" when he has nothing to

BOTH   "forget"

FRANK   He took that lie detector test voluntarily didn't he

EMILY   Oh there he is weight lifting, I don't remember who took that picture?

FRANK   When you are the actual parents you see them every day, you don't form judgments.

VOICE   In every household in America albums of family lovingly preserved, many Baby Books of course Those without children elect to have pets: a billion-dollar industry Many young people of our time faced with rising costs in housing prefer to remain in the parental home And how is your son employed, Mr. and Mrs. Kaminsky? Excuse me: Gulick.

FRANK   Up until Christmas he was working in This butcher shop in East Orange

EMILY   . . . it isn't easy, at that age

FRANK   Before that, loading and unloading

EMILY   at Sear's at the mall

FRANK   No: that was before, that was before the other

EMILY   No: the job at Sear's was

FRANK   . . . Carl was working for that Italian, y'know that

EMILY   the lawn service

FRANK   Was that before? or after Oh in this butcher shop his employer
EMILY   yes there were hard feelings, on both sides
FRANK   Look: you can't believe a single thing in the newspaper or TV
EMILY   it's not that they lie
FRANK   Oh yes they lie
EMILY   not that they lie, they just get everything wrong
FRANK   Oh they do lie! And it's printed and you can't stop them.
EMILY   In this meat shop, I never wanted him to work there
FRANK   In this shop there was pressure on him to join the union.
EMILY   Then the other side, his employer did not want him to join. He's a
sensitive boy, his stomach and nerves He lost his appetite for weeks, he'd
say "oh if you could see some of the things I see" "the insides of things"
and so much blood
VOICE   There was always a loving relationship in the household?
EMILY   . . . When they took him away he said, he was so brave he said Mama
I'll be back soon I'll be right back, I am innocent he said I don't know
how she came to be in our house I don't know, I don't know he said I
looked into my sons eyes and saw truth shining His eyes have always been
dark green, like mine.
VOICE   On the afternoon of February twelfth you have told police that no one
was home in your house?
EMILY   I, I was . . . I had a doctor's appointment, My husband was working,
he doesn't get home until
FRANK   Whoever did it, and brought her body in
EMILY   No: they say she was they say it, it happened there
FRANK   No I don't buy that, He brought her in carried her whoever that was,
I believe he tried other houses seeing who was home and who wasn't and
then he
EMILY   Oh it was like lightning striking
VOICE   Your son Dennis was at Lakepointe High School attending a meeting
of the yearbook staff, your son Carl has told police he was riding his motor
scooter in the park,
FRANK   They dragged him like an animal put their hands on him like Like Nazi
Germany,
EMILY   it couldn't be any worse
FRANK   And that judge it's a misuse of power, it's
EMILY   I just don't understand
VOICE   Your son Carl on and after February twelfth did not exhibit (in your
presence) any unusual sign of emotion? agitation? guilt?
EMILY   Every day in a house, a household is like the other days. Oh you never
step back, never *see*. Like I told them, the police, everybody. *He did not.*

Lights down.

SCENE 5

Lights up. Screen shows snapshots, photographs, of the murdered girl Kaminsky. Like Carl Gulick, she is anyone at all of that age: white: neither strikingly beautiful nor unattractive.

VOICE   Sometime in the evening of February twelfth of this year forensic reports say fourteen-year-old Edith Kaminsky daughter of neighbors 2361 Cedar Street, Lakepointe, New Jersey multiple stab wounds, sexual assault strangulation An arrest has been made but legally or otherwise, the absolute identity of the murderer has yet to be

EMILY   Oh it's so unjust,

FRANK   the power of a single man That judge

EMILY   Carl's birthday is next week Oh God he'll be in that terrible cold place

FRANK   "segregated" they call it How can a judge refuse to set bail

EMILY   oh I would borrow a million dollars if I could

FRANK   Is this America or Russia?

EMILY   I can't stop crying

FRANK   . . . we are both under medication you see but

EMILY   Oh it's true he wasn't himself sometimes.

FRANK   But that day when it happened, that wasn't one of the times.

VOICE   You hold out for the possibility that the true murderer carried Edith Kaminsky into your house, into your basement thus meaning to throw suspicion on your son?

FRANK   Our boy is guiltless that's the main thing, I will never doubt that.

EMILY   Our body is innocent . . . What did I say?

FRANK   Why the hell do they make so much of Carl lifting weights, his muscles. He is not a freak.

EMILY   There's lots of them and women, too, today like that,

FRANK   He has other interests he used to collect stamps play baseball

EMILY   Oh there's so much misunderstanding

FRANK   actual lies Because the police do not know who the murderer *is* of course they will blame anyone they can.

Lights down.

SCENE 6

Lights up. Screen shows the exterior of the Gulick house seen from various angles; then, the interior (the basement, evidently, and the "storage area" where the young girl's body was found).

VOICE   If, as is believed, "premeditated" acts arise out of a mysterious sequence of neuron discharges (in the brain) out of what source do "unpremeditated" acts arise?

EMILY   Nobody was down in, in the basement until the police came. The storage space is behind the water heater, but

FRANK   My God if my son is so shiftless like people are saying just look: he helped me paint the house last summer

EMILY   Yes Carl and Denny both,

FRANK   Why are they telling such lies, our neighbors? We have never wished them harm,

EMILY   I believed a certain neighbor was my friend, her and I, we we'd go shopping together took my car. Oh my heart is broken

FRANK   It's robin's-egg blue, the paint turned out brighter than when it dried, a little brighter than we'd expected

EMILY   *I* think it's pretty

FRANK   Well. We'll have to sell the house, there's no choice the legal costs Mr. Filco our attorney has said

EMILY   He told us

FRANK   he's going to fight all the way, he believes Carl is innocent

EMILY   My heart is broken.

FRANK   *My* heart isn't, I'm going to fight this all the way

EMILY   A tragedy like this, you learn fast who is your friend and who is your enemy

FRANK   Nobody's your friend.

VOICE   The Gulicks and Kaminskys were well acquainted?

EMILY   We lived on Cedar first, when they moved in I don't remember: my mind isn't right these days

FRANK   Oh yes we knew them

EMILY   I'd have said Mrs. Kaminsky was my friend, but that's how people are

FRANK   Yes

EMILY   Carl knew her, Edith I mean, we all did

FRANK   but not well,

EMILY   just neighbors Now they're our declared enemies, the Kaminskys

FRANK   well, so be it.

EMILY   Oh! that poor girl if only she hadn't, I mean, there's no telling who she was with, walking home walking home from school I guess

FRANK   Well she'd been missing overnight,

EMILY   yes overnight

FRANK   of course we were aware

FRANK   The Kaminskys came around ringing doorbells,

EMILY   then the police,

FRANK   then they got a search party going, Carl helped them out

EMILY   Everybody said how much he helped

FRANK he kept at it for hours They walked miles and miles, he's been out of work for a while,

EMILY he'd been looking in the *help wanted* ads but

FRANK . . . He doesn't like to use the telephone.

EMILY People laugh at him he says,

FRANK I told him no he was imagining it.

EMILY This neighborhood:

FRANK you would not believe it.

EMILY Call themselves Christians

FRANK Well, some are Jews.

EMILY Well it's still white isn't it a white neighborhood, you expect better.

VOICE The murder weapon has yet to be found?

FRANK One of the neighbors had to offer an opinion, something sarcastic I guess

EMILY Oh don't go into *that*

FRANK the color of the paint on our house So Carl said, You don't like it, wear sunglasses.

EMILY But, he was smiling.

VOICE A young man with a sense of humor.

FRANK Whoever hid that poor girl's body in the storage space of our, basement well clearly it obviously it was to deceive to cast blame on our son.

EMILY Yes if there were fingerprints down there,

BOTH that handprint they found on the wall

FRANK well for God's sake it was from when Carl was down there

BOTH helping them

FRANK He cooperated with them,

EMILY Frank wasn't home,

FRANK Carl led them downstairs

EMILY Why they came to our house, I don't know. Who was saying things I don't know, it was like everybody had gone crazy casting blame on all sides.

VOICE Mr. and Mrs. Gulick it's said that from your son's room Lakepointe police officers confiscated comic books, military magazines, pornographic magazines a cache of more than one dozen knives including switchblades plus a U.S. Army bayonet (World War II) Nazi memorabilia including a "souvenir" SS helmet (manufactured in Taiwan)

VOICE a pink plastic skull with light bulbs in eyes a naked Barbie doll, badly scratched numerous pictures of naked women and women in magazines, their eyes breasts crotches cut out with a scissors Do you have any comment Mr. and Mrs. Gulick?

FRANK Mainly they were hobbies,

EMILY I guess I don't,

FRANK we didn't know about

EMILY   Well he wouldn't allow me in his room, to vacuum or anything

FRANK   You know how boys are.

EMILY   Didn't want his mother

FRANK   poking her nose in

EMILY   So. . . . *(EMILY upsets glass of water.)*

VOICE   Police forensic findings (bloodstains, hairs, semen) and the DNA "fingerprinting" constitute a tissue of circumstance linking your son to the murder but cannot rise to revelation?

EMILY   Mr. Filco says it's all pieced together Circumstantial evidence, he says.

FRANK   *I* call it bullshit. *(Laughs.)*

EMILY   Oh Frank

FRANK   *I* call it bullshit. *(Laughs.)*

VOICE   Eyewitnesses seem to disagree, two parties report having seen Carl Gulick and Edith Kaminsky walking together in the afternoon, but a third party a neighbor claims to have seen the girl in the company of a stranger at approximately four-fifteen P.M. And Carl Gulick insists he was riding his motor scooter all that afternoon.

FRANK   He is a boy

EMILY   not capable of lying.

FRANK   Look: I would discipline him sometimes,

EMILY   you have to, with boys

FRANK   Oh yes you have to, otherwise

EMILY   He was always a good eater

FRANK   He's a quiet boy

EMILY   you can't guess his thoughts

FRANK   But he loved his mother and father

EMILY   always well behaved at home. That ugly picture of him in the paper,

FRANK   that wasn't him.

EMILY   You can't believe the cruelty in the human heart.

FRANK   Giving interviews

EMILY   telling such cruel lies

FRANK   his own teachers from high school

VOICE   Mr. and Mrs. Gulick you had no suspicion no awareness you had no sense of the fact that the battered and mutilated body of fourteen-year-old Edith Kaminsky

VOICE   was hidden in your basement in a storage space wrapped in plastic garbage bags for approximately forty hours, no consciousness of any disharmony in your household?

EMILY   Last week at my sister's where we were staying, we had to leave this terrible place in Yonkers I was crying, I could not stop crying downstairs in the kitchen three in the morning I was standing by a window and there was suddenly it looked like snow! it was moonlight moving in the window and there came a shadow I guess like an eclipse? was there an eclipse? Oh

I felt so, I felt my heart stopped Oh but I, I wasn't scared I was thinking I was seeing how the world is how the universe *is* it's so hard to say, I feel like a a fool I was gifted by this, by seeing how the world *is* not how you see it with your eyes, or talk talk about it I mean names you give to, parts of it No I mean how it *is* when there is nobody there.

VOICE   A subliminal conviction of disharmony may be nullified by a transcendental leap of consciousness; to a "higher plane" of celestial harmony, would you comment Mr. and Mrs. Gulick?

EMILY   Then Sunday night it was,

FRANK   this last week

EMILY   they came again

FRANK   threw trash on our lawn

EMILY   screamed *Murderers!* they were drunk, yelling in the night *Murderers!*

FRANK   There was the false report that Carl was released on bail that he was home with us,

EMILY   Oh dear God if only that was true

FRANK   I've lost fifteen pounds since February

EMILY   Oh Frank has worked so hard on that lawn, it's his pride and joy and in the neighborhood everybody knows, they compliment him, and now Yes he squats right out there, he pulls out crabgrass by hand Dumping such such ugly nasty disgusting things Then in the A & P a woman followed me up and down the aisles I could hear people *That's her, that's the mother of the murderer* I could hear them everywhere in the store *Is that her, is that the mother of the murderer?* they were saying Lived in this neighborhood, in this town for so many years we thought we were welcome here and now *Aren't you ashamed to show your face!* a voice screamed What can I do with my face, can I hide it forever?

FRANK   And all this when our boy is innocent.

VOICE   Perceiving the inviolate nature of the Universe apart from human suffering rendered you happy, Mrs. Gulick is this so? for some precious moments?

EMILY   Oh yes, I was crying but not because of no I was crying because I was happy I think

Lights down.

SCENE 7

Lights up. Screen shows neurological X rays, medical diagrams, charts as of EEG and CAT-scan tests.

VOICE   Is it possible that in times of fracture, of evolutionary unease or, perhaps, at any time human behavior mimics that of minute particles of light? The atom is primarily emptiness the neutron dense-packed The circuitry of the human brain circadian rhythms can be tracked but never, it's said comprehended. And then in descent from "identity" (Memory?) to tissue to cells to cell particles electrical impulses axon-synapse-dendrite and beyond, beneath to subatomic bits Where is "Carl Gulick"?

(The GULICKS turn to each other in bewilderment. Screen flashes images: Kitchen interior; weightlifting paraphernalia; a shelf of trophies; photographs; domestic scenes, etc.)

VOICE   Mr. and Mrs. Gulick you did not notice anything unusual in your son's behavior on the night of February twelfth or the following day, to the best of your recollection?

EMILY   . . . Oh we've told the police this so many many times

FRANK   Oh you forget what you remember,

EMILY   That night, before we knew there was anyone missing I mean, in the neighborhood anyone we knew

FRANK   I can't remember.

EMILY   Yes but Carl had supper with us like always

FRANK   No I think, he was napping up in his room

EMILY   he was at the table with us:

FRANK   I remember he came down around nine o'clock, but he did eat.

EMILY   Him and Denny, they were at the table with us

FRANK   We've told the police this so many times, it's I don't know any longer

EMILY   I'm sure it was Denny too. Both our sons. We had meatloaf ketchup baked on top, it's the boy's favorite dish just about isn't it?

FRANK   Oh anything with hamburger and ketchup!

EMILY   Of course he was at the table with us, he had his usual appetite.

FRANK   . . . he was upstairs, said he had a touch of flu

EMILY   Oh no he was there.

FRANK   It's hard to speak of your own flesh and blood, as if they are other people it's hard without giving false testimony against your will.

VOICE   Is the intrusion of the "extraordinary" into the dimension of the "ordinary" an indication that such Aristotelian categories are invalid? If one day fails to resemble the preceding what does it resemble?

FRANK   . . . He has sworn to us, we are his parents He did not touch a hair of that poor child's head let alone the rest. Anybody who knew him, they'd know

EMILY   Oh those trophies! he was so proud one of them is from the, I guess the Lakepointe YMCA there's some from the New Jersey competition at Atlantic City two years ago?

FRANK   no, he was in high school the first was, Carl was only fifteen years old

EMILY   Our little muscle man!

VOICE   Considering the evidence of thousands of years of human culture of language art religion the judicial system "The family unit" athletics hobbies fraternal organizations charitable impulses gods of all species is it possible that humankind desires not to know its place in the food cycle?

EMILY One day he said

VOICE Mr. and Mrs. Gulick . . .

EMILY he wasn't going back to school, my heart was broken.

FRANK Only half his senior year ahead but you can't argue, not with

EMILY oh his temper! he takes after, oh I don't know who

FRANK we always have gotten along together in this household haven't we

EMILY yes but the teachers would laugh at him he said girls laughed at him he said stared and pointed at him he said and there was this pack of oh we're not prejudiced against Negroes, it's just that the edge of the Lakepointe school district well

FRANK Carl got in fights sometimes in the school cafeteria and I guess the park?

EMILY the park isn't safe for law-abiding people these days they see the color of your skin, they'll attack some of them are just like animals yes they *are*

FRANK Actually our son was attacked first it isn't like he got into fights by himself

EMILY Who his friends are now, I don't remember

FRANK He is a quiet boy, keeps to himself

EMILY he wanted to work he was looking for work

FRANK Well: our daughter Judith was misquoted about that

EMILY also about Carl having a bad temper she never said that the reporter for the paper twisted her words Mr. Filco says we might sue

FRANK Look: our son never raised a hand against anybody let alone against

EMILY He loves his mother and father, he respects us

FRANK He is a religious boy at heart

EMILY He looked me in the eyes he said Mama you believe me don't you? and I said Oh yes he's just my baby

FRANK nobody knows him

EMILY nobody knows him the way we do

FRANK who would it be, if they did? I ask you.

Lights down.

SCENE 8

Houselights come up, TV screen shows video rewind. Sounds of audio rewind. Screen shows GULICKS onstage.

VOICE Frank and Mary Gulick we're very sorry something happened to the tape we're going to have to re-shoot Let's go back just to, we're showing an interior Carl's room the trophies I will say, I'll be repeating Are you ready? *(Houselights out, all tech returns to normal.)* Well Mr. and Mrs. Gulick your son has quite a collection of trophies!

FRANK   . . . I, I don't remember what I

EMILY   . . . yes he,

FRANK   Carl was proud of he had other hobbies though

EMILY   Oh he was so funny, didn't want his mother poking in his room he said

FRANK   Yes but that's how boys are

EMILY   That judge refuses to set bail, which I don't understand

FRANK   Is this the United States or is this the Soviet Union?

EMILY   we are willing to sell our house to stand up for what is

VOICE   You were speaking of your son Carl having quit school, his senior year? and then?

EMILY   . . . He had a hard time, the teachers were down on him.

FRANK   I don't know why,

EMILY   we were never told And now in the newspapers

FRANK   the kinds of lies they are saying

EMILY   that he got into fights, that he was

FRANK   that kind of thing is all a distortion

EMILY   He was always a quiet boy

FRANK   but he had his own friends

EMILY   they came over to the house sometime, I don't remember who

FRANK   there was that one boy what was his name

EMILY   Oh Frank Carl hasn't seen him in years he had friends in grade school

FRANK   Look: in the newspaper there were false statements

EMILY   Mr. Filco says we might sue

FRANK   Oh no: he says we can't, we have to prove "malice"

EMILY   Newspapers and TV are filled with lies

FRANK   Look: our son Carl never raised a hand against anybody let alone against

EMILY   He loves his mother and father,

FRANK   he respects us

VOICE   Frank and, it's Emily isn't it Frank and Emily Gulick that is very moving.

Lights down.

SCENE 9

Lights up. Screen shows GULICKS *in theater.*

VOICE   The discovery of radioactive elements in the late nineteenth century enabled scientists to set back the estimated age of the Earth to several billion years, and the discovery in more recent decades that the Universe is expanding, thus that there is a point in time when the Universe was tightly compressed smaller than your tiniest fingernail! thus that the age of the Universe is many billions of years uncountable. Yet humankind resides in Time, God bless us. Frank and Emily Gulick as we wind down *our* time together *What are your plans for the future?*

FRANK   . . . Oh that is, that's hard to that's hard to answer.

EMILY   It depends I guess on

FRANK   Mr. Filco had advised

EMILY   I guess it's, next is the grand jury

FRANK   Yes: the grand jury. Mr. Filco cannot be present for the session to protect our boy I don't understand the law, just the prosecutor is there swaying the jurors' minds Oh I try to understand but I can't,

EMILY   he says we should be prepared we should be prepared for a trial

VOICE   You are ready for the trial to clear your son's name?

FRANK   Oh yes . . .

EMILY   Yes that is a way of, of putting it Yes. To clear Carl's name.

FRANK   . . . Oh yes you have to be realistic.

EMILY   Yes but before that the true murderer of Edith Kaminsky might come forward. If the true murderer is watching this *Please come forward.*

FRANK   . . . Well we both believe Carl is protecting someone, some friend another boy

EMILY   the one who really committed that terrible crime

FRANK   So all we can do is pray. Pray Carl will come to his senses give police the other boy's name, or I believe this: if it's a friend of Carl's he must have some decency in his heart

VOICE   Your faith in your son remains unshaken?

EMILY   You would have had to see his toes, his tiny baby toes in his bath. His curly hair, splashing in the bath. His yellow rompers or no: I guess that was Denny

FRANK   If your own flesh and blood looks you in the eye, you believe

EMILY   Oh yes.

VOICE   Human personality, it might be theorized, is a phenomenon of memory yet memory built up from cells, and atoms does not "exist": thus memory like mind like personality is but a fiction?

EMILY   Oh remembering backward is so hard! oh it's,

FRANK   it pulls your brain in two.

EMILY   This medication the doctor gave me, my mouth my mouth is so dry In the middle of the night I wake up drenched in

FRANK   You don't know who you are until a thing like this happens, then you don't know.

EMILY   It tears your brain in two, trying to remember, like even looking at the pictures Oh you are lost

FRANK   in Time you are lost

EMILY You fall and fall, . . . ever since the, the butcher shop he wasn't always himself but who he was then, I don't know. But it's so hard, remembering why.

FRANK Yes my wife means thinking backward the way the way the police make you, so many questions you start forgetting right away it comes out crazy. Like now, right here I don't remember anything up to now I mean, I can't swear to it: the first time, you see, we just lived. We lived in our house. I am a, I am a post office employee I guess I said that? well, we live in our, our house. I mean, it was the first time through. Just living. Like the TV, the picture's always on if nobody's watching it you know? So, the people we were then, I guess I'm trying to say those actual people, me and her the ones you see *here* aren't them. *(Laughs.)* I guess that sounds crazy,

VOICE We have here the heartbeat of parental love and faith, it's a beautiful thing Frank and Molly Gulick, please comment?

FRANK We are that boy's father and mother. We know that our son is not a murderer and a, a rapist

EMILY We know, if that girl came to harm there is some reason for it to be revealed, but

EMILY They never found the knife, for one thing

FRANK or whatever it was

EMILY They never found the knife, the murderer could tell them where it's buried, or whatever it was. Oh he could help us so if he just would.

VOICE And your plans for the future, Mr. and Mrs. Gulick of Lakepointe, N.J.?

FRANK . . . Well. I guess, I guess we don't have any.

(Long silence, to the point of awkwardness.)

VOICE . . . Plans for the future, Mr. and Mrs. Gulick of Lakepointe, N.J.?

FRANK The thing is, you discover you need to be protected from your own thoughts sometimes, but who is there to do it?

EMILY God didn't make any of us strong enough I guess.

FRANK Look: one day in a family like this, it's like the next day and the day before.

EMILY You could say it *is* the next day, I mean the same the same day.

FRANK Until one day it isn't

Lights out.

JOHN OSBORNE

A Bond Honored

CHARACTERS

LEONIDO
TIZON   *His servant.*
DIONISIO   *His brother-in-law. Husband of Marcela.*
MARCELA   *Sister of Leonido.*
GERARDO   *His father.*
BERLEBEYO   *Moorish king.*
ZULEMA   *A Moor.*
ZARRABULLI   *A Moor.*
LIDORA   *A Moorish lady.*
MAID

SCENE 1

All the actors in the play sit immobile in a circle throughout most of the action. When those who are all in the same scene rise to take part in it, they all do so together. Long cloaks should be worn. The acting style is hard to discover or describe. I will just say: It must be extremely violent, pent-up, toppling on and over the edge of animal howlings and primitive rage. At the same time, it should have an easy, modern naturalness, even in the most extravagant or absurd moments. It requires actors like athletes who behave like conversationalists. It is not impossible or as difficult as it sounds. We English are more violent than we allow ourselves to know. That is why we have the greatest body of dramatic literature in the world.

Sicily. GERARDO's *garden by the sea.* TIZON, *a servant, lies asleep.*

VOICE OFF   Tizon! Tizon! *(Enter* LEONIDO.*)*
LEONIDO   Tizon! Tizon—why, of course, of course asleep. All easy, aren't you, snoozing? Like a basket of old laundry, mucky and no use to anyone. Wake up! Up!

TIZON   Master! I fell asleep.

LEONIDO   Tizon, when you sleep, you should do it under cover, in a hole or some cellar. Your sleeping's like your eating and most other things about you. It's better not looked on. When you just swallow a glass of wine the effect's like the dead stink of a bat dropped into a well. As for your other functions, I daren't think of them. But to find you *asleep*, all mess and remains like some decomposing beast, by the roadside, is so hateful to anyone awake to life itself, itself—you're lucky I didn't kill you.

TIZON   Forgive me.

LEONIDO   I can't forgive what I can't remake. Asleep! Why! You watch me when it suits your book.

TIZON   It was late, my lord.

LEONIDO   It's not late by my clock, and that is the one *you* live by. My heartbeat's the one you pay heed to. Your own's not worth keeping up for. You keep up for mine. It's more than you deserve, but it's what you've got and then you go and leave me when I'm alone and awake and waiting. Why? Eh?

TIZON   I was tired.

LEONIDO   Tired. Why? Tizon?—Are you tired?

TIZON   I don't know.

LEONIDO   No, you don't. Why should you be tired, you onlooker? You do nothing. And you're not furniture—nor decoration. There's no sweat in watching. I—I live for you, Tizon. You have nothing to do, nothing to expend. Busy little lard bundles should keep awake during the intervals and dull bits. Hear me! Keep awake and stay with me. And give me that wine. Is Dionisio gone yet?

TIZON   He's still with your father.

LEONIDO   How do you know, you don't even know you stink, you rumbling, drowsy equivocator?

TIZON   I—

LEONIDO   You don't. You're flailing, aren't you?

TIZON   I am sure—

LEONIDO   No. Not *am* sure.

TIZON   I was watching—

LEONIDO   Am *not* sure.

TIZON   Master—

LEONIDO   You're dishonest, treacherous and you even botch treachery worse than most other men. Not *am* sure, Tizon.

TIZON   Yes.

LEONIDO   What?

TIZON   Yes, master.

LEONIDO   Yes, to what? What? Yes? You don't know. You back it as easily as "no" if you think it'll come up. Don't know. Not watching—for once. The thing one should at least demand from a fool is stamina. Get up! *(Kicks him.)* Tell me, no, not why, how, how can you sleep so much? Hey? When I've not slept for three nights?

TIZON   I don't know.

LEONIDO   Three nights since I slept and then only for a few minutes before I was tipped out by my sister.

TIZON   Sh!

LEONIDO   Sh what! Tipped out before her closing-up time at dawn. What is it, why are you squinting and winking like some bit of bridal bait in the dark?

TIZON   My lord!

LEONIDO   You're like my sister. Ah, there's her light. Gone to bed already to get away from the tedium of her betrothed. Bridal bait. Marcela! Marcela! Gone to bed? Bridal bait!

TIZON   My lord, I beg you!

LEONIDO   Her maid's drawn her curtain. She sees herself as a bride guard, too. What are you begging?

TIZON   Be circumspect.

LEONIDO   About?

TIZON   What may or may not in the past, that is, have occurred between you and your sister. Now that she's to be a bride—

LEONIDO   Not may or may not have. Has. Did. Is. Not was, might, may. *Is.* Well?

TIZON   It's unkind to pollute Dionisio's opinion of his bride. As well as your father's affection for his daughter—

LEONIDO   As for Dionisio's minced opinions about my sister or any other object —they could only interest my father by their enormity of dullness.

TIZON   Then think of yourself, Leonido.

LEONIDO   Leonido, is it?

TIZON   Your reputation. I'm sorry.

LEONIDO   Don't be. Leonido was good for a moment. You almost creaked into life there, old fat bones, blown-up bones, yes, they are, why your bones have turned, so they have, they've simmered into gristle and jelly there, from all that sleep. From sleep that babyish dreaming in the belly that fishy swimming in mother's old moorings.

TIZON   Stop!

LEONIDO   Stop! Does your mother know you're back in there again?

TIZON   What is it? Do you want no man's good opinion.

LEONIDO   Not yours!

TIZON   No! Not mine.

LEONIDO   Good! First Leonido, now some more exertion. Is it only what the world thinks that stops your bones bubbling eh?, in their dull stew and gets you to your feet? And answer me back? Now: Nothing I have done has ever made me feel that anyone is better than I am. Though I was brought up to believe the reverse. See if Dionisio's still with my father. Why is it that of what they call the five Hindu hindrances you have only one: sloth? I have all the other four, craving, ill will, perplexity, and restless brooding? I think that's right? Yes.

TIZON They're still talking together.

LEONIDO I could do with your sloth. Talking dowries and property and being important over my sister's body and disposing of it—as they think. So they think.

TIZON If you have betrayed *Marcela's* virtue, you must keep it to yourself.

LEONIDO You're as full of ifs as you are fleas. I've a harsh heart, Tizon, but don't sidle up to it or walk backwards away from it like my father does. That numb old nag now—he never took a difficult fence in his life, either.

TIZON He's an old man.

LEONIDO He was born an old man. So was Dionisio. And you. All born dotards, and overarmored. You need no protection from me.

TIZON Need but not expect.

LEONIDO Good. Don't expect. As for Marcela, she is the best part of the world for me. But she's not virtuous. No, not virtuous.

TIZON She isn't now.

LEONIDO She never was. I don't know what virtue is. Can you tell me? I have never had any myself, and I never observed any in others, either. You've none.

TIZON You don't mean this.

LEONIDO I *have* watched myself for signs of it, I promise you. I am purblind to the needs of others just as they are to mine. Your laughter may be my pleasure, but your howlings might be, too. I've set traps and tried to catch myself out in a virtuous act, but I've never done what people call a good thing that didn't give me pleasure. What ill service can I do myself? What affection have I ever felt that didn't run home back to me at the end of the day? *Who* do I like? Or love? No one. Myself? A little. But not much, I'm not much lovable. Although I *am* preferable to anyone that is. For me I detest clever men and dullards. I could roast and baste them slowly myself and read a book at the same time or top and tail a virgin. Or something. Simple men are too content and ambitious men are ambitious and ambitions too simple to be tolerated, tolerated or countenanced by *anyone*—at least who has ever sat down quietly and consistently and decently schooled themselves in pain. For their own pleasure? Well—there's more mettle in painful pleasure even than, than the restraints of overprotected and feeble men like them—those two there. You see, there, it all flies back to *pleasure*, like stooping falcon. Pleasure in self, shallow self, cracked and wormy as I may be. You're the same, Tizon. Surprised. We're no different, you and I. I *am* somewhat swifter at the kill. Always and every time. Will be. And forever more. There is no disinterest in nature. And good and evil are men's opinions of themselves.

TIZON   Dionisio's leaving.

LEONIDO   Good. *Why* do you watch me, Tizon?

TIZON   I am your servant.

LEONIDO   Can you, can you tell me the truth?

TIZON   I try.

LEONIDO   How can you be honest? You are cursed with dishonest eyes. Yes. It should be a handicap in a servant, but! Daresay it gets overlooked. Not noticed. They're full of blood, as usual. Have you looked at them? Poor pink, pink, not red, mark you pink lines. And meanness and envy, envy most of all. The will to wound but no will, lackey's eyes, traced indelicately, not attractively. Loaded with shame, shame and the dread of punishment. . . . No wonder I avoid your eyes. Why do you watch me?

TIZON   No servant tells the truth.

LEONIDO   Right! Nor could. Is the old man gone to bed?

TIZON   Yes.

LEONIDO   Very well. I think then . . . I shall go up to my sister. Well? Servant. Were you about to say something?

TIZON   No, my lord.

LEONIDO   My lord again. And what will *you* do while I am awake upstairs? Niffy dormouse?

TIZON   I shall wait.

LEONIDO   Not doze?

TIZON   No.

LEONIDO   No? Dozy?

TIZON   No.

LEONIDO   You'll doze. One day you *shall*. And who knows when that is? And perhaps you'll want to then? However . . . wait. You may get some more pleasure from me before then. So my sister's waiting. . . . Her light burns. Not overbrightly, but it burns. Just about to put it out . . . but I'll be there before then. Sisters are there to be trapped, Tizon. Tripped up. And over she goes. We'll talk again soon? I doubt I'll be sleeping much tonight, or if I do, something will waken me. Try not to doze. (*He goes.* TIZON *stays awake.*)

SCENE 2

MARCELA's *bedchamber.* MARCELA *in her nightgown with her* MAID. *The* MAID *looks out of the window.*

MAID   He's gone.

MARCELA   Who? (*Enter* LEONIDO.)

LEONIDO   Why, Dionisio.

MAID   My lord!

LEONIDO   Gone. And so may you be now. Get along.

MAID   My lady is about to sleep.

LEONIDO   My lady is about to talk.

MAID   Sir!

LEONIDO   With me! We are not strangers to one another. You must know that
there's a matter of blood between us. And between *us*? Please: the door.

MAID   Good night, lady! *(He thrusts her out.)*

LEONIDO   Good night. And how *is* my lady, then?

MARCELA   Prepared for sleep.

LEONIDO   Well, prepare yourself for bed first. All this sleeping. Your betrothed
has gone off—to sleep, too, no doubt.

MARCELA   I would rather you did not bawl up at my window.

LEONIDO   Bawl?

MARCELA   Ay! Bawl! Bridal bait!

LEONIDO   Bridal bait! This is your brother, chicken. Come along! Look at me
now. What is it? Aren't I allowed to bait you?

MARCELA   Leave me.

LEONIDO   Make me.

MARCELA   You bait to kill.

LEONIDO   Not you.

MARCELA   Yes. Me. You were never playful.

LEONIDO   I have played with you, Marcela, since the day you were born.

MARCELA   To win or wound. Which you always do.

LEONIDO   How did you leave your betrothed?

MARCELA   Well.

LEONIDO   And easily?

MARCELA   He's angry with you.

LEONIDO   I may sleep tonight yet. The thought of Dionisio's anger would make
an owl yawn. Well?

MARCELA   He complains you have lied all over Sicily that he's a bastard. That
his mother was a whore and a crone and the only woman who has died
in childbed of old age.

LEONIDO   Does this sound like my invention?

MARCELA   Yes.

LEONIDO   There! It made you smile.

MARCELA   Well: He has not the edge himself to make such a fancy, I admit.

LEONIDO   I may have said something.

MARCELA   Something? What was it?

LEONIDO   I don't know. About old bitches dropping runts only. But bastard no.
Dionisio is *legitimate*. He's lawful as an endless sermon. That's not to say
proceedings shouldn't be taken up against him for being born at all. No,

for certain he is in the common run of legitimacy. A bastard's common, too, but a bastard you see's separate, a weed, often strong, quite powerful. Like your Charlemagne, your King Arthur, your Gawain, your Roland, and your Irish kings. There! You're smiling at me. It *is* fun, not repentance, makes remission of sins.

MARCELA There's none of either in you. Or ever will be. *(He mauls her.)* Go to your own bed, Leonido! You are mad.

LEONIDO This is one of my lucid patches. *(They kiss. She stops struggling.)*

MARCELA Stop! You have a tongue like a lizard.

LEONIDO There are a great many flies in your gullet. They should be got out. Otherwise, you will choke. *(He kisses her again.)*

MARCELA Blow out the light . . . that's better.

LEONIDO Now you're close to me again, Marcela. Marcela . . . When you look coldly on me, I think my bowels will break. . . . Marcela . . . Marcela. . . .

MARCELA Yes?

LEONIDO I can't see your face. . . . What defect is there in me? I find beauty and comfort . . . and sustenance . . . only . . . in you. There's no light from the sea tonight. I can't see your face. I don't care what people may speculate. I do *not* want them to know. Not words or movements or moments. Those are for our pleasure, only. Marcela? Secrecy *is* the nerve of love. Can you see me? Marcela? Are you asleep? . . .

SCENE 3

GERARDO's garden. DIONISIO sits with his bride, MARCELA, on the terrace by the sea. TIZON lies drunk among the flowers. Enter GERARDO with LEONIDO, who kicks TIZON as he passes.

GERARDO I cannot understand you.

LEONIDO Or young men like me.

GERARDO Or young men like you.

LEONIDO Whoever *they* may be. Only old men seem to have the good fortune to meet them.

GERARDO What?

LEONIDO Go on, Father, you talk endless doggerel as if it were the poetry of revealed doctrine. But go on. It's your privilege.

GERARDO *You* are too privileged. In my time—

LEONIDO As if now wasn't his time—

GERARDO —time it was all war and uncertainty. Now everything is easy come by, and you and those like you hang about sniffing blood ungratefully and harrying everyone and everything in your rancorousness.

LEONIDO Old men inhabit what are clear for miles as fortresses all their lives and talk as if they were pigging it in mud huts.

GERARDO   What?

LEONIDO   There's no cutting a way through your hairy old ear. Is there? I say that clapper tongue of yours has deafened you inside that hollow bell. Hollow bell.

GERARDO   Bell. Wedding bell?

LEONIDO   Bedding well. Yes. Very soon from the look of them. Your head, Father, the top, there, where your cap screws on, you rancid old jar.

GERARDO   You are too full of contempt.

LEONIDO   I take in a fresh stock twice weekly and whenever I am with *you*.

GERARDO   Do you hear?

LEONIDO   Alas, my ears are *not* overgrown with old man's moss. Could you not clean up that old garden to your brain one day, Father? It might not be easier to enter, but it might be more pleasant for the rest of us.

GERARDO   You tread upon your sister's bridal gown. You abuse her husband. You hiss dislike and envy at the priest. I think your midriff and your backbone must be full of—serpents.

LEONIDO   They'd be useful worms for dim dogs like the priest—or, indeed, you, Father. I say! At least, they stop me growing fat on commonplaces.

GERARDO   See, there. Look there. Your sister still weeps at the remembrance of your cruelty. All her days, I daresay. And on her wedding day.

LEONIDO   Or at the yawning expectation of her wedding night. Or the expectation of her yawning wedding night. Tizon? What? Retiring already, Marcela!

MARCELA   I am tired and unwell.

LEONIDO   Who has made you unwell, then? Dionisio?

DIONISIO   You shall not come near her again, Leonido. I have told her. Nor enter our house ever.

LEONIDO   Not welcome? Nowhere? Marcela?

MARCELA   Nowhere.

LEONIDO   Never?

MARCELA   No.

GERARDO   Come, child. Take her to bed, Dionisio. It's best. Your brother has not altogether blighted this day for you, and thank heavens, the night is not in his hands. My blessings on you both and be at peace together while you may. And remember Father Augustine.

MARCELA   "Our heart is restless till it finds itself in thee."

GERARDO   Good, child. Take her, Dionisio.

LEONIDO   Why, you've been busy, bride, you've been gospeling and swapping pieties with the priest.

MARCELA   We prayed together.

DIONISIO   All night.

LEONIDO   You'll not be up so long, so don't hurry. So! This is why you are so feverish—from sitting out in a devotional draft. That's why her bed was empty!

MARCELA I was not seeking your permission. And, Leonido, listen from this time: I obey only my husband.

GERARDO There, Leonido. Embrace it, and off with you.

MARCELA Good night, Father.

GERARDO Good night, my child. *(They turn.)*

LEONIDO Marcela? *(Pause.)* Good night. *(She stares coldly, grasps DIONISIO's hand and goes into the house. GERARDO regards him for a moment, then follows them. Music. LEONIDO stands stricken. Presently, TIZON hands him a flagon of wine to drink from. LEONIDO takes it and drinks.)* So. Rome has spoken. The matter is settled.

TIZON That's the way of it, my lord. That's the way of it.

LEONIDO What's the way of what? Must you look out at the sea and not here? There's nothing stirring out there.

TIZON Quietly, my lord. They are joined together now—

LEONIDO And by what dishonest mortar.

TIZON You must accept it.

LEONIDO I accept nothing. Nothing is offered.

TIZON Her light is on.

LEONIDO Not for me . . . it isn't . . . being looked on as a good bargain . . . Gerardo! Do you hear me now! I always worked for passion rather than for profit, for the salt pearls that ran down the knots of her spine. Marcela! *(He stares up at MARCELA's window. More music. TIZON drops off. LEONIDO draws his sword. He strikes him with it. TIZON is brought to his feet by the sudden pain.)*

LEONIDO Draw! Draw! *(Confused, TIZON does so. They duel. LEONIDO's rage helps him to beat TIZON quickly, and he has his sword pointing at his belly.)* There! *(TIZON goes.)* One day, one day of your lifetime I shall kill you with this sword. Now? No. Tonight or tomorrow or in a year. Whenever you affront me most or I'm most impatient. Don't misjudge the time by my mood. It may be when I'm gasping for want of enemies or running idly up to a joke. . . . See how alert you must be! You'd better keep awake while you can. After all, that alone, that incessant discipline, will add to your span. It must do so. Now, isn't that a fierce, energetic structure for a man to be alive in. That'll keep you awake. It'll keep you *occupied*. You won't *dare* sleep. Or perhaps you will. We'll see. It may not matter to you, it may come, it may not. Now you're breathing, now you're bleeding. Ah! *Never* turn your back on me. Or look away. *Watch* me, Tizon. And now I shall spoil the bride's sleep. You may as well wait a while. Relax yourself a little. *(He takes a lamp and goes, leaving TIZON to wipe the blood from his face.)*

SCENE 4

MARCELA's bedchamber. Enter LEONIDO with lamp. MARCELA in bed.

MARCELA Dionisio?

LEONIDO No—Leonido!

MARCELA I beg you to leave me. Brother, you have had the best of me.

LEONIDO And you of me.

MARCELA Well! Now leave the rest to Dionisio. It's little enough but the best for all of us.

LEONIDO At last! You confess it was the best!

MARCELA I confess it to flatter you, to be rid of you before my husband returns.

LEONIDO Are you so hot for this husband's—*hus*band—husband's jobbery? Is there no more, sweetheart? Please?

MARCELA Ask me no explanations. There is no more. I have nothing for you.

LEONIDO Marcela. We have been conspirators. Can you deny it? We have never thought of winning—only of each other. I thought of us only as two children together. *(She laughs.)* Anything, any excess is preferable to this miserable subordination, this imposture, this—

MARCELA Go!

LEONIDO This low,—low, uterine appeasement!

MARCELA Dionisio!

LEONIDO It is only in you that I see a foot ahead of me and my heartbeat recovers. What is it now? A life of scavenging for slops of your attention. Eh? Upturned from the window to your bedchamber? Remember, my mouth, my mouth, your mouth, Marcela.

MARCELA A man cannot make a wife of his sister. It's bane for both of them. Don't ask me why. Ask the world or God, or what, but there's law and nature against you in their battalions. Now go, my dear, I am afraid enough already.

LEONIDO Marcela, I am a woman's son. Your mother's son. I love women. Shall I *tell* you? No? Why? Sister: when did you ever look for me as I looked for you?

MARCELA Always.

(They kiss.)

Dionisio! He's coming!

LEONIDO Sister, what has this man done . . . to you? He has laid his mark on you. You are healed somehow and hardened. Where's your blood now? Your lap is as wooden as a bench. You *will* not, no, *not*, sweetheart, not deprive me? Take off your shift. . . .

(LEONIDO begins stripping MARCELA, who screams. DIONISIO enters.)

MARCELA Dionisio! My God, *help* me!

(The men duel. DIONISIO falls. LEONIDO strikes MARCELA with his sword and goes.
MARCELA goes to DIONISIO as he recovers.)

SCENE 5

GERARDO's garden. Enter LEONIDO with bloody sword. He grins at TIZON.

LEONIDO It's done.

TIZON But not well. Was it?

LEONIDO No, not well this time, but let's say we celebrated all the occasions
past when it was well done.

TIZON Have you no feeling? Even for reckoning?

LEONIDO I have God's credit for the moment. Let him settle up for me, and
send in his account when he wants to. He must know my credit's good,
indeed. He has never—in his eternal life—had a client with better prospects
or security. Nor ever will have. Come. I'm bored here. Let's go.

TIZON Where?

LEONIDO We'll have a late stroll in the marketplace. You'll enjoy that. And
you will sleep all the better for it.

TIZON You want to show off your sister's blood in the marketplace.

LEONIDO Oh, you think I killed her?

TIZON Didn't you?

LEONIDO No. I added a few grace notes to her face.

TIZON God gave her one face and a good one, and you add to it! Like mine.
Don't you think you'll pay for all this handiwork of yours.

LEONIDO I'll tell you: send the bill in to God. I'll settle with him later. Don't
concern yourself, Tizon. You'll lose your sleep.

TIZON For the final settling up! I will stay awake. I promise you.

LEONIDO Good, Tizon. I do believe I've smoked out your torpor. For tonight
run! With me! Come! Here's the old man with the other. Oh—breathless
with survival, too. *(They hide. Enter GERARDO and DIONISIO.)* Nasty pala-
verer. He's woken the old pudding from his prayers.

DIONISIO How can I tell you?

LEONIDO How indeed?

DIONISIO I came upon them together. Together, my wife, his sister, and both
of them your children. It's quite famous the kind of man he is, but I
thought I was secure on this occasion. But I was wrong. Señor. I blame
you. Yes, you. You have not checked him as you could have done, and
now we all suffer for it. He has stolen from us all, from you, from his sister,
and now from me. Look at my face!

GERARDO Marcela. Did she defend herself?

DIONISIO   As well as she could. And now she has a striped face like mine to show for it.

GERARDO   Oh, Leonido!

DIONISIO   Nothing will change him. I shall hunt him down. *(LEONIDO appears.)*

LEONIDO   Hunt me down, then.

GERARDO   What have you done with my daughter?

DIONISIO   Not what he set out for.

LEONIDO   Not on *this* evening. However, it is true I have left some equipment somewhere—sometime—in that particular warren.

(DIONISIO draws.)

It is true, Father, I tried to rob her—honor on this special night. Not because she wanted me to but because that is how *I* was born. By the same brutality. As you well know. With any good fortune I shall still insult her blood and yours, too, and take away what little honor you have creasing beneath your mattress. I did it not because it was good but interesting. I am glad to see it's painful to both of you.

GERARDO   Leonido. Why must you do these things to us? You are pillaging my heart. For all his mercy, the good God must punish you with the miseries of hell. Oh, if I could be wrong in that.

LEONIDO   Then be comforted. The precedents for your prognostications are most encouraging. *(DIONISIO lunges at LEONIDO.)* Out of the way, old man.

GERARDO   You call me old man because you have darkened the name father. Because you know you deserve no father nor even to mouth the word.

LEONIDO   So! You want my attention! *(He strikes him. GERARDO cries out.)*

DIONISIO   Father, you'll be revenged.

LEONIDO   If I fix a place, will you trust me?

DIONISIO   Yes, even you.

LEONIDO   You must not expect more or better of me. . . . My fingers are like quills. Read the message on your face. . . . Very well. I can't bear to look on that any longer. If it's revenge, then, let us say sunset. By the seashore. Tonight.

(He goes.)

GERARDO   Humble him, oh, God! I am too infirm. Let some Moorish lance skewer my own son. May they drag him on a halter into Tunis, a bruised litter of flesh strung behind some fleeing camel!

DIONISIO   Be calm, Father. You have a new son here. In me. Take a little pleasure in your son and daughter and what's to come from both of them. Let me lift you. There. On my shoulder. There.

GERARDO   Let's go to see your wife, my daughter. Your grief is mine just as she is mine.

DIONISIO   There, Father. Come.

GERARDO   Let the world judge these two men. I ask no more of it. Nothing.

SCENE 6

Sicily. A beach. LEONIDO *lies sleeping. Enter* KING BERLEBEYO, ZULEMA, *and* ZARA-BULLI.

KING   Praise Allah. Sicilian sand! Feel it.

ZULEMA   As you commanded, o King.

ZARRAB.   We can snare all the Christians we can carry home here, and then back off to Tunis.

KING   I wish they'd appear. If it were not for Lidora, I'd be at home. Where are we?

ZULEMA   This is the port of Alicarte. And this is the beach of Saso. Christians come here, I promise you, my king.

ZARRAB.   Take care you are not converted. They are great wheedlers.

ZULEMA   Here's one; he's asleep.

KING   Take his sword.

ZULEMA   Ah! *(He takes it.)*

KING   Now wake him.

LEONIDO   Why, you black lard!

KING   Tie his hands.

LEONIDO   I can see, sir, you have not been to Sicily before. Here then. *(He grabs a branch from a tree.)*

KING   *Kill* him, Zulema! Kill the Christian!

LEONIDO   Kill the Christian! Kill the Moor! *(They fight.* LEONIDO *fights like a madman and disarms them all.)*

KING   I surrender! Surrender! I never, anywhere, saw such strength. I am your slave, and if it is your pleasure, I think it will be mine. Who are you?

LEONIDO   I will tell you. But drink this wine first.

KING   I don't drink wine.

LEONIDO   Drink: King. *(He drinks.)* Well, Moor. King Berlebeyo, oh, I know you. I was born in Alicarte, by the river Saso near the mountains of Petralia. They say that when my mother gave birth to me, the whole island heard it and her breasts were covered in blood, as a sign of hatred, you see, and Etna, yes, Etna erupted, and the only contented soul here was my own. They were frightened of me from the first. Not that I killed anyone. Only wished to. They were all consumed with process. Had no idea of the unique. Me, I had an overstrong instinct, you understand, and this is an island of overprotected people. The range of possibilities in living here shrinks with every year. Soon it will be every week, then daily. I am a liar.

Lying is inescapable to me. I understand a liar and I cherish a thief. I think I have raped thirty women, and I don't include my mother, who hardly resisted. My sister took to it regularly and easily except on her wedding night. Why, I don't know. Something is wrong. God or myself. But then: I stabbed her twice in the face, oh, yes, and her husband. I could fatten *him* up for you. And then there was the man who calls himself my father, but no more, I dare say. That pleased me more than all the rest. So, you see, proud Moor, *you* are the tail end.

KING   Valiant and noble Leonido, by the sacred temple where lies the holy and divine body of Mahomet, although I am ashamed of capture and am heir to a kingdom, I rejoice in being your captive. I come here to please a Moorish lady whom I long for. Her name is Lidora and she asked me for a Sicilian Christian, even though she has more than she knows what to do with. So I come. And found my master.

LEONIDO   Then we shall take you back to Lidora, eh? All of us. Drink. Go on.

KING   If I do—Mahomet will punish me.

LEONIDO   Refer him—to me. *(He drinks.)* There—we shall get on. Now, give me a cloak and turban. *(Enter* TIZON. *He watches in horror.)* Ah, Tizon. Help me with these.

ZARRAB.   Master! It is *my* task. *(*ZARRABULLI *and* ZULEMA *robe him in Moorish costume. The others watch.)*

LEONIDO   What do you think, Tizon? *(He lunges.)* Dozing, Tizon! Do I make a good Moor? When do you think you'll die?

TIZON   You make a grand Turk. A Suleiman—

LEONIDO   Go and tell my father this—I renounce his blood. Also his God, his law, the baptism and the sacraments, oh, yes, and the Passion and Death. I think I shall follow Mahomet.

TIZON   Leonido! How can you ask me? I dare not take such a message.

LEONIDO   Dare not! Well, then—

TIZON   No—I'll take it.

LEONIDO   Yes.

KING   May you wear this and live forever, Leonido!

LEONIDO   And you, too. And now let us go and see this Lidora.

KING   I am your slave.

LEONIDO   And my master.

TIZON   I will go, then. Think on this, Leonido.

LEONIDO   I don't think. But I shall observe my processes as well as I can.

TIZON   I'll take this long cloak of yours and hat as witnesses of what's happened. Remember: You have a debt to pay to heaven.

LEONIDO   And remember also: I have the best bond. Let the Good Lord pay pound for pound. I'll settle later. *(Exits.)*

SCENE 7

Tunis. Enter LEONIDO *in Moorish costume. With him* LIDORA, *a Moorish lady.*

LIDORA   Stop.

LEONIDO   Why?

LIDORA   Turn and face me.

LEONIDO   But I've no wish to face you.

LIDORA   You are cruel.

LEONIDO   It comes easily if you apply yourself to it.

LIDORA   I love you.

LEONIDO   Me?

LIDORA   You.

LEONIDO   Or my cruelty is it? What if I'm not for the asking?

LIDORA   I shall die.

LEONIDO   Now or later?

LIDORA   On your account.

LEONIDO   So you keep saying.

LIDORA   Great Argolan!

LEONIDO   Lidora?

LIDORA   Won't you love me?

LEONIDO   I've no need, nor the energy or curiosity.

LIDORA   Oh, you are cruel.

LEONIDO   Yes, and you're a fool. I am only one of them, but you can be both.

LIDORA   Dearest!

LEONIDO   I am weary of your Moorish yapping and haggling. Now leave me.

LIDORA   Does my beauty mean nothing to you?

LEONIDO   The sun hasn't burned up my head even if it has yours. To me you are no more beautiful than some overheated whelp trailing strangers in the bazaar. I have loved oh, many women, Lidora, or performed, I suppose, the rituals of it passably well. I allow then that you're beautiful, and you can take some pride in that, though not much. Beauty is just one of many wells you might have been dropped in when your mother bore you. And all Moorish women bore me. Oh, there's a great deal of display in you, but I think it promises too much. There's a trick in there, possibly hundreds of them, and that, Lidora, is repellent. To me.

LIDORA   I am Moorish, but I, too, hate Moors. I have much to give you. I know it. Love me, Argolan. *(Enter the* KING.*)*

KING   Is this how you observe the king's law?

LIDORA   When did I not heed your law?

KING   Why, by trying to enlist proud Argolan here as one of your lovers. Now.

LIDORA   What offense is there in that, then?

KING   There is this offense: You swore that when I brought you a Christian you would love me.

LIDORA   True. But you are not betrayed yet. Besides, for all that, what Christian did you bring back? You brought back a *Moor*, and I am in love with him. I would give him my heart's blood if he asked for it.

LEONIDO   Don't be rash, Lidora. Heart's blood adds relish to a dull, many a dull, dish.

LIDORA   I would give him more than relish. I love him even for the clothes he wears and his renunciation. If he were still Christian, I should love him. *(Exits.)*

KING   Well, Argolan. What do you say?

LEONIDO   It's a common pattern. The more she protests, the less I want to hear about it. When I love this woman, Mahomet will no longer be a holy prophet, Berlebeyo.

KING   For this favor you are doing me, Argolan, you shall see the true art and scope of the great love I bear for you. Tunis is yours. Demand whatever you want of it. My kingdom is yours.

LEONIDO   I don't want someone else's kingdom.

KING   Try on my crown.

LEONIDO   I'll not go shares. *If* I wear your crown one day, it shall be in my own kingdom.

KING   Are you mad? Remember: You have left your own homeland behind.

LEONIDO   A sprightly old cock will crow anywhere he likes. Call on your government, King. Call on your city. Call out Mahomet. I am going to eat you! Out, Moor, out with your sword!

KING   Lidora! *(Enter LIDORA.)*

LIDORA   What's this?

LEONIDO   The one you love. I shall bust your law, break your city, strike at friendship and kill your king. I'll wait for you by the river. *(Exits.)*

KING   Rot you, you dog!

LIDORA   Wait. Wait, noble Berlebeyo. Check yourself.

KING   What?

LIDORA   Swallow your bitterness. It's acid that runs through dwarfs. For the love of me, and yourself, pardon him.

KING   If you wish it. But only then, then I will. I cannot see for anger, nor can I now, only you and your love can rein me in. Hold me in. Hold me. There!

LIDORA   May Mahomet strengthen you forever. *(Enter ZARRABULLI.)*

ZARRAB.   Lidora, what is the reward for good news?

KING   Bargains after.

LIDORA   Tell us.

ZARRAB.   Zulema is at the gates with as many Christian prisoners as you'd wish for.

LIDORA   Oh! Is it true?

ZARRAB. They are Sicilians.

LIDORA Tell him to come in.

ZARRAB. He is very Pompey.

KING He's a fine soldier. *(Enter ZULEMA, GERARDO, TIZON, and MARCELA —prisoners.)*

ZARRAB. Come in, Christians. Kiss King Berlebeyo's feet. And you, my lord, put your foot in their mouths. And in mine.

LIDORA Oh, you have excelled yourself! Tell me what has happened.

ZULEMA I have been lucky, as you shall see.

LIDORA Tell me.

ZULEMA Lidora, I set out happily from Tunis, with no thought but of your pleasure, with a hundred Moors. After weeks on the water, I made out the high walls of Sicily, packed with those people who follow this cross, followers of the naked prophet, who they say is on nodding terms with God. I landed, split my men into bands, and looked for the quarry. In the darkness we saw nothing, but at dawn on the foreshore Allah rewarded us for the night with three men and one woman. One of the men I spliced with my cutlass to clear the air and the remainder are here before you. Three fine Sicilians for your pleasure.

LIDORA You have pleased me so much, so exceedingly, I can think of only one gift adequate.

ZULEMA Lidora: you offer me more than any conquest I have ever made.

LIDORA You're worthy of it.

KING Divine Mahomet. Do you give yourself to anyone for a gift.

ZULEMA I think, great lord, *your* claim is undisputed. Forgive me. Let Lidora keep this gift. I remain your slave. I meant only to give you, my lord, delight through her.

KING She does not deserve Christians for servants but Mahomet himself. Zulema, I present this ring to you. Take it, but not for payment. As a sign of affection.

ZULEMA On another expedition I will do better. For you both. You shall have the Eastern church on one hand, the Western on the other. Roman and Eastern shall touch the soles of your feet.

TIZON So much talk and no wine with it, ever.

LIDORA With your leave, lord, I'll send for Argolan.

KING Wait till I have gone.

ZULEMA Have you fallen out?

LIDORA It is over now. Argolan is coming back to us.

ZULEMA Then he can meet his countrymen.

KING Find him.

ZULEMA I shall go. I only wish to serve you.

LIDORA I know how you should be repaid. *(He goes.)*

KING I will leave you alone. I've no fancy for any of these. *(He goes.)*

John Osborne / *385*

LIDORA   What is the matter? Why are you weeping? Remember you don't yet know whose power you have fallen into. Even though you are prisoners, you must not look like this. Your face is beautiful. Let me look at it.

MARCELA   O, noble and beautiful Moor. It is not for myself. What moves me is the condition of this old man. His dignity and wisdom are the world's luck. If I should serve you, it'll not matter. I know how to bear things, and I hope you will be patient with me. But how can this man serve you when he has such a short time to live. How, señora, can he be of use when he is worn out. What pleasure can you take in these powdery bones? He is certain to displease and irritate. Punish me for his fault, I beg you, even twice as much. If the father errs, then let the daughter pay, señora, let the daughter pay.

LIDORA   No more. Now I beg *you*. Wipe your eyes. What is your name?

MARCELA   Marcela.

LIDORA   Calm yourself, Marcela. Your father may be a prisoner, but he has found another daughter.

MARCELA   Señora.

LIDORA   Old man. Embrace me, old man. *(GERARDO weeps.)* Our love is clasped in this for good. Hold me closer. Ask him for me, Marcela, for he will listen to you. Even if all Tunis rises up, I will affirm today that I have met my father. Are you happy to be father to me?

GERARDO   I will be your slave.

LIDORA   Put up a front before the Moors and lift your head a little. Stop crying, Marcela. We are sisters. Truly.

TIZON   What about me? Who lifts my head for me? *(Enter LEONIDO.)*

LEONIDO   Well? Ah, Tizon! You have woken in a strange place.

LIDORA   I wanted only to please you, Argolan.

LEONIDO   And I wished to please you. So?

MARCELA   Dear God, what have I done to you to set me under him again!

LIDORA   I wanted to show how much I adore you, Argolan. These prisoners, all Christians, have just been given to me by Zulema. They all serve me, and I want you to know, they will serve you with me. *(GERARDO goes to kiss the soles of LEONIDO's feet.)* May it please Allah!

LEONIDO   I will treat you all as you deserve. Are you honored to be at my feet? Heaven casts you down just as it casts me up. You at my feet, yes, you paltry old toad. I'll not have your mouth near any shoe of mine, or I'll have to burn it afterwards. Get up! You're a brave groveler. Own the earth do you? Do you? *(He kicks GERARDO in the mouth.)* Get up!

GERARDO   Oh, divine heaven!

TIZON   You struck him on his knees.

LEONIDO   Why not. It's his natural posture.

GERARDO   This is what a good father suffers from a bad son.

LIDORA Father, get up, get up. I put myself in your hands. What is happening between you?

GERARDO Oh, bad son.

LEONIDO I your son? Utter the name son again to me and I'll hook your jaw to the rafters.

LIDORA What have I done to you, Leonido?

LEONIDO Do you know me?

MARCELA I never knew you! Why don't you kill me—Moor?

LEONIDO Mahomet will have his vengeance on you both. You won't find protection here.

LIDORA Father, sit down, sit down in this chair.

MARCELA *Moor*, do as you like. Do as you like.

LEONIDO Oh, Marcela. I've waited for you.

MARCELA But take care.

LIDORA Come to my arms, señor.

GERARDO Do not weep, child. I am better. *(Sits.)*

MARCELA Take care, Leonido. *(LEONIDO takes out his dagger.)*

LEONIDO Father? Father?

GERARDO Yes?

LEONIDO Do your old eyes see this?

GERARDO They do.

LEONIDO Then they still see very well. *(He strikes GERARDO in the eyes. GERARDO covers them with a cloth.)*

MARCELA Lidora, hold him!

LEONIDO Now you can see less than you ever chose to see.

LIDORA What jungle did you spring from. Oh!

LEONIDO Kiss this blade, old man. Down, go on! Your daughter wants me to kill you in her own way. Marcela, do your duty by me. Yes? Or watch the old toad croak.

MARCELA There's no answering you. I can't.

GERARDO Don't be doubtful, Marcela. Better that I should die than you should be his lover.

LEONIDO Does either matter?

GERARDO I will not have her dishonored.

LEONIDO Answer?

MARCELA Kill him.

LEONIDO So!

MARCELA Wait!

GERARDO Don't lose heart, Daughter.

LEONIDO He'd best die. I assure you.

MARCELA Die, then! No!

LEONIDO Speak up, Sister.

MARCELA   I want him to die.

LEONIDO   Ah!

MARCELA   Not to die!

LEONIDO   You're in some difficulty? *(She covers her eyes, but LEONIDO makes her watch.)* Now!

MARCELA   Now?

LEONIDO   And on your daughter's head!

GERARDO   Follow him, Marcela. Follow him.

MARCELA   Then do it.

LEONIDO   Do it?

MARCELA   Yes.

LIDORA   Argolan! *(She holds him back.)*

LEONIDO   By the Koran, Argolan will have you for dessert. But Tunis shall burn first. *Tunis first. (He goes.)*

SCENE 8

Tunis. Enter LEONIDO, distracted, like a madman. A voice interrupts now and then as he speaks.

LEONIDO   Marcela!

VOICE   Lidora.

LEONIDO   Marcela. I feel the bond tightening. Yes, it's tightening.

VOICE   Calm.

LEONIDO   Beyond logic so beyond doubt. Marcela, miserable, deluded, and deluding family. Where are you? Where's your timorous Dionisio? Where is your *memory* of me? It shall soon fail. My imprint will have died out of all hearts inside a month. Discard. A discard. I have been mostly, a fair mixture of intelligence, mostly, self-criticism and, yes, gullibility. Yes, that's a hesitating assessment.

VOICE   Hesitate.

LEONIDO   But there's a hint in it.

VOICE   Hint.

LEONIDO   Allah! God! Marcela. Gullibility, self-criticism. Such people are always identifying, scrabbling for their stars, for signs in themselves, in the latest philosophy twice a week. If you have no dreams or portents for the day, they will knock one up for you. If you have not hit your wife or thought of killing your father. Mother. Daughter. Son. They will think you impoverished, or insensible. You will be made to dream again. I want no more dreams.

VOICE   For that which I do.

LEONIDO   I allow not. For what I would, that I do not. But what I hate, that I do. I know that in me.

VOICE   In my flesh.

LEONIDO   There is no good thing. For the will is present in me. But how to perform what is good. I find . . .

VOICE   Not.

LEONIDO   For the good thing I would, I do not. . . . But the evil: That I do. So then I find the law. When I do good, evil is present in me. For I delight in the law of God after the inward man. But I see another law in my members, warring against the law of my mind, and bringing me into captivity.

VOICE   To the law of sin.

LEONIDO   Which of my members? Who shall deliver me? *(Enter SHEPHERD, barefoot.)*

SHEPHERD   Cannot a hard heart soften?

LEONIDO   Ay, soften. That will do. Soften is the course.

SHEPHERD   Curse.

LEONIDO   It's you. You, who spoke. Who are you?

SHEPHERD   I am a shepherd.

LEONIDO   Where are you going?

SHEPHERD   Doing shepherd's work.

LEONIDO   What are sheep to you? Or you to sheep even? Leave them. Let them die as they want to.

SHEPHERD   No. As I want.

LEONIDO   Have you called out?

SHEPHERD   It won't hear.

LEONIDO   Not?

SHEPHERD   So I grieve for it.

LEONIDO   You don't look like grief. Give up.

SHEPHERD   It was too costly for me. I am afraid he shall die.

LEONIDO   Who shall die?

SHEPHERD   Why, the sheep.

LEONIDO   Damn your ignorant sheep! What are you? A Moor?

SHEPHERD   I am no Moor.

LEONIDO   You have the look of one. They are the mercenaries of Allah. They are all cutthroats, and stall holders with prayers on their lips and all the time graft at their elbow.

SHEPHERD   *You* are dressed as a Moor.

LEONIDO   I was once dressed as a Sicilian. Christian. But neither Sicilian nor Christian meant anything to me. Who are you? Why are you loitering? What do you want? Alms? Go away.

SHEPHERD   I want no alms. But the debt you owe must be recovered.

LEONIDO   Perhaps you are a thief. I am a thief myself, and I know the signs of a thief. Just as I know a liar. Go away, lunatic.

SHEPHERD   In this meager pouch is what you owe me.

LEONIDO   Give it to me. I'll look at it. But let me warn you: If you are making game of me, I shall kill you.

SHEPHERD   I hear you. *(Hands him the pouch.)*

LEONIDO   I can hardly hold it.

SHEPHERD   It is harder still to carry.

LEONIDO   Ah, a conjurer's bag. I knew you had a look of the bazaar about you. Let's look inside. First dip: There's a lucky one. A crown. I shall wear that. It will look better on me. I feel calmer. Emptying this loon's pouch, perhaps. Oh, delightful! A tunic. Oh, yes. And with lash marks on it. It looks like a motto, is it your motto, some device? Are the lashes my motto? Why? Do you think I'm a slave? Like you? What else is there? A rope. That's good. I may lash you with this. So this is your bond. What are these things? More clothes. *(He takes out a cross.)* Why are you mocking me? If you were God himself, you'd get no reprieve from me. I am going to kill you. *(He falls to the ground.)*

SHEPHERD   Why are you afraid, Leonido? Who are you thinking of? Your mother? Gerardo? Marcela?

LEONIDO   Marcela!

SHEPHERD   Think of your sister's body. Then look into my heart. Think of your father's eyes. Then look into mine. Tell me, Leonido, what are you waiting for? What? Now that the debt is due, what are you thinking of paying with? Today, Leonido, I have to collect everything you have spent. I paid for all of them, but this is the reckoning. And I am here for it.

LEONIDO   I am overspent. It's not in your interest to believe me. But it is the case. I always knew it would be so. You will get, if you are so fortunate, a bankrupt's farewell, which is somewhat less than a penny in the pound. So be it, then. You will have had access to my books, so there is nothing for me to do but acknowledge each item, which might give satisfaction to you as a kind of divine lawyer's fee, but as wearisome to me as the hell I go to and the hell I came from. You shall have my life, which is what you came for. It's no more than fluff at the bottom of the pocket. *(Gives him fluff.)*

SHEPHERD   Let me embrace you.

LEONIDO   Kill me first. *(The SHEPHERD goes.)* I'll go to such extremes the world will use me as an example. Let's off, first with the scimitar. Cloak, hood. And turban. Tunic, yes, better than the Moorish for a debtor of my proportions. It's a good garment to stand trial in. We don't expect acquittal, do we? Perhaps *they* do, though. He looked uncertain. No, we want a harsh tribunal and the full exercise of justice. You, crown, you sit between my ears, like a child above the crowd. Tears from ears, tears from the heart, there's a wad of tears. And rope, rope, you shall need me, too. If I'm to settle up. Be made to seem to settle up.

(Moves off. Blackout. Lights up. Enter ZULEMA and the KING.)

KING   Know this, Zulema. Do not be surprised at Leonido's reversal. A bad Christian was never a good Moor. When he followed his own heavenly father, he never kept his limits. Tunis was no different to him. The man who jeers at his three for one in God will gob in Mahomet's eye for sixpence.

ZULEMA   There he is. What's he doing?

KING   Kneeling. Go on, bind him.

ZULEMA   I will try.

LEONIDO   Come, Moor, come all of you. Leonido is no longer the same man, but he will flog you a little like he did before. And then you shall have me. You shall have your man, defeated as I am. The liar you found so difficult will become a dismal lamb. *(They fight. Brutally. Then LEONIDO throws in his hand.)* Now you may take me.

ZULEMA   It's a trick.

LEONIDO   No more than all the rest, Zulema. Come along, take this rope around my neck. Grab it, go on. I am a mule now. Or lamb or what you want of me. If you want pickings from Mahomet, here's one for you.

KING   Leave him to me, Zulema. *I* want the slaughtering of this butcher. *(Chase. LEONIDO laughs. Dances.)* Got him! Got! You! *(They bind him with the rope.)* Let's go. To Tunis.

LEONIDO   To Tunis. Christ support me!

(Blackout. Lights up. LIDORA and TIZON.)

LIDORA   Go on! You are so lethargic. I want to catch up.

TIZON   Yes, ah, the articles, well, you know those already.

LIDORA   And our Father and the Credo.

TIZON   The Ave Maria.

LIDORA   Go on! Go on!

TIZON   Listen, then, señora. I will teach you the precepts which we must observe if we are to enjoy God's favor.

LIDORA   How many are there?

TIZON   No more than ten.

LIDORA   Do you mean a Christian's salvation depends only on ten commandments?

TIZON   That's all.

LIDORA   Tell me what they are quickly. It seems a bargain. But first tell me again how he died. I am confused here. How can man be mortal and immortal at once? How can he die and yet have eternal life?

TIZON   You have grasped the spike of it. Listen: For the first sin which Adam committed against God, for eating the fruit of the world, we are all of us condemned without hope or remedy. Now, because this was a sin against immense God, immense, you see, only another immense being could atone for it. Being God, as he was immortally powerful, like his Father in heaven, he could not die. Could not.

LIDORA   Most interesting. And the next?

TIZON   The next? Well: So he took on the form of a human. Human form, you see.

LIDORA   Yes, I see.

TIZON   And then, being born of a virgin, he was better than any man. Naturally.

LIDORA   I see that.

TIZON   That is the Virgin Mary, well known, where I come from, for the comfort of the afflicted, refuge of sinners, and so on and so forth and what have you. She gave birth, you see, to this little fellow, in a most unsalubrious sort of place, and, well, there it is, in the end he was crucified and suffered as you heard in the Credo. Is that all?

LIDORA   Tell me, Tizon: Shall *I* be able to see God?

TIZON   That's a difficult question, as you'd appreciate, madam. No, I would say no. You are of mortal flesh, and therefore I don't see how you could be expected to. None of us do. Do you have any wine? This talk makes me—

(Enter GERARDO, DIONISIO and MARCELA.)

MARCELA   Lidora! Lidora, my beloved husband. My husband Dionisio is back here among us!

LIDORA   Dionisio! Marcela, how is this?

DIONISIO   One day, Lidora, when your Tunisian troops came to Alicarte, God must have either wanted me to suffer or to be able to see you. My wife, her father, a servant and myself were walking by the shore when the Moors found us. They took the others and left me for dead in the sand. They took my wife from me and this old man, the most respected head in Alicarte. But it was heaven's wish, beautiful Moor, that I should recover, as you can see. Recover to find my father without sight and my wife all but blinded by what she has seen, what no one should see. It is a wicked reunion, I tell you, Moor.

LIDORA   I can think of nothing to say to comfort you. Tizon? I am sure God does not wish Gerardo to see what his son does. For if he did, he would die. Have you come to ransom them?

DIONISIO   I have sold all I can to cover it.

LIDORA   If only I could give them to you, Dionisio, but I cannot. It is true I became their mistress and they serve me, but I myself am subject to the King. I am helpless.

GERARDO   It is not my wish to leave you, Lidora. I would rather stay than leave you. In you, Marcela has a sister, a true sister. (*Enter the* KING *and* ZULEMA, *dragging* LEONIDO *by a rope.*)

MARCELA   Now we are reunited. Take care, Dionisio. I have never looked on this man without some loss to myself or others.

ZARRAB.   See! A slave!

LEONIDO   I have a debt to pay. Father, sister. Oh, and you, Dionisio. The runt has survived. And Tizon awake at this hour? And Lidora picking up Christian crumbs and comfort from the servants' table?

KING   Lidora, I have done what you asked for. He's brought in. I did it only to please you. He's about to die. Or, if you say so, not about to die.

LIDORA   He is your prisoner. Just as I am yours.

LEONIDO   Father, I am at your feet, can you feel me? At your feet. Can you hear me call you father? You wished it once. Before I die, Father, note this, note I am your son.

GERARDO   Son.

LEONIDO   By my mother, naturally. And naturally raped, raped was the word I said, by you. As I raped her in her turn. These are uneasy times. Is that not what you would say, Father? We live in troubled times, an age without faith, the young go their sweet wild et cetera ways. You cannot understand? Well, then: Ah, Mother. She was pregnant. It was beyond *your* doing. You were born old, like Dionisio here. If Marcela drops another of us, it will be mine. My daughter. You see. I will explain. It's simple enough before the bond's honored. We shall get there. Oh: First, she gave birth to a little girl who was carried off in the jaws of a she-bear. Ask me not how, but it is true. I wanted to go after them, but I didn't. My mother was crying out. I left the she-bear and went back to her and found there—Marcela. Newborn and on the rock. Our daughter. My sister. (MARCELA *collapses.*) Mark this. Marcela!

GERARDO   No—no more!

LEONIDO   It is quite enough. I am telling you so that you may know what you have to ask pardon for. For, oh, yes, then I stabbed our wife, our mother. You see. That, Father, is what happened. Your tiny heart will not deny me absolution?

KING   Zarrabulli! Take him where I told you.

LEONIDO   Lidora: I entrust all my family to you. You will be busy. But you'll not mind. Remember me a little longer. (ZARRABULLI *drags him out.*)

MARCELA   Where has he gone?

KING   You will soon know, Lidora, I have given him to you. Now, keep your word.

LIDORA   Very well, King. I am yours. (*The* KING *goes to take* LIDORA *in his arms.*)

ZULEMA   Wait, Berlebeyo, before you do this, listen to me. Before he died, your father the king gave me this paper. I was to entrust it to no one, and I have not. You must read it before you are betrothed.

KING   Read it. (*ZULEMA opens the charter.*)

ZULEMA   It is in his father's own hand, Lidora. It reads, "Son, I hear of your wanting Lidora. I must tell you she is not your equal. When I was hunting Christians some sixteen years ago on the shores of Alicarte in Sicily, I rescued her from the mouth of a she-bear. She is a Christian and no match for my son. If you should marry her, our great Prophet Mahomet will rage against you. May Allah preserve you. Your father, Amete, Sultan."

KING   What? Oh, divine Allah!

GERARDO   Divine heaven!

TIZON   If there's a pope in Tunis, he'll give him dispensation.

GERARDO   Quiet, fool! Lidora, you are really my daughter. This story tallies too well with Leonido's.

TIZON   Or well enough.

LIDORA   Oh, Gerardo. I have never known a father; it is better than the kingdom of Tunis.

MARCELA   My dearest!

KING   Damn *all* fathers! Well, I am still king of Tunis. Tizon, bring Leonido here. If it is not too late. I think you should all be set free. And, well, persuaded to live together. It should be instructive. (*Enter ZARRABULLI.*)

ZARRAB.   Oh, King, it is Argolan! See! (*LEONIDO hangs from a tree.*)

LEONIDO   All of you . . . king, famous king. For you pay me like a king.

MARCELA   Leonido.

LEONIDO   Little sister.

GERARDO   My son.

LEONIDO   Bless you. Old toad!

GERARDO   Tizon, lead me to his body, my sight is returning.

LEONIDO   Give him his sight. Tizon? Too drowsy? (*TIZON stabs him.*) Ah! If there is remembrance—I shall remember you.

LIDORA   Berlebeyo, if you will let us, we will take this body with us.

KING   Take it. Go. Bloody Christians, all of you. Go. Back to Alicarte and your blood and Sicily. Help them take him. (*ZARRABULLI and TIZON take up LEONIDO.*)

TIZON   Well, King, he played a good tune on vituperation. It may not be a bond honored, but it's a tune of sorts to end with. (*They drag him off.*)

Curtain.

JAMES PURDY

Heatstroke

LILY MAE, about forty, walks about a large, brightly illuminated room with her pink parasol up, although she is not standing in the direct sunlight, which is fierce and penetrating from the tropical day outside. There are two chairs, one on stage left and one on stage right. A small table on center stage contains a vase of fresh flowers. LILY MAE holds a large handkerchief to her nose at times, and this almost causes her to lose hold of her parasol. She is elegantly dressed.

LILY   Oh, I wish I could believe in him! Believe or not, I think of nothing but him. And he's not a doctor. Not at all. I don't know how I ever got it into my head he was. He always wears white, and as I passed by this large dwelling place so often, I just fancied he was an M.D. And I am an American, and he is, too, and we are both in this dreadful tropical place. Stuck! . . . And he talked to me like a doctor that first meeting. . . . I rushed right in and began talking to him as if this were a professional consulting room. . . . Soon I had told him everything, yes, everything and he had listened to me like a doctor. Well, almost everything. A lot certainly. Too much!

(Enter DOUGLAS STURMS from stage left. He is about forty, very fair complexioned, almost gaunt, with penetrating blue eyes.)

DOUGLAS   Did you put the witch hazel on your nipples as I advised?

LILY   Oh, you startled me!

DOUGLAS   Put down your parasol, Lily, we are inside.

LILY   I like to hide under it. *(She very slowly puts down and closes the parasol.)* The sun is so disastrous to fair complexions. You have very light skin yourself.

DOUGLAS   Lily, we are not outdoors. There is no sun in this room. And we are facing north.

LILY   There is no north in this godforsaken country. Only south. The sun is everywhere. It shines, I am sure, at night also. *(She looks over at the fresh-cut flowers.)*

DOUGLAS   About the witch hazel.

LILY   *(Pouting.)* No, I did not. . . . You and your outlandish remedies . . . I don't want to look at my . . . nipples, anyhow. I can remember them . . . when they were like rosebuds.

DOUGLAS   Did you ever hear of putting codeine in a vase of roses that were dying, Lily? Or if not codeine, aspirin. . . .

LILY   Is that what they did to flowers in Detroit? You did come from there, I recall you saying.

DOUGLAS   *(Insistent, almost speaking syllable by syllable.)* Witch hazel will give color and body to your tired nipples. . . . Then you'll be happy.

LILY   I made such a terrible mistake coming to you that day. Rushing in!

DOUGLAS   There are no mistakes. I told you that many times.

LILY   Are you a theosophist?

DOUGLAS   I am me. Douglas Jason Sturms. Not an M.D. Not a theosophist. Me.

LILY   From Detroit! . . . Just the same, you saved my life. . . . I had decided to do away with myself that day.

DOUGLAS   Oh, well, you thought you *decided*.

LILY   No, I am certain I could have done it had I not barged into your ample living quarters. *(She looks about now.)*

DOUGLAS   Something else would have stayed your hand. You're not the violent type.

LILY   *(Pleading.)* You must have some real remedies, Doctor.

DOUGLAS   Only the one I told you.

LILY   *(Vexed.)* Oh, that again! Why, my own mother used witch hazel, come to think of it. Along with camphor. The poor thing used to soak her linen handkerchief in one or the other of them and cry after Papa died. I can't bear the smell of them to this day.

DOUGLAS   *(Bearing down.)* But your nipples can bear the smell, Lily. Keep that in mind. And it will freshen and perk up your whole body.

LILY   You're indecent! And you're mocking me.

DOUGLAS   I must tell you again, I'm not a doctor, but I did study medicine. Almost . . . graduated.

LILY   I knew it!

DOUGLAS   *(As if alone, or forgetful of anything but past time.)* But when it came to cutting up the cadavers . . . I couldn't. Later on, of course . . . in the war I lay down with the dead night after night. Day after day. Day and night, the dead. But I didn't have to cut them up.

LILY   So you know medicine. I was not wrong.

DOUGLAS   What did he die of? *(Seeing she has lost the thread, he prompts her.)* Your papa.

LILY   *(Coming back from her own thoughts.)* Oh, Papa.

DOUGLAS How did he . . . go?

LILY (Angry, belligerent.) He shot himself! In the greenhouse.

DOUGLAS I thought so.

LILY (Very irritated.) Yes? Well, I wish you wouldn't ask me any more of those questions.

DOUGLAS You'll let all your secrets out in time, and then you'll use the witch hazel, see if I'm not right. Camphor is useless in your case.

LILY I've always used castor oil on my hair and eyebrows and a tiny bit of it in the shells of my ears. (She touches her ears.) As a result, my hair is still very glossy and thick, and I've not lost my hearing.

DOUGLAS I bet that was your papa's remedy.

LILY How did you know. Yes, Papa had luxuriant hair, and his hearing was perfect. He could hear me talking to my beaux from the top of the house . . . yes, castor oil. His favorite hair dressing.

DOUGLAS And your mother was partial to the witch hazel and the camphor.

LILY (As if she had not heard.) I wish I were well! (Turns to look at him.) I can tell you!

DOUGLAS There's nothing wrong with you that you can't let go of.

LILY What do you mean? My headaches are nothing? The stiffness in my spine? Nothing? I wish you could stand one of my nights of pain!

DOUGLAS I know pain. The trick is to let go of it.

LILY (Again thinking her own thoughts.) You spoke of codeine for roses. Do you have any of it for people?

DOUGLAS I've told you. I have no medicine of any kind. I don't even have any witch hazel or camphor or castor oil.

LILY I never forgave Papa for leaving us. For dying like he did.

DOUGLAS You never forgive anybody. You hold and hold and hold. (He makes as if to take her hands, and she moves away.)

LILY Watch your tongue. I mean it!

DOUGLAS I used to watch it, but it only made me sick. Now I say anything that pops into my head. That's why you keep coming here every afternoon. To a private house. Because my tongue runs on.

LILY (Walking about.) I don't know where to get witch hazel in this god-forsaken place.

DOUGLAS Go to the nearest farmacia. Ask for hamamelis.

LILY (Not having heard.) I want so to be happy. I still do! Laugh all you like! (She sobs.)

DOUGLAS I'm not laughing . . . but don't cry. I am unmoved by women's tears.

LILY What about men's?

DOUGLAS I might be interested if I saw one of them cry, but I never did. Not real tears.

LILY Never saw a man cry?

DOUGLAS   Never. Not real crying.

LILY   Ah, well, come to think of it. *(She lapses again into other thoughts.)*

DOUGLAS   Lily Mae, is the rumor true?

LILY   Don't start that now! Don't, please.

DOUGLAS   *(Hard.)* Did you kill him? Your lover. Or your husband, whoever he was.

LILY   *(Offers to go.)* I'm leaving.

DOUGLAS   If you go, maybe I won't be here when you pay me your next visit.

LILY   *(Frightened in spite of herself.)* What do you mean?

DOUGLAS   What do I mean! Just that. I'll have flown the coop.

LILY   *(Bitter.)* And where could *you* fly to? After all!

DOUGLAS   Oh, some other hot place in this area.

LILY   I know you cannot go home. *(She sits down all at once.)*

DOUGLAS   I guess I'd better not try. *Everybody* knows I killed a man. I don't have to bother about rumors. But the reason I'm here is we had a hung jury back there. Just the same, I didn't want to risk the chance of a new trial in Detroit. So, here I am.

LILY   I killed *him* because . . .

DOUGLAS   "He needed killing."

LILY   *(Caught in spite of herself.)* Ah, well.

DOUGLAS   I killed the man I killed because he ridiculed me. Because he said I deserted my country and desecrated the flag.

LILY   *(Harsh.)* And did you?

DOUGLAS   Yes, I suppose so. But you see, I didn't desert my country in my heart, and I love the flag. Still! I couldn't stand the stink of the rotting dead! That's all. And I only burned the flag by mistake when I tried at last to set fire to some of the corpses. I was dishonorably discharged only for one reason and one reason alone. I went over the hill. I ran! I ran. . . .

LILY   Oh stop! Stop. It's too grim.

DOUGLAS   But I could go home. If I wanted to, I could.

LILY   Forgive me for saying what I did.

DOUGLAS   For a long time I could smell the dead, whether they were in the rotting stage or I was burning up what was left of them in the jungle. I used camphor like your mother when she remembered the smell of your father's suicide!

LILY   I can't hear this. I can't. I'll leave. *(She rises.)*

DOUGLAS   After a while, down here where there's so much jasmine and hibiscus and tiny orchids, or flowers I don't know the names for . . . the smell of the dead gradually *don't* reach me anymore. . . . *(He touches his nostrils.)*

LILY   *(As if alone.)* I killed him because he said I wasn't young and pretty anymore. He slept with girls off the street. He said I could live with him forever, but he would never regard me as a woman from then on. . . . I don't know why the jury acquitted me. They felt he had abused me. But I never minded his beatings. It was him not thinking me pretty hurt so.

DOUGLAS *(Sarcastic.)* It was because you looked like quality they let you off.

LILY *(Seeing it all before her.)* I disobeyed my lawyer, too. I looked right at the jury as I said he told me I was not desirable and he would as soon sleep with a blind mule. The jury was almost all women. Then the lawyer showed them photos of where he burned me with cigar butts.

DOUGLAS My lawyer read my medical record at the trial. The army medical record. Then he had me take off my shirt and pants right there in the courtroom and show them how many times I had been wounded. Eighteen times. I had medals galore for bravery before I deserted. The women in the jury looked at my scars, but the guys looked away. I can still hear the defense lawyer's voice: "He killed a man who had taunted him time and again, night and day insulted and goaded one who fought and bled for his country! Didn't he ask for it, to call a hero a traitor, and one of the bravest of men a coward!"

LILY *(Rising.)* Oh, you've helped me. Douglas. I can't tell you how much. I have a funny feeling I can go on.

DOUGLAS Don't count on it.

LILY *(Hurt, disappointed.)* You spoil everything finally, don't you?

DOUGLAS Lily, listen for a minute. Hear me out. Better than witch hazel is to have a pair of human lips lightly touch you there . . . dry, hot lips. No moisture. Burning lips.

LILY I don't need that, and you know it.

DOUGLAS Are you crazy? Everybody needs it.

LILY What are you proposing! Tell me. *(She is becoming hysterical.)*

DOUGLAS I will show you something that will make you well. *(He takes hold of one of her hands very languidly.)*

LILY You wouldn't dare!

DOUGLAS I've dared more than any other man on or off the battlefield. Can I help it nobody remembers it? Even the army said before they gave me a dishonorable discharge I had the true thing, that a hundred medals could never—if it covered every inch of me, speak out for what I done. . . . But only yesterday *(He looks around.)* comes a letter from my lawyer, they may change my *dishonorable* to *honorable.* But I'm also a man, Lily, with burning lips . . . burning, healing lips.

LILY *(Breaks away.)* You're mocking me! You're driving me back into the shadows where I came from!

DOUGLAS Just the opposite, Lily. *(He takes both her hands and leads her to the back of the stage very slowly now. She allows him to take off her blouse and then her bra. He leans over and touches her nipples with his lips. A long silence while he caresses her.)*

LILY *(As if trying to awaken from deep slumber.)* Oh, my God, my God in heaven.

(DOUGLAS leaves her, and very slowly she puts back on her bra and blouse. Seeing him seated in the chair, she returns to the front of the stage.)

I don't know what came over you!

DOUGLAS Lily, go home and take a look at yourself in the mirror. Look in the looking glass.

LILY *(Queer.)* Why?

DOUGLAS Because you're different now, Lily. You've changed. You'll see.

LILY What will I see?

DOUGLAS You'll see you are as fresh and firm as a rosebud. And then you will find somebody who will think so, too.

LILY Who?

DOUGLAS Somebody, Lily. Go on home now and stand in front of the looking glass, why don't you.

LILY I don't know what it is! I feel as if the entire last twenty years had been rolled away, like a big stone had fallen from my back and chest and let me go free.

DOUGLAS Go on, Lily, go on home.

LILY *(Not looking at him.)* And do you want me to come back?

DOUGLAS Don't forget your parasol. It's hot outside, remember.

LILY I said *Shall I come back? (Still does not look at him.)*

DOUGLAS You won't have to, Lily. Almost everybody out there is waiting to greet you in the sun. Greet you and your young breasts.

LILY I didn't hear that last! And I will go right home. Good-bye, Douglas. Take care of your health and thank you. Thank you, I said. Many thanks. *(He barely looks at her as she goes out, raising her parasol and opening it.)*

DOUGLAS *(Stares at the vase with the flowers. He goes slowly over to it and bends down and kisses the flowers. He takes them out of the vase. Comes over and sits down in the chair. Holding the flowers in one hand, he loosens his shirt. He presses the flowers to his lips and then to his own uncovered breast.)* They are so cool in all this heat. Like under cold mountain water.

JONATHAN REYNOLDS

Lines Composed a Few Miles Above Tintern Abbey, Part II
or
How We Got America's Most Wanted and the New York Post

This sketch was written when Rupert Murdoch owned the Post *and had just bought Fox Broadcasting and New Yorkers were being served a daily diet of violence and mayhem.*

Lights come up on the richly decorated conservatory of an extremely expensive Victorian mansion in Adelaide, South Australia.

The time is 1938.

We discover three attractive young boys dressed as Little Lord Fauntleroys: NIGEL, *six,* ANDREW, *eight, and* RUPERT, *nine, as they are addressed by their mother,* LADY ELIZABETH MURDOCH, *also attractive and thirty-five, and their father,* SIR KEITH MURDOCH, *a rugged individualist, forty.*

LADY MURDOCH   Now, boys, today is the day we've been practicing for for six months, and Mrs. Fairchilderdern has finally arrived in town and is on her way here. You may not think admission to Harrow and Eton means much right now, but to your father and me it means everything. The one thing we've never had is a Murdoch at Eton or a Murdoch at Harrow. Unfortunately, Eton and Harrow allow only one Australian student per decade— they'd prefer it one student per millenium, they hate us so—but this is the year. And if two of you are brilliant, positively brilliant with Mrs. Fairchilderdern, as I know you can be, there is the tee-ninsiest chance you might be accepted. So, please, try your absolute best.

THREE BOYS   *(Perfect children.)* Yes, Mummy!

(A maid enters.)

MAID   The woman from Eton and Harrod's has arrived!
SIR KEITH   Harrow, not Harrod's. Tell her to wait a moment.

(The maid exits.)
SIR KEITH   I'm going to sweeten the pot. Whoever gets accepted into these schools, I'll give you anything you want. Andy?
ANDREW   Anything I want?
SIR KEITH   Yes.
ANDREW   All right. I'd like a Stutz Bearcat with wire wheels, a 3.2 turning base, and a resale value of 55,000 dollars American.
SIR KEITH   But you can't even drive!
ANDREW   I'll learn.
SIR KEITH   Very well. Nigel?
NIGEL   Well, Papa, what I'd really like is my own manse. Something much smaller than this—say twenty-six rooms on five thousand acres?
SIR KEITH   Hmm. Well, I see you boys have a firm grasp of material worth. Rupert? Quick now—more than anything.
RUPERT   More than anything? A puppy. *(The parents and brothers are stunned.)*
NIGEL   *(Disgusted.)* Rupert!
LADY MURDOCH   A puppy?
ANDREW   Oh, Rupert!
SIR KEITH   You, Rupert Murdoch, want . . . a puppy? Is that all?
RUPERT   Well, and everything that goes with a puppy—the love and cuddliness, the genuine warmth and companionship, the happy feelings all round!

(SIR KEITH and LADY MURDOCH make disparaging noises.)

LADY MURDOCH   Come on, son, something a little more than just a puppy!
RUPERT   All right—two puppies! Then I'll have twice the love and cuddling and genuine companionship! Oh, please, please, Papa, may I?
SIR KEITH SR   *(Disgusted.)* What have we raised here, some little wretched Beatrix Potter character? Oh, yes, yes, you can have your wretched puppy —a deal's a deal. Though frankly, if one of you has to lose, I certainly hope it's you. Now, Matriciana, let's have Mrs. Fairchilderdern.

(The maid enters, followed by MRS. FAITH FAIRCHILDERDERN, fifty-five and a very proper Englishwoman dressed in the conservative clothes of a preceding period. She has great contempt for the Murdoch family.)

MAID   The woman from Eton and Harrod's, Mrs. Faith Fairchilderdern!
SIR KEITH   Not Harrod's—Harrow!
MRS. FAIRCHILDERDERN   Introductions aren't necessary—I know you all by snapshot. And I must say you're an attractive family, particularly for

Australians. You are to remember, though, that while good, you are not English, just British. Nothing you can ever do will make you English. But you *will* always be British. This is a land of escaped convicts, wild 'roos and beer and always will be. And though your parents are doing their best to educate you in the English manner, because of your environment, your education can only be, at best, alas, merely British. But that's certainly better than most and miles ahead of the Frogs. And perhaps, depending on your Wordsworth, one of you might be the one in ten thousand we have to take at Eton or Harrow.

LADY MURDOCH   *(Obsequiously.)* Oh, Mrs. Fairchilderdern, we hope so. We so respect your country and realize our lowly position must grate at all—

MRS. FAIRCHILDERDERN   Now you, Sir Keith, as the king insists you be called, you have something to do with stationery, don't you.

SIR KEITH   Newspapers.

MRS. FAIRCHILDERDERN   Grubby business, grubby. But then someone has to work with his hands. All right, lads, you know the drill. "Lines Composed a Few Miles Above Tintern Abbey." Andrew? *(She takes out a book to grade in.)*

ANDREW   *(Brilliantly.)* "Five years have past; five summers, with the length
Of five long winters! and again I hear
These waters, rolling from their mountain springs
With a soft, inland murmur.—Once again
Do I behold these steep and lofty cliffs,
That on a wild secluded scene impress
Thoughts of more deep seclusion; and connect
The landscape with the quiet of the sky."

MRS. FAIRCHILDERDERN   *(Impressed.)* My goodness, what a recitation! Interpret.

ANDREW   A gentleman, returning to a splendid site, recalls a previous visit and reflects on it philosophically, employing a pastoral use of personification to describe the wooded clave which exemplifies the romantic style of the late eighteenth–early nineteenth centuries.

(MRS. FAIRCHILDERDERN is even more impressed, makes a mark in her book. SIR KEITH and LADY MURDOCH beam.)

MRS. FAIRCHILDERDERN   The boy is eight? I am quite impressed! Nigel.

NIGEL   *(Brilliantly.)* "The day is come when I again repose
Here, under this dark sycamore, and view
These plots of cottage-ground, these orchard-tufts,
Which at this season, with their unripe fruits,
Are clad in one green hue, and lose themselves
'Mid groves and copses."

MRS. FAIRCHILDERDERN   *(Again impressed.)* But the boys are brilliant! What a red-letter day for Eton and Harrow! Nigel, interpret.

NIGEL   Here, the laureate deepens the experience of his previous visit, yet views it with a newfound peace and maturity. Note also the repetition of f-t sounds, viz my brother's excellent recitation "steep and lofty cliffs" and cf. in my own more humble presentation, "cottage-ground, these orchard-tufts, their unripe fruits," et cetera.

MRS. FAIRCHILDERDERN   I've been up and down this hairy armpit of a country, or continent or whatever you call it, and have never seen such promising meat for the public schools of Britain! Sir Keith and Lady Murdoch, you must be very proud!

LADY MURDOCH   Oh, yes, Mrs. Fairchilderdern, we are, thank you so very much, your worship—

MRS. FAIRCHILDERDERN   Rupert.

RUPERT   God, I love this poem! It says everything I feel about the woods, the green coolness— *(The others ad-lib their displeasure.)*

MRS. FAIRCHILDERDERN   Well, yes, it's nice to be enthusiastic, but—

RUPERT   Have you ever had puppies, Mrs. Fairchilderdern?

MRS. FAIRCHILDERDERN   What does that have to do with—

SIR KEITH   The poem, lad!

RUPERT   Oh, yeah. Uh . . . *(Haltingly; a bad recitation:)*
"Once again, I see . . . uh . . . uh . . .
These hedge-rows, hardly hedge-rows, little lines
Of sportive wood run wild: these pastoral farms . . . *(He skips.)*
For thou art with me here upon the banks,
Of this fair river; thou my dearest Friend,
My dear, dear Friend,
My dear, dear Sister—

MRS. FAIRCHILDERDERN   *(Horrified.)* You skipped! You skipped!

RUPERT   I forgot the lines, but it's what the poem's about.

MRS. FAIRCHILDERDERN   *(All ice.)* You skipped.

SIR KEITH   *(To the rescue.)* Of course, Mrs. Fairchilderdern, he's always been the problem student, overly sentimental and profound, always delving too deeply into philosophies and subtleties. I urge you to focus on our other boys! Nigel's bracing recitation, Andrew's incisive interpretation! *(To boys, confidentially:)* I see a Stutz Bearcat in the drive, a manse in the north orchard!

RUPERT   And my puppies?

SIR KEITH   No, I don't think there'll be any puppies, Rupert.

RUPERT   No puppies? Not even one?

SIR KEITH   You gave an extremely awkward and humiliating recitation. No puppies.

RUPERT   *(Crying.)* Wahh! Wahh!

SIR KEITH   *(Flustered.)* Well, oh, well, maybe a 'roo.

RUPERT   I don't want a 'roo! I hate 'roos! Everybody's got 'roos!

MRS. FAIRCHILDERDERN *(Very sternly.)* Rupert! Stop that caterwauling at once!
(He tries to stop.) Now, Rupert, your interview isn't over till I say it is.
Interpret.

RUPERT Well, the poem is about a lot of things . . . *(The grown-ups ad-lib their
displeasure: they want a single interpretation.)* It's about nature and reflection
and spirituality . . . No puppies?

SIR KEITH No puppies!

RUPERT *(Suddenly furious.)* Well, then *this* is what your poem's about. *(At the
top of his lungs—with anger and relish.)* A repressed old fart returns to isolated
woods to get away from his boil-covered wife who has terminal smelly
diseases and lives in a slum apartment littered with excrement and
dirty pages of the London *Times*! Following birth of pregnant fetus, he kills
her with an ax in the forehead and returns to the pretty spot where he
gang-raped his sister, blood still all over him, wild-eyed and terrible, he
throws up on a tree, jerks off, and stabs himself with glass shards, blood
spurting from all the pores not already filled with pus while roving gangs
of eighteenth-century pro-Commie thugs threaten a decrepit old woman
with spikes, then bash her head in! Is no one safe!

(Lights up sensationally. The actors shout the following headlines:)

"Elvis Was a Lesbian, and I Was Her Lover"

"Pregnant Fetus of English Couple speaks German at Birth"

"Jessica Hahn Still a Virgin, Gyno Declares"

"Birth Control Pill Thrown into Angry Mob Kills Nine"

"Glenn Close Throws Own Illicit Love Child to Man on Burning
Building"

"Koch Kills Cuomo with Ax in Forehead: I was just kidding, quips
Mayor."

"How to Strip for Your Man"

"Kiddie Porn Ring Discovered in New Jersey: Five-Year-Olds Kidnap
Adults and Molest Them. They forced us to have sex with them, say
Morgan Fairchild and Heather Thomas."

"Clive Barnes, World's Most Famous Drama Critic, Jailed for Babbling
in Seat"

"Glenn Close Mauled at Tractor Pull"

"AIDS Kills All Journalists Who Write About It"

"Katie Kelly Kills Kitty Kelly, Then Kitty Kelly Corpse Kisses Kilted
Kelly McGillis—Shocking Pictures!"

"Little Children Everywhere Drool on Pope"

(Lights return to normal. Everyone onstage—except RUPERT—is dumbfounded.)

MRS. FAIRCHILDERDERN *(Gagging.)* That's what you see in the poem?

RUPERT Yup.

(LADY MURDOCH rushes to MRS. FAIRCHILDERDERN, sinks to her knees.)

LADY MURDOCH   Please, Mrs. Fairchilderdern, don't let him affect what you think of Nigel and Andrew—they're such different boys entirely.

MRS. FAIRCHILDERDERN   Don't worry, Lady Murdoch, I shan't. I've been interviewing young boys for too long to be misguided by one worm in an otherwise healthy apple. Andrew and Nigel are admitted to Harrow and Eton.

LADY MURDOCH   *(On the verge of tears.)* Oh, thank you, your grace, oh, thank you—

MRS. FAIRCHILDERDERN   And Sir Keith?

SIR KEITH   I'm grateful as well. And impressed.

MRS. FAIRCHILDERDERN   Impressed?

SIR KEITH   In addition to Eton and Harrow, this boy gets the Stutz, this boy gets his huge new house, and this boy . . . this boy . . .

MRS. FAIRCHILDERDERN   Yes, Sir Keith?

LADY MURDOCH, ANDREW, and NIGEL *(together)*   Yes, Papa?

SIR KEITH   *(Happier than he's ever been.)* This boy gets the newspapers!

(They all protest, but RUPERT and his father become locked in thought. They stroll out left, and we hear:)

SIR KEITH   Now listen, lad, just remember, never put the girl in the bikini on the front page. She goes on page three, put the blood on page one. Remember our motto: Blood before Nudity. And never forget, your main task is to put fear in the heart of the city. . . .

(Father and son have found each other, and during this exchange we slowly fade to black.)

Curtain.

MILCHA SANCHEZ-SCOTT

The Cuban Swimmer

CHARACTERS

MARGARITA SUÁREZ   *The swimmer.*
EDUARDO SUÁREZ   *Her father, the coach.*
SIMÓN SUÁREZ   *Her brother.*
AÍDA SUÁREZ   *The mother.*
ABUELA   *Her grandmother.*
VOICE OF MEL MUNSON
VOICE OF MARY BETH WHITE
VOICE OF RADIO OPERATOR

SETTING

The Pacific Ocean between San Pedro and Catalina Island.

TIME

Summer.

Live conga drums can be used to punctuate the action of the play.

SCENE 1

Pacific Ocean. Midday. On the horizon, in perspective, a small boat enters upstage left, crosses to upstage right, and exits. Pause. Lower on the horizon, the same boat, in larger perspective, enters upstage right, crosses and exits upstage left. Blackout.

SCENE 2

Pacific Ocean. Midday. The swimmer, MARGARITA SUÁREZ, is swimming. On the boat following behind her are her father, EDUARDO SUÁREZ, holding a megaphone, and SIMÓN, her brother, sitting on top of the cabin with his shirt off, punk sunglasses on, binoculars hanging on his chest.

EDUARDO   *(Leaning forward, shouting in time to MARGARITA's swimming.)* Uno, dos, uno, dos. *Y uno, dos* . . . keep your shoulders parallel to the water.

SIMÓN   I'm gonna take these glasses off and look straight into the sun.

EDUARDO   *(Through megaphone.) Muy bien, muy bien* . . . but punch those arms in, baby.

SIMÓN   *(Looking directly at the sun through binoculars.)* Come on, come on, zap me. Show me something. *(He looks behind at the shoreline and ahead at the sea.)* Stop! Stop, *Papi!* Stop!

(AÍDA SUÁREZ and ABUELA, the swimmer's mother and grandmother, enter running from the back of the boat.)

AÍDA and ABUELA   *Qué? Qué es?*

AÍDA   *Es un* shark?

EDUARDO   Eh?

ABUELA   *Que es un* shark *dicen?*

(EDUARDO blows whistle. MARGARITA looks up at the boat.)

SIMÓN   No, *Papi,* no shark, no shark. We've reached the halfway mark.

ABUELA   *(Looking into the water.) A dónde está?*

AÍDA   It's not in the water.

ABUELA   Oh, no? Oh, no?

AÍDA   No! *A poco* do you think they're gonna have signs in the water to say you are halfway to Santa Catalina? No. It's done very scientific. *A ver, hijo,* explain it to your grandma.

SIMÓN   Well, you see, Abuela— *(He points behind.)* There's San Pedro. *(He points ahead.)* And there's Santa Catalina. Looks halfway to me.

(ABUELA shakes her head and is looking back and forth, trying to make the decision, when suddenly the sound of a helicopter is heard.)

ABUELA   *(Looking up.)* Virgencita de la Caridad del Cobre. *Qué es eso?*

(Sound of helicopter gets closer. MARGARITA looks up.)

MARGARITA   Papi, Papi!

(A small commotion on the boat, with EVERYBODY *pointing at the helicopter above. Shadows of the helicopter fall on the boat.* SIMÓN *looks up at it through binoculars.)*

Papi—qué es? What is it?

EDUARDO   *(Through megaphone.)* Uh . . . uh . . . uh, *un momentico . . . mi hija.* . . . Your *papi*'s got everything under control, understand? Uh . . . you just keep stroking. And stay . . . uh . . . close to the boat.

SIMÓN   Wow, *Papi!* We're on TV, man! Holy Christ, we're all over the fucking U.S.A.! It's Mel Munson and Mary Beth White!

AÍDA   *Por Dios!* Simón, don't swear. And put on your shirt.

*(*AÍDA *fluffs her hair, puts on her sunglasses and waves to the helicopter.* SIMÓN *leans over the side of the boat and yells to* MARGARITA.*)*

SIMÓN   Yo, Margo! You're on TV, man.

EDUARDO   Leave your sister alone. Turn on the radio.

MARGARITA   *Papi! Qué está pasando?*

ABUELA   *Que es la televisión dicen? (She shakes her head.) Porque como yo no puedo ver nada sin mis espejuelos.*

*(*ABUELA *rummages through the boat, looking for her glasses. Voices of* MEL MUNSON *and* MARY BETH WHITE *are heard over the boat's radio.)*

MEL'S VOICE   As we take a closer look at the gallant crew of *La Havana* . . . and there . . . yes, there she is . . . the little Cuban swimmer from Long Beach, California, nineteen-year-old Margarita Suárez. The unknown swimmer is our Cinderella entry . . . a bundle of tenacity, battling her way through the choppy, murky waters of the cold Pacific to reach the Island of Romance . . . Santa Catalina . . . where should she be the first to arrive, two thousand dollars and a gold cup will be waiting for her.

AÍDA   Doesn't even cover our expenses.

ABUELA   *Qué dice?*

EDUARDO   Shhhh!

MARY BETH'S VOICE   This is really a family effort, Mel, and—

MEL'S VOICE   Indeed it is. Her trainer, her coach, her mentor, is her father, Eduardo Suárez. Not a swimmer himself, it says here, Mr. Suárez is head usher of the Holy Name Society and the owner-operator of Suárez Treasures of the Sea and Salvage Yard. I guess it's one of those places—

MARY BETH'S VOICE   If I might interject a fact here, Mel, assisting in this swim is Mrs. Suárez, who is a former Miss Cuba.

MEL'S VOICE   And a beautiful woman in her own right. Let's try and get a closer look.

(Helicopter sound gets louder. MARGARITA, *frightened, looks up again.)*

MARGARITA   *Papi!*

EDUARDO   *(Through megaphone.) Mi hija,* don't get nervous . . . it's the press. I'm handling it.

AÍDA   I see how you're handling it.

EDUARDO   *(Through megaphone.)* Do you hear? Everything is under control. Get back into your rhythm. Keep your elbows high and kick and kick and kick and kick . . .

ABUELA   *(Finds her glasses and puts them on.) Ay sí, es la televisión . . . (She points to helicopter.) Qué lindo mira . . . (She fluffs her hair, gives a big wave.) Aló América! Viva mi Margarita, viva todo los Cubanos en los Estados Unidos!*

AÍDA   *Ay por Dios,* Cecilia, the man didn't come all this way in his helicopter to look at you jumping up and down, making a fool of yourself.

ABUELA   I don't care. I'm proud.

AÍDA   He can't understand you anyway.

ABUELA   *Viva . . . (She stops.) Simón, comó se dice viva?*

SIMÓN   Hurray.

ABUELA   Hurray for *mi Margarita y* for all the Cubans living *en* the United States, *y un abrazo . . . Simón, abrazo . . .*

SIMÓN   A big hug.

ABUELA   *Sí,* a big hug to all my friends in Miami, Long Beach, Union City, except for my son Carlos, who lives in New York in sin! He lives . . . *(She crosses herself.)* in Brooklyn with a Puerto Rican woman in sin! *No decente . . .*

SIMÓN   Decent.

ABUELA   Carlos, *no decente.* This family, *decente.*

AÍDA   Cecilia, *por Dios.*

MEL'S VOICE   Look at that enthusiasm. The whole family has turned out to cheer little Margarita on to victory! I hope they won't be too disappointed.

MARY BETH'S VOICE   She seems to be making good time, Mel.

MEL'S VOICE   Yes, it takes all kinds to make a race. And it's a testimonial to the all-encompassing fairness . . . the greatness of this, the Wrigley Invitational Women's Swim to Catalina, where among all the professionals there is still room for the amateurs . . . like these, the simple people we see below us on the ragtag *La Havana,* taking their long-shot chance to victory. *Vaya con Dios!*

(Helicopter sound fading as family, including MARGARITA, *watch silently. Static as* SIMÓN *turns radio off.* EDUARDO *walks to bow of boat, looks out on the horizon.)*

EDUARDO   *(To himself.)* Amateurs.

AÍDA   Eduardo, that person insulted us. Did you hear, Eduardo? That he called us a simple people in a ragtag boat? Did you hear . . . ?

ABUELA   *(Clenching her fist at departing helicopter.) Mal-Rayo los parta!*

SIMÓN   *(Same gesture.)* Asshole!

(AÍDA follows EDUARDO as he goes to side of boat and stares at MARGARITA.)

AÍDA   This person comes in his helicopter to insult your wife, your family, your daughter . . .

MARGARITA   *(Pops her head out of the water.) Papi?*

AÍDA   Do you hear me, Eduardo? I am not simple.

ABUELA   *Sí.*

AÍDA   I am complicated.

ABUELA   *Sí, demasiada complicada.*

AÍDA   Me and my family are not so simple.

SIMÓN   Mom, the guy's an asshole.

ABUELA   *(Shaking her fist at helicopter.)* Asshole!

AÍDA   If my daughter was simple, she would not be in that water swimming.

MARGARITA   Simple? *Papi . . . ?*

AÍDA   *Ahora,* Eduardo, this is what I want you to do. When we get to Santa Catalina, I want you to call the TV station and demand an apology.

EDUARDO   *Cállete mujer! Aquí mando yo.* I will decide what is to be done.

MARGARITA   *Papi,* tell me what's going on.

EDUARDO   Do you understand what I am saying to you, Aída?

SIMÓN   *(Leaning over side of boat, to MARGARITA.)* Yo Margo! You know that Mel Munson guy on TV? He called you a simple amateur and said you didn't have a chance.

ABUELA   *(Leaning directly behind SIMÓN.) Mi hija, insultó a la familia. Desgraciado!*

AÍDA   *(Leaning in behind ABUELA.)* He called us peasants! And your father is not doing anything about it. He just knows how to yell at me.

EDUARDO   *(Through megaphone.)* Shut up! All of you! Do you want to break her concentration? Is that what you are after? Eh?

(ABUELA, AÍDA and SIMÓN shrink back. EDUARDO paces before them.)

Swimming is rhythm and concentration. You win a race *aquí.* *(Pointing to his head.)* Now . . . *(To SIMÓN.)* you, take care of the boat, Aída y *Mama* . . . do something. Anything. Something practical.

(ABUELA and AÍDA get on knees and pray in Spanish.)

Hija, give it everything, eh? . . . *por la familia.* Uno . . . dos. . . . You must win.

(SIMÓN goes into cabin. The prayers continue as lights change to indicate bright sunlight, later in the afternoon.)

SCENE 3

Tableau for a couple of beats. EDUARDO *on bow with timer in one hand as he counts strokes per minute.* SIMÓN *is in the cabin steering, wearing his sunglasses, baseball cap on backward.* ABUELA *and* AÍDA *are at the side of the boat, heads down, hands folded, still muttering prayers in Spanish.*

AÍDA and ABUELA   *(Crossing themselves.)* En el nombre del Padre, del Hijo y del Espíritu Santo amén.

EDUARDO   *(Through megaphone.)* You're stroking seventy-two!

SIMÓN   *(Singing.)* Mama's stroking, Mama's stroking seventy-two. . . .

EDUARDO   *(Through megaphone.)* You comfortable with it?

SIMÓN   *(Singing.)* Seventy-two, seventy-two, seventy-two for you.

AÍDA   *(Looking at the heavens.)* Ay, Eduardo, *ven acá,* we should be grateful that *Nuestro Señor* gave us such a beautiful day.

ABUELA   *(Crosses herself.)* Sí, gracias a Dios.

EDUARDO   She's stroking seventy-two, with no problem *(He throws a kiss to the sky.)* It's a beautiful day to win.

AÍDA   *Qué hermoso!* So clear and bright. Not a cloud in the sky. *Mira! Mira!* Even rainbows on the water . . . a sign from God.

SIMÓN   *(Singing.)* Rainbows on the water . . . you in my arms . . .

ABUELA and EDUARDO   *(Looking the wrong way.)* Dónde?

AÍDA   *(Pointing toward* MARGARITA.*)* There, dancing in front of Margarita, leading her on . . .

EDUARDO   Rainbows on . . . *Ay coño!* It's an oil slick! You . . . you . . . *(To* SIMÓN.*)* Stop the boat. *(Runs to bow, yelling.)* Margarita! Margarita!

(On the next stroke, MARGARITA *comes up all covered in black oil.)*

MARGARITA   *Papi! Papi . . . !*

(Everybody goes to the side and stares at MARGARITA, *who stares back.* EDUARDO *freezes.)*

AÍDA   *Apúrate,* Eduardo, move . . . what's wrong with you . . . *no me oíste,* get my daughter out of the water.

EDUARDO   *(Softly.)* We can't touch her. If we touch her, she's disqualified.

AÍDA   But I'm her mother.

EDUARDO   Not even by her own mother. Especially by her own mother. . . . You always want the rules to be different for you, you always want to be the exception. *(To* SIMÓN.*)* And you . . . you didn't see it, eh? You were playing again?

SIMÓN   *Papi,* I was watching . . .

AÍDA   *(Interrupting.)* Pues, do something Eduardo. You are the big coach, the monitor.

SIMÓN   Mentor! Mentor!

EDUARDO   How can a person think around you? *(He walks off to bow, puts head in hands.)*

ABUELA   *(Looking over side.)* Mira como todos los little birds are dead. *(She crosses herself.)*

AÍDA   Their little wings are glued to their sides.

SIMÓN   Christ, this is like the La Brea tar pits.

AÍDA   They can't move their little wings.

ABUELA   *Esa niña tiene que moverse.*

SIMÓN   Yeah, Margo, you gotta move, man.

(ABUELA and SIMÓN gesture for MARGARITA to move. AÍDA gestures for her to swim.)

ABUELA   *Anda niña, muévete.*

AÍDA   Swim, *hija*, swim or the *aceite* will stick to your wings.

MARGARITA   *Papi?*

ABUELA   *(Taking megaphone.)* Your *papi* say "move it!"

(MARGARITA with difficulty starts moving.)

ABUELA, AÍDA and SIMÓN   *(Laboriously counting.)* Uno, dos . . . uno, dos . . . anda . . . uno, dos.

EDUARDO   *(Running to take megaphone from ABUELA.)* Uno, dos . . .

(SIMÓN races into cabin and starts the engine. ABUELA, AÍDA and EDUARDO count together.)

SIMÓN   *(Looking ahead.)* Papi, it's over there!

EDUARDO   Eh?

SIMÓN   *(Pointing ahead and to the right.)* It's getting clearer over there.

EDUARDO   *(Through megaphone.)* Now pay attention to me. Go to the right.

(SIMÓN, ABUELA, AÍDA and EDUARDO all lean over side. They point ahead and to the right, except ABUELA, who points to the left.)

FAMILY   *(Shouting together.)* Para yá! Para yá!

(Lights go down on boat. A special light on MARGARITA, swimming through the oil, and on ABUELA, watching her.)

ABUELA   *Sangre de mi sangre*, you will be another to save us. En Bolondron, where your great-grandmother Luz Suárez was born, they say one day it rained blood. All the people, they run into their houses. They cry, they pray, *pero* your great-grandmother Luz she had cojones like a man. She run outside. She look straight at the sky. She shake her fist. And she say to the evil one, "Mira . . . *(Beating her chest.)* coño, Diablo, aquí estoy si me quieres." And she open her mouth, and she drunk the blood.

Blackout.

SCENE 4

Lights up on boat. AÍDA *and* EDUARDO *are on deck watching* MARGARITA *swim. We hear the gentle, rhythmic lap, lap, lap of the water, then the sound of inhaling and exhaling as* MARGARITA'*s breathing becomes louder. Then* MARGARITA'*s heartbeat is heard, with the lapping of the water and the breathing under it. These sounds continue beneath the dialogue to the end of the scene.*

AÍDA   *Dios mío.* Look how she moves through the water. . . .

EDUARDO   You see, it's very simple. It is a matter of concentration.

AÍDA   The first time I put her in water she came to life, she grew before my eyes. She moved, she smiled, she loved it more than me. She didn't want my breast any longer. She wanted the water.

EDUARDO   And of course, the rhythm. The rhythm takes away the pain and helps the concentration.

(Pause. AÍDA *and* EDUARDO *watch* MARGARITA.*)*

AÍDA   Is that my child or a seal. . . .

EDUARDO   Ah, a seal, the reason for that is that she's keeping her arms very close to her body. She cups her hands, and then she reaches and digs, reaches and digs.

AÍDA   To think that a daughter of mine . . .

EDUARDO   It's the training, the hours in the water. I used to tie weights around her little wrists and ankles.

AÍDA   A spirit, an ocean spirit, must have entered my body when I was carrying her.

EDUARDO   *(To* MARGARITA.*)* Your stroke is slowing down.

(Pause. We hear MARGARITA'*s heartbeat with the breathing under, faster now.)*

AÍDA   Eduardo, that night, the night on the boat . . .

EDUARDO   Ah, the night on the boat again . . . the moon was . . .

AÍDA   The moon was full. We were coming to America. . . . *Qué romantico.*

(Heartbeat and breathing continue.)

EDUARDO   We were cold, afraid, with no money, and on top of everything, you were hysterical, yelling at me, tearing at me with your nails. *(Opens his shirt, points to the base of his neck.)* Look, I still bear the scars . . . telling me that I didn't know what I was doing . . . saying that we were going to die. . . .

AÍDA   You took me, you stole me from my home . . . you didn't give me a chance to prepare. You just said we have to go now, now! Now, you said. You didn't let me take anything. I left everything behind. . . . I left everything behind.

EDUARDO Saying that I wasn't good enough, that your father didn't raise you so that I could drown you in the sea.

AÍDA You didn't let me say even a good-bye. You took me, you stole me, you tore me from my home.

EDUARDO I took you so we could be married.

AÍDA That was in Miami. But that night on the boat, Eduardo. . . . We were not married, that night on the boat.

EDUARDO *No pasó nada!* Once and for all get it out of your head, it was cold, you hated me, and we were afraid. . . .

AÍDA *Mentiroso!*

EDUARDO A man can't do it when he is afraid.

AÍDA Liar! You did it very well.

EDUARDO I did?

AÍDA *Sí.* Gentle. You were so gentle and then strong . . . my passion for you so deep. Standing next to you . . . I would ache . . . looking at your hands I would forget to breathe, you were irresistible.

EDUARDO I was?

AÍDA You took me into your arms, you touched my face with your fingertips . . . you kissed my eyes . . . *la esquina de la boca y* . . .

EDUARDO *Sí, sí,* and then . . .

AÍDA I look at your face on top of mine, and I see the lights of Havana in your eyes. That's when you seduced me.

EDUARDO Shhh, they're gonna hear you.

(Lights go down. Special on AÍDA.)

AÍDA That was the night. A woman doesn't forget those things . . . and later that night was the dream . . . the dream of a big country with fields of fertile land and big, giant things growing. And there by a green, slimy pond I found a giant pea pod and when I opened it, it was full of little, tiny baby frogs.

(AÍDA crosses herself as she watches MARGARITA. We hear louder breathing and heartbeat.)

MARGARITA Santa Teresa. Little Flower of God, pray for me. San Martín de Porres, pray for me. Santa Rosa de Lima, *Virgencita de la Caridad del Cobre,* pray for me. . . . Mother pray for me.

SCENE 5

Loud howling of wind is heard, as lights change to indicate unstable weather, fog and mist. FAMILY on deck, braced and huddled against the wind. SIMÓN is at the helm.

AÍDA   *Ay Dios mío, qué viento.*

EDUARDO   *(Through megaphone.)* Don't drift out . . . that wind is pushing you out. *(To* SIMÓN.*)* You! Slow down. Can't you see your sister is drifting out?

SIMÓN   It's the wind, *Papi.*

AÍDA   Baby, don't go so far. . . .

ABUELA   *(To heaven.) Ay Gran Poder de Dios, quita este maldito viento.*

SIMÓN   Margo! Margo! Stay close to the boat.

EDUARDO   Dig in. Dig in hard. . . . Reach down from your guts and dig in.

ABUELA   *(To heaven.) Ay Virgen de la Caridad del Cobre, por lo más tú quieres a pararla.*

AÍDA   *(Putting her hand out, reaching for* MARGARITA.*)* Baby, don't go far.

*(*ABUELA *crosses herself. Action freezes. Lights get dimmer, special on* MARGARITA. *She keeps swimming, stops, starts again, stops, then, finally exhausted, stops altogether. The boat stops moving.)*

EDUARDO   What's going on here? Why are we stopping?

SIMÓN   *Papi,* she's not moving! Yo Margo!

(The family all run to the side.)

EDUARDO   *Hija!* . . . *Hijita!* You're tired, eh?

AÍDA   *Por supuesto* she's tired. I like to see you get in the water, waving your arms and legs from San Pedro to Santa Catalina. A person isn't a machine, a person has to rest.

SIMÓN   Yo, Mama! Cool out, it ain't fucking brain surgery.

EDUARDO   *(To* SIMÓN.*)* Shut up, you. *(Louder to* MARGARITA.*)* I guess your mother's right for once, huh? . . . I guess you had to stop, eh? . . . Give your brother, the idiot . . . a chance to catch up with you.

SIMÓN   *(Clowning like Mortimer Snerd.)* Dum dee dum dee dum ooops, ah shucks . . .

EDUARDO   I don't think he's Cuban.

SIMÓN   *(Like Ricky Ricardo.) Oye,* Lucy! I'm home! Ba ba lu!

EDUARDO   *(Joins in clowning, grabbing* SIMÓN *in a headlock.)* What am I gonna do with this idiot, eh? I don't understand this idiot. He's not like us, Margarita. *(Laughing.)* You think if we put him into your bathing suit with a cap on his head . . . *(He laughs hysterically.)* You think anyone would know . . . huh? Do you think anyone would know? *(Laughs.)*

SIMÓN   *(Vamping.) Ay, mi amor.* Anybody looking for tits would know.

*(*EDUARDO *slaps* SIMÓN *across the face, knocking him down.* AÍDA *runs to* SIMÓN'*s aid.* ABUELA *holds* EDUARDO *back.)*

MARGARITA   *Mía culpa! Mía culpa!*

ABUELA   *Qué dices hija?*

MARGARITA   *Papi,* it's my fault, it's all my fault. . . . I'm so cold, I can't

move. . . . I put my face in the water . . . and I hear them whispering
. . . laughing at me. . . .

AÍDA   Who is laughing at you?

MARGARITA   The fish are all biting me . . . they hate me . . . they whisper about
me. She can't swim, they say. She can't glide. She has no grace. . . .
Yellowtails, bonita, tuna, man-o'-war, snub-nose sharks, *los baracudas*
. . . they all hate me . . . only the dolphins care . . . and sometimes I hear
the whales crying . . . she is lost, she is dead. I'm so numb, I can't feel.
Papi! Papi! Am I dead?

EDUARDO   *Vamos,* baby, punch those arms in. Come on . . . do you hear me?

MARGARITA   *Papi . . . Papi . . .* forgive me. . . .

*(All is silent on the boat. EDUARDO drops his megaphone, his head bent down in
dejection. ABUELA, AÍDA, SIMÓN, all leaning over the side of the boat. SIMÓN slowly
walks away.)*

AÍDA   *Mi hija, qué tienes?*

SIMÓN   Oh, Christ, don't make her say it. Please don't make her say it.

ABUELA   Say what? *Qué cosa?*

SIMÓN   She wants to quit, can't you see she's had enough?

ABUELA   *Mira, para eso. Esta niña* is turning blue.

AÍDA   *Oyeme, mi hija.* Do you want to come out of the water?

MARGARITA   *Papi?*

SIMÓN   *(To EDUARDO.)* She won't come out until *you* tell her.

AÍDA   Eduardo . . . answer your daughter.

EDUARDO   *Le dije* to concentrate . . . concentrate on your rhythm. Then the
rhythm would carry her . . . ay, it's a beautiful thing, Aída. It's like yoga,
like meditation, the mind over matter . . . the mind controlling the body
. . . that's how the great things in the world have been done. I wish you
. . . I wish my wife could understand.

MARGARITA   *Papi?*

SIMÓN   *(To MARGARITA.)* Forget him.

AÍDA   *(Imploring.)* Eduardo, *por favor.*

EDUARDO   *(Walking in circles.)* Why didn't you let her concentrate? Don't
you understand, the concentration, the rhythm is everything. But no,
you wouldn't listen. *(Screaming to the ocean.)* Goddamn Cubans, why,
God, why do you make us go everywhere with our families? *(He goes to
back of boat.)*

AÍDA   *(Opening her arms.)* Mi hija, ven, come to *Mami. (Rocking.)* Your *mami*
knows.

*(ABUELA has taken the training bottle, puts it in a net. She and SIMÓN lower it to
MARGARITA.)*

SIMÓN   Take this. Drink it. *(As* MARGARITA *drinks,* ABUELA *crosses herself.)*
ABUELA   *Sangre de mi sangre.*

(Music comes up softly. MARGARITA *drinks, gives the bottle back, stretches out her arms, as if on a cross. Floats on her back. She begins a graceful backstroke. Lights fade on boat as special lights come up on* MARGARITA. *She stops. Slowly turns over and starts to swim, gradually picking up speed. Suddenly as if in pain she stops, tries again, then stops in pain again. She becomes disoriented and falls to the bottom of the sea. Special on* MARGARITA *at the bottom of the sea.)*

MARGARITA   *Ya no puedo* . . . I can't. . . . A person isn't a machine . . . *es mi culpa* . . . Father forgive me . . . *Papi! Papi!* One, two. *Uno, dos. (Pause.) Papi! A dónde estás? (Pause.)* One, two, one, two. *Papi! Ay, Papi!* Where are you . . . ? Don't leave me. . . . Why don't you answer me? *(Pause. She starts to swim, slowly.) Uno, dos, uno, dos.* Dig in, dig in. *(Stops swimming.) Por favor, Papi! (Starts to swim again.)* One, two, one, two. Kick from your hip, kick from your hip. *(Stops swimming. Starts to cry.)* Oh God, please. . . . *(Pause.)* Hail Mary, full of grace . . . dig in, dig in . . . the Lord is with thee. . . . *(She swims to the rhythm of her Hail Mary.)* Hail Mary, full of grace . . . dig in, dig in . . . the Lord is with thee . . . dig in, dig in. . . . Blessed art thou among women. . . . *Mami,* it hurts. You let go of my hand. I'm lost. . . . And blessed is the fruit of thy womb, now and at the hour of our death. Amen. I don't want to die, I don't want to die.

*(*MARGARITA *is still swimming. Blackout. She is gone.)*

SCENE 6

Lights up on boat, we hear radio static. There is a heavy mist. On deck we see only black outline of ABUELA *with shawl over her head. We hear the voices of* EDUARDO, AÍDA, *and* RADIO OPERATOR.

EDUARDO'S VOICE   La Havana! Coming from San Pedro. Over.
RADIO OPERATOR'S VOICE   Right, DT6-6, you say you've lost a swimmer.
AÍDA'S VOICE   Our child, our only daughter . . . listen to me. Her name is Margarita Inez Suárez, she is wearing a black one-piece bathing suit cut high in the legs with a white racing stripe down the sides, a white bathing cap with goggles and her whole body covered with a . . . with a . . .
EDUARDO'S VOICE   With lanolin and paraffin.
AÍDA'S VOICE   *Sí . . . con lanolin and paraffin.*

(More radio static. Special on SIMÓN, *on the edge of the boat.)*

SIMÓN   Margo! Yo Margo! *(Pause.)* Man don't do this. *(Pause.)* Come on. . . . Come on. . . . *(Pause.)* God, why does everything have to be so hard?

(Pause.) Stupid. You know you're not supposed to die for this. Stupid. It's his dream and he can't even swim. *(Pause.)* Punch those arms in. Come home. Come home. I'm your little brother. Don't forget what Mama said. You're not supposed to leave me behind. *Vamos*, Margarita, take your little brother, hold his hand tight when you cross the street. He's so little. *(Pause.)* Oh, Christ, give us a sign. . . . I know! I know! Margo, I'll send you a message . . . like mental telepathy. I'll hold my breath, close my eyes, and I'll bring you home. *(He takes a deep breath; a few beats.)* This time I'll beep . . . I'll send out sonar signals like a dolphin. *(He imitates dolphin sounds.)*

(The sound of real dolphins takes over from SIMÓN, *then fades into sound of* ABUELA *saying the Hail Mary in Spanish, as full lights come up slowly.)*

SCENE 7

EDUARDO *coming out of cabin, sobbing,* AÍDA *holding him.* SIMÓN *anxiously scanning the horizon.* ABUELA *looking calmly ahead.*

EDUARDO   *Es mi culpa, sí, es mi culpa. (He hits his chest.)*
AÍDA   *Ya, ya viejo* . . . it was my sin . . . I left my home.
EDUARDO   Forgive me, forgive me. I've lost our daughter, our sister, our grand-daughter, *mi carne, mi sangre, mis ilusiones. (To heaven.) Dios mío*, take me . . . take me, I say . . . Goddammit, take me!
SIMÓN   I'm going in.
AÍDA and EDUARDO   No!
EDUARDO   *(Grabbing and holding* SIMÓN, *speaking to heaven.)* God, take me, not my children. They are my dreams, my illusions . . . and not this one, this one is my mystery . . . he has my secret dreams. In him are the parts of me I cannot see.

*(*EDUARDO *embraces* SIMÓN. *Radio static becomes louder.)*

AÍDA   I . . . I think I see her.
SIMÓN   No, it's just a seal.
ABUELA   *(Looking out with binoculars.) Mi nietacita, dónde estás? (She feels her heart.)* I don't feel the knife in my heart . . . my little fish is not lost.

(Radio crackles with static. As lights dim on boat, VOICES OF MEL and MARY BETH *are heard over the radio.)*

MEL'S VOICE   Tragedy has marred the face of the Wrigley Invitational Women's Race to Catalina. The Cuban swimmer, little Margarita Suárez, has reportedly been lost at sea. Coast Guard and divers are looking for her as we speak. Yet in spite of this tragedy the race must go on because . . .
MARY BETH'S VOICE   *(Interrupting loudly.)* Mel!

MEL'S VOICE   *(Startled.)* What!

MARY BETH'S VOICE   Ah . . . excuse me, Mel . . . we have a winner. We've just
   received word from Catalina that one of the swimmers is just fifty yards
   from the breakers . . . it's, oh, it's . . . Margarita Suárez!

(Special on family in cabin listening to radio.)

MEL'S VOICE   What? I thought she died!

(Special on MARGARITA, taking off bathing cap, trophy in hand, walking on the water.)

MARY BETH'S VOICE   Ahh . . . unless . . . unless this is a tragic . . . No . . . there
   she is, Mel. Margarita Suárez! The only one in the race wearing a black
   bathing suit cut high in the legs with a racing stripe down the side.

(Family cheering, embracing.)

SIMÓN   *(Screaming.)* Way to go, Margo!

MEL'S VOICE   This is indeed a miracle! It's a resurrection! Margarita Suárez,
   with a flotilla of boats to meet her, is now walking on the waters, through
   the breakers . . . onto the beach, with crowds of people cheering her on.
   What a jubilation! This is a miracle!

(Sound of crowds cheering. Lights and cheering sounds fade.)

Blackout.

SAM SHEPARD

Excerpts from *Slave of the Camera*

MARCH 15, HOTEL TAJIN:

It's six A.M. and Phillipe is knocking very politely on my door, telling me it's time to go to work. The car is ready, but I can't get out of bed. Can't figure out where I am or how I got here. There's tequila all around me. Surrounded by empty bottles. The shower's running. A constant trickle hitting the tile and gurgling down the drain. Turkeys are gobbling. Voices from the zoccolo. I can't seem to swing my legs out. The blanket's stuck to my chest. I've been sweating in the night. Sleeping in my clothes. My boots are still on. I stare at my boots. I remember where I bought them. I remember the face of the man who sold them to me, in Gallup, New Mexico. How he wanted to sell me a more expensive pair made out of belly ostrich hide. He was wearing a pair himself and highly recommended them. Gallup. The El Rancho Hotel with old black-and-white photographs of Alan Ladd, John Wayne, Andy Devine, William Holden, lining the staircase of the lobby. They'd all stayed there in the old days when they were shooting John Ford westerns or Howard Hawks westerns or somebody's westerns. It was a landmark place—the El Rancho. Phillipe knocks again, even more politely, and I tell him I'll be right down, but I still can't swing my legs out. I'm waiting for a signal from myself, but nothing comes. I'm waiting for an idea—a thought that connects me to this place and time. I remember Gabby Hayes. That's what comes. The thought of Gabby Hayes.

    I was seven years old and drove out with my father to a place on the Mojave called Shadow Mountain. We'd been looking at a little patch of desert that he'd bought out there. We'd spent all afternoon shooting rusty cans with a .22 pistol and looking for snakes. He'd wanted to bring a rattlesnake back with him to show my mother. A "Green Mojave." "Just to prove we were out here," he'd said. "Sometimes I get the feeling she doesn't believe me. Thinks I'm off tomcatting or some foolishness."

    "Is that the reason you brought me along?" I'd said.

"Is what the reason?"

"So she'd think you weren't tomcatting?"

"You're not even sure what tomcattin' means, are you? You're seven years old. How could you be sure what that means?" He turned his back on me and walked away, kicking an empty can and reloading the chamber of the pistol. I could tell he was pissed off for me having asked him that. He tossed a can in the air and fired. He missed. He emptied the whole pistol into the sky and missed every time he threw the can. I got embarrassed for him and pretended I hadn't seen this. I found a stick of manzanita and started drawing circles in the sand. He looked over his shoulder at me and reloaded the pistol. "So what's your thought on this little piece of desert here? Think I made a smart deal?" he asked me. "The two of us oughta just pick up stakes and move out here. Just forget about the women altogether." He laughed and fired again at a can on the ground. I wasn't sure if he hit it or not because I wasn't looking and I didn't hear any metal ring. I was hoping he did hit it, though, because I thought it would help to calm him down some. He kept taking sips from a fifth wrapped in a paper bag that he had stuffed in his hip pocket. He tried to get friendlier with me, and the more he tried, the more separated I felt from him. He seemed to sense this, too, but there was nothing he could do about it. "Sometimes it's good just to get off by yourself someplace," he said. "To have a spot like that, all tucked away. Don't you think?" He fired again at a jackrabbit but didn't come anywhere near it. "That's what I had in mind for this place. A little desert hideaway. Can't always be the family man. Me and you could build a bottle house, maybe. What do you think about that?"

"Sure," I said, still fiddling with the stick.

"Keep a couple a burros. Take hikes and find some treasure. There's lots to find out here. This is undiscovered territory yet."

"You mean we'd just live out here?" I asked him.

"Well, not permanent. Not on a permanent basis. Just have it as a kind of retreat. Nobody'd know about it except you and me. Be our little secret. Have to bring water to it, of course. That's the chief problem out here is water."

"We'd never bring Mom?"

This question seemed to piss him off again. He kicked at the sand and spun the chamber of the .22. "She's not the desert type," he said. "Forests is her game. Woods and lakes. Midwestern stuff." He fired into an old kerosene can that was so big he couldn't miss. "She likes it where it's all closed in and you can't see the sky. Not my cup a tea."

We drove across the sand back to the blacktop highway and stopped at a Date Shack advertising Date Shakes. He asked for directions to the Shadow Mountain Inn—some kind of country club he'd remembered from his air force days. We shared a box of dates stuffed with coconut shavings, and he kept licking his fingers and saying, "Better than a Hershey bar!" We parked in front of the country club and he wrapped the .22 up in a newspaper and stuffed it under the front seat. He took one more hit from his bottle and hid that in the glove compartment underneath some highway maps. As we crossed the parking lot, he told me this was a very exclusive club and we should act like we belonged here.

"It's all in the way you present yourself. If you go in there acting like you don't belong, they're going to sense that right off the bat. Just act natural and relaxed."

We sat at the bar and he ordered a martini and a bowl of peanuts. I'd never seen him drink a martini before, but I guess he ordered that to impress the bartender. I got a cherry Coke with a slice of lemon. That's when I saw Gabby Hayes. He was sitting in a corner booth with a black string tie and a tuxedo. It was the middle of the afternoon, and he had on a tuxedo. There were two young blond women with him dressed in slinky cocktail dresses. They kept feeding him shrimp dipped in red sauce and nibbling on his ears. "That's Gabby Hayes!" I whispered to my father. He turned stiffly on his stool and looked over at the corner booth and then turned back to his drink. "That's what fame and fortune'll get you," he said. "Couple a blond chippies and a shrimp cocktail. How 'bout that." I kept staring at Gabby Hayes's beard and watching his mouth chomp down on the shrimp. It seemed like he had teeth now. On TV he never had teeth. On TV he was subservient to Roy Rogers. He was the sidekick. He always spoke to Dale Evans like a demented hired hand with a gummy mouth. He was stepping out of character here, and it confused me. It never crossed my mind that Gabby Hayes might be somebody else.

MARCH 18, EL PASO

I see Simmons come into the bathroom combing his blond hair and heading for a mirror. I duck into one of the toilet stalls and lock the door. I'm just standing inside there, hiding from Simmons. I don't know why. I keep hearing Irene's voice: "Don't you want to meet up?" How could she ask me something like that? A trucker in the next stall lets out a long, rolling fart and then shouts out to the whole bathroom at large: "Spur it! Spur the sonabitch!" The whole place bursts into laughter and whistles and hooting. "Barn sour! That's what it is! Hairless little bastard!" the trucker yells out. He's right in the next stall to me. He's making this performance with his voice. Nobody can see him. It's a *"mucho macho"* kind of a deal. His audience is on a roll. Another trucker yells out to the one in the stall: "Whad'ya expect! You sit on the little shit for fifteen hundred miles at a stretch! He's bound to object!" More exploding laughter and rebel yells. I can picture Simons trying to comb his surfer hair in the midst of all this. I sit down on the toilet with my pants on and stare at the metal door. Somebody's scratched a sentence into the metal finish with a Buck knife: *"I'm so horny not even the crack of dawn is safe!"* That's what it says. The performance goes on: "What's the difference between an asshole and an enchilada?" They all start hooting so loud that I miss the punch line. The guy in the stall next to me starts unrolling miles of toilet paper. He's laughing so hard he starts to cough and choke. Someone's banging on his stall door, asking him if he's dying. Should they call the rescue squad. The guy keeps laughing and choking and unwinding toilet paper. Slowly, all the truckers leave, and there's only me and this choking farting guy left. I just stay in the stall staring at the graffiti, listening to him groan as he wipes his butt and recovers from his laughing seizure. Suddenly, he speaks to me. He's right next door. He can see my feet, I guess. "Where'd you get them boots, pardner?" I'm not sure what to do. I'm obliged to answer him, I guess, since we're the only ones left in the men's room.

"Gallup," I say. "Gallup, New Mexico."

"Oh, yeah. Drunkest town in America. Yer not a Navajo, are ya?"

"Nope. I'm a white guy."

"Yer not a faggot, are ya?" he says.

"Nope, I'm just a white guy."

"Lotta faggots in New Mexico now. You noticed that?"

"Haven't been there for a while."

"Faggots and New York Jews. Place is crawlin' with 'em."

"I guess."

"I dunno what made 'em ever figure they'd be able to mix with the Navajo."

"Beats me," I say.

"Where you headed?" he says, and I can hear him hitching up his jeans and zipping and buckling. He sounds like one of those grizzly bear types.

"L.A.," I say.

"L.A. and yer not a faggot?" He laughs.

"Nope."

"Wish to hell that place'd just break off and float away into the Pacific. Country'd be better off."

"Probably so."

"No Americans out there anymore. Japs and Vietcong and God knows what all. What the hell you live out there for? They don't even speak English anymore, do they?"

"I don't live there," I say. "I work there."

"What line a work do you follow?"

"I'm an actor."

"An actor!" he says. "In the movies?"

"Yeah."

"What movies you been in? What's yer name?"

"Spencer Tracy," I say.

"Spencer Tracy? I heard a him. You're an old guy, then, huh?"

"Yeah, I'm old."

"You don't sound old to me. Must keep yerself in pretty good shape."

"I'm fit as a fiddle."

"And yer sure yer not a faggot?"

"Well, nobody's ever sure, are they?" There's a silence. The guy starts to speed up his movements. He flushes. He leaves the stall and goes to a sink. The water's turned on. I can hear him splashing his face and gargling. Then he starts brushing his teeth. He spits and speaks very calmly between more brushing and spitting. He's speaking to me, a complete stranger who he can't see and knows nothing about except the color of my boots.

"I'll tell ya what, pal. It's a sad day in the morning for this country. I don't much care what a man does in his private time. Ain't none a my business. But when it starts to move out into the middle a things and infect the public at large, then I got one or two things to say about it. You know they got truckstop hookers in Lincoln Nebraska now with AIDS? You realize that? They got twelve-year-old niggers on the streets of St. Louis, Missouri, sellin' crack. And you know where them niggers originally come from? They ain't from St. Louis, I'll tell ya that much. They're from Brooklyn and Queens. Places like that. They call 'em 'mules,' and they get dumped off by their big brothers and bastard fathers just for the sole purpose of infecting St. Louis with dope. They run around with beepers strapped to their belts and nine-millimeter automatics. I seen 'em. Out there plain as day. Twelve-year-old killers. Nobody in St. Louis sees 'em, but I see 'em. Nobody's got their eyes open in this country anymore. The rug's being pulled out right from underneath us, and nobody gives a flying shit about it. The Japs own everything now. You know that. Any fool knows that. The sneaky Japs. They've bought it all up while we were napping. Hotels, motels, huge tracts of land—wilderness land—land that was deeded to us by Teddy fuckin' Roosevelt! Can you believe that? Government land. The fuckin' B.L.M.. Bunch a two-timing, double-dealing bastards. Sellin' our land to the Japs. They ought to hang 'em up by the short hairs and cut their fuckin' balls off. I'm from pioneer stock myself. I don't know about you, but I'm from pioneer stock. My people stuck it out in sod houses cut right out of the Great Plains. North Platte country. Stuck it out through drought and dust storms, fuckin' Arapaho Indians shootin' arrows at 'em. Diggin' for potatoes. Scrounging around for firewood. They stuck it out. And now the Japs own it. Goddamn camel jockeys own the gas stations. Can't buy a fuckin' plaid shirt anymore that ain't made in Taiwan or Hong Kong or some goddamn place. And this is what my people suffered their nuts off for? To have the whole thing taken over by a bunch a sleazy foreigners. It's a sad day in the mornin', pal." And then he leaves. I hear the door flapping behind him. The electric hand dryer is still blowing, but that's the only sound. I'm alone here in this toilet. I hear Irene's voice. It's sad and sweet: "I want to see you," she says. "I want to see you."

MARCH 19, TUCSON

Still living some Neal Cassady kind of life out in the Bay Area. Shacked up with two women who he somehow manages to balance while holding down his job as a shuttle driver for Avis. I first met John in New York City on St. Mark's Place, right next to the old Five Spot. He was married, and still is, to a red-haired woman named Rose whose daughter I was greatly attracted to in those days. Her name was Toola Brian—now my ex-wife. John and I were about the same age, and Rose, who was a good nine years older, maintained a youthful sexuality about her that made you think she might be Toola's older sister. I was sort of dating Toola back then, and since she lived with her mother, I was always running into Johnny Day. The two of us struck it off right away when we found out we'd both had ambitions to become veterinarians at an early age. In fact, we discovered we both had the same "History of the Dog" chart pinned to our wall which showed the whole evolution of the species from some strange prehistoric ratlike creature down through a family tree that branched off into the St. Bernard, the German shepherd, and every recognized American Kennel Club breed of the fifties. Although he was from Newark, New Jersey, and I was from out west, we both had lots in common. One of our strongest links was an overwhelming appreciation for Kerouac and, subsequently, Benzedrine, crystal Methedrine, and almost any pill that kept us up and going without sleep for days at a time.

"Hello, John? It's Clayton."
"Who?"
"Clayton. Clayton Moss."
"Say it again."
"Clayton Moss! It's me."
"You don't sound like him."
"Well, it's been a while."
"It has been that. How long's it been?" he says.
"I haven't kept track."
"Where are you now?"
"Arizona. Somewhere outside Tucson."
"Well, I'm in bed," he says.
"It's daytime there, isn't it?"
"Far as I can tell."
"Are you sick or something?"

"Nope. Just no reason to get up. I'm conducting all my business from here. It's great. Angel just made me a vodka tonic, and I'm working on my tapes."

"Which tapes?"

"Well, right now I'm working on my soundtrack tapes from famous chase scenes. You remember *Bullitt*? Steve McQueen. Just finished that one. You wanna hear it? Listen. Listen to this." He starts playing me the music from *Bullitt*, where McQueen is flying over the San Francisco hills in his Ford Mustang, burning rubber and firing some super magnum pistol out the window.

"John! Hey, Johnny! I'm in a pay phone at a Texaco here, and I haven't got much change! John!"

"What's the matter?" he says.

"I'm in a pay phone. I'm low on change."

"I thought you were a movie star now. How come you're low on change?"

"I just haven't got a lot on me."

"What're you doing in Tucson, playing cowboys and Indians again?"

"I'm just going through on my way to L.A. I wanted to talk to you for a second."

"Good. Maybe we could meet up when you get down there to L.A."

"That'd be great, but I've gotta' meet Irene there, too. She's coming."

"How come she's not with you?"

"We're going through a bad spell."

"Aw, that's too bad. I hate those. Just went through one of those myself."

"You did?"

"Yeah. Just got over it, in fact. Pure torture. That's part of why I'm in bed. It's exhausting."

"Yeah. It is."

"Thought I was dying there for a while. I'd just collapse and pray for death."

"But Angel's with you, right?"

"Yeah, Angel's right here. She just made me a great vodka tonic with a twist of lime. Rose is here, too. They're both here."

"How's that working out?"

"It has its ups and downs. Like I said, we just went through a slump, but we're back on top of it now. They're best friends again. Oh! That reminds me —I had this thought before and I've been trying to remember what it was and just now—something about what you just said reminded me of it. Maybe that's the reason you called."

"Maybe what's the reason?"

"In order to remind me of this thought."

"Yeah. Maybe. But I wanted to talk to you about Irene."

"Good. Let me just tell you this before I forget it again. I don't want to lose this. And maybe it pertains to your situation."

"Okay. Just a second. I gotta drop more quarters in."

"Go ahead." As I'm dumping another buck and a half's worth of quarters into the phone I see J.T. taking a picture of Simmons sitting on the hood of the Aerovan in his dark designer glasses. Then J.T. hands the camera to Simmons, and Simmons hands the dark glasses to J.T. They swap places, and Simmons now takes a picture of J.T. sitting on the hood of the Aerovan.

"Are you still there?" I say to Johnny Day.

"Yeah. You can always count on me, pal. But, listen—I'd just gone through this whole jealousy thing with Angel. I mean *her* jealousy, not mine. We were just coming through the worst part of it and I thought maybe I should give her a line that was a kind of Sterling Hayden kind of a line. Maybe that would work, I thought. So I said to her—I said—'If you loved me you'd be blind to all my faults.' That's what I said. And just as I said that, I caught myself trying to be somebody else. Maybe it was Sterling Hayden. It felt like something I do a lot, and I could see for the first time what was behind it— this trying to be somebody other than who you actually are—like walking into a bar and presenting yourself as this certain type of guy. A gangster, maybe. But what I saw behind it was this real basic feeling that I'm not good enough as I am—that I would be better if I could be this other type—somebody else. Sterling Hayden, maybe Charles Laughton—anybody but myself. And then, when I saw that, I saw that this was all in my thoughts, but in actual fact I *am* Sterling Hayden."

"John, listen—"

"No, look, I don't mean that I think I'm Sterling Hayden. That's not it. I'm saying that I *am* the person in my daydreams. That's all. That it's not a mistake. I'm actually here and this adventure is mine and I don't need to be somebody else. The pretending is all part of it. You see what I mean?"

"Yeah. But, look—"

"The other way it's like not seeing the movie that you're in. Thinking you're not in a similar situation to the movie. The hero lays in bed with the girl, just like me and Angel are now."

"You're *both* in bed now?"

"Yeah, sure. She's crawled right in here with me."

"Well, look—maybe I should try you some other time."

"No! Are you kidding. No time like the present! But look. You see this scene in the movie—the guy and girl in bed. They're at her place and it's dark and they're looking out through the cloudy windows and he's smoking a Camel. It's a scene. You've seen it a million times. And when you pay your five bucks and you go in and sit down in the dark and you're watching this scene, you say, 'God! I wish I had that! I wish my life was like that.' But what you're not realizing is that your ordinary life *is* that. I'm not talking about playing a part. I'll leave that up to you actors. I'm saying that the part that you're actually living is just like the one you're playing. So that means you don't have to feel the pressure of playing a role if you can just remember that you're already in the drama on a day-to-day basis. This is your movie. This is it!"

"Yeah. Right. I just thought maybe I could ask for some—uh—advice."

"I mean, I *am* that guy laying in the dark with the beautiful girl, looking out the cloudy window and smoking the Camel and drinking the vodka tonic. That's me! But I don't ordinarily recognize it. I keep yearning for what I already have. Suddenly, a possibility opens up. A new light! I see my life as a real adventure. I actually experience it in that way you experience a movie. The soundtrack surrounds me. Even a scene in a movie where the hero is in his kitchen and he's frying eggs and the camera's moving in—tracking slowly, very ominous, and there's spooky music in the background which supposedly the hero can't hear, only the audience can hear it—but basically he's just in his kitchen doing something very ordinary and banal like frying a couple eggs. And you're there in the audience, transfixed by this situation, and yet you never have that kind of feeling when you're in your own kitchen frying your own eggs. But we're actually the heroes of our own kitchen, Clay! Do you realize that? We are the heroes of our very own kitchens! It's just a matter of being creative. Don't you think? Just a question of daily creativity, that's all."

"Yeah, well, look—I'm going to have to call you when I get to L.A., I guess. I've got these two guys waiting for me in a car."

"You're on the road again! Well, lackaday! It was good hearing you, Clayton, old boy."

"You, too."

"Don't buckle under the weight of a heavy heart! That's my advice to you, bucko! Never surrender!"

"I'll call you when I get there."

"You do that. I'll roll on down Highway Five in the Buick and give you a visit."

"*Adios.* Say hi to Rose for me."

"I'll do that."

PERRY SOUCHUK

The Pleasure of Detachment

CHARACTERS

WOMAN IN BED
MAID
YOUNG MAN
VOICE

SETTING

A room with a bed and a chair. Three tall windows hang upstage of bed. Curtains flow out from windows, frozen in space.

VOICE   Picture this: a long white day with no fuzzy thinking, a hammock in a grove of palm trees. Picture this: a play with no beginning or end, a play that grows from a kind of reverie. *(Lights up to half. WOMAN stands at windows, looking out.)* First there was the image of the curtains, which, in its stillness, was like a photograph. But what does it signify? Does the stillness of the curtain mean that we are looking at a play where time is frozen? Can time be frozen? If one definition of time is the way thoughts flow, then time can be frozen if we record an idea. The curtain is a reminder of time . . . the way thoughts flow . . . the possibility of freezing an idea in the space and time of a play. *(WOMAN moves slowly to bed, lies down, slips hands into straps attached to bedposts.)* This is a play about an exercise in limitation, a self-imposed bondage; self-bondage as a meaningful self-test. In her reverie, the woman, her own test subject, discovers the consolation of stillness. When the ritual of self-bondage ends, the mind is again set in motion, then the body, then the world. *(Music fades. Lights up full.)*

WOMAN   (*Leaning forward.*) In order not to move I had to know I couldn't move! Human nature, human nature.

(*MAID enters with fresh sheets, etc.*)

MAID   How are we doing today?

WOMAN   Pretty well. (*Thoughtfully, rearranging herself in bed.*) Did you know that Toussaint L'Ouverture said that nature speaks in louder tones than philosophy or self-interest?

MAID   (*Humoring her.*) No, I didn't know that. (*Carefully.*) The doctor will be here this afternoon.

WOMAN   But I just saw the doctor yesterday!

MAID   (*Assuringly.*) And he said you are doing very well.

WOMAN   Did he also say that as I was leaving he asked me out for a drink?

(*MAID turns, surprised.*)

WOMAN   I asked him, "Would you ask me out if I wasn't well?" And he answered, "I don't think so." (*Pause.*) He's my doctor, but he's not my medicine.

(*MAID exits.*)

VOICE   Some facts about the woman: She led a life not dominated by facts. She was wide-eyed only when alone. She had dreams where all she had to do was turn around to see a different world.

WOMAN   Who doesn't?

VOICE   Her goal was never to be hidden or veiled.

MAID   (*Entering with water pitcher and glass.*) What's on the agenda for today?

WOMAN   I think I'll start my new story today.

MAID   Lovely! (*Pause.*) Am I in it?

WOMAN   (*Pausing, surprised.*) I don't know!

VOICE   How about the story of a woman obsessed with the idea of turning her obsessions into something concrete? Or the story of a woman whose biggest dilemma is an excess of joy? Or a woman who enjoys a certain detachment, a certain pleasure, the pleasure of detachment?

(*YOUNG MAN enters carrying valise. Sees WOMAN in bed.*)

YOUNG MAN   (*Flustered, uneasy.*) Hhhhello. (*Staring at WOMAN.*) The doctor sent me over to see if you might need anything today.

WOMAN   (*Delighted, curious.*) If I might need anything! Like what?

YOUNG MAN   (*Uneasily.*) I I don't know.

MAID   (*Turning to YOUNG MAN.*) I thought the doctor was coming today?

WOMAN   But I don't need the doctor today!

VOICE   No, what the woman *needs* is an answer. She's looking for an answer to a very tricky question.

WOMAN   (*Startled.*) Excuse me?

(MAID and YOUNG MAN stare at WOMAN.)

VOICE   The question is: how do you tell the difference between anxiety and desire?

(Pause.)

WOMAN   I give up!

VOICE   The difference between anxiety and desire is that desire is influential. Desire is like a tattoo which only shows when you want it to. You see, a tattoo draws a person in for a closer look. Desire attracts, anxiety repels.

WOMAN   *(Looking at MAID and then at YOUNG MAN.)* How do you get rid of a tattoo?

YOUNG MAN   *(Trying to be helpful.)* I read somewhere that you can get rid of a tattoo by rubbing salt into it!

WOMAN   *(To YOUNG MAN.)* And what does one do with an unwanted . . . desire?

(Flustered, YOUNG MAN turns away from bed.)

VOICE   The unwanted desire becomes an open wound just waiting for a pinch of salt!

WOMAN   Ouch!!

VOICE   Try this: write down a few ideas. Digest those ideas with the juices of past experience.

YOUNG MAN   *(Moving closer to bed.)* Are you really writing a story?

WOMAN   As we speak!

YOUNG MAN   What's it about?

WOMAN   *(Mysteriously.)* It's . . . kind of a travel book.

VOICE   She plans a trip by reading about different places, and the reading becomes the trip.

WOMAN   *(As a confession, to no one in particular.)* When I travel by train, I say to myself, While I'm on this train every thought is a jumping-off place! *(Pause.)* When I got back from my last trip I could only recall three words: weather, wonder, and whatcha-ma-call-its! I remember . . . I was in a car driving through Missouri. My aunt was with me, and her German welder friend was driving. He was a welder and she was a writer.

VOICE   Oh, so you mean they understood each other?

YOUNG MAN   *(Moving closer to MAID.)* Did she say Missouri or misery? *(MAID ignores YOUNG MAN. Still absorbed in WOMAN's story, she rises and moves closer to bed.)*

WOMAN   He asked me if I liked motorcycles, and I looked at him and said: *(Turning to look at YOUNG MAN, self-satisfied.)* It depends who's driving!

(YOUNG MAN, shocked, drops into chair.)

VOICE   The woman acquires a certain mystery, simply by the fact that we have come to see her. Who is she? She is an actress who rehearses lines and movements in order to get an idea across. And the audience works to understand the idea. The actress works with a director in order to get the right inflection. The audience's rehearsal is life outside the play. The ideal play is written by the audience and the writer and the actor. The greater the audience's imagination, the greater the play.

WOMAN   *(Twisting to look out windows, hands still in straps.)* I looked out the window and saw a bubble floating by. The sky was an unseeable blue, a depthless blue! A great shimmering lake spread out in front of me. I watched pink and silver fish crisscrossing in the air.

VOICE   *(Gently.)* In telling a story, you must give the listener the feeling of listening. Don't tell me so easily what you know.

WOMAN   Every morning I wake up and feel the world spreading out, starting over. *(Leaning forward.)* I run after ideas like a rabbit with a carrot in front of his nose!

(WOMAN settles back into bed. Music begins softly under dialogue.)

VOICE   She gazed out the window at the November sky.

WOMAN   *(Startled. Turning away from windows.)* Is it November already?

MAID   *(Soothingly.)* Of course it's November! Now you just relax. *(MAID examines straps, then freezes.)* *(To YOUNG MAN.)* I think I've tied the straps too tight! *(She starts to undo strap. YOUNG MAN jumps up, unties other strap.)*

(Pause.)

YOUNG MAN   She's bleeding!

VOICE   The talent of blood to coagulate itself, stopping the flow to the outside in order to preserve the flowing on the inside. Not unlike the flowing of mental activity, the talent of the brain to compound the flow, idea upon idea, until the brain has made a kind of story. The writer wills the cells of his body to seek out the nutrition of new ideas. But there is a sadness in translating sensation into words. The writer feels the inadequacies of his expression. *(WOMAN gets out of bed, goes to windows.)* This is a play about the way thoughts flow in and out of stories. Tonight, the woman is looking for her own story.

(YOUNG MAN moves to WOMAN, opens valise.)

YOUNG MAN   *(Fishing around in valise.)* I have a collection of rocks you might like to see. It's a small collection really. *(Pause.)* Actually, I only have one rock. But it's very beautiful. *(Takes out rock, puts it in WOMAN's hand. WOMAN holds rock, turns to look out windows. Lights fade to black.)*

TOM STOPPARD
AND
CLIVE EXTON

The Boundary

SCENE 1: LEXICOGRAPHERS' LIBRARY

We are aware that from nowhere in particular comes the modulated well-bred sound of a TV cricket postmortem.

We discover the room empty but cluttered with the paraphernalia of the life work of our heroes. Meanwhile paper is everywhere. But the disorder seems exaggerated. And as we see more, we realize that chaos reigns. It seems that the place has been turned over: piles of paper on the floor, over the furniture, etc. A drift, like a snowdrift, of paper against the door. The door is pushed open inward and JOHNSON, who is an old man, enters knee-deep in slips of paper. He registers the unwelcome fact that his room has been pillaged and is becoming more and more concerned and horrified. He picks slips of paper up here and there and mutters to himself. . . .

JOHNSON   Tannin . . . Therefore . . . Talismanical . . . Tortoise . . . Telephone . . .

(He searches in a mound of paper, scoops up an armful, revealing a small television set, a cricket match going on. The same time . . . announcing triumphantly. . . .)

JOHNSON   Telephone . . .

(We become aware of the source of the sound. He taps on top of the TV set with his hand.)

JOHNSON   Operator . . . ! Operator . . . ! *(Realizing his mistake, he drops the papers back on the TV set. He then begins searching for the phone under another pile of papers. Lifts up another armful, revealing a telescope on a tripod. He pauses and studies it for a moment. He's puzzled; he has lost track of his thought. He puts his eye to the telescope, which is pointing through the window in a slightly downward direction, and there in hideous close-up is a cricketeer, a batsman. Immediately afterward he realizes that he still has the wrong implement, drops the papers over the telescope, his mind clears. An old-fashioned telephone is sitting in the middle of the table. He puts the receiver to his ear, thinks for a moment, dials three digits. . . .)*

OPERATOR *(Crackle.)* Telegrams.

JOHNSON I wanted directory inquiries.

OPERATOR *(Crackle.)* A telegram to directory inquiries.

JOHNSON No, I'd rather speak to them if that's possible.

OPERATOR *(Crackle.)* Directory inquiries is 192.

JOHNSON Thank you. *(Hangs up—dials again.)*

OPERATOR *(Crackle.)* Directory. Which town?

JOHNSON Can you get me the telephone number of the police.

OPERATOR *(Crackle.)* Is it an emergency?

JOHNSON Emergency. Well, yes.

OPERATOR *(Crackle.)* Dial 999.

JOHNSON Thank you. *(Replaces the receiver and dials 999.)*

OPERATOR *(Crackle.)* Emergency. Which service?

JOHNSON Now look here, my name is Johnson. I seem to have been bungled. *(Pause.)* Just a moment. *(He hangs up absentmindedly. Crosses to a pile of galley proofs, rummages among it, comes up with the one he wants and remarks victoriously. . . .)* Burgled. *(And he turns back to the 'phone, but before he reaches it, the door opens, and in Bunyans enters.)* Burglars.

BUNYANS I beg your pardon.

JOHNSON Look.

BUNYANS *(Softly to himself.)* Buggar.

JOHNSON Burglars.

BUNYANS Anything missing? *(They look around at the chaos.)*

JOHNSON Not at first glance, but even so . . . the year's work . . . *(In despair he picks up galley proof.)*

BUNYANS Any sign of entry?

JOHNSON *(Glancing at galley proof.)* Yes, that's here. *(Reading.)* Entry . . . Entune . . . Enturret . . . Entwine . . .

BUNYANS No, I mean . . .

JOHNSON Ah . . . The door wasn't locked.

BUNYANS It's not necessarily a burglary.

JOHNSON No. No. Possibly housebreaking if the act was committed during the hours of daylight.

BUNYANS *(Turns aside, picks up handful of papers, and reads them.)* Triangle . . . Tuffett . . . Tendon . . .

JOHNSON   What are you doing?

BUNYANS   Refiling.

JOHNSON   As if nothing had happened?

BUNYANS   How else would we know if anything is missing? *(Picks up slip.)* Tactile . . . Taclobo to Tailor. . . . Taclobo to Tailor. . . . *(He wanders around the room repeating Taclobo to Tailor until he finds the box—holds it aloft triumphantly and puts it on the long table in the center of the room. He carefully puts the slip of paper into it. JOHNSON meanwhile has picked up another slip of paper from the floor. . . .)*

JOHNSON   Tardel.

BUNYANS   No. No. We're looking for *Taclobo to Tailor.*

JOHNSON   Ah. *(He allows the slip of paper to flutter to the ground. Bunyans is picking up slips and letting them drop again.)*

BUNYANS   Telpher . . . Tie-wigged . . . Take-off . . . Tentative . . . Tush . . . Tea-time . . . Thyration . . . Toadstool . . . Titanic . . . *(He picks up the end of a piece of paper, which is uniquely long, reads of it.)* The . . . *(JOHNSON is staring, puzzled at the mess.)*

JOHNSON   Terrible.

BUNYANS   Tercel-Gentel to Tazkere.

JOHNSON   No, I mean, it's just terrible, who can have done this? *(They both stop what they're doing and shake their heads, puzzled.)*

BUNYANS   It's a mystery.

JOHNSON   . . . religious truth known only from divine revelation?

BUNYANS   I think not. More prosaic. . . . Matter unexplained or inexplicable. A riddle or enigma. *(He picks up another slip.)*

BUNYANS   Telinga. *(He drops it.)*

JOHNSON   This is the wrong method. We must collect the boxes and then pick up at random.

BUNYANS   Oh. Of course! The boxes first. *(He starts to collect boxes. JOHNSON helps him.)*

JOHNSON   Put them in order on the table. T to Tacky: Taclobo to Tailor: Tailorage to Talent. . . .

BUNYANS   Tales to Tampon. *(They start to assemble the boxes in the long row on the table.)*

BUNYANS   Where's Brenda?

JOHNSON   Breezey to Brethren.

BUNYANS   No. No. Your wife. *(JOHNSON stops working and looks at BUNYANS suspiciously.)*

JOHNSON   Why? *(BUNYANS, who has gone on working, now stops and looks at JOHNSON guiltily.)*

BUNYANS   Nothing. No reason. I wondered. One wonders. *(He picks up another box insouciantly.)* Tell to Temptress.

JOHNSON   *(Angrily.)* What do you imply?

BUNYANS *(Shows the box.)* The box.

JOHNSON *(Sarcastically.)* Conveniently to hand.

BUNYANS *(Wearily.)* Oh—Johnson . . . The boxes. The boxes. *(They both go back to their work.)*

JOHNSON We had a spat at lunch.

BUNYANS Spawn of oyster? And a glass of Hock?

JOHNSON Not at all. We'd already had a spat over breakfast.

BUNYANS A pair of spats . . . Abbreviation of spatterdash, seventeenth century . . . short gater covering instep at lunch, and another at breakfast.

JOHNSON Tiff.

BUNYANS What was it about?

JOHNSON "O."

BUNYANS Oh, what?

JOHNSON Her "O." You saw her "O"?

BUNYANS Oh, "O"—her "O." No.

JOHNSON She got Osculate down as a moving staircase.

BUNYANS Did you tell her?

JOHNSON I showed her.

BUNYANS What did she say?

JOHNSON She said Chambers was a fool, and Webster taken in by Chambers.

BUNYANS *(Picks up slip.)* Trollop.

JOHNSON *(Bridling.)* What?

BUNYANS *(With another slip.)* Tart. . . .

JOHNSON By God no, now look here . . .

BUNYANS *(Calmly with third slip.)* Transsubstantiation. *(They continue to work.)*

BUNYANS You had a spat or tiff. She went off in a huff. Next thing we know chaos and no Brenda.

JOHNSON Are you implying?

BUNYANS You know Brenda as well as I do.

JOHNSON *(Bridling.)* Rather better, I trust.

BUNYANS Oh, much better. Much, much, much better. *(Intimately.)* That's my point—inside leg—job. This was obviously an inside job.

JOHNSON You really think Brenda could have done this? Out of spite?

BUNYANS Hell hath no fury like a . . . *(He pauses, forgetting the quotation.)*

JOHNSON Woman.

BUNYANS No—begins with "S."

JOHNSON Scorned.

BUNYANS Scorned.

JOHNSON Scorned? *(Accusingly.)* Have you been scorning Brenda?

BUNYANS Never constantly.

JOHNSON When did you scorn her?

BUNYANS I am scorning her all the time, that's why she's done this. All that American rubbish she wanted in. Remember last year, splashdown. It was

I who scorned her splashdown, and I was very scornful with it. . . . And go.

JOHNSON Go?

BUNYANS (*Witheringly.*) 1969. When she put in go as a noun. We have go.

JOHNSON (*Suddenly.*) You said "inside breast."

BUNYANS No, I didn't. I said leg. I mean, job—inside job.

JOHNSON (*Accusingly.*) Tassanova.

BUNYANS (*Puzzled.*) Tassanova?

JOHNSON VE night. . . .

BUNYANS Tulipomania.

JOHNSON What?

BUNYANS Obsession with tulips. Mainly Dutch.

JOHNSON You surprise me.

BUNYANS Astonish. Amaze.

JOHNSON Pedant. (*He picks up another slip.*)

JOHNSON Train.

BUNYANS Tra chelipod to Traitor. Box 28. (*JOHNSON puts the slip into the box. He stands for a moment looking down at it in a reverie.*)

JOHNSON Brenda used to love trains.

BUNYANS Used to?

JOHNSON During the war. The blacked-out windows. The dim blue lights. Rocking through the night. (*Tartly.*) But you know all about that, of course.

BUNYANS Not at all.

JOHNSON Gammon! Bosh! Tingle-tangle.

BUNYANS I know nothing of trains.

JOHNSON Oh, no! Oh, no! Does Brize Norton mean nothing to you? The Goat and Whistle?

BUNYANS Nothing.

JOHNSON And what about VE night?

BUNYANS Nothing.

JOHNSON I searched for you. I searched high and low for you.

BUNYANS Nothing!

JOHNSON I stopped sailors in the street to inquire after your whereabouts.

BUNYANS We were in the amusement arcade. After we lost you in the hokey-cokey, we went to the amusement arcade.

JOHNSON Well-named indeed. And then?

BUNYANS We waited an hour and a half and then I took her home.

JOHNSON Twaddle!

BUNYANS She was at home when you got there, wasn't she?

JOHNSON At three in the morning certainly, feigning sleep. I have turned a blind eye, Bu'Nyons, to your lasciviousness for the sake of the dictionary. I had hoped that you, too, might share my joy in its creation and that we might carry out bats together to the end of the innings. But you've gone too far now with your greasy denials of your knowledge of trains and Brize Norton.

BUNYANS   It happened thirty years ago, Johnson.

JOHNSON   What happened?

BUNYANS   *(Helplessly.)* Nothing happened. Oh, Johnson. . . .

JOHNSON   Don't Johnson me, Bunyans. *(He pronounces it like the edible rounded bulb of* allium cepa.*)*

BUNYANS   *(Bridling.)* Have a care, Johnson.

JOHNSON   Bunyans. Bunyans. Bunyans.

BUNYANS   Bu'Nyans.

JOHNSON   Bunyans. And there's an end to it.

JOHNSON   Transparent.

BUNYANS   Box thirty.

JOHNSON   *(With another slip.)* Trampoline. An elastic contrivance resembling a spring mattress. Oh, God! Oh, God! *(He hurls the slip from him and collapses into a sitting position on the floor, rocking back and forth and weeping noisily.)*

JOHNSON   Oh, God! Oh, God! *(BUNYANS looks discomfited.)*

BUNYANS   Oh, Fowler. . . . come on F. Oh, Johnson. . . . come on Johnson. . . . It was nothing.

JOHNSON   Oh, God in heaven, help me! *(BUNYANS crosses to him awkwardly, leans down and pats his head.)*

BUNYANS   Nothing.

JOHNSON   Look around you, Bu'Nyans, a year's work. We can never reassemble it in time! *(BUNYANS crouches beside JOHNSON and puts a hand on his shoulder.)*

BUNYANS   What's a year?

JOHNSON   I'm not young. Who did this to us, Bu'Nyans? *(BUNYANS shakes his head.)*

BUNYANS   Come on, Johnson—take heart. You know you can lean on me.

JOHNSON   Very well—yes, my dear chap—*(JOHNSON leans on BUNYANS.)*—your support has always been—*(Down they go in a heap.)*

JOHNSON   Now, then.

BUNYANS   I'm sorry. *(He gets stiffly to his feet.)* I'm sorry. *(He extends a hand down to help Johnson.)*

JOHNSON   I'll just stay here for a bit. Until I feel up to the mark.

BUNYANS   Good. Take a rest. You've been overdoing it. *(He goes back toward the central table and starts picking up slips again. JOHNSON lies quite still for a moment and then picks up a slip that lies on a pile about eighteen inches from his nose.)*

JOHNSON   *(Reading.)* Tit. *(He groans and throws it aside. In moving this slip he has revealed something that puzzles him. He squinnies at it. He can't make it out. Without otherwise moving, he moves another slip. A woman's foot is revealed wearing an open-toed sandal—the foot having bunions. The toe is pointing at the ceiling. JOHNSON looks nervously across at BUNYANS, who has his back to him.)*

JOHNSON *(To himself.)* Bunions . . .

BUNYANS Bu'Nyans . . . *(JOHNSON covers the foot. Casually picks up a galley off the floor.)* Here are some more of her O's.

JOHNSON *(Cautiously.)* Did Brenda have bunions?

BUNYANS Yes.

JOHNSON How would you know?

BUNYANS It's the talk of Bognor during the shrimping season. Good God, I see what you're getting at. *(Reading off a galley proof.)* "Octaroon—small biscuit of ground almonds, white of egg, sugar . . ." *(He throws away the galley proof violently.)* I could kill her.

JOHNSON I've just had a terrible thought. Where's the *Ms? (They both search the galleys.)* I thought as much—"Macaroon: noun—a wheaten paste made into long, thin tubes and dried—Italian. Eighteenth-century dandy." *(JOHNSON looks further up the proof and reads off.)* "Macaroni—small American film star, male, twentieth century." *(They stare at each other, aghast.)*

BUNYANS *(Faintly.)* You don't think . . . ?

JOHNSON We'd better look. *(BUNYANS searches for the "R" for Rooney proof while JOHNSON more alert to BRENDA's foibles, takes down the "M" proof.)*

BUNYANS No, it's all right, it goes straight from Roomy to Roop. *(JOHNSON meanwhile has found it.)*

JOHNSON No, it's here—run together as one word. *(He reads.)* "Mickey Rooney: a small egg-shaped wind instrument with a terra-cotta body; a whistlelike mouthpiece and finger holes." *(Pause.)* Ocarina!

BUNYANS *(Reading off galley.)* "Person of one-eighth Negro blood." This is where we came in—octaroon.

JOHNSON It could be an honest mistake. This is where we came in, octaroon.

BUNYANS *(Furious.)* This is deliberate sabotage. We've probably only scratched the surface of her lexicographic caprice—it is you and I on our own from now on.

JOHNSON That is all too evident, Bu'Nyans, but somewhat extreme as a solution.

BUNYANS Your trouble, Johnson, has always been sentimentality.

JOHNSON No doubt, but common, human decency—

BUNYANS *(Picking up slip.)* Troglodyte, thigh. *(He puts it in a box.)*

JOHNSON *(Picks up slip.)* Tremor. *(Pauses.)* The fact of the matter is, Bu'Nyans, we're better off without her. I'll tell you something I've never told anyone before, Bu'Nyans.

BUNYANS Yes.

JOHNSON *(Sidetracked with cricket diversion.)* There's a window broken. *(We see the broken window.)*

JOHNSON It's those damned bounders.

BUNYANS *(Correcting.)* Boundaries.

JOHNSON *(Bitterly.)* Hooked over square leg.

BUNYANS Bouncers.

JOHNSON Damn cricket. *(End of cricket diversion.)* She never liked . . . you know what.

BUNYANS She loved it.

JOHNSON What?

BUNYANS You know. A well-timed hook through the leg trap.

JOHNSON I've never told that to anyone before. And she used to imitate me behind my back, as I discovered by periodically turning on my heel as I left the room. And the way she ate her salad. She was a nibbler, was Brenda.

BUNYANS I was surprised by it myself.

JOHNSON Astonished.

BUNYANS No, surprised, it happened when I least expected it. She went at it like rabbits.

JOHNSON *(Desperately.)* But what are we going to do?

BUNYANS I have asked myself that question my whole life, and I have invariably replied, lexicography. *(Picks up slip.)* Tumescent.

JOHNSON Box forty-two.

BUNYANS Teleautograph.

JOHNSON Box nine. *(BUNYANS delving for slips uncovers the same foot pause.)*

BUNYANS Tut. Tut.

JOHNSON Box forty-five.

BUNYANS *(Reconcealing the foot.)* Tsk. Tsk.

JOHNSON I'm not sure that I could lend my name to what is, after all, hardly more than a click of the tongue.

(BUNYANS has heard nothing since discovering the body and he says thoughtfully:)

BUNYANS I see there is more in you, Johnson, than is dreamt of in our lexicography.

JOHNSON You know you are absolutely right. Ate salad just like a rabbit.

JOHNSON The first time I saw her eating celery, I experienced an appalling sense of loss.

BUNYANS Was it your celery? *(JOHNSON glowers at him.)*

JOHNSON You misunderstand me. Is it deliberate?

BUNYANS By no manner of means.

BUNYANS What kind of shoes was she wearing?

JOHNSON Oh—this is some twelve years ago, you must remember. . . .

BUNYANS No. No. Today. At lunch. When you and Brenda had a rift within your lute.

JOHNSON *(Vaguely evasive.)* Oh . . . our spat.

BUNYANS   Not that it's of any consequence.

JOHNSON   *(Hysterically.)* What's wrong with you, Bunyans? Why this talk of shoes and celery? We're wasting time, man!

BUNYANS   You brought up the celery.

JOHNSON   Never mind who brought it up—we have to get on! We have to start! We have to finish! I'm going mad!

BUNYANS   Get a grip on yourself, Johnson! I've never known you to crack like this before.

JOHNSON   I'm dying!

BUNYANS   Why?

JOHNSON   I'm old!

BUNYANS   You're not.

JOHNSON   We must work.

BUNYANS   We have to clear all this first. *(He indicates the piles of slips still scattered around the room.)*

JOHNSON   Well, then. *(Panting, he bends down and heaves an armful of slips from the floor and dumps them on the table.)* There.

BUNYANS   It's no good just . . . *(But JOHNSON does it again.)*

JOHNSON   Yes! There!

(BUNYANS unwillingly joins him in gathering armfuls of slips and dumping them.)

BUNYANS   Oh, Johnson, this is not the methodical man I used to know.

JOHNSON   I've been methodical too long. We must finish. *(He looks around him. They have cleared some of the floor now so that the mound that covers BRENDA stands in isolation.)*

JOHNSON   Isn't that better?

BUNYANS   *(Doubtfully.)* Ye-es. But . . .

JOHNSON   No. No "buts." To the typewriter.

BUNYANS   We won't have all the words.

JOHNSON   Can either of us type?

BUNYANS   Not that I know of. *(There is silence as they avoid each other's eyes.)*

BUNYANS   She used to do that.

JOHNSON   *(Irritably.)* Yes, yes, yes, yes, yes. There's no need to. . . .

BUNYANS   I'll . . .

JOHNSON   One can but try. *(He approaches the typewriter warily. He looks down at it—he looks up at Fowler, then quickly away again.)*

BUNYANS   *(In a rush.)* There's those over there.

JOHNSON   What? Oh, yes. Good heavens. Oh . . .

BUNYANS   A couple, no more.

JOHNSON   Too many. Get into those and . . .

BUNYANS   We'd never get finished.

JOHNSON   Leave them, leave them. Have we not got enough? *(He indicates the boxes expansively.)*

BUNYANS   Too many.

JOHNSON   Exactly. What do they think we are. We must start. We must finish. *(BUNYANS sits at the typewriter. JOHNSON takes the first card from the first box.)*

JOHNSON   "T." The twentieth letter from the English and other modern alphabets. The nineteenth of the ancient Roman alphabet, corresponding in form to the Greek tau, from the Phoenician and ancient Semitic . . .

BUNYANS   Wait, wait, wait! *(JOHNSON looks up from the slip.)*

JOHNSON   What is it?

BUNYANS   You're going too fast.

JOHNSON   Where have you gotten to?

BUNYANS   "T."

JOHNSON   Is that all? Dear Christ, is this the pace at which we shall proceed?

BUNYANS   I am unfamiliar with the organization of the keyboard. It's eccentrically arranged.

JOHNSON   It has letters of the alphabet, I presume?

BUNYANS   But not in order. 'Qwertyuiop.'

JOHNSON   Dear God in heaven, a faulty machine!

BUNYANS   We need a typist. We need . . . *(He breaks off awkwardly.)*

JOHNSON   No, no, no. Certainly not. You mustn't. . . . To tell the truth, I like it better without her. I mean . . . well . . . it's quieter.

BUNYANS   Certainly. One could hear a pin drop.

JOHNSON   You remember how she used to jabber? I used to wonder what she found to talk about.

BUNYANS   What did she talk about? *(JOHNSON shrugs.)*

JOHNSON   I never listened. *(In despair.)* What are we going to do?

BUNYANS   *(Succinctly.)* Get a typist. A male typist. Or at least androgynous. Tomorrow. *(Grandly.)* It doesn't make any difference to me, I must say, her not being here.

JOHNSON   Nor me. I never liked her. Not per se. I *liked* her well enough early on in our relationship. But latterly . . . I wouldn't mind if she was . . . how does one say it?

BUNYANS   Not here?

JOHNSON   Departed.

BUNYANS   Defunct.

JOHNSON   Demised.

BUNYANS   Deceased.

JOHNSON   Stiff.

BUNYANS   Kicked the bucket.

JOHNSON   Dead.

(A collective sigh is heard from the small crowd out of sight. A batsman has skied a ball. BUNYANS and JOHNSON look at the window where the man on the square leg boundary

who has figured in the play as an intermittent white-flanneled sentinel outside the library windows starts positioning himself under the catch, which we see him take cleanly. There is applause from without. The two men turn away and continue.)

Tizzy.

BUNYANS That's a start. Box twenty-three. Titoki to Toggery.

(In the following passage the two men cravenly attempt to establish that each is willing to condone the other. But they get nowhere and end in a silent morass of mutual bafflement.)

JOHNSON I am not a violent man in point of fact.

BUNYANS Of course you're not. I know that.

JOHNSON Nor are you a violent man—I know that—if you ever did a violent thing, then there would be a good reason— I mean, I would understand —see the other fellow's predicament—tolerance—

BUNYANS Live and let live. . . .

BUNYANS and JOHNSON *(Simultaneously.)* So to speak.

BUNYANS And were *you* ever to be even momentarily violent—

JOHNSON Which I wouldn't, but I would be understanding were *you*, due to the impulsiveness of youth, to be momentarily violent.

BUNYANS Though I am not a violent man.

JOHNSON As I well know.

BUNYANS In other words.

JOHNSON Exactly my point. *(Pause.)*

BUNYANS *(Picks up a slip; glumly without passion.)* This is one of hers. "Tampon —iron plate with spikes for walking on ice." *(He throws it away, more in sorrow than in anger.)* I blame you for this, Johnson.

JOHNSON *(Defensively.)* I couldn't be looking over her shoulder all the time.

(BUNYANS has picked up another galley proof.)

BUNYANS "Crampon . . . thin griddle cake made of flour, beaten egg, and milk . . ." We're ruined. We're going to have to go back over everything.

JOHNSON I'm sorry, but when I proposed to Brenda all those years ago, it was with the promise—the dream—of sharing everything, working side by side. . . .

BUNYANS You should have had the grace to share *her* work and not let her share *ours*.

JOHNSON *(Angrily.)* How could I be a money changer in a pinball parlor?

BUNYANS Pinball . . . ?

JOHNSON I got a double first in . . . . what the hell was it?

BUNYANS *(Shouts.)* Pinball machines. . . .

JOHNSON *(Shouts.)* Rubbish. . . .

BUNYANS No—we went from pinaster to pince-nez.

JOHNSON (Stopped in his tracks.) By God, you're right. Take this down. Pinball machine. American, twentieth cent.—a machine. . . .

BUNYANS A device . . .

JOHNSON A device consisting of—God help us. . . .

BUNYANS An automatic bagatelle board in which the players by releasing . . .

JOHNSON Projecting . . .

BUNYANS Propelling . . .

JOHNSON By means of a spring-controlled plunger . . .

BUNYANS Balls. Goddamn it.

JOHNSON The fact of the matter is she used the same teabag three or four times, five in the case of my aged and inoffensive sister. Did you know that?

BUNYANS No—I knew about her ear wax, but not about the teabags.

JOHNSON She was a slut. . . .

BUNYANS A boring old baggage. . . .

JOHNSON (With contempt.) And the way she was always trying to adulterate the dictionary—

BUNYANS Moronic bunny—slippered slag. . . .

JOHNSON . . . spurious words . . . cosmodrome . . . payload . . . aerospace . . . bleep . . . blip . . . megadeath . . .

BUNYANS Refusing to shave . . .

JOHNSON (Contemptuously.) We have go—

BUNYANS And her drawers—never found anything in them.

JOHNSON And she was less than scrupulous about her feet to boot.

BUNYANS Her bu'nyons. If you hadn't done it, I would have done it.

JOHNSON And I would have if you hadn't.

BUNYANS So would I.

JOHNSON But you did.

BUNYANS No, you did. This is no time for shilly-shallying, Johnson. The teabags alone condone your action. Condemned out of her own spout.

JOHNSON You are rambling, man. Raving. Corybantic. Maddened, no doubt, by guilt, you have suffered the loosening of a screw.

BUNYANS Guilt?

JOHNSON At killing my wife. My dear fellow—think nothing of it. . . .

BUNYANS You killed her. I saw her foot. No doubt in jealous rage . . .

JOHNSON You said yourself you could kill her—because of the octaroon with ground almonds. . . . (From under the papers comes a cry.)

BRENDA Enough! (They stare at the paper, which convulses, and BRENDA emerges.)

BRENDA Enough of this virago.

BUNYANS Brenda—you're alive!

JOHNSON (Mutters.) It was bunglers. (Up.) My sugar dumpling.

BRENDA Don't try to sweet-shop me, you sea-lion old taxicographer!

JOHNSON Brenda—I assure you—

BRENDA   I returned from a state of inconsequence several minutes ago . . . eardropping on your conversation as I drifted back from the barn from which no traveler returns, back from the valley of the chateau of death, I heard every syllabub of your farinaceous attack on my parson.

JOHNSON   You were dreaming.

BRENDA   Liar! Lying hypnotist.

JOHNSON   Your personal hygiene is immaculate, your breasts are like twin roses.

BRENDA   Philatelist!

JOHNSON   And your scholarship—your range—how shall I put it?

BRENDA   Syncopated groveler.

JOHNSON   Your grasp of—to put it in plain English—*le mot juste*.

BRENDA   I want go.

JOHNSON   If you want go, you shall have go.

BUNYANS   I'll help you pack.

JOHNSON   And I'll carry your boring old baggage.

BRENDA   I will not stand here and be pillarized and vitrified. I have demoted my life to toxicology and slavering over a hot stove and this is the thanks I get. My late lamentable mother saw you for the hypocritical greasy piccolo that you have proved yourself to be. But you incinerated yourself into my affectations with your swarthy talk, and I succumbed to your brandysnaps. I could have made a tureen for myself. You thought you could pack me up and cast me aside like a wartime truss. There was more to me than that before taxidermatory and Bognor Regis wore me down to my eccles, I can insure you. Even on VE night you disbanded me during the hunky-dory. *(Indicating* BUNYANS.*)* Not that he's any better. He's no gentlemen. Corsetry—he doesn't know the meaning of the word—and don't think there weren't a frenzy of other suitors, but I was never a croquette. I have been fidelitous to a fault. And now I am repaid by a vivacious blow on the head by a man whom I have allowed to play ducks and drakes with my body for thirty years.

JOHNSON and BUNYANS   *(Simultaneously.)* I deny it.

BRENDA   *(Rubbing her head.)* I still have the confusion to show for it.

JOHNSON   We entered and found you lying under the papers. The whole place was in chaos.

BRENDA   It was perfectly tidy when I entered this room in search of the crampon, which I recalled leaving half-finished with my elevenses. *(Show half-eaten crumpet.)* Ah, I remember now. I saw it on the bookshelf. *(She moves toward the bookshelf.)* I took one pace toward it and suddenly . . .

(A crash of breaking glass. All three heads jerk toward the cricket window. We get a close-up of a second broken pane. We cut back to BRENDA, *now lying on the floor with the ball rolling to a stop. The two men look at her and then look at the window, which is a French window; the cricketeer from before is opening this French window. Immedi-*

ately there is a noise of wind, and papers begin blowing everywhere. A snowstorm. The cricketeer has meanwhile walked into the room, picked up the ball, and with a furtive look at the chaos he has (for the second time) unwittingly caused, he leaves the room by the window, which closes behind him.)

ANDREW VACHSS

Placebo

A Monologue

I know how to fix things. I know how they work. When they don't work like they're supposed to, I know how to make them right.

I don't always get it right the first time, but I keep working until I do.

I've been a lot of places. Some of them pretty bad—some of them where I didn't want to be.

I did a lot of things in my life in some of those places. In the bad places, I did some bad things.

I paid a lot for what I know, but I don't talk about it. Talking doesn't get things fixed.

People call me a lot of different things now. Janitor. Custodian. Repairman. Lots of names for the same thing.

I live in the basement. I take care of the whole building. Something gets broke, they call me. I'm always here.

I live by myself. A dog lives with me. A big Doberman. I heard a noise behind my building one night—it sounded like a kid crying. I found the Doberman. He was a puppy then. Some freak was carving him up for the fun of it. Blood all over the place. I took care of the freak; then I brought the puppy down to my basement and fixed him up. I know all about knife wounds.

The freak cut his throat pretty deep. When the stitches came out, he was okay, but he can't bark. He still works, though.

I don't mix much with the people. They pay me to fix things—I fix things. I don't try and fix things for the whole world. I don't care about the whole world. Just what's mine. I just care about doing my work.

People ask me to fix all kinds of things—not just the boiler or a stopped-up toilet. One of the gangs in the neighborhood used to hang out in front of my building, give the people a hard time, scare them, break into the mailboxes, petty stuff like that. I went upstairs and talked to the gang. I had the dog with me. The gang went away. I don't know where they went. It doesn't matter.

Mrs. Barnes lives in the building. She has a kid, Tommy. He's a sweet-natured boy, maybe ten years old. Tommy's a little slow in the head, goes to a special school and all. Other kids in the building used to bother him. I fixed that.

Maybe that's why Mrs. Barnes told me about the monsters. Tommy was waking up in the night screaming. He told his mother monsters lived in the room and they came after him when he went to sleep.

I told her she should talk to someone who knows how to fix what's wrong with the kid. She told me he had somebody. A therapist at his special school —an older guy. Dr. English. Mrs. Barnes couldn't say enough about this guy. He was like a father to the boy, she said. Took him places, bought him stuff. A real distinguished-looking man. She showed me a picture of him standing next to Tommy. He had his hand on the boy's shoulder.

The boy comes down to the basement himself. Mostly after school. The dog likes him. Tommy watches me do my work. Never says much, just pats the dog and hands me a tool once in a while. One day he told me about the monsters himself. Asked me to fix it. I thought about it. Finally I told him I could do it.

I went up to his room. Nice big room, painted a pretty blue color. Faces out the back of the building. Lots of light comes in his window. There's a fire escape right off the window. Tommy tells me he likes to sit out there on nice days and watch the other kids play down below. It's only on the second floor, so he can see them good.

I checked the room for monsters. He told me they only came at night. I told him I could fix it but it would take me a few days. The boy was real happy. You could see it.

I did some reading, and I thought I had it all figured out. The monsters were in his head. I made a machine in the basement—just a metal box with a row of lights on the top and a toggle switch. I showed him how to turn it on. The lights flashed in a random sequence. The boy stared at it for a long time.

I told him this was a machine for monsters. As long as the machine was turned on, monsters couldn't come in his room. I never saw a kid smile like he did.

His mother tried to slip me a few bucks when I was leaving. I didn't take it. I never do. Fixing things is my job.

She winked at me, said she'd tell Dr. English about my machine. Maybe he'd use it for all his kids. I told her I only fixed things in my building.

I saw the boy every day after that. He stopped being scared. His mother told me she had a talk with Dr. English. He told her the machine I made was a placebo, and Tommy would always need therapy.

I go to the library a lot to learn more about how things work. I looked up "placebo" in the big dictionary they have there. It means a fake, but a fake that somebody believes in. Like giving a sugar pill to a guy in a lot of pain and telling him it's morphine. It doesn't really work by itself—it's all in your mind.

One night Tommy woke up screaming and he didn't stop. His mother rang my buzzer and I went up to the apartment. The kid was shaking all over, covered with sweat.

He saw me. He said my machine didn't work anymore.

He wasn't mad at me, but he said he couldn't go back to sleep. Ever.

Some guys in white jackets came in an ambulance. They took the boy away. I saw him in the hospital the next day. They gave him something to sleep the night before and he looked dopey.

The day after that he said he wasn't afraid anymore. The pills worked. No monsters came in the night. But he said he could never go home. He asked if I could build him a stronger machine.

I told him I'd work on it.

His mother said she called Dr. English at the special school, but they said he was out for a few days. Hurt himself on a ski trip or something. She couldn't wait to tell Dr. English about the special medicine they were giving the boy and ask if it was all right with him.

I called the school. Said I was with the State Disability Commission. The lady who answered told me Dr. English was at home, recuperating from a broken arm. I got her to tell me his full name, got her to talk. I know how things work.

She told me they were lucky to have Dr. English. He used to work at some school way up north—in Toronto, Canada—but he left because he hated the cold weather.

I thought about it a long time. Broken arm. Ski trip. Cold weather.

The librarian knows me. She says I'm her best customer because I never check books out. I always read them right there. I never write stuff down—I keep it in my head.

I asked the librarian some questions, and she showed me how to use the newspaper index. I checked all the Toronto papers until I found it. A big scandal at a special school for slow kids. Some of the staff were indicted. Dr. English was one of the people they questioned, but he was never charged with anything. Four of the staff people went to prison. A few more were acquitted. Dr. English, he resigned.

Dr. English was listed in the phonebook. He lives in a real nice neighborhood.

I waited a couple of more days, working it all out in my head.

Mrs. Barnes told me Dr. English was coming back to the school next week. She was going to talk to him about Tommy, maybe get him to do some of his therapy in the hospital until the boy was ready to come home.

I told Tommy I knew how to stop the monsters for sure now. I told him I was building a new machine—I'd have it ready for him next week. I told him when he got home I wanted him to walk the dog for me. Out in the back where the other kids played. I told him I'd teach him how.

Tommy really liked that. He said he'd try and come home if I was sure the new machine would work. I gave him my word.

I'm working on the new machine in my basement now. I put a hard rubber ball into a vise and clamped it tight. I drilled a tiny hole right through the center. Then I threaded it with a strand of piano wire until about six inches poked through the end. I knotted it real carefully and pulled back against the knot with all my strength. It held. I did the same thing with another ball the same way. Now I have a three-foot piece of piano wire anchored with a little rubber ball at each end. The rubber balls fit perfectly, one in each hand.

I know how to fix things.

When it gets dark tonight, I'll show Dr. English a machine that works.

WENDY WASSERSTEIN

Tender Offer

A girl of around nine is alone in a dance studio. She is dressed in traditional leotards and tights. She begins singing to herself, "Nothing Could be Finer Than to Be in Carolina." She maps out a dance routine, including parts for the chorus. She builds to a finale. A man, PAUL, *around thirty-five, walks in. He has a sweet, though distant, demeanor. As he walks in,* LISA *notices him and stops.*

PAUL   You don't have to stop, sweetheart.

LISA   That's okay.

PAUL   Looked very good.

LISA   Thanks.

PAUL   Don't I get a kiss hello?

LISA   Sure.

PAUL   *(Embraces her.)* Hi, Tiger.

LISA   Hi, Dad.

PAUL   I'm sorry I'm late.

LISA   That's okay.

PAUL   How'd it go?

LISA   Good.

PAUL   Just good?

LISA   Pretty good.

PAUL   "Pretty good." You mean you got a lot of applause or "pretty good" you could have done better.

LISA   Well, Courtney Palumbo's mother thought I was pretty good. But you know the part in the middle when everybody's supposed to freeze and the big girl comes out. Well, I think I moved a little bit.

PAUL   I thought what you were doing looked very good.

LISA   Daddy, that's not what I was doing. That was tap-dancing. I made that up.

PAUL   Oh. Well it looked good. Kind of sexy.

LISA   Yuch!

PAUL   What do you mean "yuch"?

LISA   Just yuch!

PAUL   You don't want to be sexy?

LISA   I don't care.

PAUL   Let's go, Tiger. I promised your mother I'd get you home in time for dinner.

LISA   I can't find my leg warmers.

PAUL   You can't find your what?

LISA   Leg warmers. I can't go home till I find my leg warmers.

PAUL   I don't see you looking for them.

LISA   I was waiting for you.

PAUL   Oh.

LISA   Daddy.

PAUL   What?

LISA   Nothing.

PAUL   Where do you think you left them?

LISA   Somewhere around here. I can't remember.

PAUL   Well, try to remember, Lisa. We don't have all night.

LISA   I told you. I think somewhere around here.

PAUL   I don't see them. Let's go home now. You'll call the dancing school tomorrow.

LISA   Daddy, I can't go home till I find them. Miss Judy says it's not professional to leave things.

PAUL   Who's Miss Judy?

LISA   She's my ballet teacher. She once danced the lead in *Swan Lake,* and she was a June Taylor dancer.

PAUL   Well, then, I'm sure she'll understand about the leg warmers.

LISA   Daddy, Miss Judy wanted to know why you were late today.

PAUL   Hmmmmmmmm?

LISA   Why were you late?

PAUL   I was in a meeting. Business. I'm sorry.

LISA   Why did you tell Mommy you'd come instead of her if you knew you had business?

PAUL   Honey, something just came up. I thought I'd be able to be here. I was looking forward to it.

LISA   I wish you wouldn't make appointments to see me.

PAUL   Hmmmmmmm.

LISA   You shouldn't make appointments to see me unless you know you're going to come.

PAUL   Of course I'm going to come.

LISA   No, you're not. Talia Robbins told me she's much happier living without her father in the house. Her father used to come home late and go to sleep early.

PAUL   Lisa, stop it. Let's go.

LISA   I can't find my leg warmers.

PAUL   Forget your leg warmers.

LISA   Daddy.

PAUL   What is it?

LISA   I saw this show on television, I think it was WPIX Channel 11. Well, the father was crying about his daughter.

PAUL   Why was he crying? Was she sick?

LISA   No. She was at school. And he was at business. And he just missed her, so he started to cry.

PAUL   What was the name of this show?

LISA   I don't know. I came in in the middle.

PAUL   Well, Lisa, I certainly would cry if you were sick or far away, but I know that you're well and you're home. So no reason to get maudlin.

LISA   What's maudlin?

PAUL   Sentimental, soppy. Frequently used by children who make things up to get attention.

LISA   I am sick! I am sick! I have Hodgkin's disease and a bad itch on my leg.

PAUL   What do you mean you have Hodgkin's disease? Don't say things like that.

LISA   Swoosie Kurtz, she had Hodgkin's disease on a TV movie last year, but she got better and now she's on *Love Sidney*.

PAUL   Who is Swoosie Kurtz?

LISA   She's an actress named after an airplane. I saw her on *Live at Five*.

PAUL   You watch too much television; you should do your homework. Now, put your coat on.

LISA   Daddy, I really do have a bad itch on my leg. Would you scratch it?

PAUL   Lisa, you're procrastinating.

LISA   Why do you use words I don't understand? I hate it. You're like Daria Feldman's mother. She always talks in Yiddish to her husband so Daria won't understand.

PAUL   Procrastinating is not Yiddish.

LISA   Well, I don't know what it is.

PAUL   Procrastinating means you don't want to go about your business.

LISA   I don't go to business. I go to school.

PAUL   What I mean is you want to hang around here until you and I are late for dinner and your mother's angry and it's too late for you to do your homework.

LISA   I do not.

PAUL   Well, it sure looks that way. Now put your coat on and let's go.

LISA   Daddy.

PAUL   Honey, I'm tired. Really, later.

LISA   Why don't you want to talk to me?

PAUL   I do want to talk to you. I promise when we get home we'll have a nice talk.

LISA   No, we won't. You'll read the paper and fall asleep in front of the news.

PAUL   Honey, we'll talk on the weekend, I promise. Aren't I taking you to the theater this weekend? Let me look. *(He takes out appointment book.)* Yes. Sunday. *Joseph and the Amazing Technicolor Raincoat* with Lisa. Okay, Tiger?

LISA   Sure. It's Dreamcoat.

PAUL   What?

LISA   Nothing. I think I see my leg warmers. *(She goes to pick them up, and an odd-looking trophy.)*

PAUL   What's that?

LISA   It's stupid. I was second best at the dance recital, so they gave me this thing. It's stupid.

PAUL   Lisa.

LISA   What?

PAUL   What did you want to talk about?

LISA   Nothing.

PAUL   Was it about my missing your recital? I'm really sorry, Tiger. I would have liked to have been here.

LISA   That's okay.

PAUL   Honest?

LISA   Daddy, you're prostrastinating.

PAUL   I'm procrastinating. Sit down. Let's talk. So. How's school?

LISA   Fine.

PAUL   You like it?

LISA   Yup.

PAUL   You looking forward to camp this summer?

LISA   Yup.

PAUL   Is Daria Feldman going back?

LISA   Nope.

PAUL   Why not?

LISA   I don't know. We can go home now. Honest, my foot doesn't itch anymore.

PAUL   Lisa, you know what you do in business when it seems like there's nothing left to say? That's when you really start talking. Put a bid on the table.

LISA   What's a bid?

PAUL   You tell me what you want and I'll tell you what I've got to offer. Like Monopoly. You want Boardwalk, but I'm only willing to give you the Railroads. Now, because you are my daughter I'd throw in Water Works and Electricity. Understand, Tiger?

LISA   No. I don't like board games. You know, Daddy, we could get Space Invaders for our home for thirty-five dollars. In fact, we could get an Osborne System for two thousand. Daria Feldman's parents . . .

PAUL   Daria Feldman's parents refuse to talk to Daria, so they bought a computer to keep Daria busy so they won't have to speak in Yiddish. Daria will probably grow up to be a homicidal maniac lesbian prostitute.

LISA   I know what that word prostitute means.

PAUL   Good. *(Pause.)* You still haven't told me about school. Do you still like your teacher?

LISA   She's okay.

PAUL   Lisa, if we're talking try to answer me.

LISA   I am answering you. Can we go home now, please?

PAUL   Damn it, Lisa, if you want to talk to me . . . Talk to me!

LISA   I can't wait till I'm old enough so I can make my own money and never have to see you again. Maybe I'll become a prostitute.

PAUL   Young lady, that's enough.

LISA   I hate you, Daddy! I hate you! *(She throws her trophy into the trash bin.)*

PAUL   What'd you do that for?

LISA   It's stupid.

PAUL   Maybe I wanted it.

LISA   What for?

PAUL   Maybe I wanted to put it where I keep your dinosaur and the picture you made of Mrs. Kimbel with the chicken pox.

LISA   You got mad at me when I made that picture. You told me I had to respect Mrs. Kimbel because she was my teacher.

PAUL   That's true. But she wasn't my teacher. I liked her better with the chicken pox. *(Pause.)* Lisa, I'm sorry. I was very wrong to miss your recital, and you don't have to become a prostitute. That's not the type of profession Miss Judy has in mind for you.

LISA   *(Mumbles.)* No.

PAUL   No. *(Pause.)* So Talia Robbins is really happy her father moved out?

LISA   Talia Robbins picks open the eighth-grade lockers during gym period. But she did that before her father moved out.

PAUL   You can't always judge someone by what they do or what they don't do. Sometimes you come home from dancing school and run upstairs and shut the door, and when I finally get to talk to you, everything is "okay" or "fine." Yup or nope?

LISA   Yup.

PAUL   Sometimes, a lot of times, I come home and fall asleep in front of the television. So you and I spend a lot of time being a little scared of each other. Maybe?

LISA   Maybe.

PAUL   Tell you what. I'll make you a tender offer.

LISA   What?

PAUL   I'll make you a tender offer. That's when one company publishes in the newspaper that they want to buy another company. And the company that publishes is called the Black Knight because they want to gobble up the poor little company. So the poor little company needs to be rescued. And then a White Knight comes along and makes a bigger and better offer so the shareholders won't have to tender shares to the Big Black Knight. You with me?

LISA   Sort of.

PAUL   I'll make you a tender offer like the White Knight. But I don't want to own you. I just want to make a much better offer. Okay?

LISA   *(Sort of understanding.)* Okay. *(Pause. They sit for a moment.)* Sort of, Daddy, what do you think about? I mean, like when you're quiet what do you think about?

PAUL   Oh, business usually. If I think I made a mistake or if I think I'm doing okay. Sometimes I think about what I'll be doing five years from now and if it's what I hoped it would be five years ago. Sometimes I think about what your life will be like, if Mount Saint Helen's will erupt again. What you'll become if you'll study penmanship or word processing. If you speak kindly of me to your psychiatrist when you are in graduate school. And how the hell I'll pay for your graduate school. And sometimes I try and think what it was I thought about when I was your age.

LISA   Do you ever look out your window at the clouds and try to see which kinds of shapes they are? Like one time, honest, I saw the head of Walter Cronkite in a flower vase. Really! Like look don't those kinda look like if you turn it upside down, two big elbows or two elephant trunks dancing?

PAUL   Actually still looks like Walter Cronkite in a flower vase to me. But look up a little. See the one that's still moving? That sorta looks like a whale on a thimble.

LISA   Where?

PAUL   Look up. To your right.

LISA   I don't see it. Where?

PAUL   The other way.

LISA   Oh, yeah! There's the head and there's the stomach. Yeah! *(LISA picks up her trophy.)* Hey, Daddy.

PAUL   Hey, Lisa.

LISA   You can have this thing if you want it. But you have to put it like this, because if you put it like that it is gross.

PAUL   You know what I'd like? So I can tell people who come into my office why I have this gross stupid thing on my shelf, I'd like it if you could show me your dance recital.

LISA   Now?

PAUL   We've got time. Mother said she won't be home till late.

LISA   Well, Daddy, during a lot of it I freeze and the big girl in front dances.
PAUL   Well, how 'bout the number you were doing when I walked in?
LISA   Well, see, I have parts for a lot of people in that one, too.
PAUL   I'll dance the other parts.
LISA   You can't dance.
PAUL   Young lady, I played Yvette Mimimeux in a *Hasty Pudding Show*.
LISA   Who's Yvette Mimimeux?
PAUL   Watch more television. You'll find out. *(PAUL stands up.)* So I'm ready. *(He begins singing.)* "Nothing could be finer than to be in Carolina."
LISA   Now I go. In the morning. And now you go. Dum-da.
PAUL   *(Obviously not a tap dancer.)* Da-da-dum.
LISA   *(Whines.)* Daddy!
PAUL   *(Mimics her.)* Lisa! Nothing could be finer . . .
LISA   That looks dumb.
PAUL   Oh, yeah? You think they do this better in *The Amazing Minkcoat?* No way! Now you go—da da da dum.
LISA   Da da da dum.
PAUL   If I had Aladdin's lamp for only a day, I'd make a wish. . . .
LISA   Daddy, that's maudlin!
PAUL   I know it's maudlin. And here's what I'd say:
LISA and PAUL   I'd say that "nothing could be finer than to be in Carolina in the moooooooooooornin'."

EUDORA WELTY

Bye-Bye Brevoort

CHARACTERS

MILLICENT FORTESCUE
VIOLET WHICHAWAY
AGATHA CHROME
EVANS Miss Fortescue's maid.
DESMOND DUPREE
FIRST WRECKER
SECOND WRECKER
THIRD WRECKER

MISS FORTESCUE's *sitting room in the Brevoort, a room not yet reached by wreckers dismantling the building and obviously occupied by her.*

Set marked off perhaps by one collapsible wall and one folding screen. A window, heavily looped with curtains. A large dark oil painting of a lady ancestor in ornate frame, which can fall. Crowded and abundant Victorian furnishings, two scrolled wicker high-backed chairs and a wicker settee, a tea table down front big enough to load with china and service and fixed so as to shudder or shimmy with every crash outside as the Brevoort is being torn down, so that some dishes and a flower vase eventually fall off. Right, a stand with old-fashioned telephone on it, a big sea shell, and a large silver dish with a mountain of calling cards in it. In rear, a dumbwaiter. Other things might be stacked albums, a fishnet full of postcards and Valentines, at least one musical instrument. Plant stands with luxuriant growth appropriately placed. Door, down left.

Curtain rises to show FORTESCUE, WHICHAWAY, *and* CHROME, *three old Brevoort relics, in* FORTESCUE's *sitting room, each playing her own game of solitaire—one on the as yet unlaid tea table, the other two perhaps on checkerboards on their knees.*

The old ladies are dressed de rigueur. *Suggest* FORTESCUE *in lace,* CHROME *in velvet or in floral silk,* WHICHAWAY *in tweeds with white shoes and stockings. A lace parasol will be available for* FORTESCUE. *All wear hearing aids, though* WHICHAWAY may prefer the trumpet. CHROME and WHICHAWAY, who come from across the hall, may wear their hats throughout. EVANS will wear an elaborate maid's uniform, starched and winged, with frilled cotton drawers as seen. DESMOND DUPREE, for whom the extra chair waits, is an old sport in a chesterfield, with a furled umbrella (as he goes out to the park) and yellow gloves.

The moment before curtain rise, a few bangs and a dull thud. The wreckers dismantling the building are coming closer and closer as skit proceeds. Noises come intermittently, sometimes a hoarse shout. The ladies do not hear, or else they ignore these crude sounds. But a moment after curtain rise: A faint tinkle. Ladies all hear that. They sit bolt upright in polite, pleased anticipation. All speak up in high, carrying voices.

FORTESCUE *(Waving her battery gaily.)* Tea time! Tea time! Four o'clock! Did you notice I'd had an alarm put in my hearing aid? Tiffany's sent a man down. To work by the *hour*, my dears.

WHICHAWAY *Et tu,* Tiffany.

FORTESCUE *(Calling out.)* Tea, Evans! Isn't Evans back?

CHROME *(As crash, off, dies away. Without flinching.)* I haven't heard even a little mouse.

FORTESCUE I sent her to Charles'—for petit fours. Desmond's coming, with his appetite.

CHROME Our Thursday Tiger!

WHICHAWAY Desmond! Shall we go back to our rooms for our hats?

FORTESCUE You have on *something*, dear.

WHICHAWAY *(Touching up top.)* Chances are it hasn't been removed since *yesterday*'s tea. Simpler. *(Tinkle again, from hearing aid.)*

FORTESCUE There goes the second bell. If Evans isn't back soon, I'll telephone down and have the Brevoort search Sixth Avenue.

(Enter EVANS, from door left, in cape, parcel in both hands and purse swinging from teeth. She is riding a bicycle. They don't turn to see her.)

EVANS *(Speaking through teeth.)* The cheese straws from Charles's, mum.

FORTESCUE Evans: don't—hiss.

(EVANS dismounts. With faint clicking sound as she walks, goes with burdens behind screen, comes out in her elaborate apron, and begins business of setting the tea table for high tea. Brings from behind screen a linen cloth and napkins, elaborate tea service, which seems to overflow the whole set, covered dishes, several pots, silver and china, cake stand with half a tiered cake. Whenever the pounding or a crash occurs off, all this shakes.)

CHROME *(Sharply clapping her hand to her back as if shot by an arrow.)* Oh! There's a draft! It struck me!

WHICHAWAY For thirty-nine years I've said the Brevoort had a draft. And have mentioned it Downstairs. *(Meaningly.)* They know it.

FORTESCUE We should simply *avoid* the *corridors*.

EVANS   *(In normal voice, since they won't hear. As she bends over to set a bud vase with rose and fern on tea table, as final touch.)* Draft, they call it. We're living in a fool's Swiss cheese.

FORTESCUE   *Evans!*

EVANS   *(Bending over, arrested motion.)* Mum?

FORTESCUE   You've come in with your bicycle clips on. *How* did you come through the lobby?

EVANS   *(Proudly.)* Sidesaddle.

FORTESCUE   *(To others.)* And *yesterday*, she came in on skates!

EVANS   *One* skate.

CHROME   Millicent—is *Evans* slipping—or the *Brevoort*? *(A large crash, off.)*

EVANS   *(Sitting down hard, with the rose.)* We'll go down together.

FORTESCUE   And as you came scorching through the lobby, Evans, tell me— did anyone budge?

EVANS   No one saw me downstairs, mum, except some persons with axes and the persons with dynamite to blow up the building.

FORTESCUE   No one with lorgnettes? Then thank your lucky stars.

CHROME   Must we wait for Desmond?

FORTESCUE   Dear Desmond! So dashing! Such a wreck!

CHROME   Mr. Knickerbocker says, nothing keeps Desmond in one piece but penicillin and *passe-partout*.

WHICHAWAY   Nonsense, he's always looked that way. It's only from wincing.

CHROME   He insists on going *out*, you know.

FORTESCUE   There's something gallant about him. Shine or shine, he goes forth and strolls in the park. *(They all shake their heads over it.)* And I understand the elevator isn't running past our floor. Some sort of obstruction in the passage!

EVANS   It's got the hiccups. *(Knock at door.)*

EVANS   *(Going to door and opening.)* Hold that tiger.

DUPREE   *(Entering, with EVANS behind.)* Hullo, old things.

LADIES   *(All together, gladly. All kissing.)* Desmond dear! Desmond, you're look- ing *shattered!*

DUPREE   *(EVANS trying to take his coat. Does so.)* Difficult time getting through again. Odd thing in the corridor: persons all about sawing the walls. Didn't look too savory. Can't help noticing—thing like that during *Lent*.

CHROME   *(Gives him a pat of comfort.)* Riff-raff. Best *not* to notice them.

DUPREE   *(Sinking into chair, offhand.)* They must be looking for treasure.

WHICHAWAY   Yes. Millicent, didn't you once lose an old Carolina moonstone?

FORTESCUE   *(Coldly.)* *Not* in the *corridor*.

(EVANS, busy with tea, now brings it in. As she bends over tea table, DUPREE stares.)

DUPREE   Aluminum garters? Daresay it was bound to come.

FORTESCUE   Dear Desmond. You're looking frightfully crepey.

DUPREE   Thanks, old thing. Shall we feed?
FORTESCUE   Evans!

(EVANS *skips, dropping napkins in everybody's lap and* DUPREE's *on the floor, as in drop-the-handkerchief. Goes to* FORTESCUE's *side.*)

Telephone down, Evans. Ask room service for an earthen jug of *hotter and fresher water.* Pouring, dears! (FORTESCUE *begins to pour. All the dishes start to hobble and shake as bangs and thuds begin coming louder. They bravely ignore. They call a little more loudly and at higher pitch to one another to make themselves heard. Drink tea, eat cake.*)

CHROME   Modern times! The noise of the city is frightful. The vehicles!
WHICHAWAY   Yes. Rat-a-tat—rat-a-tat.
FORTESCUE   I cawn't think why they don't make vehicles go *around* the island!
DUPREE   This cake has a marvelous texture—marvelous crumb, Millicent. Wherever did you get it?
EVANS   (*Over her shoulder. She is still at the phone, which doesn't answer.*) Hearn's, and I didn't say Hicks's.
FORTESCUE   No answer below, Evans?
EVANS   No, mum. The last we was in communication with the outside world was a week ago Saturday. A copy of the *Villager* was thrown through the window.
CHROME   (*As crash comes.*) I think they're trying it again.

(*All shudder.*)

FORTESCUE   Keep listening, Evans. I cawn't think they'd have given *me* a telephone without the other end. Thirty-nine years in the Brevoort—why, the phone should ring incessantly by this time. (*Decides.*) Hang up, and let them call *us.*
EVANS   (*Hanging up.*) I'd rather skate across the street and fill my earthen jug at the King Cole Room.
FORTESCUE   (*Offering chocolates out of enormous satin-lined candy box, requiring both hands to handle. Ladies choose, cooing.*) Desmond? The liquid cherries are in the fourteenth row—balcony.
DUPREE   (*Cramming.*) Teddibly good of you. Any quail sandwiches, or do I presume?
EVANS   (*Carrying long, old-fashioned flintlock across stage and standing it in corner.*) You presume. It's Lent—remember?
CHROME   (*Gaily.*) That last time we had a bird! Do you recall, Millicent?
FORTESCUE   (*A short scream.*) Oh! Indelibly. That was the afternoon Raymond Duncan came to tea.
WHICHAWAY   Threading his way down from the Waldorf.
CHROME   Bringing his weaving.

FORTESCUE   Saint Valentine's Day! . . . And he took the bones home in his pocket.—He *had* pockets, hadn't he?

CHROME   For the goats. The Brevoort, of course, doesn't sanction goats.

WHICHAWAY   *(Calling over noises off.)* Sanction who?

ALL THE OTHERS, WITH EVANS   *Goats*!

(The portrait falls off the wall at this extra clamor.)

EVANS   *(Gesture of announcement.)* E-o-leven! *(Then rehangs portrait. On second thought, turns it face to the wall.)*

FORTESCUE   *(Explaining to DUPREE.)* Evans is keeping count of the times Aunt Emmeline falls—*excellent* count. *(Fuller explanation.)* This was *her* home, you know.

WHICHAWAY   *(Broodingly.)* There are moments when I seem to notice something over and beyond the noise of traffic and falling portraits.

FORTESCUE   You hear the seashell, dear. Evans, hold up the seashell for Miss Whichaway.

(EVANS holds it up, and it vibrates and jerks in her hands as the noises sound. She shudders.)

FORTESCUE   See, dear? It makes Evans shudder.—That will *do*, Evans.

EVANS   *(Gesturing with seashell aloft, reciting.)*
    "It was the schooner Hesperus
    That sailed the wintry sea—"

FORTESCUE   More tea? Let's all have more hot tea. *(She begins to pour.)*

EVANS   *(Reciting with shell.)*
    "We are lost, the Captain shouted
    as he staggered down the stair."

(This makes DESMOND's hand shake; his cup falls and breaks.)

DUPREE   Seems to me at times *china* isn't lasting much better than *we* are.

(EVANS is immediately bringing him another cup.)

EVANS   Ooh, don't talk that way—Mr. Wedgewood!

FIRST WRECKER   *(Off.)* That's it! Hook a chain around her middle and drag her down!

CHROME   Did you speak, Desmond?

FORTESCUE   I think that was someone in the corridor, dealing with a maid.

EVANS   Doing it with chains now, are they? *(A large crash, off.)*

SECOND WRECKER   *(Off.)* Crack her open—ah! Chock full of termites!

WHICHAWAY   Do you feel that life's quite the same, since traffic? I say, a disrespectful element is creeping in.

CHROME   The Brevoort should do away with the taxi stand.

DUPREE   It's worse than that. I'd meant to keep it from you—but the skaters in Washington Square of late are heavily bearded.

FORTESCUE   I *do* think we should alarm the Brevoort. Evans, will you telephone below? Inform the desk that out there *bullies* are *skating.*

(EVANS goes to phone, jiggles it. A pounding right at door.)

CHROME   *(Crossing to EVANS, graciously.)* Here, Evans. Let me try. I'm awfully good with a telephone. My father played chess for years with Mr. Bell. *(Takes phone, jiggles.)* Hello? Hello? . . . There seem to be *mice* at the other end. *(She hangs up.)* *(Pounding at the door.)*

FORTESCUE   Often I console myself by pretending the traffic noises are simply pistol shots—the riffraff *murdering* one another.

DUPREE   *(Touched. Kissing her ear.)* Dear Millicent!

FIRST WRECKER   *(Just outside door.)* This door's locked! My God, whose *bicycle?*

(Crash and bicycle bell ringing.)

CHROME   The traffic seems curiously active for St. Swithin's Day.

EVANS   I'm holding out for St. Vitus's Day. *(The WRECKERS break down the door and enter. EVANS steps to the door as it falls. To the WRECKERS:)* You knocked?

FORTESCUE   Evans, we are not at home.

FIRST WRECKER   Anudder nest of 'em. You can't smoke 'em out.

SECOND WRECKER   Want to use the block and tackle on these, boss?

FIRST WRECKER   Foist we'll see if dey won't come out nice.

(Pounding outside keeps on. WRECKERS galvanized at sight of the tea table shimmying. WRECKER speaks in wheedling voice.)

Folks—how about coming outside in de nice . . . *sunshine?*

(They all rise, reel, give little cries, and cling together.)

THIRD WRECKER   *(Unwinding ropes and chains and creeping up at DUPREE.)* Ya see? Ya never loin, Leonard.

FIRST WRECKER   *(Trying again. Smiling.)* Would youse boys and goils like to come out and see my great, big, shiny—*bulldozer?*

(They cry out again.)

CHROME   Bulldozers, or any other kind, are not mentioned in the Brevoort Hotel.

(THIRD WRECKER holds up a square rule.)

FORTESCUE   I *beg* your pardon. I think you people are looking for Klein's on the Square.

(A carrier pigeon flies in window, bringing a note to FORTESCUE.)

FORTESCUE   *(Explaining brightly to WRECKERS.)* Oh, the mail. There you are, my pretty. *(Pokes cake crumb at pigeon, which flies back out window. Prettily, to*

WRECKERS.) We much prefer pigeons to the government. Always on time
—and in the end, of course, they can be eaten.

WHICHAWAY   Open your letter. Maybe it's from the Metropolitan Museum
again—insisting that we take care of ourselves.

FORTESCUE   *(Opens note, reads, gasps.)* Oh! Listen to this! *(Reads aloud.)* "The
management-in-exile of the Hotel Brevoort hereby notifies you that Wreckers are on their way to your suite. You will please receive them and carry
out their wishes."

(Horrified pause.)

DUPREE   *(Manfully.) Where's* that pigeon?

EVANS   *(Pensively.)* Their wishes?

FIRST WRECKER   Okay, boys.

*(They begin moving stuff out of the room, the plant stands, musical instruments, etc.
But leave the group at tea table for moment.)*

FORTESCUE   *(Brightly.)* Tea's what we need, my dears. Fresh tea! Do sit down.
(Flutters at tea table.)

(WHICHAWAY sits, extends cup.)

CHROME   *(Sitting.)* One must be impervious to the riffraff. Two lumps.

DUPREE   *(Remains standing, thoughtfully.)* Yes. But still, I cawn't think too
highly of those old women knitting on the roof of Wanamaker's.

FORTESCUE   Desmond, dear—room service! *You* can get them. Tell them *fresh
hot tea* on the dumbwaiter instantly.

(Dumbwaiter signals.)

Why, here it is! Evans—tea!

*(WRECKERS still carrying out. EVANS goes through them to dumbwaiter. Lifts tray and
turns to room, showing it loaded with lighted dynamite sticks.)*

EVANS   *(Taking dashing position, with crossed feet.)* TNT is served, mum.

FORTESCUE   *(Grandly.)* Bring it on!

*(EVANS brings tray forward and sets it down on the tea table, DESMOND absentmindedly
tucking in his napkin, and they all sit there grandly. FIRST and SECOND WRECKERS
swoop down on WHICHAWAY in her wicker chair and carry her off. She snatches her
solitaire pack and deliberately plays the first card, up in the air.)*

WHICHAWAY   I *insist* there's a draft. *(WRECKERS return and pick up CHROME in her
chair.)*

CHROME   Will you dip in Suite Two for my tippet?

*(They bear her away. Return for FORTESCUE, who is on the settee. She takes up her
lace parasol and opens it over her head. Rides out with it over her, as in a howdah.)*

MILLICENT   *(Aloft.)* Shall I tell you what I think about Life, all? I think there's
    something of *elegance* gone.

*(She is borne off. EVANS jumps up on the back of the remaining WRECKER and rides
out piggyback, showing her bicycle clips attached to her long drawers. She prods him
in the back.)*

EVANS   *What* wishes?

(WRECKERS return and surround DUPREE. A fusillade of crashes, off.)

DUPREE   *(Stiffly.)* I can go unaided, thank you.

*(He opens his collar and bares his throat, as one going to the guillotine. Suffers the
WRECKERS to light his cigarette, or a long cheroot, for him with a dynamite stick. To
sounds of wrecking, mingled with a strain of the "Marseillaise," he goes nobly out ahead
of WRECKERS. Last WRECKER out lifts Aunt Emmeline's portrait and carries it under
his arm. Aunt Emmeline's fingers are in her ears. Explosion and walls collapse as
curtain falls.)*

TENNESSEE WILLIAMS

The Chalky White Substance

TIME AND PLACE

A century or two after our time and possibly an almost equal time after the great thermonuclear war. Against a cyclorama of sky that is cloudless and yet faintly blurred by tiny granules of something like old powdered bones, there is an up-and-down thrust, a promontory, downstage center.

At rise.

    A youth named LUKE, *about twenty years of age, sits on this promontory with an air of perplexed and anxious waiting. Upstage and to the left of him is seated a young man, about eight years older, watching him with an enigmatic fixity of expression. He will be called* MARK.

    After some moments MARK *rises and slides stealthily off his upstage perch, disappearing from sight for a minute, during which* LUKE *removes from a pocket a small metal bottle containing water and a cloth which he dampens and with which he carefully and gently cleans his face. No sooner has he returned the bottle and cloth into the pocket than* MARK *appears silently behind him and stoops to clasp his large, powerful hands over* LUKE's *eyes.*

    LUKE *sits upon the precipitous verge of a chasm over what is presumably a dried-up riverbed. (It is called, now, Arroyo Seco.) He has a pure and luminous quality in his face when the hood of his monklike robe is thrown back. Throughout the brief play there is a wind that rises and falls, always infinitely sad in its implication as much as in its actual sound, for this is the wind that constantly blows about an earth as shriveled and desiccated as a terminally sick being.*

MARK   *(In a prolonged, deep growl.)* Whoooo?
LUKE   Youuuuuuu! —You can disguise your voice but not your hands. What makes you so late?

MARK   Boys are inquisitive, aren't they? What, why? I wasn't late. If you'd turned around, you'd have seen me sitting back there on that boulder behind you.

LUKE   Why?

MARK   I thought to myself, "It could be the last time I'll observe him, sitting here, waiting for me?"

LUKE   You're planning to go away? Somewhere? Without me?

MARK   Make a departure? From you? From this precipice over the Arroyo Seco, this desolation, so beautiful through the continual screen provided by the —chalky white substance? No, I'm making no departure. But how do I know that you're not?

LUKE   A secret departure? One I'd not mentioned to you?

MARK   Don't you know departures can be made without warning? You don't say you're going, you don't even know you're going, then *(Snaps his fingers.)* you're gone. Life's full of sudden departures; what a pity death isn't. *(MARK removes his hands from the youth's eyes.)*

MARK   Don't pull that cowl over your face.

LUKE   It protects my eyes from the dust always blowing, blowing constantly —from where?

MARK   The shrinking earth's a desert and barren mountains. In our part of it, the vicinity here, most of the chalky white stuff is provided by the Arroyo Seco, down there. I've heard that once, a few hundred years ago, there was a river in it—there's nothing drier and dustier than an arroyo in which there was once a river that's now dried up.

(The youth lowers the cowl over his head; MARK draws it back up.)

LUKE   I thought you admired my eyes for being so clear, not inflamed?

MARK   This evening let me have a long look at your face, memorize it, as if I might never be going to see it again.

LUKE   You said you weren't going away, and I told you I wasn't, either. — I still don't understand why you kept me waiting here while you were right back there all that time.

MARK   You learn a great deal about someone you care for by observing him without him knowing you are. You notice whether he waits indifferently, or with increasing concern as it gets later, oh, you learn many things you'd never know otherwise.

LUKE   What did you observe you didn't already know?

MARK   More and more tension in you as the sky started to fade.

LUKE   You know I'm afraid of the dark when I'm alone at night. If it had gotten a bit darker, I would have started home and missed our meeting.

MARK   —Fear, that's a bad thing to feel.

LUKE   A natural thing to feel. Now that women are so much fewer than men, there are bands of nomads that will seize a boy after dark and—

MARK I know. Ravage him. And when their lusts are satiated, they leave no witness, just the lifeless body. —Lean back.

(LUKE leans into his embrace.)

It always amazes me, the smoothness of your skin under the robe, not granulated at all by the chalky white substance.

LUKE I know you like the touch of smooth skin, so I keep mine smooth for your pleasure.

MARK How do you do that?

LUKE Before I go to meet you here, I bathe myself and then immediately I put on my robe.

MARK You bathe once a day before you come here to meet me, not just at night, as we're ordered to do?

LUKE I bathe twice, once for you and again at night, Mark.

MARK Bathe twice? Did you say twice? But that would mean that you disregard the water restrictions as if they didn't exist. —You know, this confirms my suspicions that you have another protector, one in a high position in the regime, you little—cheater, yes, you get by with violating the restrictions because you give yourself at night to someone of great power among the—

LUKE I've never had more than one protector at a time. That one protector now is you.

MARK Before me, you had others.

LUKE They were necessary. I hardly remember my parents. I'll tell you something that'll amuse you. On the wall at my place I have a colored picture of the lady that was called the Madonna.

MARK Those old mythological pictures are a rarity now and could be sold to the center for special privileges, you know.

LUKE I'd rather keep the picture on my wall.

MARK What were you going to tell me that will amuse me? Something about the picture of the Madonna?

LUKE Once I had a protector. When I woke up one morning, he was standing there staring at the picture. He said, "Is this your mother?"

MARK Thought that the Madonna was your mother . . .

LUKE The funny thing is that I said, 'Yes, that is, that was my mother." —Women were a comfort. —Why are they disappearing? Do they succumb more quickly to the chalk all about us now?

MARK The earth's not able to support its shrinking population. There's little food, and even less water. I've heard that a man will use a woman awhile, and then, when she's no longer desirable to him, not as she was before, he's likely to destroy her. You see, Luke, the battle between people that happened so long ago that it's barely recorded, I understand that it had a brutalizing effect. Do you understand me?

LUKE   Brutalizing—?

MARK   Opposite effect from the care of a Madonna.

LUKE   So that now we have only each other.

MARK   Have I told you that I have a woman at home?

LUKE   A mother? A Madonna?

(MARK laughs harshly.)

MARK   No, what remains of a girl, the remnant of her, used too much, not able now to excite me nor even to—serve . . . only to stagger about, looking more and more frightened. I suspect she knows.

LUKE   You suspect she knows what?

MARK   That her withering, frightened look, her choking sounds at night—

LUKE   From the disease? She has it?

MARK   She's breathed too much of the chalk. I think she knows that soon it will be necessary to relieve myself of her presence in my place.

LUKE   I don't think you'll do that. No, you couldn't do that.

MARK   You haven't sat for an hour observing me waiting for you, and so you know me less.

LUKE   Since I know you completely—

MARK   Are you sure that you do?

LUKE   I feel secure with you, Mark. And as for the woman you've never mentioned before, have you told her about us?

MARK   I say nothing to her now but, "Oh, are you still here? Go lie down in that corner over there and don't cough and don't crawl toward me."

LUKE   You're making all this up, I know it's not true.

MARK   You know so little, boy. You know dangerously little. You don't know enough to distrust.

LUKE   Oh, I distrust them all except you, Mark.

MARK   That might be a mistake. The worn-out girl at my place, she—trusted me once as you do. But when I go home tonight, if she's still there—out she'll go, I'll throw the door open, and kick her living or dead body into the wind she can't stand against, that will sweep her away and bury her in white dust. No, don't trust. So. —You said you bathe twice a day, before you come here to meet me and again at night, violating the water restrictions?

LUKE   When I was very young—

MARK   Younger than now?

LUKE   Little more than a child. I had a protector, my first, who was very clever, very wise, at secret, mechanical things. Did I say that right?

MARK   Perfectly. Go on.

LUKE   One day he put his ear to the earth.

MARK   In or out of the house?

LUKE   Both in and out, and he discovered that not far under the earth, running under the house, there was water, he said a stream of it, not wide, not deep, but—

MARK   Ohhh . . .

LUKE   He was a strong man, he dug and dug down to it and built steps down with stones.

MARK   But when the house is inspected by the—

LUKE   Inspectors, no. You see, the opening to the steps is covered over with an old, dry animal skin, and even if the inspectors looked under this ragged leather—you know their eyes are bad, half-blinded by the chalk—they wouldn't notice the width of the cracks.

MARK   By which you can lift the cover to the underground spring of water? —How very foolish of you!

LUKE   He did it all, not I.

MARK   But he's gone now, and you have it all to yourself, for your own private and—illegal—use. You are not at all wise.

LUKE   (Shrugging.) I must live, and to live I must please.

MARK   But you mustn't talk about it.

LUKE   Of course not. To no one but you.

MARK   No, not even to me, because by talking about it to me, you make me a conspirator with you, as criminal as you are.

LUKE   Oh, but—you—

MARK   Would bear the same penalty you would, knowing what you've told me and not—informing.

LUKE   Whom would you—

MARK   Inform? The ones you inform to. The rulers, the authorities of the regime. (Pause.)

LUKE   You believed that story? You didn't know that it was all made up? Just an invention, like yours about the woman and what you'll do to her tonight?

MARK   That was no invention. And neither was what you told me about the underground spring.

LUKE   You're holding me so tight it's hard to breathe.

MARK   You're a light-footed boy. You might suddenly spring up and take to your heels.

LUKE   From you?

MARK   Of course, now that you realize that you've made such a dangerous mistake. I suspected something. And now I know.

LUKE   But I know something, too.

MARK   What?

LUKE   You've told me how completely you love me.

MARK   A thing that I also told the woman when she was desirable to me.

LUKE   She doesn't still attract you. I do. Don't I? Mark?

MARK   You've put in my possession a secret that to keep from the authorities would expose me to the same penalty you're exposed to. You know what such penalties are?

LUKE   A term of imprisonment, but—

MARK   A long, long term, and even if you're alive when it expires, you'd be—unrecognizable, Luke.

LUKE   I'd be disfigured, you mean?

MARK   By more than time, by more than the terminal effect of the chalky white substance.

(He clamps his arms tighter about LUKE.)

LUKE   What are you, why are you—!

MARK   I must deliver you to them and repeat your confession and—receive the bounty. Did you know there's a bounty offered for turning in a person who violates the laws, the restrictions? The authorities regard him with more respect, he's given a title, sometimes, and his licenses are extended. The inspectors pay his house a—respectful visit, they smile at him and say, "The place needs some improvements in keeping with your new position. We'll see to that right away."

LUKE   The authorities are vicious.

MARK   I understand that's always been their nature, even before the people of the earth divided into two or three hostile parts that battled for ownership and rule with the great explosive devices. —Who won? —Nobody. *Nobody!*

(The italicized word is echoed, after a couple of moments, from the opposite side of the chasm.)

—Hear that? Know what that was? As if somebody called back? That was an echo. So many of the old words have dropped out of use and aren't known anymore. *(Pause.)*

LUKE   The authorities are corrupt, but we don't have to imitate them.

MARK   To save our skins we do.

LUKE   Would they still be worth saving?

MARK   I understand that there used to be considerations called moral. And for these considerations, morality, a thing such as the betrayal of someone you love, would be held in contempt. But that was once, long before I remember. Stop struggling. I'm hard and strong. What's the use? You can't escape. Light's faded. We must get going.

LUKE   Where? The cave? Or my place?

MARK   Neither this evening, Luke. We're going to the *cabildo* where you will stay confined till long outused, to the end of your time. —*Time!*

(The pause; the echo.)

LUKE   Then kill me. Kill me, Mark!

MARK   And sacrifice the reward? *(Wind rises. LUKE thrashes impotently in the grasp of MARK.)* Call him, the great protector called God. No breath? I'll call Him for you. *Pro-tec-tor!*

(Pause; the echo.)

> What a huge creature, what an immense beast He must have been to have left such enormous white bones when He died . . . Endlessly long ago, the bones of Him now turned to powder that blows and blows about His broken—creation . . .

(He bears LUKE, futilely struggling, down the upstage declivity, and the stage darkens.)

AUGUST WILSON

Testimonies

Four Monologues

HOLLOWAY

It ain't that he don't want to work. He don't want to haul no bricks on a construction site for three dollars a hour. That ain't gonna help him. What's he gonna do with twenty-five dollars a day. He can make two or three hundred dollars a day gambling . . . if he get lucky. If he don't, somebody else will get it. That's all you got around here is niggers with somebody else's money in their pocket. And they don't do nothing but trade it off on each other. I got it today and you got it tomorrow. Until sooner or later as sure as the sun shine . . . somebody gonna take it and give it to the white man. The money go from you to me to you and then . . . bingo, it's gone. From him to you to me, then . . . bingo, it's gone. You give it to the white man. Pay your rent, pay your telephone, buy your groceries, see the doctor . . . bingo. It's gone. Just circulate it around till it find that hole then . . . bingo. Like trying to haul sand in a bucket with a hole in it. Time you get where you going the bucket empty. That's why that twenty-five dollars a day ain't gonna do him no good. A nigger with five hundred dollars in his pocket around here is a big man. But you go out there where they at . . . you go out to Squirrel Hill, they walking around there with five thousand dollars in their pocket trying to figure out how to make it into five hundred thousand.

People kill me talking about niggers is lazy. Niggers is the most hardworking people in the world. Worked three hundred years for free. And didn't take no lunch hour. Now all of a sudden niggers is lazy. Don't know how to work. All of a sudden when they got to pay niggers, ain't no work for him to do. If it wasn't for you the white man would be poor. Every little bit he got he got standing on top of you. That's why he could reach so high. He give you three dollars a hour for six months and he got him a railroad for the next hundred years. All you got is six months' worth of three dollars an hour.

It's simple mathematics. Ain't no money in niggers working. Look out there on the street. If there was some money in it . . . if the white man could figure out a way to make some money by putting niggers to work, we'd all be working. He ain't building no more railroads. He got them. He ain't building no more highways. Somebody done already stuck the telephone poles in the ground. That's been done already.

The white man ain't stacking no more niggers. You know what I'm talking about stacking niggers, don't you? Well, here's how that go. If you ain't got nothing . . . you can go out here and get you a nigger. Then you got something, see. You got one nigger. If that one nigger get out there and plant something . . . get something out the ground . . . even if it ain't nothing but a bushel of potatoes . . . then you got one nigger and a bushel of potatoes. Then you take that bushel of potatoes and go get you another nigger. Then you got two niggers. Put them to work and you got two niggers and two bushels of potatoes. See, now you can go buy two more niggers. That's how you stack a nigger on top of a nigger. White folks got to stacking . . . and I'm talking about they stacked up some niggers! Stacked up close to fifty million niggers. If you stacked them on top of one another they make six or seven circles around the moon.

I always said I was gonna get me a dart board and put Eli Whitney's picture on one side and the boll weevil on the other. Eli Whitney invented the cotton gin and put niggers to work and the boll weevil come along and put them out of work. Eli Whitney and the boll weevil the cause of all the problems the colored man is having now. Man invented the cotton gin and they went over to Africa and couldn't find enough niggers. It's lucky the boat didn't sink with all them niggers they had stacked up there. It take them two extra months to get here cause it ride so low in the water. They couldn't find you enough work back then. Now that they got to pay you they can't find you none. If this was a different time wouldn't be nobody out there on the street. They'd all be in the cotton fields.

HOLLOWAY

West's wife been dead twenty years. Died right after the war. Two or three years after that. He buried her himself. Say he didn't want nobody touching her when she was living . . . he didn't want nobody else touching her when she was dead. She died and he ain't had nothing else to live for. He married Joe Westray's daughter. People say they was cousins. I don't know the truth of that but I know he ain't been the same since his wife died. See, I know West. I know him from way back. West used to be a gangster. West wasn't above breaking the law. He wasn't always Johnny B. Goode. This is way back in the thirties I'm talking about. This before you come up here. I been here since twenty-seven.

I know West before he got to be an undertaker. West used to gamble, chase women, bootleg, and everything else. He always kept him four or five hundred dollars in his pocket. West used to carry a gun. See, Wolf don't know this . . . but West used to run numbers for the Alberts. Him and Big Dave used to run around together. Big Dave got killed holding up that insurance company and West went in the undertaking business. Opened that funeral home there down on Centre. Had four or five viewing rooms and tried to keep somebody in all of them. I remember one time he had two niggers laid out in the hallway and one on the back porch. Most of them had welfare caskets but West didn't care cause the government pay on time. He might have to worry his money out of some of them other niggers but the government pay quicker than the insurance companies. Come time to bury them, West would tell John D. to carry them niggers out there and dump them out and bring the casket on back. This is what John D. told me. Say West went out there and took the suits off the corpse. Bring them back to bury somebody else in. West was burying niggers so fast you couldn't keep up with him. Every nigger in Pittsburgh at some time or another was walking up handing West some money. He done buried their cousin . . . their uncle. Their mother. Started out with two cars and ended up with seven. Every year he'd buy him seven new Cadillacs—wear them out— and buy him seven more the next year. You could have fed everybody in the neighborhood on the checks West was getting from the government. Man worked twenty hours a day. Up at four and to bed at midnight. It got so every nigger looked alike to him. He couldn't tell one from the other. West got tired of seeing niggers. Niggers dying from pneumonia. Niggers dying from tuberculosis. Niggers getting shot. Niggers getting stabbed to death with ice picks. Babies dying. Old ladies dying. His wife dying. That's the only thing West ever loved. His wife. That's the only thing he understood. The rest of life baffled him.

MEMPHIS

That's what half the problem is . . . these black-power niggers. They got people confused. They don't know what they doing themselves. These niggers talking about freedom, justice, and equality and don't know what it mean. You born free. It's up to you to maintain it. You born with dignity and everything else. These niggers talking about freedom. But what you gonna do with it? Freedom is heavy. You got to put your shoulder to freedom. Put your shoulder to it and hope your back hold up. And if you around here looking for justice, you got a long wait. Ain't no justice. That's why they got that statue of her and got her blindfolded. Common sense would tell you anybody need to see she do. There ain't no justice. Jesus Christ didn't get justice. What makes you think you gonna get it? That's just the nature of the world. These niggers talking about they want freedom, justice, and equality. Equal to what? Hell, I might be a better man than you. What I look like going around here talking about

I want to be equal to you? I don't know how these niggers think sometimes. Talking about black power with their hands and their pockets empty. You can't do nothing without a gun. Not in this day and time. That's the only kind of power the white man understand. They think they gonna talk their way up on it. In order to talk your way you got to have something under the table. These niggers don't understand that. If I tell you to get out my yard and leave my apples alone, I can't talk you out. You sit up in the tree and laugh at me. But if you know I might come out with a shotgun . . . that be something different. You'd have to think twice about whether you wanted some apples.

You could take it to the round table if you had one. Sit down and talk it out. But the white man and the black man ain't got no round table. Ain't never had none. The white man don't want you to have the chairs if you did have a table. You can't sit down with him. You always standing up in front of him. And he shaking his finger at you. You ain't got no right to sit down at the table with him. That's what the problem is. If you take it to the round table, you might be able to work something out. But he ain't gonna sit down with you as long as he got you under control. He sit and shake his finger at you and tell you what you better do.

These niggers around here talking about they black and beautiful. I been black all my life. And gonna be black till I die. You can't change that. If you live to be a hundred years you can't change that. I was black the day I was born. I didn't get black yesterday. These niggers crazy. Talking about they black and beautiful. Sound like they trying to convince themselves. When I was coming along, we knew that white people ran the world, but that didn't make us ugly. We was just the low man on the pole. Why you got to go around telling everybody you beautiful? That's some kind of trick the white man done put these people in. He got them thinking like they do. Every nigger they see is uglier than the next. Everything was alright till the white man got to separating the niggers like separating the wheat from the chaff telling them, "It ain't how you look, it's how you do. You do ugly. If you change the way you do, you won't be ugly. If you change, we'll let you be like us. Otherwise you stay over there and suffer." That's when niggers got to thinking they was ugly. You got to think you ugly to run around shouting you beautiful. You don't hear me say that. Hell, I know I look nice. Got good manners and everything.

MEMPHIS

I don't know how much they was gonna give me cause we didn't get that far. I didn't wait to find out when they started out like that. I told them I got a clause too. They ain't the only one got a clause. My clause say they got to give me what I want for it. It's my building. If they wanna buy it they got to meet my price. That's just common sense. I raised so much hell the judge postponed it . . . told me talk to my lawyer. The lawyer looked at the deed and told me that they was right. I told him, I don't need you no more. Fired him on the spot. He supposed to be on my side. They left it like that till I could get me another lawyer. He ain't even looked at the paper good . . . talking about they right. I don't care what the paper say. He supposed to fix it so they meet my price. I left out of there and called me one of them white lawyers, which is what I should have done in the first place. Fellow named Joseph Bartoromo.

I'll be glad to get rid of this old place. I can't make no money. At one time you couldn't get a seat in here. Had the jukebox working and everything. Time somebody get up somebody sit down before they could get out the door. People coming from everywhere. Everybody got to eat and everybody got to sleep. Some people don't have stoves. Some people don't have nobody to cook for them. Men whose wives done died and left them. Cook for them thirty years and lay down and die. Who's gonna cook for them now? Somebody's got to do it. I order four cases of chicken on Friday and Sunday it's gone. Fry it up. Make a stew. Boil it. Add some dumplings. You couldn't charge more than a dollar. But then you didn't have to. It didn't cost you but a quarter. I done seen everything. Patchneck Red sat right there. He sat right down there and ate a bowl of beans. I seen him here and I seen him over there across the street. I seen him both places. Mr. Samuels, the blind man . . . he sat right over there. He could find that table in his sleep. I seen him both places, too. People come from all over. The man used to come twice a week to collect the jukebox. He making more money than I am. He pay seventy-five cents for the record and he make two hundred dollars off of it. If it's a big hit, he's liable to make four hundred. The record will take all the quarters you can give it. It don't never wear out. The chicken be gone by Sunday.

People come in crying . . . you didn't have to ask what it was about. West right across the street. They come here for awhile and go back over there. I done seen that a lot. People arguing about who's gonna bury who . . . arguing over the insurance money. And I done seen a lot of love. People caring for and caring about each other. Touching each other. Right there in that booth I have seen grown men cry. And after they cry I seen them laugh and order another bowl of beans. It ain't nothing like that now. I'll be glad when they tear it down. But they gonna meet my price. See, they don't know. The half ain't never been told. I'm ready to walk through fire. I don't bother nobody. The last person I bothered is dead. My mama died in fifty-four. I said then I wasn't going for no more draws. They don't know I feel just like I did when my mama died. She got old and grey and sat by the window till she died. She must have done that cause she ain't had nothing else to do. I was gone. My brother was gone. Sister gone. Everybody gone. My daddy was gone. She sat there till she died. I was staying down on Logan Street. Got the letter one day and telegram the next. They usually fall on top of one another . . . but not that close. I got the letter say, if you wanna see your mother you better come home. Before I could get out the door the telegram came saying it's too late . . . your mother gone.

I was trying to borrow some money. Called the train station and found out the schedule and I'm trying to borrow some money. I can't go down there broke. I don't know how long I got to be there. I ain't even got the train fare. I got $2.63 cents.

I got the telegram and sat down and cried like a baby. I could beat any new born baby in the world crying. I cried till the tears all run down in my ears. Got up and went out the door and everything looked different. Everything had changed. I felt like I had been cut loose. All them years something had a hold of me and I didn't know it. I didn't find out till it cut me loose. I walked out the door and everything had different colors to it. I felt great. I didn't owe nobody nothing. The last person I owed anything to was gone. I borrowed fifty dollars from West and went on down to her funeral. I come back and said everybody better get out my way. You couldn't hold me down. It look like then I had somewhere to go fast. I didn't know where but I damn sure was going there. That's the way I feel now. If there's an Aunt Ester I'm going up there to see her. See if she can straighten this out . . . cause they don't know I got a clause of my own. I'll get up off the canvas if I have to. They can carry me out feet first . . . but my clause say, I ain't going for no more draws.

LANFORD WILSON

The Moonshot Tape

SETTING

A room at the Ozark Cabins Motel in Mountain Grove, Missouri. It is late on a drizzling spring afternoon. The set is a motel bed and nothing else. A pair of motel pillows and a motel bedspread. DIANE *has an ashtray, a notebook, a pen, a Bic lighter, and a package of cigarettes. There is a motel glass on the floor and a bottle of no-name vodka beside it. The light is from motel lamps that we can't see, and toward the end perhaps the hint of a light from a sign outside blinking: Red, blue, lavender, off. Red, blue, lavender, off.*

DIANE is thirty-five. She has short hair, jeans and a T-shirt, socks, no shoes. When she reads, she uses dime-store reading glasses. She speaks to an interviewer, who would be sitting against the fourth wall. She is trying to be cordial, but she has a "to hell with it, let the chips fall where they may" directness that hides a natural warmth and also masks a pain and grievance of which she is only partially aware.

DIANE   *(Sitting cross-legged in the middle of the bed, reading a typed list. After a moment she takes off the reading glasses and folds them.)* Well, that covers all the usual bases, I think. I'm sorry, I was reading, what did—oh, sure, smoke, use a tape recorder by all means, I usually won't be interviewed without, do whatever it takes—

(She puts her glasses back on and looks at the list again. Reading.)

"How did living in a small town, essentially a rural area, prepare you for a career and living in a metropolitan area. Or not?" "When did you leave Missouri?" "Where do you get your ideas for stories?" "How much of an influence has Mountain Grove been on your writing, your life?" "What is your favorite of your own work? Why?" "What do you think is the current state of short story writing?" "What do you see as the future of S. S. Writing?" That sounds like a steamship. Stories are a little skiff. "Why are your stories so downbeat?" "Do you plan to write a novel?" Now, *that's* a steamship. S.S. *Madame Bovary;* S.S. *The Sun Also Rises.* That male chauvinist, anti-Semitic closet case. He says the same about me.

(Pause. She is probably thinking of the questions unasked. She comes out of it slowly and looks at her interviewer.)

I like the way you do your hair. When I was in school here we were all hippies and wore our hair down to our ass. We just washed it and brushed it—in public—as nature intended. Consequentially, I never learned how to do anything with it and am insecure about my hair. Anyone over thirty was untrustworthy. You wore a suit, you were the enemy. Everything was visible, you knew immediately where you stood; black and white. No gray areas like now, everywhere is a gray area now, isn't it? I was mightily ashamed of the excitement I felt watching Neil Armstrong walk on the moon. He was there, but he was still an American Establishment Pig. "One small step for Man, one giant leap for Mankind." Which means *nothing.* He had obviously rehearsed it to say "One small step for *a* man," but he fucked it up. And then lied about it, which was perfect. It was a, I guess, sophomore. The surgeon general had just issued his warning that cigarette smoking was hazardous to our health, so I'd started to smoke. *(Pause.)* It was over, of course. We didn't know. The writing was on the ol' wall if we'd taken the trouble to learn to read. I went to my cousin's eighth-grade graduation, the thirteen-year-olds were Yuppies already, rebelling against either our parents, who were still stuck relieving Dunkirk and Saipan and buying new refrigerators, or their older siblings. God knows we must have looked like we definitely didn't have the answer. All the little thirteen-year-old girls were done up like Donnie or Marie, whichever one is the girl. I was class of '71, that'd make them class of '75, that's about right. You don't have any idea what I'm talking . . . doesn't matter, you would have been about a year old. All those names that were burned into our skin back then are . . . William Calley, My Lai, Alan Shepard, the Native Americans who took over Alcatraz to be a what? Cultural center I think, God help us. Rest in peace.

(She looks over the list a second, then takes off her glasses again, breaking off; preoccupied.)

I'm expecting a call from mother, so— She's going to call me when Edith leaves. That's one of my stepfather's kids. I said I was—well, I was meeting you—I said I had to work, that's always my excuse. We—Edith and I, my stepsister and I—how to say this in the briefest possible—hated each other. So Mom's going to call me when she clears out. She's just dropping through from wherever she lives now, wherever it is that her husband has been sent to assistant manage the new Pizza Hut or Burger King. Someplace, Kansas. She's busy packing up photo albums and pots and pans and sweaters and sheets and quilts and refrigerator jars. I don't know where she'll put—add them to what is already one of the world's largest private collections of Tupperware.

(Looking around.)

This isn't bad, this joint. I used to wonder about it. I passed it every day on the way to school. We lived down on Church Street. I mean, there couldn't be more than what? Ten rooms? Who's going to stop at a moldy little Masonite motel just an hour from Springfield where there's an actual Great Western? You wouldn't even come here for a rendezvous, it's too crummy. How to end a liaison. I mean, you know, as it turns out, the rooms are perfectly adequate, they're clean, the heat's a little eccentric, but there's a bathroom with at least a shower. Luckily, it's only—you know, it's just a mile up the hill to the nursing home, so it couldn't be more convenient. I've triangulated that trip: here, to the house, to the nursing home, back to here, about forty times in the last two days. I'd imagined I'd stay at home, but Mom, ever ahead of schedule, had my bed taken apart, tied together and stacked out in the yard with most of the other contents. The home lets you keep a dresser and bed table from your belongings, so— But all those years I passed this place I couldn't imagine who stayed here. Now I know.

(Looking toward the window.)

If this damn weather wasn't so typically foul, we could walk. That wouldn't make your job any easier, but I only have five days, and I want to spend as much time with Mother as possible. I won't even get a chance to see the town. I haven't been here in . . . God! Well, Mom likes to travel, and I hate it, I get enough of it, so I try to bring her to New York once a year. I'm not going to have time to look up—you know how many kids from my graduating class still live here? Exactly two. Out of thirty-six, which we thought was an enormous class back then. Well . . .

(She puts her glasses back on and looks at the list.)

"How did living in a small town, essentially a rural area, prepare you for a career and living in a metropolitan area. Or not?" *(Pause. She stares at the paper.)* "How did living in a small town, essentially a *rural* area, prepare you for a career and living in a *metropolitan* area. Or not?"

(Pause. She continues to stare at the list. Finally.)

"When did you leave Missouri?" We graduated on June eleventh, the day the federal marshals took over Alcatraz—so much for the Native Americans' cultural center—and I left for Boston the next day. Early. I'd been staying most of the year at a girlfriend's place; I'd had my bags packed for a month. I got to Boston, saw what they were wearing, or not wearing, and threw everything away. I'd been accepted at B.U. I flew from Springfield to St. Louis to Boston, found the room I'd arranged for, found the campus, took this huge sketch pad and an assortment of pencils to the Lobster Claw, ordered a beer, and hung out for three months. Till the fall semester started. I was going to be a painter, you understand. My drawings, and the few paintings I'd done, about ten, swung wildly from doe-eyed but determined young women with flowers in their hair to what I imagined the apocalypse would look like.

(She breaks off and looks around her bed for a moment.)

I've managed to build a nest here without the foresight to get another bottle of vodka. With things as they are, half a bottle is definitely not going to do it. Long as I pick one up before they close—at eight-thirty if you believe it. The evening sessions, getting Mom to sleep, take it out of you. It was her idea to go there, insisted on it, looked forward to it almost, but . . .

(Pause.)

Half the inmates are insane or senile or *some*thing. Some ex-telephone operator rolls up and down the halls looking helplessly lost, yelling, I swear to God, "Operator? Operator? Help me. Operator, help me." The lady in Mom's room—she asked for a roommate and she drew this gal who can't remember from one minute to the next anything that's happened before in her life. She doesn't know if she has to go to the bathroom, if she's eaten, if she's slept. So she says, "Lady? Lady? Lady? Whatta I do now? Lady? Whatta I do now?"

(Pause.)

That's going to wear thin, I can tell. Even for Mom, who has the patience of the angels.

(She looks at the list.)

"Where do you get your ideas for stories?"

(She sighs, then thinks seriously.)

Well, why not? To begin with, most of my critics would have you believe I've never *had* an idea for a story. And, you know, for all I know or care, they're right. "Where do I get" . . . I'm gonna try to answer this truthfully. I've lied to dozens of interviewers about it. A lot of the time they're flat-out portraits of people I know; things in their lives they've been foolish enough to tell me or I've witnessed or surmised. Then I swear it isn't them; how could they think I'd do that? Or, you know, sometimes it's just raw speculation. You see someone, you start making up a story about them. That's a little old woman, probably lives with fifty cats. That guy is a wife beater. Someone on the subway, it's a game, you know, I've always done it. Like the song:

(Singing conversationally.)

"Laughing on the bus, playing games with the strangers." You said the man in the gabardine suit was a spy. I said, "Be careful, his bow tie is really a camera . . ." It makes them less of a stranger. Or at least it's easier than the trouble it would take to meet them. It's a good exercise to get the imagination going. And sometimes it ends with a story. Or, you know, sometimes—well, it's *always*, unfortunately, just yourself you're writing about, but sometimes they're *blatantly* autobiographical. My side of the story, that's always fun. Never underestimate the power and excitement of revenge.

(Without a beat she breaks off.)

What in the hell is Edith taking so much—probably dishing me to filth. In that superior Christian tone. She's what? Holy Roller, whatever it is, there's a name for it. No lipstick, no movies. Probably married him just so she'd have a legitimate excuse not to read my work. Fiction, good God forbid, the devil's door; and salacious fiction at that. They don't know the half of it. I could curl her toes good, but what's the point? Mom married Edith's dad when Edith was about two; I was eleven. Tom, Edith's dad, was a case. Well, actually he was only about three six-packs. And half a fifth of J. W. Daunt. The smell still turns my gut. It didn't keep me from drinking, but it kept me from drinking J. W. Daunt. "Where do I get my ideas?" Sometimes I start writing something, it turns into a piece that's been kicking me around forever; and I think, *Oh, good, I'm finally doing that.* Then I'll go months with nothing. One thing I haven't done, at least in years, is sit in front of a blank sheet of paper—or now a blank PC screen —and force myself to write. "Now is the time for all good women to come to the aid of their party." If they had one. I always wait till I'm—well, I started to say inspired, that's a little sweeping—at least until I have some*one* or some incident or some place or some event in mind. Like if you weren't here now I might be writing a story about a girl coming home to help her mother move into a nursing home. Or just coming back for a visit and seeing the town or someone from school or any of the things coming back home does to you. Being invaded by those memories, those times, those voices, the pictures. The moonshot, watching it on TV, imagining that silence, that airlessness, weightlessness, kicking up that dust that hadn't been kicked up before and doesn't settle immediately because of the weak gravity. That barren place. Or graduation; *that* barren place. Or being interviewed by a terminally shy young high school reporter and filling her tape with maundering stories of the first moonshot. And the various lies you tell of your history to protect the guilty. But probably coming back to this particular town I'd just be getting drunk so don't feel you're usurping my time; no other interviewer has. I'd more likely be watching TV. We get channels two, seven and almost ten. So.

(She looks at the paper again, tired of this, exasperated, almost pissed.)

"How much of an influence has Mountain Grove been on your writing comma your life?" Buckets. Whole bucketsful.

(Pause.)

I'm sorry. You've caught me at low ebb, or a bad time. I have all these feelings, guilt trips, ghosts, bombarding me here. How much of an influence has Mountain Grove been? Never underestimate that, either, and in little ways. The first boyfriend I had at B.U.—for all our free love talk in high school I'd managed to remain a virgin, squirming out from under basketball players in the backseats of Camaros. I can't imagine *why*. What kind of morality is that? It's all right to be felt up till you're literally raw, french-kiss all night, jerk 'em off even, if that's what it takes, but preserve the integrity of your hymen at all costs. Oh, Lord. For all the flaws in our design, and with Mother lately, I'm beginning to realize the human body is not nearly the miracle it seems when you're eighteen, but as for the hymen: *Think* of the sweeping changes it would make in the history of Man if Woman had never been designed with that particular membrane. Anyway, I had this boyfriend for about a month. We went on a picnic, walking through the woods. The poor guy had never been in the country before in his life. I'm stomping through the underbrush, I look back, and this bastard is getting slapped in the face with every sapling in the forest. He had no idea how to walk in the woods. So I lost some respect for him in that hidden place where we judge men and didn't see him much after that. I'd say over, over by the oak tree, and he'd say, Which one is that? No. I couldn't seriously consider someone who can't tell a birch from a beech. I was thankful that he took my virginity with him, but that was about it. And introducing me to Swinburne, which was important to me then. And tells you quite a bit about both of us.

(Suddenly remembering.)

Oh! The sketch pad that I took to the Claw to draw in. It was too dark, just the light on my table, so I started writing in it. Started out a diary and ended up my first story, that first day in Boston. And by the time the fall semester rolled around, I matriculated as an English major, minor in art history. All my life I'd said I was going to be a painter. Made all the protest signs: "The Draft Sucks!" Charming things like that. After that afternoon, if anyone had asked, I would have said I write stories; I'm a story writer. And saying makes it so. Sympathetic magic. If you want it to rain, make the sound of rain.

(Pause.)

I'm going to have to go up there if Edith doesn't leave, and I have no desire to see her. She's had three kids in four years and lords them over anyone who hasn't. Her dad died, my stepfather, Tom, about four years ago. I thought I'd seen the last of her at his funeral. Well, she's taking Mom's giving up of the house—she's studying to be a nurse, she didn't go to college, so she had to take all this other crap, aside from equivalency tests, math courses, civics for God sake. And actually she does care about people. One of the few Christians I know who takes her religion seriously, which doesn't make her any easier to be around but will surely get her into heaven. And of course after I left, Edith was still at home; she was only about nine, so Mom's her mother, too. Mother says the vilest things behind her back, but that's behind her back, and she shouldn't, but—well, fuck it, never mind.

(She picks up the list, puts on her glasses, and reads without looking up, quite pissed now at this imposition.)

"What is your favorite of your own work?" The one I'm working on at the time. "Why?" Because it might actually be good. "What do you think is the current state of short-story writing?" I don't read other people's work, not fiction. I read mysteries to keep my mind off writing and life and nonfiction. "What do you see as the future of steamship writing?" I couldn't tell you where it's going, I don't know where it's been. "Do you plan to write a novel?" Why not? Plans are easy.

(She stares off. Pause.)

Oh, brother. There are good days and bad days, and then there are days when some nice girl from your high school comes to interview you for the *Mountain Grove Sentinel*! I wrote for the *Sentinel*, you know. I started a continuing saga about—God knows. No, even God wouldn't remember this one. Anyway, I didn't finish it. It ended with "to be continued." And I suppose was.

(Pause. She looks back at the list.)

"How did living in a small town, essentially a rural area, prepare you for a career and living in a metropolitan area? Or not?"

(Pause.)

Living in one place is very much like living in another. You see, the environment tries to work its way with you—the verdant hills, the necessity to plow the land, the perk of stealing honey or making sugar from sugarcane. The closeness of the cows—I mean the emotional closeness, but what the environment has to work with is human nature and the human being. And human beings have not evolved much in the last several thousand years, so we are what we are, which is a pretty hard sell, and all environmental constraints do is make us more or less wily, and though I could pick a mess of greens in Central Park and quote chapter and verse from the Bible, unless we are reared in an area of particularly hazardous waste, and maybe I was, we are not going to be nearly as deftly molded by the environment as we are by the People. Who. Inhabit. It.

(Pause.)

As for instance, my father left Mom and me when I was five. Mom didn't remarry until I was eleven: Tom and Edith and little Sam, who was three and a half and never spoke, and if he did, Tom told him to shut up. Or as for instance Tom.

(Pause.)

Mom was frail and quite a bit older than Tom and always the peacemaker; nothing was to upset the order of the household, the sanctity of the home we hear so much about. Just put a lid on it and let it boil. And Tom was the quietly expansive, friendly type that everyone loved. Good job at the cheese factory, nothing flashy or threatening, just a good ol' Joe who started coming into my room sometime during that first year. Edith and Sam had a room on one side of the bathroom, and I had a room on the other. The house hadn't been built that way; my room was added. Tom built it—with intent, I'm sure now. After all, I was eleven, nearly twelve, I had to have my privacy.

(Pause.)

He'd stand by the side of my bed in the dark, pull the covers back and feel my breasts, rub his enormous dick against my cheek, turn my head over, and fuck my face. Or stick his dick in my mouth and come. Then he'd cover me up and go to the door. Stand there, very quiet, forever . . . I never knew why . . . then go back to bed.

(Pause.)

That was only when he drank. Maybe once every three weeks. The room would reek from him. Cigarette sweat and boilermakers. I thought, of course, that it was some sort of punishment. You can't imagine how good I was. I'd help in the kitchen, set the table, do the dishes, wipe the counter, clean the refrigerator, do my homework for the next month, read all the elective outside-reading assignments, fall asleep, and in a few hours I'd wake up with his hand brushing my forehead and lie very still. The two or three times I tried to turn my head he yanked it back with such violence I thought he'd break my neck. So. Eleven, twelve, thirteen, fourteen, fifteen, *sixteen*. If you believe it. I put a lock on my door when I was fourteen; he took it off. I went to Mom, said, "Mom, at night, after you're asleep, Tom comes into my room"—and she slapped me halfway across the house. Told me never to lie again. All I thought was, *My God, you really do see stars, just like in Looney Tunes*. So most of my last year in school I lived at a friend's house. Moved in with her. Used Edith as an excuse. Said I'd kill her if I had to live with her. But really I was gonna kill Tom. Which I didn't by the by, he died of emphysema about four years ago. So. "How did living in a small town, essentially a rural area, prepare you for a career and living in a metropolitan area? Or not?" and "How much of an influence has Mountain Grove been on your writing comma your life?" Coping with Tom was my adolescence. Anything else was peripheral. He was a good-looking man. Tall, thin, blond, younger, nearly ten years, than Mom. All the girls were crazy about him. I never told them. Well, even after I was in high school, I still thought it was some discipline. Had to be some reason. I was looking at it from my point of view, of course, not Tom's. But from his the act is still degrading. I didn't realize that it made me feel dirty—well, fuck it, who am I kidding, it didn't. Or the amount that it did I could cope with, with those endless resources we have at your age.

(Pause.)

At B.U., having been a virgin for eighteen years, I tried very hard to make up for lost time. After the lousy Boy Scout candidate I slept around most of the Big East. Actually most of the eastern seaboard. The current cry was "Make Love, Not War," and of course I leapt at the opportunity, ripped my clothes off with the least provocation, desperately angry that I had missed Woodstock by four years, making it up as I went along. The usual trip: acid, mushrooms, vodka. Then, as you may know, I was published by the time I was a sophomore, so I was writing a lot and milling with my gang, trying hard to be one of the crowd, not stand out, don't be above anything. And God knows I wasn't. I spent my college years either at my typewriter, marching, or on my back. First position, second position, third position. Didn't go home once in those four years. Talked to Mom on the phone; always when Sam and Edith would be in school and Tom would be at work, making cheese and whey.

(Pause.)

All that fucking, of course, was a search, but I didn't know it. Tangled in the blankets, beating the bushes. This goes back to feeling a little dirty, or only a little dirty. I rationalized that I was striving to cleanse myself, put my adolescence behind me.

(Pause.)

So, I didn't come back here till our class reunion. Our fifth. I'd moved to New York by then, got a job as a copy editor, left it, started writing advertising copy, quit that, finally realizing that I didn't want a job where I had to write someone else's bidding, so I worked—office temp, legal, medical—until the first collection came out and I was like: Oh, wow, discovered! By which I mean two stories were sold as movies, and I bought a brownstone and began to move in the literary circles, still moving in circles. So I didn't really know I hadn't been trying to cleanse myself with semen, or douche—I'd been trying to get myself dirty again. And very unsuccessfully. So I came back here, for our fifth high school reunion, contrived to get everyone but Tom out of the house one Sunday afternoon. Tom was very respectful. I was important, of course, and an adult now. And Tom had found God. So I showed him how the police tied us up to take us off to jail—they hadn't actually, and as a matter of fact, I was never in jail, but it comes in handy from time to time to be able to tell a story. Which he told me later was just lying and getting away with it. So there he was, with his feet belted together and his hands tied behind his back, lying on the middle of the living-room floor. I wish you could have seen it gradually . . . dawn on him that he was helpless. . . .

(Pause. She lights a cigarette. Maybe she pours a couple of fingers of vodka and has a belt as well.)

Never underestimate the power and excitement of revenge.

(Pause.)

I wandered into the kitchen, got myself a soda from the fridge. Tom started calling, "Diane? Where'd you go, honey? Diane, this ain't funny, sweetheart." I looked around the kitchen, some of the drawers. I hadn't realized, Lord above, Mom had a regular slaughterhouse in her knife drawer. Mallets and cleavers and a collection of butcher knives that was absolutely *sobering.* But I selected the weapon of my trade—an indelible, permanent-ink, felt-tip pen that Mom used to mark packages of meat for the locker plant or deep freeze, and I went back into the room with Tom. He was thinking very fast, but he didn't say anything. So I sat down beside him on the floor and very slowly started unbuttoning his shirt and pants, with him starting to say now, "Oh, don't do that, Diane, honey, I'm gonna tell your mother," if you can believe it. I went back into the kitchen, got the

Lanford Wilson / 489

scissors, scared him to death, but only to cut his clothes off him, around the rope and my belt and his belt that I had hogtied him with. Which *really* pissed him off—his Sunday suit pants and good new Arrow shirt. I just said, "Tom, don't tell me you've forgot all our nights together." I was stroking his stomach and his dick. You've never seen anyone struggle so hard not to get an erection. I just said, "You're coming into my room, it's dark and quiet and smells like Evening in Paris body powder. You pull the covers down off my perky little breasts." He's yelling, "I don't know what you're talking about, you just dreamed that." I said, "Why, Daddy, that's every little girl's dream—in the minds of men." And, "Oh, there, finally, is that big ol' fat stubby hard dick with the pointy head I been lookin' for." He's trying to roll over, so I straddled him. He's saying, "Don't do nothin', whatta you doin'?" I told him, "Now, Tom, Peepin' Tom, you taught me about love in the village, I'm gonna show you how we do it downtown." And I got him up in me—he's going, "Oh, God, no, oh, God forgive her." Maybe if he'd said, Oh, God, forgive *me*— and I told him, "And I'm gonna write you a little story, Tom—that I want you to treasure, 'cause I get about three thousand dollars for something like this." And I took that nice indelible pen and took his shirt and wiped the sweat off his pretty blank white hairless chest and wrote: "Once there was a little girl whose guardian came to see her in the night." Keeping my hips going and writing was like trying to rub your stomach and pat your head. He's bucking around, yelling, "You're not really writin' that, don't mark me up." I said, "Oh, honey, you marked me up." My story went something like—I'm saying it aloud, writing: "He liked to put his hands on her adolescent breasts to excite himself, and he liked to rub his hot dick on her red cheeks—her cheeks must have felt like flames. And when he got so hot and hard he couldn't stand it any longer, he'd put it in her mouth to cool himself off and pump till he came. And that's how he took care of his little ward. And that's how his little ward took care of him."

(Pause.)

Probably a little more Dickensian than most of my work. Of course, he was screaming and bucking. I wasn't proud of my penmanship, but under the circumstances—and I went slow enough to make sure it was legible. Then he was trying not to come. Saying, "Stop it, don't do that. I don't do that anymore. I was drunk. It was the devil, darlin'," wailing like a revivalist, and I said, "When you come, Daddy, let's both yell, 'Oh, yes,'" but I yelled, "Oh, yes," and he yelled, "Oh, God!" I lay down, stretched out, against his chest. I told him, "All those other times were for you, Daddy, but this one was for me."

(Pause.)

CONTRIBUTORS

KOBO ABE was born in Japan and grew up in Mukden, Manchuria. He is the author of *The Face of Another, The Box Man, Secret Rendezvous,* and *The Woman in the Dunes,* which won the Yomiuri Prize for literature in 1960. He lives in Tokyo where he directs his own theatre company.

EDWARD ALBEE is the author of *Who's Afraid of Virginia Woolf* (1962) and other plays, most recently *Finding the Sun* (1983). He has twice received the Pulitzer Prize and was awarded the Gold Medal in Drama from the American Academy and Institute of Arts and Letters in 1980.

LYNNE ALVAREZ is the author of two books of poetry and eight full-length plays. *The Wonderful Tower of Humbert Lavoignet* received the Le Comte de Nouy Award and the FDG/CBS Award in 1985. She is currently working on an adaptation of Boccaccio's *Decameron* for the Classic Stage Company in New York.

ROBERT AULETTA grew up in New York and received an MFA from the Yale School of Drama. Two one-act plays, *Stops* and *Virgins,* received Obie Awards. He teaches at the School of Visual Arts in New York City and at Harvard University.

AMIRI BARAKA is a poet and playwright. He has been awarded a Whitney Fellowship, a Guggenheim Fellowship, and grants from the Rockefeller Foundation and the National Endowment for the Arts, among other honors. He has taught at Columbia and Yale, and currently lives in Newark. *The LeRoi Jones/Amiri Baraka Reader* is due out this spring from Thunder's Mouth Press.

VERA BLACKWELL resides in New York as a broadcaster, writer, and researcher. She was the first to translate Vaclav Havel's work into English. Since 1964 she has translated all of his major plays, up to and including the three *Vanek* one-act plays, of which *Protest* is the last.

JANE BOWLES, wife of composer and writer Paul Bowles, lived for many years in Tangier, Morocco. A collection of her work, *My Sister's Hand In Mine* (The Ecco Press), includes the Broadway play *In The Summer House.* She died in 1973.

CHRISTOPHER DURANG's plays include *A History of the American Film, Beyond*

Therapy, *The Marriage of Bette and Boo*, and *Sister Mary Ignatius Explains it All for You*. A collection of his work, *Christopher Durang Explains It All For You*, will be re-published by Grove Press. He is also one-third of the cabaret act, "Chris Durang and Dawne."

CLIVE EXTON, a scriptwriter and playwright, has written numerous TV plays and series, including *No Fixed Abode* (1959), *The Rainbirds*, and *Dick Barton— Special Agent*. A stage play, *Have You Any Dirty Washing, Mother Dear?* was written in 1970. His latest film is *The Awakening*.

RICHARD FORD's most recent novel, *Wildlife* (1990), is published by Atlantic Monthly Press. He is the author of three other novels and a collection of stories, *Rock Springs*. He lives in New Orleans.

MARIA IRENE FORNES is the author of more than two dozen plays; her most recent work, the quartet *And What of the Night?*, appeared at Trinity Repertory Theatre in early 1990. She teaches in New York and Los Angeles.

EDWARD GOREY's latest theatre pieces, *Useful Urns* and *Stuffed Elephants*, were done this past summer at opposite ends of Cape Cod.

RICHARD GREENBERG is the author of *Eastern Standard* and several other full-length and one-act plays. His work has appeared in *Best Plays 1988–89*, and in *Best Short Plays* (1987, 1989).

JOHN GUARE is the author of *The House of Blue Leaves*, which won the New York Drama Critics Circle Award for the Best American play of 1971. His most recent play, *Six Degrees of Separation*, is currently at Lincoln Center.

A.R. GURNEY, JR. is a playwright and novelist. His most recent plays are *The Cocktail Hour* and *Love Letters*. His three novels are *The Gospel According To Joe*, *Entertaining Strangers*, and *The Snow Ball*. He is currently working on a fourth while on leave from twenty years of teaching literature at M.I.T.

DAVID HARE is a filmmaker and the author of over a dozen plays, including *Plenty*, which won the New York Critics Circle Award in 1983, *A Map of the World*, *Pravda*, and *The Secret Rapture*. *Wetherby*, his first film as director and writer, was awarded the Golden Bear at Berlin in 1985 for Best Film. His most recent play, *Racing Demon*, opened at the National Theatre in London in 1990.

VÁCLAV HAVEL is the author of *The Garden Party*, *The Memorandum*, *Largo Desolato*, *Temptation* and three one-act plays, *Audience*, *Private View*, and *Protest*. Havel has always been politically active and is currently president of Czechoslovakia.

BETH HENLEY wrote the screenplay for her first full length play *Crimes of the Heart*, for which she was nominated for an Academy Award. She also wrote the screenplay for her second play, *The Miss Firecracker Contest*. Among her other plays her most recent are *Abundance* and *Signature*. *Abundance* opened at the Manhattan Theatre Club in October, 1990.

GERT HOFMANN was born in Germany and has taught in Yugoslavia, Scotland,

and the United States. *Our Man in Madras* was presented in tandem with *Vacationing In Miami* at the ANTA Matinee Series in New York.

TINA HOWE is the author of seven plays, including *The Nest* and *Painting Churches*. Awards and grants include Obie and Outer Critics Circle awards in 1983, and a Guggenheim fellowship in 1990. She teaches at NYU.

DONALD KEENE has translated Yukio Mishima's *Five Modern Noh Plays* and has published three volumes of an expected four volume history of Japanese literature. His most recent book, *Travelers of a Hundred Ages*, appeared in 1989. Mr. Keane is currently University Professor and Shincho Professor of Japanese at Columbia University.

GARRISON KEILLOR's most recent book is *We Are Still Married*. He received a Grammy Award for his recording of excerpts from his novel, *Lake Wobegon Days*. For thirteen years he was the host of the popular radio show, "A Prairie Home Companion." In 1989 he returned to Public Radio with "The American Radio Show," which is broadcast live from The Lamb's Theatre in Manhattan.

ADRIENNE KENNEDY won an Obie award in 1960 with her first play, *Funnyhouse of a Negro*. In 1987, a memoir, *People Who Led to My Plays*, was published by Knopf. She has received two Rockefeller Foundation Grants and a Guggenheim Fellowship.

HARRY KONDOLEON is the author of over 13 plays, a book of poems, *The Death of Understanding*, and a novel, *The Whore of Tjampuan* (PAJ Publications/ Farrar Straus Giroux). His many honors include Fulbright, Rockefeller, Guggenheim and National Endowment for the Arts fellowships, and Drama-Logue, Oppenheimer and Obie awards.

ARTHUR KOPIT's most recent play, *Road To Nirvana*, premiered in spring 1989 at the Louisville Humana Festival. A new play, *Discovery of America*, is forthcoming. He lives in Connecticut with his wife, writer Leslie Garis, and their children.

CAROL S. LASHOF teaches English and Drama at St. Mary's College in California. Her plays, which include *The Story* and *Fraulein Dora*, have been produced by the Magic Theatre of San Francisco, by Palo Alto TheatreWorks, and for National Public Radio.

ROMULUS LINNEY is the author of three novels and eighteen plays. His many awards include two National Critics Awards, an Obie Award, and the Mishima Prize for fiction. He lives in New York City.

DAVID MAMET is a playwright, screenwriter and essayist. His first book of poetry, *The Hero Pony*, was published last fall by Grove Press.

GRACE McKEANEY has worked in television and film, as Artistic Coordinator of Baltimore's Center Stage Theatre Wordplay program, which teaches playwriting in elementary and secondary schools, and as a lecturer in playwriting at Northwestern University. In 1987, her play *How It Hangs* was published in *Best Short Plays* and she was awarded a National Endowment Grant. *Chicks* was performed at the Actor's Theatre of Louisville in 1985.

TERRENCE McNALLY's most recent play, *The Lisbon Traviata,* was awarded the Dramatist Guild's Hull-Warriner Award. His other recent works include *Frankie And Johnny in the Claire De Lune, It's Only a Play* and an adaptation of Bronson Howard's 19th Century American farce, *Up in Saratoga.*

JOSEPH McPHILLIPS is the headmaster of the American School in Tangier. This is his first publication.

CASSANDRA MEDLEY's Off-Broadway musical *A. . . . My Name is Alice* received the 1984 Outer Drama Critics Circle Award. Other plays include *terrain* and *Ma Rose.* She is a recipient of a 1990 National Endowment for the Arts Grant in Playwriting, among other awards, and currently teaches playwriting at Sarah Lawrence College. *Waking Women* was produced in The Ensemble Studio Theatre Marathon '87.

ARTHUR MILLER is the well-known author of numerous plays, including *Death Of A Salesman,* which won the 1949 Pulitzer Prize, *The Crucible, All My Sons,* and *A View From the Bridge,* short stories and essays, a novel and two books of reportage. His autobiography, *Timebends,* was published in 1987.

JOYCE CAROL OATES's most recent novella, *I Lock My Door Upon Myself,* was published in October by The Ecco Press. *Tone Clusters* was produced at the 1990 Actors Theatre of Louisville New Play Festival, and is a co-winner of the 1990 Heidemann Award for one-act plays.

JOHN OSBORNE, author of *Look Back In Anger* (1956), began writing plays while a repertory actor in the 1950s and won an Oscar for his screenplay of *Tom Jones* (1962). He has written numerous other plays, including *Hotel In Amsterdam,* which won the Best Play of the Year Award in 1968, and *Watch It Come Down.* His adaptation of Lope de Vega's *A Bond Honoured* was produced in 1966.

JAMES PURDY's plays are frequently performed at the Theater for the New City under the direction of John Uecker. He has published numerous stories and novels. He recently completed two full-length plays, *Ruthanna Elder* and *Zeal of My House.*

JONATHAN REYNOLDS has written for television, film and theatre. *Lines Composed a Few Miles Above Tintern Abbey, Part II* was written in 1987, when Rupert Murdoch owned the New York Post. A New Yorker for forty years, Reynolds now lives in North Carolina with his wife and two children.

MILCHA SANCHEZ-SCOTT's work is represented in the *Best Short Plays of 1986. The Cuban Swimmer* won a Le Compte de Nouy Foundation Award. Her forthcoming play is entitled *The Architect Piece.*

SAM SHEPARD's most recent play is *A Lie of the Mind* (1985). His plays have won 11 Obies and a Pulitzer Prize. His film work includes the screenplay for *Paris, Texas* and performances in *The Right Stuff* and *Country.*

PERRY SOUCHUK's work has been presented in New York City at Franklin

Furnace, the Ohio Theatre, BACA Downtown and Theatre Club Funambules. He is a recipient of a Playwriting Fellowship from the Edward Albee Foundation.

TOM STOPPARD is a former freelance journalist and the author of a novel, radio dramas, and several plays, including *The Right Thing*. He wrote the screenplay and directed the film version of his play *Rosencrantz and Guildenstern Are Dead*, and most recently, wrote the screenplay for *The Russia House*.

ANDREW VACHSS is a New York City attorney and the author of five novels, two nonfiction books on child abuse and juvenile delinquency, and numerous short stories and articles. His novel *Strega* was awarded the Falcon Award in 1988 by the Maltese Falcon Society of Japan.

WENDY WASSERSTEIN won the 1989 Pulitzer Prize and a Tony Award for Best Play for *The Heidi Chronicles*. Her plays include *Any Woman Can't, Montpelier Pa-Zazz, Isn't It Romantic*, and *When Dinah Shore Ruled the Earth* (co-authored with Christopher Durang) among others. She is the recipient of a Guggenheim Fellowship and a National Endowment for the Arts grant for playwriting. She has also written for periodicals, public television and film.

EUDORA WELTY was born and still resides in Mississippi. She is the author of numerous books, including: *One Writer's Beginnings, Delta Wedding*, and *The Optimist's Daughter. The Eye of the Story*, a collection of essays and reviews, was recently released by Vintage.

TENNESSEE WILLIAMS was awarded the Gold Medal for Literature by the American Academy of Arts and Letters in 1969. His complete works, *The Theatre of Tennessee Williams*, are published in seven volumes by New Directions. He died in New York on February 25, 1983.

AUGUST WILSON is the author of *Ma Rainey's Black Bottom, Fences, Joe Turner's Come and Gone*, and *The Piano Lesson*. His most recent play, *Two Trains Running*, premiered at the Yale Repertory Theatre in March, 1990, and will be published by Summit Books. He is the recipient of two Pulitzer Prizes and numerous other awards, including the New York Drama Critics' Circle Award, Tony Award, Drama Desk Award, Outer Critics' Circle Award and the American Theatre Critics' Association Award, as well as fellowships from the Bush and Guggenheim Foundations. He is a member of New Dramatists of New York.

LANFORD WILSON received the 1980 Pulitzer Prize for Drama and the New York Drama Critic's Circle Award for *Talley's Folly*. He has won awards for his other plays, which include *The Hot L Baltimore, 5th of July*, and *Angels Fall*. His latest play, *Burn This*, opened on Broadway in 1987 and he is currently writing the screenplay for the film version. He is a founding member of Circle Repertory Company and makes his home in Sag Harbor, New York.

NOTES

The Problem may be given stage presentation by amateurs in theatres seating less than 500 upon payment of a royalty of Fifteen Dollars for the first performance, and Ten Dollars for each additional performance. Please note: for amateur productions in theatres seating over 500, write for special royalty quotation, giving details as to ticket price, number of performances and exact number of seats in your theatre. Royalties are payable one week before the opening performance of the play, to Samuel French, Inc., at 45 W. 25th St., New York, NY 10010; or at 7623 Sunset Blvd., Hollywood, CA 90046, or to Samuel French (Canada), Ltd., 80 Richmond St. East, Toronto, Ontario, Canada M5C 1P1.

Royalty of the required amount must be paid whether the play is presented for charity or gain and whether or not admission is charged. Stock royalty quoted on application to Samuel French, Inc. For all other rights than those stipulated above, apply to Samuel French, Inc. Particular emphasis is laid on the question of amateur or professional readings, permission and terms for which must be secured in writing from Samuel French, Inc.

Copying from this play in whole or in part is strictly forbidden by law, and the right of performance is not transferable. Whenever the play is produced the following notice must appear on all programs, printing and advertising for the play: "Produced by special arrangement with Samuel French, Inc." Due authorship credit must be given on all programs, printing and advertising for the play.

recitation, lecturing, public reading, radio broadcasting, television, and the rights of translation into foreign languages, are strictly reserved. Particular emphasis is laid upon the question of readings, permission for which must be secured from the author's agent in writing. All inquiries concerning rights should be addressed to the author's agent, Bridget Aschenberg, International Creative Management, 40 West 57th Street, New York, N.Y. 10019.

She Talks to Beethoven copyright © 1990 by Adrienne Kennedy
CAUTION: Professionals and amateurs are hereby warned that *She Talks to Beethoven* is subject to a royalty. It is fully protected under the copyright laws of the United States of America, and of all countries covered by the International Copyright Union (including the Dominion of Canada and the rest of the British Commonwealth), and of all countries covered by the Pan-American Copyright Convention and the Universal Copyright Convention, and of all countries with which the United States has reciprocal copyright relations. All rights, including professional, amateur, motion picture, recitation, lecturing, public reading, radio broadcasting, television, and the rights of translation into foreign languages, are strictly reserved. Particular emphasis is laid upon the question of readings, permission for which must be secured from the author's agent in writing. All inquiries concerning rights should be addressed to the author's agent, Bridget Aschenberg, International Creative Management, 40 West 57th Street, New York, N.Y. 10019.

Linda Her copyright © 1991 by Harry Kondoleon. All rights reserved.
Produced by the Second Stage in New York City in 1984.
CAUTION: Professionals and amateurs are hereby warned that *Linda Her* is subject to a royalty. It is fully protected under the copyright laws of the United States of Americas, and all countries covered by the International Copyright Union (including the Dominion of Canada and the rest of the British Commonwealth), and of all countries with which the United States has reciprocal copyright relations. All rights, including professional and amateur stage performing, motion picture, recitation, lecturing, public reading, radio broadcasting, television, video or sound taping, all other forms of mechanical or electronic reproduction, such as information storage and retrieval systems and photocopying, and the rights of translation into foreign languages, are strictly reserved. All inquiries concerning performing rights should be addressed to William Morris Agency, Inc. 1350 Avenue of the Americas, New York, New York 10019, Attn: George Lane.

CAUTION: Professionals and amateurs are hereby warned that *Prelude and Liebestod* by Terrence McNally is subject to a royalty. It is fully protected under the copyright laws of the United States of America, and of all countries covered by the International Copyright Union (including the Dominion of Canada and the rest of the British Commonwealth), and of all countries covered by the Pan-American Copyright Convention and the Universal Copyright Convention, and of all countries with which the United States has reciprocal copyright relations. All rights, including professional, amateur, motion picture, recitation, lecturing, public reading, radio broadcasting, television, video or sound taping, all other forms of mechanical or electronic reproduction, such as information storage and retrieval systems and photocopying, and the rights of translation into foreign languages, are strictly reserved. Particular emphasis is laid upon the question of readings, permission for which must be secured from the author's agent in writing. Inquiries concerning all performance rights should be addressed to Gilbert Parker, c/o William Morris Agency, Inc., 1350 Avenue of the Americas, New York, NY 10019.

Camp Cataract copyright © 1991, a play by Joseph A. McPhillips, III adapted from the story by Jane Bowles. All Rights Reserved.
CAUTION: Professionals and amateurs are hereby warned that *Camp Cataract* being fully protected under the Copyright Laws of the United States of America, the British Commonwealth, including the Dominion of Canada, and all other countries of the Berne and Universal Copyright Conven-

The Modern Dramatists Series

Series Editors: Bruce King and Adele King

Modern Dramatists is an international series of introductions to major and significant nineteenth- and twentieth-century dramatists, movements and new forms of drama in Europe, Great Britain, America, as well as new sources of drama, such as Nigeria and Trinidad. The series includes volumes on many dramatists, such as writers of farce, who have created theater "classics" while remaining neglected by literary criticism, and discusses contemporary authors and recent trends in the theater.

Alan Ayckbourn
Second Edition
Michael Billington
1990/ISBN 0-312-04242-6 $24.95

Joe Orton
Maurice Charney
1990/ISBN 0-333-29203-0 $11.95 pb.

Harold Pinter
Second Edition
Bernard F. Dukore
1990/ISBN 0-333-48435-5 $11.95 pb.

George Bernard Shaw
Arthur Ganz
1990/ISBN 0-333-28919-6 $11.95 pb.

Edward Bond
David L. Hirst
1990/ISBN 0-333-32032-8 $11.95 pb.

Theatre for the Young
Alan England
1990/ISBN 0-312-03459-8 $24.95

Federico Garcia Lorca
Reed Anderson
1990/ISBN 0-333-31888-9 $9.95 pb.

Feminist Theatre
An Introduction to the Plays of Contemporary British and American Women
Helene Keyssar
1990/ISBN 0-312-04129-2 $12.95 pb.

Samuel Beckett
Charles R. Lyons
1990/ISBN 0-333-29466-1 $11.95 pb.

Jean Genet
Jeanette L. Savona
1990/ISBN 0-333-29224-3 $11.95 pb.

Anton Chekhov
Lawrence Senelik
1990/ISBN 0-333-30882-4 $11.95 pb.

To order books, or to receive a free Literature catalog, write or call 1-800-221-7945!

St. Martin's Press
Scholarly and Reference Division ❖ 175 Fifth Avenue ❖ New York, NY 10010

Yale University Press
92A Yale Station
New Haven, CT 06520

NEW DIRECTIONS BOOKS
Spring 1991

JACQUES BARZUN
AN ESSAY ON FRENCH VERSE—FOR READERS OF ENGLISH POETRY. A brilliant and amusing essay about the English prejudice against French poetry. $22.95 & $11.95. (Apr.).

CARMEL BIRD
THE BLUEBIRD CAFÉ. A delightful novel/fantasy from the Australian author. $19.95 & $10.95. (Apr.).

KAY BOYLE
THREE SHORT NOVELS. *The Crazy Hunter. The Bridegroom's Body. Decision.* Startling and brilliant. *A Revived Modern Classic.* $10.95 pbk. (Jan.).

VEZA CANETTI
YELLOW STREET. Tr. by Ian Mitchell. A novel set in Vienna in the 1930's. $18.95 & $10.95. (Apr.).

MAURICE COLLIS
SHE WAS A QUEEN. *A Revived Modern Classic.* An extremely witty and vivid rags-to-riches saga set in 13th century Burma. $11.95 pbk. (June).

JUDY GAHAGAN
DID GUSTAV MAHLER SKI? A stunning fictional debut. 12 short stories. $18.95 & $9.95. (May).

MARTIN GRZIMEK
SHADOWLIFE. Tr. B. Mitchell. Intriguing and blackly amusing anti-utopian novel. $22.95 & $11.95. (March).

DEBORAH LARSEN
STITCHING PORCELAIN. *After Matteo Ricci in Sixteenth-Century China.* "Bewitching poetry..." —Jonathan Spence. $8.95 pbk. (Apr.).

HERBERT LEIBOWITZ
FABRICATING LIVES. *Explorations in American Autobiography.* Self-portraits examined from Ben Franklin to Gertrude Stein. $14.95 pbk. (June).

MICHAEL McCLURE
REBEL LIONS. McClure's first book of poetry since the retrospective *Sel. Poems* (ND, '86). $10.95 pbk. (May).

HENRY MILLER
LETTERS TO EMIL. Miller's correspondence (1921-1934) with his friend Emil Schnellock. *Now* in pbk. $12.95 pbk. (June).

JOYCE CAROL OATES
THE RISE OF LIFE ON EARTH. A beautiful short novel about a nurse's aide. $16.95. (Apr.).

OTA PAVEL
HOW I CAME TO KNOW FISH. Tr. by Badal and McDowell. Stories about a beloved Czech childhood and its annihilation by the Nazis. $9.95 pbk. (May).

OCTAVIO PAZ (1990 Nobel Laureate)
THE COLLECTED POEMS OF OCTAVIO PAZ, 1957-1987. Tr. by E. Weinberger. Bilingual. *Now* in pbk. $15.95 pbk. (Apr.).

STENDHAL
THREE ITALIAN CHRONICLES. Tr. by C.K. Scott-Moncrieff. Intro. by Richard Howard. *A Revived Modern Classic. The Charterhouse...* in miniature. $9.95 (Feb.).

TENNESSEE WILLIAMS
BABY DOLL & TIGER TAIL. A reissue of the screenplay for the provocative Elia Kazan movie and later stage version. $23.95 & $11.95. (May).

NEW DIRECTIONS   80 Eighth Ave., New York, NY 10011